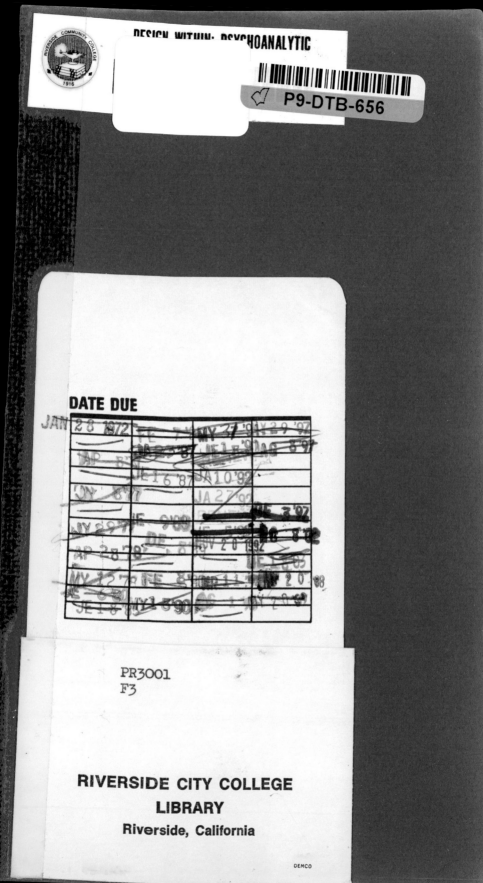

DESIGN WITHIN: PSYCHOANALYTIC

P9-DTB-656

THE
DESIGN
WITHIN
Psychoanalytic
Approaches
to Shakespeare

The Design Within

Psychoanalytic
Approaches
to Shakespeare

M. D. Faber

Science House
New York
1970

Library of Congress Catalog Card Number: 76-89690
Standard Book Number: 87668 024 4

Manufactured by Haddon Craftsmen, Inc. Scranton, Pennsylvania *for Kathleen*

Acknowledgments

I have a distinct feeling of futility as I begin this little section, for I simply cannot, with words, adequately express my indebtedness to Dr. Edwin S. Shneidman of the National Institute of Mental Health and to Professor Robin Skelton of the University of Victoria. It was the inspiration and assistance of Dr. Shneidman and Professor Skelton that made this book possible. I want also to single out Professor Norman N. Holland of the State University of New York, Buffalo. Professor Holland was kind enough to read the manuscript and to make many valuable suggestions. Too, I must acknowledge my indebtedness to Professor John J. McLaughlin of Clemson University, Professor Michael Steig of Simon Fraser University, Dr. Norman L. Watkins, Mr. Sidney Field, and Miss Peggy Wheeldon for helping me in small but crucial ways. Nor can I overlook the staff of the Library of the University of Victoria, especially those in the Reference and Inter-Library Loan Divisions.

Table of Contents

Introduction

As even a cursory examination of the bibliographies will demonstrate, we are witnessing in the twentieth century all sorts of revolutions in the study of Shakespeare. Critics have been calling our attention to the significance of the playwright's sources, to the significance of his images, his theater, his company, his audience, his religion, his politics, his ethics, his handwriting, and even his printers—the individuals who set up the type for the quarto and folio editions. Commentators deeply committed to folklore and historical anthropology have stressed the mythic or "mythopoeic" aspect of the plays; existentialists have stressed the existential aspect; Marxists the Marxian aspect; Zen Buddhists the Zen Buddhist aspect; Thomists the Thomistic aspect. Perhaps partly in reaction to all of this, the group we call, or used to call, the New Critics has emphasized the danger of leaving the "universe of the play," of going outside the text for inspiration, of depending upon anything but the linguistic content of the work—its words—as a critical starting point. And as this introduction is being written, a number of digital computers in various parts of the world are being primed for the cybernetic assault upon *Hamlet* and *King Lear*.

One cannot but marvel—marvel not only that the works of a single author should so fascinate, so *drive,* a sizable portion of the world's thinking men and women (the annual bibliography published by *Shakespeare Quarterly* has recently been listing well over a thousand items), but marvel too that such a multiplicity of approaches can be taken to a relatively small body of plays and poems. As sciences are born, as methods of research become increasingly sophisticated, as new syntheses of various slants on the human experience are forged in the minds of the truly creative scholars, so fresh approaches to Shakespeare's works—which surely must hold the mirror to nature or we are all of us involved in a very wild goose chase—are thought out and made known to the world. But there is one approach we have not mentioned and to which we must now turn our attention.

I

The psychoanalytical interpretation of Shakespeare's works began officially in 1900 when Freud, in *The Interpretation of Dreams,* pointed out the similarities between Hamlet and Oedipus and thus opened the way to an oedipal reading of Shakespeare's play, a reading that many regard as psychology's chief contribution to Shakespearean criticism. But Freud's observation did not, as the idiom has it, "come out of nowhere." Long before Freud was born, the conception of Shakespeare as the world's foremost poet-psychologist was current among western intellectuals; this conception was in large part responsible for Freud's monumental insight. Dryden, Pope, Johnson, Coleridge, Goethe, Lessing, the Schlegels—critics such as these had stressed the playwright's uncanny ability to depict "the Passions," to render upon the stage the "mind's realities," to afford us the "truths of the heart": "He is not so much an Imitator, as an Instrument, of Nature; and 'tis not so just to say that he speaks from her, as that she speaks thro' him. His *Characters* are so much Nature her self, that 'tis a sort of injury to call them by so distant a name as Copies of her . . . [;] every single character in Shakespeare is as much an Individual, as those in Life itself." So said Pope in 1725.[1] By 1859 John Charles Bucknill (like Freud, a medical man) could express himself, in a treatise called *The Psychology of Shakespeare,* "astonished" at the "exactness" of Shakespeare's "psychological knowledge," and A. O. Kellogg by 1866 could maintain in *Shakespeare's Delineations of Insanity, Imbecility, and Suicide* that the poet's knowledge "extended far beyond the range of ordinary observation, and comprehended subjects such, as in our day, and we may suppose in his, were regarded as strictly professional." Kellogg continued: "To suppose that Shakespeare obtained his knowledge of insanity and medical psychology from his contemporaries, or from works on these subjects extant in his day, is simply absurd, for there were none in existence worthy of mention, and all the ideas of his contemporaries were vague and undigested. Yet, notwithstanding all this, after . . . two centuries and a half, we have little to add to what Shakespeare appears to have known." Two decades after Kellogg, Karl Elze wrote simply (and this is Schmitz's translation of the German) that Shakespeare understood "all the varied emotions which move the human heart and mind."[2]

Thus Freud was born into a Europe that regarded Shakespeare as the fountainhead of psychological insight, that stressed again and again the playwright's godlike understanding of the emotions. This tradition can be regarded as the formal cause of Freud's undying fascination with and worship of Shakespeare (or more properly, the man he believed to be Shakespeare)—a fascination that led, in turn, to his critical observations and to the critical observations of his followers.

But European psychology before Freud, at least as far as it can be called psychology at all, was primarily *descriptive,* primarily devoted to noting meticulously the symptoms of the mentally ill and then giving those symptoms such impressive names as "dementia praecox" or "folie circulaire." Not that this work proved ultimately fruitless; on the contrary, it turned out to be quite helpful. It did, however, lack an empirical method of discovering *origins* and was therefore given to explanations of aberrant behavior that were, to put it as mildly as possible, something less than scientific. Thus, the psychological criticism of Shakespeare before Freud was largely a matter of pointing out the degree to which Shakespeare's "madmen," say, resembled the actual "madmen" in Victorian asylums, mulling over the resultant correspondences in a couple of hundred pages punctuated periodically with ecstatic outbursts of astonishment and wonder, and finally, speculating upon the causes of the "lunacy" or "affliction."

Freud's psychology, on the other hand, put aside classification, and he and his followers devoted themselves to establishing empirically—in the actual psychoanalytic setting of doctor and patient—the genesis of mental disease and the inner working of the "psychical apparatus." As Bromberg expresses it: "Dynamic psychotherapy"—that is, therapy based upon Freud's psychoanalytic psychology—"is that type of mental healing most closely identified with modern psychotherapy. For many it is the only rational type of healing through mental means worthy of the name. For dynamic therapy is essentially *causal* in viewpoint, and, it is hoped, final in its aim, since it attempts to understand and remove the effects of antecedent pathogenic emotional elements in the development of the illness."[3] Because of Freud's discovery of a dynamic unconscious mental life and the importance he and his followers gave to it, psychoanalytic psychology took a direction that can only be described as "all its own" and that produced an approach to Shakespeare, indeed to literature as a whole, as original and provocative as anything we have yet seen.

That approach is multifaceted because the men who developed it had a multiplicity of interests. These men were interested in the work of art as the formal expression of its creator's unconscious fantasies and emotional struggles, as a way to understand the artist's psychic life. Implicit in this, of course, is the belief that works of art *are* in large measure formalized embodiments of the mind's unconscious preoccupations, or, to put it somewhat differently, that works of art are coherent dreams—wish fulfillments that make "conscious sense" or "ego sense" in spite of the fact that they come largely from the unconscious, where the "laws of reality" are suspended in the service of infantile needs. This interest in the artist's mind has ultimately given rise to the enormous number of analytic writings on the man we call William Shakespeare, on his childhood, his parents, his adolescence, his marriage, his separation, his fatherhood, and so forth, or on his works as the expression of these things. This interest has created for us a thoroughly modernistic case history, or file, on a long-dead English actor-playwright who seems to have been unwilling to write anything about himself that was nonliterary in nature—something that has opened all sorts of speculative doors for Freudian critics who are especially fond of supporting what they find in a play with "facts" from Shakespeare's life, or indeed, of using those "facts" as guideposts to the unconscious material ostensibly revealed in the text of the play itself.

Psychoanalytic critics, when they approach a Shakespeare play from this particular perspective, are thus free to place the emphasis upon the man or upon the work. That is to say, they can approach the work primarily as an illustration of an unconscious struggle, presumably Shakespeare's, or they can approach Shakespeare's unconscious struggles through the avenue of the work. When the emphasis falls upon the work side of this symbiotic scheme (invariably it is a question of emphasis) the result is apt to be closer to what we normally regard as literary criticism than when it falls on the man side.

Freud and his followers were interested not only in the mind of the individual artist and in the work as the expression of that mind but also in what might be called the racial or mythic or collective origins of artistic productions. It must be remembered that psychoanalysis got under way in the golden age of cultural anthropology, the age of Frazer and Robertson-Smith, and that psychoanalysis was deeply influenced by the theories and discoveries that the new science of anthropology was making known to the world. Of greatest importance is that Freud came to believe that the customs and behavior of ancient and/or savage peoples reveal the emotive predilections of modern Europeans, which, because of the repressive pressures of civilization, are difficult to get at (we eat gingerbread men instead of men, for example), and that the individual human experience consists of a number of *universal* human experiences that are manifested close to the surface in ancient and/or savage society and under a variety of guises in civilized society. One of these guises is literature. That is to say, a "story" or a "plot," which at first glance seems to have nothing to do with anything other than itself, may actually constitute a variation upon a timeless human experience (the Oedipus complex, for example) and may derive its fundamental aesthetic strength from an appeal to our own unconscious participation in that very experience. (An author may, of course, be working out *his* individual role in this experience in the work he is creating.) From mythology, from the writings of the pioneer anthropologists, from the researches of his brilliant disciple Otto Rank, and from his own data as well, Freud gathered a substantial body of material that led him to compose not only such milestones as *Totem and Taboo* and *Civilization and Its Discontents* but also such literary pieces as *The Theme of the Three Caskets* in which he attempts to explain the root origin and ultimately the timeless attraction of plays such as *King Lear* and *The Merchant of Venice* by delving into the mythic or collective experiences they embody.

From these early efforts—and we must in all fairness single out Rank as well as Freud—there has arisen a body of critics and an entire critical literature that attempts to clarify the work of art and the appeal of the work of art in what Jung and his followers would probably call "archetypal terms" and in what we call universal or cross-cultural or mythic terms. This aspect of psychoanalytic criticism, we should note, is gaining considerable favor among critics of purely literary persuasions. While the first kind of criticism, the kind that reads from the work to the man or vice versa, does not clarify, at least in any direct or obvious fashion, the way the work works as literature, the second kind of criticism does shed light upon the reason(s) why the text of a specific work affects a specific audience in the way it does. In other words, to find the mythic or archetypal attraction of *King Lear* is to find out something about the play *King Lear* and not about Shakespeare's mother or what Shakespeare "had to" sublimate. It follows that to treat the whole play in mythic terms is perforce to treat individual characters in these terms. Creations such as Edgar, or Kent, or Cordelia become for the mythic interpreter not "real" but "psychically real," not "actual individuals" but embodiments of timeless human tendencies—in a sense, allegorical figures.

There is still another side to the psychoanalytic criticism of Shakespeare, a side that is ultimately very different from the one at which we have just glanced. Writing about the impact of the Christian religion upon the pagan authors and transmitters of *Beowulf,* J. R. R. Tolkien says that "new Scripture and old tradition touched and ignited."[4] That is good, not only in and of itself, but also because it describes so vividly what happened when psychoanalysis, the "new Scripture," came into contact with the character-oriented approach to Shakespeare, the "old tradition." By the time of Freud's discoveries it had become traditional to explain, or to criticize, the works of Shakespeare almost exclusively in terms of the characters they contained. The Tragedies were regarded as tragedies of character, and the way to understand them was to understand "the character" of the tragic hero; the Comedies afforded us a wonderful procession of "comic characters," characters such as Bottom the jolly weaver or Malvolio the self-inflated steward; the Histories demonstrated to all the world the great influence of character upon the fortunes of a nation. The most famous and brilliant of the many critical works committed to this view is, of course, A. C. Bradley's *Shakespearean Tragedy* (a book that can still bring us closer to Shakespeare's genius than much of the material published in our scholarly journals and on our university presses); I need hardly add that everyone on this planet who thinks about Shakespeare or writes about Shakespeare is at least to some extent working in this tradition. But the characters that Shakespeare gave us were not like the characters given us by "ordinary" authors. They were more lifelike, more complete, more emphatic—and even more mysterious and more puzzling; in other words, they were characters so incredibly arresting and human as to invite a variety of impressions and interpretations. This is where psychoanalysis comes in.

For psychoanalysis, too, was interested in character and was to become increasingly so. Indeed, from one standpoint, the whole business of psychoanalysis in its early stages was to explore the kinds of development that lead to the kinds of character that lead to neurotic, wasteful, and even tragic kinds of lives. With the publication of Freud's work on the Oedipus complex, on infantile sexuality, and on anality, along with the pioneering achievements of Reich and Abraham, it became common in analytic circles to speak of an anal character or an oral character or a masochistic character or a narcissistic character. Because the interest of Freud and his followers in the work of the world's greatest poet-psychologist continued (and continues) unabated, there arose a body of analytic criticism devoted to exploring Shakespeare's "great characters" (and even some of the minor ones) in analytic and, to differentiate this kind of criticism from the mythic kind, realistic terms. Controversial or puzzlng characters such as Brutus or Iago or Hamlet or Coriolanus were meticulously examined under the bright light of psychoanalytic science. Those who did the examining felt not only that they were aiding the world in understanding great literature but also, and quite rightly, that they were working within the accepted traditions of Shakespearean criticism.

But Shakespearean criticism was changing, and changing fast. Even before the publication of Jones's classic *Hamlet and Oedipus,* it was being objected that Shakespeare's characters were not "real people" but "linguistic phenomena" and that to talk of Hamlet's Oedipus complex or Shylock's anal eroticism was to "read into" the play all sorts of things that were not there and were not intended to be there. Increasingly, as Shakespeare's works came to be regarded as "aesthetic contraptions," as "extended metaphors," as "symbolic actions," and as emphasis came to be placed not upon the "content" of the play but upon its "form," its "structure" (one thinks here of G. Wilson Knight, Francis Fergusson, William Empson, Kenneth Burke, Caroline Spurgeon, and others), it came to be suspected that the whole business of character analysis sidetracked people, taking them away from an appreciation of the *real* Shakespeare. Character analysis made people

think of Shakespeare as a psychologist, a heart-reader, a soul-plumber
—something that he was, but not exclusively or even primarily. Instead, the new critics said, people should appreciate Shakespeare the
master creator of atmospheres, extender of metaphors, designer of
structures.

The current tendency to widen our appreciation and understanding
of Shakespeare by concentrating on all kinds of textual matters that
were not being concentrated upon sixty or seventy years ago is a salu-
brious and laudable tendency that should be encouraged by everyone
involved in the teaching and criticism of Shakespeare. After all, should
we *narrow* our scope? However, to maintain, as many now do, that
the analysis of character is pernicious and, more significantly, uncritical is another matter about which a few words must be said.

Everyone will agree, of course, that character analysis as it was
practiced by, shall we say, the lesser commentators of the Victorian
age has not a great deal to be said for it. To talk of Rosalind's girl-
hood, to explain Hamlet's emotional problems (assuming he has some)
by discussing his adolescence as it *probably* occurred, to probe the
relationship of Iago and Othello prior to the first act and first scene
of the tragedy—all this is indefensible because it goes outside the
text, where any man's guess is as good as another's and where responsible literary criticism has no business. But this sort of dreaming is
not at issue here, for although the authors that make up the psychoanalytic school of Shakespearean criticism are on occasion guilty of
this fault (as are other authors), they are in the overwhelming majority of instances what we may call responsible; that is, they derive their
observations from specific passages of the text and they discuss the
preplay existences of characters only when the text of the play would
put those existences in the audience's mind through specific, concrete
allusions to the past. (A great deal is said in *Coriolanus,* for example,
about the hero's boyhood and upbringing.)

But to say that even *this* analysis of character, grounded as it is in
the text of the play itself, is uncritical because a play's characters are
not "real," is to go, I think, too far.[5] For let us note, in the first place,
that Shakespeare strives to make his characters "real" and that he
does this in a very special way. I mean that as a dramatist Shakespeare
is able to show us only a part or an aspect of every dramatis persona
because every dramatis persona must perform some special function

in the play. As much as we would like to, we simply cannot be allowed to view the good Horatio in the Elsinore kitchen breakfasting upon Danish rolls and cream because such a view, however delightful, would have nothing to do with the overall conception that informs the play. But the part or aspect of the dramatis personae with which Shakespeare chooses to present us should be, indeed must be, "real," and not only real but also full enough or rich enough to give us the impression of a whole or real person standing, as it were, behind the presented part or aspect. In other words, Shakespeare must, and does, give us that which is essential to enable us to realize in our own minds a full, rounded character. It is precisely this essential "stuff" that allows us to treat a dramatis persona in a manner that might be called realistic or psychological. In "real life" we do not have to know everything about a personality to understand its essential quality. If one is familiar with the basic or most revealing aspects of a particular "real person," one is quite justified in describing that person as egocentric or aggressive or infantile or dependent or whatever. The rest, in fact, can go by the board. Thus, Shakespeare, by *having* to hold information back, by *having* to manipulate character in such a way as to service the design of the total drama, is actually in an aesthetic position especially conducive to "realistic" or "essential" portraiture through actions and words. It is as if Shakespeare is asking us to believe that he has already examined the "person" as a whole and is giving us what he has taken to be a "real" aspect of that person, and that if he did present Cordelia as the wife of France, which he never does, or Hamlet as a student in Wittenberg, which he never does, there would be nothing in the presentation that would be inconsistent with the "essential" presentation that he has been "forced" to give us in the text. Thus, the critic who looks at Hamlet as a real person *outside the text* is making the mistake of trying to see what only Shakespeare saw: the whole person.

In this way, then, psychological criticism of character is not only consistent with but necessary to what we think of as the New or Modern approach to the playwright's work. For if the dramatis personae are not "real people" but "characters in plays" and if Shakespeare presents us with only an aspect or side of the character to the end of preserving a unity of structure or a poetic intention, then we must be able to grapple meaningfully, even scientifically if you will allow that, with the aspect or side of the character that Shakespeare has chosen to present. The superficial, homespun psychology that informs so much Shakespearean criticism, and the antiquated medicine lore of the Elizabethan "doctors" that turns up in so many historical treatises, will no longer do the job, and that is all there is to it. As for the objection (often heard) that since Freud lived after Shakespeare the latter could hardly have been aware of psychoanalytic findings, we might consider this comment by Griffin: "The implication would be that Freud created men instead of studying them, or that Shakespeare was not a man as other men are, or that he was incapable of registering his own impressions of his fellowmen."[6]

Then too, and from a much more commonsensical perspective, there is the whole business of identification and theater reality; that is to say, we might as well not go to the play at all unless we can feel ourselves in the presence of "real people," unless we can *identify* with the stage personages offered us. True, one *can* respond to a character as a "function" and view the play as an "aesthetic contraption," as a kind of erector set, and there are probably three or four in the audience who are capable of repressing their feelings to such an extent that they can do this. But Shakespeare did not write his plays for such individuals; he wrote them, rather, for people who came to the theater to *feel,* to identify, to escape themselves and enter the *reality* of the stage universe. It is surely of prime importance to discuss what there is in a specific character that allows us to identify with him in this or that way or to suspect this or that about him, as long as our discussion is grounded firmly in the text. This kind of criticism does not open the door to every sort of personal reaction, to ungovernable impressionism and indefensible subjectivism; on the contrary, it opens the door to a meaningful examination of the *text* and the sorts of creatures the text is creating in the minds of the audience and the audience is creating from the text before them. It opens the door, in short, to a correct understanding of Shakespeare.

But realistic character analysis must not be regarded as something that can be pursued only in a monistic or isolated way, a way that overlooks the broader and perhaps more significant question of the total drama. On the contrary, one of the most remarkable advances in the psychoanalytic study of Shakespeare derives from the analytic critic's growing ability to demonstrate the importance of a particular character trait or character aspect to the poetic fabric, or sructure, of the drama as a whole. Such essays as Norman Holland's *Romeo's Dream and the Paradox of Literary Realism* or David Barron's *The Babe That Milks: An Organic Study of "Macbeth"* make plain not only the influence of the New and neo-New Criticism on psychoanalytic criticism, but also the propensity of the psychoanalytic critic, preoccupied as he is with problems of character and realistic portrayal of psychic phenomena, to employ his analytic insights in such a way as to illuminate the dramatic and metaphoric unity of the entire Shakespearean conception.

II

These, then, are the methods of psychoanalytic criticism, as well as some of the pros and cons that swirl about them. A great deal more could be said, of course, for they are methods that admit of many many nuances, which have afforded us all manner of comments upon the playwright and upon the playwright's work, and which have provoked any number of heated critical discussions from individuals in both the literary and psychological worlds. Why the heat? It can be attributed, in part at least, to the extreme, or even the irresponsible, analytic criticisms that are sometimes marshaled forth in the quarterlies and reviews and in books upon Shakespeare and psychology. Surely we can understand the "average scholar's" dismay at hearing that Hamlet is "actually" Shakespeare's small son Hamnet and that the action of the play revolves around this child's anger at the entrance of siblings into the Shakespeare household, an anger that takes the form of a refusal to defecate, or that the poison in the ear speaks not only of murder but also of homosexuality, or that Shakespeare wrote tragedies because he saw his father butcher domestic animals, or that Falstaff wanted to look upon his parents in bed, or that Timon of Athens is suffering from syphilis, "and so forth."

But every school of criticism has its extremists; every school of criticism can and does on many occasions go astray; it's just that when psychoanalytic criticism appears to go astray it appears to go very much astray as a result of its tendency to see the latent in the manifest, to translate the literal into the symbolic, in a word, to penetrate appearances. But we surely cannot condemn the whole school because of its extremists. As this volume will demonstrate, the psychoanalytic critics have a great many important and illuminating things to tell us about the works of the world's greatest playwright. It is simply unfortunate (and very human) that extreme or radical criticisms are particularly able to attract attention and provoke critical fury and thus make guilty by association views that are healthy and valuable. To say, as Harley Granville-Barker does, that Freud's influence on the study of Shakespeare is "damnable"[7] is not only to display a misunderstanding of what the best and the most responsible of the psychoanalytic critics are trying to do, but also to speak too broadly. One only regrets that such a man as Granville-Barker should have been betrayed, as it were, into making such a statement.

Nor should one be fooled by the occasional commentator who says that the psychoanalytic school of criticism has yet to present a convincing defense of its method to the scholarly world.[8] For what such a commentator means is that since the methods that stand behind the psychoanalytic approach to literature differ from his own methods and from the methods of some of his colleagues, psychoanalytic criticism has no right to call itself criticism at all. That is all he means. For the day has not yet arrived when what is critical and what is uncritical is "writ down for all to see," and when a disagreement with a critical approach turns out to be the negation of that approach. Perhaps the fairest statement comes from Miss Mabel Collins Donnelly, who writes: "The kind of interpretation that sensitive use of Freud's method can make is a valuable one. . . . Let the psychologist and psychiatrist learn more about literary conventions and the literary critic learn more about psychology, and in time we shall have one of the greatest syntheses, lacking miracles."[9]

This volume can further such a synthesis. It gathers together many of the most important of the psychoanalytic pieces that place the emphasis upon the work rather than upon the man. Not always, however, is this selection a clear-cut matter, and in a few instances the reader will have to untangle the more strictly biographical from the more strictly critical remarks, trusting that the critical insights are worth the effort—which they are. By "most important" is meant not only the pieces that may be regarded as among the best that psycho-analytic criticism has to offer (though there could hardly be full agree-ment on such a matter), but also the pieces that have turned out to be especially influential, the pieces that have opened up new avenues of approach to the playwright's work, the pieces that have carried on most interestingly and most effectively the kind of criticism that arose in Vienna around the turn of the century. The book's format is de-signed to lead the reader, when it is possible to do so, from the original or germinating work on each play to the developing and expanding work that followed, and which is being added to even now.

Again, not every selection here is "pure and unadulterated" psycho-analysis, if there is such a thing. Freud's ideas traveled in many direc-tions and came into contact with the ideas of such authors as Jung, Reich, Adler, Horney, and Sullivan, and with the ideas of *their* fol-lowers as well. As a result, a good many pieces on Shakespeare that are ultimately psychoanalytic in nature are nevertheless touched with ideas from the various schools of psychoanalytic thought, and a num-ber of those pieces are presented in this anthology. It should also be stressed—and this is amplified in the interstitial material—that Shake-speare's works have not been accorded equal and impartial treatment by psychoanalytic critics. Indeed, the overwhelming emphasis has been (and apparently still is) upon the Tragedies, especially *Julius Caesar, Hamlet, Othello, King Lear, Macbeth,* and *Coriolanus,* and upon a few of the Comedies and Histories, including, most notably, *Richard III, Henry IV Part I, Henry IV Part II, The Merchant of Venice,* and *The Tempest.* The emphasis upon the Tragedies can be explained, in large part, by calling to mind the early and persistent tendency of psychoanalysis to concern itself almost exclusively with neurotic, tragic, self-damaging behavior. This is changing somewhat. For psychoanaly-sis today, through the efforts of such men as Heinz Hartmann, David Rapaport, and Erik Erickson, to name but three, is paying increased, explicit attention to the problem of what makes for healthy, produc-tive, vigorous, "normal" conduct. From the perspective of psycho-dynamics, the Comedies are harder to analyze than the Tragedies, perhaps because the behavior expressed in them is more formalized, more "social," and therefore less realistic than the behavior expressed in the other genre. As for the Sonnets, which seem always to figure into psychoanalytic discussions of Shakespeare, they have been examined primarily as an avenue to the poet's unconscious and, as a result, have yet to be analytically explored as works of literature.[10]

But enough in the way of introductory remarks. It is time the psychoanalytic critics spoke for themselves.

Notes

(Indented notes are from the author's Introduction to the book or from his introductory statements preceding each article. All other notes are from the reprinted articles.)

Introduction

1. ALEXANDER POPE, "Preface to Shakespeare," in D. NICHOL SMITH (ed.), *Shakespeare Criticism: A Selection (1623–1840)* (London: Oxford University Press, 1958), p. 43.
2. J. C. BUCKNILL, *The Psychology of Shakespeare* (London, 1859), p. viii; A. O. KELLOGG, *Shakespeare's Delineations of Insanity, Imbecility, and Suicide* (New York, 1866), pp. 1, 9; KARL ELZE, *William Shakespeare, A Literary Biography,* trans. Schmitz (London, 1888), p. 437.
3. WALTER BROMBERG, *The Mind of Man: A History of Psychotherapy and Psychoanalysis* (New York: Harper and Brothers, 1959), p. 167.
4. J. R. R. TOLKIEN, *Beowulf: The Monsters and the Critics* (London: Oxford University Press, 1958), p. 27.
5. See, for example, ELMER EDGAR STOLL, *Shakespeare Studies, Historical and Comparative in Method* (New York: The Macmillan Company, 1927), pp. 118-127; BERNARD BECKERMAN, *Shakespeare at the Globe, 1599–1609* (New York: The Macmillan Company, 1962), chap. 4.
6. WILLIAM J. GRIFFIN, "Uses and Abuses of Psychoanalysis in the Study of Literature," *Literature and Psychology,* *1*:10, 1951.
7. HARLEY GRANVILLE-BARKER, *The Study of Drama* (Cambridge: Cambridge University Press, 1934), p. 53.
8. NORMAN RABKIN (ed.), *Approaches to Shakespeare* (New York: McGraw-Hill Book Company, 1964), p. x.

9. MABEL COLLINS DONNELLY, "Freud and Literary Criticism," *College English, 15*:158, 1953.
10. There are a couple of exceptions here, neither of which invalidates my statement. GORDON ROSS SMITH's "Note on Shakespeare's Sonnet 143," *American Imago,* 14 (1957), is fine as far as it goes, but, because of its severely restricted scope, it simply does not go very far. CLARISSA RINAKER's "Some Unconscious Factors in the Sonnet as a Poetic Form," *International Journal of Psycho-Analysis, 12*:167-187, 1931, devotes very little space to an explicit examination of Shakespeare's work and is almost too speculative to be meaningful.

Suggestions for Further Reading

The following list of works, arranged as this book is arranged, should not be regarded as a comprehensive bibliography of psychoanalytic writings on Shakespeare. For comprehensive bibliographical treatments, see Gordon Ross Smith, *A Classified Shakespeare Bibliography* (University Park: Pennsylvania State University Press, 1958); Norman N. Holland, *Psychoanalysis and Shakespeare* (New York: McGraw-Hill Book Company, 1966).

General

HOLLAND, NORMAN N. *Psychoanalysis and Shakespeare.* New York: McGraw-Hill Book Company, 1966. (Particularly comprehensive.)
LUCAS, F. L. *Literature and Psychology* (1951). Ann Arbor: University of Michigan Press, 1957.
STEWART, J. I. M. *Character and Motive in Shakespeare.* London: Longmans, Green, 1949.

Romeo and Juliet

MENNINGER, KARL A. *Man Against Himself.* New York: Harcourt, Brace, and Co., 1938, pp. 320-321.
REIK, THEODORE. *Psychology of Sex Relations.* New York: Farrar and Rinehart, 1945, pp. 88-89.
VREDENBURGH, JOSEPH L. "The Character of the Incest Object: A Study of Alternation between Narcissism and Object Choice," *American Imago, 14*:45-52, 1957.

Julius Caesar

FABER, M. D. "Freud and Shakespeare's Mobs," *Literature and Psychology, 15*:238-255, 1965.

———. "Lord Brutus' Wife: A Modern View," *Psychoanalytic Review, 52*:108-115, 1965-1966.

FELDMAN, HAROLD. "Unconscious Envy in Brutus," *American Imago, 9*:307-335, 1952-1953.

LUNDHOLM, H. "Mark Antony's Speech and the Psychology of Persuasion," *Character and Personality, 6*:293-305, 1935.

SMITH, GORDON ROSS. "Brutus, Virtue, and Will," *Shakespeare Quarterly, 10*:367-379, 1959.

Hamlet

CAMPBELL, OSCAR J. "What's the Matter with Hamlet?" *Yale Review, 32*:309-322, 1942.

ERIKSON, ERIK H. "Youth: Fidelity and Diversity," *Daedalus, 91*:5-27, 1962.

FEINSTEIN, HOWARD M. "Hamlet's Horatio and the Therapeutic Mode," *American Journal of Psychiatry, 123*:803-809, 1967.

HELLER, LORA and ABRAHAM. "Hamlet's Parents: The Dynamic Formulation of a Tragedy," *American Imago, 17*:413-421, 1960.

JOFEN, JEAN B. "Two Mad Heroines: A Study of the Mental Disorders of Ophelia in *Hamlet* and Margarete in *Faust*," *Literature and Psychology, 11*:70-77, 1961.

LUCAS, F. L. *Literature and Psychology* (1951). Ann Arbor: University of Michigan Press, 1957, pp. 32-51.

MacCURDY, JOHN T. "Concerning Hamlet and Orestes," *Journal of Abnormal Psychology, 13*:250-260, 1918-1919.

SLOCHOWER, HARRY. "Hamlet: The Myth of Modern Sensibility," *American Imago, 7*:197-238, 1950.

WADSWORTH, FRANK W. "Hamlet and the Methods of Literary Analysis; A Note," *American Imago, 19*:85-90, 1962.

WERTHAM, FREDERIC. *Dark Legend: A Study in Murder*. New York: Duell, Sloan and Pearce, 1941.

Othello

AUDEN, W. H. "The Alienated City: Reflections on *Othello*," *Encounter*, August, 1961, pp. 3-14.

BODKIN, MAUD. *Archetypal Patterns in Poetry* (1934). 2nd ed. New York: Vintage Books, 1958, pp. 211-218.
FELDMAN, A. BRONSON. "The Yellow Tragedy: Short Studies of Five Tragedies of Jealousy," *Literature and Psychology*, 6:38-52, 1956.
HAGOPIAN, JOHN V. "Psychology and the Coherent Form of Shakespeare's *Othello*," *Papers of the Michigan Academy of Science, Arts, and Letters*, 45:373-380, 1960.
STEWART, J. I. M. *Character and Motive in Shakespeare*. London: Longmans, Green, 1949, Ch. V.

King Lear

BODKIN, MAUD. *Archetypal Patterns in Poetry* (1934). 2nd ed. New York: Vintage Books, 1958, pp. 14-17 and 273-276.
FABER, M. D. "Some Remarks on the Suicide of King Lear's Eldest Daughter," *University Review*, 33:313-317, 1967.
FROST, WILLIAM. "Shakespeare's Rituals and the Opening of *King Lear*," *Hudson Review*, 10:577-585, 1957-1958.
PAUNCZ, ARPAD. "Psychopathology of Shakespeare's *King Lear*," *American Imago*, 9:55-77, 1952-1953.
SHARPE, ELLA FREEMAN. "From *King Lear* to *The Tempest*," *Collected Papers on Psycho-Analysis*, ed. Marjorie Brierley. London: The Hogarth Press, 1950, pp. 214-241.

Macbeth

CORIAT, ISADOR H. *The Hysteria of Lady Macbeth* (1912). 2nd ed. Boston: Four Seas Co., 1920.
ROBERTSON, P. L. "The Role of the Political Usurper: Macbeth and Boris Godounov," *American Imago*, 23:95-109, 1966.
STRONG, L. A. G. "Shakespeare and the Psychologists." *Talking of Shakespeare*, ed. John Garrett. London: Hodder and Stoughton, 1954, pp. 187-208.

Antony and Cleopatra

WEISINGER, HERBERT. "The Myth and Ritual Approach to Shakespearean Tragedy," *Centennial Review of Arts and Science*, 1:142-166, 1957.

Coriolanus

BARRON, DAVID B. "*Coriolanus*: Portrait of the Artist as Infant," *American Imago*, 19:171-193, 1962.

PUTNEY, RUFUS. "Coriolanus and His Mother," *Psychoanalytic Quarterly, 31*:364-381, 1962.

Richard III

ADLER, CHARLES A. "Richard III—His Significance as a Study in Criminal Life-Style," *International Journal of Individual Psychology, 2*:55-60, 1936.
WILE, IRA S. "Some Shakespearean Characters in the Light of Present Day Psychologies," *Psychiatric Quarterly, 16*:62-90, 1942.

Richard II

WANGH, MARTIN. "A Psychoanalytic Commentary on Shakespeare's *The Tragedie of King Richard the Second*," *Psychoanalytic Quarterly, 37*:212-238, 1968.

I and II Henry IV

ALEXANDER, FRANZ. "A Note on Falstaff," *Psychoanalytic Quarterly, 2*:592-606, 1933.
REIK, THEODORE. *The Haunting Melody.* New York: Farrar, Straus and Young, 1953, pp. 137-145.
STEWART, J. I. M. *Character and Motive in Shakespeare.* London: Longmans, Green, 1949, pp. 132-139.

Comedy of Errors

FELDMAN, A. BRONSON. "Shakespeare's Early Errors," *International Journal of Psychoanalysis, 36*:114-133, 1955.

A Midsummer Night's Dream

GUI, WESTON A. "Bottom's Dream," *American Imago, 9*:251-305, 1952-1953.
JACOBSON, DONALD F. "A Note on Shakespeare's *Midsummer Night's Dream*," *American Imago, 19*:21-26, 1962.

The Merchant of Venice

CORIAT, ISADOR H. "Anal-Erotic Character Traits in Shylock," *International Journal of Psycho-Analysis, 2*:354-360, 1921.
JEKELS, LUDWIG. "On the Psychology of Comedy" (1926), trans. I.

Jarosy. *Selected Papers*. New York: International Universities Press, 1952, pp. 97-104.

MIDGLEY, GRAHAM. *"The Merchant of Venice:* A Reconsideration," *Essays in Criticism, 10*:119-133, 1960.

RANK, OTTO. *Psychology and the Soul* (1932), trans. William D. Turner. Philadelphia: University of Pennsylvania Press, 1950, pp. 60-70.

ROSS, THOMAS ARTHUR. "A Note on *The Merchant of Venice,"* British *Journal of Medical Psychology, 14*:303-311, 1934.

The Merry Wives of Windsor

REIK, THEODORE. *The Secret Self*. New York: Farrar, Straus and Young, 1953, pp. 63-75.

All's Well That Ends Well

ADAMS, JOHN F. *"All's Well That Ends Well:* The Paradox of Procreation," *Shakespeare Quarterly, 12*:261-270, 1960.

Twelfth Night

SCOTT, W. I. D. *Shakespeare's Melancholiacs*. London: Mills and Boon, 1962, pp. 57-60.

SEIDEN, MELVIN. "Malvolio Reconsidered," *University of Kansas City Review, 28*:105-114, 1961.

As You Like It

EMDE BOAS, CONRAD VAN. "The Connection between Shakespeare's Sonnets and His 'Travesti-Double' Plays," *International Journal of Sexology, 4*:67-72, 1950.

SCOTT, W. I. D. *Shakespeare's Melancholiacs*. London: Mills and Boon, 1962, pp. 61-72.

Pericles

FELDMAN, A. BRONSON. "Imaginary Incest," *American Imago, 12*:117-155, 1955.

The Tempest

MANNONI, OTHAR. *Prospero and Caliban,* trans. Pamela Powesland. New York: Frederick A. Praeger, 1956, pp. 97-109.

Sonnets

RINAKER, CLARISSA. "Some Unconscious Factors in the Sonnet as a Poetic Form," *International Journal of Psychoanalysis, 12*:167-187, 1931.

SMITH, GORDON ROSS. "A Note on Shakespeare's Sonnet 143," *American Imago, 14*:33-36, 1957.

Venus and Adonis

WEBSTER, PETER DOW. "A Critical Fantasy or Fugue," *American Imago, 6*:297-309, 1949.

Tragedies

The Ritual Origin of Shakespeare's "Titus Andronicus"

Although its authorship has been disputed, *Titus Andronicus* is generally considered to be the first, and perhaps the worst, of Shakespeare's tragedies, a play that caters almost shamelessly to the Elizabethan appetite for lust and murder, and whose sole claim upon our serious critical attention lies in its lucid structure, its sense of dramatic direction and flow. Writing in Alfred Harbage's recent anthology, *Shakespeare: The Tragedies,* H. T. Price remarks:

> If we could acquit Shakespeare of being an accomplice in *Titus,* we should all be glad to do so. But it is attributed to him by close colleagues who presumably knew Shakespeare well enough to be aware of what they were doing. At any rate they knew him much better than we do. All the tests of affinities, parallels, resemblances, and methods of technique point definitely to Shakespeare. No convincing evidence has been brought forward which would connect *Titus* with any other dramatist. The horrors of the play are undeniable. But if scholars would refrain from still harping upon these horrors and would instead consider the play on its merits as an excellent piece of stagecraft, they might see in it something not unworthy of the young Shakespeare.[1]

William H. Desmonde's psychoanalytic essay on the play, an essay that obviously has *its* origin in psychoanalysis' preoccupation with mythological material, is of particular interest because it calls to mind further reasons for regarding *Titus Andronicus* as a worthy and logical starting point for the youthful tragedian named Shakespeare. Desmonde demonstrates not only that *Titus Andronicus* contains a number of mythic elements such as a cannibalistic banquet, a struggle for kingship between two royal sons following an old king's death, a rape at a pit in the woods, and a human sacrifice—elements Shakespeare may well have inherited from Ovid—but also that the heart of the plot, which consists of the struggle for kingship, the eating of Chiron and Demetrius, and the elevation of Lucius to Emperor, bears a striking resemblance to Freud's conception of the "primal crime," in which the brothers rise up and slay and eat the all-powerful father. In a word, Desmonde demonstrates that the tragedy of *Titus Andronicus* is rooted in the soil of the "oedipal conflict," which recurs, as he puts it, "in each succeeding generation." Thus, when he wrote this play the youthful Shakespeare not only was aware of formal and technical matters but also sensed the powerful dramatic appeal that lay in what we might call the fundamental human struggle. Shakespeare was interested in the oedipal conflict from the very beginning.

M. F.

he survival of ritual forms in literature and in the drama is well known to scholars. Lord Raglan has conjectured that such traditions as those of Robin Hood, the Norse Sagas, Hengist and Horsa, Cuchulainn, and the story of Troy have originated in religious ceremonies,[1] and Jessie Weston has offered the hypothesis that the Holy Grail stories originated in Mithraism.[2] It has been shown by Dieterich,[3] Ridgeway,[4] Jane Harrison,[5] Gilbert Murray,[6] and Cornford[7] that theatrical forms are traceable to the religious rituals of ancient Greece.

G. Wilson Knight has suggested that Shakespearian tragedy is essentially a reworking of ancient religious ceremonies connected with the sacrifice of the mass. Shakespeare's kings, he states, are to be compared with the ritual kings of pagan cultures.[8] This essay seeks to show the existence of a ritual pattern in the tragedy *Titus Andronicus*.

In a recent article on the Eleusinian Mysteries[9] I discussed the psychoanalytic significance of primitive puberty rites. They represent, according to the hypothesis offered, a social institution devised, no doubt over a long period of time, by the older men. The purpose of this institution was both to rid the adolescents of their oedipal ambivalence, freeing their energies for higher cultural activities, and to provide an outlet for the hostility of the tribal fathers against their sons.

The essential feature of these rituals consists of being shown the tribal mysteries, dramatic portrayals of the killing and resurrection of the neophyte. Originally, according to Freud's hypothesis, the separa-

"The Ritual Origin of Shakespeare's *Titus Andronicus*," by William H. Desmonde. Reprinted with permission from the *International Journal of Psychoanalysis*, XXXVI (1955), 61-65.

tion of the son from the mother was carried out by the killing, castrating, or driving out of the male offspring. Frequently, puberty rituals for girls consist of a defloration ceremony.

In the course of social development, these mysteries often survive under the direction of organizations of priests, who conduct the dramatic-magical rites of the group. The religious mysteries of ancient Greece arose from the barbaric rituals of the primitive Aegean, according to Webster,[10] Andrew Lang,[11] Van Gennep,[12] and Jane Harrison;[13] and it is well known that Greek ritual had a great influence upon the Roman drama, from which Shakespeare derived many of his plots.

The Tragedy of "Titus Andronicus"

I propose to demonstrate here that the plot of the tragedy *Titus Andronicus* was derived by Shakespeare or one of his contemporaries[14] from a Roman play or myth stemming from Greek ritual origins, and ultimately from tribal puberty rites.

The persistence of this ritual pattern in an Elizabethan play is to be regarded not as accidental, but as resulting from the recurrence of the oedipal conflict in each succeeding generation, along with the necessary social defenses against the nonresolution of these antisocial impulses. For this reason, the initiatory theme is continually found in folklore, games, literature, and other similar phenomena. The artist seizes upon this motif because he inwardly realizes the basic emotional significance of these themes for all members of the culture.

The play *Titus Andronicus* is unusually rich in material for psychoanalytic investigation. However, in this essay, I shall confine myself merely to the psychoanalytic study of the play's origin, and will not treat such material as the relation of this tragedy to the playwright's personality, or the effect of the play upon audiences.

The story of *Titus Andronicus* opens with an impending struggle for the kingship between Saturninus and Bassianus, the two sons of the dead emperor. The brothers agree to submit their dispute to Titus Andronicus, a popular general, now returning to Rome from a victorious war with the Goths.

Andronicus enters, wearing laurel boughs, and sorrowfully relates that, of his twenty-five sons, all but four have been killed in wars for Rome. Against the anguished entreaties of Tamora, the captured

Queen of the Goths, Andronicus agrees to the sacrifice of her son, in order to propitiate the soul of his own son, recently killed in battle.

Titus Andronicus names Saturninus as emperor. Saturninus chooses Lavinia, Titus' daughter, for his wife, but she is stolen by Bassianus, who claims her as rightfully his. In attempting to thwart the abduction, Andronicus kills Mutius, his son. Saturninus marries Tamora, who seeks vengeance upon Andronicus. Demetrius and Chiron, sons of Tamora, plot to seduce Lavinia; and Aaron, Tamora's paramour, devises a scheme to aid them.

Bassianus and Lavinia discover Tamora and Aaron at a secret tryst near a pit. Demetrius and Chiron kill Bassianus, and rape Lavinia, after which they cut off her hands and her tongue, to prevent her from revealing the identity of the criminals. Meanwhile, Aaron leads two of Andronicus' sons to the pit where Bassianus' body lies. The emperor discovers them there, and believes them to have commited the murder. Aaron tells Andronicus that his two sons will not be executed if he sends his hand. Titus permits his hand to be cut off, but receives only the heads of his sons in return.

Lucius, the last surviving son of Titus Andronicus, is banished from Rome. Raising an army among the Goths, he marches on Rome; on the way, he captures Aaron with Tamora's illegitimate child.

Andronicus invites Saturninus and Tamora to a banquet. Titus has meanwhile killed Demetrius and Chiron, and has baked them into a pie, which is served and eaten by Tamora, their mother. After the killing of Lavinia, Tamora, Andronicus, and Saturninus, the only remaining son of Titus, Lucius, becomes emperor of Rome.

The following major episodes occur in the tragedy of *Titus Andronicus:* the struggle between two princes for the kingship, following the death of the old king; a human sacrifice to propitiate the dead soul; a marriage by capture in which a son is killed; a rape near a pit in the ground; and a cannibalistic meal. Furthermore, all of Titus' sons are gradually killed, with the exception of the last, who succeeds to the kingship.

The Ritual Origin of the Play

I shall now attempt to show that this plot can be traced back to the ancient Greek myths of Pelops and the Rape of Persephone, both of which were enacted frequently in antiquity as ritual dramas.

In the story of Pelops, related by Pindar, Pelops engages in a chariot race, in order to win his bride, the daughter of the king Oinomaos. Oinomaos has already killed thirteen suitors, but he is overcome by Pelops, who carries off his daughter in a chariot.

In Francis Macdonald Cornford's interpretation,[15] the myth of Pelops is composed of at least two distinct ritual features: the contest between the old and the new king, ending in the death of the older, and the succession of the younger to the kingdom; and the carrying off of the bride, with the aim of escaping the pursuing father, i.e., a flight, such as often occurs in marriage by capture.

Both of these features are present in *Titus Andronicus*.

Oinomaos, interpreted by Cornford as a magician-king controlling the rain and the weather, is analogous to the King of the Wood at Nemi, who mated with the mother goddess and defended his office against all comers, until finally defeated and superseded by a successful combatant. The first kings were simply the fathers, and the struggle for the kingship was the oedipal conflict.[16]

Thus, the above similarity between the myth of Pelops and the plot of *Titus Andronicus* takes us back to the primal horde. The death of most of Titus' sons, one of whom he kills himself, fits in with this material.

The parallelism between the plot of *Titus Andronicus* and the primal crime and puberty rites is increased when we consider the last part of the legend of Pelops, which contains a story of the banquet of Tantalus.

Invited by the gods to eat nectar and ambrosia at their table, Tantalus asked them in return to a banquet. Tantalus, as the last course, served the flesh of his son Pelops, whom he had cut in pieces and boiled in a cauldron. The deities were taken unaware; and one of them, Demeter, ate of the horrible dish. Zeus then ordered that the flesh should be put back into the cauldron, and the child restored whole and healthy.

The eating of children continually recurs in connection with the succession to the kingdom in the house of Tantalus. There is reason to believe that the Feast of Tantalus was Kronian in nature, commemorating how Kronos became king. These religious ceremonies survived in the myths and dramas of the Romans, particularly in Seneca, providing a source for plots for Elizabethan playwrights.

This would explain the fact that in *Titus Andronicus* the cannibalistic meal is followed by the death of Andronicus, and the accession of his son to the kingship.

Cornford interpreted the Tantalus feast as a ritual of New Birth, as the second birth of the child, following purification at puberty. Such initiation rituals formed the core of the cult of the Great Mother and her attendant Kouretes, which was widespread all along the coast of Asia Minor, and which was also established at the hill of Kronos at Olympia. Initiated men were also called the "Bacchoi." The cult of the Kouretes, the religion of Dionysos, and the ritual of Zagreus are substantially one. As has been stated, the mock slaying, dismemberment, and eating of the neophyte is a phenomenon frequently encountered in tribal initiation ceremonies all over the world.

Cornford concluded that the entire Pelops story stems from a ritual to determine who was to be the next year-god. The Feast of Tantalus was part of the victor's inauguration ceremony, consisting of his death and resurrection, followed by a sacred marriage, the King and Queen embodying the powers of fertility in nature.

All of these features are to be found in *Titus Andronicus*. In particular, the struggle for the kingship, the eating of Demetrius and Chiron, and the proclaiming of Lucius as emperor, closely parallel the ancient Greek ritual. Indeed, many writers have contended that the form of the tragedy itself arose from the primitive enactment, in early Greece, of the death and resurrection of Dionysos. According to Cook, "the boiling and eating of Pelops were for centuries regarded as among the most popular of all tragic themes."[17]

Psychoanalytically, the plot of *Titus Andronicus* may be interpreted from either of the two following standpoints: (1) as a dramatic re-enactment of the circumstances in the primal horde, in which the father kills all of his male progeny, until vanquished by the youngest, who then comes into possession of the females and becomes leader of the horde, after murdering and eating the father; or (2) as the survival, through the centuries, of the primitive death-and-resurrection ceremony at an initiation or inauguration. Possibly we may regard the rituals from which *Titus Andronicus* stemmed as overdetermined, in which case both interpretations would be simultaneously correct. Or, following Theodor Reik's hypothesis in "The Puberty Rites of Savages," we might regard the dramatic ceremonies at initiation rites as

reenactments of the primal crime, but with the son, in the later Dionysian rites, taking the place of the father, and atoning for the guilt
of the brother-horde:

> The powerful motive which struggles for expression in the
> Dionysian celebrations and in the earliest Greek tragedy,
> namely, the rebellion, based on incestuous impulses, of the
> son against the father and its tragic expiation, has remained
> the real theme of all dramatists from the *Oedipus* of Sopho-
> cles up to the present day.[18]

The rape of Lavinia at a pit in the woods also has its counterpart
in ancient Greek ritual. The story runs that the youthful Persephone
was in the meadow, when the earth gaped open, and Pluto issued forth
from the abyss, and carried her off to the gloomy subterranean world.
Her mother, Demeter, sorrowfully sought her in vain, and the corn
would grow no more, until Zeus commanded Pluto to return Persephone.

This myth was regularly enacted in the sacred dramas at Eleusis.
Most authorities regard Persephone as a personification of the corn,
which spends part of the year under the ground, and the remainder
of the time with the living. The fact that, in the Shakespearian tragedy,
the rape of Lavinia is carried out near a pit presents a striking similarity to the ancient ritual, in which Persephone is ravished, and taken
to the underworld by Pluto. According to Gaster, seasonal ceremonies
form the basic nucleus of dramatic forms.[19] In my paper on the Eleusinian Mysteries, I offered the hypothesis that the Persephone ritual
was a survival, in ancient Greece, of primitive female puberty rites,
in which defloration took place. I also sought to connect these adolescent defloration rituals with Freud's hypothesis of the primal crime
and with Reik's work on puberty rites.

All of the salient features of *Titus Andronicus* are now seen to have
been present in the two Greek rituals which have been mentioned.
Both religious rites were popular and widespread dramas. What is
particularly remarkable is the fact that the rituals of the Rape of
Persephone and the death and resurrection of Dionysos comprised the
sacred dramas regularly performed in the Eleusinian Mysteries.

The Eleusinian Mysteries, which exerted an enormous influence upon the development of Christianity,[20] consisted of two separate rituals. The first, enacted in Agra, reenacted the myth of Zagreus (Dionysos). The second, called the Greater Mysteries, whose basis was the story of Persephone and Demeter, was celebrated at Eleusis. Both mysteries, Lesser and Greater, constituted a single initiatory process, the Lesser Mysteries being necessary before full initiation at Eleusis. *Titus Andronicus* is thus the survival of a male and female puberty rite of primitive origins, which survived in classical Greece in the Eleusinian Mysteries.

Ovid's "Metamorphoses"

According to the hypothesis offered here, Shakespeare or one of his contemporaries drew the plot of *Titus Andronicus* either from a classical writer or from an Italian play. It is quite possible that Ovid may have been this source, since the *Metamorphoses* is mentioned in Act IV, Scene 1 of the tragedy. Indeed, Book IV of Ovid's *Metamorphoses* contains a good deal of material on the basis of which an Elizabethan could have constructed the plot of *Titus Andronicus*. In one of the recounted stories, King Tereus raped his wife's sister, Philomela, and tore out her tongue to prevent her from revealing his identity. Philomela, kept hidden by Tereus, managed to send a message to her sister, Procne, who searched for her. As revenge upon the king, Procne cut the throat of Tereus' son:

> . . . and they cut up the body still warm and quivering with life. Part bubbles in brazen kettles, part splutters on spits; while the whole room drips with gore.

Procne then served this meal to her husband who unknowingly ate it. Here, then, we have the main episodes of *Titus Andronicus*—the rape and cutting out of the ravished girl's tongue, and the serving to the king of his sons in a banquet. Other stories in Book VI of the *Metamorphoses* bear similarities to other incidents in the Shakespearian play.

If *Titus Andronicus* was based on Ovid, may we still presume a ritual origin for its plot? The answer is affirmative. The above tale from Ovid obviously bears a strong resemblance to the Greek rituals we have spoken of. Cook said that it is very probable that Ovid drew upon earlier sources for many of the stories in his *Metamorphoses*.[21] Halliday definitely regards the Philomela story as a reworking of early Greek cannibalistic ritual.[22]

If Ovid derived the story of Tereus and Philomela from the Rape of Persephone and the dismemberment of Zagreus, we might expect to find traces of this ritual origin in his writings. The fact is that Ovid himself placed the scene of the Tereus and Philomela tale at the time of the Bacchic rites. When Procne, like Demeter, went in search of the ravished and hidden virgin she was clad in the ritual attire of the Dionysian revels. Her quest took place, wrote Ovid:

> . . . when the Thracian matrons were wont to celebrate the triennial festival of Bacchus. Night was in their secret; by night Mount Rhodope would resound with the shrill clash of brazen cymbals, so by night the queen went forth from her house and joined in the orgies of the god, arrayed for the mad revels.

Since the ravishment and mutilation of the virgin, as well as the cannibalistic banquet, occur in Ovid at the time of the Dionysian rites, it is likely that these ancient mysteries were the ultimate source for the stories in Book VI of the *Metamorphoses,* from which Shakespeare may have obtained the plot of his tragedy.

Notes

1. H. T. PRICE, in ALFRED HARBAGE (ed.), *Shakespeare: The Tragedies* (Englewood Cliffs, N.J.: Prentice-Hall, 1964), pp. 26-27.

1. LORD RAGLAN, *The Hero* (London: Watts and Co., 1949).
2. JESSIE WESTON, *From Ritual to Romance* (Cambridge: Cambridge University Press, 1920; New York: Peter Smith, 1941).
3. ALBRECHT DIETERICH, "Die Entstehung der Tragödie," *Archive für die Religionswissenschaft,* 2:163-193, 1908.

4. WILLIAM RIDGEWAY, *The Dramas and Dramatic Dances of Non-European Races* (Cambridge: Cambridge University Press, 1915).

5. JANE HARRISON, *Themis* (Cambridge: Cambridge University Press, 1927).

6. GILBERT MURRAY, "Excursus on the Ritual Forms Preserved in Greek Tragedy," in HARRISON, *op. cit.*, pp. 341-363.

7. FRANCES MACDONALD CORNFORD, "The Origin of the Olympic Games," in HARRISON, *op. cit.*, pp. 212-259.

8. G. WILSON KNIGHT, *Principles of Shakespearean Production* (New York: The Macmillan Company, 1936).

9. WILLIAM H. DESMONDE, "The Eleusinian Mysteries," *Journal of the Hillside Hospital, 1*:204-218, 1952. The psychoanalytic interpretations made in this paper are written from the standpoint of Reik's theory of the significance of puberty rites. However, this does not preclude the possibility of interpretations from alternative points of view, as for example those expressed in BRUNO BETTELHEIM's *Symbolic Wounds* (Glencoe, Illinois: The Free Press, 1954).

10. HUTTON WEBSTER, *Primitive Secret Societies* (New York: The Macmillan Company, 1908).

11. ANDREW LANG, *Myth, Ritual and Religion*, II (London: Longmans, 1906).

12. A. VAN GENNEP, *Les Rites de Passage* (Paris: Librairie Critique, 1909).

13. HARRISON, *op. cit.*

14. Shakespeare's authorship of the play has been contested.

15. CORNFORD, *op. cit.*

16. I have discussed the ritual for the succession to the kingship in the grove of Diana at Nemi in terms of the oedipal conflict in more detail in the paper "Psycho-Analysis and Legal Origins," *International Journal of Psycho-Analysis, 34*:52-62, 1953.

17. ARTHUR BERNARD COOK, *Zeus*, I (Cambridge: Cambridge University Press, 1914), p. 679.

18. THEODOR REIK, *Ritual: Psychoanalytic Studies* (New York: Farrar, Straus and Company, 1946), p. 163.

19. THEODOR H. GASTER, *Thespis: Ritual, Myth and Drama in the Ancient Near East* (New York: Henry Schuman, 1950).

20. V. D. MACCHIORO, *From Orpheus to Paul* (London: Constable, 1930).

21. COOK, *op. cit.*, p. 675.

22. W. R. HALLIDAY, *Indo-European Folk Tales and Greek Legend* (Cambridge: Cambridge University Press, 1933), p. 102.

The Credibility of Shakespeare's Aaron

Although the mythic and ritualistic aspects of *Titus Andronicus* have begotten the interest of three or four psychoanalytic critics, critics such as Rank, Flügel, and Desmonde,[1] the character aspects of the play have begotten almost no interest at all. This is hardly surprising, for the characters that *Titus* offers us hardly call to mind "the common progeny of mankind," and indeed, often behave so woodenly, so "suddenly," as it were, as to beget a general reaction of incredulity or even amusement. It is especially interesting, in the light of this, to examine Gordon Ross Smith's approach to the character of Aaron, not only because Mr. Smith's provocative treatment unquestionably makes a case where many have despaired of making one, but also because the blackamoor Aaron in his "inexplicable villainy" looks forward to such "inexplicable" Shakespearean villains as Iago or Goneril. Just as Mr. Desmonde's essay brings out aspects of *Titus Andronicus* that merit the close attention of those interested in Shakespeare's overall development, Mr. Smith's essay makes it clear that even where early Shakespearean characterization appears on the surface to be naïve and improbable there may be valid (and fascinating) explanations of behavior rooted firmly in the text of the play. I am not, of course, suggesting that the jump from Aaron to Iago is a small one; I am suggesting, rather, that it may be more accurate to speak not of a jump but of a development.

What Smith contends is essentially this: The terrible, remorseless villainy that Aaron indulges in throughout much of the action is not incompatible with the tender, fatherly affection he displays toward his bastard son, and the reason for this lies in Aaron's color. That is to say, because the universe of *Titus Andronicus* automatically couples black and bad together, Aaron can behave villainously and at the same time fulfill rather than disappoint the expectations of those around him, the disappointment of expectation being to psychoanalysis the source of guilty feelings. Thus the total absence of conscience and the presence of real devotion are in Aaron's case compatible. And not only compatible, but even reminiscent of actual cases described in the writings of the European criminologist, Hans Brennecke.

M. F.

he usual opinion of *Titus Andronicus* has been that it is crowded with grotesque characters and senseless horrors which destroy the dramatic illusion and divert the audience into an amused suspension of belief. Professor Stoll's comment upon Aaron is typical: "Fee, faw, fum! A completer product there could not be of . . . dualistic . . . thinking. . . . This is man . . . thrust beyond the pale of the species."[1]

It is not my intention here to try to reverse the general opinion. The faults of the play are too many and obvious. Rather, I should like only to suggest that the character of Aaron may be worth more serious attention than has commonly been given it.

In spite of the opinions of such distinguished twentieth-century critics as E. E. Stoll and Wilson Knight, I still think it a legitimate function of criticism to determine the nature of the characters in a dramatic work. The extravagance of some nineteenth-century critics in analyzing character from a succession of dubious inferences and the extreme divergence of conclusion exhibited by such writers as Georg Brandes and Stopford Brooke have to many people made the character approach seem spurious and futile. But although this particular function of criticism has been driven out of fashion, it remains a practical necessity during the production of a Shakespearian play, as the work of Granville-Barker shows clearly enough, and it cannot be an irrelevant approach unless one has abandoned the principle that comedy and tragedy should be believable. To abandon that principle is to reduce all drama to the levels of power and significance characteristic

"The Credibility of Shakespeare's Aaron" by Gordon Ross Smith. Reprinted with permission from *Literature and Psychology*, X (1960), 11-13.

of farce and spectacle. Such an attitude seems to me essentially frivolous, and while I don't mind a critic's being frivolous, I will not admit that his position carries with it an inherent aesthetic superiority.

The character of Aaron is usually thought of as two incompatible layers ill-laminated under the arbitrary pressure of dramaturgic incompetence. Evident first is an infinite capacity for senseless evil-doing. Aaron is the energetic mastermind implementing Tamora's ill-will. Tamora has her reasons, evident enough to the audience, but Aaron is apparently evil without cause. But when Aaron is presented with his child, the audience is presented with his other layer. He loves the child and its color right off, cuddles the infant, protects it, hides it, and finally, to preserve it, confesses his crimes, apparently with considerable enjoyment.

Such a combination of qualities in a dramatic figure may seem insulting to reason and common sense, but on the other hand we haven't enough evidence from the text for reason to be insulted unless the reasoner himself supply certain assumptions about human character that essentially beg the question. As for common sense, that is merely what we are used to; it has no authority over and against empirical evidence.

Empirical evidence for a character type not identical with but certainly comparable to Aaron has been presented by the European criminologist Hans Brennecke. His lengthy report has been summarized by the American criminologist Walter Reckless as follows:

> The particular case . . . is that of a primitive unfeeling personality, who has lost respect for property and life. Without remorse he passed through police and court handling, made no confession, and defended himself coolly. He showed no trace of guilty feelings and shame. After he was freed from detention, he committed thefts and declared to his accomplices that he would commit a new murder. After exposure of his career and life at home, he went away, found work, married, and became a father. In the new circumstances nobody was suspicious of him, but after much mental conflict he finally confessed the deed to his wife. Brennecke tries to explain why, and in so doing turns to psychoanalytic formulations. Was it the love of the child and his father-love which caused the remorse? Brennecke thinks so. The

psychic breakdown and the mental depression following his confession show how great was his repression. But after this period, the man relapses into his original character, cold and unfeeling.[2]

Objectively speaking, a character in a play is only a group of ideas, not a living person. But the character of a living person is largely a mystery, even to himself, and in dealing with living persons we deal chiefly with our ideas of them. We speculate about the character and motivations of relatives, friends, and acquaintances, even while we know that we may be only half right, or quite mistaken, and we are often forced by the nature of human knowing to respond not to a person as he really is (something we cannot know), but to our ideas of him. In our thinking about living people we deal not with demonstrable entities but with disconnected scraps of evidence that achieve coherence and meaning only through the operation of our own ideas; our "knowledge" of a living person is therefore only a system of ideas. Similarly, a dramatic character is some kind of group of ideas—perhaps only a personification of an abstract idea, perhaps a satiric idea, perhaps the dramatist's report of someone he has encountered, perhaps an amalgam of his observations of several types he has seen or read of. A dramatic character may be quite as "real" a group of ideas; i.e., may have as close a correspondence in objective reality as any we entertain of someone we think we know but don't. On the grounds of the desirability of always dealing with reality, one may as legitimately speculate about a dramatic figure as about a living person; in both cases we are dealing with ideas of people, not with people, and in either case the ideas may or may not have a correspondence in those objective realities that confront but ultimately elude us. I therefore offer the following interpretation of Aaron not as the sole right or possible one but as an interpretation of Shakespeare's dramatic conception which would justify our thinking the character of Aaron to have some objective truth as a portrait of an infrequent but recurrent human type. Certainly any of several other interpretations might also be selected by an actor undertaking the role.

Like Brennecke's criminal, Aaron feels no guilt over his crimes and wishes to commit more, is much affected by the birth of his child, makes a subsequent confession, and thereafter continues his criminal indifference. But Aaron differs in showing no remorse, and the reason he shows none can be inferred from Hamlet's "mole of nature" speech (*Hamlet,* I. iv. 23-38), and can be speculatively elaborated from more modern knowledge.

The text of the play does not oblige us to accept Aaron's evil-doing as motiveless. To a medieval or Elizabethan audience the devil had commonly been represented as black, and by backward association we may suppose a black man a devil. Certainly the other characters of the play, good and bad alike, despise and loathe Aaron's color and call him a fiend. Although Aaron has been detested for his color by the other characters and derided to his face, he himself justifies and accepts his color. But along with his blackness supposedly went ill-doing, and he accepted that too, thereby at once conforming to what was thought of him and revenging himself on those who had thought it and who by so doing had excluded him from social acceptance just as surely as Shylock had been excluded. His love for his child and the military future he plans for it also demonstrate some such attitudes. The only good and all the evil in his character spring from these same circumstances of his being. The pattern thus becomes the well-known phenomenon of a person's becoming what he was thought by the people around him to be. Aaron could not change his blackness, and so he accepted himself for what he was—an attitude in itself and thus far a mentally healthy one. But since evil-doing was universally thought to go along with blackness, he was obliged by the principle of the looking-glass image to accept both. In Hamlet's words, Aaron did also "in the general censure take corruption/From that particular fault." Black and bad were what he was. Because for him they were right and proper, no punishment of ego by superego could occur, and hence no remorse.

Whether Shakespeare could have so understood Aaron is relevant only if one supposes that Shakespeare could not make a report of a character he had encountered or could not incorporate a recollection of some living character into his dramatic fabric. No grounds exist for any such supposition. To think that a character presented on the stage before the time of Freud cannot be analyzed in Freudian terms is no more reasonable than to suppose that the appearance of disease caused by bacterial infection could not have been described before the time of Pasteur. Surface appearances can be described even though underlying causes be unknown. The objection to Freudian analysis of Shakespearian characters formerly sprang from a denial of the validity of Freudian concepts and a neglect or ignorance of the empirical bases of Freudian formulations. More recent objections have usually been generalized from some far-fetched application of Freudian theory that does not itself invalidate the Freudian approach. How much of the foregoing analysis Shakespeare consciously understood, how much he vaguely sensed, how much he hit upon by sheer accident we cannot know. All we have is a character who, however bizarre, still stands up, wobblingly erect from some kind of truth in him.

Whether this interpretation would be effective upon a stage would depend upon the skill of the actor playing the part, the size of the theater, the possibility of conveying nuances, the interests of the audience, whether naïvely antiquarian or modern, and if the latter, whether sophisticated or popular, and certainly much else besides. For some people this interpretation would be reprehensible and "not Shakespeare." For others it might be the only way to make Aaron once again alive. But whether one accept the foregoing speculations or not, it must be granted that the character of Aaron roughly parallels the surface of the character reported by Brennecke and therefore that Aaron is not merely an impossible fabrication beyond the pale of the species.

Notes

1. OTTO RANK, *Das Inzest-Motiv in Dichtung und Sage* (1912) (2nd ed.; Leipzig: Franz Deuticke, 1926), pp. 209, 367n.; J. C. FLÜGEL, "A Note on the Phallic Significance of the Tongue and of Speech," *International Journal of Psycho-Analysis,* 6:209-215, 1925.

1. ELMER EDGAR STOLL, *Shakespeare Studies, Historical and Comparative in Method* (New York: The Macmillan Company, 1927), p. 345.
2. WALTER RECKLESS, *Criminal Behavior* (New York: McGraw-Hill Book Company, 1940), pp. 212-213.

Romeo's Dream and the Paradox of Literary Realism

Although *Romeo and Juliet* is one of Shakespeare's most popular plays, and although it contains elements that would seem to be of considerable interest to psychoanalysis (I am thinking here of the suicides and the parent-child conflicts generally), it has not attracted much attention from analytic critics. Menninger commented upon the lovers' impulsiveness; Reik analyzed briefly the nature of Romeo's love for Juliet; Fliess dissected a couple of the play's speeches for psychoanalytic significances,[1] and that is about as far as it went until Norman N. Holland decided to turn his attention to the play.

Focusing upon what he calls "one of the least conspicuous of the invented dreams in literature," Holland raises a number of conspicuous questions: Does a dream in literature lend itself to analysis in the way that "an ordinary" dream does? How is it possible, without the tools available to the professional interpreter under normal circumstances, to correctly interpret a literary dream? Is the literary critic with analytic interests wise enough to explicate such dreams realistically? Precisely what is the significance of *this* dream of Romeo's in *this* play of Shakespeare's?

Holland supplies answers to the first two of these questions, by pointing out that Romeo's dream does in fact manifest all of the characteristics ordinarily associated with dreams in real life and by demonstrating that the dream can be approached from two perspectives commonly used in analytic practice, namely, associations known to the analyst, which the dreamer does not supply, and the interpretation of symbolism. In answering his final two queries, Holland lifts some critical mists and brings us closer to the essence of Shakespeare's conception. He states, in the first place, that realistic interpretation of psychological phenomena in literature, phenomena such as Romeo's dream, is of prime importance insofar as it can help us to know how the members of the audience (who respond to plays realistically whether we allow them to or not) will understand the text that is being presented to them. And in short, Holland realizes, as too few critics do, that a play is not simply a made thing but a performed thing as well and that we cannot hope to criticize it thoroughly until we understand the way in which it functions in performance. Secondly, he demonstrates that Romeo's dream, analytically interpreted, throws light not only upon Romeo's character but also, through its ironic reversal of reality, upon the ironic essence of the tragedy as a whole. Holland makes his psychoanalytic data *interpretive* in the broadest sense and thus highlights the way in which psychoanalytic findings can, ideally, work.

M. F.

nvented dreams can be interpreted in the same way as real ones." That statement of Freud's seems natural enough, I suppose, once we have gotten used to the idea of a continuum between the making of dreams in sleep and the processes of waking creativity. Yet, from a literary point of view, it remains an astonishing statement. A real dream preserves sleep, expresses a wish, and fulfills it in fantasy; its form and content are biologically and psychologically determined in the mind of the dreamer. A dream in literature, however, serves typically to give a prophecy or insight, to introduce a symbol or theme, or any of a dozen purposes quite alien to those of a real dream. Unlike a real dream, an invented dream is determined not by the wishes of the "dreamer," or only secondarily and indirectly so, but by the author's imagination. Yet, Freud insists, invented dreams can be interpreted like real ones—as though a realism forced itself willy-nilly on a writer once he decided to invent a dream for one of his characters, surely a very odd idea.

Like so many odd ideas, it began with Jung. In the summer of 1906, Jung called Freud's attention to a novel in which there were a number of dreams and fantasies attributed to the hero, and Jung raised the question whether these invented or artificially constructed dreams could be analyzed in the same way as ordinary dreams. Freud took up the challenge, and the result was his study published in 1907, *Delusion and Dream in Wilhelm Jensen's "Gradiva"* in which he showed that the fictional dreams did indeed function like real dreams. In a 1909 footnote to *The Interpretation of Dreams,* in his *History of the Psy-choanalytic Movement* (1914), in his *Autobiographical Study* (1925),[1] he repeated his statement that artificial dreams could be analyzed or interpreted in the same way as regular ones, making it clear that this insight was one of the original paths from his under-standing of the dream-work to his analysis of artistic creativity and imaginative writing. All right, then. Invented dreams stand as one of the key points in the continuum between dreaming and the creative imagination in general; but why should the dream in a work be realistic when (often) the whole work is not?

One of the least conspicuous of the invented dreams in literature is Romeo's three-line recounting of a dream just before he learns of Juliet's supposed death. A tidy little dream, it raises precisely the question of realism involved. That is, *Romeo and Juliet* is a highly stylized play, not formally realistic (in Ian Watt's sense) like a mod-ern novel (say, *Gradiva*) where an invented dream would indeed be likely to resemble a real one. Rather, *Romeo and Juliet* gives us a pair of teen-agers capable of composing (jointly!) an impromptu son-net as they meet. It is hardly likely so talented a poet as Romeo would content himself with a mere ordinary dream. He tells it, in any case, in iambic pentameters, and few psychoanalysts, I expect, are lucky enough to have such poetic patients.

Nevertheless, according to Freud, we can consider such a dream realistically. To do so, however, we will need to know its background. We must establish both the context in which the dreamer dreamed the dream and a timetable of the events which may appear in it as day-residue.

Considered realistically, our dreamer finds himself in a cultural situ-ation which puts a premium on aggressive, hostile behavior. The cul-tural group with which he is most closely identified is preoccupied with sex, but rather as a topic for amusement, as something fit for servants, crude, low, funny. Romeo is exactly and squarely on the outs with this cultural pattern. A rather dreamy character, he seems to care only for romantic love, not for the fighting, quarreling, and fornication which are the local amusements in Verona. And his friends, Benvolio and Mercutio, and his mentor, Friar Laurence, ridicule and criticize him for this dreamy, romantic quality.

Romeo dreamed the dream in question on a Tuesday night. As of Sunday morning, he was in love with Rosaline, who, unfortunately for him, had taken a vow of chastity. Sunday night, he crashed the Capulets' party where he met Juliet and promptly fell in love with her. Knowing that their families would disapprove of the match, he and Juliet plan to marry secretly the next day, Monday. They do so, but on his way home from this secret marriage ceremony, Monday afternoon, Romeo fails to avoid a fight with one of his wife's relatives, kills him, and as a result is banished. He stays around long enough, however, to consummate the marriage on Monday night, and he makes his getaway Tuesday morning.

On Tuesday night, he has this dream:

> If I may trust the flattering truth of sleep,
> My dreams presage some joyful news at hand:
> My bosom's lord sits lightly in his throne;
> And all this day an unaccustom'd spirit
> Lifts me above the ground with cheerful thoughts.
> *I dreamt my lady came and found me dead;*
> Strange dream, that gives a dead man leave to think!
> *And breath'd such life with kisses in my lips,*
> *That I reviv'd, and was an emperor.*
> Ah me! how sweet is love itself possess'd,
> When but love's shadows are so rich in joy!
> (V.i.1-11)

At this point his servant turns up, and Romeo cries:

> News from Verona! How now, Balthasar!
> Dost thou not bring me letters from the friar?
> How doth my lady? Is my father well?
> How fares my Juliet?
> (V.i.12-15)

Balthasar tells him of Juliet's supposed death, and, after one more request, "Hast thou no letters to me from the friar?" Romeo resolves—

> Well, Juliet, I will lie with thee tonight.
> Let's see for means: O mischief! thou art swift
> To enter in the thoughts of desperate men.
> I do remember an apothecary, . . .
> (V.i.34-37)

And the tragedy proceeds to its medicinal catastrophe.

The normal way to interpret a dream is through the dreamer's free associations, but in trying to interpret an invented dream, we, of course, cannot have Romeo's associations. In such a case, Freud (in the *Gradiva* study) suggests, "We shall have to content ourselves with referring to his impressions, and we may very tentatively put our associations in place of his."[2] Dr. Robert Fliess in *The Revival of Interest in the Dream* notes that an analyst can contribute, independently of the dreamer's associating, two elements to the interpretation of a dream: (1) associations known to the analyst which the dreamer—for whatever reason—may not supply; (2) the interpretation of symbolism.[3]

Romeo's dream seems to have almost all the properties a dream could have. For one thing, it is prophetic, but in a special way. As any good Elizabethan could have told Romeo, the "flattering truth of sleep" is likely to be just that. Since Romeo has had a joyful dream, he should be on the lookout for trouble, but Romeo is foolish in this as in most other things; and, in Act V, we find him drinking the poison he has bought from the apothecary—he dies, saying, "Thus with a kiss I die," an exact reversal of the dream. And Juliet, when she wakes up in the tomb, tries to kiss poison from Romeo's lips, another reversal of the dream-image in which she breathed life into his lips.

The dream is also a wish-fulfillment in the most simple, direct sense. That is, the dream enables Romeo to have Juliet with him, instead of her being in Verona while he is in Mantua. The dream makes him an important, powerful man—an emperor—who would outrank not only the two fathers whose enmity has interfered with his love, but also the Prince who has banished him. The dream is a wish-fulfillment in yet another sense: it is precisely because of his romantic behavior that Romeo becomes an emperor (Juliet breathes *"such"* life in his lips "that I revived and was an emperor"), a reversal of the real situation where it is precisely Romeo's romantic love that has turned him into a stateless outcast. The dream is also a sleep-preserving dream in the sense that it gives a substitute awakening ("I revived and was an emperor") instead of letting Romeo actually wake up from what must be quite disturbing dream-thoughts: the dread of his death, the separation from Juliet, thoughts of his own helpless situation.

The striking feature of the manifest dream is Romeo's passivity. He does nothing; Juliet does everything; but he becomes an emperor precisely in doing nothing. Theodor Reik has pointed out that Romeo shows the principal characteristic of this kind of sudden, adolescent romantic attachment, a wish to replace one's self by a new self built up out of the loved person:[4]

> Call me but love, and I'll be new baptized;
> Henceforth I never will be Romeo.
>
> (II.ii.50-51)

And this building up of a new self is exactly what Romeo does in the dream: he takes a new, more powerful existence—being an emperor—out of "such life" as Juliet breathes into him.

Freud suggests that the emperor in a dream is likely to symbolize the father,[5] which entitles us to guess that the new life which Romeo takes involves some kind of identification with the father or replacing of him. Perhaps, in view of the fact that Romeo has just consummated his marriage, there is a wish quite literally to do what fathers do. Yet, we should remember that both the women Romeo loves during the course of the play, Rosaline and Juliet, are taboo—Rosaline because she has taken a vow of chastity; Juliet because she is a Capulet. It would seem that Romeo is drawn to women who are forbidden to him, either by a vowed-to God or his father's feud. In this context, Romeo's being found dead in the dream becomes the price he pays for equaling or becoming his father, for his relationship with Juliet, for having—and being had by—a forbidden woman.

Yet his being dead is a price both paid and unpaid by the dream, for "I revived." In terms of associations, Romeo's first thought when his servant arrives is of the friar, whom Romeo usually calls in the play "my ghostly father," "holy father." Further, once this servant has told him of Juliet's death, Romeo has a real "free association."

> Let's see for means: O mischief! thou art swift
> To enter in the thoughts of desperate men.
> I do remember an apothecary. . . .
>
> (V.i.35-37)

In the context of the play as a whole, the apothecary is an "unholy father," the friar's opposite number: both men are poor; both are associated with herbs; each gives a lover "poison." In effect, Romeo, after he has recounted the dream, submits himself to these two fathers (as well as his real one: "Is my father well?" he asks his servant). Before recounting the dream, he had said, "My bosom's lord sits lightly in his throne." "Bosom's lord" literally means the heart (or perhaps Cupid), but the phrasing "lord" hints (like "emperor") at a father—the heart as "king of the organs." In effect, before recounting the dream, Romeo had shaken off his father; the dream enabled him to wear his father's domination "lightly," he having, through his dreamed death, paid (and unpaid) the price of sexually "becoming a man."

Freud points out that "judgments made *after waking* upon a dream that has been remembered, and the feelings called up in us by the reproduction of such a dream, form part, to a great extent, of the latent content of the dream and are to be included in its interpretation."[6] In this dream, Romeo interrupts his account of it to comment that it is a "strange dream." He speaks of it beforehand as "the flattering truth of sleep" and afterward as "love's shadows." Freud suggests that when we come across this kind of discounting or ridicule of one's own dream, it leads back to a motif of criticism or ridicule in the dream-thoughts.[7] And Romeo has indeed been criticized and ridiculed for being a romantic, dreamy individual (most notably by Mercutio, but also by Benvolio and his parents). The dream reverses this criticism; Romeo himself becomes the ridiculing critic.

Another quality of the dream is its "thinness," its abstract quality, the lack of sensory detail or imagery. "My lady," "such life," "revived," are all rather abstract words and phrases. "Was an emperor" has no supporting detail. This thinness suggests (to me, at least) almost a reluctance to dream, an alliance of the dream-work with the ridiculing motif, as though the dream itself embodied a wish not to dream. The thinness, in effect, fulfills Romeo's wish that he were not such a dreamy person, as does his waking judgment that his own dream was "strange" and the fact that he wakes up in the dream.

Surely, though, it must be an important part of the underlying dream-thoughts that this young man, who had been a virgin as of Monday afternoon (see III.ii.13), consummated his marriage on Monday night. In describing the dream, Romeo says,

> . . . all this day an unaccustomed spirit
> Lifts me above the ground with cheerful thoughts,
>
> (V.i.4-5)

almost as though his association to the dream, his reaction to it, were itself a kind of flying dream, as though in some sense (to follow Federn's suggestion quoted by Freud) the dream signified an erection.[8] Perhaps, then, the dream involves a body-penis symbol, where the idea, "I revived and was an emperor," suggests the penis arising in an erection to its all-powerful state. "My bosom's lord sits lightly in his throne." In such a case, the kisses which breathe life into the body-penis might suggest the act of love, which so far from exhausting this inexperienced lover, gives his body-penis new life. This symbolism might seem crude indeed were there not a considerable basis for it in the play.

In a rather crucial scene, the one in which Romeo learns that he is being banished, he collapses. The bawdy Nurse looks at him lying on the ground and says,

> Stand up, stand up: stand, an you be a man:
> For Juliet's sake, for her sake, rise and stand;
> Why should you fall into so deep an O?
> (III.iii.89-90)

This should all be taken as double-entendre, the standing up standing for an erection, the "O" a quite explicit and conscious symbol for a vagina about which a number of jokes were made in this play and others.[9] Romeo has fallen into it, and he should stand up again. Later, almost the last words that Juliet says to Romeo as he leaves after their wedding-night are:

> Methinks I see thee, now thou art so low,
> As one dead in the bottom of a tomb.
> (III.v.55-56)

This, after their wedding-night, echoes not only the body-penis symbolism, but also the symbol of sexual consummation as a falling or dying, repeated over and over again in this tragedy of a "death-marked love." Earlier, for example, the friar has said,

> The earth that's nature's mother is her tomb.
> What is her burying grave, that is her womb.
> (II.iii.9-10)

This same "womb-tomb" equation occurs in Romeo's line as he plans suicide immediately after recounting the dream: "Well, Juliet, I will lie with thee tonight." Again, in the final scene, Romeo looks at Juliet's tomb and speaks of it as

> Thou detestable maw, thou womb of death,
> Gorg'd with the dearest morsel of the earth, . . .
>
> (V.ii.45-46)

His linking of womb and tomb and maw or mouth reminds us that there is a considerable oral element in Romeo's dream. A mother is an obvious person for giving life into the lips of an infant, and Romeo's term, "my lady," for Juliet could refer to his mother as well as to his later love. In other words, we could say that Romeo's dream represents still another kind of reversal. The dream of his own death reverses his coming death and turns Romeo into one newly born, receiving life (milk) in his lips. We can see this facet most clearly by one of the techniques of interpretation Freud suggests: reversing the temporal sequence of the manifest dream.[10] At first, Romeo would be the demanding child-emperor; then, his "mother" responds by giving "life" into his lips; then he relaxes into sleep—is "dead." And this oral element of the dream would illustrate Bertram Lewin's recent construct: the dream-screen—the idea that the act of dreaming is itself an hallucination of the breast and the act of waking up (here, "I revived") is a relinquishing of the breast.[11]

In short, Romeo's dream can be analyzed with all the armamentarium of modern psychoanalytic dream-interpretation—it is as real a dream as a dream can be, although it occurs in one of the most formal, stylized, and artificial of Shakespeare's plays. And this is the paradox of literary realism, that highly realistic events can exist in the highly formal, unreal atmosphere of a work of art: an imaginary garden with real toads in it, as though an early creative movement toward shaping and order were canceled by a subsequent impulse toward verisimilitude.

The above analysis is something, too, in the nature of a recantation if so large, even pompous, a term can be applied to a matter both so small and so personal. That is, I have argued rather strenuously in the past[12] that to use psychological techniques derived from real persons and real life in analyzing fictional characters is to confuse art with life. Yet that is exactly what the analysis has done: apply psychoanalytic techniques to Romeo's dream as though he were a real person. In fact, by inferring such matters as the events of the wedding-night or Romeo's unstated fear of his father, I have violated the most basic rule of reason all self-respecting New and neo-New Critics follow—do not go beyond the words on the page.

Despite this reversal, I still feel that the proper place to apply psychoanalytic techniques is to the real minds of the audience, but I have come to accept the fact that part of that real response of the audience is to the fictional characters and events as though they were real,[13] whether or not such a response is consistent with the style of the play or the canons of New Criticism. Hence, to apply psychoanalytic techniques to the characters' minds is in fact to apply them to the audience. Verisimilitude, like beauty, is in the eye of the beholder. Realism of dream or work lies in the response, not the words of the text. We can respond to the dream as realistic even if we do not find the work as a whole realistic. Why not?

Yet it seems doubtful that any audience but one composed entirely of psychoanalytic critics would respond, consciously or unconsciously, to Romeo's dream in terms so elaborate and complicated as these. Realistic Romeo's dream may be, but surely not *this* realistic.

But equally surely, the psychoanalytic critic is entitled to his response just as much as the more conventional critic of, say, imagery is entitled to his Byzantine web woven of dozens of half-lines in subtle warp and woof. And surely the average playgoer is entitled to his response, innocent of all such subtleties, either psychoanalytic or imagistic. These responses are all legitimate, and yet, clearly, some responses must not be. There must be (to borrow a term from Ernst Kris) "stringencies" which define and limit in such analyses as this one what is idiosyncratic to the critic and what is "in the play."

In general, it now seems to me, describing individual literary characters psychologically is legitimate, provided that the description is controlled and informed by an understanding of the work as a whole. The ingenious excursions of critics psychoanalytic, historical, or imagistic must at some point return and touch the base of text. That is vague—a more exact and convenient test is to see whether the psychological description of the character (or event) can be phrased in words that can apply to the total work, be they ordinarily critical language or the technical terms of psychoanalysis.

For example, in this paper, it is a little silly to analyze Romeo's dream and come up with an interpretation that it represents a wish for unlimited sexual potency. Such a statement, by itself, has no bearing on the tragedy; it is simply a psychological curio. What would save this paper would be a final paragraph or two stating the psychology of Romeo's dream in words that can also describe the play as a whole.

In *Romeo and Juliet* as a whole, dream, as such, is an important concern, most obviously in Mercutio's "Queen Mab" speech with its view of dreams as wish-fulfilling fantasies. Further, to some extent, the entire relationship of Romeo and Juliet is treated as a dream. Their affair mostly takes place at night, for example, the balcony scene with its

> O blessèd, blessèd night! I am afeard,
> Being in night, all this is but a dream,
> Too flattering-sweet to be substantial;
> (II.ii.139-141)

and the love of Romeo and Juliet has no place in the gray morning on which the Montagues and Capulets make up. The analysis of Romeo's dream as wish-fulfilling is not at all inappropriate to the role of dreams in *Romeo and Juliet* as "the flattering truth of sleep."

There is, however, another way in which even a very elaborate account of Romeo's dream in psychoanalytic terms returns to the play as a whole. Romeo's dream prophesies (by reversal) his own death, "Thus with a kiss I die." It is also a wish-fulfillment which reverses his present precarious and loveless situation: he becomes an "emperor," a father, reversing his usual passivity. By his remarks on his own dream, he becomes himself the ridiculing critic of his own passivity and dreamless, again, a wishful reversal of his usual situation. In terms of sexual symbolism, his dream gives him an inexhaustible potency, in which intercourse simply produces new erections—presumably a reversal of his behavior on the wedding night. Finally, at the deepest level, the dream turns Romeo's own death into being newly born. He is the emperor-child-father whose mother thrusts life into his lips. In short, at every level, the dream operates by the process of reversal. It is a dream, we could say, about the power of dreams to reverse. And such an understanding must accord even with the innocent theatergoer's: to him, too, this happy dream, coming as it does just before Romeo learns of his love's death, must seem a reversal.

But the tragedy as a whole—its psychological effect—is also a reversal, for what is *Romeo and Juliet* but the most exquisite expression of the child's inverted wish for love, "Wait till I'm gone. *Then* they'll be sorry." And all through the tragedy we find oxymora and reversals: "It was the nightingale, and not the lark." Or, Capulet's lament,

> All things that we ordained festival,
> Turn from their office to black funeral;
> Our instruments to melancholy bells,
> Our wedding cheer to a sad burial feast,
> Our solemn hymns to sullen dirges change,
> Our bridal flowers serve for a buried corse,
> And all things change them to the contrary.
> (IV.v.84-90)

Friar Laurence, the *raisonneur,* sums it up:

> For naught so vile that on the earth doth live
> But to the earth some special good doth give;
> Nor aught so good but, strained from that fair use,
> Revolts from true birth, stumbling on abuse.
> (II.iii.17-20)

The action of the tragedy is the young love of Romeo and Juliet reversing their families' old hate. "My only love, sprung from my only hate!" says Juliet, and then, at the end,

> Capulet, Montague,
> See what a scourge is laid upon your hate,
> That heaven finds means to kill your joys with love.
> (V.iii.291-293)

Love springs from hate; then the love of Romeo and Juliet reverses the families' hate. The action of the tragedy is itself a reversal; its psychological effect on the audience is as well. In short, then, that one term brings into meaningful interplay Romeo's tragedy, Romeo's audience, Romeo's dream—and the reversal worked in this essay.

Notes

1. KARL A. MENNINGER, *Man Against Himself* (New York: Harcourt, Brace and Co., 1938), pp. 320-321; THEODOR REIK, *The Psychology of Sex Relations* (New York: Farrar and Rinehart, 1945), pp. 88-89; ROBERT FLIESS, *Erogeneity and Libido* (New York: International Universities Press, 1957), pp. 263-264, 274.

1. SIGMUND FREUD, *Complete Works,* ed. James Strachey (London: Hogarth Press, 1953), IV, p. 97; XIV, p. 36; XX, p. 65.
2. *Ibid.,* IX, p. 73.
3. ROBERT FLIESS, *The Revival of Interest in the Dream* (New York: International Universities Press, 1953), pp. 123-124.
4. THEODOR REIK, *A Psychologist Looks at Love* (New York: Farrar and Rinehart, 1944), p. 69.
5. FREUD, *op. cit.,* V, p. 353.
6. *Ibid.,* p. 445.
7. *Ibid.,* pp. 434-435, 444-445.
8. *Ibid.,* p. 394.
9. ERIC PARTRIDGE, *Shakespeare's Bawdy* (New York: E. P. Dutton, 1960), s. v. "O".
10. FREUD, *op. cit.,* IV, p. 328.
11. See, for example, BERTRAM D. LEWIN, "The Forgetting of Dreams," in Rudolph Loewenstein (ed.), *Drives, Affects, Behavior* (New York: International Universities Press, 1953), pp. 191-202; or, by the same author, "Reconsiderations of the Dream Screen," *Psychoanalytic Quarterly, 22*:174-199, 1953.
12. NORMAN N. HOLLAND, "Realism and the Psychological Critic: or, How Many Complexes Had Lady Macbeth?" *Literature and Psychology, 10*:5-8, 1960; "The Next New Criticism," *The Nation, 192*:339-341, 1961; "Shakespearean Tragedy and the Three Ways of Psychoanalytic Criticism," *Hudson Review, 15*:217-227, 1962.
13. See SIMON O. LESSER, *Fiction and the Unconscious* (Boston: Beacon Press, 1957), chap. VIII.

On "Julius Caesar"

It is an interesting coincidence that just as the tragedy of *Julius Caesar* appears to be constructed in two parts, so do the psychoanalytic readings of the play lend themselves to a twofold classification: the early readings focus upon the events in the first part of the play —namely, Brutus' involvement in the conspiracy and the murder of Caesar—and tend to regard these events in the light of the oedipal conflict; the later readings concentrate intensively upon the personality structure of the play's characters (especially Brutus') from the stand-point of what is best termed "ego psychology."

Of the earlier readings, which clearly reflect the overwhelming pre-occupation of the founders of psychoanalysis with the universality of the Oedipus complex, Ernest Jones's is perhaps the most suggestive and the most complete. Building upon the work of Otto Rank,[1] Jones begins by asserting that the murder of Caesar by Brutus is a variation upon the murder of the father by the son. (The king-as-father symbol is best expressed in Freud's *Group Psychology and the Analysis of the Ego* and is basic to a great many analytic readings of Shakespeare.) Jones then proceeds to point out that whereas in *Hamlet* the original father is transformed into three fathers, one good, two bad (the ghost, Claudius, and to a lesser extent Polonius are intended here), with Hamlet expressing the various attitudes of the son toward the father, in *Julius Caesar,* Caesar alone represents the original father, and the Roman nobles represent the various attitudes of the son. (Antony speaks for piety, Cassius for remorsefulness, and Brutus for rebelliousness.) Thus *Julius Caesar* becomes for Jones a "simple" play in terms of the father substitute and a "complex" play in terms of the son's behavior toward the father—a view that tends to support the majority of recent literary interpretations. Again, Jones finds it highly interesting that Shakespeare chose to suppress the many passages in his source material that indicated that Brutus was Caesar's illegitimate son and explains this suppression by referring to Shakespeare's own ambivalent attitudes. Finally, Jones postulates that the absence of the sexual element in the play is only apparent, that Brutus' love of Rome is the unconscious equivalent of his love for the mother, and that his hatred of Caesar is therefore grounded in his feeling that the mother is being abused and tyrannized over. Needless to say, Jones's reading indicates the direction from which the audience's involvement in the action may stem and demonstrates Shakespeare's continuing exploitation of oedipal themes, an exploitation that began, as we have seen, with the first of the tragedies, *Titus Andronicus*.

M. F.

he play that Shakespeare wrote next after *Hamlet* was probably *Measure for Measure,* the main theme of which Masson considers to be "mutual forgiveness and mercy."[1] *Julius Caesar,* which was probably composed the year before *Hamlet,* calls for some special consideration. Here we have a drama apparently devoid of any sexual problem or motive, and yet it has been shown, in Otto Rank's excellent analysis,[2] that the inspiration of the main theme is derived from the same complex as the one we have studied in *Hamlet.* His thesis is that Caesar represents the father, and Brutus the son, of the typical Oedipus situation. Psychoanalytic work has shown that a ruler, whether king, emperor, president, or what not, is in the unconscious mind a typical father symbol, and in actual life he tends to draw on to himself the ambivalent attitude characteristic of the son's feelings for the father. On the one hand, a ruler may be piously revered, respected, and loved as the wise and tender parent; on the other, he may be hated as the tyrannical authority against whom all rebellion is justified. Very little experience of life is enough to show that the popular feelings about any ruler are always disproportionate, whether they are positive or negative. The most complete nonentity may, if only he finds himself in the special position of kingship, be regarded either as a model of all the virtues, to whom all deference is due, or as a heartless tyrant whom it would be a good act to hurl from his throne. We have pointed out earlier the psychological origin of revolutionary tendencies in the primordial re-

"On *Julius Caesar*" by Ernest Jones. Reprinted from *Hamlet and Oedipus* by Ernest Jones, M.D. By permission of W. W. Norton & Company, Inc. Copyright © 1949 by Ernest Jones.

bellion against the father, and it is with these that we are here mainly concerned. In Hamlet the two contrasting elements of the normal ambivalent attitude towards the father were expressed towards two sets of people; the pious respect and love towards the memory of his father, and the hatred, contempt, and rebellion towards the father-substitutes, Claudius and Polonius. In other words, the original father has been transformed into two fathers, one good, the other bad, corresponding with the division in the son's feelings. With Caesar, on the other hand, the situation is simpler. He is still the orginal father, both loved and hated at once, even by his murderer. That the tyrant aspect of Caesar, the Caesar who has to be killed by a revolutionary, was in Shakespeare's mind associated with Polonius, another "bad" father who has to be killed, is indicated by a curious identification of the two in the *Hamlet* play: Polonius when asked what part he had ever played answers "I did enact Julius Caesar: I was killed i' the Capitol; Brutus killed me" (III.ii.8-9). Those who always underestimate the absolute strictness with which the whole of our mental life is determined will pass this by; to those, however, who are accustomed to trace out the determining factors in unsparing detail it serves as one more example of how fine are the threads connecting our thoughts. Polonius might have quoted any other part on the stage, but it is an unescapable fact that he chose just this one.

Appropriate estimates disclose the curious fact, first pointed out by Craik,[3] that Shakespeare made more frequent allusions to Caesar in his works than to any other man of all past time; of all men in the range of history Caesar seems to have been the one who most fascinated his imagination. There are so many passages mocking at Caesar's hook nose and tendency to brag that Masson[4] concludes these must have constituted special features in Shakespeare's recollection of him. These exhibitionistic symbols accord well with the fact that the boy's "repressed" antipathy towards his father always centers about that part of his father whose functioning most excites his envy and jealousy.

That the two noble characters of Hamlet and Brutus have a great deal in common has often been remarked.[5] The resemblances and differences in which the "son's" attitudes toward the "father" come to expression in the two plays are of very great interest. In *Julius Caesar* they are expressed by being incorporated in three different "sons."

Thus, as Rank points out,[6] Brutus represents the son's rebelliousness, Cassius his remorsefulness, and Antony his natural piety,[7] the "father" remaining the same person. In *Hamlet,* on the other hand, the various aspects of the son's attitude are expressed[8] by the device of describing them in regard to three different "fathers," the love and piety towards his actual father, the hatred and contempt towards the father-type Polonius, and the conflict of both towards his uncle-father, Claudius (conscious detestation and unconscious sympathy and identification, one paralyzing the other).[9] The parricidal wish in Shakespeare is allowed to come to expression in the two plays by being concealed in two different ways. In *Hamlet* it is displaced from the actual father to the father-substitutes. In *Julius Caesar* there is supposed to be no actual blood relation between the two men, the "son" and "father" types. But a highly significant confirmation of the interpretation here adopted is the circumstance that Shakespeare in composing his tragedy entirely suppressed the fact that Brutus was the actual, though illegitimate, son of Caesar;[10] this fact is plainly mentioned in Plutarch, the source of Shakespeare's plot, one which he almost literally followed otherwise.[11] Even Caesar's famous death-cry "Et tu, mi fili, Brute!" appears in Shakespeare only in the weakened form "Et tu, Brute!" Rank comments on the further difference between the two plays that the son's relation to the mother, the other side of the whole Oedipus complex, is omitted in *Julius Caesar,* whereas as we have seen, it is strongly marked in *Hamlet.* Yet even of this there is a faint indication in the former play. In his great speech to the citizens Brutus says "Not that I loved Caesar less, but that I loved Rome more" (III.ii.8-9). Now it is not perhaps altogether without interest in this connection that cities, just like countries, are unconscious symbols of the mother[12]—this being an important source of the conscious feeling of patriotism—so that the passage reads as if Brutus, in a moment of intense emotion, had revealed to his audience the unconscious motive from which his action sprang: to kill the Father who is thought to be ill-treating and tyrannizing over the Mother.

It is appropriate that in both plays the ghost of the murdered ruler appears, in one to the actual murderer (Brutus), and in the other to the avenger, i.e., would-be murderer (Hamlet). In both cases their actions lead to self-destruction. Although dramatically the ghost is another being, psychologically it represents the remorseful conscience of the murderer; in Hamlet's case they both bear the same name (an alteration in the original story introduced by Shakespeare).

Besides Shakespeare's obvious interest in Caesar, noted above, there is another set of considerations, some of which were presumably known to Shakespeare, connecting Brutus and Hamlet, and it seems likely that they constituted an additional influence in determining him to write the one play so soon after the other. They are these. Belleforest[13] pointed out some striking resemblances between Saxo's story of Amleth and the Roman legend of the younger Brutus (Lucius Junius Brutus), and it is probable that Saxo derived much of his story from the Latin sources.[14] Both Plutarch and Belleforest were certainly accessible to Shakespeare. In both cases a son has to avenge a father who had been slain by a wicked uncle who usurped the throne—for the usurper Tarquinius Superbus had slain his brother-in-law, Brutus' father, as well as Brutus' brother[15]—and in both cases the young man feigned madness in order to avoid arousing the suspicions of the tyrant, whom in both cases he finally overthrew. Of further incidental interest, though of course not known to Shakespeare, is the fact that the name Hamlet[16] has the same signification as that of Brutus, both words meaning "doltish," "stupid". . . .

There are numerous other indications of the influence of his Oedipus complex throughout Shakespeare's works, especially in the earlier ones —there are actually son-father murders in *Henry VI* and *Titus Andronicus*—but since this subject has been dealt with so exhaustively by Rank in his work *Das Inzest-Motiv in Dichtung und Sage* it is not necessary to repeat his discussion of it here.

Notes

1. OTTO RANK, *Das Inzest-Motiv in Dichtung und Sage* (1912) (Leipzig: Franz Deuticke, 1926), chap. 6.

1. D. MASSON, *Shakespeare Personally* (1914), p. 133.
2. OTTO RANK, *Das Inzest-Motiv in Dichtung und Sage* (1912) (Leipzig: Franz Deuticke, 1926), pp. 204-209.

3. GEORGE L. CRAIK, *The English of Shakespeare* (3rd. ed.; London: Chapman and Hall, 1864).

4. MASSON, *op. cit.*, p. 177.

5. See, for instance, GEORGE M. C. BRANDES, *William Shakespeare* (Copenhagen: Gyldendalske Boghandels Forlag, 1896), p. 456.

6. RANK, *op. cit.*, p. 209.

7. Against our treating Brutus, Cassius, and Antony as types in this way it may be objected that they were after all actual historical personages. But we are discussing them as they appear in Shakespeare, to whom they owe most of their life; what we know of them historically is colorless and lifeless by comparison.

8. That is, in the main. As is indicated elsewhere in the text, certain "son" aspects are also depicted by, for instance, Laertes.

9. Hamlet's contrast of the two pictures in the bedroom scene is a perfect delineation of the "good father" and "bad father" as melodramatically imagined by the infant.

10. Shakespeare's suppressed knowledge, however, seems to leak through in Brutus' apology to Antony for the murder of Caesar (III.i): "Our reasons are so full of good regard that were you, Antony, the son of Caesar [i.e., as I am], you should be satisfied."

11. DELIUS, "Cäsar und seine Quellen," *Shakespeare-Jahrbuch*, 17.

12. See, for instance, OTTO RANK, "Um Städte werben," *Zeitschrift für Psychoanalyse, 2*:50.

13. I quote from YORK POWELL in Elton's translation of Saxo's Danish history, 1894, pp. 405 ff.

14. Saxo's two main sources were the Roman ones (Livy and Valerius Maximus' "Memorabilia") and the Icelandic Hrólf Saga.

15. DIONYSIUS HALIC, *Antiquitates Romanae, 4*:67, 77, 1885.

16. See DETTER, *Zeitschrift für Deutsches Altertum, 6*:1 ff., 1892.

A Psychological Approach to "Julius Caesar"

Andrew M. Wilkinson's essay shares with the work of Jones (and ultimately with the work of Rank) one basic characteristic: a preoccupation with disguised motivation. Obviously an oedipal reading of *Julius Caesar* is going to comment significantly upon the difference between what characters *appear* to be doing and what they are *really* doing, and this is, to a large extent, precisely what Mr. Wilkinson explores. Again, if Jones's work reflects the overwhelming absorption of early psychoanalytic thinking with what we can now call the "classical Oedipus complex," then Wilkinson's essay is clearly an outgrowth of later psychoanalytic emphases on disorders of character and mechanisms of defense, emphases that ultimately led to what we presently call "ego psychology." Nor can we fail to note in an ancillary way the close connection between Mr. Wilkinson's reading of the character of Brutus, and finally of the play, and other analytic treatments such as Feldman's *Unconscious Envy in Brutus*[1] and Smith's *Brutus, Virtue, and Will*,[2] which devote themselves almost exclusively to exploring the appearance-reality motif and which underscore much in the way of self-deceptive behavior.

Wilkinson begins by suggesting that the tendency to regard Shakespearean characters exclusively in terms of their functions and to negate any psychological approach to character has simply gone too far. What was wrong with much of the psychological criticism of the past and what justified the harsh reaction to it, says the author, was that psychological critics did not really know or understand psychology. Wilkinson concludes the first section of his paper by suggesting that a psychological approach to *Julius Caesar* can provide what he calls a "unity of character."

Turning first to Caesar, Wilkinson stresses his strongly paranoid tendencies, his egocentric view of life, his fancies of persecution, his projection of guilt, his repressed homosexuality, and finally his sentimentality toward mankind, "where he is not committed." In Caesar, writes Wilkinson, the superego has become dissociated from the reality principle so that conscience is devoted to justifying the pursuit of the ego ideal that turns out to be Caesarism itself. Wilkinson goes on to point out that there is a similar lack of relationship between ideal and reality in Brutus—the ego ideal turns out to be honor, which is synonymous with Brutus's own name. No less than Caesar, the author maintains, Brutus brings about his downfall by adhering to an ideal role that he has created for himself. He believes he can support the murder and yet avoid the evil associated with it because his conscience is so egocentric, but his conscience ultimately betrays him. As for Cassius, he is in large part "the ego," the one who advances all the practical considerations; yet, and this is the point, he requires for his actions the authority that the superego provides. Thus he is overruled again and again by Brutus in a manner that would be remarkable were it not for the fact that Brutus represents to him "Rome" and the ancient virtues that he both respects and repudiates. Of the play's chief characters, only Antony is alive at the end. He survives, says Wilkinson, because he is free from the superego conflicts in which the others are involved.

M. F.

After two hundred years the Great Disintegrators were eventually discredited. It was generally felt that Shakespeare's plays were all of a piece, and that Shakespeare had probably written them. But no sooner were the Great Disintegrators out of the way than a new race of critics appeared, much more deadly because much more efficient, the Great Dismemberers. Their target was not the plays themselves but the characters in the plays.

Before they began work the plays were a throbbing menagerie of human life; they were peopled with "real men and women, fellow humans with ourselves," Falstaff's page was a "little friend to laugh with and be sorry for"; Hamlet was "a recently deceased acquaintance."[1] The Dismemberers began a fairly systematic assassination of those characters, but their knives encountered no flesh; no blood rushed out when they plucked away the cursed steel. This did not surprise them; they had suspected it all along, for "character" to them was the sum total of a number of functions, playing a part in the total effect of a play.

Thus after, say, 1930, when the *Wheel of Fire* was published, it became impossible to think of character in naturalistic terms. The girl you met at a party could not possibly be Goneril, for Goneril was a "personification," one single element in the projection of a poetic vision. Discussion from then on, insofar as it concerned character, centered on its functions. A Shakespearean character could no longer be said to act "inconsistently" for that implied a psychological unity in him which he was no longer required to possess. A man in his time

"A Psychological Approach to *Julius Caesar*" by Andrew M. Wilkinson. Reprinted with permission from *Review of English Literature*, VII (1966), 65-78.

plays many parts, and certainly the Shakespearean character had to do so. He might have a strictly specialized view of his role; if so he had better forget it, for he was now a jack of all trades. If a choric comment had to be made, a bit of narrative inserted, a symbolic attitude struck; if the curtain had to be rung up or rung down; if some scenery had to be word painted; or some particularly shameless piece of plot passed off; then he had to do it. Worst of all, by an embarrassing device known as "dramatic self-explanation"[2] he was expected to reveal his motives or future course to an audience, though his *alter ego* might well be unaware of these things.

But of course the point was that this ego, this "real self," could scarcely be said to exist any longer. Characters were thought of in terms of "layers" or "modes."[3] There was an attempt to realize imaginatively through the findings of scholarship the experience of the original audiences; and thus it was possible to discuss character in terms of the psychology of humors, or as figments in a morality pattern, but not in terms of psychological naturalism. The rediscovery of the conventions and dramatic devices of the Elizabethan Theater was, ironically enough, in danger of producing a view of character which was out of touch with the theatrical experience of a modern audience. At least in the theater the physical presence of the actor, who is visibly the same person throughout the play, provides a unity for character which neither a discredited naturalism, nor the more modern description in terms of function, seems able to do effectively.

Clearly a large debt is owed to the Great Dismemberers; those fat fleshy rioters in Dowden and Bradley had it coming. It was impossible to get a clear view of the plays for them. Nevertheless one wonders whether the reaction against any psychological approach at all hasn't gone too far. Certainly the psychological naturalists pushed their interpretations over hard in one direction—in attempting to discover the number of Lady Macbeth's children, for instance.[4] But it is arguable that in another direction they did not go far enough; that what was wrong with the psychological critics is that they did not know enough psychology; and that they equated psychology with rationalized common sense without realizing that the concepts of common sense are often many generations behind the scientific discoveries and observations on which they are based. Certainly it is worth while to look at Shakespeare in the light of more recent psychological and psychiatric theory; the example of Ernest Jones with Hamlet has been too little regarded. The present paper suggests that, for one play at least, *Julius Caesar,* this approach provides a unity of character which is part of one's experience in the theater but which eludes one in so much criticism.

Of all the characters in the play, that of Caesar himself has suffered most from the attention of the Great Dismemberers. It has been found very hard to see him as one man. There is on the one hand the stage tradition which requires a "thrasonical" Caesar; how do you reconcile this with the expectations, apparently of many members of the original audiences,[5] that he would be presented as "the noblest man who ever lived in the tide of times"? Clearly there are two Caesars here. Schücking would attempt to describe them in terms of function: that by the technique of direct self-explanation, Caesar's boasts are not so much boasts as statements of fact, the most obvious way of telling us that he *is* brave and fearless, information that in a modern play might emerge in the conversation of others about him. In criticizing Schücking, J. I. M. Stewart comes back firmly to the two Caesars: "In these modifications [of Plutarch] it appears to me that Shakespeare is creating his *two* Caesars, the popular and the deeper Caesar."[6] Two Caesars, however, is very few; in his "The Problem of *Julius Caesar"* Ernest Schanzer gives us no less than seven:

> Throughout the first half of the play then, we are given a series of images of Caesar none of which bear much resemblance, though some of them are not irreconcilable with each other. There are the two Caesars of Cassius, there is Casca's Caesar, Brutus' Caesar, Artemidorus' Caesar, and finally Antony's Caesar. But doubt is thrown in one way or another on the validity of most of these images, and to these Shakespeare adds his own presentation of Caesar, a presentation so enigmatic and ambiguous that none of the others are really dispelled by it.[7]

And yet one is emphatically not concerned to criticize the various shrewd observations outlined above; rather to look for an approach which may unify them, and Caesar. To put it another way Shakespeare

may have intended to cater for contrary renaissance expectations about
Caesar; he certainly inherited self-explanation techniques and used
them; he may well as Foakes suggests have wanted to give us seven
views of the same man (human beings are "many-sided" as we say),
but at the same time he is creating a character from all these elements,
not describable merely in terms of function, but in terms of modern
clinical psychology. In such terms Caesar is of strongly paranoid
tendency.

Paranoia[8] in its extreme state is characterized by the retention of
the logical and intellectual faculties, which create systems of delusion.
Once the fallacious premises are accepted the conclusions are inescapable; often the sufferer appears quite normal until the subject of
his delusions is touched upon. He takes an impossibly egocentric view
of life and conceives himself as having great power or importance.
He is often subject to fancies of persecution; and the guilt for his
own faults and the world's he foists off on other people, on external
events or objects. Freud considered that paranoia was characterized
primarily by repressed homosexuality, and the observed behavior of
paranoiacs in their strong reactions to their own sex, their frequent
impotence or frigidity, their poor material adjustments, bears this out.
On the other hand, towards mankind in general, where they are not
committed, they often exhibit a maudlinly sentimental benevolence.

The first scene in which Caesar appears brilliantly establishes several
of these tendencies in him. He proclaims publicly that it is Calpurnia,
not he, who has failed in their marriage:

> Forget not, in your speed, Antonius,
> To touch Calpurnia; for our elders say,
> The barren, touched in this holy chase,
> Shake off their sterile curse.

> (I.ii.6-9)

These words, Caesar's opening ones, indicate overanxiety to disclaim
responsibility; they are humiliating for a woman, and from a husband
whose friendship with a young man, Antony, has much greater significance. The "ceremony" begins, but is stopped immediately by
Caesar who has heard a voice, that of the Soothsayer, calling him.
The Soothsayer is not, obviously, a figment of his imagination, as
might be in the case of a paranoid patient; nevertheless it is notable

that Caesar is tuned to hear such a voice, even above all the din. In a sense he is his own persecutor. This hint of the persecution he expects is developed quite clearly as the procession returns. Furious that he has had to reject the crown and thus frustrated in his drive for absolute power, Caesar looks for someone on which to vent his irritation, and—in effect—on whom to pin responsibility. He sees Cassius, and the triviality of his first complaint against him—that he is not fat enough, and thinks too much—indicates the irrationality of his irritation. Antony knows what to do: in the phrase "Fear him not Caesar . . ." he tries to check Caesar's anxiety, by suggesting that it is possible for him to fear, and turn him to his other obsession by using the name "Caesar" (the actor should give it appropriate subtle emphasis). Caesar immediately assumes the role of superhuman ruler which the name represents to him, and considers the situation as a hypothesis.

> Yet if my name were liable to fear
> I do not know what man I should avoid
> So soon as that spare Cassius.
>   (I.ii.196-198)

In this way he objectifies what is really his own dilemma:

> Such men as he be never at heart's ease
> Whiles they behold a greater than themselves.
>   (I.ii.205-206)

Even so, his talk of Cassius has worried him; he is compelled to remind himself once again of his own immunity:

> I rather tell thee what is to be fear'd
> Than what I fear, for always I am Caesar.
>   (I.ii.208-209)

The fear is not laid to rest; he does not believe Antony's assurances, and asks him for his real opinion: "Tell me truly what thou think'st of him." This line is usually used as an exit line only; one has not seen a performance in which the actor stresses "truly" as a sign of Caesar's nagging anxieties. The next time we see Caesar he has been disturbed by Calpurnia's dream and seeks assurance from the augurers. By the time she appears however he has in effect put on the robes of Caesar, and identified himself with the public image of Caesarism, "Caesar shall forth." He is one of the "valiant" who never taste of death but once; he is surprised that ordinary men fear. When the bad news comes from the augurers, he becomes even more confident:

> . . . Danger knows full well
> That Caesar is more dangerous than he.
> (II.ii.44-45)

But Calpurnia's fears coincide with unacknowledged ones on Caesar's part; he allows her to prevail; and this accounts for his outburst when Decius presses him for a reason:

> The cause is in my will: I will not come;
> That is enough to satisfy the Senate.
> (II.ii.71-72)

Decius skilfully feeds Caesar's grandiose delusions and persuades him easily enough, not only by a new interpretation of the dream (the obvious flaw in which, that a whole body does not spout forth blood, passes Caesar by); but also by playing on Caesar's fear, and his fear of being thought fearful. Calpurnia gets the blame; and Caesar prepares for the Senate.

There is little need to describe in detail Caesar's conduct in the murder scene. The grand delusions of the paranoiac are all too obviously present; the claim to be the exception to the rule,

> I could be well mov'd if I were as you;
> (III.i.58)

and the assumption of Godlike status,

> I am constant as the northern star,
> (III.i.60)

and

> Hence! Wilt thou lift up Olympus?
> (III.i.73)

The identification of the man with the Caesar image he has created is complete; he refers to himself in the first person or as "Caesar" indifferently in the typical unconscious self-dramatizations of the paranoiac. Even at the moment of his death his cry is not "you have killed me" but "then fall Caesar."

For the rest what we know about Caesar comes through the mouths of the other characters. The suggestion that what we learn from these characters is in some way incompatible with what we see of Caesar is a recurring theme in criticism of the play, and leads to descriptions of the two or even the seven Caesars. Cassius suggests that Rome is coming to share Caesar's image of himself:

> Why, man, he doth bestride the narrow world
> Like a Colossus; . . .
>
> (I.ii.135-136)

He attempts to belittle him by showing him up as a poor specimen physically—as a swimmer who failed, and as a "god" who shook when he had a fever on him. In psychological terms there is no contradiction between physical weakness and great moral and intellectual drive; the one is often a form of compensation for the other. In poetic terms Caesar's physical and his mental disorder are appropriately parallel. Casca's report of the "falling sickness" contributes to the impression: Casca also speaks of Caesar's actions in refusing the crown and in offering his throat to be cut:

> If the tag-rag people did not clap him and hiss him, according as he pleased and displeased them, as they use to do the players in the theatre, I am no true man.
>
> (I.ii.255-258)

Caesar's play-acting is part and parcel of the man; it is exactly what one would expect.

Brutus knows Caesar well; he claims to be his "best lover"; his motives are disinterested. If there is another Caesar to be seen Brutus will surely disclose him to us. But his estimate is quite incredibly out of touch with the reality of Caesar as we see him.

> to speak truth of Caesar,
> I have not known when his affections sway'd
> More than his reason. . . .
>
> (II.i.19-21)

It shows us the blindness of Brutus. But the question arises, has Caesar always been so; did that "lowliness" which Brutus sees in him never form part of the character of Caesar? For Cassius says quite specifically that there has been recently a deterioration in Caesar's reason:

> he is superstitious grown of late,
> Quite from the main opinion he held once
> Of fantasy, of dreams, and ceremonies.
> (II.i.195-197)

Criticism in terms of function, in terms of spatial concepts, in terms of imagery, often pays little regard to the dimension of time; in terms of psychology everyone has a past. If one wishes to talk about the "two Caesars" one may perhaps more profitably do so in terms of the past and present Caesar.

Certainly Antony wishes to remind the people of Caesar's past achievements: "the day he overcame the Nervii" for instance. It is from Antony that we receive the most favorable impression of Caesar; and yet there is nothing in what he says about him which is in any sense fundamentally contradictory to the picture we have built up above. Further, Antony is pleading a case, and is not concerned to be scrupulous about it: he moves the people mainly by an appeal to their greed and to their pity at the sight of the wounds. His proof that Caesar was not ambitious (because he thrice refused the crown) is a false reasoning; for the rest Antony claims:

> He was my friend, faithful and just to me:
>
> He hath brought many captives home to Rome,
> Whose ransom did the general coffers fill:
>
> When the poor have cried, Caesar hath wept.
> (III.ii.87, 90-91, 93)

One may accept Caesar's friendship for Antony, whilst placing it in context of the strongly homosexual atmosphere[9] of the play; and the relationship this has to Caesar's mental disorder. Caesar's generosity to the people, both with his ransoms and in his will, is the other side of his desire for deification as the father of the people—Decius' interpretation of Calpurnia's dream which so flattered him. Caesar's weeping over the Roman poor is doubtless sincere; but it is not incompatible with the sentimentality one finds in people of paranoid tendency towards the agonies of man in general. Even without allowing for the temporal dimension Caesar is demonstrably the same person throughout the play; within that dimension the unity of his character is, one would suggest, indisputable.

> The Super, the Ego, and the dirty old Id,
> The all liv'd together in my uncle Sid;
> And through their wild incessant strife
> He led, poor man, a dreadful life.[10]

To state what happens to Caesar in more specifically psychoanalytic terms: the superego has become dissociated from the ego or reality principle, so that Caesar is indifferent to the real conditions of human life and to his own safety. The one subsystem of the superego, the ego-ideal, is equated with Caesarism, the other subsystem, conscience, is concerned to justify the pursuit of the ego-ideal. Although the conspiracy is building up against him, Caesar has several opportunities to escape, but by consulting each time the superego, not the ego, he throws them away. In the Calpurnia scene he counters her pleas with a series of sententious or boastful phrases, reflecting the attitude of an idealized self-image:

> Danger knows full well
> That Caesar is more dangerous than he.
> (II.ii.44-45)

Decius only has to appeal to this image to get his own way. Even en route to the Senate Caesar is given another chance: Artemidorus wants him to read a schedule which touches him near. The opportunity for the fine Caesarean sentiment is too tempting. With

> What touches us ourself shall be last serv'd
> (III.i.8)

Caesar places himself in the power of those who are to serve him last.

There is a similar lack of relationship between ideal and reality in the character of Brutus. Brutus has the same habit of referring to himself in the third person ("Brutus had rather be a villager . . ." etc.): his ego-ideal is "honour," which is synonymous with his own name:

> I love
> The name of honour more than I fear death
> (I.ii.88-89)

And the general opinion men hold of him confirms this:

> When you do find him, or alive or dead,
> He will be found like Brutus, like himself.
> (V.iv.24-25)

Yet Brutus' great decision, one which sets the whole action of the murder in motion, is one in which the ego triumphs over the superego.

> And, since the quarrel
> Will bear no colour for the thing he is,
> Fashion it thus; that what he is, augmented,
> Would run to these and these extremities;
> And therefore think him as a serpent's egg
> Which, hatch'd, would, as his kind, grow mischievous,
> And kill him in the shell.
> (II.i.28-34)

This decision having been made, however, the superego reasserts itself with a force which is all the more intense from the guilt of the decision. Brutus thinks that he can support the deed and yet avoid the evil associated with it; time and again practical considerations are rejected—there is to be no oath; Antony is not to be killed with Caesar; Antony is to be permitted to speak in the marketplace; no money is to be obtained for the troops "by vile means"; the battle is to be forced at Philippi. Brutus' grasp on reality is faint, typified by the infantile fantasy:

> O! that we then could come by Caesar's spirit,
> And not dismember Caesar. . . .
> (II.i.169-170)

No less than Caesar Brutus brings disaster by adherence to the ideal role which he has cast for himself.

In some sense Cassius is the ego as Brutus is the superego. It is Cassius who advances all the practical considerations, who knows the realities of Roman politics, who has no illusions. Caesar says of him:

> He is a great observer, and he looks
> Quite through the deeds of men; . . .
> (I.ii.202-203)

He does not succumb to the myth of Caesar's superego, but regards him as a "poor man," physically infirm whom only the shortcomings of the Romans have permitted to attain a quite undeserved stature. He knows how to play on Brutus, and recognizes that his "honour" is not all it seems to be:

> Well Brutus, thou art noble; yet, I see,
> Thy honourable metal may be wrought
> From that it is disposed: . . .
> (I.ii.312-314)

Each man has his price, not only Lucius Pella (IV.iii.2) but Antony himself:

> Your voice shall be as strong as any man's
> In the disposing of new dignities.
> (III.i.177-178)

For Cassius the appetite, acting prudently under the guidance of the ego, is king.

And yet Cassius needs that authority for his actions which the superego gives. He turns to Brutus as a father figure:

> O! you and I have heard our fathers say,
> There was a Brutus once that would have brook'd
> The eternal devil to keep his state in Rome,
> As easily as a king.
> (I.ii.158-159)

The conspirators are desperately anxious for approval, for "good opinion" (II.i. 114-115). Cinna (I.iii. 140-141) and Caius Ligarius (II.i.316-317) express the common yearning for Brutus. Under the circumstances it is not surprising that Cassius, whom Caesar describes as impatient of rule (I.ii.208-209), becomes more and more under the power of Brutus. He is overruled repeatedly in a way which would seem quite remarkable were it not for the fact that Brutus exemplifies for him "Rome" and the patriarchal virtues which he so honors and so denies. It is this conflict which incapacitates him; he becomes, to modify the phrase, but a limb of Brutus.

Of the four principal figures in the play Antony is the only one alive at the end. He has survived, and triumphed, because he is the best equipped to do so in the jungle that is imperial Rome. Caesar is dominated by his own superego—"Caesar"; Brutus by his—"Brutus/honour"; Cassius by that of Brutus. But Antony lacks this superego,[11] he consults the ego only, and thus he is free from the conflicts the others are involved in, which bedevil their judgment. He is not better in moral terms for this; on the contrary. But he is better in the sense of being freer to act, more efficient, more deadly. Not for him the compulsive self-dramatization; when he puts on a public face, as he does before the conspirators and the people, he is fully conscious, in a way the other three are not, of what he is doing. The role he assumes, e.g., as "friend of Caesar," are roles he can put off at pleasure, whereas their roles are a necessary part of their psychological make-up.

It has been suggested in the foregoing:

1. That descriptions of "character" in terms of function have their validity, but tend to disintegrate the characters, so that their central unity disappears.

2. That, although old "commonsense psychology" is incompetent to supply this unity, yet an approach based on modern clinical psychology may in fact do so, at least in certain cases.

3. That one such case is that of Julius Caesar, where explanations of him in terms of, for instance, "direct self-explanation," or traditional layers—"the popular and the deeper Caesar"—or audience expectations, find their place in a greater unity. For instance, in clinical terms, Caesar's boasts are more than self-explanation; they are a compulsive assertion of his ego-ideal; the "two Caesars," the one we see, the one Antony tells us of, are related in a temporal dimension.

4. That, as far as the play Julius Caesar is concerned, the unity lies in character, viewed in modern psychoanalytic terms, particularly in the manifestations of the superego in public affairs. In our age, when every director, dictator, and adman is violently concerned with the "public image," this approach to the play has a particular topicality.

5. That if one pleads:

> O! that we could come by Caesar's spirit,
> And not dismember Caesar
>
> (II.i.169-170)

the only reply possible is emphatically *not* that of the Great Dismemberers:

> But, alas,
> Caesar must bleed for it.
> (II.i.170-171)

Notes

1. HAROLD FELDMAN, "Unconscious Envy in Brutus," *American Imago, 9*:307-335, 1952-1953.
2. GORDON ROSS SMITH, "Brutus, Virtue, and Will," *Shakespeare Quarterly, 10*:367-379, 1959.

1. Quotations from SHAHANI, *Times Literary Supplement,* and HARTLEY COLERIDGE in L. C. KNIGHT, "How Many Children Had Lady Macbeth?" *Explorations* (1946).
2. L. L. SCHÜCKING, *Character Problems in Shakespeare's Plays* (New York and London, 1922), chap. I.
3. See, for instance, J. DOVER WILSON, *The Fortunes of Falstaff* (Cambridge: Cambridge University Press, 1935).
4. KNIGHT, *op. cit.*
5. The "thrasonical" Caesar is supported by J. DOVER WILSON in his New Cambridge edition, but D. S. BREWER argues that this was not the traditional view in "Brutus' Crime: A Footnote to *Julius Caesar,*" *Review of English Studies,* 3: January, 1952.
6. J. I. M. STEWART, *"Julius Caesar* and *Macbeth:* Two Notes on Shakespearean Technique," *Modern Language Review, 40*:169, 1945.
7. ERNEST SCHANZER, "The Problem of *Julius Caesar,*" *Shakespeare Quarterly, 6*:305, 1955.
8. See, for instance, T. W. RICHARDS, *Modern Clinical Psychology* (New York: McGraw-Hill Book Company, 1946), pp. 205 ff.; M.

CULPIN, *Mental Abnormality: Facts and Theories* (New York: Rinehart and Company, 1948), pp. 158 ff.; O. FENICHEL, *The Psychoanalytic Theory of Neurosis* (New York: W. W. Norton and Company, 1945), pp. 424 ff.

9. G. WILSON KNIGHT, *The Imperial Theme* (New York: The Macmillan Company, 1931), is the only critic to comment that "All people are 'lovers' " but does not press home the implications of this (chap. 4).

10. From "The Ballad of My Uncle Sidney," by PETER GURNEY.

11. In contrast, in *Antony and Cleopatra* the ego-ideal of "Antony himself" with his "Roman thoughts" exists, but largely as a creation of his followers; but this is material for a paper in itself.

On Hamlet and Oedipus

Virtually every facet of the tragedy of *Hamlet* has at one time or another fired the imagination of the psychoanalytic critic: He has taken up specifically the poison in the ear, the play within the play, the Ghost, the King, the Queen, the Gravediggers, Hamlet's madness, Ophelia's doubtful death, Osric, the Pyrrhus speech, the bonny sweet Robin song, the bodkin (both bare and otherwise), and any number of things besides. The result has been a body of material so enormous that it probably outweighs, quantitatively at least, the psychoanalytic writings on all of Shakespeare's other works combined. It should be pointed out, however, that the bulk of this material is devoted to what we can call with impunity, The Problem—namely, why does Hamlet hesitate to kill the King?—and that in this regard it contributes to a current of criticism that psychoanalysis did not originate but which psychoanalysis profoundly affected. Nor can we fail to underscore for a second time that it was in attempting to answer the problem of Hamlet's procrastination that the psychoanalytic school of Shakespearean criticism originated.

On October 15, 1897, Sigmund Freud, in a letter to Wilhelm Fliess, announced that he had found in his own development all the symptoms of the Oedipus complex and that he was coming to consider "love of the mother and jealousy of the father" to be "a general phenomenon of early childhood." He then proceeded to apply his idea to Sophocles' *Oedipus Rex* and to *Hamlet*. Three years later Freud brought forward an extended version of his insight in his monumental *Interpretation of Dreams;* that is the version reproduced below. *Hamlet*, Freud asserts, "has its roots in the same soil as *Oedipus Rex*." Because Hamlet is suffering from an Oedipus complex, because in his own subconscious mind he has nourished a desire to do precisely what his uncle has done, he is unable to carry out his initial resolution. Were he to destroy Claudius, the man who shows him "the repressed wishes of his own childhood," then he would also have to destroy himself. Hamlet's melancholic self-abuse springs from the realization that he is no better than his uncle. Freud also suggests (and this is perhaps the most brilliant stroke) that the difficulty critics have had in discovering the explanation for Hamlet's curious behavior lies in the "secular advance of repression in the emotional life of mankind"; in other words, in the critics' own unwillingness to consciously recognize the role that the oedipal conflict has played in their own lives. Finally, by stating that the tragedy of *Hamlet* gives expression to Shakespeare's own personal problems, Freud opens up an area of psychobiographical investigation that has occupied scores of minds and resulted in hundreds of pages of ingenious speculation.

M. F.

edipus Rex is what is known as a tragedy of destiny. Its tragic effect is said to lie in the contrast between the supreme will of the gods and the vain attempts of mankind to escape the evil that threatens them. The lesson which, it is said, the deeply moved spectator should learn from the tragedy is submission to the divine will and realization of his own impotence. Modern dramatists have accordingly tried to achieve a similar tragic effect by weaving the same contrast into a plot invented by themselves. But the spectators have looked on unmoved while a curse or an oracle was fulfilled in spite of all the efforts of some innocent man: later tragedies of destiny have failed in their effect.

If *Oedipus Rex* moves a modern audience no less than it did the contemporary Greek one, the explanation can only be that its effect does not lie in the contrast between destiny and human will, but is to be looked for in the particular nature of the material on which that contrast is exemplified. There must be something which makes a voice within us ready to recognize the compelling force of destiny in the *Oedipus,* while we can dismiss as merely arbitrary such dispositions as are laid down in [Grillparzer's] *Die Ahnfrau* or other modern tragedies of destiny. And a factor of this kind is in fact involved in the story of King Oedipus. His destiny moves us only because it might have been ours—because the oracle laid the same curse upon us before our birth as upon him. It is the fate of all of us, perhaps, to direct our first sexual impulse towards our mother and our first hatred and

"On Hamlet and Oedipus" by Sigmund Freud. Reprinted from *The Interpretation of Dreams,* Standard Edition, IV, pp. 264-266, with permission of George Allen and Unwin Ltd. and Basic Books, Inc.

our first murderous wish against our father. Our dreams convince us that that is so. King Oedipus, who slew his father Laius and married his mother Jocasta, merely shows us the fulfillment of our own childhood wishes. But, more fortunate than he, we have meanwhile succeeded, insofar as we have not become psychoneurotics, in detaching our sexual impulses from our mothers and in forgetting our jealousy of our fathers. Here is one in whom these primaeval wishes of our childhood have been fulfilled, and we shrink back from him with the whole force of the repression by which those wishes have since that time been held down within us. While the poet, as he unravels the past, brings to light the guilt of Oedipus, he is at the same time compelling us to recognize our own inner minds, in which those same impulses, though suppressed, are still to be found. The contrast with which the closing Chorus leaves us confronted—

> . . . Fix on Oedipus your eyes,
> Who resolved the dark enigma, noblest champion and most
>   wise.
> Like a star his envied fortune mounted beaming far and wide:
> Now he sinks in seas of anguish, whelmed beneath a raging
>   tide . . .[1]

—strikes as a warning at ourselves and our pride, at us who since our childhood have grown so wise and so mighty in our own eyes. Like Oedipus, we live in ignorance of these wishes, repugnant to morality, which have been forced upon us by Nature, and after their revelation we may all of us well seek to close our eyes to the scenes of our childhood.[2]

There is an unmistakable indication in the text of Sophocles' tragedy itself that the legend of Oedipus sprang from some primeval dreammaterial which had as its content the distressing disturbance of a child's relation to his parents owing to the first stirrings of sexuality. At a point when Oedipus, though he is not yet enlightened, has begun to feel troubled by his recollection of the oracle, Jocasta consoles him by referring to a dream which many people dream, though, as she thinks, it has no meaning:

> Many a man ere now in dreams hath lain
> With her who bare him. He hath least annoy
> Who with such omens troubleth not his mind.[3]

Today, just as then, many men dream of having sexual relations with their mothers, and speak of the fact with indignation and astonishment. It is clearly the key to the tragedy and the complement to the dream of the dreamer's father being dead. The story of Oedipus is the reaction of the imagination to these two typical dreams. And just as these dreams, when dreamt by adults, are accompanied by feelings of repulsion, so too the legend must include horror and self-punishment. Its further modification originates once again in a misconceived secondary revision of the material, which has sought to exploit it for theological purposes. . . . The attempt to harmonize divine omnipotence with human responsibility must naturally fail in connection with this subject-matter just as with any other.

Another of the great creations of tragic poetry, Shakespeare's *Hamlet*, has its roots in the same soil as *Oedipus Rex*.[4] But the changed treatment of the same material reveals the whole difference in the mental life of these two widely separated epochs of civilization: the secular advance of repression in the emotional life of mankind. In the *Oedipus* the child's wishful phantasy that underlies it is brought into the open and realized as it would be in a dream. In *Hamlet* it remains repressed; and—just as in the case of a neurosis—we only learn of its existence from its inhibiting consequences. Strangely enough, the overwhelming effect produced by the more modern tragedy has turned out to be compatible with the fact that people have remained completely in the dark as to the hero's character. The play is built up on Hamlet's hesitations over fulfilling the task of revenge that is assigned to him; but its text offers no reasons or motives for these hesitations and an immense variety of attempts at interpreting them have failed to produce a result. According to the view which was originated by Goethe and is still the prevailing one today, Hamlet represents the type of man whose power of direct action is paralyzed by an excessive development of his intellect. (He is "sicklied o'er with the pale cast of thought.") According to another view, the dramatist has tried to portray a pathologically irresolute character which might be classed as neurasthenic. The plot of the drama shows us, however, that Hamlet is far from being represented as a person incapable of taking any action. We see him doing so on two occasions: first in a sudden outburst of temper, when he runs his sword through the eavesdropper behind the arras, and secondly in a premeditated and even crafty fashion, when, with all the callousness of a Renaissance prince, he sends the two courtiers to the death that had been planned for himself. What is it, then, that inhibits him in fulfilling the task set him by his father's ghost? The answer, once again, is that it is the peculiar nature of the task. Hamlet is able to do anything—except take vengeance on the man who did away with his father and took that father's place with his mother, the man who shows him the repressed wishes of his own childhood realized. Thus the loathing which should drive him on to revenge is replaced in him by self-reproaches, by scruples of conscience, which remind him that he himself is literally no better than the sinner whom he is to punish. Here I have translated into conscious terms what was bound to remain unconscious in Hamlet's mind; and if anyone is inclined to call him a hysteric, I can only accept the fact as one that is implied by my interpretation. The distaste for sexuality expressed by Hamlet in his conversation with Ophelia fits in very well with this: the same distaste which was destined to take possession of the poet's mind more and more during the years that followed, and which reached its extreme expression in *Timon of Athens*. For it can of course only be the poet's own mind which confronts us in Hamlet. I observe in a book on Shakespeare by Georg Brandes (1896) a statement that *Hamlet* was written immediately after the death of Shakespeare's father (in 1601),[5] that is, under the immediate impact of his bereavement and, as we may well assume, while his childhood feelings about his father had been freshly revived. It is known, too, that Shakespeare's own son who died at an early age bore the name of "Hamnet," which is identical with "Hamlet." Just as *Hamlet* deals with the relation of a son to his parents, so *Macbeth* (written at approximately the same period) is concerned with the subject of childlessness. But just as all neurotic symptoms, and, for that matter, dreams, are capable of being "over-interpreted" and indeed need to be, if they are to be fully understood, so all genuinely creative writings are the product of more than a single motive and more than a single impulse in the poet's mind, and are open to more than a single interpretation. In what I have written I have only attempted to interpret the deepest layer of impulses in the mind of the creative writer.[6]

Notes

The notes below have been reproduced from the *Standard Edition* of Freud's works; they represent Strachey's treatment of the original material.

1. SOPHOCLES, *Oedipus Rex,* trans. Lewis Campbell, lines 1524 ff.
2. (Footnote added 1914): None of the findings of psychoanalytic research has provoked such embittered denials, such fierce opposition—or such amusing contortions—on the part of critics as this indication of the childhood impulses toward incest which persist in the unconscious. An attempt has even been made recently to make out, in the face of all experience, that the incest should only be taken as "symbolic."—Ferenczi (1912) has proposed an ingenious "overinterpretation" of the Oedipus myth, based on a passage in one of Schopenhauer's letters.—(Added 1919): Later studies have shown that the "Oedipus complex," which was touched upon for the first time in the above paragraphs in the *Interpretation of Dreams,* throws a light of undreamt-of importance on the history of the human race and the evolution of religion and morality. (See my *Totem and Taboo,* 1912-13 [Essay IV].)—[Actually the gist of this discussion of the Oedipus complex and of the *Oedipus Rex,* as well as of what follows on the subject of *Hamlet,* had already been put forward by Freud in a letter to Fliess as early as October 15, 1897 (see Freud, 1950a, Letter 71). A still earlier hint at the discovery of the Oedipus complex was included in a letter of May 31st, 1897 (*ibid.,* Draft N).—The actual term "Oedipus complex" seems to have been first used by Freud in his published writings in the first of his "Contributions to the Psychology of Love" (1910h).]
3. SOPHOCLES, *op. cit.,* lines 982 ff.
4. This paragraph was printed as a footnote in the first edition (1900) and included in the text from 1914 onward.
5. Brandes' statement is probably inaccurate. Evidence suggests that *Hamlet* was begun before the death of Shakespeare's father. This, however, does not necessarily negate Freud's argument: an imminent death can be very influential, as can an illness (Editor's note).
6. (Footnote added 1919): The above indications of a psychoanalytic explanation of *Hamlet* have since been amplified by Ernest Jones and defended against the alternative views put forward in the

literature of the subject. (See Jones, 1910*a* [and, in a completer form, 1948].)—(Added 1930) : Incidentally, I have in the meantime ceased to believe that the author of Shakespeare's works was the man from Stratford (see Freud, 1930*e*).—(Added 1919) : Further attempts at an analysis of *Macbeth* will be found in a paper of mine (Freud, 1916*d*) and in one by Jekels (1917).—[The first part of this footnote was included in a different form in the edition of 1911 but omitted from 1914 onwards: "The views on the problem of *Hamlet* contained in the above passage have since been confirmed and supported with fresh arguments in an extensive study by Dr. Ernest Jones of Toronto (1910*a*). He has also pointed out the relation between the material in *Hamlet* and the myths of the birth of heroes discussed by Rank (1909)."—Freud further discussed *Hamlet* in a posthumously published sketch dealing with "Psychopathic Characters of the Stage" (1942*b*), probably written in 1905 or 1906.]

"Hamlet": The Psychoanalytical Solution

Perhaps the most accurate way to characterize the commonly expressed notion that Ernest Jones's *Hamlet and Oedipus* is a restatement and amplification of Freud's earlier conclusions about the Prince, the play, and the poet is to say paradoxically that such a view is at once correct and incorrect. For while it is true that Jones adds little in the way of new discoveries to what Freud had said already, his work ultimately constitutes far more than a restatement or even an amplification. By carefully sifting the writings of other critics in an effort to throw every conceivable light upon the matter; by meticulously examining the historical materials that might have influenced the playwright; by probing the tragedy for dramatic themes related to the central problem; in short, by taking the whole business up inch by inch, Jones succeeds in replacing Freud's astonishingly insightful but finally passing remarks with a fully developed critical edifice.

I would not want to suggest, however, that *Hamlet and Oedipus* is the last word in the psychoanalytic criticism of Shakespeare (as it is often, sadly, taken to be), or that it is a book without critical trouble spots. While one cannot deny its effectiveness, one cannot deny also certain objections to its methods and assumptions, objections that this volume presents in detail in the essay titled *On the Mutuality of the Oedipus Complex: Notes on the Hamlet Case.*

Jones's accomplishment was long in the building. What we know today as a book first appeared as an essay of some forty pages titled *The Oedipus Complex as an Explanation of Hamlet's Mystery: A Study in Motive.*[1] In substantially the same form it underwent a number of printings until it became in 1947 the introduction to an edition of *Hamlet.*[2] Two years later it attained its present form as *Hamlet and Oedipus.*[3] I have chosen to reproduce here what can be regarded as the core of Jones's argument. After demonstrating that Hamlet fails to present us with a fully satisfactory explanation for his procrastination, that he is a man of action rather than a man of inaction, and that his failure to destroy the King does not result from an inability to actually get close to him, Jones proceeds to make a number of crucial observations. First, he points out that Hamlet's obvious tendency to rationalize argues convincingly for the presence of hidden motives, and he underscores this idea with a reference to the rationalizations of Iago. Second, he points out that Hamlet's violent reaction to the remarriage of his mother attests to the depth of his attachment to her and thus reaffirms from another perspective the validity of Freud's conclusions. Again, he asserts that Claudius' crime has the effect of reawakening in Hamlet impulses that Hamlet had successfully repressed for a good many years. In other words, Hamlet cannot kill Gertrude's husband because to do so would be, from the standpoint of the subconscious, to commit the very crime he has kept himself from committing for so long. Jones also maintains that the timeless fascination of *Hamlet* is rooted in the play's appeal to repressed material in the minds of the audience, and in this way he reminds us again of Shakespeare's persistent exploitation of oedipal themes.

M. F.

e are compelled . . . to take the position that there is some cause for Hamlet's vacillation which has not yet been fathomed. If this lies neither in his incapacity for action in general, nor in the inordinate difficulty of the particular task in question, then it must of necessity lie in the third possibility—namely, in some special feature of the task that renders it repugnant to him. This conclusion, that Hamlet at heart does not want to carry out the task, seems so obvious that it is hard to see how any open-minded reader of the play could avoid making it. . . .

Hamlet's hesitancy may have been due to an internal conflict between the impulse to fulfill his task on the one hand and some special cause of repugnance to it on the other; further, the explanation of his not disclosing this cause of repugnance may be that he was not conscious of its nature; and yet the cause may be one that doesn't happen to have been considered by any of the upholders of this hypothesis. In other words, the first two stages in the argument may be correct, but not the third. This is the view that will now be developed, but before dealing with the third stage of the argument it is first necessary to establish the probability of the first two—namely, that Hamlet's hesitancy was due to some special cause of repugnance for his task and that he was unaware of the nature of this repugnance.

A preliminary obstruction to this line of thought, based on some common prejudices on the subject of mental dynamics, may first be considered. If Hamlet was not aware of the nature of his inhibition,

"Hamlet: The Psychoanalytical Solution" by Ernest Jones. Reprinted from *Hamlet and Oedipus* by Ernest Jones, M.D. By permission of W. W. Norton & Company, Inc. Copyright © 1949 by Ernest Jones.

doubt may be felt concerning the possibility of our penetrating to it. This pessimistic thought was expressed by Baumgart as follows: "What hinders Hamlet in his revenge is for him himself a problem and *therefore* it must remain a problem for us all."[1] Fortunately for our investigation, however, psychoanalytic studies have demonstrated beyond doubt that mental trends hidden from the subject himself may come to external expression in ways that reveal their nature to a trained observer, so that the possibility of success is not to be thus excluded. Loening has further objected to this hypothesis that the poet himself has not disclosed this hidden mental trend, or even given any indication of it.[2] The first part of his objection is certainly true— otherwise there would be no problem to discuss, but we shall presently see that the second is by no means true. It may be asked: Why has the poet not put in a clearer light the mental trend we are trying to discover? Strange as it may appear, the answer is probably the same as with Hamlet himself—namely, he could not because he was unaware of its nature. We shall later deal with this question in connection with the relation of the poet to the play.

As Trench well says: "We find it hard, with Shakespeare's help, to understand Hamlet: even Shakespeare, perhaps, found it hard to understand him: Hamlet himself finds it impossible to understand himself. Better able than other men to read the hearts and motives of others, he is yet quite unable to read his own."[3] I know of no more authentic statement than this in the whole literature on the Hamlet problem. But, if the motive of the play is so obscure, to what can we attribute its powerful effect on the audience, since as Kohler asks, "Who has ever seen Hamlet and not felt the fearful conflict that moves the soul of the hero?"[4] This can only be because the hero's conflict finds its echo in a similar inner conflict in the mind of the hearer, and the more intense is this already present conflict the greater is the effect of the drama.[5] Again, it is certain that the hearer himself does not know the inner cause of the conflict in his own mind, but experiences only the outer manifestations of it. So we reach the apparent paradox that the hero, the poet, and the audience are all profoundly moved by feelings due to a conflict of the source of which they are unaware.

The fact, however, that such a conclusion should appear paradoxical is in itself a censure on popular ignorance of the actual workings of the human mind, and before undertaking to sustain the assertions made in the preceding paragraph it will first be necessary to make a few observations on the prevailing views of motive and conduct in general. The new science of clinical psychology stands nowhere in sharper contrast to the older attitudes towards mental functioning than on this very matter. Whereas the generally accepted view of man's mind, usually implicit and frequently explicit in psychological writings and elsewhere, regards it as an interplay of various processes that are for the most part known to the subject, or are at all events accessible to careful introspection on his part, the analytic methods of clinical psychology have on the contrary decisively proved that a far greater number of these processes than is commonly surmised arises from origins that he never even suspects. Man's belief that he is a self-conscious animal, alive to the desires that impel or inhibit his actions, is the lost stronghold of that anthropomorphic and anthropocentric outlook on life which has so long dominated his philosophy, his theology, and above all, his psychology. In other words, the tendency to take man at his own valuation is rarely resisted, and we assume that the surest way of finding out why a person commits a given act is simply to ask him, relying on the knowledge that he, as we ourselves would in a like circumstance, will feel certain of the answer and will almost infallibly provide a plausible reason for his conduct. Special objective methods of penetrating into the more obscure mental processes, however, disclose the most formidable obstacles in the way of this direct introspective route, and reveal powers of self-deception in the human mind to which a limit has yet to be found. If I may quote from a former paper: "We are beginning to see man not as the smooth, self-acting agent he pretends to be, but as he really is, a creature only dimly conscious of the various influences that mould his thought and action, and blindly resisting with all the means at his command the forces that are making for a higher and fuller consciousness."[6]

That Hamlet is suffering from an internal conflict the essential nature of which is inaccessible to his introspection is evidenced by the following considerations. Throughout the play we have the clearest picture of a man who sees his duty plain before him, but who shirks it at every opportunity and suffers in consequence the most intense remorse. To paraphrase Sir James Paget's well-known description of hysterical paralysis: Hamlet's advocates say he cannot do his duty, his detractors say he will not, whereas the truth is that he cannot will. Further than this, the deficient will-power is localized to the one question of killing his uncle; it is what may be termed a *specific aboulia*. Now instances of such specific aboulias in real life invariably prove, when analyzed, to be due to an unconscious repulsion against the act that cannot be performed (or else against something closely associated with the act, so that the idea of the act becomes also involved in the repulsion). In other words, whenever a person cannot bring himself to do something that every conscious consideration tells him he should do—and which he may have the strongest conscious desire to do—it is always because there is some hidden reason why a part of him doesn't want to do it; this reason he will not own to himself and is only dimly if at all aware of. That is exactly the case with Hamlet. Time and again he works himself up, points out to himself his obvious duty, with the cruellest self-reproaches lashes himself to agonies of remorse —and once more falls away into inaction. He eagerly seizes at every excuse for occupying himself with any other matter than the performance of his duty—even in the last scene of the last act entering on the distraction of a quite irrelevant fencing-match with a man who he must know wants to kill him, an eventuality that would put an end to all hope of fulfilling his task: just as on a lesser plane a person faced with a distasteful task, e.g., writing a difficult letter, will whittle away his time in arranging, tidying, and fidgeting with any little occupation that may serve as a pretext for procrastination. Bradley even goes as far as to make out a case for the view that Hamlet's self-accusation of "bestial oblivion" is to be taken in a literal sense, his unconscious detestation of his task being so intense as to enable him actually to forget it for periods.[7]

Highly significant is the fact that the grounds Hamlet gives for his hesitancy are grounds none of which will stand any serious consideration, and which continually change from one time to another. One moment he pretends he is too cowardly to perform the deed, at another he questions the truthfulness of the Ghost, at another—when the opportunity presents itself in its naked form—he thinks the time is unsuited, it would be better to wait till the King was at some evil act and then to kill him, and so on. They have each of them, it is true, a certain plausibility—so much so that some writers have accepted them at face value; but surely no pretext would be of any use if it were not plausible. As Madariaga truly says: "The argument that the reasons given by Hamlet not to kill the king at prayers are cogent is irrelevant. For the man who wants to procrastinate cogent arguments are more valuable than mere pretexts."[8] Take, for instance, the matter of the credibility of the Ghost. There exists an extensive and very interesting literature concerning Elizabethan beliefs in supernatural visitation. It was doubtless a burning topic, a focal point of the controversies about the conflicting theologies of the age, and moreover, affecting the practical question of how to treat witches. But there is no evidence of Hamlet (or Shakespeare!) being specially interested in theology, and from the moment when the ghost confirms the slumbering suspicion in his mind ("O, my prophetic soul! My uncle!") his intuition must indubitably have convinced him of the Ghost's veridical nature. He never really doubted the villainy of his uncle.

When a man gives at different times a different reason for his conduct it is safe to infer that, whether consciously or not, he is concealing the true reason. Wetz, discussing a similar problem in reference to Iago, truly observes: "Nothing proves so well how false are the motives with which Iago tries to persuade himself as *the constant change in these motives.*"[9] We can therefore safely dismiss all the alleged motives that Hamlet propounds as being more or less successful attempts on his part to blind himself with self-deception. Loening's summing-up of them is not too emphatic when he says: "They are all mutually contradictory; *they are one and all false pretexts.*"[10] The alleged motives excellently illustrate the psychological mechanisms of evasion and rationalization I have elsewhere described.[11]

The whole picture presented by Hamlet, his deep depression, the hopeless note in his attitude towards the world and towards the value of life, his dread of death,[12] his repeated reference to bad dreams, his self-accusations, his desperate efforts to get away from the thoughts of his duty, and his vain attempts to find an excuse for his procrastination: all this unequivocally points to a *tortured conscience,* to some hidden ground for shirking his task, a ground which he dare not or cannot avow to himself. We have, therefore, to take up the argument again at this point, and to seek for some evidence that may serve to bring to light the hidden countermotive.

The extensive experience of the psychoanalytic researches carried out by Freud and his school during the past half century has amply demonstrated that certain kinds of mental process show a greater tendency to be inaccessible to consciousness (put technically, to be "repressed") than others. In other words, it is harder for a person to realize the existence in his mind of some mental trends than it is of others. In order therefore to gain a proper perspective it is necessary briefly to inquire into the relative frequency with which various sets of mental processes are "repressed." Experience shows that this can be correlated with the degree of compatibility of these various sets with the ideals and standards accepted by the conscious ego; the less compatible they are with these the more likely are they to be "repressed." As the standards acceptable to consciousness are in considerable measure derived from the immediate environment, one may formulate the following generalization: those processes are most likely to be "repressed" by the individual which are most disapproved of by the particular circle of society to whose influence he has chiefly been subjected during the period when his character was being formed. Biologically stated, this law would run: "That which is unacceptable to the herd becomes unacceptable to the individual member," it being understood that the term herd is intended here in the sense of the particular circle defined above, which is by no means necessarily the community at large. It is for this reason that moral, social, ethical, or religious tendencies are seldom "repressed," for, since the individual originally received them from his herd, they can hardly ever come into conflict with the dicta of the latter. This merely says that a man cannot be ashamed of that which he respects; the apparent exceptions to this rule need not be here explained.

The language used in the previous paragraph will have indicated that by the term "repression" we denote an active dynamic process. Thoughts that are "repressed" are actively kept from consciousness by a definite force and with the expenditure of more or less mental effort, though the person concerned is rarely aware of this. Further, what is thus kept from consciousness typically possesses an energy of its own; hence our frequent use of such expressions as "trend," "tendency," etc. A little consideration of the genetic aspects of the matter will make it comprehensible that the trends most likely to be "repressed" are those belonging to what are called the innate impulses, as contrasted with secondarily acquired ones. Loening seems very discerningly to have grasped this, for, in commenting on a remark of Kohler's to the effect that "where a feeling impels us to action or to omission, it is replete with a hundred reasons—with reasons that are as light as soap-bubbles, but which through self-deception appear to us as highly respectable and compelling motives, because they are hugely magnified in the (concave) mirror of our own feeling," he writes: "But this does not hold good, as Kohler and others believe, when we are impelled by *moral* feelings of which reason *approves* (for these we admit to ourselves, they need no excuse), only for feelings that arise from our *natural* man, those the gratification of which is *opposed by our reason.*"[13] It only remains to add the obvious corollary that, as the herd unquestionably selects from the "natural" instincts the sexual one on which to lay its heaviest ban, so it is the various psychosexual trends that are most often "repressed" by the individual. We have here the explanation of the clinical experience that the more intense and the more obscure is a given case of deep mental conflict the more certainly will it be found on adequate analysis to center about a sexual problem. On the surface, of course, this does not appear so, for, by means of various psychological defensive mechanisms, the depression, doubt, despair, and other manifestations of the conflict are transferred on to more tolerable and permissible topics, such as anxiety about worldly success or failure, about immortality and the salvation of the soul, philosophical considerations about the value of life, the future of the world, and so on.

Bearing these considerations in mind, let us return to Hamlet. It should now be evident that the conflicting hypotheses discussed above, which see Hamlet's conscious impulse towards revenge inhibited by an unconscious misgiving of a highly ethical kind, are based on ignorance of what actually happens in real life, since misgivings of this order belong in fact to the more conscious layers of the mind rather than to the deeper, unconscious ones. Hamlet's intense self-study would speedily have made him aware of any such misgivings and, although he might subsequently have ignored them, it would almost certainly have been by the aid of some process of rationalization which would have enabled him to deceive himself into believing that they were ill-founded; he would in any case have remained conscious of the nature of them. We have therefore to invert these hypotheses and realize—

as his words so often indicate—that the positive striving for vengeance, the pious task laid on him by his father, was to him the moral
and social one, the one approved of by his consciousness, and that the
"repressed" inhibiting striving against the act of vengeance arose in
some hidden source connected with his more personal, natural instincts.
The former striving has already been considered, and indeed is manifest in every speech in which Hamlet debates the matter: the second
is, from its nature, more obscure and has next to be investigated.

This is perhaps most easily done by inquiring more intently into
Hamlet's precise attitude towards the object of his vengeance, Claudius, and towards the crimes that have to be avenged. These are two:
Claudius' incest with the Queen,[14] and his murder of his brother. Now
it is of great importance to note the profound difference in Hamlet's
attitude towards these two crimes. Intellectually of course he abhors
both, but there can be no question as to which arouses in him the
deeper loathing. Whereas the murder of his father evokes in him indignation and a plain recognition of his obvious duty to avenge it,
his mother's guilty conduct awakes in him the intensest horror. Furnivall remarks, in speaking of the Queen, "Her disgraceful adultery and
incest, and treason to his noble father's memory, Hamlet has felt in
his inmost soul. Compared to their ingrain dye, Claudius' murder of
his father—notwithstanding all his protestations—is only a skin-deep
stain."[15]

Now, in trying to define Hamlet's attitude toward his uncle we have
to guard against assuming off-hand that this is a simple one of mere
execration, for there is a possibility of complexity arising in the following way: The uncle has not merely committed *each* crime, he has
committed *both* crimes, a distinction of considerable importance, since
the *combination* of crimes allows the admittance of a new factor, produced by the possible interrelation of the two, which may prevent the
result from being simply one of summation. In addition, it has to be
borne in mind that the perpetrator of the crimes is a relative, and an
exceedingly near relative. The possible interrelationship of the crimes,
and the fact that the author of them is an actual member of the family,
give scope for a confusion in their influence on Hamlet's mind which
may be the cause of the very obscurity we are seeking to clarify.

Let us first pursue further the effect on Hamlet of his mother's misconduct. Before he even knows with any certitude, however much he

may suspect it, that his father has been murdered he is in the deepest depression, and evidently on account of this misconduct. The connection between the two is unmistakable in the monologue (I.ii.), in reference to which Furnivall writes: "One must insist on this, that before any revelation of his father's murder is made to Hamlet, before any burden of revenging that murder is laid upon him, he thinks of suicide as a welcome means of escape from this fair world of God's, made abominable to his diseased and weak imagination by his mother's lust, and the dishonour done by her to his father's memory."[16]

But we can rest satisfied with this seemingly adequate explanation of Hamlet's weariness of life only if we accept unquestioningly the conventional standards of the causes of deep emotion. Many years ago Connolly, a well-known psychiatrist, pointed out the disproportion here existing between cause and effect, and gave as his opinion that Hamlet's reaction to his mother's marriage indicated in itself a mental instability, "a predisposition to actual unsoundness"; he writes: "The circumstances are not such as would at once turn a healthy mind to the contemplation of suicide, the last resource of those whose reason has been overwhelmed by calamity and despair."[17] In T. S. Eliot's opinion, also, Hamlet's emotion is in *excess* of the facts as they appear, and he specially contrasts it with Gertrude's negative and insignificant personality.[18] Wihan attributes the exaggerated effect of his misfortunes to Hamlet's "Masslosigkeit" (lack of moderation), which is displayed in every direction.[19] We have unveiled only the exciting cause, not the predisposing cause. The very fact that Hamlet is apparently content with the explanation arouses our misgiving, for, as will presently be expounded, from the very nature of the emotion he cannot be aware of the true cause of it. If we ask, not what ought to produce such soul-paralyzing grief and distaste for life, but what in actual fact does produce it, we are compelled to go beyond this explanation and seek for some deeper cause. In real life speedy second marriages occur commonly enough without leading to any such result as is here depicted, and when we see them followed by this result we invariably find, if the opportunity for an analysis of the subject's mind presents itself, that there is some other and more hidden reason why the event is followed by this inordinately great effect. The reason always is that the event has awakened to increased activity mental processes that have been "repressed" from the subject's consciousness. His mind has been specially prepared for the catastrophe by previous mental processes with which those directly resulting from the event have entered into association. This is perhaps what Furnivall means when he speaks of the world being made abominable to Hamlet's "diseased imagination." In short, the special nature of the reaction presupposes some special feature in the mental predisposition. . . .

Shakespeare's extraordinary powers of observation and penetration granted him a degree of insight that it has taken the world three subsequent centuries to reach. Until our generation (and even now in the juristic sphere) a dividing line separated the sane and responsible from the irresponsible insane. It is now becoming more and more widely recognized that much of mankind lives in an intermediate and unhappy state charged with what Dover Wilson well calls "that sense of frustration, futility and human inadequacy which is the burden of the whole symphony"[20] and of which Hamlet is the supreme example in literature. This intermediate plight, in the toils of which perhaps the greater part of mankind struggles and suffers, is given the name of psychoneurosis, and long ago the genius of Shakespeare depicted it for us with faultless insight.

Extensive studies of the past half century, inspired by Freud, have taught us that a psychoneurosis means a state of mind where the person is unduly, and often painfully, driven or thwarted by the "unconscious" part of his mind, that buried part that was once the infant's mind and still lives on side by side with the adult mentality that has developed out of it and should have taken its place. It signifies *internal* mental conflict. We have here the reason why it is impossible to discuss intelligently the state of mind of anyone suffering from a psychoneurosis, whether the description is of a living person or an imagined one, without correlating the manifestations with what must have operated in his infancy and is *still operating*. That is what I propose to attempt here.

For some deep-seated reason, which is to him unacceptable, Hamlet is plunged into anguish at the thought of his father being replaced in his mother's affections by someone else. It is as if his devotion to his mother had made him so jealous for her affection that he had found it hard enough to share this even with his father and could not endure to share it with still another man. Against this thought, however, suggestive as it is, may be urged three objections. First, if it were in itself a full statement of the matter, Hamlet would have been aware of the jealousy, whereas we have concluded that the mental process we are seeking is hidden from him. Second, we see in it no evidence of the arousing of an old and forgotten memory. And, third, Hamlet is being deprived by Claudius of no greater share in the Queen's affection than he had been by his own father, for the two brothers made exactly similar claims in this respect—namely, those of a loved husband. The last-named objection, however, leads us to the heart of the situation. How if, in fact, Hamlet had in years gone by, as a child, bitterly resented having had to share his mother's affection even with his own father, had regarded him as a rival, and had secretly wished him out of the way so that he might enjoy undisputed and undisturbed ᵗhe monopoly of that affection? If such thoughts had been present in his mind in childhood days they evidently would have been "repressed," and all traces of them obliterated, by filial piety and other educative influences. The actual realization of his early wish in the death of his father at the hands of a jealous rival would have stimulated into activity these "repressed" memories, which would have produced, in the form of depression and other suffering, an obscure aftermath of his childhood's conflict. This is at all events the mechanism that is actually found in the real Hamlets who are investigated psychologically.[21]

The explanation, therefore, of the delay and self-frustration exhibited in the endeavor to fulfill his father's demand for vengeance is that to Hamlet the thought of incest and parricide combined is too intolerable to be borne. One part of him tries to carry out the task, the other flinches inexorably from the thought of it. How fain would he blot it out in that "bestial oblivion" which unfortunately for him his conscience contemns. He is torn and tortured in an insoluble inner conflict. . . .

We are now in a position to expand and complete the suggestions offered above in connection with the Hamlet problem.[22] The story thus interpreted would run somewhat as follows.

As a child Hamlet had experienced the warmest affection for his mother, and this, as is always so, had contained elements of a disguised erotic quality, still more so in infancy. The presence of two traits in the Queen's character accord with this assumption, namely her markedly sensual nature and her passionate fondness for her son. The former is indicated in too many places in the play to need specific reference, and is generally recognized. The latter is also manifest: Claudius says, for instance (IV.vii.), "The Queen his mother lives almost by his looks." Nevertheless Hamlet appears to have with more or less success weaned himself from her and to have fallen in love with Ophelia. The precise nature of his original feeling for Ophelia is a little obscure. We may assume that at least in part it was composed of a normal love for a prospective bride, though the extravagance of the language used (the passionate need for absolute certainty, etc.) suggests a somewhat morbid frame of mind. There are indications that even here the influence of the old attraction for the mother is still exerting itself. Although some writers, [23] following Goethe,[24] see in Ophelia many traits of resemblance to the Queen, perhaps just as striking are the traits contrasting with those of the Queen. Whatever truth there may be in the many German conceptions of Ophelia as a sensual wanton[25]—misconceptions that have been questioned by Loening[26] and others—still the very fact that it needed what Goethe happily called the "innocence of insanity" to reveal the presence of any such libidinous thoughts demonstrates in itself the modesty and chasteness of her habitual demeanor. Her naïve piety, her obedient resignation, and her unreflecting simplicity sharply contrast with the Queen's character, and seem to indicate that Hamlet by a characteristic reaction towards the opposite extreme had unknowingly been impelled to choose a woman who should least remind him of his mother. A case might even be made out for the view that part of his courtship originated not so much in direct attraction for Ophelia as in an unconscious desire to play her off against his mother, just as a disappointed and piqued lover so often has resort to the arms of a more willing rival. It would not be easy otherwise to understand the readiness with which he later throws himself into this part. When, for instance, in the play scene he replies to his mother's request to sit by her with the words "No, good mother, here's metal more attractive" and proceeds to lie at Ophelia's feet, we seem to have a direct indication of this attitude; and his coarse familiarity and bandying of ambiguous jests with the woman he has recently so ruthlessly jilted are hardly intelligible unless we bear in mind that they were carried out under the heedful gaze of the Queen. It is as if his unconscious were trying to convey to her the following thought: "You give yourself to other men whom you prefer to me. Let me assure you that I can dispense with your favors and even prefer those of a woman whom I no longer love." His extraordinary outburst of bawdiness on this occasion, so unexpected in a man of obviously fine feeling, points unequivocally to the sexual nature of the underlying turmoil.

Now comes the father's death and the mother's second marriage. The association of the idea of sexuality with his mother, buried since infancy, can no longer be concealed from his consciousness. As Bradley well says: "Her son was forced to see in her action not only an astounding shallowness of feeling, but an eruption of coarse sensuality, 'rank and gross,' speeding post-haste to its horrible delight."[27] Feelings which once, in the infancy of long ago, were pleasurable desires can now, because of his repressions, only fill him with repulsion. The long "repressed" desire to take his father's place in his mother's affection is stimulated to unconscious activity by the sight of someone usurping this place exactly as he himself had once longed to do. More, this someone was a member of the same family, so that the actual usurpation further resembled the imaginary one in being incestuous. Without his being in the least aware of it these ancient desires are ringing in his mind, are once more struggling to find conscious expression, and need such an expenditure of energy again to "repress" them that he is reduced to the deplorable mental state he himself so vividly depicts.

There follows the Ghost's announcement that the father's death was a willed one, was due to murder. Hamlet, having at the moment his mind filled with natural indignation at the news, answers normally enough with the cry:

> Haste me to know't, that I with wings as swift
> As meditation or the thoughts of love,
> May sweep to my revenge.

> (I.v.29-31)

The momentous words follow revealing who was the guilty person, namely a relative who had committed the deed at the bidding of lust.[28] Hamlet's second guilty wish had thus also been realized by his uncle, namely to procure the fulfillment of the first—the possession of the mother—by a personal deed, in fact by murder of the father. The two recent events, the father's death and the mother's second marriage, seemed to the world to have no inner causal relation to each other, but they represented ideas which in Hamlet's unconscious phantasy had always been closely associated. These ideas now in a moment forced their way to conscious recognition in spite of all "repressing forces," and found immediate expression in his almost reflex cry: "O my prophetic soul! My uncle?" The frightful truth his unconscious had already intuitively divined, his consciousness had now to assimilate as best it could. For the rest of the interview Hamlet is stunned by the effect of the internal conflict thus reawakened, which from now on never ceases, and into the essential nature of which he never penetrates.

One of the first manifestations of the awakening of the old conflict in Hamlet's mind is his reaction against Ophelia. This is doubly conditioned by the two opposing attitudes in his own mind. In the first place, there is a complex reaction in regard to his mother. As was explained above, the being forced to connect the thought of his mother with sensuality leads to an intense sexual revulsion, one that is only temporarily broken down by the coarse outburst discussed above. Combined with this is a fierce jealousy, unconscious because of its forbidden origin, at the sight of her giving herself to another man, a man whom he had no reason whatever either to love or to respect. Consciously this is allowed to express itself, for instance after the prayer scene, only in the form of extreme resentment and bitter reproaches against her. His resentment against women is still further inflamed by the hypocritical prudishness with which Ophelia follows her father and brother in seeing evil in his natural affection, an attitude which poisons his love in exactly the same way that the love of his childhood, like that of all children, must have been poisoned. He can forgive a woman neither her rejection of his sexual advances nor, still less, her alliance with another man. Most intolerable of all to him, as Bradley well remarks, is the sight of sensuality in a quarter from which he had trained himself ever since infancy rigorously to exclude it. The total reaction culminates in the bitter misogyny of his outburst against Ophelia, who is devastated at having to bear a reaction so wholly out of proportion to her own offense and has no idea that in reviling her Hamlet is really expressing his bitter resentment against his mother.[29] "I have heard of your paintings too, well enough; God has given you one face, and you make yourselves another; you jig, you amble, and you lisp, and nickname God's creatures, and make your wantonness your ignorance. Go to, I'll no more on 't; it hath made me mad" (III.i.148-154). On only one occasion does he for a moment escape from the sordid implication with which his love has been impregnated and achieve a healthier attitude towards Ophelia, namely at the open grave when in remorse he breaks out at Laertes for presuming to pretend that his feeling for her could never equal that of her lover. Even here, however, as Dover Wilson has suggested,[30] the remorse behind his exaggerated behavior springs not so much from grief at Ophelia's death as from his distress at his bad conscience that had killed his love—he acts the lover he fain would have been. . . .

The intensity of Hamlet's repulsion against woman in general, and Ophelia in particular, is a measure of the powerful "repression" to which his sexual feelings are being subjected. The outlet for those feelings in the direction of his mother has always been firmly damned, and now that the narrower channel in Ophelia's direction has also been closed the increase in the original direction consequent on the awakening of early memories tasks all his energy to maintain the "repression." His pent-up feelings find a partial vent in other directions. The petulant irascibility and explosive outbursts called forth by his vexation at the hands of Guildenstern and Rosencrantz, and especially of Polonius, are evidently to be interpreted in this way, as also is in part the burning nature of his reproaches to his mother. Indeed, towards the end of his interview with his mother the thought of her misconduct expresses itself in that almost physical disgust which is so characteristic a manifestation of intensely "repressed" sexual feeling.

> Let the bloat king tempt you again to bed;
> Pinch wanton on your cheek; call you his mouse;
> And let him, for a pair of reechy kisses,
> Or paddling in your neck with his damn'd fingers,
> Make you to ravel all this matter out, . . .
>
> (III.iv.182-186)

Hamlet's attitude towards Polonius is highly instructive. Here the absence of family tie and of other similar influences enables him to indulge to a relatively unrestrained extent his hostility towards what he regards as a prating and sententious dotard.[31] The analogy he effects between Polonius and Jephthah is in this connection especially pointed.[32] It is here that we see his fundamental attitude towards moralizing elders who use their power to thwart the happiness of the young, and not in the overdrawn and melodramatic portrait in which he delineates his father: "A combination and a form indeed, where every god did seem to set his seal to give the world assurance of a man."

It will be seen from the foregoing that Hamlet's attitude towards his uncle-father is far more complex than is generally supposed. He of course detests him, but it is the jealous detestation of one evil-doer towards his successful fellow. Much as he hates him, he can never denounce him with the ardent indignation that boils straight from his blood when he reproaches his mother, for the more vigorously he denounces his uncle the more powerfully does he stimulate to activity his own unconscious and "repressed" complexes. He is therefore in a dilemma between on the one hand allowing his natural detestation of his uncle to have free play, a consummation which would stir still further his own horrible wishes, and on the other hand ignoring the imperative call for the vengeance that his obvious duty demands. His own "evil" prevents him from completely denouncing his uncle's, and in continuing to "repress" the former he must strive to ignore, to condone, and if possible even to forget the latter; *his moral fate is bound up with his uncle's for good or ill.* In reality his uncle incorporates the deepest and most buried part of his own personality, so that he cannot kill him without also killing himself. This solution, one closely akin to what Freud has shown to be the motive of suicide in melancholia,[33] is actually the one that Hamlet finally adopts. The course of alternate action and inaction that he embarks on, and the provocations he gives to his suspicious uncle, can lead to no other end than to his own ruin and, incidentally, to that of his uncle. Only when he has made the final sacrifice and brought himself to the door of death is he free to fulfill his duty, to avenge his father, and to slay his other self—his uncle.

There are two moments in the play when he is nearest to murder, and it is noteworthy that in both the impulse has been dissociated from the unbearable idea of incest. The second is of course when he actually kills the King, when the Queen is already dead and lost to him for ever, so that his conscience is free of an ulterior motive for the murder.

The first is more interesting. It is clear that Hamlet is a creature of highly charged imagination; Vischer, for instance, quite rightly termed him a "Phantasiemensch."[34] As is known, the danger then is that phantasy may on occasion replace reality. Now Otto Rank, who uses the same term, has plausibly suggested that the emotionally charged play scene, where a nephew kills his uncle, and when there is no talk of adultery or incest, is in Hamlet's imagination an equivalent for fulfilling his task. It is easier to kill the King when there is no ulterior motive behind it, no talk of mother or incest. When the play is over he is carried away in exultation as if he had really killed the King himself, whereas all he has actually done is to warn him and so impel him to sign a death warrant. That his pretext for arranging the play—to satisfy himself about Claudius' guilt and the Ghost's honesty —is specious is plain from the fact that *before* it he had been convinced of both and was reproaching himself for his neglect. When he then comes on the King praying, and so to speak finds him surprisingly still alive, he realizes that his task is still in front of him, but can only say "Now *might* I do it" (not "will"). He then expresses openly the unconscious thoughts of his infancy—the wish to kill the man who is lying with his mother ("in th' incestuous pleasure of his bed")—but he knows only too well that his own guilty motive for doing so would always prevent him. So there is no way out of the dilemma, and he blunders on to destruction.

The call of duty to kill his stepfather cannot be obeyed because it links itself with the unconscious call of his nature to kill his mother's husband, whether this is the first or the second; the absolute "repression" of the former impulse involves the inner prohibition of the latter also. It is no chance that Hamlet says of himself that he is prompted to his revenge "by heaven and hell."

In this discussion of the motives that move or restrain Hamlet we have purposely depreciated the subsidiary ones—such as his exclusion from the throne where Claudius has blocked the normal solution of the Oedipus complex (to succeed the father in due course)—which also play a part, so as to bring out in greater relief the deeper and effective ones that are of preponderating importance. These, as we have seen, spring from sources of which he is quite unaware, and we might summarize the internal conflict of which he is the victim as consisting in a struggle of the "repressed" mental processes to become conscious.

The call of duty, which automatically arouses to activity these unconscious processes, conflicts with the necessity of "repressing" them still more strongly; for the more urgent is the need for external action the greater is the effort demanded of the "repressing" forces. It is his moral duty, to which his father exhorts him, to put an end to the incestuous activities of his mother (by killing Claudius), but his unconscious does not want to put an end to them (he being identified with Claudius in the situation), and so he cannot. His lashings of self-reproach and remorse are ultimately because of this very failure, i.e., the refusal of his guilty wishes to undo the sin. By refusing to abandon his own incestuous wishes he perpetuates the sin and so must endure the stings of torturing conscience. And yet killing his mother's husband would be equivalent to committing the original sin himself, which would if anything be even more guilty. So of the two impossible alternatives he adopts the passive solution of letting the incest continue vicariously, but at the same time provoking destruction at the King's hand. Was ever a tragic figure so torn and tortured!

Action is paralyzed at its very inception, and there is thus produced the picture of apparently causeless inhibition which is so inexplicable both to Hamlet[37] and to readers of the play. This paralysis arises, however, not from physical or moral cowardice, but from that intellectual cowardice, that reluctance to dare the exploration of his inmost soul, which Hamlet shares with the rest of the human race. "Thus conscience does make cowards of us all."

Notes

1. ERNEST JONES, "The Oedipus Complex as an Explanation of Hamlet's Mystery: A Study in Motive," *American Journal of Psychology*, 21:72-113, 1910.
2. WILLIAM SHAKESPEARE, *Hamlet,* ed. Ernest Jones (New York: The Viking Press, 1947).
3. ERNEST JONES, *Hamlet and Oedipus* (New York: W. W. Norton and Company, 1949).

1. HERMAN BAUMGART, *Die Hamlet-Tragödie und ihre Kritik* (Königsberg: Koch, 1877).

2. RICHARD LOENING, *Die Hamlet Tragödie Shakespeares* (Stuttgart: Cotta, 1893).

3. W. F. TRENCH, *Shakespeare's* Hamlet: *A New Commentary* (London: Smith, Elder, 1913).

4. JOSEF KOHLER, *Shakespeare vor dem Forum der Jurisprudenz* (Würzburg: Stahel, 1883), p. 195.

5. It need hardly be said that the play, like most others, appeals to its audience in a number of different respects. We are here considering only the main appeal, the central conflict in the tragedy.

6. "Rationalization in Every Day Life," *Journal of Abnormal Psychology* (1908), p. 168.

7. A. C. BRADLEY, *Shakespearean Tragedy* (London: The Macmillan Company, 1905).

8. S. DE MADARIAGA, *On Hamlet* (London: Hollis and Carter, 1948).

9. WILHELM WETZ, *Shakespeare vom Standpunkt der vergleichenden Litteraturgeschichte* (Worms: Reitz, 1890), Vol. I, p. 186.

10. LOENING, *op cit.,* p. 245.

11. "Rationalization in Every Day Life," p. 161.

12. LUDWIG TIECK saw in Hamlet's cowardly fear of death a chief reason for his hesitancy in executing his vengeance (*Dramaturgische Blätter,* 2:1826). How well Shakespeare understood what this fear was like may be inferred from Claudio's words in *Measure for Measure:*

> The weariest and most loathed worldly life
> That age, ache, penury and imprisonment
> Can lay on nature is a paradise
> To what we fear of death.
>
> (III.i.31-34)

13. LOENING, *op. cit.,* pp. 245, 246.

14. Had this relationship not counted as incestuous, then Queen Elizabeth would have had no right to the throne; she would have been a bastard, Katherine of Aragon being still alive at her birth.

15. F. J. FURNIVALL, *Introduction to the "Leopold" Shakespeare* (London: Cassell), p. 72.

16. *Ibid.,* p. 70.

17. JOHN CONNOLLY, *A Study of Hamlet* (London: Moxon, 1963), pp. 22, 23.

18. T. S. ELIOT, *Selected Essays* (London: Faber and Faber, 1932).

19. Josef Wihan, "Die Hamletfrage," *Leipziger Beiträge zur englischen Philologie* (1921), p. 89.

20. Dover Wilson, *What Happens in* Hamlet (Cambridge, England: Cambridge University Press, 1925).

21. See, for instance, Wulf Sachs, *Black Hamlet* (London: Bles, 1937).

22. Here, as throughout this essay, I closely follow Freud's interpretation given in the footnote previously referred to. He there points out the inadequacy of the earlier explanations, deals with Hamlet's feelings toward his mother, father, and uncle, and mentions two other matters that will presently be discussed, the significance of Hamlet's reaction against Ophelia and of the probability that the play was written immediately after the death of Shakespeare's own father.

23. For example, Georg Brandes, *William Shakespeare* (London: Heinemann, 1898), remarks that Hamlet's talk to Ophelia could be translated as "You are like my mother; you could behave like her" (Vol. II, p. 48).

24. Johann Wolfgang von Goethe, *Wilhelm Meister*, IV, 14: "Her whole being hovers in ripe, sweet voluptuousness." "Her fancy is moved, her quiet modesty breathes loving desire, and should the gentle Goddess Opportunity shake the tree the fruit would at once fall."

25. For instance, D. B. Storffrich, *Psychologische Aufschlüsse über Shakespeares Hamlet* (Bremen: Kauhtman, 1859), p. 131; Karl Dietrich, *Hamlet, der Konstabel der Vorsehung; eine Shakespeare-Studie* (Hamburg: Nolte, 1883), p. 129; Tieck, *op. cit.,* pp. 85 ff.

26. Loening, *op. cit.,* chap. 13, "Charakter und Liebe Ophelias."

27. Bradley, *op. cit.,* p. 118.

28. It is not maintained that this was by any means Claudius' whole motive, but it was evidently a powerful one and the one that most impressed Hamlet.

29. His similar tone and advice to the two women show plainly how closely they are identified in his mind. Cf. "Get thee to a nunnery: why wouldst thou be a breeder of sinners?" (III.ii.122-123), with "Refrain tonight;/And that shall lend a kind of easiness/To the next abstinence" (III.iv.165-167).

The identification is further demonstrated in the course of the play by Hamlet's killing the men who stand between him and these women (Claudius and Polonius).

30. Wilson, *op. cit.,* p. 270.

31. It is noteworthy how many producers and actors seem to accept

Hamlet's distorted estimate of Polonius, his garrulity being presumably an excuse for overlooking the shrewdness and soundness of his worldly wisdom. After all, his diagnosis of Hamlet's madness as being due to unrequited love for Ophelia was not so far from the mark, and he certainly recognized that his distressful condition was of sexual origin.

32. What Skakespeare thought of Jephthah's behavior toward his daughter may be gathered from a reference in *Henry VI, Part III* (V.i.). See also on this subject CHARLES WORDSWORTH, *On Shakespeare's Knowledge and Use of the Bible* (London: Elder, 1864), p. 67.

33. SIGMUND FREUD, "Trauer und Mealcholie," *Vierte Sammlung kleiner Schriften* (1918), chap. 20.

34. F. T. VISCHER, "Hamlet, Prinz von Dänemark," *Shakespeare Vorträge,* I:1899.

35. OTTO RANK, "Das Schauspiel in Hamlet," *Imago,* 4:45. There is a delicate point here which may appeal only to psychoanalysis. It is known that the occurrence of a dream within a dream (when one dreams that one is dreaming) is always found when analyzed to refer to a theme which the person wishes were "only a dream," that is, not true. I would suggest that a similar meaning attaches to a "play within a play," as in *Hamlet.* So Hamlet (as nephew) can kill the King in his imagination since it is "only a play" or "only in play."

36. The situation is perfectly depicted by Hamlet in his cry

> I do not know
> Why yet I live to say "this thing's to do,"
> Sith I have cause, and will, and strength, and means,
> To do't.

(IV.iv.43-46)

With greater insight he could have replaced the word "will" by "pious wish," which, as LOENING (*op. cit.,* p. 246) points out, it obviously means. Oddly enough, WILLIAM ROLFE, in his Introduction to KARL WERDER, *The Heart of Hamlet's Mystery,* trans. Elizabeth Wilder (New York: G. Putnam and Sons, 1907), p. 23, quotes this very passage in support of Werder's hypothesis that Hamlet was inhibited by the thought of the external difficulties of the situation, which shows to what straits the supporters of this untenable hypothesis are driven.

The Matricidal Impulse:
Critique of Freud's Interpretation of "Hamlet"

Few criticisms of literature have provoked a reaction so widespread and so passionate as the one provoked by the Freud-Jones view of *Hamlet*. From quarters inhabited by analysts and by critics with psychoanalytic leanings came numerous expressions of belief and gratitude: The mystery had been solved and hats off to those who had solved it. From literary circles, however, came a great many statements of disbelief and shock, as well as critical assaults that aimed at pointing up the erroneousness of regarding Hamlet in the Freud-Jones manner. The Prince, went the assaults, is not a real person but a character in a play and it is mistaken to treat him as a real person; moreover, the theater-reality of the tragedy is a far cry from the intricacies of psychoanalytic speculation. The play's the thing the critic should consider, not the Prince. Of course this is all vastly general. The camps were not—and are not—so clearly divided and armed, though one still runs the risk of being branded an iconoclast by the majority of literary Shakespeareans when he announces his belief in the psychoanalytic solution to The Problem. Nor would it be correct to suggest that the objections to the Freud-Jones view came exclusively from areas outside psychoanalysis. On the contrary, the accuracy of that view was seriously challenged within orthodox psychoanalysis itself, and it is to such developments that we must now turn our attention.

Although it is true that Frederic Wertham's matricidal approach to the tragedy (1941) was foreshadowed in the writings of Erich Wulffen (1913),[1] it was Wertham who really worked out the idea. Objecting to the view that "repressed death wishes against the father, a patricidal drive, is the theme of *Hamlet*," Wertham maintains that the text of the play bears out the interpretation that Hamlet's primary emotional struggle is with his impulses "to take revenge on and punish the mother." The play affords us no evidence of Hamlet's hostility against the real father, but it does afford us plenty of evidence of his hostility against the mother. Moreover, as Hamlet's matricidal tendencies develop, they call to Wertham's mind actual instances from his own clinical experience, not only in terms of general characteristics, but also in terms of specific details. "The real basis of Freud's interpretation is his theory that the Oedipus complex is a universal, biological, normal, unavoidable inheritance of the human race. In the very case of Hamlet, it can be demonstrated—and for the first time in a concrete case analyzed by Freud—that this theory has to be modified." It is not the "Oedipus complex" but the "Orestes complex" that is at

M. F.

ccording to Freud, Shakespeare's *Hamlet* deals with the theme of patricide.[1] He published this for the first time in *The Interpretation of Dreams* in 1900. Wittels has succinctly summarized this interpretation: "Hamlet cannot love Ophelia because he has a mother fixation. He cannot revenge his father, cannot fulfill the Ghost's command to kill his (Hamlet's) stepfather, because the murder of his father was a deed which Hamlet himself has long harbored as a design in his unconscious. Hence his irresolution."[2]

Ernest Jones developed Freud's interpretation in a monograph.[3] According to his formulation, "the main theme of this story is a highly elaborated and disguised account of a boy's love for his mother and consequent jealousy of and hatred towards his father."

What supports Freud's interpretation that repressed death wishes against the father, a patricidal drive, is the theme of *Hamlet?* There are at least six points to be considered.

1. The first is the Ghost's "command to kill his [Hamlet's] stepfather." If you will look up the text of Hamlet, you will find that this command is nonexistent. Neither in his first appearance, on the platform, nor in his second appearance, in the Closet Scene, does the Ghost say one word about killing Claudius.[4]

The Ghost does give a command. It is directed against the mother, and not at the father. And it is a negative one: Do not harm your mother!

"The Matricidal Impulse: Critique of Freud's Interpretation of *Hamlet*" by Frederic Wertham. Reprinted with permission from *Journal of Criminal Psychopathology*, II (1941) 455-464.

"Let not thy soul contrive against thy mother aught!"

According to fundamental psychoanalytical tenets, such a prohibition would not be expressed by the father if there were no psychological need for it in the son's mind.

2. The dead father appears to the son as a ghost. But this cannot be taken as an indication of repressed hostility against the father on the part of the son.

The apparition of the Ghost must be interpreted, of course, as if it were a dream image. Very frequently, the appearance of a dead person in dreams is the assertion of one part of the dreamer's ego. The ghost of the father is that part of Hamlet's personality which identifies itself with the father. It is the self-assertion within the son of the patriarchal father.

The ghost of the father appears as a friend, and makes the son his representative. He tells him in effect: You take my place; you have the patriarchal right and duty to guard the mother, but do not hurt her physically.

3. Freud's interpretation takes it for granted that the revenge on Claudius is Hamlet's main impulse throughout the play. The text does not bear this out.

The revenge—as the text abundantly shows—is primarily a revenge for the adultery of the mother with the uncle, and is only secondarily for the murder of the father. Hamlet lays the chief blame for this adultery on the mother and not on Claudius. Throughout the play, his hatred for Claudius plays a role subordinate to the emotional struggle with his impulse to take revenge on and punish the mother.

Hamlet kills Claudius only after his mother is dead. Even then he does not do it unprompted. At the very end of the play Laertes has to draw his attention expressly to the king:

> The king, the king's to blame.
>
> (V.ii.331)

It is only then that Hamlet finally stabs Claudius.

4. Hamlet expresses in the play his great love and admiration for his father. That this feeling *may* be accompanied by ambivalence must be conceded. But there is no evidence of this hostility against the real father in the text, and certainly no evidence either in the text or in the whole psychological setting of the story, that this assumed hostility is

so strong and far-reaching that it can serve as the main explanation of Hamlet's behavior.

5. Freud has taken from Georg Brandes' biography of Shakespeare the statement that *Hamlet* was written after the death of Shakespeare's father. But there is no historical evidence for that assumption.

On the contrary, the available evidence to date suggests that *Hamlet* was written before that event. The source of Shakespeare's *Hamlet* was a play, now lost, that existed in 1594. The death of Shakespeare's father is recorded in the Parish Register of Stratford for September 8, 1601. The first entry of *Hamlet* in the Stationers' Register is dated July 26, 1602. Quite apart from historical allusions in the text of *Hamlet,* it is unjustified to assume that Shakespeare conceived, planned, and wrote his *Hamlet* in these few intervening months.

Even if it were so, Shakespeare's reaction to the death of his father is entirely unknown to us. It therefore cannot be used as confirmation of any interpretation of *Hamlet*.

6. Finally, there is the Oedipus complex. Freud has spoken of an "identity" between Hamlet and Oedipus. However, in his interpretation of *Hamlet,* the Oedipus complex is not only reached as a conclusion; it is assumed as a starting-point in the beginning. This is the crux of the whole matter. The real basis of Freud's interpretation is his theory that the Oedipus complex is a universal, biological, normal, unavoidable inheritance of the human race. In the very case of Hamlet, it can be demonstrated—and for the first time in a concrete case analyzed by Freud—that this theory has to be modified.

A number of years ago I observed a young man whose case had a remarkable similarity to *Hamlet*. After his father's death, this young man's mother had relations with his uncle. The uncle usurped this patient's possessions. Like Hamlet, he remembered and harped on the happy love relationship that had existed between his parents and was shocked at the brief interval between his father's death and his mother's transfer of affection to the uncle. His dead father, like the Ghost of *Hamlet,* appeared to him. The patient had a dream in which his father drew his attention to his mother's behavior: "Look at your mother; see what she's doing!"

He was intensely preoccupied with thoughts of revenge, but hesitated and delayed. At one time, like Hamlet in the Prayer Scene, he had his uncle at his mercy and could have killed him, but refrained from doing so. Rank explains the Play-Within-The-Play in Hamlet as symbolizing sexual spying upon the parents.[5] My patient actually carried this out. He went home one day stealthily and surprised his mother and her lover in the compromising situation of the *Ur-Szene*.

He had daydreams in which he threatened his mother with a gun and then recited to her all her sexual misdeeds. You will remember that Hamlet actually carries this out when he says to his mother:

> Come, come, and sit you down . . . I set you up a glass
> Where you may see the inmost part of you.
> (III.iv.18-20)

Immediately before going to his mother's bedroom my patient did not arrange—as Hamlet did before the Closet Scene—for a play to be performed, but went to a movie which depicted the pursuit of a successful revenge. Finally, in his mother's bedroom he did not restrain himself—as Hamlet did in the Closet Scene—and merely threaten and upbraid his mother; he stabbed her to death.

When I attempted to collect the literature on matricide, I found that there is no literature to collect. No systematic study of the subject exists, criminological, psychiatric, or psychoanalytic. My study, the results of which are only outlined here, is apparently the first and only one.

Matricide is not so exceedingly rare as the absence of scientific investigations might lead one to believe. From time to time new cases are reported. The murderers are usually very young, between fifteen and the middle or late twenties. They have no previous criminal or delinquent records. They are apt to be hypermoral rather than immoral. For the murder they use knives, hammers, hatchets, guns, but never poison. Frequently they are excessively attached to their mothers, are "unusually fond of her." They show little interest in the other sex. Concealment of their deed is apt to be perfunctory, and they usually make a full confession. Nearly always the murder takes place in the mother's bedroom.

Reexamination of Shakespeare's text shows that not a "patricidal" drive, but a consuming hostility against the *mother* and an emotional struggle with the impulse to matricide is the underlying pattern of *Hamlet*.

Although repressed and disguised, the matricidal theme can be demonstrated from the text. This pattern can be only briefly outlined here.

Immediately before going to his mother's closet, Hamlet warns himself not to "use" "daggers" against his mother and exclaims:

> Let not ever the soul of Nero enter this firm bosom.
>
> (III.ii.411-412)

The "soul of Nero" has and can have only one meaning here. Nero is the classical symbol of matricide. In the Closet Scene Hamlet does not discuss his father's murder or any revenge on his uncle.[6] He violently upbraids his mother for her sexual misdeeds. He threatens her so menacingly that she cries out:

> What wilt thou do? Thou wilt not murder me?
>
> (III.iv.21)

Following the Closet Scene and the second appearance of the Ghost —which is the high point of the play—the matricidal "soul of Nero" becomes less dreaded. But until the end of the play Hamlet never speaks of the murder of his father—about which his mother knew nothing—or the revenge on his uncle, without connecting them with the sexual guilt of his mother. Throughout the play his bitterest reflections are directed against her.

In a scene following the Closet Scene there is a curious passage. Hamlet's mother is not present. Hamlet addresses the King:

> Farewell, dear mother.
>
> *King.* Thy loving father, Hamlet.
>
> *Ham.* My mother; father and mother is man and wife,
> Man and wife is one flesh, so my mother.
>
> (IV.ii.50-55)

Neither Freud nor any other commentator has explained this seemingly nonsensical passage. Yet it is Freud who gave us the key in his "Psychopathology of Everyday Life."

Hamlet's slip in saying "mother" instead of father reveals his suppressed hostile preoccupation with his mother even when confronting the usurper. In an earlier scene the King, speaking to the Queen about Hamlet, actually warns her against the danger of matricide:

His liberty is full of threats to all,
To you yourself. . . ."
(IV.i.14-15)

In the Nunnery Scene Hamlet says to Ophelia:

I say we will have no more marriages; those that are married
already, all but one shall live; the rest shall keep as they are. . . .
(III.i.154-157)

In the Freudian interpretation—and in all others—it is taken for
granted that the line "All but one shall live" is a thrust at the King.
But the context itself shows beyond doubt that this murderous threat
is directed against the mother. For Hamlet speaks here only about
women: they paint their faces, they jig, amble, and make their wantonness ignorance.

Hamlet is being watched in this scene by the King and Polonius, who
are hiding behind a curtain. In modern productions stage directions
have been introduced according to which Hamlet would know that he
is being watched. But there is no authority for such stage business,
either in the texts or in the stage history of the play. Hamlet speaks in
this scene with deep earnestness and not for the information of eaves-
droppers. His words "All but one shall live" are the keynote of the
play. They refer to the mother.

In the Play-Within-The-Play Scene Hamlet's attention is more on
his mother than on his uncle-stepfather. And all through the play his
expressions of hostility are more often and more clearly directed
against his mother than against his uncle. This is not inference; it is
the naked evidence of the text.

From the Play Scene, Hamlet goes to his mother's closet to do

. . . such bitter business as the day would quake to look on.
(III.ii.409-410)

Neither for Hamlet, nor for an Elizabethan audience, nor for Shakespeare (on the evidence of his other plays) would such strong words
be applicable to revenge on the murderer of his father. They refer
to his matricidal impulse.

Hamlet's mother does not die at his hand. But he alone initiates
the circumstances that lead to her death.[7] When he finally stabs

Claudius, his last words to the King show again his underlying matricidal trend. He reproaches the King not for the murder, but for the "incest" and then exclaims:

> Follow my mother.
> (V.ii.338)

The basis of Hamlet's hostility against his mother is his overattachment to her, just as it is in the matricidal patient with whom I have compared him. But this overattachment to the mother need not necessarily lead to hatred against the father or the father-image. It turns into a violent hatred toward the mother, while the image of the father is a friendly one.

Just as the Oedipus complex may be most clearly manifest in cases of patricide, so the situation of "son against mother" is most clearly manifest in overt cases of matricide. While these overt cases are rare, their psychological equivalents are not infrequent. I have collected a considerable number of cases: matricidal ideas appearing in dreams or as the content of psychotic symptoms; sons who have an obsessive fear of injuring their mothers with a knife or a fountain pen, or by leaving the gas turned on, and who on analysis have an excessive attachment to their mothers; a nine-year-old boy who attempted to stab his mother in a somnambulistic state of which he had no memory; schizophrenic patients who satisfy their hostility against the mother by a delusional denial of her existence, or who hear hallucinatory commands to kill her.

In suitable cases the mode of development of this central hostility against the mother can be demonstrated. While the roots of opposition between mother and son may go back to childhood, the ambivalence becomes acute and manifests itself in open antagonism and conflict when the distorted mother image stands in the way of the son's adolescent or mature striving toward a psychologically adequate love object. The psychological distortion of the mother image—to which usually correspond contradictions in the social position of the mother within the family and within society—is the operative principle in the chain of events. It is my thesis that excessive attachment toward the mother can be transformed directly ino a violent hostility against her. There are many cases of adults and children that cannot be understood without a knowledge of this typical psychological constellation, its multiform disguises, and the forms of adjustment by which it is overcome. This variety of parent complex which centers on the mother, and more specifically on hostility toward her, can be designated as the Orestes complex.

Orestes killed his mother Clytemnestra and her lover, his father's kinsman, Aegisthus. The legend of Orestes, which historically marks a turning point in the social position of the mother, has far more similarity to the story of Hamlet than has the story of Oedipus.

Notes

1. ERICH WULFFEN, *Shakespeares Hamlet ein Sexualproblem* (Berlin: Carl Duncker, 1913).
2. It should be noted that ERNEST JONES, in Chapter V of the 1949 edition of *Hamlet and Oedipus,* comments upon Wertham's point of view.

1. S. FREUD, *Dostojewski and Patricide,* in *Collected Papers* (Leipzig: Franz Deuticke, 1934).
2. F. WITTELS, *Sigmund Freud* (Vienna: E. P. Tal, 1924).
3. E. JONES, *Essays in Applied Psycho-Analysis* (London: International Psycho-Analytic Press, 1923).
4. This is not a candid reading. Wertham is stretching things a bit here to make his case (Editor's note).
5. O. RANK, "The 'Play-Within-the-Play' in *Hamlet*," *Imago,* 4:1915.
6. But the Ghost appears, and its appearance may be related to the problem of patricide (Editor's note).
7. Again Wertham appears to be stretching things a bit (Editor's note).

On the Mutuality of the Oedipus Complex:
Notes on the Hamlet Case

The Freud-Jones view of *Hamlet* encountered in the work of Frederic Wertham is a frontal attack upon its accuracy as criticism and its validity as science. This sort of confrontation, however, does not represent the general trend of psychoanalytic approaches to *Hamlet* after 1910, the year in which Jones's essay first appeared. Although some rumbling was noticeable within orthodox circles, the overall tendency was to build upon or modify the original position and to incorporate into it the new insights of the day. Freud, it seems, did not simply originate a tradition in which his science commented upon The Problem and attempted to resolve it; he also originated a tradition in which commentators looked to *Hamlet* (as Freud obviously did) in an effort to ascertain new truths about the human situation. From one perspective, it would be fair to say that Freud's actual criticisms of literature resulted from a *return* to materials that aided him in formulating the ideas ultimately employed as critical tools. Generally speaking, this symbiotic activity was carried on by Freud's successors. Yet, so numerous are the discussions that develop or modify the Freud-Jones view that one is forced to choose somewhat arbitrarily from among them and to hope that his judgement is able to select an outstanding example that is not only interesting in itself but also indicates significant trends in the science and in the criticism.

The work of Neil Friedman and Richard M. Jones suggests that the "classical" approach to *Hamlet,* the approach embodied in the work of Freud and Ernest Jones, needs to be modified. Such a suggestion is hardly surprising in view of the important changes that psychoanalysis has undergone in the past half century, and while this is obviously no place to chart these changes in an exhaustive way, it might be said generally that the crucial development lies in the area of psychosocial investigation, in the growing tendency of analysts to dwell not so much upon strictly intrapsychic phenomena as upon the give-and-take between the individual and his environment. Indeed, recent trends in psychoanalysis—the work of Hartmann, Rapaport, Kris, and particularly Erik Erikson—strongly suggest that Freud's original model of the mind, an intrapsychic model, needs to be altered to take into account the earliest stage in development when mother and child constitute a symbiotic unit; in later development, the whole social environment succeeds to the mother's role.

As students of Erikson, and as investigators in their own right, Friedman and Jones complain that the "classical" approach to the play fails to see Hamlet's behavior "in an adaptive perspective." They would shift the analysis from the "psychodynamic to the psychosocial level." It is not enough to say simply that Hamlet has an Oedipus complex and that for five acts he wriggles helplessly in its clutches. Such a view is ultimately static and ignores the very real fact that something *is* rotten in the State of Denmark and that Hamlet's problem is to a very great extent determined by that rottenness. Friedman and Jones see Hamlet as an individual who is struggling to grow, to mature, to achieve a meaningful, masculine identity; but they do not see the impediments to this development primarily in the psychodynamics of the protagonist himself; they see them in the State of Denmark as a whole, and this is where the rottenness comes in. Hamlet's world is corrupt and psychologically crippling because the people who make it up are, one and all, victims of "a system of tacit intrigue and unabashed spying by the older generation into the private affairs of the younger generation." All the members of the *Hamlet* universe (even the Ghost) are caught up in an atmosphere of oedipal rivalry, of parent-sibling conflict, an atmosphere that negates the possibility of open, honest action and, most of all, that negates the possibility of achieving a consistent, coherent identity. Hamlet becomes an actor and an equivocator because he lives in a world of acting and equivocating. He fails to accomplish his task because he fails to achieve the integrated, adult personality that such a task demands. The work of Friedman and Jones, apart from the new and valuable light it throws upon *Hamlet,* makes it abundantly clear that the "inter-fertilization between great intuitive and great rational discourses" need not diminish as "rational" or theoretical developments are made known.

M. F.

hat the poet anticipates the theorist is well seen in the relation of Shakespeare to Freud. A rare sensitivity to the misloyalties of sons and fathers made of *Julius Caesar* something more than a perceptive political drama. *Macbeth* comes from a hand as equipped to write with authority of unconscious designs as of conscious ones. King Henry's retort to his son who, thinking the old man dead, has taken his crown, "Thy wish was father, Harry, to that thought," is as nice an example of making the unconscious conscious as will be found in many a therapeutic adventure. And of *Hamlet,* to say that its author's articulation of the paradoxes of familial loves was clinically precise is but to embarrass clinicians. If Freud adds meaning to Hamlet for some, Hamlet lends meaning to Freud for many.

But Shakespeare was not simply a pre-Freudian. The constant temptation of Psychological Man is to reinterpret alien geniuses as mere Freudian forerunners. Freud himself was no stranger to the temptation. In a letter to Fliess (May 31, 1897) he wrote that his own analytic work substantiated the Bard "in his juxtaposition of poetry and madness."[1] Freud saw preconfirmation for his own *sometimes* reductive view of the artist in Theseus' famous speech from *Midsummer Night's Dream:*

> The lunatic, the lover, and the poet,
> Are of imagination all compact.
> (V.i.7-8)

"On the Mutuality of the Oedipus Complex: Notes on the Hamlet Case" by Neil Friedman and Richard M. Jones. Reprinted with permission from *American Imago,* XX (1963), 107-131.

Freud here accepts Theseus as Shakespeare's voice and so adds the Bard to his own lineage. The fallacy is that Theseus and Bottom are the literal-minded minority spokesmen in a play which suggests that fancy is as real as reality. What size are the fairies in *Midsummer Night's Dream*? Life-size. The play incorporates within itself an ironic parallel plot which is meant to highlight by contrast the play's main action but which succeeds here only in tripping up the investigator intent on planting a family tree.

And this is ironic. For the method of the parallel plot highlights a formal linkage between Freud and Shakespeare which has, so far as we can tell, been overlooked in the search for contextual similarities. Writing about Hamlet, Francis Fergusson notes:

> It has been well established by now that the Elizabethan "double plot," at its best, is more than a device for resting the audience . . . the various stories with their diverse casts of characters are analogous and . . . the drama is therefore "one by analogy" only.[2]

And so it is with any of the Freudian masterpieces. The whole is not developed by a single line of reasoning or causality; instead the final fabric is woven from extended analogies. Like Shakespeare, Freud sees reverberations throughout various realms. He uses the dreamer, the neurotic, the child, the artist, the primitive, the sexual, the sublime to comment upon one another. Like Shakespeare's, Freud's imagination never isolates. It "holds the mirror up to nature." Freud and Shakespeare live in many worlds. They exploit various levels of experience, interweave and learn from them all. His dramatic imagination allows Freud to sample diverse worlds, remain a sojourner in each, and then leave with incisive perceptions to be alloyed with perceptions gathered from other areas. In *Henry IV* Shakespeare moved between the worlds of Falstaff and Pistol, Glendower and Hotspur, king and queen, that is, between tavern, battlefield, and court. Similarly, in the center of any of the Freudian masterworks may be the primitive, or the group, or the dreamer, or the artist, but the dramatic scene is constantly shifting to let Freud bring in from the wings data from some of his other realms.[3]

The above briefly suggests a promising area of investigation—the complex relation of poet and theorist—which has so far been done little justice by most psychoanalytic sorties into literature. The carelessness, moreover, has run both ways. Psychoanalytic interpreters of Hamlet mistake Shakespeare for Freud, while literary critics mistake Freud for Shakespeare. Interfertilization between great intuitive and great rational discourses has thereby been jeopardized, unnecessarily. In what follows, our major supposition shall be that while Freud continues to explicate Shakespeare, Shakespeare continues to implicate Freud. Specifically we shall endeavor to show that far from "resisting" the standard oedipal interpretation of Prince Hamlet, Shakespeare can be instrumental in broadening the psychoanalytic theory of the Oedipus complex itself.

Jones and Hamlet

> Mother, for love of grace,
> Lay not that flattering unction to your soul
> That not your trespass, but my madness speaks.
> It will but skin and film the ulcerous place,
> Whiles rank corruption, mining all within,
> Infects unseen.
>
> (*Hamlet*, III.iv.144-149)

The standard psychoanalytic interpretation of Hamlet is that he suffers from an Oedipus complex. As a child he had resented having to share his mother's affection, had therefore regarded his father as a rival, had wished him out of the way, and had repressed this wish. When the play opens his Uncle Claudius has murdered Hamlet's father and is sleeping with Hamlet's mother. The uncle has thus perpetrated in reality the two acts which are inextricably intertwined in Hamlet's unconscious fantasy. The accomplished usurpation further resembled the imaginary one in being incestuous. The similarity by association reactivates a noxious childhood fantasy which leads to Hamlet's subsequent depression and suffering. Hamlet cannot kill Claudius, for Claudius represents the most buried part of his own personality. He therefore becomes enmeshed in obsessional and self-destructive procrastination in his endeavor to fulfill his father's demand for revenge.

We have briefly summarized Ernest Jones' treatment of Hamlet, the most extensive in psychoanalytic literature.⁴ We shall show the inadequacy of this view by (1) locating its metapsychology within the history of psychoanalytic theory; (2) examining its exclusion of Hamlet's, and (3) of Shakespeare's historical contexts; (4) questioning its implied standard of right action; and (5) making clear that it leads to a false estimation of the role of Polonius in the play.

1. In his first chapter Jones advances credentials for embarking on a Freudian analysis of a literary subject. He contends that no previous psychological student of an artistic topic could plumb the depths because no previous student had had access to those depths which reveal themselves only in the cases of psychoneuroses: *"Depth psychology has perforce to be medical psychology."*⁵

Jones then notes an obvious objection to this approach:

> ... any conclusions reached by such investigations have their general validity vitiated by their origin in the study of the "abnormal."⁶

But he does not consider the objection decisive:

> This quite logical objection, however, lost its force when it was discovered that the neurotic symptoms that had given rise to the suffering proceed from primordial difficulties and conflicts inherent in every mind, and that they are merely one of the many ways in which attempts are made to cope with these.⁷

Jones adds, in his own defense, a concluding key sentence:

> ... the character traits and peculiarities of the *so-called "normal"* person, for instance, which are *commonly defensive* in nature, proceed from exactly the same source as do neurotic symptoms.⁸

This sentence circumscribes Jones's theoretical perspective. It serves both to date it within the history of psychoanalytic thought and to uncover its limitation. Jones's thinking comes out of the reductionistic period of psychoanalysis in which, as Rapaport puts it, "even crucial ego functions were conceived of in terms of instinctual drives,"[9] in which the ego's sole function was pictured as defensive. This theoretical preoccupation disqualified Jones from seeing Hamlet's behavior in an adaptive perspective; the perspective, that is, of a depth psychology which is not exclusively a medical psychology:

> If I had to describe such a condition as Hamlet's in clinical terms—which I am not particularly inclined to do—it would have to be as a severe case of hysteria on a cyclothymic basis.[10]

He is not inclined to do so, but he does. Hamlet the Prince is dissolved into Hamlet the Case. When Jones writes that his conclusions about Hamlet's psychic state are verified by their correspondence with the mechanisms found in the real Hamlets who are investigated psychologically, he glosses over the fact that Hamlet is on the stage, not on the couch. Psychoanalytic practice (necessarily medical) is here misused to buttress psychoanalytic metapsychology (necessarily ontological). It is one thing to "extrapolate from psychopathology what may be of benefit to normal psychology."[11] It is quite another to try to reduce all behavior to the vocabulary derived from the study of the abnormal.

2. To see Hamlet's behavior in an adaptive perspective is to move from the psychodynamic to the psychosocial level of analysis. The lever to be used is the question of the play's main concern. Jones writes:

> The play is mainly concerned with a hero's unavailing fight against what can only be called a disordered mind.[12]

In contrast to this view Francis Fergusson writes:

> The Oedipus complex does not account for the fact that Hamlet, besides being a son, is also a dispossessed prince; nor that Claudius, besides being a father symbol, is also the actual ruler of the state. But the actual movement of the play—to say nothing of its ultimate meaning—depends upon such objective facts and values as these . . .[13] The main action of Hamlet may be described as the attempt to find

and destroy the hidden "imposthume" which is poisoning the life of Claudius' Denmark . . .[14] We see that the welfare of Denmark . . . is the matter of the play as a whole, rather than Hamlet's individual plight.[15]

Thus Fergusson sees that a fundamental fact of the play is not only Hamlet's guilty conscience but also that something *was* rotten in the State of Denmark. The time *was* out of joint, such that Hamlet *was* cursed by his birth to set it right. Erik Erikson alludes to a society in which the confirming rituals no longer have the power and purity to enlist the talents and devotions of its youth. This was a society in need of rejuvenation.[16] And Denmark's rituals? From the martial changing of the guard, to the hypocrisy of the almost contiguous marriage and funeral, to the speciousness of Claudius's first court, to Polonius's "hugger-mugger" funeral at which the only ceremony was the convocation of politic worms, to Ophelia's "maimed rite," and finally to the black mass of Claudius' final court, they are all variations on a single theme. They are all "lamps lighting the rottenness of Denmark."[17]

It is this social malignancy—and a more basic one, which we shall soon indicate—that Jones overlooks in his idiopathic reading of the play. It is only through recognition of this malignancy that we can appreciate the adaptive achievement of Hamlet's actions. The other members of the court have chosen to "play along" and profit from Claudius' usurpation. They do not question the corrupt rituals. Only Hamlet's ultimate revenge remains as a revivifying force in the rotten universe of the play.

3. Fergusson also offers evidence that in terms of the society in which the play was first produced these ritual elements cannot be overlooked. The lever to be used here is the question of the source of the play's appeal. Jones traces the appeal of *Hamlet* to the empathy which one sufferer from an Oedipus complex feels for a fellow sufferer depicted on the stage.[18] Fergusson, on the other hand, shows that, like the Greek Theater of which it was the heir, the Elizabethan Theater was essentially a theater of ritual drama. Through his use of the parallel plot Shakespeare is able to widen his play to encompass all orders and levels of the community:

> . . . the toe of the peasant comes so near
> the heel of the courtier,
> he galls his kibe.
>
> (V.i.152-154)

Thus, Jones's exclusion from purview of the historical setting of *Hamlet* becomes multiply ahistorical if one considers the theater for which it was first produced. Shakespeare's audience came to see something more than a guilty son reacting to a guilty mother. That audience would have put much more weight than we, in an age of musical comedy, can know on the ritual occasions that elude Jones's focus. Shakespeare's audience came to be "purged" through witnessing the purification of a state, as well as to empathize with the tormented imagination of an individual.

4. Let us return from the problem of *Hamlet* to the problems of Hamlet. Jones quotes approvingly F. Harris:

> Why did Hamlet hate his mother's lechery? *Most men* would hardly have condemned it, certainly would not have suffered their thoughts to dwell on it beyond the moment. . . .[19]

and also Connolly, who

> pointed out the disproportion here existing between cause and effect, and gave as his opinion that Hamlet's reaction to his mother's marriage indicated in itself a mental instability, "a predisposition to actual unsoundness. . . ."[20]

Jones here shows no acumen for the psychology of young adulthood with its concern for fidelity and devotion. He also reveals a reactionary ethical sense. In viewing the malcontent as merely defensive and pathological, Jones aligns himself with the adjustment psychologists of the court of Elsinore:

Queen. Good Hamlet, cast thy nighted color off,
　　　And let thine eye look like a friend on Denmark.
　　　Do not forever with thy veiled lids
　　　Seek for thy noble father in the dust:

> Thou know'st 'tis common; all that lives must die,
> Passing through nature to eternity.
> *Ham.* Ay, madam, it is common.

(I.ii.69-74)

The play upon the double meaning of "common" is the perfect answer to Jones. For in real life "common" men are seldom so noble as Hamlet; few have such a sense of justice, such a penetrating and indignant perception of "carnal, bloody, and unnatural acts." *Most men* are willing to compromise both themselves and others, to make hay of the slings of outrageous fortune, to make their meek peace with existing villainy. When Jones proceeds to measure Hamlet by the rod of *most men* he threatens to accept a statistical definition of morality.

5. Finally, witness the untenable extreme to which Jones's single-minded psychiatry draws him in his view of Polonius, the prize specimen in Shakespeare's retinue of pretentious old prattlers. In his notes on the acting of Hamlet, Jones writes:

> Polonius is commonly turned into a buffoon, and his children, who certainly respect and obey him, are mistakenly made to snigger at him during his advice speech. It is *only* Hamlet who takes an unfavorable view of him, and that for reasons of his own which are far from objective.[21]

Jones's point is that Hamlet can indulge his hostility toward Claudius only by displacing it onto Polonius. This makes the latter "but a substitute for the step-father."[22] To Hamlet, Polonius is a prating and sententious doltard; but to Jones he constitutes a figure who is sympathetic "to those who compassionately recall his bygone capacities and services,"[23] a court leader to be noted for "the soundness and shrewdness of his worldly wisdom."[24]

But Hamlet is not, as Jones asserts, alone in his unfavorable view of Polonius:

> *Pol.* My liege, and madam, to expostulate
> What majesty should be, what duty is,
> Why day is day, night night, and time is time,
> Were nothing but to waste night, day, and time.

Therefore, since brevity is the soul of wit,
And tediousness the limbs and outward flourishes,
I will be brief. Your noble son is mad:
Mad call I it; for, to define true madness,
What is't but to be nothing else but mad?
But let that go.
Queen. *More matter, with less art.*

(II.ii.86-95)

And, as for his loyal services, have they not amounted to actually abetting in the usurpation of the throne?

King. You cannot speak of reason to the Dane,
And lose your voice; what would'st thou beg, Laertes,
That shall not be my offer, not thy asking?
The head is not more native to the heart,
The hand more instrumental to the mouth,
Than is the throne of Denmark to thy father.

(I.ii.44-49)

Lastly, transfixed as we tend to be by the majesty of Shakespeare's language, it is tempting to read "wisdom" into the following banalities:

Pol. And these few precepts in thy memory
See thou character. Give thy thoughts no tongue,
Nor any unproportion'd thought his act.
Be thou familiar, but by no means vulgar;
The friends thou hast, and their adoption tried,
Grapple them to thy soul with hoops of steel;
But do not dull thy palm with entertainment
Of each new-hatch'd, unfledg'd comrade. Beware
Of entrance to a quarrel, but being in,
Bear't that the opposed may beware of thee.
Give every man thine ear, but few thy voice;
Take each man's censure, but reserve thy judgment.
Costly thy habit as thy purse can buy,
But not express'd in fancy; rich, not gaudy;
For the apparel oft proclaims the man,
And they in France of the best rank and station
Are most select and generous, chief in that.

> Neither a borrower nor a lender be:
> For loan oft loses both itself and friend,
> And borrowing dulls the edge of husbandry.
> This above all: to thine own self be true,
> And it must follow, as the night the day,
> Thou canst not then be false to any man.
>
> (I.iii.58-80)

But the intent of the characterization cannot be lost when Shakespeare has this champion of truth and honor dispatch a spy to oversee the recipient of this advice, with instructions on how to remedy probable misdemeanors. Let us here suggest that in his views of Polonius Jones's countertransference is notably in evidence, and return from Hamlet to *Hamlet*.

Erikson and Hamlet

> For 'tis sport to have the enginer
> Hoist with his own petar.
> (*Hamlet*, III.iv.206-207)

What *was* the "hidden imposthume" that made of Claudius's Denmark "a prison"? What had set the time so out of joint? What social excesses existed that only the psychological excesses which rankled Hamlet sufficed to set them right? As we have seen, Fergusson notes phenotypical signs of societal decay. But he is vague as to their genotypical source. Again, Fergusson sees, as Jones cannot, that only Hamlet's integrity, over and above his neurosis, prevailed as an adaptive revivifying force in the rotten universe of the play. However, the question remains to be asked of this conclusion why Hamlet delayed so long. If Fergusson draws our attention to the weakness of Jones's psychology on these points, he proposes none of his own.

Toward such a psychology we begin by inquiring of the play into the child-rearing practices typical of the times. The reply is definite: The prevailing educational assumptions supported a system of tacit intrigue and unabashed spying by the older generation into the private affairs of the younger generation. The adults of the play are paternal rather than parental. Children are to be watched over, seen into, and so controlled.

Examples abound. We have noted one instance in Polonius's sending of his "bait of falsehood" on the very heels of his instruction to his son on how not to be false to any man:

> See you now;
> Your bait of falsehood takes this carp of truth;
> And thus do we of wisdom and of reach,
> With windlasses and with assays of bias,
> *By indirections find directions out.*
>
> (II.i.62-66)

A more flagrant example is to be noted in the devastating candor with which Polonius in all innocence administers the psychological *coup de grace* to his daughter Ophelia, having just enlisted her services as an instrument in her lover's betrayal:

> How now Ophelia!
> You need not tell us what Lord Hamlet said;
> *We heard it all.*
>
> (III.i.86-88)

But though he is the archspy, Polonius only embodies a predictable pattern that has deep roots in the society of the play. Claudius wants Hamlet, "Here, in the cheer and comfort of *our eye.*" Mothers, while not always active participants in these intrigues, are nevertheless sanctioning parties to them:

> *King.*   Sweet Gertrude, leave us too;
> For we have closely sent for Hamlet hither,
> That he, as 'twere by accident, may here
> Affront Ophelia.
> Her father and myself, *lawful espials,*
> Will so bestow ourselves, that, seeing unseen,
> We may of their encounter frankly judge,
> And gather by him, as he is behav'd,
> If't be the affliction of his love or no
> That thus he suffers for.
> *Queen. I shall obey you.*
>
> (III.i.28-37)

And the ghost of Hamlet's father will return in the bedroom scene to whet his son's almost blunted purpose and watch over his actions.[25]

Excessively watched children become, as we know, excessively wary adults. Thus:

Ham. What man dost thou dig it for?
Clown. For no man, sir.
Ham. What woman, then?
Clown. For none, neither.
Ham. Who is to be buried in't?
Clown. One that was a woman, sir; but, rest her soul,
    she's dead.
Ham. *How absolute the knave is! We must speak by the card, or*
    equivocation will undo us. By the Lord, Horatio, this three
    years I have taken note of it; the age is grown so picked that
    the toe of the peasant comes so near the heel of the courtier,
    he galls his kibe.

(V.i.141-154)

We surmise from this that the repeated finding out of directions by means of indirections has spawned a folkway of directness "by the card"—a reaction well known to children who are used to dealing with rude authority.

The King's question to Gertrude, "Where is your son?" is therefore not an innocent expression of curiosity but a key to the corruption of Denmark—the relation of the generations. There can be no mutual trust; only control and exploitation as against petty compliances and evasions. There is no sense of the young being allowed (or even expecting) privacy; there is only "lawful espial," an intrusion which is held to be neither an infringement on the rights of the young nor a transgression of the role of adults.

Pol. By heaven, it is as *proper* to our age
    To cast beyond ourselves in our opinions
    As it is for the younger sort
    To lack discretion.

(II.i.114-117)

The invasion of youthful privacy is but a custom—a custom against which Hamlet alone articulates uncustomary outrage:

Why, look you now, how unworthy a thing you make of
me. You would play upon me; you would seem to know my

stops; you would pluck out the heart of my mystery; you would sound me from my lowest note to the top of my compass; and there is much music, excellent voice, in this little organ, yet cannot you make it speak. 'Sblood! do you think I am easier to be played on than a pipe? Call me what instrument you will, though you can fret me, you cannot play upon me.

(III.ii.379-389)

The psychology with which we choose to formulate this generational conflict is that of Erik H. Erikson.[26] His psychosocial developmental scheme will comprehend both the matters which Fergusson leaves open.

In terms of Erikson's theory of the succession of phase-specific life crises, the child-rearing patterns described above lead us to look for a characteristic resolution of the autonomy/shame-doubt crisis in very early life. In terms of his theory of the universally sequential roots of virtue, we would expect the young of this society to grow up with weakened will and blunted purpose.[27] And so the ease with which Laertes, Ophelia, Rosencrantz, and Guildenstern become mere extensions of their elders' intrigues.

The role of the young man Hamlet can likewise best be understood through Erikson's developmental spectrum. As the play opens we see Hamlet in early adulthood still enmeshed in the identity crisis of late adolescence, and showing the fundamental timidity of will to be expected of any son of Denmark in oppositional dealings with his elders. His identity crisis is intensified by social conditions in Denmark's family.

Erikson designates "fidelity" as the human virtue central to the formation of ego identity in late adolescence. It is this quality of ego strength—or its absence—to which the youth approaching maturity is most keenly sensitive, in himself and in others. This is the nexus of ego development which stirs the young man or woman in all cultures to expect of himself no less than true personal growth, and, as he approaches independence, to settle for no less than a history of the same in those on whom he has thus far been *de*pendent. Thus the often painful scrutiny to which parents are held at this time. Thus too the "adolescent rebellions" as, generation by generation, the inequities of infantile superego formations are partially redeemed in the slow evolution of human conscience.

In the play the theme of Hamlet's tortured and unenjoined fidelity in relation to himself and others equals in emphasis his ambivalent struggle for revenge. The specific infidelity of his mother and the general infidelity between the outer appearances and the inner meanings of rituals and social relations in this society intensifies the crisis. Nothing is as it "seems." ("I know not 'seems,'" says Hamlet.) "Are you honest?" becomes Hamlet's calling card. For lack of anything genuine to become—no syntonic role being provided by the society—Hamlet assumes a negative identity. He takes a place outside his society. But the negative identity always "fits" umbilically the society in which it was formed. Hamlet becomes an actor. In a society in which one is constantly being spied upon, the putting on of an "antic disposition" buffers the intruding activity of adults. In a society in which sham and pretense are accepted and expected, becoming an actor realizes to its limits the unconscious tendency of that society. A society of actors is "purged" by an actor.

But if Hamlet the Prince has here hoisted the enginery with his own petar, Hamlet the Man has not gained by the exercise. He forfeits his life and leaves no heirs. We are obliged after all, therefore, to reconstruct Hamlet the Child. Insofar as the man inherited neurotic tendencies from the child, little has been left unsaid by Jones. But what of the ghost at whose instigation the revenge was hatched? Was this really an "honest ghost?" We judge this question to be crucial to any psychological analysis of the play which aspires to hold its own with the deep intuitive sense of personal tragedy typically inspired in the playgoer. Unmitigated neurosis is, after all, a bore.

From the psychosocial vantage it cannot go unnoticed that in his initial encounter with Hamlet—as in his second visitation—the Ghost does embody the paternalistic pattern seen in this corrupt state. Beyond this, let us examine at length the first interchange between Hamlet and the Ghost, inferring what we can from between the lines as to the specific undercurrents of this father-son relation:

Ghost.   My hour is almost come,
    When I to sulphurous and tormenting flames
    Must render up myself.
Ham. Alas! poor ghost.
Ghost. Pity me not, but lend thy serious hearing
    To what I shall unfold.

Ham. Speak, I am bound to hear.
Ghost. So art thou to revenge, when thou shall hear.
Ham. What?

(I.v.2-8)

Having forsworn pity, the Ghost continues to invite it:

Ghost. I am thy father's spirit;
      Doom'd for a certain term to walk the night,
      And for the day confined to fast in fires,
      Till the foul crimes done in my days of nature
      Are burnt and purg'd away. But that I am forbid
      To tell the secrets of my prison-house,
      I could a tale unfold whose lightest word
      Would harrow up thy soul, freeze thy young blood,
      Make thy two eyes, like stars, start from their spheres,
      Thy knotted and combined locks to part,
      And each particular hair to stand on end,
      Like quills upon the fretful porpentine.
      But this eternal blazon must not be
      To ears of flesh and blood. List, list, O, list!
      If thou didst ever thy dear father love—
Ham. O God!

(I.v.9-25)

We wonder here whether the doubt which the father casts on his son's love is not more than a rhetorical device, so consistent is it with the system of paternal exploitation previously outlined.

Ghost. Revenge his foul and most unnatural murder.
Ham. Murder!
Ghost. Murder most foul, as in the best it is;
      But this most foul, strange, and unnatural.
Ham. Haste me to know't, that I, with wings as swift
      As meditation or the thoughts of love,
      May sweep to may revenge.
Ghost.   I find thee apt:
      And duller should'st thou be than the fat weed
      That roots itself in ease on Lethe wharf,
      Woud'st thou not stir in this. Now, Hamlet, hear:
      'Tis given out that, sleeping in my orchard,

> A serpent stung me; so the whole ear of Denmark
> Is by a forged process of my death
> Rankly abused; but know, thou noble youth,
> The serpent that did sting thy father's life
> Now wears his crown.
> *Ham.*   O my prophetic soul!
>   My uncle!
>
>   (I.v.26-41)

Neither the son's trust nor the father's right is questionable, and yet the appeal is negative. *Mis*integrity of mind would be seen in Hamlet's *not* responding as desired. We know Hamlet in other contexts to be ultrasensitive to appeals of this ilk, and to possess great skill in turning them back upon their perpetrators. In this context, however, oedipal bias does lay its claim, and Hamlet is caught:

> *Ghost.* Ay, that incestuous, that adulterate beast,
>   With witchcraft of his wit, with traitorous gifts,
>   O wicked wit and gifts, that have the power
>   So to seduce! won to his shameful lust
>   The will of my most seeming-virtuous queen.
>   O Hamlet! what a falling-off was there;
>   From me, whose love was of that dignity
>   That it went hand in hand even with the vow
>   I made to her in marriage, and to decline
>   Upon a wretch whose natural gifts were poor
>   To those of mine!
>   But virtue, as it never will be moved,
>   Though lewdness court it in a shape of heaven,
>   So lust, though to a radiant angel link'd,
>   Will sate itself in a celestial bed,
>   And prey on garbage. . . .
>   O, horrible! O, horrible! most horrible!
>   *If thou hast nature in thee, bear it not;*
>   Let not the royal bed of Denmark be
>   A couch for luxury and damned incest.
>
>   (I.v.42-57, 80-83)

Again the negative appeal: *if* you love me, you will do as I say; *if* you are not a dullard . . . .—and now: *"if* thou hast nature in thee . . . ." Bear in mind that this is the prince for whom "the stamp of but one defect" is not lightly to be carried. Presumably the father knows his son. Presumably, also, he cannot simply trust what he knows.

We are inclined, in short, to approach this ghost in his own manner: *If* he was all as good as he says he was then why the negative appeals? A father does not invoke superego sanctions in a son in whom mature loyalty is obvious, unless he has something himself to hide. We shall theorize later as regards what this may have been, but here it warrants emphasis that it was in particular response to a father's ghost that Hamlet's usual perceptiveness failed him—as he uttered these famous last words:

> Remember thee!
> Ay, thou poor ghost, while memory holds a seat
> In this distracted globe. Remember thee?
> Yea, from the table of my memory
> *I'll wipe away all trivial fond records,*
> All saws of books, all forms, all pressures past
> That youth and observation copied there,
> And thy commandment all alone shall live
> Within the book and volume of my brain,
> Unmixed with baser matter.
>
> (I.v.95-104)

Repression, the tragedy that psychoanalysis best knows, thus guides the motive for revenge from the outset. Henceforth, Hamlet the Child is dead (and, therefore, Hamlet the Man, already done) and we may interpret the many consequent hesitations between the father's injunction and the son's eventual compliance with it as overdetermined by (1) the fundamentally blunted strength of will heretofore mentioned, (2) unconscious oedipal guilt, per Jones, and (3) a preconscious reluctance to forfeit identity to identification with a less than honest ghost. This precarious balance persists through the play until Hamlet's sense of fidelity allies itself regressively with oedipal hostility, and—directed by his negative identity to the last—the actor commits the ultimate act.

On the Mutuality of the Oedipus Complex

... and a little child shall lead them ....
(Isaiah 11:6)

We promised to show that so far from "resisting" the oedipal interpretation of Hamlet Shakespeare responds by broadening oedipal interpretations. What we have in mind is this: Erikson's concept of "mutuality" has yet, it seems to us, to come into its own in systematic psychoanalysis. Readers of *Childhood and Society* tend to be much taken with the observation that children bring up their parents as much as they are brought up by them.[28] Too often this has been regarded as a happy little sentiment conspicuous in its utterance by a psychoanalyst. It is more than that: it represents a basic shift in psychoanalytic theory, from the principle of infantile determinism to a principle of life cycle relativism, i.e., from genetic to epigenetic causality in the development of persons and societies.

With respect to the Oedipus complex, for example, what does it mean to speak of its "mutuality"? Parents do not usually seduce their children. (That was Freud's first answer). Nor do the more enlightened of them crudely threaten castration. And yet the child's Oedipus complex is not solely determined by his imagination. It is not just intrapersonal. (That was Freud's second answer.) It is interpersonal.

Therefore it will help us to review the irreducible prime factors of the oedipal situation from the child's point of view *and* from the parents'. From the child's point of view these are (1) comparative physical inadequacy, especially in regard to interpersonal sexuality; (2) superiority of imagination, especially in regard to interpersonal sexuality; and (3) a resultant urgency to feel in control of sexual desires (necessarily incestuous), which, paradoxically, the child could hardly consummate in any event of reality. To the extent that the child can develop this feeling of control without forfeiture of either his present imaginative or his future physical prowess he is said to develop an enduring sense of initiative. To the extent that he is constrained to forfeit some of both he does so by developing an enduring potential for guilt. The resultant ratio determines whether we say he enters middle childhood with a successfully or unsuccessfully resolved Oedipus complex. All of this is said to depend on the extent to which the child-parent relationships are governed by patterns of mutual regulation as against the extent to which they are governed by patterns of mutual duress.

What of the parents' point of view? Normal young married couples are not singularly dedicated to their children's Oedipus complexes (save, perhaps, those militant converts to psychoanalysis for whom garden variety conviction has come to seem an affliction). The parents are presumably engaged in continuing to live everyday lives of their own. Psychoanalysis in its haste to grind adulthood *into* childhood rather than to ground it *in* childhood has neglected to speak of these everyday adult circumstances. And yet if we wish to specify the mutuality of the Oedipus complex, we must start there: in the lives which are the parents' own.

With Erikson we assume the parents of first-born oedipal-age children to be focally involved in the normal life crisis of "intimacy vs. isolation." Turning our attention to the irreducible prime factors of *this* complex we find an exact complement to the Oedipus complex: (1) physical primacy, especially as regards interpersonal sexuality; (2) constricted imagination, especially as regards interpersonal sexuality; and (3) a renewed attempt to liquidate, in an adult partnership, left over oedipal debts of their own.

In other words, parents whose bodies and sentiments have been charted into the highways, by-ways, one-way streets, and dead ends which are the "civilized" sexual organizations, and whose imaginations have been schematized according to the clichés of everyday experience are faced with a clever devil who can still love with *all* of himself and gain pleasure from *all* his body's orifices and surfaces, and whose lively imagination is still unfettered by irrational conscience, or by identification with his parents. In his doctor games the child conceives ways of being intimate (ways of knowing another) which have long become taboo for his parents through the institutions of basic repression (the oedipal superego) and of surplus repression (education, religion, morality, etc.). The child has the gleam but lacks the wherefore; the adult has the wherefore but lacks the gleam.[29]

The child thus presents both a potential threat and a potential model to the parents, at the very time when for converse reasons the parents present the same dual specter to the child. Insofar as the child comes to associate his parents with controlled sexuality, to that extent he is strengthened by his identification with them in a matter of crucial developmental concern to him. Insofar as he comes to associate his parents with uncontrolled (*which includes too controlled*) sexuality, to that extent he is weakened via the same route. On the parents' side, insofar as they can admit to their conception of parenthood a recognition of the child's easier accessibility to imaginative behavior, to that extent may they admit a potentially rejuvenating influence into *their* lives, in a matter of critical developmental concern to *them*. For, indeed, the intimacy/isolation crisis will be the arena in which the oedipal consciences of adults will either be replaced by identity sanctions or reign supreme. Insofar, however, as marital bonds become intimacy barriers, and the piston-pure sexuality of the modern mechanized body causes these consciences to be more honored than the weak purposes of oedipal children, to that extent must the child be perceived as a threat to the sanity of established houses—and dealt with accordingly by one pattern or another of household defense.

We have examined the defensive pattern evolved by the House of Denmark. Intimacy between adults would be near impossible in a society in which basic patterns of interaction had hardened into ennobled forms of showing off. A substitute gratification would then have to be found to mask the default. We propose that the substitute in Denmark was none other than its ennobled forms of looking on— and into—the intimacies of its children. In this manner does personal retardation become social corruption, and lock itself into history.

Ultimately of course, defensive patterns are erected against *internal* rather than external dangers, which reminds us that we have omitted the id from the parental segment of our oedipal mutuality paradigm. Shakespeare, we think, did not, when he had Claudius clamor for:

> The present death of Hamlet. Do it, England;
> For like the *Hectic* in my blood he rages,
> And thou must cure me. Till I know 'tis done,
> Howe'er my haps, my joys were *ne'er begun*.
> (IV.iii.68-71)

(This is the crux of the potential threat posed by the imaginative child to the isolated adult: that his joys will be seen—too late—not to have begun.)

Or, more to the point (as usual) with Hamlet:

Ham. O Jephthah, judge of Israel, what a treasure hadst thou!
Pol. What a treasure had he, my lord?
Ham. Why,
> One fair daughter, and no more,
> The which he loved passing well.

Pol. (Aside) Still on my daughter.
Ham. Am I not i' the right, old Jephthah?
Pol. If you call me Jephthah, my lord, I have a daughter that I love passing well.
Ham. Nay, that follows not.
Pol. What follows then, my lord?
Ham. Why,
> As by lot, God wot,

and then, you know
> It came to pass, as most like it was.

The first row of the pious chanson will show you more; for look where my abridgement comes.

(II.ii.423-439)

The abridgement comes at a passage which describes an incestuous *and infanticidal* elder, and his ultimate downfall at the hands of the children of Israel.

We shall put down then, as the noxious parental wish which is symbiotic with the child's incestuous wish, and against which household defense patterns are ultimately constructed, that of infanticide. For the traditionally desirable Greek credentials, need we mention Medea? Electra, too, would serve. Nor, for this purpose, need we ever leave the first act of *Oedipus Rex*. Laius and Oedipus both have an Oedipus complex, wrote Geza Roheim. Now with the help of the Bard, we can update that foresight.

In conclusion we suggest that adult intimacy was precluded in Denmark by forces of social inertia. Therefore (1) children became increasingly threatening, (2) infanticidal wishes became increasingly pressing, and (3) the need for intimacy gratification went underground, seeking substitute outlets. The cultural superego, with the economy typical of neurotic symptom formation, then settled on an enduring missolution: It is as if it (the cultural superego) said to parents: "Now hear this, the thing to do is to spy on your children.

See how it works: (1) you get to be in on matters intimate, (2) you control the clever devils, and (3) *you get to kill your children!"* For Denmark, that is, no less than for Hamlet, the pattern was present from which neurosis follows: a repressed impulse deviously expressed by the very defenses erected against it. For, we submit that Hamlet the child was as surely put to death by Denmark as was Denmark by Hamlet the Prince.

As for Hamlet the Man, we can only say, with Fortinbras, that:

> . . . he was likely, *had he been put on,*
> to have prov'd most royally . . .
>   (V.ii.408-409)

Notes

1. SIGMUND FREUD, *The Origins of Psychoanalysis* (New York: Doubleday, 1957), p. 212.

2. FRANCIS FERGUSSON, *The Idea of a Theatre* (New York: Doubleday, 1949), pp. 114-115.

3. This question of the relation of Freud the scientist to the artist has caused many a psychoanalytic historian to come a cropper. Freud did say that he thought the highest source of resistance to his ideas would be to call him an artist. He did likewise say that the artist was comparable to the daydreamer. He did likewise say that only science is no illusion while art is but a substitute gratification. And so Ira Progoff concludes that Freud was a rational burgher of his time. And so psychoanalysts of smaller stature delight in laying bare the banal meanings of art works. Jones, we suspect, in a far less vulgar way than the contemporary financially pressed psychoanalytic specialist shared this disposition. (See GOMBRICH, *Psychoanalysis and Art History*.) But Freud also wrote admiringly of the poets, "who with hardly an effort do salve from the whirlpool of their own emotions the deepest truths, to which we others have to force our way, carelessly groping amid torturing uncertainties" (*Civilization and Its Discontents,* p. 122). We throw in our lot with that sentiment, and offer the poetry of Shakespeare, as against the chatter of psychoanalytic journals, in evidence.

4. ERNEST JONES, *Hamlet and Oedipus* (New York: Doubleday, 1949), p. 18.

5. *Ibid.*

6. *Ibid.*

7. *Ibid.*

8. *Ibid.*

9. DAVID RAPAPORT, "A Historical Survey of Psychoanalytic Ego Psychology," *Psychological Issues, 1*:7, 1959.

10. JONES, *op. cit.*, p. 76.

11. Attributed to Freud and quoted by ERIK ERIKSON, "The Problem of Ego Identity," *Psychological Issues, 1*:121, 1959.

12. JONES, *op. cit.*, p. 18.

13. FERGUSSON, *op. cit.*, p. 123.

14. *Ibid.*, p. 117.

15. *Ibid.*, p. 113.

16. ERIK ERIKSON, *Young Man Luther* (New York: W. W. Norton and Company, 1958), p. 114.

17. FERGUSSON, *op. cit.*, p. 132.

18. JONES, *op. cit.*, pp. 25, 57.

19. *Ibid.*, p. 133.

20. *Ibid.*, p. 71.

21. *Ibid.*, p. 182.

22. *Ibid.*, p. 154.

23. *Ibid.*

24. *Ibid.*, p. 99.

25. One must differentiate here between two levels of spying: There is the reaction to the specific threat raised by Hamlet, "Madness in great ones cannot unwatched go." But for unmad lesser ones the watching is there still. It is the thing to do in Denmark.

26. Erikson has at least three charts which have yet to be synthesized. One is a chart of low level theorizing to be found on pp. 83-84 of *Childhood and Society*. This related body zones to social modalities. A second, to be found facing p. 121 of *Psychological Issues*, Vol. 1, No. 1, is more longitudinal in scope, relating a succession of phase-specific developmental crises from birth to death to the derivatives of each crisis for identity formation. The third and newest work chart can be found in the paper, "Roots of Virtue." This links the source of human virtues to the developmental scheme of the second chart. Part of our task in this paper has been to link the crisis (autonomy-shame) to the mode (intrusiveness) to the virtue (will, purpose) and finally to project these results into the later crisis (identity) with its own virtue (fidelity) and its social structural complement (ritual). A theory which can do this is quite a theory. For someone more interested

in polishing up theory than in rewriting applications, the systematic dovetailing and explicating of these three charts—there is a fourth—remains in front of us.

27. And, conversely, a show of autonomy on the part of a child would be stigmatized as a socially aberrant display of will:

Claudus: 'Tis sweet and commendable in your nature, Hamlet,
   To give these mourning duties to your father;
        . . . but to persever
   In obstinate condolement is a course
   Of impious stubborness; 'tis unmanly grief;
   It shows a will most incorrect to heaven, . . .
              (I.ii.87-88, 92-95)

28. ERIK ERIKSON, *Childhood and Society* (New York: W. W. Norton and Company, 1950).

29. Basically we are suggesting a level of concordance between the works of NORMAN BROWN, *Life Against Death;* HERBERT MARCUSE, *Eros and Civilization;* and ERNEST SCHACHTEL, *Metamorphosis.* The three share a turning to childhood faculties as a source of utopian imagery—for Brown and Marcuse as the exemplar of nonrepressions, for Schachtel as the exemplar of a nonembedded world openness. We believe that Erikson shares this new (and romantic) bias, as exemplified by the sentence, "We must learn to be more childlike if we are to avoid utter cosmic childishness." The intersections of these four theorists and their relation to the previous generation of psychoanalysts (Fromm, Horney, and others), is a topic deserving of mention and further contemplation.

The Dramatic Device: A Play Within A Play

As was pointed out earlier, not every psychoanalytical reading of *Hamlet* is devoted to explaining The Problem; it is unfortunate that literary scholars are apt to believe that when they have read a few pages of Jones or perhaps a brief review of some work that presents his view in a slightly modified form, they have exhausted not only the analytic readings of *Hamlet* but also the field of psychology and Shakespeare as well. This anthology as a whole demonstrates, of course, that that field is wide, and varied, and truly challenging—and probably that it offers the student of Shakespeare many criticisms that are better as criticisms than the work of Jones himself. The following paper by Alexander Grinstein reflects the interest of analytic critics in the play within the play. Indeed, it should be mentioned that with the overwhelming exception of The Problem, and with the possible exception of Hamlet's "antic disposition," the play within the play has called forth most of the analytic commentaries on Shakespeare's tragedy.

Grounding his observations in Freud's *Interpretation of Dreams,* and building upon the earlier work of Rank,[1] Jones,[2] and Eissler,[3] Grinstein suggests that the play within the play may be compared to a dream within a dream. Because dreams are wish fulfillments, a dream that one is dreaming signifies (1) that the dreamer is wishing the thing described as a dream "had never happened" and (2) that the dreamer is confessing disguisedly that it *did happen*. With regard to Hamlet, the play within the play gives expression to his wish (1) that his father had not been murdered (something that happened) and (2) that his father's murder had not aroused his oedipal desires (something that *also* happened). With regard to Claudius, the Mouse Trap makes him wish he had not murdered his brother. After making these initial points, Grinstein goes on to take up a matter that has puzzled critics of all persuasions, namely, why does not the King "blench" during the dumb show? Why is it only later that he "starts away"? In his reply to this question, Grinstein not only puts forward a stimulating and cogent solution, but also sheds light upon the way in which the Mouse Trap, as a dramatic device, prepares the audience emotionally for the tragedy's resolution.

M. F.

he dramatic device of a play within a play has proved very effective and has been successfully employed in many plays. Its use, although frequently dictated by technical considerations, may actually be considered to be related to a familiar psychological mechanism seen in dream work, namely, a dream within a dream.

Freud, in discussing this subject, wrote: "What is dreamt in a dream after waking from the 'dream within a dream' is what the dream wish seeks to put in the place of an obliterated reality. It is safe to suppose, therefore, that what has been 'dreamt' in the dream is a representation of the reality, the true recollection, while the continuation of the dream, on the contrary, merely represents what the dreamer wishes. To include something in a 'dream within a dream' is thus equivalent to wishing that the thing described as a dream had never happened. In other words, if a particular event is inserted into a dream as a dream by the dream work itself, this implies the most decided confirmation of the reality of the event—the strongest *affirmation* of it."[1]

It is impossible, in this brief communication, to go into great length with regard to either any number of plays or even the complex details of any single one of them. In order to elucidate my point, therefore, I shall limit the paper to one dramatic work which is well known to everyone, namely, *Hamlet*.

We find here an interesting situation in which Hamlet contrives with the players to stage a performance which would test the truth of the Ghost's assertions.

"The Dramatic Device: A Play Within A Play" by Alexander Grinstein. Reprinted with permission from *Journal of the American Psychoanalytic Association*, IV (1956), 49-52.

> . . . the play's the thing
> Wherein I'll catch the conscience of the King.
>
> (II.ii.638-639)

He enlists Horatio's assistance to observe his uncle's reaction to the play.

> I prithee, when thou seest that act afoot,
> Even with the very comment of thy soul
> Observe my uncle; . . .
> . . . Give him heedful note;
> For I mine eyes will rivet to his face,
> And after we will both our judgments join
> In censure of his seeming.
>
> (III.ii.83-85, 89-91)

The actual play within the play is preceded by a brief dumb show, the instructions of which are as follows:

> *Enter a King and a Queen, very lovingly; the Queen embracing him, and he her. She kneels, and makes show of protestation unto him. He takes her up, and declines his head upon her neck; lays him down upon a bank of flowers: she, seeing him asleep, leaves him. Anon comes in a fellow, takes off his crown, kisses it, and pours poison in the King's ears, and exits. The Queen returns; finds the King dead, and makes passionate action. The Poisoner, with some two or three Mutes, comes in again, seeming to lament with her. The dead body is carried away. The Poisoner woos the Queen with gifts: she seems loath and unwilling awhile, but in the end accepts his love.*
>
> (III.ii.between 145 and 146)

If we now apply Freud's observations to this play within a play, we find that indeed it does in effect represent the *historical* reality, in so far as we know it from the Ghost (Hamlet's father) who described the details of his assassination to Hamlet:

> . . . Sleeping within my orchard,
> My custom always in the afternoon,
> Upon my secure hour thy uncle stole,

With juice of cursed hebenon in a vial,
And in the porches of my ears did pour
The leperous distilment; . . .
Thus was I, sleeping, by a brother's hand
Of life, of crown, of queen, at once dispatched.

(I.v.59-63, 74-75)

It is also true here, as in the dream, that to include something in a dream within a dream is equivalent to wishing it had never happened. Hamlet certainly wished on one level, that his father had not been murdered nor that he would be required to avenge him. After the Ghost Scene he exclaims:

The time is out of joint: O cursed spite,
That ever I was born to set it right!

(I.v.189-190)

This wish that his father had not been murdered contains, on a deeper layer, the wish of not being confronted with an overt expression of his own oedipal strivings.

Viewed from the standpoint of Claudius, Hamlet's uncle, one may see here too that the play within the play confirms the historical reality of the King's murder. The proof for this is that after the play within the play he admits his deed in a soliloquy:

O! my offence is rank, it smells to heaven;
It hath the primal eldest curse upon 't;
A brother's murder!

(III.iii.36-37)

Claudius, in the prayer scene, clearly demonstrates not only his guilt but also his wish (at least in part) to undo his deed.

There is another point here which is interesting, namely that Claudius does not shown any sign of emotional disturbance on viewing the dumb show. The reason for this may be that, although a murder of a king is portrayed, and in the manner that he himself presumably killed his brother, the identity of the murderer still remains unspecified. In the play within the play, however, which profoundly upsets him, and makes him leave, the murderer is Lucianus, who is the *nephew* of the *King*. The play within the play thus implies a direct threat to him, namely, that Hamlet would kill him in the same manner *(lex talionis)* as he (Claudius) murdered his brother.[2] If we now attempt to apply the parallel to the dream within the dream, we find that, as far as the *historical reality* is concerned, Hamlet had not murdered his uncle. The play within the play, however, *presages* what is to develop in the play itself, namely, that Hamlet will kill him in the end. In addition, including this murder in a play within the play expresses his wish that it would not have to happen. The reason for this lies in the fact that the uncle is too closely identified in his mind with his own father, so that killing him would stir up intolerable guilt feelings and expose him also to the incestuous dangers from his mother.

If, in summary, we compare the dream within a dream to the play within the play, as it occurs in *Hamlet* and in other dramatic works which were studied, such as Shakespeare's *Midsummer Night's Dream,* Shaw's *Fanny's First Play* and others, we may outline the following parallels. The dream within a dream deals with a historical reality in the life history of the dreamer; the play within the play represents something which has happened or *will happen* in the life history of one or more of the characters of the play. The dream within a dream usually deals with a reality *event* in the life of the dreamer which the dreamer wishes had never happened, which he wishes were really not so. The play within the play, too, deals with reality events, as well as with *psychic* reality, including basic conflicts or problems of the hero, or, whoever, in the play, represents an important facet of his personality. These conflicts, being intolerable to part of the ego, are those with which the hero wishes he were not compelled to struggle, which he, like the dreamer, wishes were really not so. Dealing with the material in this manner serves to prepare the audience emotionally for what is to happen in the resolution of the conflicts presented in the play and thus helps them participate more fully in the play itself.

Notes

1. OTTO RANK, "Das 'Schauspiel' in *Hamlet,*" *Imago,* 4:41-51, 1915.

2. ERNEST JONES, *Hamlet and Oedipus* (New York: W. W. Norton and Company, 1949).

3. K. R. EISSLER, "On *Hamlet*," *Samiska*, 7:85-132, 155-202, 1953.

1. SIGMUND FREUD, *The Interpretation of Dreams* (1900), Standard Edition, Volume IV (London: Hogarth Press, 1953), p. 338.

2. Jones expressed a similar idea. "There is a delicate point here which may appeal only to psychoanalysts. It is known that the occurrence of a dream within a dream (when one dreams that one is dreaming) is always found when analyzed to refer to a theme which the person wishes were 'only a dream,') that is, not true. I would suggest that a similar meaning attaches to a 'play within a play'; as in *Hamlet*. So Hamlet (as nephew) can kill the King in his imagination since it is 'only a play' or 'only in play.'" (ERNEST JONES, *Hamlet and Oedipus* [New York: W. W. Norton and Company, 1949], p. 89.) It may be seen, however, that his remarks pursue a different direction from the thesis presented in this paper.

"Othello": The Tragedy of Iago

The psychoanalytic criticism of *Othello*—and there is a good deal of it—resembles the psychoanalytic criticism of earlier Shakespearean tragedies in that it busies itself with what can best be called motivational problems, namely, the mainspring for Iago's fiendish behavior and the reason for Othello's sudden fall. We shall begin with Iago.

Very few of Shakespeare's characters have provoked and puzzled critics to the extent that Iago has. Indeed, a recent book by Marvin Rosenberg suggests that for three centuries critics and actors alike have been engaged in a "search" for "Iago's identity."[1] The most famous pronouncement that this search has produced (and perhaps the shrewdest one, too) is Coleridge's, which holds that Othello's ancient is driven by a "motiveless malignity."[2] And there is also, of course, Stoll's view that since *Othello* contains "fictions" and not people and that since it works perfectly well upon the stage, we need not trouble our heads about the "real reasons" for Iago's conduct.[3] As for the psychoanalytic critics, their approach to the problem is twofold. On the one hand, they consider *Othello* from a mythic or folkloric perspective and regard Iago as a variation upon the Devil archetype. What this means, of course, is that Iago is not a realistic character in the strict sense, but that he embodies very real tendencies in men. The work of Stewart and Bodkin should be mentioned in this connection.[4] Nor can we fail to note in passing that their work, and work like it, calls to mind recent literary-historical studies that meticulously trace the development of the Morality Vice from the late medieval stage to the stage of Shakespeare's England and regard the character of Iago as an outgrowth of that development.[5] On the other hand, psychoanalytic critics of *Othello* approach the character of Iago from a strictly realistic standpoint. They are in agreement with Coleridge that Iago is driven by what can loosely be called a "malignity," but they are not in agreement with him that this malignity is "motiveless." On the contrary, they devote themselves to analytic readings of the play that develop in detail the psychological factors that stand behind Iago's behavior. Two of these readings, one a continuation and expansion of the other, will be presented here.

Like innumerable critics before him, Martin Wangh is unconvinced by the explanations that Iago himself puts forth upon the stage. Not only does the villain repeatedly shift ground, but he also offers us motives that do not "jibe." "There is no direct relation between them; nor does either lead logically to the shocking murder of Desdemona." Beneath the "apparent motivation," then, there must be a "basic motivation" that speaks "directly to the unconscious of every spectator" and in which "the magic of the play lies." Wangh finds the "basic motivation" in Iago's deep, homosexual attraction to Othello and in the paranoiac jealousy that springs therefrom. Iago's rapid shifting of ground and the contradictory attitudes that he offers us at certain points in the action come to make sense when we view them in the light of psychoanalytic discoveries about various neurotic mechanisms such as reversal and projection which commonly occur in jealousy, paranoia, and homosexuality.

M. F.

n "Certain Neurotic Mechanisms in Jealousy, Paranoia and Homosexuality," Freud makes distinction between competitive or normal jealousy, projective jealousy, and delusional jealousy.[1] To illustrate projective jealousy, he quotes Desdemona's song from Shakespeare's Othello.

> I called my love false love; but what said he then? . . .
> If I court moe women, you'll couch with moe men.
>
> (IV.iii.55,57)

Othello's mounting anguish under the impact of Iago's scheming is very moving, and the irrationality of the Moor's jealousy is obvious to every spectator. Many clues are given in the play as to why Othello is so easily afflicted by such a consuming passion. He says of himself, "I am black . . . declined into the vale of years;" elsewhere he declares "the young affects" are in him "defunct." The Moor's jealousy and conflict fill the foreground of the tragedy; nevertheless it is always clear that Othello is only a victim and the tool of Iago's machinations. It is Iago who starts the action of the play, sets its pace, and keeps it moving. It should, therefore, be rewarding to seek the motives of this villain who goads a man to murder his wife.

The hero of the drama is a noble Moor who has done great service for Venice as a general. Desdemona, daughter of the Senator Brabantio, falls in love with him and the pair elope. Othello's aide, Iago,

"Othello: The Tragedy of Iago" by Martin Wangh. Reprinted with permission from *Psychoanalytic Quarterly*, XIX (1950), 202-212.

angered by the fact that one Cassio has been given preferment over
him, is overwhelmed with hatred for the two men, and thenceforth
devotes his energies to destruction. First he plots to displace Cassio,
then to stimulate Othello's jealousy and goad him until the maddened
Moor strangles his beloved and loving bride.

Shakespearean criticism has always held the motivation for Iago's
destructive hatred to be too slight. Critics of all lands have spoken of
Iago's "motiveless malignity."[2] Some have called him "monster;"[3]
others, the proponent of evil. To none has it seemed that the provocation was sufficient for the pitiless revenge.

One thing, however, has impressed all critics—the repeated shifting of Iago's ground. At first Iago is enraged by the slight he has suffered through Cassio's preferment. Soon the motive shifts to cuckoldry.
Iago suspects that Othello and Cassio have slept with Emilia, Iago's
wife, and this suspicion grows to a certainty.

Clearly, the two motives do not jibe. There is no direct relation
between them; nor does either lead logically to the shocking murder
of Desdemona. If the first motivation is the true one, then the play
should end in the second act with the displacement of Cassio. If the
second motivation is the true one, why is it not presented at once?
Why does it not lead to revenge by cuckoldry rather than by murder?
How explain Iago's hatred for Desdemona, when it is desire that
should animate him? How, also, explain the hold this "illogical" play
has maintained upon the imagination of three and a half centuries of
playgoers?[4]

We can conclude only that the apparent motivation is not the basic
motivation. The magic of the play lies in its hidden content, which
speaks directly to the unconscious of every spectator.

Jealousy grown to the proportion of paranoia is a clinical condition,
sufficient to effect the murder of Desdemona. Although it is Othello
whom Shakespeare depicts as the person afflicted, I should like to
present the view that the prime sufferer is Iago. It is he who is
jealous of Desdemona and hates her. Iago loves Othello. This is never
expressed in so many words, but its opposite is repeatedly stressed.
From the beginning it is clear that Iago has only disdain for women.
He is "nothing if not critical" of the entire sex. As he puts it to Desdemona and Emilia:

> . . . you are pictures out of doors,
> Belles in your parlours, wild cats in your kitchens,
> Saints in your injuries, devils being offended.
> Players in your housewifery, and housewives in your beds. . . .
> Nay, it is true, or else I am a Turk:
> You rise to play, and go to bed to work.
>
> (II.i.110-113, 115-116)

I should like to consider the tragedy first from the standpoint of the action and its timing, then to follow the emotional conflicts of the character, Iago; for, although the play is called *Othello,* it is Iago who is the absorbing personality, the evil genius of the play.

In listening to a patient's account of his illness, we are accustomed to pay special attention to the situation immediately preceding the onset of the symptoms. What then are the precipitating factors in Iago's psychopathology? Apparently, before the action of the play Iago has had no conflicts. He has been Othello's trusted aide, very much in the general's confidence, and seemingly deserving it. Suddenly he is thrown into an explosive frenzy. The first scene finds Iago shouting, "Thief, thief," under Brabantio's window. Iago thus spectacularly acquaints Desdemona's father with his daughter's elopement with the Moor.

It is night; the town is sleeping when Iago raises his outcry. The disturbance, moreover, occurs immediately after Othello's marriage. Iago has sped to Brabantio's house knowing that Othello and Desdemona have retired to the marriage chamber. We can assume that Iago, being Othello's trusted aide, knew about the plans for the wedding; yet he did not warn Brabantio beforehand.[5] Only when the marriage is about to be consummated does Iago create an uproar.

We should be warranted in reserving judgment were this the only indication of a triangle. But the action is repeated—not once but twice—and each time the uproar has the similar effect of disturbing the marital, sexual relationship. On the night of Othello's arrival in Cyprus, and again later, the couple are roused from bed by the tumult following Rodrigo's attacks on Cassio, both instigated by Iago. The conclusion is inescapable that in disturbing the marital relation Iago has achieved his immediate aim.

So far we can assume only that a triangle exists. On the face of it,

Desdemona may be the object of Iago's affection. It may be simply an instance of competitive jealousy based upon the Oedipus. Since Othello is a paternal authority, especially for Iago, the Moor's withdrawal to the marriage chamber reawakens the oedipal conflict in Iago. Three times there is a reproduction of the primal scene.

There is further evidence to support this interpretation. *Othello* is based on a tale called "The Moor of Venice," a short story in the *Hecatommithi* of Cinthio.[6] This story also features the death of Desdemona, but not at the hands of the Moor. It is Iago who kills her, and the weapon is a stocking filled with sand. Significantly, Iago hides in a closet while Othello is in bed with Desdemona.[7]

If Iago be motivated by projective jealousy, the object of that jealousy should be his own wife, Emilia; and the manner of revenge should be one of two: Iago should either cuckold Othello or kill him. Since neither of these happens, we are left with delusional jealousy as the final possibility.

Delusional jealousy, Freud says, ". . . represents an acidulated homosexuality and rightly takes its position among the classical forms of paranoia. As an attempt at defense against an unduly strong homosexual impulse it may, in a man, be described in the formula: 'Indeed I do not love him, *she* loves him.' "[8]

In his study of the Schreber case, Freud states that the principal forms of paranoia can all be represented as contradictions of the single proposition: "I (a man) love him (a man)."[9] The first contradiction is: "I do not love him; I hate him." A second contradiction may be: "It is not I who love the man; she loves him." In consonance with these contradictions the sufferer suspects the woman's relation to all the men he himself is tempted to love.

In the very opening lines of the play the first contradiction, "I do not love him, I hate him," is spoken by Rodrigo, a disappointed suitor for Desdemona's hand. Quoting Iago, he says: "Thou told'st me thou dist hold him in thy hate." (I.i.7)

It is noteworthy that in Cinthio's story of the Moor of Venice there is no character Rodrigo. Iago is the unrequited lover, and the drive to murder is ascribed to hurt pride. Shakespeare splits Cinthio's Iago into two characters. Rodrigo represents normal competitive jealousy, expressive of the positive oedipal relationship between Iago and Desdemona; Iago is the pathological counterpart, present under the surface in Cinthio's version as well.

Iago's declaration of his hatred of Othello is stated repeatedly.

> Though I do hate him as I do hell-pains,
> Yet, for necessity of present life,
> I must show out a flag and sign of love,
> Which is indeed but sign.
>
> (I.i.55-58)

> I have told thee often, and I re-tell thee again and again I hate the Moor: . . .
>
> (I.iii.372-373)

In an ensuing soliloquy a significant motivation for his hatred is first stated.

> . . . I hate the Moor,
> And it is thought abroad that 'twixt my sheets
> He hath done my office: I know not if't be true,
> But I, for mere suspicion in that kind,
> Will do as if for surety.
>
> (I.iii.392-396)

Before accepting these expressions of hate as paranoid, we must, of course, rule out the possibility that there is rational basis for Iago's hatred. But the fact that the protestations are so obsessively repeated would lead us to believe that we are dealing with what Fenichel calls a "cramped emotion."

What evidence is there that Iago denies his love by projecting the part onto a woman? What indication is there that he suspects the woman's relation to all the men he himself is tempted to love?

The evidence for the first is overwhelming. Iago's assertions that Desdemona loves the Moor are too numerous to quote. With respect to the second, it is out of the substitution of Emilia for Desdemona that the thought of Cassio as Desdemona's lover is born. The substitution of Emilia for Desdemona is easy, for their relationship is that of mistress and maid.

Iago reiterates his suspicions of being cuckolded. "I do suspect," he says, "the lusty Moor hath leap'd into my seat" (II.i.304-305). From this suspicion Iago jumps to another equally unfounded: "I fear Cassio with my night-cap too" (II.i.316). This groundless conjecture is preceded by Iago's suspicion that Cassio loves Desdemona and that she returns his love.

> That Cassio loves her, I do well believe it;
> That she loves him, 'tis apt and of great credit.
> (II.i.294-295)

Such rapid shifts are possible for Iago notwithstanding his previous assertion that Desdemona loves the Moor—possible because Iago is so tormented by Othello's love for Desdemona. Iago is driven to separate the pair and, the wish being father to the thought, he accomplishes it by asserting that Desdemona and Othello must tire of each other and that Desdemona must love Cassio. "She must change for youth," he says, "she must have change, she must." It is an obsession with him.

This shift from Othello to Cassio certainly resembles a need to suspect the woman in relation to all the men Iago himself is tempted to love. The woman is Emilia who is interchangeable with Desdemona. And so in consonance with the second paranoid contradiction we have a situation in which Iago suspects Desdemona's relation to the two men, Othello and Cassio, whom he is himself tempted to love.

Iago's various projections may be summarized: the Moor has lain with Emilia; therefore Cassio has lain with Emilia; Emilia equals Desdemona; therefore Cassio has lain with Desdemona. All of these serve the function of warding off anxiety and enable Iago to deny by projection his homosexual drive to lie with the Moor.

By the third act the drama has advanced to the point where Othello has been goaded into an intolerable state of jealousy and anxiety. He demands proof that Desdemona is unfaithful, and Iago offers him three. The second of these contains the evidence we need. With mock reluctance Iago pours the following invention into Othello's ready ear.

> . . . I lay with Cassio lately;
> And, being troubled with a raging tooth,
> I could not sleep. . . .
> In sleep I heard him say, 'Sweet Desdemona,

Let us be wary, let us hide our loves!'
And then, sir, would he gripe and wring my hand,
Cry 'O, sweet creature!' and then kiss me hard,
As if he pluck'd up kisses by the roots,
That grew upon my lips; then laid his leg
Over my thigh, and sigh'd, and kiss'd; and then
Cried, 'Cursed fate that gave thee to the Moor!'
                    (III.ii.413-415, 419-426)

Lies have a psychoanalytic interest similar to fantasies and dreams. A lie told about a dream combines two of these categories. In this instance it is accurate to consider the dream to be a lie and the lie a dream.

Clearly the first and unmistakable purpose of the fabrication is to goad Othello into further jealousy; but behind this there is another, an unconscious motive. Iago's fantasy is an invention to satisfy his own unconscious strivings. We can, then, with confidence assume Iago's fiction to have quite another meaning. The lie can be interpreted as a product of the censorship of the dream, a censorship which contents itself with simple denial.

We feel justified in concluding that Cassio and Othello are equated in function on the accepted evidence that the person to whom a dream is told is himself involved in the dream. In telling the dream to Othello, Iago plainly says: "I dreamt of you." It has already been noted that Cassio and the Moor become interchangeable when Iago's jealousy is aroused. At first Iago suspected that the lusty Moor had leaped into his seat, and from this suspicion he immediately jumped to "I fear Cassio with my night-cap too." Iago's dream, then, means: "I lay with you, Othello, and you made love to me, as you do to Desdemona." The last line, 'Cursed fate that gave thee [Desdemona] to the Moor' should be reread, 'Cursed fate that gave thee [Desdemona, not me] to the Moor.'

Let us examine the details of Iago's dream and see how far they confirm this interpretation. Since the characters and the dream are the invention of a playwright, our analysis has to be on the basis of symbolism and analogy to the dreams of patients.

The dream begins with an imagined toothache which prevented Iago from sleeping. A tooth is one of the commoner universal symbols of the penis in dreams. "A raging tooth" would then indicate sexual excitement. Iago's saying that he was "troubled" with a raging tooth has two meanings: first, of censorship—resistance to his homosexual excitement; second, the wish for and the fear of castration. "Kisses plucked up by the roots" can be similarly understood as a phrase heavy with castration symbolism, and the whole fantasy is replete with oral erotism. We can conclude that it is in part a fantasy of fellatio. "He laid his leg over my thigh" is self-explanatory.

These considerations give ample confirmation to the thesis that Iago's dream is a homosexual wish fulfilment, and they are thus strong supporting evidence for the opinion that the basic motivation of the play is Iago's delusional jealousy.

Let us now trace the development of this paranoid condition and review the clinical course of Iago's illness as if the play were a case history.

The sudden onset of his disturbance is most comparable to a state of homosexual panic. In the course of the illness Iago tries to reestablish the countercathexis against the repressed homosexuality. He tries at first to rationalize his excitement. He insists that his jealousy is caused only by his failure to attain the post he desired and by its having been conferred on Cassio instead. However, the basic conflict is revealed in Iago's choice of words: "Preferment goes by letter and affection, and not by the old gradation" (I.i.36). The words preferment and affection point up the fact that Iago's hurt stems not only from a blow to professional pride, but from a rupture in his love relationship—another has been taken into favor in his stead.

The pathological conflict is hidden behind the verbalization of reasonable ambition. But at the next moment there is a return of the repressed, and Iago next attempts to curb his intolerable torment by denying the need for a love object; he tries to turn his love for Othello into love of himself. "I never found a man," he says, "that knew how to love himself. Ere I would say I would drown myself for the love of a guinea-hen, I would change my humanity with a baboon" (I.iii.315-319). But this is whistling in the dark. The regression into narcissism fails and Iago is found bolstering resolution by calling on intellect to control emotion. "Our bodies," he says, "are our gardens, to the which our wills are gardeners" (I.iii.323-325).

Now the need to destroy takes possession of Iago. "Nothing can or shall content my soul till I am even with him wife for wife" (II.i.307-308). Cuckolding, however, is not what he wants. Utterly frustrated, at last he makes Desdemona the object of his hate. Much more than Cassio, Desdemona is the rival to be destroyed. Iago will so work upon him that the Moor himself will destroy the hated rival, Desdemona: "So will I turn her virtue into pitch, and out of her own goodness make the net that shall enmesh them all" (II.iii.66-68). His intellectual and emotional awareness apart, he has succeeded in turning over the weight of his intolerable jealousy to Othello, and having projected it thus becomes free to declare his love for Othello. Now he can openly say to the Moor: "My lord, you know I love you" (III.iii.117). From now on he seizes every opportunity to pour out his hate for Desdemona. In a compelling crescendo he vilifies her, triumphs over each occasion when he has brought the Moor to express distaste for his rival. When finally the Moor says, "Damn her, lewd minx" (III.iii.476), and in the next breath grants Iago the coveted lieutenancy, Iago lets go completely: "I am your own forever" (III.iii.480).

The play moves relentlessly toward the murder of Iago's rival. Devoted, innocent, helpless, Desdemona, caught in the heavy web of Iago's intrigue, is unable to produce the handkerchief Othello gave her as a gift. In his frenzied state of jealousy this is evidence enough to convince Othello that his bride is faithless.

That Desdemona is the real adversary and that her murder is the objective toward which Iago works is still more clearly represented in the Cinthio version of the story in which Desdemona is murdered by Iago. Othello, to be sure, is an accomplice to the deed, but Iago himself beats her to death with a sand-filled stocking.

In Shakespeare's version the fatal stabbing of Emilia by Iago follows immediately on the murder of Desdemona. It is as though Shakespeare used this means to point up the fact that Iago is the real culprit and that Desdemona and Emilia in his mind are one. In Cinthio's story, a postscript states that Othello dies through an act of revenge by Desdemona's family, and Iago's death is due to injuries following torture by order of a court of justice. That the torture consists of stringing him up by the neck is a direct parallel to Desdemona's death by strangulation in Shakespeare's play.

At this point one might well ask: whence comes the driving power of Iago's devouring jealousy? Many writers have given us the key.[10] They have traced jealousy to its outgrowth from oral envy. In addition to the oral imagery of Iago's dream invention in Shakespeare's play, in Cinthio's version of the tale it is not Emilia but Iago who steals the handkerchief from Desdemona and, significantly, he does this while Desdemona is holding his child in her lap. This is the classic situation of the envious older child.[11] The handkerchief, on which the tragedy hinges, has long been identified as a fetish, the child's substitute for the breast.[12] In this instance, the symbolism is doubly clear. The handkerchief is embroidered with strawberries, easily recognizable symbols of the nipples.[13]

Summary

Shakespeare's *Othello* is studied as a case history of the psychopathology of Iago. His struggle is against his feminine identification with Desdemona, Othello's wife. The power of the repressed homosexuality causes his jealousy, and drives him to contrive the death of Desdemona, his rival. Several mechanisms of defense are described in Iago's frantic attempts to maintain repression. The tragedy occurs for the very reason that Iago must hide the unacceptable truth from himself. Safety for Iago lies only in ignorance and denial; the affliction is too deep to be resolved. His last words are a final closing of the door.

> Demand me nothing: what you know, you know:
> From this time forth I never will speak word.
> (V.ii.303-304)

Notes

1. MARVIN ROSENBERG, *The Masks of Othello: The Search for the Identity of Othello, Iago, and Desdemona by Three Centuries of Actors and Critics* (Berkeley and Los Angeles: University of California Press, 1961).
2. See TERENCE HAWKES (ed.), *Coleridge's Writings on*

Shakespeare (New York: Capricorn Books, 1959), p. 171.
3. E. E. STOLL, *Art and Artifice in Shakespeare* (1933) (New York: Barnes and Noble, 1962), chap. 2.
4. J. I. M. STEWART, *Character and Motive in Shakespeare* (London: Longmans, Green, 1949), chap. 5; MAUD BODKIN, *Archetypal Patterns in Poetry* (1934) (New York: Random House, 1958), pp. 211-218.
5. See, for example, BERNARD SPIVACK, *Shakespeare and the Allegory of Evil* (New York: Columbia University Press, 1958).

1. SIGMUND FREUD, "Certain Neurotic Mechanisms in Jealousy, Paranoia and Homosexuality," *Collected Papers,* Vol. II (Leipzig: Franz Deuticke, 1934).
2. SAMUEL TAYLOR COLERIDGE, *Lectures and Notes on Shakespeare and Other English Poets* (London: G. B. Bell and Sons, 1884), p. 388.
3. LYTTON STRACHEY, *Characters and Commentaries* (New York: Harcourt, Brace and Company, 1935), p. 295.
4. S. A. BROOKE, *Ten More Plays of Shakespeare* (New York: Henry Holt and Company, 1913), p. 175: "The improbability of the whole affair is shocking."
5. This kind of argument is suspect. One should not go outside the text of the play to assume something so specific as this (Editor's note).
6. GIOVANNI BATTISTA GIRALDI CINTHIO, *Hecatommithi Decca Terza,* Novella VII, *Il Moro di Venezia* (Venice: G. B. Pulciani, 1608), p. 213.
7. This is not the best kind of argument: Shakespeare wasn't shackled to his sources and often altered them considerably. The next paper by Gordon Ross Smith deals, in part, with this problem (Editor's note).
8. FREUD, *op. cit.,* p. 234.
9. SIGMUND FREUD, "Psychoanalytic Notes Upon an Autobiographical Account of a Case of Paranoia," *Collected Papers,* Vol. III (Leipzig: Franz Deuticke, 1934).
10. RICHARD STERBA, "Eifersüchtig auf," *Psychoanalytische Bewegung, 2*:1930; RUTH MACK BRUNSWICK, "Die Analyse eines Eifersuchtwahnes," *Internazionale Zeitschrift für Psychoanalyse, 14*:1928; JOAN RIVIERE, "Jealousy as a Mechanism of Defense," *International*

Journal of Psycho-Analysis, 13:1932; OTTO FENICHEL, "Beitrag zur Psychologie der Eifersucht," *Imago, 21*:1935.

11. CINTHIO, *op. cit.*

12. M. WULFF, "Fetishism and Object Choice in Early Childhood," *Psychoanalytic Quarterly, 15*:1946.

13. JACOB ARLOW, personal communication.

Iago the Paranoiac

On the one hand, the following essay by Gordon Ross Smith continues and expands the line of thought originally developed by Martin Wangh. Smith returns to the work of Freud to discover further evidence in support of Wangh's analysis of Iago's motivation, and, in addition, enlarges upon Wangh's insights into the possible role of "the handkerchief" in the behavior of the main characters. On the other hand, Smith presents us with much more than a continuation and an expansion. His concern with the *implications* of a realistic interpretation of Iago's character, with the *pertinence* of such an interpretation to an overall determination of the nature of *Othello* as tragedy, leads him to demonstrate that Iago's paranoia is not simply a psychological curio within a larger whole, but that it lends to *Othello* a psychological coherence that allows us to participate in the tragic happenings on an immediate, common sense level. "One may, if he wish, continue to consider *Othello* a poetic melodrama creakily hinging upon an inexplicable villain and trivial mischance, but the sense of tragedy cannot be brought about by such elements unless the spectators manage to suspend their critical common sense. Within Wangh's interpretation such suspension is not necessary. All the major figures of *Othello* become possible people caught in a net of circumstance from which their characters make them unable to escape. Through psychoanalytic understanding the play becomes again, as it presumably also was three centuries ago, a tragedy." As will be seen, Smith constructs his discussion in such a way as to make it, ultimately, a kind of running commentary upon the validity and meaningfulness of the psychoanalytic approach to Shakespeare.

M. F.

ome years ago Dr. Martin Wangh discussed Shakespeare's Iago as a paranoiac who disdains women, who loathes Desdemona for usurping the place he coveted in Othello's affections, and who rationalizes with incompatible excuses his conscious hatred (unconscious love) for Othello and Cassio.[1] Wangh suggested homosexual panic in Iago precipitated by Othello's marriage, pointed out how three times Iago interrupts what he imagines to be Othello's connubial proceedings, and showed how Iago's behavior illustrates two of the four masks of homosexuality described by Freud.[2] Wangh also discussed the raging-tooth dream as a fantasy of fellatio and the strawberry handkerchief as a breast symbol.

Aside from automatic listing in the standard annual Shakespeare bibliographies, Dr. Wangh's article has gone unnoticed or at least uncommented upon by Shakespearean scholars. Perhaps the chief reason lies in the disinclination of most literary historians to acquaint themselves with psychoanalytic theory, for which phenomenon there are in turn many other reasons. A second reason may lie in certain undemonstrated assumptions of "historical" literary criticism in recent decades, namely, that Shakespeare was bookish and disinclined to use his own direct observation; although Hardin Craig recently remarked that "An unimpeded observation of life" seems to have been Shakespeare's habit of mind,[3] Professor Craig's view has not yet been generally accepted by conservative editors or professors of literature.

Three further reasons for the general lack of notice are that Dr. Wangh's essay (1) did not cite all of the textual evidence that will

"Iago the Paranoiac" by Gordon Ross Smith. Reprinted with permission from *American Imago*, XVI (1959), 155-167.

support his point of view, (2) did not distinguish explicitly enough between evidence and inference, and (3) did not show the relevance of his interpretation to the dramatic functions of such a work of art. This last can be fatal to the possibilities of general acceptance of a psychoanalytic interpretation of a classic, for without it a faint and figurative "So what?" tends to echo down the academic corridors. It is my intention here to discuss these three aspects of Dr. Wangh's article.

Further Evidence

Of Freud's four masking contradictions of homosexual love Wangh cited the first and third: that the paranoiac hates the object of his unconscious love (Othello and Cassio), and that it is not the paranoiac who loves the man or men, but rather, some woman. As evidence of the first contradiction Wangh's cited Iago's statements of hatred for Othello but failed to mention Iago's comparable expressions toward Cassio as an incompetent book soldier and a drunkard improperly advanced before himself, his scheming to get Cassio murdered, and most interesting of all, the ambivalence and self-condemnation in Iago's remark,

> He hath a daily beauty in his life
> That makes me ugly; . . .
>   (V.i.19-20)

As evidence of Freud's third contradiction Wangh pointed out that Iago suspects Cassio with both Emilia and Desdemona—although the play gives no evidence elsewhere to justify such suspicions—and Othello with Emilia as well as with Desdemona. Of these four relationships, which exhaust all the possible combinations of the four principals concerned, only one is not a complete delusion.

Freud's second and fourth masking contradictions were that the paranoiac hates the object of his unconscious love because the latter persecutes him and that the paranoiac loves no one or else only himself. Iago illustrates both of these also, the former because of his reaction to Othello's advancement of Cassio as lieutenant and in his suspicions of their both having made him a cuckold, the latter in such explicit statements as these:

>   . . . Others there are
> Who . . .
> Keep yet their hearts attending on themselves, . . .
>   . . . these fellows have some soul;
> And such a one do I profess myself. . . .
> Heaven is my judge, not I for love and duty,
> But seeming so, for my peculiar end: . . .
>   (I.i.49-60)

> . . . I never found a man that knew how to love
> himself. Ere I would say I would drown
> myself for the love of a guinea-hen, I would
> change my humanity with a baboon.
>   (I.iii.315-318)

> I thank you for this profit, and from hence
> I'll love no friend, sith love breeds such offence.
>   (III.iii.379-380)

The first and third of these remarks serve certain dramatic functions of exposition and deceit, but those functions could have been as readily served by remarks that did not parallel the independent self-love of the second. We are rather obliged to conclude that Shakespeare conceived Iago as one who would repeatedly declare he loved only himself.

Iago's violations of logic presumably occasioned by his believing one or another of these masking propositions are several, only some of which were pointed out by Wangh; Iago's ambivalence toward Cassio already cited also exists toward Othello:

> The Moor, howbeit that I endure him not,
> Is of a constant, loving, noble nature.
>   (II.i.297-298)

(To call such repeatedly juxtaposed contradictions mere exposition within a primitive dramatic technique, as various twentieth-century scholars have done, is to give them a categorical label but is *not* to prove they belong in such a category within an art in so many other respects so calculated and so consummate.) In the first scene Iago tells Roderigo he hates Cassio and Othello because Cassio had been made lieutenant. If this were the chief grievance, then presumably Othello's subsequent removal of Cassio (II.iii.248-249) would have removed Iago's animus also; instead, as Wangh noted, we find it unabated. If we must understand his animus as produced by his suspicions of Othello's and Cassio's having seduced Emilia, then, the fuss over the lieutenancy becomes irrelevant. So far as Othello and Emilia are concerned, there are further difficulties: when voicing his suspicions, Iago describes Othello as "lusty" (II.i.304-308); yet both before and after this occasion he describes Othello as defective in appetite, loveliness, sympathy, manners, and beauties (II.i.229-233) and weak in sexual function (II.iii.351-354). Othello declares:

> . . . the young effects
> In me defunct, . . .
> (I.ii.264-265)

and himself

> . . . declin'd
> Into the vale of years, . . .
> (III.iii.265-266)

Iago admits he has no grounds for his suspicions except that

> . . . It is thought abroad that 'twixt my sheets
> He has done my office; . . .
> (I.iii.393-394)

a suspicion that Emilia scorns (IV.ii.145-147), and that no one else anywhere in the play so much as hints. Yet Iago continues,

> . . . I know not if 't be true,
> Yet I, for mere suspicion in that kind,
> Will do as for surety. . . .
> (I.iii.394-396)

Here, surely, is an explicit dramatic statement of a will instead of a reason to believe.

The same will to believe is made apparent in Shakespeare's handling of Iago's suspicions of Cassio with Desdemona. Initially he suggests the liaison as a means of revenge upon Othello (I.iii.398-404), but on the second occasion he appears more nearly convinced. With typical paranoid delusions of reference such as were described by Freud,[4] he misinterprets Cassio's courtesies to Desdemona to his own psychic ends:

> He takes her by the palm;

[Iago presumes Cassio did so to see if it was moist, since a moist palm was thought indicative of an amorous disposition]

>   ay, well said, whisper;
> with as little a web as this will I ensnare
> as great a fly as Cassio. Ay, smile upon her, do;
> I will gyve thee in thine own courtship.

[there is no evidence that Cassio or anyone else thought these courtesies were courtships]

> You say true, 't is so, indeed. If such tricks
> as these strip you out of your lieutentantry,
> it had been better you had not kissed your three
> fingers so oft, which now again you are most
> apt to play the sir in. Very good; well kissed!
> an excellent courtesy! 't is so, indeed.

[i.e., that Cassio is her paramour]

>   Yet
> again your fingers to your lips? would they
> were clyster-pipes for your sake!
>   (II.i.167-179)

Iago's comparison of Cassio's fingers to "clyster-pipes" is one of those Shakespearean figures with multiple meanings. A clyster-pipe was a syringe—an obvious phallic symbol—and especially one used for administering an enema. Since Iago mentions Cassio's fingers being at his lips, the allusion to clyster-pipes suggests both fellatio and pederasty, as does the raging-tooth fantasy later on. Shortly after this scene on the quays, Iago talks Roderigo into accepting his calumny (II.i.220-290), and has apparently convinced himself:

> That Cassio loves her, I do well believe it;
> That she loves him, 't is apt and of great credit.
>   (II.i.295-296)

He quite evidently enjoys the idea (II.iii.363, 394-396; IV.i.1-4, 33-34, 71-73, 85-87).

In brief, it is not logic or acute observation that leads Iago to the conscious beliefs that seem to animate him, but delusions of reference and a will to believe, although in violation of logic. S. T. Coleridge's description of these processes has become one of his most famous phrases: "the motive-hunting of a motiveless malignity." Literary criticism could go no farther, and it wasn't until the appearance of Wangh's article that the portrait of Iago was shown to be parallel to a recurrent type of human behavior.

Evidence and Inference

Essentially the case for Iago as a paranoiac must rest upon the above evidence, whether newly presented here or reviewed from Wangh's article. These are the things indisputably in the play and indisputably parallel to psychoanalytic observation. If the case be accepted as the proper frame of reference for the interpretation of the play, then a great many otherwise unrelated details in the play come into a new kind of focus. These I shall discuss presently, but *not* before pointing out how they are *consequences* of the interpretation, not evidences for it, unless by convergence of evidence, which is a method always leaving some question, since much of the evidence can converge quite as effectively within a totally different frame of reference and since the internal consistency of a system is no proof of its validity. On the other hand, convergence is the method that every usual frame of reference for Shakespearean criticism has always been obliged to employ. Confronted as we are with no record whatever of Shakespeare's theories, intentions, objectives, or interpretations, no other method is available.

Wangh's procedure might be divided into four steps. The first consists of the citation of actions and ideas in Shakespeare's text. The second consists of clear parallels between psychoanalytic formulations and those actions and ideas. The third consists of the inferences drawn immediately from the interaction of steps one and two. The fourth consists of further inferences arrived at by the application of more analytic concepts against the inferences of step three. The first three steps seem to me to be reasonably sound, but the fourth must by its nature consist of inferences about events or characters for which the text gives no support. They therefore depend for their validity upon their degree of positive correlation with the basic pattern which the text does allow us to infer—in this case, but still tentatively, the paranoia of Iago. It is the presence of the type of evidence arrived at in this fourth step that has so often prevented general acceptance of a psychoanalytic interpretation of a classic that in other respects may be very worthy of general attention.

The point may be clearer if I illustrate from Wangh's article. He suggests that Iago's symptoms had their onset suddenly and just before the play begins and that they were precipitated by Othello's unexpected marriage to Desdemona. But what hypothetically might have taken place before the play began does not constitute evidence. We could as reasonably say instead that the paranoia was brought on by Iago's failure to get the coveted and expected lieutenancy, that this failure in the man's world was psychically disastrous, as Sulzberger recently testified it can be.[5] If we restrict ourselves to what can be demonstrated, we cannot say either, for the text of the play gives us no clues.

Similarly with the strawberry handkerchief: We have no precise description of it and cannot know what it looked like. Wangh suggests that the strawberries are symbols of the nipples and that Iago is the envious older child. I should like to suggest as an alternative that since breast and penis symbols are often interchangeable, as Rodrique, Lewinsky, and Winterstein have all testified,[6] the strawberries might equally well or better have been penis symbols, or even actual representations of the glans, enwreathed in "curious" hair-like leaves. If so, we can understand why a gay young soldier like Cassio should want a copy of it (III.iv.180-190) and why Bianca with her pretensions to respectability (V.i.122-123), should show such furious indignation at being asked to make the copy (IV.i.153-161). Moreover, if the strawberries are either symbols or representations of the glans penis, then why the handkerchief should be a symbol of happy matrimony (III.iv.58-60), why its loss should presage marital alienation (III.iv.60-63), why Othello gave it to Desdemona (III.iii.291; III.iv.63-65), why he attaches such importance to the gift (III.iii.294; III.iv.55, 66-75), why Iago produces the fantasy of having seen Cassio wipe his beard (and mouth?) with it (III.iii.437-439), and why Othello is so furious when he hears Iago's lie about an intrinsically trivial object (III.iii.439-450) all fall into place as parts of the larger pattern. Thus the strawberry handkerchief, upon which the whole intrigue seems so trivially to turn, would become the perfect symbol for the central psychological conflicts of the play. If we accept this interpretation, many other seemingly mechanical details acquire dramatic and symbolic significations they did not previously have: Desdemona's inability to bind Othello's aching head with the handkerchief, and its falling to the ground immediately after (III.iii.285-288), symbolize both the inadequacy of their sexual relationship with its attendant trust to undo Iago's damage and the consequent cessation of sexual intimacy; Iago's seizure of it (III.iii.310-320) symbolizes both his baleful influence over their marital relationship and his own repressed homosexual desires; the repeated bickering about it that ensues symbolizes the warfare of sexual interests and finally, Othello's reference to it as a "recognizance and pledge of love" (V.ii.214), together with his accompanying mention of his mother and father, Cassio, and himself and Desdemona, indicates that sexual elements are the only important parts of the symbolism of the handkerchief. But all of these ideas, however consistent with each other, are *consequences* of interpreting the play as a tale of paranoia and attendant sexual turmoil. They cannot be considered evidence, except by convergence, as I said above.

A third reservation about Wangh's article is his use of Shakespeare's source as evidence of the implicit content of the play. Shakespeare was so free with his sources, especially when they were contemporaneous rather than ancient, that we can never conclude that anything in his source is consequently implicit in his play. Something in his source *may* be explicit in the play, *may* be implicit, *may* be merely absent, or *may* be replaced by its complete opposite. It is with sources and contemporaneous ideas as it is with psychoanalytic parallels: what we can suppose present depends primarily upon what we can find in the text.

In brief, Wangh's or any psychoanalytic approach to Shakespeare should base itself exclusively upon the text, should demonstrate the parallels to analytic literature point to point, should consider and dispose of all the counterevidence, and should clearly label as speculative those ideas which are based not directly upon the text but rather upon intermediate inferences.

Relevance of This Interpretation

If with the above reservations we accept the chief outlines of Wangh's interpretation, we find various consequences broadening out from revisions of the interpretation and acting of individual lines and parts in *Othello* to the nature of tragedy in this play and its position within Shakespearean tragedy in general. I shall indicate only briefly the nature of these consequences.

A considerable number of remarks, especially by Iago, acquire additional meanings. Thus his early declaration, "I am not what I am" (I.i.65), which ought to be phrased, "I am not what I seem," if it were simple, objective self-description, can be seen to express the fundamental conflict in Iago's mind: his denial of his own homosexual impulses. His remark somewhat later, "Men should be what they seem" (III.iii.126), illustrates the split even better. Superficially it represents, like the former one, his hypocritical pose as an honest man, but on deeper levels of self-description it may be considered an expression of his superego which would say, "Men should [i.e., ought to or must] be heterosexual who seem so." On a still deeper level it expresses the contradictory id impulses and as such may be translated, "Men who are homosexual should seem [i.e., be] so." As an ego-product the remark is a wonder, for it expresses or deals with all of what Freud called the ego's three harsh masters.[7]

After Iago gets Cassio drunk and Othello asks how the ensuing brawl had come about, Iago answers:

> I do not know; friends all but now, even now,
> In quarter and in terms like bride and groom
> Devesting them for bed; . . .
>
> (II.iii.179-181)

If we interpret the play within a so-called historical frame of reference that considers Iago merely the stage convention of the Machiavel or calumniator believed, the simile here is aimless. Within Wangh's frame of reference we can easily see its homosexual undertones and understand such an image as psychically determined, a shadow cast on the surface from the impulses below. This montagelike quality of human thinking Shakespeare has elsewhere shown himself well aware of, (e.g., *II Henry IV*, IV.v.93).

In the long scene where Iago swears loyalty and at last becomes lieutenant, such overtones recur like luridly flickering lights. Wangh has pointed out how the last line, Iago's "I am your own forever" (III.iii.479), expresses Iago's deepest feelings toward Othello. But the whole middle of the scene is patterned upon courtship and the conclusion, upon the marriage ceremony. The overtones of courtship were apparent to the nineteenth-century actor Edwin Booth, who during the raging tooth passage had Iago holding Othello's hand, "which Othello [drew] with disgust from his grasp."[8] The grim parody of the marriage ceremony begins where Othello kneels and exclaims,

> . . . Now by yond marble heaven,
> In due reverence of a sacred vow
> I here engage my words.
> (III.iii.460-462)

Iago promptly joins him:

> Do not rise yet. (*Kneels.*)
> Witness, you ever-burning lights above!
> You elements that clip us round about!
> Witness that here Iago doth give up
> The execution of his wit, hands, heart,
> To wrong'd Othello's service! Let him command,
> And to obey shall be in me remorse,
> What bloody business ever.
> (III.iii.461-469)

Modern editors usually gloss the word "remorse" to mean "solemn obligation," and this interpretation derives from the 1911 *Shakespeare Glossary* of C. T. Onions, which in turn is derived from the Oxford *New English Dictionary*. But the *N.E.D.* declares this use of the word obsolete and rare and cites this line from *Othello* as the only extant representative of such meaning. It follows that this meaning for the word is not certainly established. I should like to suggest that the proper meaning here may be its most common one—pity, compassion, and that Iago's use of it here means, superficially, the "pity of it" (IV.i.206), which Othello somewhat later mentions to him, but more significantly, it indicates Iago's deep internal regret that he is soon to destroy the persons he most wants to love. Such a feeling in the depths of his mind is also suggested by the use of the word "clip," which superficially means "surround" but more commonly meant embrace as a lover.

Subsequently Othello falls down before Iago in what is reportedly his second (IV.i.52) fit. Especially noteworthy is the tone—formerly thought diabolical, now, psychotic—that Iago takes:

> Oth. . . . Pish! Noses, ears, and lips. Is 't possible?
> Confess!—Handkerchief!—O devil! (*Falls in a trance.*)
> Iago. Work on,
> My medicine, work!
>
> (III.iv.44-47)

Superficially "my medicine" is the deceit Iago has fed Othello, but on a deeper level of Iago's mental life his working medicine is the semen that his repressed homosexuality so longed to deliver to the prostrate figure before him. Freud has cited a comparable instance.[9] Iago has earlier referred to his machinations as "my poison" (III.iii.325), an epithet that conveys all the preceding plus the censorship that kept his homosexuality repressed.

Many other passages of the play can be found to yield additional and comparable meanings within Wangh's frame of reference. Iago's incessant allusions to sexual matters suggest curtailment of satisfactory outlet, and Emilia's generalizations upon husbands suggest that he had permanently left her bed:

> 'T is not a year or two shows us a man:
> They are all but stomachs, and we all but food:
> They eat us hungrily, and when they are full
> They belch us.
>
> (III.iv.103-106)

Her own frequently loose remarks, as in the willow-song scene, suggest that she too lacks adequate sexual satisfactions. Certainly Iago nowhere shows her any affection.

We should certainly note here that for none of these foregoing interpretations is it necessary to suppose that Shakespeare clearly anticipated psychoanalytic ideas upon the etiology of paranoia. Neither here nor elsewhere does he give us any systematic theory of personality. Instead, he presents us with various facets of the *surface* of characters whom we can recognize as specific types and whom we can therefore suppose he reported from his own observation. It is not his prosodic or dramatic art but rather his remarkable insight and consequent capacity for the selection of bafflingly convincing surface details that make certain of Shakespeare's characters so lifelike and that mark Falstaff, Brutus, Hamlet, Iago, Cleopatra, and various others as the creations of the same inimitable master. That Shakespeare anticipated Freud's systematic formulations is doubtful; that in *Othello* he shows some knowledge of the configuration we call paranoia, of its suspicion, its destructiveness, and its relation to homosexuality, seems more than likely, but whether he arrived at such knowledge by introspection and intuition, or by some other means must for the present remain a speculation.

A second consequence of the interpretation is that it can provide a controlling central idea that is intelligible to a modern audience and that is therefore capable of restoring to the realms of tragedy what by the general changes of taste and understanding had become for many people merely an improbable and ornate melodrama. This is not a proposal to "improve" Shakespeare by violating his text. Rather, it is a proposal to exploit what is already there and was very possibly put there for the understanding of the "judicious," as Dr. Johnson called them. Certainly it is necessary for the achievement of tragic feeling that the characters and plot of a drama must be at least believable enough for us to accept them as possible. We might reasonably give less attention to interpretations more suitable to attract and hold the ignorant wonder of the long-departed groundlings and give more attention to developing through the actors the character insights implicit in the text.

A third consequence is that *Othello* as a tragedy leaves the category of poetic melodrama to which many critics have relegated it and joins certain other Shakespearean tragedies, particularly *Julius Caesar, Hamlet, Macbeth,* and *Antony and Cleopatra,* as plays in which the catastrophic events issue not from trivial accidents or occasional errors of judgment but from the deep, involuntary parts of character. There lies the essence of these tragedies: the people come to grief not casually or by mistake, but by repeated acts that issue from the deepest parts of themselves; for reasons within only themselves they cannot avoid their own predicaments. Tragedy resides in the heart of character. Its inescapable quality is justified by what responsibility each person ultimately carries for what he has become, but its tragic qualities derive from the helplessness of people to escape from what they essentially are.

One may, if he wish, continue to consider *Othello* a poetic melodrama creakily hinging upon an inexplicable villain and trivial mischance, but the sense of tragedy cannot be brought about by such elements unless the spectators manage to suspend their critical common sense. Within Wangh's interpretation such suspension is not necessary. All the major figures of *Othello* become possible people caught in a net of circumstance which their characters make them unable to escape. Through psychoanalytic understanding the play becomes again, as it presumably also was three centuries ago, a tragedy.

Notes

1. MARTIN WANGH, *"Othello:* The Tragedy of Iago," *Psychoanalytic Quarterly, 19*:202-212, 1950.
2. SIGMUND FREUD, *On the Mechanism of Paranoia,* Standard Edition, Vol. III (London: Hogarth Press, 1962), pp. 444-466.
3. HARDIN CRAIG, "Shakespeare and the Here and Now," *Publications of the Modern Language Association, 67*:87-94, 1952.
4. SIGMUND FREUD, "Certain Neurotic Mechanisms in Jealousy, Paranoia, and Homosexuality," *Collected Papers,* Vol. II (Leipzig: Franz Deuticke), pp. 232-243.
5. CARL FULTON SULZBERGER, "An Undiscovered Source of Heterosexual Disturbance," *Psychoanalytic Review, 42*:435-437, 1955.
6. EMILIO RODRIGUE, "Notes on Symbolism," *International Journal of Psycho-Analysis, 37*:147-158, 1956; HILDE LEWINSKY, "The Closed Circle," *International Journal of Psycho-Analysis, 37*:290-297, 1956; ALFRED WINTERSTEIN, "On the Oral Basis of a Case of Male Homosexuality," *International Journal of Psycho-Analysis, 37*:298-302, 1956.
7. SIGMUND FREUD, *New Introductory Lectures in Psycho-Analysis* (New York: W. W. Norton and Company, 1933).
8. EDWIN BOOTH, *Prompt-Book of Othello* (1878), quoted in FURNESS, *Variorum* edition of *Othello* (Philadelphia: Lippincott, 1886).
9. FREUD, *On the Mechanism of Paranoia.*

Othello's Desdemona

The transformation of Othello from noble Moor to frenzied murderer is one of Shakespeare's swiftest and most radical transformations
and one that has called forth explanatory criticisms from ten generations. Johnson called Othello "artless" and "credulous."[1] Coleridge
maintained that the Moor "could not act otherwise than he did with
the lights he had"; his "belief" in Desdemona's sin was "forced upon
him" by Iago.[2] Bradley referred to Othello's "very simple" mind and
described him as "unusually open to deception."[3] More recently, R. B.
Heilman has spoken (almost psychoanalytically) of Othello's "inadequate selfhood" and "instinct" to punish others.[4] As for the psychoanalytic critics, their approach to the problem parallels their approach
to the problem of Iago's motivation. On the one hand, they regard
Othello from a mythic or folkloric perspective; its hero, consequently,
is treated not as a "real person" but as an embodiment of certain timeless tendencies in men. J. I. M. Stewart, for example, refers to that
part of the personality that is prone to project base desires onto someone else, while Miss Bodkin speaks of the side of us that would idealize
the world and its creatures.[5] On the other hand, the tragedy is regarded from a realistic standpoint and clinical, analytic explanations
are offered for its hero's behavior. The paper to follow is an example
of the second approach. ·

After summarizing briefly the psychoanalytic readings of his predecessors, Stephen Shapiro proceeds to trace Othello's fall to his subconscious hatred of Desdemona. What psychoanalytic commentators
have not noticed is that Othello is "psychically impotent." Thus, out
of the living Desdemona, he abstracts a "virginal but maternal idol to
worship." Grounding his argument in Freud's observation that the
main defense employed by men threatened by psychic impotence "consists in a psychical *debasement* of the sexual object," Shapiro contends
that Othello *"must"* hate Desdemona because she ultimately inhibits
the expression of his instincts. He is eager to hear Iago's news. What

is especially interesting about this view is, among other things, the manner in which it focuses on the realistic psychological level aspects of Othello's personality that have become an accepted part of the criticism: his incompleteness, his naïveté, his idealism. Like the work of Wangh and Smith, Shapiro's interpretation lends to the tragedy a psychological coherence and moves it from the realm of myth and melodrama to the realm of immediate, all-too-real experience.

M. F.

he last scene of *Othello* poses a difficult but crucial interpretive problem. Does Othello achieve self-awareness before he dies or does he remain the victim of his tendency
to dramatize and deceive himself? This question cannot be
answered in such a way as to remove the possibility of the alternate
solution, but a psychoanalytic exploration of the conflicts within Othello
will tend to strengthen the argument that Othello remains blind, that he
is the object of irony at the end.

The critics who have considered Othello from a psychoanalytic viewpoint have, in general, followed two lines of reasoning. The first, exemplified by Dr. Martin Wangh[1] or Professor Gordon R. Smith,[2]
explores Iago's homosexual attraction to Othello. The second, represented by Dr. A. Bronson Feldman,[3] Professor John V. Hagopian,[4]
or W. H. Auden,[5] traces Othello's doubts about his virility, or his
insecurity as a black man in a white world, and shows why Othello is
an easy prey to Iago. All of these writers concentrate on Iago. Their
points of view should, it seems to me, be supplemented by a third
one which focuses on the relationship between Othello and Desdemona.

When Othello claims that Desdemona has committed "the act of
shame/A thousand times" (V.ii.212-213) with Cassio, we know that
he is deceiving himself, that his exaggeration is a desperate and wild
attempt to justify his own actions. But when Othello speaks of himself as "one that lov'd not wisely but too well" (V.ii.344), reactions
and interpretations are mixed. Some critics accept Othello's description
of himself as an accurate one. But F. R. Leavis insists that "Othello's

too much love everywhere

"Othello's Desdemona" by Stephen A. Shapiro. Reprinted with permission
from *Literature and Psychology*, XIV (1964), 56-61.

Othello" must be distinguished from Shakespeare's Othello.[6] And R. B. Heilman suggests that Othello loved "not wisely, nor enough."[7] A third possibility, that Othello is an ironist lacerating himself, does not seem to be supported by the lines—despite the savage twist at the end of the speech. And Othello's final speech.

> I kiss'd thee ere I kill'd thee, no way but this,
> Killing myself, to die upon a kiss
>
> (V.ii.358-359)

indicates that whether "pride is purged"[8] or not, Othello believes that he *loved Desdemona as he killed her,* just as he loves her now. What Othello never sees or admits is that he *hated* Desdemona. No critic could maintain that Othello lacks dignity as he punishes himself with death. But he does lack the kind of dignity conferred by insight into the black heart of human motivations. The question whether we ought to expect this kind of insight from Othello, or whether it is necessary to a tragic effect, is outside the realm of this essay. I am primarily concerned with the textual evidence that gives us insight into the reasons for Othello's failure or refusal to acknowledge the hate in his love for Desdemona, the hate that surges out of his love and submerges it.

Several critics have commented incisively on the incompleteness of Othello's response to Desdemona. In Act I Othello seems quite tepid for a lover on his wedding night. He begs the Duke not to suspect

> I will your serious and great business scant
> For she is with me. No, when light-wing'd toys
> Of feather'd Cupid seel with wanton dulness
> My speculative and offic'd instruments,
> That my disports corrupt and taint my business,
> Let housewives make a skillet of my helm,
> And all indign and base adversities
> Make head against my estimation!
>
> (I.iii.268-275)

Othello's language, his associations, are quite revealing. He equates sensual love with "light-wing'd toys." There is scorn in his use of the terms "disports," "corrupt," and "taint." Othello is clearly more concerned with his "reputation" than with loving Desdemona.

Even if we grant that war is a serious business, and must take priority over private matters, Othello still remains curiously "detached." Desdemona is emotional:

> . . . if I be left behind,
> A moth of peace, and he go to the war,
> The rites for which I love him are bereft me, . . .
>
> (I.iii.256-258)

Othello asks that she be allowed to join him, but not

> To please the palate of my appetite,
> Nor to comply with heat, the young affects
> In me defunct, and proper satisfaction, . . .
>
> (I.iii.263-265)

He is not confessing impotence; he is simply asserting that he is not a passionate sensualist. But his "tone" is quite strange. Whereas Desdemona's speech is pregnant with her love of Othello, his is full of formal posing. Even more striking, however, is his response to the First Senator's "You must away tonight" (I.iii.279). What can one say of Othello's "With all my heart" (I.iii.279) except that he seems eager to be separated from Desdemona on their marriage night (though he is, of course, unconscious of this feeling).

In Act I Shakespeare has exposed Othello as a man concerned more with the "serious business" of war and with ceremony than with loving Desdemona. The absence of passion in Othello in Act I is connected to his attitude toward Desdemona, an attitude expressed in the following lines:

> She love'd me for the dangers I had pass'd,
> And I lov'd her that she did pity them.
>
> (I.iii.167-168)

Othello loves Desdemona for the purity of her sympathy for him. He delights in the fact that, "She gave me for my pains a world of sighs" (I.iii.159). Othello has abstracted out of the living Desdemona a virginal but maternal idol to worship.

An examination of the connection between idealization and psychic impotence will illuminate the character of Othello. Psychic impotence results from the radical separation of affection or reverence and sensuality in the lover. Of the psychically impotent, Freud has written, "Where they love they do not desire and where they desire they cannot love."[9] We have already seen that in Act I Othello reveals his profoundly divided psyche. His love for Desdemona seems naked of sexual desire. We need only turn to Antony or Benedict to see how "pure" Othello's love is. He displays no erotic awareness, beyond a kind of contempt for the corrupt and animal-trivial nature of sex.

However, *Othello* is a sex-drenched drama. Heilman has discussed the voyeuristic elements in the play, noting that what Iago, Othello, and Roderigo have in common is a tormenting but morbidly exciting vision of Desdemona having sexual intercourse with "another."[10] Clearly, Othello does not remain the statue of moderation that was undraped in Act I. In Act II Othello's suspicions outrace Iago's suggestions:

> ... he echoes me,
> As if there were some monster in his thought,
> Too hideous to be shown. Thou dost means something:
>
> . . . .
>
> And didst contract and purse thy brow together,
> As if thou then hadst shut up in thy brain
> Some horrible conceit. . . .
>
> (III.iii.106-108, 113-115)

Is the horrible monster in Iago's mind or in Othello's? Why is Othello so readily convinced that Desdemona is a whore? A psychoanalytic explanation of Othello's behavior will illuminate some of the dark and unexplored areas of his character.

Othello wants to debase Desdemona. His instincts *must* hate the virginal-maternal idol he has created because it inhibits their expression. Freud has explained that the main defense utilized by men threatened by psychic impotence, by the split in their love, "consists in a phychical *debasement* of the sexual object. . . . As soon as the condition of debasement is fulfilled, sensuality can be freely expressed. . . ,"[11] because the inhibiting fear of incest has been evaded. The inevitable complaint that psychoanalytic criticism "imposes a pattern" can be forestalled by a detailed examination of the text. Freud was not paying an idle compliment when he said that the poets discovered the unconscious.

The horror of the "brothel scene" (IV.ii) arises from Othello's reduction from a person to a repulsive animal. And, as we shall see, there is a vital connection between the brothel scene and the murder scene. In the brothel scene we can observe the intimate relationship between Desdemona's debasement and the awakening of Othello's sexuality:

> . . . O thou weed!
> Who are so lovely fair, and smell'st so sweet
> That the sense aches at thee, . . .
> (IV.ii.67-69)

"Sense" still aching, Othello calls her "public commoner" (l. 73), "impudent strumpet" (l. 81), "whore" (l. 87). Of course, Iago has told Othello that Desdemona has betrayed him with Cassio. But Othello is inventing elaborate variations on the adultery theme when he transforms Desdemona into a "public commoner." Only a very simple conception of man's psychological constitution could deny that Othello's fury is compounded partially of relish. Othello has created the brothel and the whore. He luxuriates in the fantasy he has woven out of his own perversity.

In the last scene of *Othello*, Desdemona says, "That death's unnatural that kills for loving" (V.ii.42). She thus prepares us to reject Othello's estimation of himself as "one that lov'd not wisely but too well." And Othello's protest that "nought did I in hate, but all in honour" (V.ii.295) is nothing but an evasion of self-knowledge. In Professor Heilman's terms: "Othello does not know how close hate is to love, and he has forgot the intensity of his passion to destroy."[12] The "passion to destroy" is a much more accurate description of Othello's behavior than his own self-deceiving formulation of his motivation.

Professor Brents Stirling has examined Othello's ritualization of his passion in this final scene and has indicated how Othello has fortified his delusion by transforming violence into impersonal ceremony.[13] Othello refuses to see himself as a maddened, lusting animal. He masquerades as a self-controlled priest, as a judge. This "trial scene" in which Othello is prosecutor, judge, and jury is an inversion of the fair hearing of the Brabantio claim against Othello in Act I. Similarly, Othello's strangling of Desdemona, a symbolic enactment of sexual intercourse, is an ironic consummation of the marriage of Othello and Desdemona.

Let us recall that Desdemona has ordered her "wedding sheets" (IV.ii.106) placed on the bed she is to die in. I doubt that this is a detail added simply to heighten the pathos of the murder scene. Shakespeare is deliberately identifying the marriage with the murder. But it is quite significant that before Othello kills Desdemona in bed, and dies by her side, one condition has been manufactured by Othello. He has transformed Desdemona into a whore, and has staged their chambers as a brothel. It is not psychoanalytic theory, but structural irony, that we are dealing with here.

In Act I Othello vindicates his marriage in a trial scene. He reveals little passion for Desdemona and betrays a desire to leave her on their wedding night. By the middle of the third act, Othello's moderation in love has given way to an erotically intense jealousy, made possible by the degradation of Desdemona. In Act IV he acts out a fantasy that establishes Desdemona as a whore in a brothel. This, in turn, makes possible the consummation of their marriage in death. Othello's last words,

> I kiss'd thee ere I kill'd thee; no way but this,
> Killing myself, to die upon a kiss,
>
> (V.ii.358-359)

seem full of a sense of reconciliation. But we must realize that this reconciliation has come only after Othello has expressed his desire to degrade and destroy Desdemona. The fact that he kisses Desdemona before he kills her (let us remember that "kill" is a metaphor for the sexual climax) is not to be accepted in a simple sentimental sense. The Desdemona that Othello kisses and kills is to him a whore. Love, hate, degradation, and death are fused in Othello.

However, if we return to our original problem—Othello's recognition of his responsibility for the tragedy—we are forced to observe that Othello has no awareness of the destructive elements in his being. He speaks right to the end like an innocent man who has been at worst a fool, at best the victim of Iago's diabolism. His symbolic self-transformation into a "dog" of a Turk certainly lends him the dignity of a willingness to undergo punishment. But sandwiched as it is between his conviction that he loved "too well" and his final kiss to

Also a picture of the homosexual desire toward a woman — annihilation.

Desdemona, it is inadequate to give one the sense that Othello realized that one does not kill because one loves. Othello dies blind to the fact that his fear of Desdemona's being a whore is also his desire.

But Othello is not blind alone. Roderigo is blind. Emilia is blind. Cassio is blind. Desdemona is blind. Even subtle Iago is blind to his own motivations. *Othello,* like Shakespeare's other tragedies, presents man as a creature groping in the darkness of self, misconstruing the motives of others, stumbling over unforeseen, fatal consequences. Othello says, "Certain, men should be what they seem" (III.iii.128). But he cannot see either Cassio or Iago. And he cannot distinguish between Desdemona as she "seems" to him, and Desdemona herself. When Othello "put[s] out the light" (V.ii.7) before he kills her, the darkness is deeper than he knows.

Suspicion or fear that something may come to pass is also ambiguously a desire for that thing to occur. *Othello* offers us not a simple warning against unfounded jealousy, but the opportunity to purge ourselves of the desire to degrade and destroy where we love. If we accept Othello's version of himself instead of the whole play's comment on Othello, we are, I fear, revealing that we, like Othello believe ourselves innocent of all desire to degrade and destroy.

Notes

1. W. K. WIMSATT, JR. (ed.), *Samuel Johnson on Shakespeare* (New York: Hill and Wang, 1960), p. 114.
2. TERENCE HAWKES (ed.), *Coleridge's Writings on Shakespeare* (New York: G. P. Putnam's Sons, 1959), pp. 175, 177.
3. ANDREW C. BRADLEY, *Shakespearean Tragedy* (New York: World Publishing Company, 1960), p. 155.
4. R. B. HEILMAN, "Wit and Witchcraft: An Approach to *Othello,*" in Leonard F. Dean (ed.), *Shakespeare: Modern Essays in Criticism* (New York: Oxford University Press, 1957), p. 305.
5. J. I. M. STEWART, *Character and Motive in Shakespeare* (Longmans, Green, 1949), chap. 5; MAUD BODKIN, *Archetypal Patterns in Poetry* (1934) (New York: Random House, 1958), pp. 211-218.

1. MARTIN WANGH, "Othello: The Tragedy of Iago," *Psychoanalytic Quarterly, 19*:202-212, 1950.

2. GORDON ROSS SMITH, "Iago the Paranoiac," *American Imago, 16*:155-167, 1959.

3. ABRAHAM BRONSON FELDMAN, "Othello's Obsession," *American Imago, 9*:147-163, 1952-1953; "Othello in Reality," *American Imago, 11*:147-179, 1954.

4. JOHN V. HAGOPIAN, "Psychology and the Coherent Form of Shakespeare's *Othello*," *Proceedings of the Michigan Academy of Science, Arts, and Letters, 45*:373-380, 1960.

5. W. H. AUDEN, "The Alienated City: Reflections on *Othello*," *Encounter*, August, 1961, pp. 3-14.

6. F. R. LEAVIS, "Diabolic Intellect and the Noble Hero," *Scrutiny, 6*:624, 1937.

7. ROBERT B. HEILMAN, *Magic in the Web* (Lexington, Kentucky: University of Kentucky Press, 1956), p. 168.

8. BRENTS STERLING, *Unity in Shakespearean Tragedy* (New York: Columbia University Press, 1956), p. 135.

9. SIGMUND FREUD, *On the Universal Tendency to Debasement in the Sphere of Love*, Standard Edition, Vol. XI (London: Hogarth Press, 1957), p. 183.

10. HEILMAN, *op. cit.*, p. 208.

11. FREUD, *op. cit.*, p. 183. Emphasis in the original.

12. HEILMAN, *op. cit.*, p. 184.

13. STIRLING, *op. cit.*, p. 126.

The Theme of the Three Caskets

Time and time again, *King Lear* is singled out by commentators as Shakespeare's greatest accomplishment, and perhaps the world's greatest play. In the face of this, it is somewhat surprising that *Lear* has not attracted more attention than it has from psychoanalytic critics. Not that readings are actually rare, just that they are far less numerous than one would expect. *Hamlet, Othello, Macbeth,* and even *The Merchant of Venice* have stimulated more discussion, and this is especially true in the last fifteen years. Does the explanation lie in the *Lear* universe that, for all its tragic grandeur, is somehow less inviting, somehow more harrowing to the mind and spirit, than the universe of the other plays? Dr. Johnson, it will be recalled, claimed to have been so deeply affected by the conclusion of *Lear* that he vowed never to read the drama again. And thanks to the seventeenth century's Nahum Tate, who gave the tragedy a happy ending, English audiences were virtually denied the opportunity of seeing the original Shakespearean version on the stage for over one hundred years. It may be that the death of Cordelia, or better, the entrance of Lear with his dead daughter in his arms is, as Robert Speaight put it, a *coup de theâtre,*[1] but it is a terrible *coup* and one that is not easily thought on.

Freud thought on it. Indeed, in the essay to follow he endeavored to explain whence this terrible power came by uncovering in the play an archetypal substructure with the ability to appeal directly to the unconscious of the beholder. Pointing up the similarities between the opening scene of *King Lear,* a scene in which, as it turns out, a man chooses between three women, and other scenes from myths, fairy tales, and literature generally, Freud proceeds to demonstrate that Cordelia, the mute or silent woman, is in reality a symbolic substitution for the Goddess of Death. When we watch Lear enter with his dead daughter in his arms we are actually witnessing, through "replacement by the opposite," a symbolic enactment of Lear's being carried off by Death. Only this interpretation, Freud believes, satisfactorily explains the harrowing effect of the play. Thus for Freud, *Lear* as a whole becomes a drama about an old king's resistence to death (Lear rejects Cordelia at the outset) and his desire for feminine love. As shall be seen, this overall approach to the tragedy is of great significance in understanding the realistic analyses of Lear's psychology that followed upon the appearance of Freud's mythopoeic treatment.

M. F.

wo scenes from Shakespeare, one from a comedy and the other from a tragedy, have lately given me occasion for posing and solving a small problem.

The first of these scenes is the suitors' choice between the three caskets in *The Merchant of Venice.* The fair and wise Portia is bound at her father's bidding to take as her husband only that one of her suitors who chooses the right casket from among the three before him. The three caskets are of gold, silver, and lead: the right casket is the one that contains her portrait. Two suitors have already departed unsuccessful: they have chosen gold and silver. Bassanio, the third, decides in favor of lead; thereby he wins the bride, whose affection was already his before the trial of fortune. Each of the suitors gives reasons for his choice in a speech in which he praises the metal he prefers and depreciates the other two. The most difficult task thus falls to the share of the fortunate third suitor; what he finds to say in glorification of lead as against gold and silver is little and has a forced ring. If in psychoanalytic practice we were confronted with such a speech, we should suspect that there were concealed motives behind the unsatisfying reasons produced.

Shakespeare did not himself invent this oracle of the choice of a casket; he took it from a tale in the *Gesta Romanorum*,[1] in which a girl has to make the same choice to win the Emperor's son.[2] Here too the third metal, lead, is the bringer of fortune. It is not hard to guess

"The Theme of the Three Caskets" by Sigmund Freud. Reprinted from *The Collected Papers of Sigmund Freud,* Chapter XV of Volume IV, edited by Ernest Jones, with permission of Basic Books, Inc. (1959) and Hogarth Press, Ltd. (1958).

that we have here an ancient theme, which requires to be interpreted, accounted for, and traced back to its origin. A first conjecture as to the meaning of this choice between gold, silver, and lead is quickly confirmed by a statement of Stucken's, who has made a study of the same material over a wide field. He writes: "The identity of Portia's three suitors is clear from their choice: the Prince of Morocco chooses the gold casket—he is the sun; the Prince of Aragon chooses the silver casket—he is the moon; Bassanio chooses the leaden casket—he is the star youth."[3] In support of this explanation he cites an episode from the Estonian folk-epic "Kalewipoeg," in which the three suitors appear undisguisedly as the sun, moon, and star youths (the last being "the Pole-star's eldest boy") and once again the bride falls to the lot of the third.

Thus our little problem has led to an astral myth! The only pity is that with this explanation we are not at the end of the matter. The question is not exhausted, for we do not share the belief of some investigators that myths were read in the heavens and brought down to earth; we are more inclined to judge with Otto Rank that they were projected on to the heavens after having arisen elsewhere under purely human conditions.[4] It is in this human content that our interest lies.

Let us look once more at our material. In the Estonian epic, just as in the tale from the *Gesta Romanorum,* the subject is a girl choosing between three suitors; in the scene from *The Merchant of Venice* the subject is apparently the same, but at the same time something appears in it that is in the nature of an inversion of the theme: a *man* chooses between three—caskets. If what we were concerned with were a dream, it would occur to us at once that caskets are also women, symbols of what is essential in woman, and therefore of a women herself—like coffers, boxes, cases, baskets, and so on.[5] If we boldly assume that there are symbolic substitutions of the same kind in myths as well, then the casket scene in *The Merchant of Venice* really becomes the inversion we suspected. With a wave of the wand, as though we were in a fairy tale, we have stripped the astral garment from our theme; and now we see that the theme is a human one, *a man's choice between three women.*

This same content, however, is to be found in another scene of Shakespeare's, in one of his most powerfully moving dramas; not the choice of a bride this time, yet linked by many hidden similarities to the choice of the casket in *The Merchant of Venice*. The old King Lear resolves to divide his kingdom while he is still alive among his three daughters, in proportion to the amount of love that each of them expresses for him. The two elder ones, Goneril and Regan, exhaust themselves in asseverations and laudations of their love for him; the third, Cordelia, refuses to do so. He should have recognized the unassuming, speechless love of his third daughter and rewarded it, but he does not recognize it. He disowns Cordelia, and divides the kingdom between the other two, to his own and the general ruin. Is not this once more the scene of a choice between three women, of whom the youngest is the best, the most excellent one?

There will at once occur to us other scenes from myths, fairy tales, and literature, with the same situation as their content. The shepherd Paris has to choose between three goddesses, of whom he declares the third to be the most beautiful. Cinderella, again is a youngest daughter, who is preferred by the prince to her two elder sisters. Psyche, in Apuleius's story, is the youngest and fairest of three sisters. Psyche is, on the one hand, revered as Aphrodite in human form; on the other, she is treated by that goddess as Cinderella was treated by her stepmother and is set the task of sorting a heap of mixed seeds, which she accomplishes with the help of small creatures (doves in the case of Cinderella, ants in the case of Psyche).[6] Anyone who cared to make a wider survey of the material would undoubtedly discover other versions of the same theme preserving the same essential features.

Let us be content with Cordelia, Aphrodite, Cinderella, and Psyche. In all the stories the three women, of whom the third is the most excellent one, must surely be regarded as in some way alike if they are represented as sisters. (We must not be led astray by the fact that Lear's choice is between three *daughters;* this may mean nothing more than that he has to be represented as an old man. An old man cannot very well choose between three women in any other way. Thus they become his daughters.)

But who are these three sisters and why must the choice fall on the third? If we could answer this question, we should be in possession of the interpretation we are seeking. We have once already made use of an application of psychoanalytic technique, when we explained the three caskets symbolically as three women. If we have the courage to proceed in the same way, we shall be setting foot on a path which will lead us first to something unexpected and incomprehensible, but which will perhaps, by a devious route, bring us to a goal.

It must strike us that this excellent third woman has in several instances certain peculiar qualities besides her beauty. They are qualities that seem to be tending towards some kind of unity; we must certainly not expect to find them equally well marked in every example. Cordelia makes herself unrecognizable, inconspicuous like lead, she remains dumb, she "loves and is silent."[7] Cinderella hides so that she cannot be found. We may perhaps be allowed to equate concealment and dumbness. These would of course be only two instances out of the five we have picked out. But there is an intimation of the same thing to be found, curiously enough, in two other cases. We have decided to compare Cordelia, with her obstinate refusal, to lead. In Bassanio's short speech while he is choosing the casket, he says of lead (without in any way leading up to the remark) :

> Thy paleness[8] moves me more than eloquence.
>
> (III.ii.106)

That is to say: "Thy plainness moves me more than the blatant nature of the other two." Gold and silver are "loud"; lead is dumb—in fact like Cordelia, who "loves and is silent."[9]

In the ancient Greek accounts of the Judgement of Paris, nothing is said of any such reticence on the part of Aphrodite. Each of the three goddesses speaks to the youth and tries to win him by promises. But, oddly enough, in a quite modern handling of the same scene this characteristic of the third one which has struck us makes its appearance again. In the libretto of Offenbach's *La Belle Hélène*, Paris, after telling of the solicitations of the other two goddesses, describes Aphrodite's behavior in this competition for the beauty prize:

> La troisième, ah! la troisième . . .
> La troisième ne dit rien.
> Elle eut le prix tout de meme. . . .[10]

If we decide to regard the peculiarities of our "third one" as concentrated in her "dumbness," then psychoanalysis will tell us that in dreams dumbness is a common representation of death.[11]

More than ten years ago a highly intelligent man told me a dream which he wanted to use as evidence of the telepathic nature of dreams.

In it he saw an absent friend from whom he had received no news for a very long time, and reproached him energetically for his silence. The friend made no reply. It afterwards turned out that he had met his death by suicide at about the time of the dream. Let us leave the problem of telepathy on one side;[12] there seems, however, not to be any doubt that here the dumbness in the dream represented death. Hiding and being unfindable—a thing which confronts the prince in the fairy tale of Cinderella three times, is another unmistakable symbol of death in dreams; so, too, is a marked pallor, of which the "paleness" of the lead in one reading of Shakespeare's text is a reminder.[13] It would be very much easier for us to transpose these interpretations from the language of dreams to the mode of expression used in the myth that is now under consideration if we could make it seem probable that dumbness must be interpreted as a sign of being dead in productions other than dreams.

At this point I will single out the ninth story in Grimm's *Fairy Tales,* which bears the title "The Twelve Brothers."[14] A king and a queen have twelve children, all boys. The king declares that if the thirteenth child is a girl, the boys will have to die. In expectation of her birth he has twelve coffins made. With their mother's help the twelve sons take refuge in a hidden wood, and swear death to any girl they may meet. A girl is born, grows up, and learns one day from her mother that she has had twelve brothers. She decides to seek them out, and in the wood she finds the youngest; he recognizes her, but is anxious to hide her on account of the brothers' oath. The sister says: "I will gladly die, if by so doing I can save my twelve brothers." The brothers welcome her affectionately, however, and she stays with them and looks after their house for them. In a little garden beside the house grow twelve lilies. The girl picks them and gives one to each brother. At that moment the brothers are changed into ravens, and disappear, together with the house and garden. (Ravens are spirit-birds; the killing of the twelve brothers by their sister is represented by the picking of the flowers, just as it is at the beginning of the story by the coffins and the disappearance of the brothers.) The girl, who is once more ready to save her brothers from death, is now told that as a condition she must be dumb for seven years, and not speak a single word. She submits to the test, which brings her herself into mortal danger. She herself, that is, dies for her brothers, as she promised to do before she met them. By remaining dumb she succeeds at last in setting the ravens free.

In the story of "The Six Swans"[15] the brothers who are changed into birds are set free in exactly the same way—they are restored to life by their sister's dumbness. The girl has made a firm resolve to free her brothers, "even if it should cost her her life"; and once again (being the wife of the king) she risks her own life because she refuses to give up her dumbness in order to defend herself against evil accusations.

It would certainly be possible to collect further evidence from fairy tales that dumbness is to be understood as representing death. These indications would lead us to conclude that the third one of the sisters between whom the choice is made is a dead woman. But she may be something else as well—namely, Death itself, the Goddess of Death. Thanks to a displacement that is far from infrequent, the qualities that a deity imparts to men are ascribed to the deity himself. Such a displacement will surprise us least of all in relation to the Goddess of Death, since in modern versions and representations, which these stories would thus be forestalling, Death itself is nothing other than a dead man.

But if the third of the sisters is the Goddess of Death, the sisters are known to us. They are the Fates, the Moerae, the Parcae, or the Norns, the third of whom is called Atropos, the inexorable.

We will for the time being put aside the task of inserting the interpretation that we have found into our myth, and listen to what the mythologists have to teach us about the role and origin of the Fates.[16]

The earliest Greek mythology (in Homer) only knew a single *Mõioa*, personifying inevitable fate. The further development of this one Moera into a company of three (or less often two) sister-goddesses probably came about on the basis of other divine figures to which the Moerae were closely related—the Graces and the Horae [the Seasons].

The Horae were originally goddesses of the waters of the sky, dispensing rain and dew, and of the clouds from which rain falls; and, since the clouds were conceived of as something that has been spun, it came about that these goddesses were looked upon as spinners, an attribute that then became attached to the Moerae. In the sun-favored Mediterranean lands it is the rain on which the fertility of the soil depends, and thus the Horae became vegetation goddesses. The beauty of flowers and the abundance of fruit was their doing, and they were accredited with a wealth of agreeable and charming traits. They became the divine representatives of the Seasons, and it is possibly owing to this connection that there were three of them, if the sacred nature of the number three is not a sufficient explanation. For the peoples of antiquity at first distinguished only three seasons: winter, spring, and summer. Autumn was only added in late Graeco-Roman times, after which the Horae were often represented in art as four in number.

The Horae retained their relation to time. Later they presided over the times of day, as they did at first over the times of the year; and at last their name came to be merely a designation of the hours (*heure, ora*). The Norns of German mythology are akin to the Horae and the Moerae and exhibit this time-signification in their names.[17] It was inevitable, however, that a deeper view should come to be taken of the essential nature of these deities, and that their essence should be transposed on to the regularity with which the seasons change. The Horae thus became the guardians of natural law and of the divine Order which causes the same thing to recur in Nature in an unalterable sequence.

This discovery of Nature reacted on the conception of human life. The nature-myth changed into a human myth: the weather-goddesses became goddesses of Fate. But this aspect of the Horae found expression only in the Moerae, who watch over the necessary ordering of human life as inexorably as do the Horae over the regular order of nature. The ineluctable severity of Law and its relation to death and dissolution, which had been avoided in the charming figures of the Horae, were now stamped upon the Moerae, as though men had only perceived the full seriousness of natural law when they had to submit their own selves to it.

The names of the three spinners, too, have been significantly explained by mythologists. Lachesis, the name of the second, seems to denote "the accidental that is included in the regularity of destiny"[18]—or, as we should say, "experience"; just as Atropos stands for "the ineluctable"—Death. Clotho would then be left to mean the innate disposition with its fateful implications.

202 / THE DESIGN WITHIN

But now it is time to return to the theme which we are trying to interpret—the theme of the choice between three sisters. We shall be deeply disappointed to discover how unintelligible the situations under review become and what contradictions of their apparent content result, if we apply to them the interpretation that we have found. On our supposition the third of the sisters is the Goddess of Death, Death itself. But in the Judgement of Paris she is the Goddess of Love, in the tale of Apuleius she is someone comparable to the goddess for her beauty, in *The Merchant of Venice* she is the fairest and wisest of women, in *King Lear* she is the one loyal daughter. We may ask whether there can be a more complete contradiction. Perhaps, improbable though it may seem, there is a still more complete one lying close at hand. Indeed, there certainly is; since, whenever our theme occurs, the choice between the women is free, and yet it falls on death. For, after all, no one chooses death, and it is only by a fatality that one falls a victim to it.

However, contradictions of a certain kind—replacements by the precise opposite—offer no serious difficulty to the work of analytic interpretation. We shall not appeal here to the fact that contraries are so often represented by one and the same element in the modes of expression used by the unconscious, as for instance in dreams.[19] But we shall remember that there are motive forces in mental life which bring about replacement by the opposite in the form of what is known as reaction-formation; and it is precisely in the revelation of such hidden forces as these that we look for the reward of this enquiry. The Moerae were created as a result of a discovery that warned man that he too is a part of nature and therefore subject to the immutable law of death. Something in man was bound to struggle against this subjection, for it is only with extreme unwillingness that he gives up his claim to an exceptional position. Man, as we know, makes use of his imaginative activity in order to satisfy the wishes that reality does not satisfy. So his imagination rebelled against the recognition of the truth embodied in the myth of the Moerae, and constructed instead the myth derived from it, in which the Goddess of Death was replaced by the Goddess of Love and by what was equivalent to her in human shape. The third of the sisters was no longer Death; she was the fairest, best, most desirable, and most lovable of women. Nor was this substitution in any way technically difficult: it was prepared for by an ancient ambivalence, it was carried out along a primeval line of connection which could not long have been forgotten. The Goddess of Love herself, who now took the place of the Goddess of Death, had once been identical with her. Even the Greek Aphrodite had not wholly relinquished her connection with the underworld, although she had long surrendered her chthonic role to other divine figures, to Persephone, or to the tri-form Artemus-Hecate. The great Mother-goddesses of the oriental peoples, however, all seem to have been both creators and destroyers—both goddesses of life and fertility and goddesses of death. Thus the replacement by a wishful opposite in our theme harks back to a primeval identity.

The same consideration answers the question how the feature of a choice came into the myth of the three sisters. Here again there has been a wishful reversal. Choice stands in the place of necessity, of destiny. In this way man overcomes death, which he has recognized intellectually. No greater triumph of wish-fulfilment is conceivable. A choice is made where in reality there is obedience to a compulsion; and what is chosen is not a figure of terror, but the fairest and most desirable of women.

On closer inspection we observe, to be sure, that the original myth is not so thoroughly distorted that traces of it do not show through and betray its presence. The free choice between the three sisters is, properly speaking, no free choice, for it must necessarily fall on the third if every kind of evil is not to come about, as it does in *King Lear*. The fairest and best of women, who has taken the place of the Death-goddess, has kept certain characteristics that border on the uncanny, so that from them we have been able to guess at what lies beneath.[20]

So far we have been following out the myth and its transformation, and it is to be hoped that we have correctly indicated the hidden causes of the transformation. We may now turn our interest to the way in which the dramatist has made use of the theme. We get an impression that a reduction of the theme to the original myth is being carried out in his work, so that we once more have a sense of the moving significance which had been weakened by the distortion. It is by means of this reduction of the distortion, this partial return to the original, that the dramatist achieves his more profound effect upon us.

To avoid misunderstandings, I should like to say that it is not my purpose to deny that King Lear's dramatic story is intended to inculcate two wise lessons: that one should not give up one's possessions and rights during one's lifetime, and that one must guard against accepting flattery at its face value. These and similar warnings are undoubtedly brought out by the play; but it seems to me quite impossible to explain the overpowering effect of *King Lear* from the impression that such a train of thought would produce, or to suppose that the dramatist's personal motives did not go beyond the intention of teaching these lessons. It is suggested, too, that his purpose was to present the tragedy of ingratitude, the sting of which he may well have felt in his own heart, and that the effect of the play rests on the purely formal element of its artistic presentation; but this cannot, so it seems to me, take the place of the understanding brought to us by the explanation we have reached of the theme of the choice between the three sisters.

Lear is an old man. It is for this reason, as we have already said, that the three sisters appear as his daughters. The relationship of a father to his children, which might be a fruitful source of many dramatic situations, is not turned to further account in the play. But Lear is not only an old man: he is a dying man. In this way the extraordinary premiss of the division of his inheritance loses all its strangeness. But the doomed man is not willing to renounce the love of women; he insists on hearing how much he is loved. Let us now recall the moving final scene, one of the culminating points of tragedy in modern drama. Lear carries Cordelia's dead body on to the stage. Cordelia is Death. If we reverse the situation it becomes intelligible and familiar to us. She is the Death-goddess who, like the Valkyrie in German mythology, carries away the dead hero from the battlefield. Eternal wisdom, clothed in the primeval myth, bids the old man renounce love, choose death, and make friends with the necessity of dying.

The dramatist brings us nearer to the ancient theme by representing the man who makes the choice between the three sisters as aged and dying. The regressive revision which he has thus applied to the myth, distorted as it was by wishful transformation, allows us enough glimpses of its original meaning to enable us perhaps to reach as well a superficial allegorical interpretation of the three female figures in the theme. We might argue that what is represented here are the three inevitable relations that a man has with a woman—the woman who bears him, the woman who is his mate, and the woman who destroys him; or that they are the three forms taken by the figure of the mother in the course of a man's life—the mother herself, the beloved one who is chosen after her pattern, and lastly the Mother Earth who receives him once more. But it is in vain that an old man yearns for the love of woman as he had it first from his mother; the third of the Fates alone, the silent Goddess of Death, will take him into her arms.

Notes

1. ROBERT SPEAIGHT, *Nature in Shakespearean Tragedy* (New York: Collier Books, 1962), p. 130.

1. [A medieval collection of stories of unknown authorship.]
2. GEORG BRANDES, *William Shakespeare* (Paris: 1896).
3. E. STUCKEN, *Astralmythen der Hebraeer, Babylonier und Aegypter* (Leipzig: Pfeiffer, 1907), p. 655.
4. OTTO RANK, *Der Mythus von der Geburt des Helden* (Leipzig and Vienna: F. Deuticke, 1909), pp. 8 ff.
5. See SIGMUND FREUD, *The Interpretation of Dreams* (1900), in *Complete Works*, ed. JAMES STRACHEY (London: Hogarth Press, 1953), V, p. 354.
6. I have to thank Dr. Otto Rank for calling my attention to these similarities. [Cf. a reference to this in Chapter XII of *Group Psychology* (1921), in *Complete Works*, XVIII, p. 136.]
7. [From an aside of Cordelia's, Act I, Scene 1.]
8. "Plainness" according to another reading.
9. In Schlegel's translation this allusion is quite lost; indeed, it is given the opposite meaning: "Dein schlichtes Wesen spricht beredt mich an" ["Thy plainness speaks to me with eloquence."]
10. [Literally: "The third one, ah! the third one . . . the third one said nothing. She won the prize all the same."—The quotation is from Act I, Scene 7, of Meilhac and Halévy's libretto. In the German version used by Freud "the third one" *"blieb stumm"*—"remained dumb."]
11. In W. STEKEL, *Sprache des Traumes* (Wiesbaden: Bergmann, 1911), too, dumbness is mentioned among the "death" symbols (p. 351). [Cf. *The Interpretation of Dreams*, p. 357.]
12. [Cf. FREUD's later paper "Dreams and Telepathy" (1922).]
13. STEKEL, *loc. cit.*

14. [BROTHERS GRIMM, "Die zwölf Brüder," *Die Märchen der Brüder Grimm* (Leipzig: Insel, 1918), I, p. 42.]

15. [BROTHERS GRIMM, "Die sechs Schwäne," *ibid.*, p. 217 (No. 49).]

16. What follows is taken from W. H. ROSCHER, *Ausführliches Lexikon der griechischen und römischen Mythologie* (Leipzig: Teubner, 1884-1937), under the relevant headings.

17. [Their names may be rendered: "What was," "What is," "What shall be."]

18. ROSCHER, *op. cit.*, quoting L. PRELLER, *Griechische Mythologie* (4th ed.; Berlin: Weidmann, 1894).

19. [Cf. *The Interpretation of Dreams*, p. 318.]

20. The Psyche of Apuleius' story has kept many traits that remind us of her relation with death. Her wedding is celebrated like a funeral, she has to descend into the underworld, and afterward she sinks into a deathlike sleep (Otto Rank).—On the significance of Psyche as goddess of the spring and as "Bride of Death," cf. A. ZINZOW, *Psyche und Eros* (Halle: 1881).—In another of Grimm's Tales ("The Goose-girl at the Fountain" ["Die Gänsehirtin am Brunnen"], BROTHERS GRIMM, *ibid.*, II, p. 300 [No. 179), there is, as in "Cinderella," an alternation between the beautiful and the ugly aspect of the third sister, in which one may no doubt see an indication of her double nature—before and after the substitution. This third daughter is repudiated by her father, after a test which is almost the same as the one in *King Lear*. Like her sisters, she has to declare how fond she is of their father, but can find no expression for her love but a comparison with salt. (Kindly communicated by Dr. Hanns Sachs.)

On "King Lear"

In his *Theme of the Three Caskets* Freud treats the tragedy of *King Lear* on the mythic or folkloric level, and in this respect his paper can be regarded as representative of one broad way in which psychoanalytic critics have approached the play.[1] The second approach is grounded in what we have called realistic psychology: characters are treated as "real people" and psychoanalytic findings are presented in such a manner as to illuminate what the critic considers to be the motivational issue. With regard to method, then, the psychoanalytic criticism of *King Lear* bears a general resemblance to the psychoanalytic criticism of *Othello*. And indeed, the reader may by this time be appreciating something that we suggested in the Introduction to this volume, namely, that the cleavage between the mythic and realistic methods of analysis constitutes the basic cleavage in psychoanalytic approaches to Shakespeare.

The realistic readings of *Lear* tend on the one hand to echo the conclusions Freud reached from another perspective and to regard the play's protagonist as an old man libidinously involved with his daughters, especially Cordelia; on the other hand, they tend to regard the King as a child and to view the play as an externalization of the child's frustrated longing and subsequent rage.[2] The first kind of reading is by far the more prevalent and is ably represented in the work of F. L. Lucas.

Lucas is interested, ultimately, in motivation. Unable to agree with Freud's conclusions about the symbolic identity of Cordelia, he turns his attention to, as he puts it, the "more interesting question," namely, "can psychological experience justify this old father's quarrel with his favourite daughter over the mere wording of her affection? Or the icy ruthlessness of Goneril and Regan toward their father and sister?" Or Edmund's "treatment" of his helpless, hounded parent? What Lucas suggests is that the King's quarrel with Cordelia is in the last analysis a "lover's quarrel." Although cases in which the parent is overly attached to the child are less common in psychological literature than cases in which the reverse is true, they nevertheless exist,[3] and there is every reason to believe that we have such a case here. "I do not wish to overstate; but I suggest that the first fatal scene between Lear and Cordelia becomes more intelligible, and more pathetic, when we see in it a lover's quarrel, though neither of them knows it." As for Goneril, Regan, and Edmund, they too behave in a way that is consistent with psychological findings. "Shakespeare," says Lucas, "was no novice" in these matters, and what he finally presents us with in *Lear* is "a concentrated tragedy of the jealousy between parents and children, between sisters or brothers; above all, of a father's morbid possessiveness towards a favorite daughter." Thus the playwright, it may fairly be said, has returned once again to the soil of *Oedipus Rex,* but this time in a more comprehensive way.

M. F.

amlet is the story of a son ruined by a mother; *Lear* the story of two fathers ruined by their children.

It does not, indeed, seem to me nearly so profound or penetrating a play. *Lear* contains, unlike *Hamlet,* several characters who are, Aristotle would have felt, vile and excessively vile, without that demonic poetry which half redeems Iago; the plot has at times the naïvétè of a fairy tale; and the author's own mind seems at times to lose the magnificent balance it maintains in *Hamlet, Macbeth, Othello,* or *Antony and Cleopatra.*

And yet, whatever view one takes of the place of *Lear* among Shakespeare's plays, its psychology turns out to be less fantastic, I think, than it looks. It is a tragedy of family relations—Lear and his daughters; Cordelia and her sisters; Gloucester and his sons; Edmund and his brother. First, Lear and his daughters. Here Freud, in his essay *Das Motiv der Kästchenwahl,*[1] has suggested an interpretation of the legend that, I must admit, leaves me skeptical. He compares, reasonably enough, the legend of Psyche and her two sisters, of Aschenputtel (Cinderella) and hers, of Paris and his three goddesses; and also the choice of Bassanio between the three caskets (familiar symbols for the feminine) in *The Merchant of Venice.* He suggests that in all these legends the three women are the Three Fates or Norns, and the one chosen is Death. And he points to the pale lead of Portia's casket:

"On *King Lear*" by F. L. Lucas. Reprinted from *Literature and Psychology* by F. L. Lucas, pp. 62-71, with permission of the University of Michigan Press and Cassell & Co., Ltd. Copyright © 1957 University of Michigan Press.

> . . . thou meager lead,
> Which rather threat'nest than dost promise aught,
> Thy paleness moves me more than eloquence, ...
> (III.ii.104-106)

Since in dreams all may go by opposites, Freud argues that here the man's choice of Death can symbolize Death's inevitable choice of man; by a similar interchange of contraries, in the choice of Paris the Goddess of Love replaces Death; and in *Lear,* when the old king carries off the dead Cordelia, this disguises the real situation in which Death carries off the doomed king. He has indeed found only Death still left for him; the years of woman as mother, woman as mistress, are past and gone. Hence the deep effect of Shakespeare's tragedy on our unconscious minds.

I am afraid I should find it just as convincing to explain *Lear* as a solar myth. More interesting, I think, is the question—can psychological experience justify this old father's quarrel with his favorite daughter over the mere wording of her affection? Or the icy ruthlessness of Goneril and Regan towards their father and sister?

It may be argued that it is idle to demand probability of a folk legend; but this is a play, not a fairy tale. And yet Lear's contention with Cordelia seems as fantastic as a lover's quarrel. Perhaps, in a way, that is precisely what it is.

The following case history may help.[2] The patient, an American of fifty-three, once a robust athlete, arrived pale and thin in the consulting room, with his weight fallen from 73 kilos to 53. Once he had been a successful businessman, happily married—too happily, indeed, so that he paid only grudging attention to his two sons and his daughter. He gave them an expensive education; he rewarded and punished; but his leisure, Sundays and holidays, was always devoted to his adored wife.

Then came the Slump. He retired, hoping for consolation in a calm domestic happiness with home and children. But *they* had not forgiven his early indifference. Children, it seems, will sooner forgive even tyranny in a parent than apathy.

His sons had left home. His daughter, though still there, remained icily unresponsive. And to this aging man her coldness grew intolerable

—for now she recalled to him what his wife had been in the days of their youth.

> Thou art thy mother's glasse and she in thee
> Calls back the lovely Aprill of her prime.
> (Sonnet IV.9-10)

He grew jealous of his daughter's friends, of her music, of all her interests. What did she give him but a grudging walk in her company once a week, with hardly a word spoken? And yet he was still unaware why he was in general so miserable and so ill. He dreamed— "Twenty-six could end your troubles. But twenty-six will not help." He was mystified. The number 26 meant nothing to him. "Does the date 2/VI mean anything?" Yes, that indeed was his daughter's birthday. *She* was the helper he craved in vain. When he had been brought to face his own conflict, and his daughter had travelled from home, he was at last able to recover his lost balance of mind and body.

Such cases when parent is tied to child, though less prominent in psychological literature than their converse, where child is tied to parent, remain common enough, alike in modern reality and ancient legend. In story after story we have a king who imposes dire penalties on the suitors of his daughter. The lovers of Atalanta who could not outrun her were put to death by her father, Iasus. King Oenomaus allowed his would-be sons-in-law to take his daughter Hippodameia in a chariot, gave them a start while he sacrificed a ram to Zeus, then drove after and killed them; until Pelops bribed the old king's charioteer to take the linch-pins from his chariot-wheels, so that Oenomaus crashed and was killed, breathing as he died the first of those curses that were to dog the House of Pelops, down to Agamemnon and Orestes.

More memorable still, to me, is the story of Icarius and his daughter Penelope. When she wedded Odysseus, Icarius tried to keep the young pair with him at Sparta. But Odysseus, as we might guess, would not give up his Ithaca. Then Icarius implored his daughter to remain. Even when Odysseus set her in his chariot and drove north out of Lacedaemon, the insistent father pursued Penelope along the road with his entreaties. At last Odysseus said to her, "Choose." In silence she veiled her face. Then Icarius understood what, gentler than

Cordelia, she would not say; and, resigning himself to necessity, set up by the wayside a statue of Modesty—the same, Pausanias fondly believed, as he saw there fourteen hundred years later, in the second century A.D. Such was the Greek genius for embodying eternal truths in stories almost as eternal in their grace.

Similarly, in real life Charlemagne could not bear to let his daughters marry; nor could Mr. Barrett of Wimpole Street. Mr. Barrett may seem a Victorian monstrosity. But his case is not so rare; there are only too many mothers that find no girl good enough to marry their sons; and every now and then we read of some father who has unaccountably committed suicide just at the period of his daughter's wedding.

I do not wish to overstate; but I suggest that the first fatal scene between Lear and Cordelia becomes more intelligible, and more pathetic, when we see in it a lovers' quarrel, though neither of them knows it. Lear is jealous.

> Why have my sisters husbands, if they say
> They love you all? Haply, when I shall wed,
> That lord whose hand must take my plight shall carry
> Half my love with him, half my care and duty.
> Sure I shall never marry like my sisters,
> To love my father all.
>
> (I.i.101-106)

Indeed Dr. Pauncz of New York has coined for such situations in real life the term "Lear-complex."[3]

Once more we are faced by the hidden pitfalls which civilization has introduced into the human family. Parents too fond may tangle their children in emotional leading-strings; parents not fond enough can breed in their children a rankling resentment. Life is not easy. The only solution is a fondness that does not clutch, an affection that is freedom.

> The wild hare of love
> Is alert at his feet.
> Oh the fierce quivering heart!
> Oh the heart's fierce beat!

He has tightened his noose,
    It was fine as a thread;
But the wild hare that was love
    At his feet lies dead.

Those lines of Susan Miles were not written of father and daughter, mother and son; but they well might have been. That was the tragic error committed by the parents of John Ruskin.

There is no less psychological truth in the relations of Gloucester with his son Edmund, who can never forget that he is illegitimate:

Thou, Nature, art my goddess; to thy law
My services are bound. Wherefore should I
Stand in the plague of custom. . . . ?

(I.ii.1-3)

Edmund's ruthlessness to his father, his rancor towards his brother, his scorn and hate of all established authority are much more typical—less melodramatic—than most critics realize. It is, of course, usual enough for sons to react against their fathers anyway; but with an illegitimate son there is (very understandably) a far stronger motive for hating the parent who has disgraced both the child's mother and the child itself; and for hating also the society that inflicts that disgrace.

Let us take an actual example that in fiction we should dismiss as overdrawn. A Viennese dentist had a natural son. The boy grew up ignorant of his parentage. But when he reached manhood, he discovered the secret, went to the dentist as a patient, and shot his long-lost father in his own consulting-room. Many of us may, it is true, have felt similar impulses towards our dentists; but we seldom carry them out.

Noticeable also is the tendency for a revolutionary attitude towards society to be closely linked with the revolutionary's attitude to his own father.[4] (I am speaking now of sons in general, legitimate or not. And I wish to make it quite clear that I am speaking only of things that are liable to happen, not of universal laws.) An amusing instance is provided by the son of a left-wing father, in France, who was passionately right-wing till his father died; *then* promptly switched round and became left-wing himself. A similar case, I believe, from history is our own Henry V—a far more intriguing, complicated, and sinister character in reality than Shakespeare's fifteenth-century Rupert Brooke. It seems fairly well established that the historic Henry V *was* riotous in his youth; it is certain that the antagonism between him and his father, Henry IV, grew at times acute; what is less known is that after that father's death, he became not merely a reformed character, but a ruler whose austerity was the astonishment of his age—a figure far grimmer than Shakespeare's king of Agincourt—more like another Cromwell, not only in strictness, but, unfortunately, in cruelty also, even by the standards of his day; a leader, just indeed, but pitiless. One gets the impression that, like the French politician I have just mentioned, the young Henry may have played libertine from antagonism to his father; and when that father died, swung back to a fundamental austerity of temper not uncommon in masterful characters. For such aggressive masterfulness can be turned against oneself as well as against the world. So it was with the ascetic Charles XII of Sweden.

For similar antagonism between son and father one has only to look at our own Hanoverians in the eighteenth century, or Frederick the Great, or the Prince de Ligne, or Mirabeau. More striking still is the penalty that Henry II paid for unfaithfulness and rigor towards his queen—one after the other, as they grew up, his sons made open war against him—Henry, Richard, Geoffrey, John; until the last and best-loved broke his heart. The Oedipus complex has been overworked; some of us have grown sick of the very name of it; but it exists; and those who ignore it can pay bitterly.

I can recall a distinguished colleague in the war who was in certain things subordinated to me. It soon grew clear from his comments on those above us, especially our commanding officer and the Prime Minister, that he suffered from a resentfulness that bore no relation to reality. By taking great pains to avoid anything remotely suggesting parental authority it proved possible to get through those years without incurring—at least audibly—the violence of his anathemas. Perhaps in the far future when such elementary psychology grows more widely spread, the ordinary audience that hears some zealot blowing up with all his bellows the fires of class-hatred, instead of being deceived, or dismayed, or disgusted, will burst into peals of knowing laughter. When apparently rational men find their spiritual home in Moscow or Berchtesgaden, the answer to the riddle often lies simply in reaction from the homes of their childhood.

> Yes, *Cassius;* and from henceforth
> When you are over-earnest with your *Brutus,*
> He'll think your mother chides, and leave you so.
> (*Julius Caesar,* IV.iii.122-124)

Let us not too hastily condemn Shakespeare's Edmund and his treatment of his father as overdrawn. Shakespeare was no novice in the human heart. There has been in our time a tendency to praise Shakespeare as a mere wizard of words, whose conjuring with phrases conceals commonplace ideas and mediocre psychology. I do not think he cared very much about general ideas; but I have come to think he knew a good deal more about human nature than some of us suspected —than some of us knew ourselves.

Meanwhile there is yet another psychological trait in *King Lear*— the callousness of Goneril and Regan towards their younger sister, and of Edmund towards his legitimate brother. This too may seem to a purely rational mind—or one that fondly imagines itself so—rather theatrical. Perhaps it is; but not because it is untrue to life. Long before Shakespeare, popular psychology recognized the intense hatred that can be felt by elder brothers or sisters towards younger, in stories like those of Joseph, or Cinderella.

Even with the most scrupulous parental justice elder children may hate intensely the younger arrival who inevitably deprives them in part of the attention and tenderness they monopolized before. Every year there is a steady number of cases where this jealousy leads to the actual murder of a younger child by an elder—just as queen-bees do with their sisters and Turkish sultans used to do with their brothers.

Let me tell you the tragicomic story of the lady with the cats. This patient at the age of eight or nine became jealous of a baby niece. She had heard from her nurse the horrific tale of a clergyman's cat which used to sit at table with its master; but one day the bishop came to dinner; a cat could not possibly be allowed to sit at table and look at a bishop; so it was excluded. The cat, however, was of a revengeful disposition; that night it stalked into the poor clergyman's bedroom and stifled him by the ingenious method of thrusting its tail down his throat.

Shortly after hearing this tragic tale the child came on a black cat sleeping in the baby-niece's pram. She fainted.

From that time she was haunted by cats as Orestes by the Furies. Even when grown up, she would burst into wild screams on finding a cat at the foot of her bed. She developed a power to smell cats whose presence no one else had even guessed. She would come home and refuse to enter because there was a cat. No assurances to the contrary could shake her. At length search would reveal some miserable kitten cowering under the stairs.

She tried every means of overcoming this aversion. She even kept a cat in a cage in her room. No use. The very mention of a cat was enough to make her vomit.

Her travel journal contained only references to cats—"St. Gothard Hotel—white angora." She married and was hoping to become a mother: she met a cat and miscarried.

Why? In her jealousy she had entertained death-wishes against the infant niece. When she found the black cat sitting in the pram, it seemed the very incarnation of her guilty hope that the child might perish like the unfortunate clergyman in her nurse's story. (There were other complications also—such as her father's fur coat—that need not concern us here.) Hence a lasting horror of cats as symbols of her death-wish—a horror that made her literally sick.

So much for this fantastic hatred which *can* burst out between brothers and sisters, and has given birth to so many stories and tragedies, including those Greek plays that turn on the detestation of Atreus for his brother Thyestes, whom he feasted on his own children's flesh; or of Eteocles and Polyneices, whose abhorrence was stronger even than death, so that on the funeral pyre itself the flames from their two bodies, in unconquerable loathing, turned different ways.

Lear, then, is a concentrated tragedy of the jealousy between parents and children, between sisters or brothers; above all, of a father's morbid possessiveness towards a favorite daughter. As drama I cannot myself, as I say, rank it with *Hamlet;* but my object has been not to stress a personal preference but to justify some of the psychology of the play from real life. It is *not* so naïve as it looks.

Nor is a fuller grasp of such things irrelevant to our own lives. It would be grotesque to give the impression that I regard the family as a sort of den of cannibals where every member either loathes or perversely loves every other. On the contrary, I do not believe a state can be happy where happy families grow few and rare. They are its firmest foundation. Healthy happiness at home in early years can perhaps do more than anything else to produce sane and balanced men and women. But these dangers do exist. The family is, in both senses, one of the most *primitive* features of human society.

Notes

1. See also MAUD BODKIN, *Archetypal Patterns in Poetry* (1934) (New York: Random House, 1958), pp. 14-17, 273-276; WILLIAM FROST, "Shakespeare's Rituals and the Opening of *King Lear*," *Hudson Review*, *10*:577-585, 1957-1958.
2. See, for example, ELLA FREEMAN SHARPE, "From *King Lear* to *The Tempest*" (1947) in MARJORIE BRIERLY (ed.), *Collected Papers on Psycho-Analysis* (London: Hogarth Press, 1950), pp. 214-241.
3. See ARPAD PAUNCZ, "Psychopathology of Shakespeare's *King Lear*," *American Imago*, *9*:55-77, 1952-1953.

1. SIGMUND FREUD, *Gesammelte Werke*, Vol. X, pp. 24-37.
2. WILHELM STEKEL, *L'Education des Parents*, pp. 139-145.
3. Pauncz's initial presentation of the "Lear-complex" came in "Der Learkomplex, die Kehrseite des Odipuskomplexes," *Zeitschrift für Neurologie und Psychiatrie*, *143*:294-332, 1933. (Editor's Note.)
4. See "Oedipal Patterns in *Henry IV*," pp. 429-438 of this anthology. (Editor's Note.)

Imagery in "King Lear"

Rooted firmly in the mythopoeic treatments of *Lear* that have appeared in the past half century (especially Freud's), as well as in Caroline Spurgeon's pioneering studies of dramatic imagery, the following paper by Mark Kanzer represents one of the major developments in recent psychoanalytic criticism of Shakespeare, namely, the effort on the part of the psychoanalytic commentator to reveal the interrelatedness of literary and psychological factors and to demonstrate how the critical integration of these factors can convey the overall unity and meaning of the Shakespearean conception. With regard specifically to the images in a play, Kanzer believes that "an insightful psychological orientation" can "set" them in their "dramatic context (plot, character, and audience appeal) and, if possible, in relation to their origins and functions in the creative imagination of the dramatist himself."

Kanzer begins his analysis of *Lear* by asserting that the "familiar oedipal triangle" of father, son, and daughter provides "the deeply running currents of the inner drama that moves the puppets on the surface." He then goes on to demonstrate the way in which the central image of the play, namely, "the male body in violent movement and excruciating pain," expresses on the poetic-dynamic level the forbidden attachments and sexual crimes of the chief characters as well as the suffering they must undergo for their offenses. As Lear enacts the "symbolic orgasm" on the heath, his body is tortured by the terrible storm; as Gloucester discovers the treachery of his bastard son, his eyes (testicles) are destroyed by his ruthless enemies. "Gloucester and Lear, each punished for becoming a father, fuse into Oedipus, the proud and incestuous parricide who loses regal status and external eyes, but discovers the truth within himself." Again, Kanzer regards Edgar's role in the play as an expression of the archetypal "son-as-successor" theme. By disguising himself and participating (if only on the make-believe level) in the crimes that destroy his elders, Edgar sheds his innocence and emerges as one capable of reuniting the state. Thus, as Kanzer sees it, the "birth" of the legitimate son combines with the animal imagery, the nakedness imagery, and the tortured body imagery to reveal that *Lear* as a whole embodies a kind of sadistic primal scene, and a subsequent fruition in which the forces of "legality and morality" triumph over nature. Kanzer concludes by discussing the relevance of this interpretation to the playwright's own personal history.

M. F.

he study of imagery is a potential meeting ground, but also too often a dividing line, between literary and psychoanalytic scholarship.[1] To Caroline Spurgeon, a nose is a nose and, as an organ of smell, may indicate Shakespeare's preference for flowers and the aroma of good cooking;[2] to Ernest Jones, it is uncompromisingly phallic.[3] The discovery that the idea of "dog" suggests to the dramatist the licking of sweets provides an opportunity for a spontaneous word-association test not only of the author but of the critic, who justifiably sees a natural metaphor for false flatterers, and of the psychoanalyst, who equally justifiably suspects a fellatio phantasy.

Neither the common-sense nor the poetic nor the sexual meanings need to be right or wrong or mutually exclusive. Images are stratified, patterned, and convey multiple implications which are the very essence of their origin and function. Unfortunately, literary scholar and psychoanalyst have too often been equipped to respond to and develop only one aspect of these implications and have shown indifference or even antagonism to another. This may well relate to the respective aesthetic and psychological interests involved as well as to the ambiguity of the image itself, which invites attention to a surface meaning while recessively suggesting another. Obviously, the over-all significance can be derived only from a full survey of all facets of the image—and indeed of the image pattern of the work—better still, of all the author's works, supplemented by all we know of the author (cf. Henry James's "The Figure in the Carpet"). Ultimately, the

"Imagery in *King Lear*" by Mark Kanzer. Reprinted with permission from *American Imago*, XXII (1965), 3-13.

image, like the drama of which it is part, is rooted in time, place, and person.

King Lear lends itself in various respects to such a task. It is remarkably rich in imagery. Shakespeare himself has made mental processes, in their breakdown and recovery, the subject of the play. It is the dramatist himself who introduces the clinical viewpoint into a work of art, and the literary critic is therefore tempted to venture into this field in his search for understanding. It remains only for the analyst to apply the technical rule of interpretation, "approach from the surface," to deepen through his specific knowledge the insight that the literary commentator has already achieved.

The latter has sometimes seen the point and counterpoint linking of Lear and Gloucester as representatives of mental and physical transgressions, of pride and lust, that are punished respectively and appropriately by mental and physical suffering. The analyst will suggest that they are split portions of a single personality. The difficulties of each character with his children are set forth in unmistakable parallels and also become inextricably related, as would a tale about one individual. The almost allegorical division of the two sets of children into good and bad makes possible (if not inevitable) the further corollaries: Edgar-Edmund, on the one hand, and Cordelia-Goneril-Regan, on the other, as composites of a single personality. Was not Cordelia the first of the three sisters to reject and disillusion the old man? Was not her blunt truthfulness merely an act of virtue? And did it not set off the entire train of tragic events that constitute the drama?

From this perspective, our cast is reduced to three persons: father, son and daughter. Mother is missing, but with some readily demonstrable transpositions, wrought by the unconscious processes, she emerges, as the Fool notes, from the figures of the ostensible daughters. The familiar oedipal triangle takes shape to provide the deeply running currents of the inner drama that moves the puppets on the surface. In its outlines, the drama is something like an animated fairy tale and not far removed from the child's oedipal view of reality. This fairy tale, however, also has the profundity of a nature myth, as Freud has pointed out: a variant of the choice of Bassanio among the three caskets, of the eventful judgment of Paris, and of the decision of the Prince with respect to Cinderella and her sisters.[4]

As a nature myth, the story is that the golden prince, the sun god, and the silver prince, the moon god, seek to woo the earth goddess, represented by lead. The magical world of the astrologer and the alchemist derive here from the child's projected sexual investigations. Conversely, the three sisters are also goddesses of the sun, moon, and earth. They represent the triple-headed mother goddess, the mother as the fate who determines from birth to death the course of man's life. Lear's choice of the earth goddess, Cordelia, is in fact no choice, as Freud notes: in her guise as Death, she may be temporarily avoided but will choose him in the end. A sexual fantasy adheres however to man's last moments; she is also the forbidden mother whose embrace is granted at the very end.

Freud did not follow through in the detailed application of this theme to the drama, but to do so is most illuminating. Spurgeon permits us to discern in Lear a dominant image of the male body in violent movement and excruciating pain as it is torn apart by bestial females, but she stops short of discovering here the reincarnation of the ancient legends about Dionysus and Orpheus. W. H. Clemen remarks that this imagery attains a climax in the storm on the heath, which is both the altar of the nature gods and an externalization of the aged king's mind as it loses its grasp upon external reality and sinks into universal archetypes.[5] It is precisely at this point that otherwise unmotivated references to sex and incest come to the fore. The entrance of Lear into the hovel provides a phallic climax which is followed by a restful sleep.

Robert B. Heilman draws the imagery into patterns that unmistakably reveal not only the oedipal motive but also the remarkable similarity of the play to that of Sophocles.[6] The male body reaches its ultimate torture (in immediate sequence to the symbolic orgasm on the heath) in Gloucester's loss of his eyes; it is his alter ego, Lear, who declares for both of them: "Judicious punishment! 'Twas this flesh begot those pelican daughters." Gloucester and Lear, each punished for becoming a father, fuse into Oedipus, the proud and incestuous parricide who loses regal status and external eyes but discovers the truth within himself.

The incest drive accompanies Lear from the beginning in the jealous demand that his daughters shall prefer him to the husbands whom he must choose for them. It continues as he enters in turn the homes of each of the newlyweds and demands attention and homage. The fairy-tale theme of spending a month with each daughter alternately (the zodiacal sun god in the houses of the celestial goddesses) is cover for a more mundane note which creeps in with Goneril's indignant charge that the King's knights are seeking to convert her castle into a brothel. The "month" becomes even more transparently a female as well as a lunar cycle when Lear invokes upon the sexually rejecting Goneril the curse that she shall be sterile. Then he departs to bang upon the door of Regan and Cornwall; we would interpret this as a birth-of-the-hero phantasy in which the King seeks from among his daughters the future mother of his son. More deeply, it is the primal scene for which the infantile-regressed Lear-Gloucester shall suffer castration and the loss of his home—i.e., the birth of a sibling.

But who is to be the son-sibling of this Oedipus? Here the Gloucester-Edgar-Edmund nexus attains significance: Is it to be the legitimate Edgar or the illegitimate Edmund (Fortune's spear or Fortune's hand, the allegorically named celestial twins)? Where the surface action in the play concerns the choice among the daughters, the deeper motive involves that between the sons. Drawing upon analytic experience with free association as psychically determined and applying this principle to *King Lear,* we find that the opening and closing of the play (with the traditional importance of preliminary and final associations in an analytic setting) deal with the "son-as-successor" theme.

The first lines of the play describe Lear's impending choice between two sons-in-law, Albany and Cornwall, as heirs to his realm. This preliminary choice between the one who will prove to be good and the other evil is carried over into the next "association": Gloucester introduces his son Edmund, contrasts this natural scion with Edgar, the legitimate, and makes his choice. It is Edmund who will be exiled, though he has already been banished for nine years (why nine?). Immediately thereafter, Cordelia is also chosen for exile by her own father—a link which strengthens the traditional birth-of-a-hero detail: the expulsion of the divine bride and her child by the royal grandfather.

The end of the play is marked by the triumphant return of Edgar (chosen for exile by Fate rather than by his father) and the final choice of Edgar and Albany for title and power—but not for women. Lear in death still retains Cordelia for himself. Legality and morality have won over nature; the crimes of the oedipal child, personified in

Edmund, have been punished; the details of the ancient puberty rite, perpetuated in the myths and chronicles which Shakespeare drew upon for his sources, furnish the substance of the intervening drama.

The basic construction both derives confirmation from and lends meaning to the images that have been quantitatively gleaned by Spurgeon so as to provide a spontaneous Rorschach test. There is the famous symbol of Lear bound to a wheel of fire with molten tears streaming from his eyes "like lead." This masochistically transformed fantasy of sex and birth has archetypes in the ritual death of the Winter King and is very likely a conscious portrayal by the dramatist of Jesus on the Cross.[7] There is a crown of thorns and even a lance in the form of images of wild beasts and serpents that lacerate and sting the dying monarch and represent the phallic daughters. The "lead" persists from the unconscious of mankind and the dramatist.

There is also resurrection in the form of Edgar, the son who splits with Albany the role of Summer-King. The significance of Edgar as the "ego" of the play may be overlooked amid the dramatic events that focus attention on the Winter-King. We find a similar situation in dreams, where the true ego may avoid conflicts by assuming a background position and projecting its problems into other figures. Not that Edgar is entirely spared conflicts; his final battle with Edmund is in the full-blooded tradition of the hero of righteousness, which is in fact the part assigned to him. The title bestowed upon the play in the first Folio did not belittle him; it was called "The True Chronicle Historie of the life and death of King Lear and his three daughters. With the unfortunate life of Edgar, son and heir to the Earle of Gloster, and his sullen and assumed humor of Tom of Bedlam."[8]

The themes of simulated madness and suicide and of revenge for injury to a father, as linked to Edgar, are significant in the hands of a dramatist who had written *Hamlet*. Armstrong has made a very interesting and convincing comparison of the cliff scene between Edgar and Gloucester at Dover and the battlement scene between Hamlet and his father's ghost.[9] The duel between Edgar and Edmund carries over the one between Hamlet and Laertes, so that an application of the principle that successive dreams transmit common themes reveals, when transferred to the plays, that Edgar is in fact a reincarnation of the Danish prince.

In a "happy ending" devised by Nahum Tate in 1680 and popular in England for more than 150 years, King Lear is restored to his kingdom and Cordelia marries Edgar—which is the traditional fairy-tale ending that Shakespeare himself felt the need to modify. For the dramatist, the play was one more unsatisfying solution of a repetitive and compelling theme which left his heroes without women and increasingly at a distance from a throne that had to be yielded to obscure brother figures (Fortinbras, Albany, etc.).[10] They maintain the oedipal taboos at increased tragic expense until a point of final intensity reaches self-destructive expression in Timon.

Edgar's most immediate successor in the sequence of the dramas seems to be Macduff: Much the same cast was reassembled by Shakespeare for *Macbeth* and made to go through much the same paces as in the preceding play: the three daughters become three witches spinning evil destinies for men; King Duncan and his retinue are brought to the castle to meet expected gratitude and to find betrayal—(though he did remind Lady Macbeth of her father!); Macduff and Macbeth resume the duel of Edgar and Edmund, with Malcolm emerging from obscurity to take over the kingdom. But still there is no heroine!

The true importance of Edgar, from the psychological, if not dramatic standpoint, is astutely evaluated by G. Wilson Knight, who sees in him the voice of Shakespeare's philosophy.[11] In the Last Judgment scene on the heath, he is designated to play the part of the Judge—an assignment that can be no idle fantasy. No less intriguing is the part that Edgar plays in breaking down the King's mind; as Knight shows, he externalizes through his pretended madness the products of Lear's growing psychosis so that the latter is tempted further and further beyond the limits of his reality-testing abilities and finally succumbs, under the hypnotic influence of Edgar, to complete madness.

Is Edgar here a representative of good or evil? He himself tells us that he is possessed by multitudes of demons and has committed many deadly sins. Is there some hint that it is the Prince of Darkness into whose hands Lear has fallen? There are remarkable links between Edgar and Edmund which suggest that they are alternate masks for the same person. It is Edmund whom Gloucester intends to exile—and it is Edgar who is exiled. It is Edmund who is illegitimate in the beginning—and Edgar in the heath scene who is the outlaw. It is Edmund who announces, in a soliloquy, that he will play Tom o' Bedlam and Edgar who actually plays it. How does he happen to share so well the mind of this villainous brother?

Edmund warns Gloucester that Edgar will kill him and he proves to be as correct in this matter as the oracle at Delphi in the case of Laius and Oedipus. For while Edmund is sent by Regan to slay Gloucester on the road to Dover, it is Edgar who finds him there and accomplishes the mission—inadvertently, of course, and after many demonstrations of his loyalty to the father and after having twice saved his life. Still, at the very end, he reveals his identity, tells the story of his sufferings and so moves the old man that his heart bursts "smilingly." A likely story indeed! Edgar, in encompassing his father's death, had all the alibis of Oedipus and was just as much a helpless instrument of fate—yet the Greek gods did not remit the penalty in the least.

Under closer scrutiny, Edgar scarcely emerges before the bar of justice as a helpless innocent. His capacity at short notice to simulate roles, to change his name and even his voice, and to deceive people, suggests an actor (like Shakespeare, who also had a younger brother named Edmund). His ready improvisation of tales and his manipulation of Lear and Gloucester as though they were puppets, further indicate a natural-born dramatist. At the crucial heath scene, he is the master of ceremonies—introducing it in a prologue, dominating it increasingly and bringing it to a close. From it, he sends Gloucester off to the blinding scene with the cryptic message, "Childe Rowland to the dark tower came—I smell the blood of a British man"; and he is the first to behold him again later. True, he then saves the father from suicide and from Oswald, but what shall we make of Edgar's story that the kindness of the gods had saved Gloucester from a horrible demon who stood beside him on the cliff? Only Edgar had stood beside the old man, and the demon and the kind gods seem to have been contending forces within himself as he peered into his own depths. Finally, it is Edgar who announces that Lear is dead. Psychic determinism will not permit us to overlook the practical implications of this act.

Literary scholars, while indebted to the findings of Caroline Spurgeon, have tended to adopt the viewpoint that the quantitative study of individual images, and even their "common sense" correlation, is not enough. There must be an insightful psychological orientation that will set the images in their dramatic context (plot, character, audience appeal) and, if possible, in relation to their origins and functions in the creative imagination of the dramatist himself. In *King Lear,* the profusion of animal images, nakedness images, or tortured male body images, attracts the attention of the literary commentator, but apparently it is the analysis, like the outspoken child in the tale of the Emperor's clothing, who must cry out that this is indeed a picture of the sex act.

That the storm in Lear's mind is re-echoed in the storm on the heath needs no lengthy psychoanalytic training to recognize. A specific symbol thus constitutes a point of mutual orientation. But that the storm becomes the occasion for the greatest profusion of animal images in the play, for the emergence of demons and the ushering in of a Last Judgment for sexual sinners—these are developments which do call for the analyst's special experience with the regressive widening of ego boundaries as the animal phobia of the child deepens into the world-destruction phantasy of the paranoid state.

Analysts themselves sometimes take a dubious view of the extent to which their methods and insights can be applied to the understanding of the writer's imagination and art. That Freud borrowed from the legend of Oedipus to describe his own patients and returned the debt to literature by his interpretation of Hamlet would seem to show that analytic methodology and the validity of its inferences are not limited to the couch. Psychic determinism and the operations of the unconscious prevail wherever the human mind is operative. Freud did not need to have Schreber on the couch when he used the latter's writing to prepare a lasting chart of the human mind.

The application of psychoanalysis to King Lear, used as a legitimate instrument, yields—in our opinion—a consistent and demonstrable world of fantasy intermediate between the surface events (often incongruous and even silly) and the source material on which Shakespeare is known to have drawn. It is not merely that the Oedipus triangle has once more been discovered in an author's work; specific details of his fantasies may be discerned and found to act as a propelling force that animates each character, each action, each image in the play. True, the extent to which we may postulate from the fantasies the facts about the dramatist's childhood or contemporary life (indispensable for analytic therapy) is limited—but what is left is of tremendous value, especially in relation to our understanding of the arts. The analytic commentator is no more bound to produce a final case history of Shakespeare than he is to disqualify himself from making possible contributions to literary criticism.

The dominant fantasy that we feel justified in reconstructing from *King Lear* is one of childbirth which, on a deeper layer, encloses a sadistic primal scene. There is much reversal in the roles of the sexes: the male is attacked and castrated by the female and later gives birth to the child. The problem of quantitative evaluation of images is inextricably connected with psychological insight; the symbols of intercourse and childbirth will not yield themselves either to discovery or conviction without the clinical training of the Freudian analyst. Thus, the "nine year's exile" of Edmund before the play begins, becomes a double indication of a pregnancy fantasy—both in the "nine" and in the "exile" (the latter is a familiar theme in the family romance).

We have already cited the monthly visits of the King to his daughters and the sterility that must be the penalty for a failure to receive him (sterility is also the curse of the gods for parricide in the Oedipus legend). There is the emergence of the naked Edgar from the hovel on the heath, ravenous and indiscriminate in appetite and feeble in mind like a newborn infant (he will reappear from Shakespeare's image clusters at a later date as Caliban, offspring of a witch and associated with a tempest). The double "rescue of the father" on the way to Dover and the "oceanic experience" on the cliff are again birth fantasies, as are the reunion with and death of the daughters (the hanging of Cordelia is analogous to that of Jocasta, from which it may well be taken, and derives from the significance of the navel cord attachment).

While the literary commentator will develop the philosophy of the "naked babe" image, the analyst will delve into the deeper unconscious levels from which the "babe" arises. He will be impressed with the fact that *Macbeth*, in which Freud also discovered the central role of childbirth and childlessness, was written in close sequence to *King Lear*, thus establishing one of the psychological links between the plays.[12] He will also find it pertinent to trace variants in others of Shakespeare's works, as in the controversy between Titania and the jealous Oberon over possession of a male child, or the urgency with which

Shakespeare pressed upon the recipient of the sonnets the need to procreate a son. What part did the death of Shakespeare's own son Hamnet, some nine years before *King Lear* was written, play in all this? We know only that *King John,* written soon after that loss, initiated a series of child-destroying scenes in the dramas that included the threat to Edgar's life in *Lear* and the murder of the young Macduff and attempted murder of Fleance in *Macbeth.*

These considerations all have bearing on the ultimate significance of symbols. The path from the manifest content on the stage to the deepest wish in the mind of the dramatist is one that must be transversed if the relation between the image and that which it symbolizes is to be fully understood. The relationship is not merely genetic, it is also organizational and involves intrapsychic as well as interpsychic communication. In its most archaic aspects, it is as close to the wordless affects as the cry of the newborn child that is simulated by the storm on the heath. It struggles toward definition in this animal-haunted nightmare scene, which reproduces the terror of primitive men in the presence of wild beasts and angry gods.

Dionysian fury passes into Apollonian serenity of the triumphant Edgar, the controlled and unified ego as a virtuous hero of social righteousness, fused with the superego despite the fact that he has killed his father and brother.[13] Shakespeare himself, as a dramatist, emphatically shared the hero's sufferings and the incomplete triumph that would induce him to make renewed attempts to express satisfactorily the repetitive urges whose origins he could not fathom and whose ends he could not attain. It is he, as well as Lear, who is bound to a ceaselessly revolving wheel of fortune. Art enables him to create a symbol that will tell this truth about himself; science teaches the reader the fuller truth that is hidden in the symbol.

Notes

1. MARK KANZER, "Autobiographical Aspects of the Writer's Imagery," *International Journal of Psycho-Analysis,* 40:Nos. 1-2, 1959.
2. CAROLINE SPURGEON, *Shakespeare's Imagery* (London: Cambridge University Press, 1939).

3. ERNEST JONES, *Hamlet and Oedipus* (New York: W. W. Norton and Company, 1949).

4. SIGMUND FREUD, *The Theme of the Three Caskets,* Standard Edition, Vol. XII (London: Hogarth Press, 1959).

5. W. H. CLEMEN, *The Development of Shakespeare's Imagery* (Cambridge, Massachusetts: Harvard University Press, 1951).

6. ROBERT B. HEILMAN, *This Great Stage* (Seattle: University of Washington Press, 1963).

7. *Ibid.*

8. F. E. HALLIDAY, *Shakespeare and His Critics* (London: Gerald Duckworth and Company, 1950).

9. EDWARD A. ARMSTRONG, *Shakespeare's Imagination* (London: Lindsay Drummond, 1946).

10. MARK KANZER, "The Central Theme in Shakespeare's Works," *Psychoanalytic Review, 38* :No. 1, 1951.

11. G. WILSON KNIGHT, *The Wheel of Fire* (New York: World Publishing Company, 1957).

12. SIGMUND FREUD, *Some Character Types Met with in Psychoanalytic Work,* Standard Edition (London: Hogarth Press, 1957).

13. His travails are those of the older child who reacts to the birth of a sibling with death wishes against all concerned. Still, he must accept the reality of the situation, abdicate as little king of the family, and restore his past supremacy through daydreams.

The Riddle of Shakespeare's "Macbeth"

Freud was so impressed with *Macbeth* that he included it among "the ten most magnificent works of world literature."[1] His followers, evidently, shared some of this enthusiasm, for a sizeable body of psychoanalytic criticism has grown up around the tragedy. The most interesting general fact about this criticism is that, with the exception of certain treatments of Lady Macbeth, it is written almost entirely from the standpoint of psychic realism; in other words, it deals with the play as fantasy and discovers "realistic" psychological portrayal only beneath a mythic or dreamlike surface. This fact is not especially surprising when one considers the degree to which apparitions, omens, ghosts, witches, and prophecies participate in the action, as well as the degree to which Shakespeare's poetic depiction of scene calls up a world of primeval murkiness, a kind of supernatural landscape.

The germinating comments on *Macbeth,* the comments that appear to stand behind much of the later criticism, came from the pens of Freud and Rank. While perusing Freud's essay on Hamlet and Oedipus (see pp. 79-86 of this anthology), the careful reader may have noticed a remark, made almost offhandedly in the final paragraph, to the effect that *Macbeth* deals with the theme of childlessness. This is one of the germinating insights. The other was developed by Rank in 1912 and holds that Macbeth's murder of Duncan speaks for hostility toward and resentment of the father-king, or, to use the popular expression, the "authority figure."[2] Such a view quite obviously suggests that Shakespeare is once again exploiting his audience's subconscious involvement in the oedipal conflict.

Five years after the appearance of Rank's brief commentary, Ludwig Jekels gave the tragedy its first comprehensive reading and one that can be said to have influenced all subsequent treatments. Beginning upon a ritual note, Jekels maintains that the legend of Macbeth symbolizes the process of vegetation, that it is "in reality" a vegetation myth. The hero of Shakespeare's drama corresponds to the hibernal giant "whose reign comes to an end when the May festival begins and the green wood [Birnam Wood] comes marching." Further, Freud's observation that the tragedy deals with the contrast between "sterility and fecundity" calls to Jekel's mind, among other things, the "sterility" of Elizabeth, the "Virgin Queen" who died childless, and the "fecundity" of the Kings of Scotland, from whom James was descended. In short, the play is topical as well as mythical and celebrates the ascension of James. Jekels then proceeds to treat the tragedy in two parts, the first of which is concerned with the son's (Macbeth's) rebellion against the father (Duncan), and the second with the father's (Macbeth's) maltreatment of the sons (Banquo and the lords). The play indicates, says Jekels, that a bad son makes a bad father. And too, it indicates through the character of Macduff, who also rebels against the father (Macbeth) in the second part, that a bad son "not only sacrifices his son, but, in so doing, also forfeits the blessing of a continuous descent." While Macduff achieves heroic stature through his destruction of the bad father, it is the offspring of Banquo, the good son, who ultimately preserve the clan. As for Lady Macbeth, she is the " 'demon woman' who creates the abyss between father and son." Her "vague allusion to the past refers in reality to the mother as the origin and the deepest source of hostility against the father." The three witches, in turn, become variations upon the Fatal Sisters or Norns of mythology and suggest "the three forms into which the image of the mother is cast for man in the course of his life." The brief comments of Freud and Rank, then, are developed by Jekels into a comprehensive reading of Shakespeare's play.

M. F.

A s with most of Shakespeare's plays, the date of the origin of *Macbeth* has not been established exactly. But we do know that it could not have been written before 1604, nor after 1610.[1] The later date is fixed by the first known performance of the tragedy. The earlier date, however, is derived from an important historical event: in 1604, the Scottish King, James, was crowned King of Great Britain and Ireland; the play contains an unmistakable allusion to this event.

> . . . and some I see
> That two-fold balls and treble sceptres carry.
> (IV.i.120-121)

There are still other indications that the play was composed with the King in mind. For instance, the healing power of Edward the Confessor is mentioned. As Edward himself had prophesied, this power was supposedly passed on to his descendants, including, of course, King James. The allusion is unanimously characterized by scholars as "dragged in by the hair," and is definitely out of place.

Shakespeare, moreover, elaborated the witch motif in very great detail, devoting whole scenes to a factor which is made very little of in his source (Holinshed's *Chronicle*). This procedure is obviously connected with James's interest in witchery, a preoccupation which was exceptional even in a time submerged in the belief in witchcraft. James had only recently composed a *Demonology*, and had personally interrogated an alleged witch.

"The Riddle of Shakespeare's *Macbeth*" by Ludwig Jekels. Reprinted with permission from *Psychoanalytic Review*, XXX (1943), 361-385.

The most striking evidence of the poet's concern with the King is his choice of subject. At this time, all England was familiar with the Macbeth legend. In 1605, when the King had visited Oxford, students had greeted him with a rhapsody containing elements of the legend. It seemed to be particularly well suited as an ovation for the King. Having come to Scotland and its throne only by way of wedlock, the Stuarts were particularly eager to deny their Gallic origin, and to affirm their "Scottish" ancestry by referring it to Banquo and Fleance, although both are now considered purely legendary.

The dramatist's intention to pay homage to his King is further revealed by another modification of the original material. As already noted, Shakespeare took the plot of his play from Raphael Holinshed's *Chronicle of Scottish History*. There, Banquo is depicted as an accomplice to the murder of the King, while Shakespeare shows him as a complete outsider. He did this—according to general opinion—precisely because it would have been impossible to present the King's ancestor as a bloody assassin (all the more so since the play was probably performed in James's presence). In the face of this data, it is difficult to avoid the conclusion that *Macbeth* really represented an apotheosis of James upon his accession to the throne.

Our first problem, therefore, is why the dramatist offered this homage: from what inner urge did it arise?

This question may conceal a much deeper problem than appears at first. In any case, we are fully justified in putting it, since such flattery is altogether incompatible with Shakespeare's usual habits. He had, on the contrary, been extremely chary of praise for James's predecessor, the great Elizabeth. Yet, in the course of more than ten years, she had frequently attended performances of his plays; Shakespeare had himself repeatedly appeared before her as an actor; and the playwright had achieved acknowledgement and wealth under her reign—even being raised to the peerage. Still, as Brandes points out, "Shakespeare was the only poet of the period who absolutely refused to comply with this demand" of the Queen for "incessant homage."[2]

This contrast between 'James and Elizabeth, and its intimate relation to the plot of the tragedy, has already been emphasized by Freud in his essay on *Macbeth*.[3] Despite its cursoriness, this essay is of prime importance; careful study of it was indispensable for the present paper.

Not only does it throw light on the particular question raised here, but it also clears the way for a general understanding of the play.

According to Freud, the tragedy is basically concerned with the contrast between sterility and fecundity. This follows from the fact that the weird sisters assure Macbeth "that he shall indeed be king, but to Banquo they promise that *his* children shall obtain possession of the crown."[4] In Freud's opinion, the plot is developed in accordance with this prophecy.

Furthermore, Freud points out that the same contrast between sterility and fecundity is illustrated by the historical succession to the English throne which took place, as it were, before the very eyes of the dramatist, shortly before the play was written.

"The 'virginal Elizabeth,' of whom it was rumored that she had never been capable of childbearing and who had once described herself as 'a barren stock,' in an anguished outcry at the news of James's birth, was obliged by this very childlessness of hers to let the Scottish king become her successor. And he was the son of that Mary Stuart whose execution she, though reluctantly, had decreed, and who, despite the clouding of their relations by political concerns, was yet of her blood and might be called her guest."[5]

In order to make more obvious this parallel to the historical situation which he discovered, Freud refers to Macbeth's words:

> Upon my head they plac'd a fruitless crown,
> And put a barren sceptre in my gripe,
> Thence to be wrench'd with an unlineal hand,
> *No son of mine succeeding.*
>
> (III.i.61-64)

These words repeat Elizabeth's outcry almost literally.[6]

* * *

The mythological content of the Scottish legend of Macbeth, which is the foundation of the play, seems also to corroborate Freud's conception of the basic motif. Although he dealt with the subject only in passing, he probably came very close to the psychological problem concealed in it. Even a superficial examination of the legend reveals the contrast between fertility and its opposite as the core.

According to Simrock's comments, there can hardly be any doubt that the legend symbolizes the process of vegetation, that it is in reality a vegetation myth.[7] There are actually considerable analogies with the legend of the Hessian King Grunewald as well as with that of the Giant King of Saxo Grammaticus (VII, 132). From these parallels, Simrock concludes that Macbeth, like these legendary characters, is a hibernal giant, whose reign comes to an end when the May festival begins and the green wood comes marching.

What Simrock says about the meaning of the second prophecy,

> . . . none of woman born
> Shall harm Macbeth,
>
> (IV.i.80-81)

however, is less specific. He sees in Macduff an analogy to mythical characters like Rogdai, Rustem, Woelsung, and others, men or demi-gods, who have supposedly been "ripped" from their mothers' wombs, in token of their strength and power.

This explanation of the second prophecy need not conflict with that of the Birnam wood prophecy, if we recall Simrock's hint that being "ripped from one's mother's womb" is a sign of the demigod. It would be an expression of deep reverence for the fructifying power of nature that Spring—in contrast to Winter, which is personified as purely human—be endowed with divine attributes and thus implicitly represented as victorious.

Since, however, we expect to reach a thorough explanation of this special problem in the course of our investigation, let us conclude these preliminary remarks by merely repeating that the myth of Macbeth somehow contains the contrast between sterility and generative power.

* * *

Although this theme recurs in so many aspects of the drama, it is inadequate as a basic motif—as the readers of Freud's essay will remember. It does not explain in what sense the problem of fertility or its opposite may have been meant by Shakespeare; it cannot be related to the further development of the drama; above all, it cannot elucidate the crucial psychological problem.

In the first place, this conception of the basic problem of the tragedy is remarkably weak historically. Its relation to the external historical situation, which Freud revealed in so promising a way, is only slight. It cannot establish any profound and revealing parallel.

On the other hand, Freud attempts to explain the transformation of Macbeth into a raving murderer and of his Lady into a distracted penitent by the couple's childlessness. They are understood to have conceived their disappointed hopes for children as a punishment for their crimes. This interpretation, however, failed—as will be remembered—because Shakespeare, by reducing to eight days the ten-year period which Holinshed had described between the murder of Duncan and the subsequent crimes of Macbeth (particularly the murder of Banquo), had left "no time for a long-drawn disappointment of their hopes of offspring to enervate the woman and drive the man to an insane defiance."[8] Freud is forced to conclude:

> What, however, these motives can have been which in so short a space of time could turn the hesitating, ambitious man into an unbridled tyrant, and his steely-hearted instigator into a sick woman gnawed by remorse, it is, in my view, impossible to divine. I think we must renounce the hope of penetrating the triple obscurity of the bad preservation of the text, the unknown intention of the dramatist, and the hidden purport of the legend.[9]

We shall therefore attempt to gain a deeper understanding of the problems discussed by a more detailed psychological analysis of the characters of the tragedy, of their grouping, and of their interrelations.

The psychological structure of the tragedy, which seems so bewildering at first, becomes clearer if we conceive the king as a father-symbol—a conception revealed and confirmed again and again by psychoanalysis.

We should then conclude that Macbeth's psychic function is twofold. First, like Banquo and Macduff, he is son to the father (King), Duncan. Secondly, however, when he himself has become King, he is father to Banquo and Macduff: these two come to be seen as his sons, just as they are originally conceived as Duncan's sons. Macbeth's first phase thus concerns the relationship of son to father; his second phase involves the opposite relationship, that of father to son.

In order to facilitate orientation, let us first investigate the son-father relationship. Needless to say, the murder of Duncan cannot be classified, analytically, as other than parricide.[10]

As a son, Macbeth is therefore parricidal, or—to put it less strongly —hostile, rebellious; Hecate calls him the "wayward son" (III.v.11).

The motive of the parricide, the reason for the hostility against the father, is personified in Lady Macbeth. She is the "demon-woman," who creates the abyss between father and son. We can prove the correctness of this interpretation by a number of instances. To begin with, Lady Macbeth is accomplice only to the crime Macbeth commits as son, i.e., before he had become King (father). From the moment he obtains the throne, she has no part at all in his criminal deeds: apparently she is not in on his murderous plans against either Banquo or Macduff.

Shakespearean scholars seem scarcely to have been startled by this fact. Supported by psychoanalytic insight, however, we gain the most important corroboration of our conception of Lady Macbeth from the following dialogue. (In the great seventh scene of the first act, in which she finally induces the still reluctant Macbeth to murder, the Lady refers to the past):

> . . . What beast was 't then
> That made you break this enterprise to me?
>
> · · · · · · · · · · · · · ·
>
> . . . Nor time nor place
> Did then adhere, and yet you would make both. . . .
>
> (I.vii.47-48, 51-52)

The words quoted point to abysmal psychic depths. Lady Macbeth, the "demon-woman," refers Macbeth to the past—indeed, "woman," in the guise of the three witches, had already stepped between him and the father.

A good deal has been written and argued about the witches in *Macbeth*. . . . However, Holinshed tells us plainly who these "weitches" (as he called them) are, and the dramatist himself has them name themselves the "weird sisters" (I.iii.32). "Weird" means destiny, fate; Holinshed also speaks of the witches as "goddesses of destiny."[11]

Schiller is doubtless right in concluding that the three witches represent the three Fatal Sisters, the Norns of the Edda, the Parcae of the Romans, the Moires of the Greeks. According to an essay by Freud, the same is true of Lear's three daughters, Cordelia, Regan, and Goneril, and of the three caskets in *The Merchant of Venice.*[12]

To the same engrossing essay by Freud, we owe the insight that the motif of the three sisters, which is customarily conceived as an allegory of the past, the present, and the future, also means "the three inevitable relations man has with woman," the three forms into which the image of the mother is cast for man in the course of his life: "the mother herself, the beloved who is chosen after her pattern, and finally the Mother Earth . . ."[13] Lady Macbeth's vague allusion to the past refers in reality to the mother as the origin and the deepest source of hostility against the father.

That is why the poet has the three witches meet the hero on a "blasted heath" with the prophecy that he will become Thane of Cawdor. The title of Thane of Cawdor does not mean an elevation in rank; it is rather a symbol of treason. For Ross calls the Thane a "most disloyal traitor" (I.ii.53), and Angus reports that "treasons capital, confess'd and prov'd,/Have overthrown him" (I.iii.115-116). By this detail Shakespeare implies that, through his mother, the son turns traitor to his father: Lady Macbeth, through the image of the mother, symbolizes the abyss separating father and son.

Finally, this conception of Lady Macbeth is corroborated by the character of Banquo. Having no part at all in the murder, he stands for the exact opposite of the bad son, Macbeth, and must represent the good son.[14]

In connection with the immediate subject, however, two peculiarities of Banquo are important contrasts with Macbeth: no wife is mentioned for him, and he appears to have no contact with Lady Macbeth. When the Lady exclaims,

> . . . Had he not resembled
> My father as he slept I had done 't,
> (II.ii.13-14)

she is telling us that the genii of the sexes disarm each other. At the same time, she teaches that man is urged by woman to fight his own sex, and she thus embodies the "other" sex, victorious over one's "own" sex. She stands for heterosexuality, which overpowers homosexuality.

In short, the woman—Lady Macbeth—makes Macbeth turn into a bad son, and thus the woman is the son's doom.

* * *

In his second psychic phase, Macbeth is the "father." As such, he has one son, Banquo, murdered, and also seeks the life of his other son, Macduff; consequently, he is the bad father, hostile to his sons and ready to kill them.

The validity of this interpretation is established by the great emphasis with which Macbeth orders the hired assassins not to kill Banquo alone, but also to kill his son, Fleance. When the murderers talk, after Fleance's successful flight, their stress is obviously on "son":

Third Murderer: There's but one down; the son is fled.
Second Murderer: We have lost
     Best half of our affair.
          (III.iii.19-21)

This problem of hostility against the son becomes even clearer when Macduff's little son is murdered; though we are repeatedly told that Macduff has lost *all his kith and kin,* yet the son is emphatically singled out; it is the fate of the son that Shakespeare puts into the foreground.

What is the motif of this hostility against the son?

Suffice it that we hint at the famous vision of Banquo's ghost—often interpreted and as often misunderstood—whom Macbeth sees taking his, the father's seat, just as formerly he himself had dislodged Duncan from his seat. And let us recall Macbeth's word at this moment:

   Ay, and a bold one, that dare look on that
   Which might appal the devil.
         (III.iv.59-60)

Here the poet dramatizes, with wonderful clarity, the fear of the son, now a father, upon confronting, in his own son, the same hostility he had himself harbored against his father—a motif Rank has also disclosed in Hamlet.

This *fear of requital,* a fear nourished and maintained by consciousness of the wrong committed against the father, explains Macbeth's desperate outcry at the news that although Banquo is dead, his son, Fleance, has succeeded in escaping:

> Then comes my fit again: I had else been perfect;
> Whole as the marble, founded as the rock,
> As broad and general as the casing air:
> But now I am cabin'd, cribb'd, confin'd, bound in
> To saucy doubts and fears.
>
> (III.iv.21-25)

It is the father within Macbeth, the never-silenced memories of hatred against his father and of the injury inflicted on that father in his thoughts, that nourishes suspicions of the very same feelings in the son; it is the father surviving within him that demands the death of the son. Malcolm, the cautious son, therefore speaks of

> . . . wisdom
> To offer up a weak, poor innocent lamb
> To appease an angry god.
>
> (IV.iii,15-17)

Obviously, the relation to one's son appears to the poet as strictly conditioned by the relation to one's father; one will be, as a father, as one was as a son. *Macbeth demonstrates the fact that a bad son will make a bad father.*

The same close connection of the psychical functions of son and father is revealed in other characters of the tragedy, especially in Macduff and Banquo. . . .

For Macduff must be called a bad, obstinate son, quite as much as Macbeth. Despite his love for his father (amply demonstrated for Duncan, and hinted at even for Macbeth),[15] Macduff rebels against Macbeth. He does not attend the coronation at Scone; he uses "broad words," according to Lennox (III.vi.21); and, unlike the submissive son, Banquo, who accepts unhesitatingly, Macduff refuses the invitation to the banquet offhand.

Why does he act this way?—because Macbeth has murdered Duncan, committed parricide, shown the traditional hostility against the father.

It is Macduff's rebellion against the father, however, which destroys all his kin. Persecuted by the father, he is forced to abandon them to the murderous hand, especially his son, who is stabbed to death before our very eyes. That is why he wails,

> . . . Sinful Macduff!
> They were all struck for thee. Naught that I am
> Not for their own demerits, but for mine,
> Fell slaughter on their souls. . . .
>
> (IV.iii.224-227)

Here is the same motif as in the story of Macbeth; Macduff, too, demonstrates the fact that a bad son is also a bad father.

This identical content is communicated to us, however, in two distinct dialects. Macduff's fate proclaims in an undisguised, direct manner what the character of Macbeth expresses in a veiled and therefore indirect form; the latter seems to be a symbolic presentation of the former. Analysis of Macbeth should, then, disclose a technique similar to that which is frequently used in dreams. Everyone familiar with Freud's theory of dreams knows that they discard nuances and tints and instead adopt a lapidary brevity and a violent imagery. Almost every negative emotional relation is expressed by death, for example. Macbeth's murder of the King thus corrsponds to Macduff's mere unconcern about him.[16]

The same insight is even more accurate for the female characters. Is not Lady Macduff, in her little scene (IV.ii.) but reproducing Lady Macbeth's actions in the first two acts? Macduff's wife incites her little son against his father, calling her husband a traitor who swears and does not keep his word, a man who should be hanged. She deeply degrades the child's father before him by saying how easily he could be replaced by another father. Schiller, in his translation, thought this scene so irrelevant that he left it out. But can Lady Macduff's words be symbolized more adequately than by Lady Macbeth's daggers? Hamlet, reproaching his mother with her sins, says, *"I will speak daggers to her, but use none"* (III.ii.414); even in colloquial language, "words like daggers" is a familiar figure.[17]

What could have led Shakespeare to the double presentation of this motif? . . . The character of Macduff, so poorly outlined in the legend, has been endowed so richly by Shakespeare because he saw in it a more concrete, more cleanly cut, more specific formulation of the motif which Macbeth's character expresses in a much more general way.

This may explain why he developed the Macduff nucleus of the legend, treated it separately and paralleled it to Macbeth, almost pointing out that in this case Macbeth should be understood as practically identical with Macduff.

Combing these elements, we reach a conclusion essential for the understanding of the tragedy: that *not Macbeth, but Macduff, is the true hero.* Similarly, the further development of the basic idea of the drama—the concatenation of the father function with that of the son —proceeds, not in Macbeth, but in Macduff, who becomes, as it were, the continuation of Macbeth.

* * *

Banquo is, so to speak, the positive of the picture of which Macduff is the negative. In saving himself from Macbeth's persecutions, Macduff disregards his son and sacrifices him; when Banquo is attacked by murderers, however, he gives his last thought to his son. "Fly, good Fleance, fly!" are his dying words (III.iii.17). His fate therefore symbolizes the idea treated in the play, that one's conduct as father is conditioned by one's attitude as son; here, the meaning is reversed, however, and the implication is that only a good son can become a good father.

Our original interpretation of Banquo as, notwithstanding his inner contradictions, a tractable son, is borne out if we interpret the allegory as meaning that while such a son may fall victim to his father, he will safeguard his own son. Furthermore, the apparition of the infinitely long line of Stuart kings (IV.i.112-124) shows that by saving his child a good son may expect further reward, since this action guarantees the undisturbed succession of generations: the House of Stuart originates from that same Fleance.

Applying this insight to Macbeth, *the basic idea is discovered to be that a bad son not only sacrifices his son, but, in so doing, also forfeits the blessing of continuous descent.*

* * *

This complex, we believe, this worry about the preservation of the clan, bears the main emphasis of the drama. The son is regarded primarily as a means to this end, that is, as the first-born male descendant. Although Banquo is represented in the procession of Kings, Fleance is missing.

The historical incident to which the drama can be traced also supports the supposition that the author aims principally at the problem of preservation of the line of descent. When Elizabeth died, and the Tudor dynasty was ended, the transference of the crown to the Stuarts offered an analogy with the contrasting fates of Banquo and Macduff in the tragedy. The same disappointment at the disruption of the line of descent can also be inferred from Macduff's reaction to Ross's report of the murder of

> Wife, children, servants, all
> That could be found.
> (IV.iii.212-213)

In his desperate outcry, what he bemoans is the loss of *all* his children:

> He has no children. All my pretty ones?
> Did you say all? O hell-kite! All?
> What, all my pretty chickens. . . .
> (IV.iii.216-218)

This grief is not directed to the children as such, but to their function as links in the chain of generations. Macduff's exclamation, "He has no children," which has so often been re-interpreted, may favor this interpretation. It refers to Macbeth, and, keeping the congruity of the two figures, could be replaced by a resigned, "And so I have no children." That these words, in so general a form, and in the specific situation, can only reflect on the lost prospect of continuous descent, can hardly be denied.

Notes

1. See FREUD's letter to Hugo Heller in Standard Edition, Vol. IX (London: Hogarth Press, 1959), p. 245.
2. SIGMUND FREUD, "Das Inzest-Motiv in Dichtung und Sage," *Collected Papers* (Leipzig: Franz Deuticke, 1926), pp. 209-211.

1. Recent investigations, however, have restricted this period to three years, 1604, 1605, and 1606.

2. GEORG BRANDES, *William Shakespeare,* trans. William Archer, Mary Morison, and Diana White (London: William Heinemann, 1905), p. 41.

3. SIGMUND FREUD, "Some Character Types Met with in Psycho-analytic Work" (1915), *Collected Papers* (New York, London: The International Psycho-analytic Press, 1924-1925), pp. 318-344.

4. *Ibid.,* p. 329.

5. *Ibid.,* p. 328.

6. Italics have been added in the last line of the passage quoted above.

7. KARL SIMROCK, *Die Quellen des Shakespeare* (Bonn: Marcus, 1872), pp. 255-260.

8. FREUD, *op. cit.,* p. 331.

9. *Ibid.*

10. There are lines of the text which corroborate the nature of Duncan's murder as we conceive it. Because of the basic importance of this conception for the content of the tragedy as we intend to develop it here, and because such psychoanalytic statements still meet with incredulity in many places, we quote Lennox's short speech in which parricide is mentioned repeatedly, though with ironic intent:

> *Who cannot want the thought* how monstrous
> It was for Malcolm and for Donalbain
> To kill their gracious father?
>
> (III.vi.8-10)

This quotation actually contains two negations. One is in "want," which is of rather indefinite nature, and means basically: not-to-have, to miss, to feel the lack of; this passage should therefore read: "Who can want. . . ."

Curiously enough, a second negation, "not," is appended to "want" —and this double negation leads to the affirmation and approval of the parricide.

Naturally, commentators have noticed the contradiction in this significant passage. I quote Darmesteter, *Macbeth,* Édition classique by James Darmesteter (Paris: Librairie Delagrave, 1881): "La negation est de trop dans *cannot* et ferais dire la phrase tout le contraire de ce qu'elle signifie—si le sens n'était trop claire de luimême" (*The negation in "cannot" is superfluous and would make the phrase mean the opposite of what it should*—if the sense in itself were not perfectly clear.)

This speech of Lennox is very well known among the commentators on account of its ironic content. Darmesteter calls it "un modèle d'ironie voilée" (a model of veiled irony); the remark refers particularly to Lennox's words when he says Banquo was killed because he went out late. Actually, however, the irony here does not lie in this ambiguity of motivation, but rather in the fact that the poet is telling us the truth about Macbeth's crime—doing so, however, in such a way that we do not notice it. By proposing the ridiculous motive of Banquo's going out late, the poet creates an atmosphere of absolute incredibility, into which the information about the real fact is thrown. The essential irony is that the audience is duped by receiving the truth in such a way as to be further than ever from recognizing it.

11. *Holinshed's Chronicles* (London: J. Johnson, 1808), V, p. 269.

12. SIGMUND FREUD, "The Theme of the Three Caskets" (1913), *Collected Papers,* IV, pp. 244-256.

13. *Ibid.,* p. 256.

14. Our designation of Banquo as the "good son" is a summary one, bound to rouse certain doubts, since the character does not entirely tally with it. As characterized by Shakespeare, Banquo shows a certain incompleteness, at least some indistinctness. This has been noted by several of the more serious scholars. Gervinus, arguing that imprudence causes the downfall of the minor characters, adduces the character of Banquo as another example of such poetic justice: "The same want of foresight ruins Banquo. He had been initiated into the secret of the weird sisters; pledged to openness toward Macbeth, he had opportunity of convincing himself of his obduracy and secrecy; he guesses at, and strongly suspects, Macbeth's deed; yet he does nothing against him or in self-defense" (G. GERVINUS, *Shakespeare Commentaries,* trans. F. E. Bunnètt [New York: Scribner, Welford, and Armstrong, 1875], pp. 605-606). Ulrici also describes Banquo as one who, "in self-complacent conceit, believes in the promises for his future good fortune, and thus brings destruction upon his own head" (H. ULRICI, *Shakespeare's Dramatic Art,* trans. L. D. Schmitz [London: George Bell and Sons, 1876], Vol. I, p. 474). Bodenstedt objects to Banquo's kindness, which is commonly taken for granted: "Banquo has found out all about Macbeth for a long time, but he has not done a thing to warn or to protect old King Duncan against him" [F. BODENSTADT, *Shakespeares Frauencharaktere* (Berlin: A. Holmann and Company, 1874), p. 315.] We are inclined to take this vague and compromising characterization of Banquo as simply another way of expressing psychological insight. The dramatist seems to mean that it was, after all, only the woman (the mother) who opened an unbridgeable abyss between father and son, and drove the latter into extreme hostility. All

other reasons—for example, unequal reward for equal merits (so often noticed by scholars)—could only result in vexation or indifference toward the father (Banquo confesses to "cursed thoughts" [III.i.8] against Duncan) but they could never produce the sudden turn into explicit hostility.

Still, Banquo can hardly be considered a "good" son. In reply to the King's scanty words of gratitude, he assures him, "There if I grow, The harvest is your own" (I.iv.33-34), and yet, in the next act, harbors "cursed thoughts" against him. Both suspecting and envying King Macbeth, he nevertheless submissively states, "Let your Highness command upon me, to the which my duties Are with a most indissoluble tie forever knit (III.i.15-17). Considering that Banquo thus, though wrathful in his heart, always shows himself devoted to his father, we will find the conception of him as the "submissive son" to be much more conclusive than that of the "good son." At the same time, this analysis fully retains the contrast to the "wayward" Macbeth.

16. Malcolm to Macduff: "You have lov'd him well . . ." (IV.iii. 13).

17. It is beyond the framework of this investigation to decide whether, or to what extent, such simultaneous use of the veiled and the direct manners of presenting a leading motif can be considered a basic phenomenon of dramatic composition.

18. The common external fate of the two Ladies seems to confirm the correspondence stated here: although the poet does not usually refrain from having murders acted out, both Ladies die behind the scenes.

The Babe That Milks: An Organic Study of "Macbeth"

David B. Barron's paper resembles earlier psychoanalytic treatments of *Macbeth* in two important ways. First, it views the tragedy only from the standpoint of psychic realism. The surface or action level is the level of fantasy, and it is only by delving beneath it that realistic psychological truths may be discovered. Second, it recognizes how closely Macbeth's fate is bound up with his wife's (at one point Freud and Jekels spoke of Macbeth and Lady Macbeth as the divided images of a single prototype[1]), and it recognizes, too, the way in which the treacherous or evil elements in the drama are invariably associated with things feminine. In two important ways, however, it differentiates itself. In the first place, it tends to play down the father-son conflict and to center the concern of all five acts in Macbeth's struggle to overcome his need for oral gratification, for mothering. It suggests, in other words, that Macbeth's behavior as bad son and bad father can be traced to his dependence upon his wife and to his incomplete masculinity. In the second place, it is committed to the belief that all the patterns that emerge from the play comprise a single dramatic unity and that a correct tracing of these patterns can uncover the significance of the smallest details in the text, down even to single, "isolated" images. I am not suggesting, of course, that a paper such as Jekels' "The Riddle of Shakespeare's *Macbeth*" fails to create a unified impression of the tragedy; I am suggesting that Barron goes one step further in his meticulous effort to integrate fully the literary and psychological features of the play.

Barron maintains that the theme of *Macbeth* "is not simply that woman is treacherous, but more specifically that she is treacherous in the feeding situation," and he cites a good many speeches and images in support of this. Macbeth's decision to submit himself to the female influence "implies his identification with mother rather than father, and as a result he has great qualms over his masculinity." His need to "rise" and the deeds of violence that spring therefrom can be traced to these qualms, as can his inability to distinguish between self and object that culminates in his withdrawal into a world of fantasy. Only toward the end of the play are the forces of masculinity able to emancipate the hero from the female influence that has "cabined, cribbed, confined" him for so long and to allow him to achieve, if only for a moment of dramatic time, an individual, masculine identity. And of course it is Macduff, the man of no woman born, who does the emancipating.

M. F.

hakespeare of all men has penetrated closest to the heart of man, and in the contemplation of his masterpieces we feel the possibility of absorbing something of the nature of mind and of life itself. The present study shall be based upon the premises contained in the above two mottoes—that adequate submission of our faculties to his work will enable us to discern elements of design and organic pattern, and that understanding of the pattern is to be obtained through tracing the network of relationships linking the elements to the work as a whole. No attempt shall be made to fit the data—that is, the words of the play—into a preformulated conceptual framework, but rather shall effort be focused upon tracing patterns which emerge from the play itself as crystallizations of experience. This approach is based upon the conviction that we must submit to Shakespeare rather than attempt to contain him within metapsychological formulations. The interpretations are to be derived empirically *from the play,* and are to be judged according to whether we are able, through their aid, to return *to the play* with a heightened appreciation of its wealth of meaning. The approach will resemble a thematic analysis of a work of music, in which several basic themes are found to repeat themselves in different contexts with slightly changing and ever increasing meaning, until after full development they culminate in the restatement in the finale.

The tragedy of *Macbeth,* like the tragedy of *Hamlet,* presents a very satisfying esthetic experience; but unlike *Hamlet* its plot develops so swiftly and inevitably that the audience is borne along to the end

"The Babe That Milks: An Organic Study of *Macbeth*" by David B. Barron. Reprinted with permission from *American Imago,* XVII (1960), 133-161.

of the play with no questions left hanging. However, as we assume that the play comprises an organic whole in which all of the elements are interrelated, it is possible to hold up for scrutiny any detail and hope that *full* comprehension of the detail will eventually lead to understanding the play as a whole and all the elements which in their interrelationships comprise the whole.

We shall begin our analysis with the following question: What is the significance of the witches' prophecy that "none of woman born shall harm Macbeth" (IV.i.80-81)? We learn at the end of the play that these words are equivocal: Macduff, who in fulfillment of the prophecy kills Macbeth, was not of woman born but was from his mother's womb untimely ripp'd. But why is Macbeth's destined conqueror to be not of woman born? An answer suggests itself—because Macbeth's plunge into crime was goaded by destructive female influences, of the witches and of his wife, and the man destined to overcome Macbeth is so far free from taint of woman's influence that he is not of woman born.

This answer is close to the heart of the play and requires further elaboration. Early in the play we see Macbeth in the position of having to make a choice whether to submit himself to the authority of man or woman. He has just been honored by Duncan with the title *Thane of Cawdor* (I.ii.65) and has been assured of Duncan's intentions to heap further honors upon him: "I have begun to plant thee and will labor to make thee full of growing" (I.iv.28-29). But when a few lines later Duncan proclaims his own son Malcolm heir to the throne, the ambitious Macbeth breaks from the male authority of the king and rushes to his wife to plot the murder that will fulfill the witches' intoxicating prophecy that he shall be king. His submission to female authority eventually brings about his doom.

Many lines throughout the play convey the danger in placing one's fate in the hand of woman.[1] The role of mother is gruesomely connoted in the ingredients of the witches' cauldron, which include a "finger of *birth-strangled babe* ditch-deliver'd by a drab" and *"sow's blood that hath eaten her nine farrow"* (IV.i.30-31,64-65). Woman's unreliability is suggested in the phrase "Fortune . . . showed like a rebel's whore" (I.ii.14,15). Bearing on this theme are the drunken porter's comments on the effects of drink on lechery: "Lechery, sir, it provokes, and unprovokes; it provokes the desire, but it takes away the performance. . . . it . . . makes him stand to, and not stand to: in conclusion, equivocates him in a sleep, and, giving him the lie, leaves him" (II.iii.31-40). These lines, following just after the killing of the king, are a fitting comment on the intoxicating provocations that led Macbeth to carry out the murder. Provoking effects of drink and woman are linked in the image of Lady Macbeth "pouring her spirits" in her husband's ear and summoning the murdering ministers to "come to my woman's breasts, and take my milk for gall" as she contemplates stirring her husband to the crime (I.v.48-49).

But here we come to the most appalling instance of all—the goading lines of Lady Macbeth which are not congruent with the story of the play but which are yet the epitomization of its theme:

> *. . . I have given suck, and know*
> *How tender 't is to love the babe that milks me:*
> *I would, while it was smiling in my face,*
> *Have pluck'd my nipple from his boneless gums,*
> *And dash'd the brains out, had I so sworn as you*
> *Have done to this.*[2]
>
> (I.vii.54-59)

The supreme irony in this speech lies in the tremendous force of its goad to action and the simultaneous threat of mortal danger in trusting one's fate to the mercy of the speaker. Macbeth follows her speech with a question, "If we should fail?" and his wife replies, "Screw your courage to the sticking place and we'll not fail." Her breast, with intoxicating gall in place of milk, is indeed a precarious "sticking place" (I.vii.60).

We have now further delineated the theme: it is not simply that woman is treacherous, but more specifically that she is treacherous in the feeding situation. The various lines cited above converge on the idea that witches-wife-mother can feed intoxicating dreams of glory, only to build up false hope, "make him stand to and not stand to . . . and giving him the lie, leave him." But there is another theme equally important and complementary to this—that of the greedy impatient overly ambitious son. Macbeth acknowledges his "Vaulting ambition, which o'er-leaps itself" (I.vii.27), and his depiction of the murder of the King suggests unquenchable thirst: "The wine of life is drawn, and the mere lees is left" (II.iii.100-101). Another commentator suggests a motive of destructive voracious appetite underlying the ambition of the murderer: "Thriftless ambition, that will ravin up thine own life's means" (II.iv.28-29). Only at the end is Macbeth sated, having "*supp'd full* with horrors" (V.v.13) so that his bosom is "*stuff'd*" with "perilous stuff which weighs upon the heart" (V.iii.44-45).[3] We have here a complementary picture: the provocative, faithless, nursing mother balanced against the overly ambitious, greedy child who ravins up his own life's means.

Macbeth's choosing to submit to female influence implies his identification with mother rather than father, and as a result he has great qualms over his masculinity. He is chagrined that the weird sisters "put a barren sceptre in my gripe, thence to be wrench'd with an unlineal hand" (III.i.62-63)—referring to the descendants of Banquo. The symbolic meaning of the barren sceptre is of course obvious. Throughout the play the inadequacy of Macbeth's masculinity is depicted alongside the adequacy of Banquo, who could be said to serve as a standard.[4] In the beginning we find Macbeth and Banquo as equals fighting side by side, two "cannons overcharg'd with double cracks" (I.ii.37). The distinction appears later when they confront the weird sisters, who prefer Macbeth special treatment.[5] Banquo's address to them is ignored, but Macbeth is greeted as Glamis, Cawdor, and "king hereafter." Macbeth's reaction is to grow rapt and apparently senseless, whereas Banquo is more masterful and independent: "*Speak then to me, who neither beg nor fear/Your favours nor your hate*" (I.iii.60-61). Banquo is then acknowledged "Lesser than Macbeth, and greater. . . . Thou shalt get kings, though thou be none" (I.iii.64, 67). The overtaking of Macbeth by Banquo is reflected in the changing order in which the two are finally saluted: "So all hail, Macbeth and Banquo! Banquo and Macbeth, all hail" (I.iii.68-69).

Macbeth next reveals his latent weakness when he and Banquo receive word from the king that Macbeth has been in truth appointed "Thane of Cawdor." With this partial confirmation of the witches' prophecy Macbeth again becomes rapt whereas the alert Banquo warns of danger in trusting the instruments of darkness which "win us with honest trifles, to betray's in deepest consequence" (I.iii.125-126). In Macbeth's disturbed state we see him in his strength and in his weakness. On the one hand he reflects on the announcement of his promotion as "happy prologues to the *swelling act of the imperial theme"* (I.iii.128-129), and on the other hand his *"single state of man is shaken* (I.iii.140).⁶ The shaking of his single state of man reflects a fundamental split in his orientation. He is tempted to the world of dream, in which he feels his fortunes swelling, but with the result that "function is smother'd in surmise, and nothing is but what is not" (I.iii.140-141). To the concrete presence of his friends he is unresponsive. He is horrified by the thought of murder—"my thought, whose murder yet is but fantastical" (I.iii.139)—required to make real the dream and thus bridge the cleavage in his soul between dream and reality. Banquo is not absorbed by the witches into a nightmare world but is able to deal with his surroundings, whereas Macbeth is for all practical purposes as helpless as an infant "lured with honest trifles." The remainder of the play is dominated by Macbeth's attempt to bridge the gap between his dream and external reality by deeds of blood and violence which transform his entire kingdom into a bloody nightmare,⁷ wherein Scotland "cannot be call'd our mother, but our grave" (IV.iii.165-166).

Macbeth's feeling of inadequacy disturbs him to the end and can be seen to be one of his dominating motives. Near the opening of the third act he broods over Banquo's superiority:

> . . . Our fears in Banquo
> Stick deep, and in his royalty of nature
> Reigns that which would be fear'd: 'tis much he dares,
> And, to that dauntless temper of his mind,
> He hath a wisdom that doth guide his valour
> To act in safety. There is none but he
> Whose being I do fear; and under him
> My genius is rebuk'd, as it is said
> Mark Antony's was by Caesar.⁸ He chid the sisters
> When first they put the name of king upon me,
> And bade them speak to him; then prophet-like
> They hail'd him father to a line of kings.
> Upon my head plac'd a fruitless crown
> And put a barren sceptre in my gripe,
> Thence to be wrench'd with an unlineal hand,
> No son of mine succeeding. If 't be so,
> For Banquo's issue have I fil'd my mind;

> For them the gracious Duncan have I murdered;
> Put rancours in the vessel of my peace
> Only for them; and mine eternal jewel
> Given to the common enemy of man,
> To make them kings, the seed of Banquo kings!
> (III.i.49-70)

In this speech are described the qualities of Banquo which rebuke the genius of Macbeth, that is, threaten his sense of masculinity. Chief of these is Banquo's ability to father a line of kings, whereas Macbeth is fruitless. Macbeth is disturbed to the point of irrationality, and if we can master the full significance of his feelings on this score we will be able to trace all the weird, irrational, and even supernatural occurrences that derive from them in a clear swift line of dramatic movement.

Banquo's superior masculinity is manifested in an uncanny ability to *rise*, to elevate himself above Macbeth, and this ability symbolizes his superior potency and fertility. In the speech just cited Macbeth says of Banquo *"Under him* my genius is rebuked." Macbeth orders the murder of Banquo and Fleance, father and son (III.i.135-138), for he feels he must "Cancel and tear to pieces that great bond which keeps me pale" (III.ii.49-50). Here he is concerned with the linkage between father and son by which Banquo is to be father to a line of kings but from which he is himself cut off. His mind is tortured and warped, "full of scorpions . . . that Banquo and his Fleance lives" (III.ii.36-37). He orders the death of Banquo and Fleance, but Fleance escapes and Macbeth is threatened:

> Then comes my fit again: I had else been perfect;
> Whole as the marble, founded as the rock,
> As broad and general as the casing air:
> But now I am *cabin'd, cribb'd, confin'd.* . . .
> (III.iv.21-24)

In his distressed state Macbeth perceives the ghost of Banquo, which symbolizes, as it were, the triumph of Banquo's fatherhood despite his death as father. The "great bond" has not been cancelled—its ascendency through the survival of Fleance is signalled by the rising of Banquo's ghost, which appears at Macbeth's banquet and takes the place reserved for Macbeth. In frenzy Macbeth protests:

> . . . the time has been
> That, when the brains were out, the man would die,
> And there an end; but now they *rise again,*
> With twenty mortal murders on their crowns,
> And push us from our stools: . . .
>
> (III.iv.78-82)

His sense of masculinity is shattered by Banquo's mysterious rise; and only when the ghost leaves is he *"a man again"* (III.iv.108). He rationalizes his weakness on the basis of immaturity: "My strange and self-abuse is the *initiate* fear that wants hard use: We are but *young in deed"* (III.iv.142-144).

Macbeth again seeks out the weird sisters (IV.1.48-132), and in his opening address to them we can detect the core of his maddening thoughts. He is so crazed by his sense of impotence and sterility that in desperation he would topple down all tall structures and destroy the source of all fertility:

> Though bladed corn by lodg'd and trees blown down;
> Though castles topple on their warders' heads;
> Though palaces and pyramids do slope
> Their heads to their foundations; *though the treasure*
> *Of nature's germens tumble all together,*
> *Even till destruction sicken;* answer me
> To what I ask you.
>
> (IV.i.55-61)

The apparitions then appear—the first telling him to beware Macduff, the second telling him that "none of woman born shall harm Macbeth" (IV.i.80-81). The third apparition is a child *crowned, with a tree in his hand.* We can perceive what is on the mind of Macbeth by his response:

> . . . What is this
> That *rises like the issue of a king,*
> And wears upon his baby brow the round
> And top of sovereignty?
>
> (IV.i.86-89)

The apparition replies:

> . . . take no care
>
> . . . .
>
> Macbeth shall never vanquish'd be until
> Great Birnam wood to high Dunsinane hill
> Shall come against him.
>
> (IV.i.90-94)

Macbeth rejoices:

> Rebellion's head, *rise never* till the wood
> Of Birnam rise, and our high-plac'd Macbeth
> Shall live the lease of nature . . .
>
> (IV.i.97-99)

The prophecy which links the possibility of Macbeth's downfall to the rise of Birnam wood fits into the organic context of the play; for the apparition with a tree in his hand,[10] rising like the issue of a king, and speaking of great Birnam wood coming to Dunsinane, crystallizes in Macbeth's mind the burning question: "Shall Banquo's issue ever reign in this kingdom?" (IV.i.102) Then follows the show of eight kings, some of whom carry "two-fold balls and treble sceptres"[11] and the envious, despairing Macbeth sees Banquo smile "and points at them for his" (IV.i.121, 124).

Macbeth's reaction is to resolve upon an act of utmost violence, as if this will somehow release him from the "cabin'd, cribb'd, confined" state brought on by thought of Banquo's masculine—and therein kingly—superiority. No more will he allow his single state of man to be so shaken that function is smother'd in surmise; no more will he suffer the initiate fear that wants hard use or admit himself but young in deed: "From this moment the very firstlings of my heart shall be the firstlings of my hand" (IV.i.146-148)—and the next lines reveal how by violent action he hopes to break out of his confined and smother'd state and thus prove his regality and masculinity:

> . . . And even now
> *To crown my thoughts with acts,* be it thought and done:
> The castle of Macduff I will surprise;
> Seize upon Fife; *give to the edge o' the sword*
> *His wife, his babes, and all unfortunate souls*
> That trace him in his line. . . .
>
> (IV.i.148-153)

The next scene crowns this horrible thought with the act.

The slaughtering of Macduff's wife constitutes a decisive point in the drama. It is the peak in horror. From this point on there is no more display of Macbeth's ambition—he has "supp'd *full* with horrors" (V.iii.13)—and our attention is focused on the forces of recoil which gather together to bring about his downfall. By his murderous act Macbeth has prepared the very instrument to work vengeance upon himself. Macduff, informed of the slaughtering of his family, cries out:

> *. . . front to front*
> Bring thou this fiend of Scotland and myself;
> Within my sword's length set him; . . .
> (IV.iii.232-234)

and upon this Malcolm proclaims the readiness of the forces of vengeance:

> *. . . our power is ready;*
> Our lack is nothing but our leave. Macbeth
> Is ripe for shaking, . . .
> (IV.iii.236-238)

The denouement seems to follow automatically. The forces of Malcolm and Macduff march toward Macbeth's castle in Dunsinane, fulfill the witches' prophecy by cutting themselves branches in Birnam wood (V.iv.4-7), and Macduff confronts and slays Macbeth. The last dramatic moment presents Macbeth finally overcoming his sense of deficient manhood in the moment before his death.
He warns Macduff:

> I bear a *charmed life,* which must not yield
> To one of woman born,

whereupon Macduff counters:

> *Despair thy charm;*
> And let *the angel whom thou still hast serv'd*
> Tell thee, Macduff was from his mother's womb
> Untimely ripp'd.

Macbeth's reply,

> Accursed be that tongue that tells me so.

For it hath *cow'd my better part of man:*

. . . .

               ... I'll not fight with thee
                   (V.viii.12-22)

demonstrates his essential lack of masculinity up to this point. For his acts have not been those of a mature and independent man but of a charmed and protected child dependent upon his "angel." Macduff reveals the hollowness of this protection, thereby forcing Macbeth to stand on his own. Finally, taunted as coward, Macbeth confronts destiny independent of the witches' prophecies:

> Though Birnam wood be come to Dunsinane,
> And thou oppos'd, being of no woman born,
> Yet will I try the last: before my body
> I throw my war-like shield. Lay on Macduff,
> And damn'd be him that first cries 'Hold, enough!'
>   (V.viii.30-34)

To gain the deepest understanding into the character of Macbeth and into the structure of the play we should scrutinize the high point in Macbeth's actions—the killing of Macduff's wife and little ones (IV.ii). From a rational point of view the act is completely meaningless, since the warning given Macbeth pertains to the threat of danger from Macduff but not from his family. Yet dramatically it is most meaningful: It is *the act* of Macbeth which is to *crown his thoughts.* In its position in the drama it has a meaning which transcends in importance even Macbeth's murder of the King, for the avenger who confronts Macbeth is Macduff—not the son of the murdered King.

Our first clue to the understanding of this act lies in Macbeth's resolution to kill all the unfortunate souls that trace Macduff in his line. This is a displaced outlet for his maddened envy upon seeing the ghost of Banquo smilingly pointing to his (Banquo's) crown'd issue carrying the two-fold balls and treble sceptres, as if boasting the ability to sire a line of kings.[12] Macbeth rages at his own impotence:

>   ... though the treasure
> Of nature's germens tumble all together,
> Even till destruction sicken; answer me
> To what I ask you.
>   (IV.i.58-61)

Since he cannot procreate he will destroy the treasure of nature's germins, and he attempts to realize this symbolically in the killing of a mother together with her children.[13] Yet we cannot but wonder that such an act, an attack upon a defenseless mother and her children, should constitute Macbeth's supreme attempt to achieve full manhood; and in the irony of this fact lies much of the force of the drama, as it displays Macbeth in all his desperate futility.

Why is not a man chosen as outlet for his offended masculine pride? The answer lies partly in the fact that he has already killed the most important man of his time, the King, has become king himself, and still is haunted by feelings of inadequacy. But what is the basis of these feelings? The former king is described as meek (I.vii.17) and would seem to present no threat to Macbeth's self-esteem. In valor and soldiership Macbeth is presented as at least equal to if not greater than Banquo, and it is Macbeth whose heroism is rewarded with promotion to Thane of Cawdor. The very vantages of Macbeth—his strength, his gaining the crown—highlight the hidden weakness which gnaws at him and eventually brings about his fall.

We have seen this weakness dramatized in his inability to become a father. Yet we can pursue the problem further. We can look upon his sterility not as a cause but as an effect, and then we are challenged to search for the heart of Macbeth's weakness: We must explain why Macbeth, a mighty warrior, should be unable to become a father.

The nature of Macbeth's weakness is interwoven in the entire fabric of the play. It permeates the atmosphere, imagery, and structure of the dramatic situations. Before his appearance on the scene Macbeth is described as being overwhelmingly active in his defense of his king: "His brandish'd steel, which smoked with bloody execution" (I.ii. 17-18). He and Banquo have fought as "cannons overcharged with double cracks" as they "doubly redoubled strokes upon the foe" (I.ii.38-39). But when Macbeth first appears upon the stage he is being drawn from the world of bright reality into a murky world having the blurred and vaporous quality of a dream, in which "the earth hath bubbles, as the water has," and what seems corporal melts "as breath into the wind" (I.iii.79, 82). Macbeth expresses his helplessness in the situation as he asks himself: "Why do I *yield* to that suggestion whose horrid image doth unfix my hair?" (I.iii.134-135). The "blasted heath" (I.iii.77), on which the temptation takes place, reflects the rent in Macbeth's inner nature which renders him open to evil and uncanny influences. His first line in the play indicates confusion: "So *foul and fair* a day I have not seen" (I.iii.38). Furthermore, these words indicate that he is already succumbing to the strange influence of the weird sisters even though he has not encountered them till now, for in the opening scene the witches had indicated the prevailing atmosphere: *"Fair is foul, and foul is fair"* (I.i.11).

The effect of the witches is intoxicating, as reflected in Banquo's query: "Have we eaten on the insane root that takes the reason prisoner?" (I.iii.84-85). We have previously noted Macbeth's rapture when he was outwardly greeted with the title of his inner dreams. *This coincidence between external event and inner wish reflects a crack in his sense of reality,* as he is tempted into the dream world in which "function is smother'd in surmise, and nothing is but what is not" (I.iii.141-142).[14] *He is tempted into passivity:* "If chance will have me king, why chance may crown me, without my stir" (I.iii.143-145). A change in role and identity, from that of vigorous defender of the king to rebel, is thrust upon him by external circumstance; for the messengers surprise Macbeth by greeting him with the title of the rebel Cawdor (I,iii), whom he had just defeated ("confronted . . . with self-comparisons, point against point rebellious" [I.ii.55-56]). Here there is not only a coincidence between internal wish and external reality but also another confusion characteristic of dream-life, a *confusion between subject and object,* between himself who has just defeated the rebel and the rebel who has been defeated.[15]

Macbeth is here portrayed as a being not fully individuated. He is the plaything of chance. Neither his words nor his role derive fully from his own identity but seem to *flow* from an external source. When Macbeth approaches the fateful act of murdering the King, we see him trying to be master of himself, trying to "bend up each corporal agent to this terrible feat" (I.vii.80). But as he is about to commit the crime, instead of showing inner determination he is led by a hallucinated dagger—"Thou marshall'st me the way that I was going" (II.i.42). And the timing of the murder is based not on inner decision but on external circumstance: "I go, and it is done: *the bell invites me"* (II.i.62). In these crucial moments *Macbeth's will is not fully his own but is involved with and dependent upon external events which upon scrutiny are seen to emanate from strange female sources.* The ringing of the bell is such an instance: Just prior to the well-known dagger speech

Macbeth instructs his servant: "Go bid my mistress, when my drink is ready, she strike upon the bell" (II.i.31-32). The bell by which his wife *simultaneously announces that his drink is ready and summons him to murder Duncan* anticipates Macbeth's later description of Duncan's death. "The wine of life is drawn" (II.iii.100); for the drink to which his wife summons him is the blood of Duncan. We recall that the helplessness of Macbeth was most apparent when his wife was goading him to murder by boasting how she could while nursing a baby "have plucked my nipple from his boneless gums and dash'd the brains out" (I.vii.57-58). The helplessness of Macbeth was here depicted in its most intense and primitive form: *helplessness in the nursing situation*. It is his wife's playing upon this kind of helplessness that determined him to murder, and it is his wife's ringing of the bell to announce that his drink is ready which summons him to perform the crime. It would logically follow that an act deriving from such helplessness and carried out in compliance with external influences would fail to confer a sense of adequacy upon the performer; and we begin to understand the reason for Macbeth's sense of masculine deficiency even after he becomes king, and why the final murder has to be the murder of a woman.

The atmosphere and texture of the woman-ruled world are plainly indicated: "Light thickens" (III.iii.50). The witches hover through "filthy air" (I.i.12). Lady Macbeth summons "thick night" (I.v.50). Fearsome ingredients are thrown into the witches' cauldron to make it "thick and slab" (IV.i.32). The thickening of these media parallels the thickening of the blood of Lady Macbeth as her milk becomes gall (I.v.44, 49).[16]

It is towards this murky, dark, mysterious world that Macbeth rushes when Duncan proclaims his son Malcolm heir. Macbeth chooses a regressive magical relationship to female figures rather than identification with his king. There is a marked contrast between the brightness of the world ruled by Duncan, in which *"signs of nobleness, like stars, shall shine* on all deservers" (I.iv.41-42), and the brooding darkness of the world of wife and witches. As Macbeth leaves the King to hasten to his wife we see him enter this latter world: "Stars, hide your fires! Let not light see my black and deep desires" (I.iv. 50-51).[17] The next lines express the dreamlike and mysterious nature of the interactions which are to replace the clear and open qualities of the world governed by conscious resolution: "The eye wink at the hand; yet let that be which the eye fears, when it is done, to see." In this speech Macbeth has again revealed the mysterious bond linking his thoughts with the dark utterances of evil women, for in the next scene Lady Macbeth expresses an identical wish: "Come, thick night, and pall thee in the dunnest smoke of hell, that my keen knife see not the wound it makes" (I.v.51-53).

The speech of Lady Macbeth containing these lines is very significant and is worthy of study in some detail. It is occasioned by a coincidence between inner wish and external reality similar to that which had precipitated the rapture of Macbeth: While she is pondering the deeds required for her husband to ascend the throne, she is informed that Duncan, the intended victim, is on his way to her castle, and she exclaims:

> . . . The raven himself is hoarse
> That croaks the fatal entrance of Duncan
> Under my battlements. Come, you spirits
> That tend on mortal thoughts! unsex me here,
> And fill me from the crown to the toe top full
> Of direst cruelty; make thick my blood,
> Stop up the access and passage to remorse,
> That no compunctious visitings of nature
> Shake my fell purpose, nor keep peace between
> The effect and it! Come to my woman's breasts,
> And take my milk for gall, you murdering ministers,
> Wherever in your sightless substances
> You wait on nature's mischief! Come, thick night,
> And pall thee in the dunnest smoke of hell,
> That my keen knife see not the wound it makes,
> Nor heaven peep through the blanket of the dark,
> To cry 'Hold, hold!'
>
> (I.v.39-55)

This speech vividly portrays some of the characteristics of the dark world: Ideas and persons are not individually delineated but are merged together in a fashion which suggests the murky mixture in the witches' cauldron and which also recalls the mysterious tie linking Macbeth to wife and witches. The thoughts of Lady Macbeth are not processes confined to her individual personality but are portrayed as magically participating with obscure "spirits that tend on mortal thoughts" and with murdering ministers who "wait on nature's mischief." A magical atmosphere clouds over the clear world of day in "the dunnest smoke of hell." This atmosphere, though presided over by women, is not a feminine one. For just as the beards of the witches prevent Banquo from considering them as women, so Lady Macbeth is *"unsexed,"* and her milk—a commodity we already know to be most unreliable—is to be taken for gall.

When the nightmare world triumphs over the sense of reality, consequences of actions are obscured, as in: "My keen knife see not the wound it makes." She later expresses a similar blurring of her sense of reality as she feels herself transported "beyond this ignorant present, and I feel now the future in the instant" (I.v.57-59). Elsewhere she assails the sensorium: ". . . memory, the warder of the brain, shall be a fume and the receipt a limbeck only" (I.vii.65-67).

The obscuring of consequences is related to the process of *unsexing* Lady Macbeth, in which *access and passage* to remorse are *stopped up,* an image which suggests the cause of her infertility.[18] In another context we find Macbeth using similar images in association with each other: He expresses apprehension over the stirring up of *"pity, like a naked new-born babe"* should the assassination fail to *"trammel up the consequence"* (I.vii.21; 2-3). Here, too, stated negatively, the blocking up of pity connotes the idea of contraception and thus parallels the unsexing of Lady Macbeth.[19] The ideas of consequential action and of reproduction are joined together in Shakespeare's use of the word *issue* which he applies to both contexts: ". . . certain issue strokes must arbitrate" (V.iv.20), and "Shall Banquo's issue ever reign?" (IV.i.102-103)—so that the stoppage of one connotes the stoppage of the other.[20]

We now gain further understanding of Macbeth's infertility: He is unable to have issue—that is, heirs—in the real world because he and his wife have chosen to dwell in the nightmare which has no real issue—that is, consequence. Once again we find Lady Macbeth and Macbeth mirroring each other. Previously we observed Lady Macbeth's depriving tendencies paralleled by her husband's greed. Now we see Macbeth's sterility paralleled by his wife's unsexed and stopped-up passages. These considerations might seem to lend support to

Freud's interpretation that Lady Macbeth and Macbeth represent a composite personality, since they are so closely united.[21] Our interpretation is, however, different. Lady Macbeth and Macbeth together do not represent a single composite personality, but they seem to do so because they have failed to differentiate from one another. There is a failure in individuation. The image in which they are to be conceived is not that of the composite personality but of a mother and son who have failed to achieve separate identities.[22]

There can be no issue, no flowing forth of consequence or progeny, because the external medium, the atmosphere, and the internal medium, the blood, are too choked up: *"Come thick night,* and pall thee in the dunnest smoke of hell." The atmosphere is permeated by murdering ministers who draw their sustenance from Lady Macbeth ("take my milk for gall") and who in turn render her blood akin to the atmosphere *("make thick my blood")* of which it is thus both source and product. It is a similar choking which caused Macbeth's function to be *"smother'd* in surmise," and which is observed in several contexts: Dark night *"strangles* the traveling lamp" (II.iv.7); seeling night is called upon to "scarf up the tender eye of pitiful day" (III.ii. 47); Macbeth is "cabin'd, cribb'd, confined." Finally, the choking off of issue is most fully realized in the *"birth-strangled babe* ditch-deliver'd by a drab" (IV.i.30-31).

We can understand Macbeth's being so desperate to *break out* of this confined state that he would "let the frame of things disjoint" (III.ii.16). Scattered throughout the play are phrases that suggest breaking and cutting. The idea of time itself cutting its way out points the way for Macbeth to break out of his rapt state: "Come what come may, time and the hour *runs through* the roughest day" (I.iii. 146-147). This idea is echoed just before the climax in the words of another speaker: "The time approaches . . . certain issue strokes must arbitrate" (V.iv.16-20). Macduff's description of the act of violence suggests a desperate search for an opening: "Most sacrilegious murder hath *broke ope* the Lord's anointed temple" (II.iii.72). Duncan's gashed stabs "look'd like a breach in nature" (II.iii.119). Macbeth determines to break out of his strangling situation through violence, to "give to the edge of the sword" the wife and babes of Macduff and thus cut his way out of the female environment which chokes and smothers him.

In yielding to the female influence Macbeth has become embedded in it so that he is unable to emerge a man. He is so entangled in the bloody atmosphere diffusing out from wife and witches that he can almost be said to be mingling with the organs of reproduction, but he is unable to reproduce because the organs are "poison'd"—just as Lady Macbeth is unsexed—and are so glutted with foul ingredients as to strangle the process of birth. In this connection it is significant that the cauldron, "thick and slab" with "poison'd entrails," is a sterile thing from which nothing fruitful can emerge; and therefore it disappears from the stage before the spirits of Banquo and his progeny make their appearance (IV.i.112-124).

Macbeth is desperate to unite sexually with a fertile woman, and in the words with which he announces his decision to murder Macduff's wife and babes he reveals his frustrated wish to propagate: "From this moment the very *firstlings* of my heart shall be the firstlings of my hand" (IV.i.147-148). Rage has transformed his reproductive instinct to destructiveness. He cannot reach the goal of sexual union with a woman so he will destroy her generative organs: "though the *treasure of nature's germens* tumble all together even till destruction sicken" (IV.i.58-60). The wife and children of Macduff are significantly referred to in images relating to egg-laying creatures—". . . egg. Young fry of treachery" (IV.ii.84-85), "pretty chickens and their dam" (IV.iii.218)—thus focusing our attention upon the female egg, which Macbeth is unable to reach and fecundate.

Trammeled up by the witches, Macbeth is as it were but one of many ingredients used to glut their cravings. This brings us to a final linkage between Macbeth and the witches: *Like Macbeth they are hungry.* They utilize and are symbolized by "sow's blood, that hath *eaten her nine farrow*" (IV.i.64-65). Their famished state is figured in their "skinny lips" (I.iii.45). One of them cannot abide the "rump-fed ronyon" who had "chestnuts in her lap, *and munch'd, and munch'd, and munch'd,*" and she is determined to seek vengeance by attacking the woman's husband: "I will drain him dry as hay" (I.iii.6, 5, 19). It would seem to require a cauldron full of entrails to staunch their fearsome appetite. Lady Macbeth also is possessed by thirst: "*Fill me, from the crown to the toe, top full* of direst cruelty" (I.v.44-45).

We are now able to derive the motive for the inciting of Macbeth to murder the king. Previously we noted Lady Macbeth to be a most unenthusiastic feeder who gives gall in place of milk. We can now perceive a hidden meaning when she reflects on her husband: "Yet do I *fear* thy nature; it is *too full the milk* of human kindness" (I.v.18-20). She fears being drained by Macbeth "as dry as hay," by his "thriftless ambition that wilt ravin up thine own life's means" (III.ii.28-29) ; so she and her witch-partners seek to divert this devouring ambition from themselves to another object, the person of the King. Macbeth is to drink not a beverage given by herself but the blood of Duncan when she summons that his drink is ready; with Duncan's blood he is to sate himself till "the wine of life is drawn, and the mere lees is left this vault to brag of" (II.iii.100-101). But intimations of the original object break through, for when Macbeth is killing the King a mysterious voice tells him that he is killing something other than the King, that he is killing sleep—a sleep which assumes the contours of mothering:

> Methought I heard a voice cry 'Sleep no more!
> Macbeth does murder sleep,' the innocent sleep,
> Sleep that *knits up the ravell'd sleave of care,*
> The death of each day's life, *sore labour's bath,*
> *Balm of hurt minds,* great nature's second course,
> *Chief nourisher in life's feast.*
>
> (II.ii.35-40)

In the end, the female attempt to divert Macbeth to a male object fails, as Macbeth turns directly upon woman in the person of Lady Macduff and "sups full with horrors." But on the other hand, the female threat to Macbeth—to "dash the brains out"—is figuratively carried out when he is beheaded by Macduff. Thus the nursing mother and the suckling babe are destroyed, and the mutually destructive fantasies of both are symbolically brought to realization.

The folly of Macbeth's ambition which ravins up his own life's means and drains the wine of life becomes quickly apparent to him as he perceives that in murdering the king he has destroyed his sustenance: "The spring, the head, the fountain of your blood is stopp'd; the very source of it is stopp'd" (II.iii.103-104). But Macbeth has another more dreadful and almost inarticulate fear which is expressed indirectly, and by indirection made more horrible. After the appearance of Banquo's ghost Macbeth is given to brooding reflection: *"It will have blood, they say; blood will have blood"* (III.iv.122). Blood, the devoured substance, will seek to eat the agent which has devoured it, as if the cannibal victim were to return to eat the cannibals. An event strikingly similar to this notion had stimulated the notion that "blood will have blood." Banquo, invited as the chief guest at Macbeth's banquet, had been admonished, *"Fail not our feast . . . it had been as a gap in our great feast"* (III.i.28; 12); which is to say that the absence of Banquo would be as a gap in the victuals. By the murder of Banquo before the feast Macbeth had sought to satisfy his ambitious appetite as he had previously by the killing of Duncan. He is thinking of this murder when he is about to propose a toast to Banquo and says "Give me some wine, *fill full*" (III.iv.88). But Banquo's ghost comes to the feast as a guest rather than as a victual, and takes the place at the table reserved for Macbeth. The return of Banquo's ghost with its *marrowless* bone and *cold blood* causes Macbeth to feel that his own blood is sought by the murdered Banquo: *Blood will have blood.* He fears being eaten, and in this he is but reflecting the fear of Lady Macbeth and the witches, with whom he is so closely involved. He tries to assuage his fear of being devoured by the thought that Banquo's young son has "no teeth for the present" (III.iv.31).

We can now add another motive to explain the driving force of desperate hunger which is felt in the frenzied pace of the entire play. He must eat up his enemies before he is himself eaten up. He is desperate to "trammel up the consequence" before he is himself trammeled. The mutual strivings of Macbeth and wife to devour each other, which is expressed in the murder of Duncan, is reflected on the night of the murder by phenomena in the animal world: Duncan's horses are said to "eat each other" (II.iv.18). Later Macbeth is fearful of the witches with their portentous "sow's blood that hath eaten her nine farrow." But fear of being eaten gives way to an awareness that he is already caught up in the witches' world. He is *cabin'd, cribb'd, confined* in the entrails of devouring woman, and must therefore cut his way out with the sword.

In the course of his crimes Macbeth progressively cuts himself off from his wife. In the beginning he murders Duncan at her instigation. He attempts the murder of Banquo and Banquo's son after giving her a mere hint. The culminating act, the killing of Macduff's wife and children, is decided upon and performed without any prior communication with his wife. By the end of the play he has been so severed from her that the report of her death elicits from him only the comment that "she should have died hereafter; there would have been a time for such a word" (V.v.17-18). After his last encounter with the witches he is through with them also: "Infected be the air whereon they ride, and damn'd all those that trust them! . . . But no more sights!" (IV.i.138-139, 155).

He attempts to act as an individuated man cut off from female influence. It is noteworthy that his attempt to "crown his thought with acts" takes the form of annihilating the family of a man who has fled to another country. Through his violent attack on Macduff's family Macbeth achieves individuation vicariously as it were, for *he creates a separated man who is as individuated—symbolically, through violence —as Macbeth himself is enmeshed in a female but unfeminine world.* And in creating this individuated man he is creating, as we have noted, the instrument that is to work vengeance upon himself. However, Macbeth's action does not actually create but rather culminates the violent individuation of Macduff. For Macduff was violently separated from woman in the process of birth: *he was from his mother's womb untimely ripp'd.* Macduff was thus triply separated in that he was ripp'd from his mother's womb, he left his wife and children behind, and they were murdered by the hirelings of Macbeth.

Paradoxically, Macduff leaves his family in the interest of familial continuity—in this case, the continuity of the most important family, that of the king. He is concerned with restoring Malcolm, the *truest issue* of Scotland, to the throne; and he is very much aware of Malcolm's family relationships even if heedless of his own. He tells Malcolm, "Thy royal father was a most sainted king: the queen that bore thee, oft'ner upon her knees than on her feet, died every day she liv'd" (IV.iii.108-111).[23] He is so devoted to the continuity of the prime male, the king, that he leaves his own family in danger; and Malcolm's question highlights this fact: "Why in that rawness left you wife and child, those precious motives, those strong knots of love?" (IV.iii.26-27).

This violent separation of Macduff emphasizes through exaggeration the necessity for individuation in the service of male continuity. Macduff's flight from wife to son of Duncan reverses the direction of Macbeth's earlier flight from Duncan to wife, and through his flight Macduff succeeds in restoring Malcolm. By the violence of his separation Macduff is peculiarly fit to overcome the witch-entrammeled Macbeth, to confront him with *"self-comparisons,* point against point rebellious, arm 'gainst arm, curbing his lavish spirit" (I.ii.55-57), as Macbeth had previously confronted Cawdor in Fife, Macduff's own territory. The results of Macduff's meeting with Malcolm anticipate his later effect on Macbeth, for in this confrontation Malcolm throws off his pose of greed and luxury and emerges as true issue of his father.

Macduff not only overcomes Macbeth; he emancipates him. For in encountering him *front to front* he dispels the female charm surrounding Macbeth's life which had made him fruitless and prevented him from fully experiencing the consequences of his actions. Before his encounter with Macduff *Macbeth had not effectively confronted an opposing male figure,* and this had left a large gap in his mastery of reality.[24] He had killed the king not in hand to hand encounter but while the latter was asleep, in compliance with his wife's suggestion: "What cannot you and I perform upon the unguarded Duncan?" (I.vii.69-70). And he was encouraged by the witches to "laugh to scorn the powers of man" (IV.i.79-80). The closing action of the play focuses our attention on the importance of confronting male opposition, for the fight between Macbeth and Macduff is the central point of a battle which serves as an ordeal of initiation for "many unrough youths that even now protest their first of manhood" (V.ii. 10-11). One of these youths becomes a man in the act of confrontation, dying with his hurts *"on the front,"* and therefore, though he "only lived but till he was a man . . . like a man he died" (V.viii.40, 43).

To be a man requires confrontation with reality, and a most important component of the confronting reality is the opposing male figure—ideally, of course, the father. It is through encountering the strength of the opposing father that one obtains a mastery of reality; for one can then feel the strength of one's own impulses and measure them against a superior force. In this way one gains insight simultaneously into inner tendencies and limiting factors of external reality.[25] Thus the father's role is of greatest importance in disengaging the son from an engulfed relationship to his mother—a relationship in which son and mother, comprising the inner and outer worlds, are magically blended together, as were Macbeth, wife, and witches. In encountering his father's opposition the son becomes individuated, and learns to distinguish between his own impulses and the forces in his environment.

The encounter with the father sheds *light* on both internal and external reality. To turn from Duncan's authority is to turn from light, and this is what happens when Macbeth abandons the King, who represents the bright world of reality, and turns to his wife, who represents the dark world of dream. The King, *"clear* in his great office" (I.vii.18), had proclaimed that "stars shall shine on all deservers." But at this point Macbeth left the presence of the King to plot with his wife how to fulfill his "black and deep desires." With the killing of the supreme male figure, the light which stood for order and clarity in the land has been extinguished, so that "confusion now hath made his masterpiece" (II.iii.71). Because Macbeth failed to confront the King in his seizure of power, his life loses masculine gravity; reality becomes less meaningful to him:

> Had I but died an hour before this chance
> I had liv'd a blessed time; for, *from this instant,*
> *There's nothing serious in mortality,*
> *All is but toys;* renown and grace is dead, . . .
>
> (II.iii.96-99)

In his diminished state at the end his title is described as a "giant's robe upon a dwarfish thief" (V.ii.21-22). Having killed the King in such unmanly fashion he is unable to experience reality or to look within himself: "I am afraid to think what I have done; look on't again I dare not. . . . To know my deed 'twere best not know myself" (II.ii.51-52, 73). The entire country over which he rules becomes, like himself and his deed, submerged in darkness, for, lacking the guiding light of a mature man at its head, it becomes "almost afraid to know itself" (IV.iii.165).

Macbeth hopes that he can avoid male challenge, but deep within he is aware that he is himself the "secret'st man of blood" who must be brought forth (III.iv.125-126); and he is finally delivered when brought "front to front" with Macduff. With the killing of Macbeth Macduff has destroyed the last vestige of the female dominated world, and Macduff now proclaims Malcolm, heir to the murdered Duncan, King of Scotland. This fulfills the establishment of the estate upon Malcolm as proclaimed by Duncan at the beginning of the play, and restores the continuity which had been breached by the violent actions of Macbeth. Thus, Duncan, who embodies the principle of male as-

cendancy, triumphs over the witches (and Lady Macbeth) who embody the principle of female ascendancy. Chaos is overcome, as the new
king, fully confronting reality, declares that whatever is needful "by
the grace of Grace we will perform in measure, time, and place"
(V.viii.72-73). The fertility of Duncan, who had vainly sought to
plant rebellious Macbeth, is harvested in his son Malcolm. The
tragedy is over, the cycle is completed, and the stage is ready for that
which would be *newly planted with the time.*

Notes

1. SIGMUND FREUD, *Some Character-Types Met with in
Psycho-Analytic Work,* Standard Edition, Vol. XIV (Lon-
don: Hogarth Press, 1957), pp. 318-324; LUDWIG JEKELS,
"The Problem of Duplicated Expression of Psychic Themes,"
International Journal of Psycho-Analysis, 14:300-309, 1933.

1. It should be clear that here and elsewhere in this paper I am
referring to *woman* as conceived in the play *Macbeth.* In following
papers I shall try to show that this image of woman has a special
significance for Shakespeare and may even be a figure of great importance in the creative process.

2. This is the only mention that Lady Macbeth has ever had any
children. That Macbeth in brooding over his lack of heirs never
mentions any previous children causes these lines to stand out all the
more and thus highlights the horror of their import.

3. Although Macbeth is here referring to the stuff'd bosom of Lady
Macbeth, he is also thinking of his own, as is indicated by his next
lines: "Throw physic to the dogs; *I'll* none of it" (V.iii.47). The
two-fold reference of the stuff'd bosom to Macbeth and Lady Macbeth
reflects their mutual devouring of each other, a theme which will be
elaborated towards the end of this paper.

4. As A. C. BRADLEY points out in his *Shakespearean Tragedy*
(New York: World Publishing Company, 1955), the character of
Banquo is pretty much that of "average human nature." Banquo, more
than Macbeth, embodies the "milk of human kindness . . . would'st not
play false, and yet would'st wrongly win" (I.v.18, 22-23). This would
seem to represent the morality of the average man, who would not

commit a crime but would not mind benefiting from it. Banquo, although suspecting false play by Macbeth, looks forward to becoming father to a line of kings, and shows no resistence to Macbeth's assumption of the throne. The average quality of Banquo suits him to serve as a standard against which Macbeth can be measured.

5. Such treatment connotes the special situation of the infant and, along with this, infantile helplessness.

6. One is reminded of the equivocal effect of intoxication upon potency: it makes him stand to and not stand to.

7. Cf. G. WILSON KNIGHT, "Macbeth and the Metaphysic of Evil," *The Wheel of Fire* (New York: Barnes and Noble, 1964).

8. It is interesting to note that Mark Antony, like Macbeth, was to become in later life unduly subject to the influence of a woman, so that one of his lieutenants is moved to say: "So our leader's led, and we are women's men" (*Antony and Cleopatra,* III.vii.70-71).

9. This use of "bond" to indicate the all-important patrilinear linkage occurs twice in *King Lear:* "With how manifold and strong a bond the child was bound to his father" (II.ii.49-50). Again, in a different context: "The bond cracked 'twixt son and father" (I.ii.119).

10. The means by which Birnam wood later moves to Dunsinane is through soldiers' carrying branches in their hands. The rising of Birnam wood thus parallels the rising of the apparition of the crowned child with a tree in his hand, symbolizing the growth potency of Banquo contrasted with the barren scepter of Macbeth. The images which reassure Macbeth are symbols of the forces which will defeat him.

11. These symbols are commonly interpreted as portending the coming of James I of Scotland, supposedly descended of Banquo, to rule over England and Scotland. But besides the idea of political power we are undoubtedly justified in believing sexual power to be symbolized in the "two-fold balls and treble sceptres." This is but one example of Shakespeare's ability to obtain concentration of meaning through overdetermined use of symbols.

12. Macduff's reflection upon hearing of the murder of his family expresses the motive of Macbeth: "He [Macbeth] has no children" (IV.iii.16). This meaning of Macduff's words was pointed out by FREUD in his essay "Some Characters Met with in Psycho-Analysis," *Collected Papers,* Vol. IV (Leipzig: Franz Deuticke, 1926). Freud emphasizes that childlessness is the dominating theme of Macbeth and Lady Macbeth.

13. The imagery of mingling the deaths of a mother and her chil-

dren is gruesomely paralleled in one of the ingredients last added to the witches' cauldron: ". . . sow's blood, that hath eaten her nine farrow" (IV.i.64-65). This image achieves final realization in the deaths of Macbeth and Lady Macbeth.

14. The domination of timeless dreams over present reality is reflected later in the transport of Lady Macbeth "beyond this ignorant prsent, and I feel now the future in the instant."

15. It is assumed by the authorities that "that Bellona's bridegroom" (I.ii.54) who has defeated Cawdor is Macbeth. Yet Macbeth refers to Cawdor as a "prosperous gentleman" (I.iii.73). The contradictory circumstances perhaps serve the purpose of spreading the atmosphere of confusion into the audience and reveal something of the nature of Macbeth's character, as we shall see. There is dramatic irony in Macbeth's taking on the borrowed robes of the rebel he has killed, for in doing so he takes on the fate of the rebel, which is to be beheaded.

16. *Thickness of the fluid greatly impedes the sucking of the babe that milks,* and choking off of the supply is perceived as an external choking around the neck, as figured in the "-strangled babe" (IV.i.30) and reflected in the last charm of all used by the witches: "grease that's sweaten from the murderer's gibbet" (IV.i.65-66)—a concentrated image which summons to mind the hardening fluid, the choking off of the supply of nourishment, and the punishment for the crime so provoked. Infantile rage at interference with feeding is a basic motive of Macbeth, and is projected in several violent images: First and foremost, of course, is the instance of Lady Macbeth speaking of plucking out her nipple and dashing the brains out. The murder of Duncan is described as an obstruction of liquid flow; the fountain is stopped. Banquo's bloody ghost appears to Macbeth to interrupt him in the midst of drinking wine. The extent of Macbeth's rage is revealed in his imprecation: "But let the frame of things disjoint, both the worlds suffer, ere we will eat our meal in fear" (III.ii.16-17). The images of fantastic hunger are also reactions to the obstruction.

17. The contrast between the two worlds is emphasized by the fact that Macbeth's hiding of the stars occurs only nine lines after Duncan bids them shine. It is poetic justice that this wished-for obscurity results in fatal consequences for Macbeth; at the end he exclaims: "Be these juggling fiends no more believ'd, that palter with us in a double sense; that keep the word of promise to our ear, and break it to our hope" (V.viii.19-22). The words of wife and witches have made him stand to and not stand to and giving him the lie have left him.

18. Freud raises the question whether the final succumbing to re-

morse of Lady Macbeth requires enough time to elapse for her to realize that her self-unsexing results in childlessness. However, in a symbolic sense she is not childless at the end, for while she is sleep-walking "pity, like a naked new-born babe" (I.vii.21) breaks through her defenses and thus triumphs over her attempts to denaturalize her feminine instincts.

19. Loss of infant, loss of pity, and choking are elsewhere associated together in *Julius Caesar:* "Mothers shall but smile when they behold their infants quarter'd with the hands of war; all pity chok'd with custom of fell deeds" (III.i.267-269). The three notions are again linked with one another in the description of the murder of the little princes in *Richard III:* " 'We smothered the most resplendent sweet work of nature, that from the prime creation 'er she framed.' Hence both are gone with conscience and remorse" (IV.iii.17-20).

20. Time itself is a fertile process in Banquo's very pregnant phrase, "the seeds of time" (I.iii.58). There could be no greater contrast with this than the sterile view of Lady Macbeth which blinds itself to the ripening effects of time, preferring to dream of the future in the instant.

21. FREUD, "Some Characters Met with in Psycho-Analysis." Freud uses this interpretation to explain the remorse of Lady Macbeth along with the lack of remorse of her husband towards the end of the play.

22. The theme of undifferentiated male and female so closely merged that they are unable to procreate is succinctly expressed in stanzas from SHAKESPEARE's "The Phoenix and the Turtle":

> So they lov'd, as love in twain
> Had the essence but in one;
> Two distincts, division none;
> Number there in love was slain.
>
> .   .   .   .
>
> Leaving no posterity:
> 'T was not their infirmity,
> It was married chastity.
>
>   (25-28,79-81)

23. How the humility of the true queen contrasts with the pride of Macbeth's "dearest partner of greatness" (I.v.12)!

24. It may be objected that, according to the descriptions of Macbeth's fighting at the beginning of the play, Macbeth had been exposed to sufficient confrontation; for his sword "smok'd with bloody execution" (I.ii.18), and he is said to have "confronted [Cawdor] with

self-comparisons" (I.ii.55). Yet after having vanquished Cawdor he refers to him as a "prosperous gentleman" (I.iii.73), as if unaware of his own victory. Either he was during the fighting too "rapt" or "charmed," or his meeting with the witches stunned him out of his awareness of consequences.

25. This process is similar in certain respects to the repetition and working through of infantile impulses in therapy; for the patient acquires insight into his impulses by measuring them aganst the interpretations which he encounters from the therapist. We might refer to this as the ordeal function of the interpretation. This would contrast with another phase of treatment, in which interpretations seem to the patient almost magical in that they seem to be mysteriously in tune with his impulses rather than confronting him as an ordeal.

The War in "Antony and Cleopatra"

The psychoanalytic criticism of *Antony and Cleopatra* resembles the psychoanalytic criticism of *Romeo and Juliet* in one important respect: there is not a great deal of it. Indeed, it may be said that Shakespeare's love tragedies, fine as they are, have yet to receive from psychoanalytic criticism (or from other criticism) the exhaustive kind of attention that has been paid such plays as *Hamlet, Othello,* and *Macbeth.* As for specific remarks on *Antony and Cleopatra,* K. R. Eissler has discussed the love death of the hero and heroine as an erotic metaphor;[1] Herbert Weisinger has treated certain elements in the action from the standpoint of myth and ritual;[2] Samuel Tannenbaum has commented upon two possible slips of the tongue in an effort to demonstrate that Shakespeare understood the subconscious significance of such slips;[3] and that, with the exception of the paper to follow, is about as far as it goes.

Cynthia Kolb Whitney's psychological analysis of *Antony and Cleopatra* achieves a remarkable comprehensiveness as a result of its integration of the external and internal levels of action. The war about which the tragedy revolves is not simply the war between Egypt and Rome; it is also the war between opposing sides of the characters' personalities, especially Antony's. These sides are expressed symbolically by the nations in conflict on the level of external action. The attempt of Antony to reconcile these worlds as they exist both within himself and on the level of events is a futile attempt because "what Rome values directly opposes what Egypt values." Moreover, the essential conflict of the play, the conflict between Egypt and Rome, "develops tragically in the dimension of time." In other words, everything that happens on the narrative level happens at the wrong time. Now as Mrs. Whitney demonstrates, this ill-timing of feelings and events also exists on the level of inner action and reveals what can be regarded as the psychological structure or essence of the tragedy.

M. F.

he war about which *Antony and Cleopatra* revolves exists on several levels and ultimately reveals a basic psychological truth. The conflict between Rome and Egypt is devastating on a huge scale. All the world is split in half and fights itself: "As if the world should cleave, and that slain men/Should solder up the rift" (III.iv.31-32).

The world thus sundered in battle is the external world, but the conflict and self-destruction reach into the inner worlds of men as well. The characters make war on themselves. Caesar contrives that "Antony may seem to spend his fury/Upon himself" (IV.vi.10-11). In Lepidus, drink raises a war between himself and his discretion (II.vii.10-11). In Octavia, duty to her husband and love for her brother make war with each other (III.vi.77-78). Agrippa notes that "nature must compel us to lament/Our most persisted deeds" (V.i.29-30). Human beings in the play seem to be made of discrete elements: honor, reason, sexuality, breeding, fidelity,—and the elements fight one another.

This war between opposing elements of character rages particularly in Antony. His experience, manhood, and honor violate themselves (III.x.23-24), and, as Enobarbus says,

> A diminution in our captain's brain
> Restores his heart: when valour preys on reason,
> It eats the sword it fights with.
>
> (III.xiii.198-200)

"The War in *Antony and Cleopatra*" by Cynthia Kolb Whitney. Reprinted with permission from *Literature and Psychology*, XIII (1963), 63-66.

Antony's Roman honor is at war with his Egyptian sexuality. Certainly the presence of Cleopatra at the war must ". . . take from his heart, take from his brain, from's time" (III.vii.12), but it adds to his sexuality. Conversely, the marriage with Octavia augments his reputation, his position, and his honor, but steals from his sexuality. Antony's internal war is as devastating as the external combat between Egypt and Rome. Antony cries out, "The shirt of Nessus is upon me" and desires the power to "subdue my worthiest self" (IV.xii,43, 47). He must break his "strong Egyptian fetters" or lose himself in dotage (I.ii.120-121); alternatively, his "self" becomes submerged in Roman honor (III.iv.22-23). Destructively, then, the elements in Antony are always in conflict; sometimes he is a Roman and sometimes an Egyptian, but never both, for two such contrary selves cannot be resolved into one.

Such a resolution is impossible because what Rome values directly opposes what Egypt values. Behavior which is almost divine to one is repugnant and silly to the other. The Roman leaders are "chief factors for the gods" (II.vi.10); Caesar is a "Jupiter of men" (III.ii.9), a god (III.xiii.60). In his Roman hours, Antony, too, is a god. He is a "Herculean Roman" (I.iii.84); he must "speak as loud as Mars" (II.ii.6). But, in his Egyptian hours, Cleopatra has the power to command him from the bidding of the gods (III.xi.60), and in doing so she makes of him—in the eyes of the Romans—a eunuch. To Caesar, speaking as a Roman, Antony

> . . . is not more manlike
> Than Cleopatra; nor the Queen of Ptolemy
> More womanly than he.
>
> (I.iv.5-7)

As a leader he is led; his men "are women's men" (III.vii.71). He is condemned, in his own words, ". . . to lack/The courage of a woman" (IV.xiv.59-60); like the eunuchs Cleopatra has about her, all of whom bear the names of once-great men, Antony is reduced from his former virility. In the opening speech of the play Philo says that Antony ". . . is become the bellows and the fan/To cool a gipsy's lust" (I.i.9-10), and at that very moment Cleopatra is carried on stage "with Eunuchs fanning her."

Nevertheless, Antony's Egyptian hours have a strong appeal of their own; they witness a kind of manhood foreign to the Roman concept of manhood, a godlike majesty foreign to the Roman concept of what is godlike, yet altogether befitting ". . . a race of heaven" (I.iii.37). The Romans conceive of a "man" as a warrior, without any reference to women; the Egyptian concept of "man" is as a sexual being, necessarily with women. The two concepts can never be reconciled. The idle wish ". . . that the men might go to wars with the women" (II.ii.65-66) can never be fulfilled.

The very earth of Egypt functions like a woman, in a most graphic way: it is periodically inundated and made fertile by the flow of the Nile, and

> . . . as it ebbs, the seedsman
> Upon the slime and ooze scatters his grain,
> And shortly comes to harvest.
> (II.vii.24-26)

Cleopatra is a mother goddess, an Isis. Roman women in the play do not have children; they have full-grown men to whom they cannot really be mothers. But Cleopatra has many children, both natural and symbolic. Even Death is ". . . my baby at my breast" (V.ii.312). Antony is her child, whom she dresses in her own "tires and mantles" (II.v.22) and also in his own armor (IV.iv.8). His heart is tied to her rudder by strings (III.xi.57) as an infant is tied to its mother by the umbilical cord. Always he returns to her to be nourished, for while ". . . other women cloy/The appetites they feed, . . . she makes hungry/Where most she satisfies" (II.ii.241-243).

Rome, by contrast, is a harsh fatherland. Every Roman in the play is known by an honorable father or some other male identity. The "Pompey" of the play is Sextus Pompeius, son of Cneius Pompeius Magnus, and "rich in his father's honour" (I.iii.50). (Octavius) Caesar is really (Julius) Caesar Junior, and much annoyed that Cleopatra's bastard, Caesarion, should also be called his "father's son" (III.vi.6). Octavia exists as Caesar's sister or Antony's wife (III.vi. 42-44), not as Octavia. In spite of his youth Caesar is the image of the unbeatable father, whose dice always obey him, whose cocks always win, whose quails always survive (II.iii.33-38). He is to be obeyed; he scorns to meet Antony in single combat, for he is "twenty men to one" (IV.ii.4). It is his will that Antony shall not have the mother-goddess, Cleopatra.

Furthermore, this, the essential conflict of the play, develops tragically in the dimension of time. In the play, as the character of a man is conquered for a time by one element or another, the man actually becomes one thing or another completely alien to what he was a moment before. Men are often not themselves: messengers are colored by the message of the moment; priests are temporarily enchanted by the wrangling queen; Antony, pleading with his soldiers to remain loyal to him, is urged not to transform them into women (IV.ii.36). Antony, especially, is always in some sense not himself, no matter what he is. He will always, says Cleopatra, "be himself" (I.i.43); yet she exults when he calls for one more "gaudy night" of revels, crying ". . . my lord is Antony again" (III.xiii.187-188). But these hours of revel are the very times "when he is not Antony" (I.i.57). The self of Antony is split in time.

Time is one of the most important themes in the play. Cleopatra is "wrinkled deep in time" (I.v.29); while the gods do not deny assistance to the "deeds of justest men," "they do delay" (II.i.2-3); time, says Lepidus, "calls upon's: Of us must Pompey presently be sought . . ." (II.ii.160-161); during all the time when Antony is absent from her, Octavia will pray to the gods (II.iii.2-3); Caesar's military advance is incredibly speedy (III.vii.21-24); Antony pleads with his followers to give him but a little more time (IV.ii.25-32); and "time is at his period" (IV.xiv.107) when death comes. There is a time of love and revel: the "soft hours" of the Egyptian Queen (I.i.44); the orgiastic feasts, when everyone ought to be "a child o' th' time" (II.vii.106). There is a time of Roman affairs, a time when Antony's hours "Were nice and lucky [and] men did ransom lives/Of me for jests" (III.xiii.180-181); a time when the hours of love seem poisoned hours (III.xiii.116-121). Life according to Egypt and life according to Rome are separated in time, and no character can exist simultaneously in both.

The essence of tragedy in this play is the ill timing of events and feelings. Everything happens at the wrong time. Antony is busy making love just when Rome needs him most (I.iv.17-33). Cleopatra decides to withdraw her warships at just the wrong time (III.x.11-24). Antony, believing Cleopatra to be dead, decides to kill himself at an ill-chosen hour (IV.xiv.55-69). Love is negligent; Antony neglects both his wives until too late, and likewise neglects his mistress (I.iii. 33-34). Fulvia is beloved only when she is gone (I.ii.126-131). Everything happens too late. In politics as well as in personal affairs, ". . . love is never link'd to the deserver/Till his deserts are past" (I.ii.193-194) ; ". . . the ebbed man, ne'er loved till ne'er worth love, /Comes dear'd by being lack'd" (I.iv.43-44). The play is made up of conflicts in time. Antony says, "My very hairs do mutiny; for the white/Reprove the brown for rashness, and they them/For fear and doting" (III.xi.13-15). The gray is something old, linked to the past, and the brown is something young, linked to the present. Gray and brown, like Rome and Egypt, attempt to mingle (IV.viii.19-20) but without success. The nature of youth and the nature of age are split irrevocably in the play. Ultimately, the basic conflict in *Antony and Cleopatra* is a war between the gray and the brown.

The essential conflict in time explains the wars within the characters and between the motherland and the fatherland. The essential conflict reveals the psychological structure of the play. In his happiest time man shares with the mother one identity, and their separate beings are mingled. He is completely the child. In the joyous hours of the play, Cleopatra puts her "tires and mantles" on Antony and dons "his sword Philippan" (II.v.22-23). The "great gap of time" that Antony is gone from Cleopatra (I.v.5) is as painful and unnatural as a gap in the air, which nature cannot sustain (II.ii.219). It is natural for a man to desire eternal uninterrupted union with the mother goddess. But man is forcibly separated from his identity with the nurturing mother by his own life span. His being is forever at the wrong time, and hence tragic. This is the tragedy not only of Antony in *Antony and Cleopatra,* but of everyman.

Notes

1. K. R. Eissler, "On *Hamlet,*" *Samiska,* 7:183, 1953.
2. Herbert Weisinger, "The Myth and Ritual Approach to Shakespearean Tragedy," *Centennial Review of Arts and Science,* 1:142-166, 1957.
3. Samuel Tannenbaum, "Slips of the Tongue," *Shakespeare Studies* (New York: The Author, 1930).

An Interpretation of Shakespeare's "Coriolanus"

The extensive psychoanalytic criticism of *Coriolanus* can be best introduced by underscoring three central points. First, since the tragedy contains numerous references to the hero's infancy and upbringing, and since it also contains a rather obtrusive mother who seems to stand behind nearly everything the hero does, psychoanalytic commentators, with obvious justification, have devoted considerable energy to exploring the play from the oedipal angle. Second, since the hero of *Coriolanus* is, to put it mildly, an arresting sort of character and the kind that one does not meet everyday, a number of analytic critics, again with obvious justification, have attempted to explain precisely what kind of a character Coriolanus is. Third, since almost all of this material is written from a realistic, even clinical perspective, the psychoanalytic criticism of *Coriolanus* as a whole can be considered the methodological opposite of the psychoanalytic criticism of *Macbeth* where dramatic action is regarded almost exclusively as fantasy and psychological truth discovered only beneath a dreamlike surface. Of course some overlapping exists: Studies from the oedipal angle suggest character types; character studies touch upon the hero's relationship with his mother; and the bulk of the criticism comments, implicitly if not explicitly, on the psychological meaning of the total drama. Nevertheless, the broad outlines remain remarkably clear.

The earliest treatments of *Coriolanus,* those developed by Rank and Towne,[1] focus on the oedipal aspect of the play. Charles K. Hofling, by contrast, grounds his approach in the character studies of Wilhelm Reich, maintaining that Coriolanus corresponds to what Reich designated as the "phallic-narcissistic" type. Coriolanus is "self-confident," "arrogant," "vigorous," "athletic," "haughty," and "derisively aggressive." His narcissism expresses itself in "the exaggerated display of self-confidence, dignity, and superiority"; yet, in spite of this narcissism, Coriolanus is capable of showing "strong attachments to people and things outside," another aspect of the phallic-narcissistic character. Again, Hofling traces the development of Coriolanus' personality to Volumnia, the "unfeminine, nonmaternal" mother. Thus the tremendous aggression that Coriolanus unleashes upon the world is ultimately rooted in his childhood frustrations. However, it becomes clear as the drama proceeds that Coriolanus' wife, the "healthy" and "feminine" Virgilia, is having a positive effect upon the hero's emotional-makeup and is to some degree offsetting the damage wrought in early childhood. In Hofling's opinion, it is the "corrective emotional experience" of marriage that explains Coriolanus' relenting in the final act. As for the tragic irony of the play, it stems from the fact that Coriolanus is destroyed just after he has become, for the first time, an emotionally mature human being. And it is doubly ironic that the word "boy," which no longer applies to him, should provoke in the hero the aggressive rage that brings about his downfall.

M. F.

To a degree probably unparalleled in Shakespeare, the interest in the play centers in the character of its hero. Coriolanus is portrayed as a man of outstanding physical courage and valor, a man of great aristocratic pride and arrogance, and a man of great honesty. He is primarily a man of action, although he can be eloquent at times. . . .

Coriolanus' patrician pride and arrogance, and specifically, his attitude toward the plebeians are brought out when he is first introduced, in Act I, Scene I. The commoners have been speaking with Menenius, who has been trying to dissuade them from outright rebellion, when Marcius enters.

> *Men.*   . . . Hail noble Marcius!
> *Mar.* Thanks. What's the matter, you dissentious rogues,
>   That, rubbing the poor itch of your opinion,
>   Make yourselves scabs?
> *First Cit.*   We have ever your good word.
> *Mar.* He that will give good words to thee will flatter
>   Beneath abhorring. What would you have, you curs,
>   That like not peace nor war? the one affrights you,
>   The other makes you proud. He that trusts to you,
>   Where he should find you lions, finds you hares;
>   Where foxes, geese: . . .
>   . . . What's their seeking?
> *Men.* For corn at their own rates; whereof, they say,
>   The city is well stor'd.

"An Interpretation of Shakespeare's *Coriolanus*" by Charles K. Hofling. Reprinted with permission from *American Imago*, XIV (1957), 407-437.

Mar.   Hang 'em! They say!
    They'll sit by the fire and presume to know
    What's done i' the Capitol: . . .
        . . .
    Would the nobility lay aside their ruth,
    And let me use my sword, I'd make a quarry
    With thousands of these quarter'd slaves, as high
    As I could pick my lance.
                    (I.i.167-176,192-196,201-204)

Yet the pride of Coriolanus has a very specific quality, relating to the satisfying of inner standards and having little to do with praise or signs of recognition from others, even from those whom Coriolanus clearly respects. In Act I, Scene IX, Cominius and Lartius, fellow patricians and comrades-in-arms, have been praising Coriolanus for his heroism against the Volscians, when he interrupts.

The characteristic of honesty is so consistently shown by Coriolanus that it scarcely requires specific quotations by way of illustration, but one very brief and pointed instance may be offered as typical. In Act I, Scene VIII, Coriolanus meets Aufidius, then his deadly enemy, in combat.

    I'll fight with none but thee; for I do hate thee
    Worse than a promise-breaker.
                    (I.viii.1-2)

The hero uniformly says what he thinks, regardless of whom he is addressing and regardless of the consequences to himself.

Speaking from the standpoint of psychiatric diagnosis, one would say that the category into which Coriolanus most nearly fits is that of phallic-narcissistic character, as originally delineated by Reich. In fact, three-fourths of Reich's description applies so closely as to seem that it could have been written about Coriolanus. A few sentences from the first portion of this description will illustrate the point.

> . . . the typical phallic-narcissistic character is self-confident, often arrogant, elastic, vigorous and often impressive . . . they most frequently belong to Kretchmer's athletic type. . . . Everyday behavior is . . . usually haughty, . . . derisively aggressive. . . . The outspoken types tend to achieve leading

positions in life and resent subordination. . . . In contrast to other characters, their narcissism expresses itself not in an infantile manner but in the exaggerated display of self-confidence, dignity and superiority . . . In spite of their narcissistic preoccupation with their selves they often show strong attachments to people and things outside. In this respect, they resemble most closely the genital character; they differ from it, however, in that their actions are much more intensively and extensively determined by irrational motives. It is not by accident that this type is most frequently found among athletes, aviators, soldiers and engineers. One of their most important traits is aggressive courage.[1]

The possibility for strong attachments to others is of great interest in the character of Coriolanus and of crucial importance to the drama. Leaving aside for the moment the matter of his relationship to his mother, one may say that Coriolanus has sincere and affectionate object-relationships with a number of persons: with his comrades-in-arms, Cominius and Lartius, with old Menenius, with his son, young Marcius, and, above all, with his wife, Virgilia. Perhaps the best evidence as to the nature of Coriolanus' feeling toward his wife which is afforded us prior to Act V is his first sentence of greeting to her on this return to Rome after the Victory at Corioli.

> My gracious silence, hail!
> (II.i.192)

The imaginative tenderness of this line is most revealing, not only of a strong affection, but of a considerable ability to see and react to Virgilia as she is. The line is devoid of pride and selfishness.

Having briefly considered the personality of Coriolanus as it is presented in the early portions of the drama, one is faced with several questions. How did it become what it is at the outset? To what extent is the action of the play explicable in terms of personality? Are there any changes in the personality as a result of the events of the play?

In similar situations of literary criticism one can often develop satisfactory answers to the two latter questions, but *Coriolanus* is unusual for a Shakespearean play in the extent to which the author has provided material relevant to answering the first question as well. This material consists largely in the portrayal of Volumnia, the mother of Coriolanus, and in unmistakable hints as to the history of this mother-son relationship.

It is interesting to note the Volumnia is not infrequently referred to in Shakespearean criticism in terms of considerable admiration.[2] She is supposed to typify the noble Roman matron of the days when the republic was young. A careful reading of the play falls short of substantiating this concept. It does reveal that Shakespeare regarded Volumnia as having exerted a definitely traumatic influence upon Coriolanus.

Volumnia is first introduced in Act I, Scene III. Her long initial speech affords a basis for considerable insight into her personality.

> I pray you, daughter, sing; nor express yourself in a more comfortable sort. If my son were my husband, I should freelier rejoice in that absence wherein he won honour than in all the embracements of his bed where he would show most love. When yet he was but tender-bodied and the only son of my womb, when youth with comeliness plucked all gaze his way, when for a day of kings' entreaties a mother should not sell him an hour from her beholding, I, considering how honour would become such a person, that it was no better than picture-like to hang by the wall, if renown made it not stir, was pleased to let him seek danger where he was like to find fame. To a cruel war I sent him; from whence he returned, his brows bound in oak. I tell thee, daughter, I sprang not more in joy at first hearing he was a man-child than now in first seeing he had proved himself a man.
>
> (I.iii.1-19)

Goddard says discerningly of Volumnia: ". . . she had been little other than an Amazon, a woman—to call her that—who so rejoiced in battle and military glory that for her vicarious satisfaction she pushed her son into blood-shed almost before he had ceased to be a child. She fairly feasted on wounds and scars. A wolf is said to have suckled Romulus and Remus. Coriolanus did not need any such nourishment. He had its human equivalent." Volumnia thus is seen to be an extremely unfeminine, nonmaternal person, one who sought to mold her son to fit a preconceived image gratifying her own masculine (actually pseudo-masculine) strivings. Her method, we learn from the above and from other speeches, was to withhold praise and the scant affection she had to give from any achievements except aggressive and exhibitionistic ones.

Volumnia gives much lip-service to "honor," but this attitude proves to be in part hypocritical. During the political crisis of Acts II and III, she urges her son to adopt craft and dissembling until he has won power. In other words, this woman is much more concerned about appearances than about honor or truth as things in themselves.

The influence of Volumnia's personality on that of her son is indicated to have been the more intense by reason of the facts that Coriolanus lost his father in infancy and, so far as we are told in the play, had no brothers or sisters. Thus, on the one hand, the boy's emotional needs had no source of satisfaction save this militant mother, and, on the other, there was no guiding influence to counterbalance hers.

The latter portion of the scene from which Volumnia's long speech has been quoted is of crucial importance in estimating the effects of the mother-son relationship. In the middle of the scene the Lady Valeria is introduced. Along with Virgilia, she serves the purpose of throwing Volumnia into contrast and showing that the latter is not merely the typical Roman matron of the period. She does more than this, however. She inquires about Coriolanus' son, little Marcius, and thus gives the audience a glimpse into the hero's own childhood.

Val. . . . How does your little son?

Vir. I thank your ladyship; well, good madam.

Vol. He had rather see the sword and hear a drum, than look upon his schoolmaster.

Val. O' my word, the father's son; I'll swear 'tis a very pretty boy. O' my troth, I looked upon him o' Wednesday half an hour together; has such a confirmed countenance. I saw him run after a gilded butterfly; and when he caught it, he let it go again; and after it again; and over and over he comes, and up again; catched it again; or whether his fall enraged him, or how 't was, he did so set his teeth and tear it. O! I warrant how he mammocked it!

Vol. One on 's father's moods. . . .

Vir. A crack, madam.

(I.iii.56-74)

Coming immediately after the passage in which Volumnia has spoken of Coriolanus' grace and comeliness as a child and of the standards she imposed upon him, this little vignette can only mean that Volumnia is attempting to repeat the process with her grandson, and that, in effect, the little boy can be taken to represent Coriolanus, himself, at a similar age. The butterfly incident shows childish curiosity, affection, and desire for mastery turning into sadism.

With consummate art Shakespeare reintroduces the butterfly theme in Act IV, Scene VI. Cominius and Menenius are describing to the tribunes the advance on Rome of Coriolanus and his Volscian Army.

> *Com.* He is their god: he leads them like a thing
> Made by some other deity than Nature,
> That shapes men better; and they follow him,
> Against us brats, with no less confidence
> Than boys pursuing summer butterflies,
> Or butchers killing flies.
>
> (IV.vi.90-95)

Thus it would seem evident that the childhood frustrations of Coriolanus stand—and are seen by Shakespeare to stand—in a cause-effect relationship to the unleashing of furious aggression in adult life.

These hints as to the early history of the hero are again in marked agreement with sequences frequently noted in the past history of the phallic-narcissist. Reich remarks: "The infantile history regularly reveals serious disappointments in the object of the other sex, disappointments which occurred precisely at the time when attempts were made to win the object through phallic exhibition. In men, one often finds that the mother was the stronger of the parents, or the father had died early or was otherwise out of the picture."[3]

Before proceeding to a consideration of the interaction between the personality of Coriolanus and the events of the drama, it seems advisable to direct special attention to the character of Virgilia, since her role, although extremely brief in number of lines, is of great significance to the action of the play.

The personality contrast between Virgilia and Volumnia is revealed quite early in the drama. When Volumnia has given the long speech quoted above about sending her son into battle at the age of sixteen, Virgilia breaks in with, "But had he died in the business, madam;

how then?" (I.iii.20). And, indeed, one gathers from Volumnia's opening line ("I pray you, daughter, sing; or express yourself in a more comfortable sort"), that Virgilia's affectionate concern for her husband's well-being prevents her from taking the unfeminine delight in his military exploits which her mother-in-law shows to excess.

In addition to its presentation of the butterfly anecdote the scene appears expressly designed to show the contrast between Virgilia and Volumnia. The women's reaction to this very story of Valeria's is illuminating. Volumnia takes unadulterated pleasure in thinking that little Marcius is developing his father's fierceness, saying, "One on's father's moods." Virgilia's pleasure at Valeria's remarks appears to be mingled with misgivings, for her comment is "A crack, madam." When Valeria invites her to go out seeking amusement, Virgilia declines, plainly out of anxiety about her husband's dangerous situation. Volumnia is all for putting on a brave front, and she insists that her daughter-in-law go, but Virgilia shows herself capable of standing up to the older woman and courteously persists in her refusal.

The contrast is again pointed out in Act II, Scene I. Just before Coriolanus's return from his victory over the Volscians, Volumnia and Virgilia are conversing with Menenius.

> *Vol.* Look, here's a letter from him: the state hath another, his wife, another; and I think there's one at home for you.
> *Men.* I will make my very house reel tonight. A letter for me!
> *Vir.* Yes, certain, there's a letter for you; I saw't.
> *Men.* A letter for me! . . . Is he not wounded? He was wont to come home wounded.
> *Vir.* O! no, no, no.
> *Vol.* O! he is wounded; I thank the gods for't.

$$(\text{II.i.118-133})$$

In addition to the obvious contrast between the reaction of Virgilia and that of Volumnia to the idea of Coriolanus' having been wounded, this scene indicates that Virgilia elicits a different response from Coriolanus than does his mother, that is, the hero has not referred to his wounds in the letter to his wife.

A few moments later, when Coriolanus has appeared, Volumnia becomes almost boisterous in her enjoyment of her son's honors and then quickly alludes to the one remaining one which she expects him to receive, the consulship. Virgilia, it may be inferred, shows quietly a much greater depth of feeling, but one altogether focused on her husband and not on his honors. Coriolanus responds to her with the speech of which the first line has previously been quoted.

> My gracious silence, hail!
> Would'st thou have laughed had I come coffin'd home,
> That weep'st to see me triumph? Ah! my dear,
> Such eyes the widows in Corioli wear,
> And mothers that lack sons.
>
> (II.i.192-196)

A final point to be made in this connection is that whereas Volumnia figures prominently in urging Coriolanus to seek the consulship and to speak hypocritically to the tribunes and plebeians in so doing, Virgilia takes no part in these maneuvers. In other words, in addition to having a greater capacity for tender affection than has Volumnia, Virgilia also exceeds her mother-in-law in certain qualities of dignity and integrity.

Thus, in summary, Virgilia appears much more feminine than does the mother of Coriolanus, less selfish in her relationship to her husband, more loving toward him, and less concerned with honors and appearances.

In a consideration of the relationship in which the action of the play stands to the personality of Coriolanus, it is convenient to divide the play into three sections: Acts I and II, Act III, and Acts IV and V. To keep within the limitations of a single paper, it will be necessary to concentrate on features of particular significance.

One such feature, which is fully developed in the early portions of the play, is the attitude of Coriolanus toward the plebeians, partly expressed in the lines previously quoted as an example of his arrogance. There is marked tension and dislike mutual between Coriolanus and his patrician friends and the plebeians and their tribunes, so much so that the play has sometimes been considered to be essentially a political one, with Coriolanus portraying a "typical tory who prefers the privileges of his class to the good of his country." Goddard points out that this view is superficially plausible, but will not stand up under close scrutiny. On the one hand, the interest in the drama is attached much more to character than to class. On the other, Coriolanus disqualifies himself as a typical tory with the following speech.

> . . . Custom calls me to't:
> What custom wills, in all things should we do't,
> The dust on antique time would lie unswept
> And mountainous error be too highly heapt
> For truth to o'er-peer. . . .
>
> (II.iii.124-128)

What, then, is the nature of Coriolanus's antipathy to the Roman plebeians, and, specifically, to the plebeians as a mob? One of his most specific statements on this point is that he sees the mob as "foes to nobleness." Since he is dedicated to a kind of nobility, this statement sounds as if the mob represents to him the personification of unacceptable impulses in his own personality. This idea is difficult to prove, but it receives some confirmation in another speech of Coriolanus.

> For the mutable, rank-scented many, let them
> Regard me as I do not flatter, and
> Therein behold themselves: . . .
>
> (III.i.66-68)

A paraphrase of the latter part of this sentence, taken just at face value, would probably be: ". . . let them give heed to me, and, since I shall tell them the truth (about themselves) without flattery, they can see what they are really like." Yet when a *double entendre* such as this exists in a speech of one of Shakespeare's characters, it is often felt by critics that the character was conceived by the author as intending both meanings. It is my impression that such is the case here. Very likely Coriolanus is not to be thought of as aware of the second, the latent meaning of the speech, but he is nevertheless betraying his identification of the mob with repressed tendencies in himself.

If this idea appears plausible, it might be of value to consider some of the accusations Coriolanus levels at the plebeians and to see if they would fit in logically as ego-alien (unconscious) tendencies in his own personality. The principal charges are that the plebeians are cowardly, covetous, parasitic, and pleasure-loving: in other words, the diametric opposites of the surface features of Coriolanus' personality. This striking contrast does not in itself prove anything, but it is compatible with what has elsewhere been demonstrated to be true of phallic-narcissists in general, namely, that their overt behavior has an important defensive value against the opposite characteristics. Here again it is of interest to note a portion of Reich's original formulation. "The phallic character does not regress. He remains at the phallic stage; more than that, he exaggerates his manifestations in order to protect himself against a regression to passivity and anality."[4]

The last-named characteristics are clearly expressed in lay terms by Coriolanus' indictment of the plebeians.

Another aspect of Coriolanus's estimate of the mob is that he considers it to be untrustworthy and childish. It is worthwhile to note that the two terms to which Coriolanus reacts with the greatest violence when applied to himself are "traitor" (III.i.162-253) and "boy" (V.v.101-117). The passages in question will be considered later, but it should be mentioned at this point that one receives a strong impression that Coriolanus is reacting on the basis of a major inner conflict at these times, inasmuch as the appellations are logically meaningless as regards his overt behavior.

A second point, closely related to the one concerning his attitude toward the mob and of crucial importance to the action of the drama, is the extreme aversion felt by Coriolanus to the prescribed behavior of begging for votes to obtain the consulship. Of this procedure the single feature most repulsive to the hero is the traditional showing to the crowd the wounds received in his country's service. Coriolanus's response to Volumnia when she first expresses the hope that he will receive the consulship reveals the close linkage between the two points.

> Know, good mother,
> I had rather be their servant in my way
> Than sway with them in theirs.
> (II.i.218-220)

During the scenes in which Coriolanus is urged to seek the office of consul and then does stand in the forum soliciting votes, it becomes rather clear that the aspect of the situation which he finds most intolerable is his being placed in the passive position. The defense-system by which his self-esteem is maintained cannot function under these conditions, whereas in the battle situation, in which the wounds were actually received, it functioned effectively.

The structural turning-point of the play occurs classically in Act III, Scene III. The preparation for the crisis has taken place during the final scene of the previous act and the first two scenes of Act III.

Although the citizens had responded to Coriolanus' solicitation by giving him their votes initially, they quickly withdrew them under the skillful suasion of the envious and fearful tribunes. An altercation ensued between the plebeians and tribunes on the one hand and Coriolanus and some patrician friends on the other, as a result of which Coriolanus was to stand trial as an enemy of the people. One is given to understand that the outcome is still very much in doubt, that reconciliation and even the consulship are still within reach for Coriolanus if he were to behave in a humble fashion at the trial. In response to his mother's plea, Coriolanus has reluctantly given his word to dissemble his pride, and at first does so.

> *Sic.*   I do demand,
> If you submit you to the people's voices,
> Allow their officers, and are content
> To suffer lawful censure for such faults
> As shall be proved upon you?
> *Cor.*   I am content.
>   (III.iii.43-47)

Menenius then speaks movingly in Coriolanus's behalf, but immediately thereafter the situation explodes.

> *Sic.* We charge you, that you have contriv'd to take
> From Rome all season'd office, and to wind
> Yourself into a power tyrannical;
> For which you are a traitor to the people.
> *Cor.* How! traitor!
> *Men.*   Nay, temperately; your promise.
> *Cor.* The fires i' the lowest hell fold-in the people!
> Call me their traitor! Thou injurious tribune!
> Within thine eyes sat twenty thousand deaths,
> In thy hands clutched as many millions, in
> Thy lying tongue both numbers, I would say
> "Thou liest" unto thee with a voice as free
> As I pray the gods.
> *Sic.*   Mark you this, people?
> *Plebeians.* To the rock! To th' rock with him!
>   (III.iii.64-75)

As mentioned above, the charges, taken literally, are rather wide of the mark. Coriolanus is not at all a contriver, and is not particularly interested in political power, *per se*. His violent reaction to the indictment is therefore the more remarkable and can only be understood as coming from powerful forces of the unconscious. The two key stimulus words for his outbreak are "Rome" and "traitor." To comprehend the hero's reaction, it appears of value to hypothesize an unconscious identification on his part of Rome with his mother, with the appellation, "traitor," then referring to an offense with regard to the mother, not Rome or its citizens. Such an identification is a fairly common one, and, in this instance, would be rendered especially likely by the patriotic posing of Volumnia, plus her emphasis on the martial virtues which were so highly regarded by the city-state.

If there does exist such an unconscious equation, the action of the drama is rendered more comprehensible. Coriolanus's entire life until Act II has involved an effort to prove that he wanted nothing from mother-Rome except to serve and defend her. During Acts II and III, and particularly in the crucial third scene of the latter, he is in the position of asking something from her. What he is asking is her full acceptance of him as consul, that is, as father-figure. Moreover the immediate circumstances of his asking have strongly passive aspects. Thus, when the tribune accuses Coriolanus of being a traitor to Rome, the defense-system by which the hero has maintained his equilibrium is dealt a severe blow. The unconscious significance of the accusation appears to be that Coriolanus' acts have been entirely selfish and that what he has really wanted is exclusive possession of the mother. The charge strikes home the more readily for its coming at a time when Coriolanus has just set partially aside his arrogant pride, a quality which constituted his main line of defense against both passive yearnings and oedipal desires.

When Coriolanus leaves Rome at the end of Act III, he does so on a subdued note, a note of pathos, yet not without dignity. The idea of his avenging return to the city in force has not yet appeared. Act IV is chiefly concerned with the development and implementation of this idea. Several subordinate considerations are also developed; the change of heart of the plebeians, who now feel that they were betrayed by the tribunes into banishing their natural leader; a further contrasting of the personalities of Volumnia and Virgilia; and the growth of an envious fear of Coriolanus on the part of Aufidius, who initially furnished the Roman with the means of revenge by placing him at the head of a Volscian army.[5] All in all, Act IV is a relatively quiet period between two emotional crises.

The intensely dramatic Act V is chiefly concerned with the successive pleas made to Coriolanus to abandon his revenge by those persons who mean the most to him: Cominius, Menenius, Virgilia, Volumnia, and little Marcius.

According to the hypothesis previously developed, the sack of Rome with the destruction of many of its inhabitants and the looting of its property would have the unconscious significance of (a regression to) sadism directed against the mother. The general impression of literary critics, that it is the long and impassioned speech of Volumnia in Scene III, a scene in which she goes down on her knees to her son, which changes Coriolanus' intention, is consonant with this hypothesis. The mother's abandoning her masculine behavior and asking her son's forgiveness and mercy could dissolve some of his unconscious hostility toward her as well as some of the conscious hostility toward Rome. . . .

The probability appears to be that Shakespeare intended us to regard Coriolanus' change of intent as the result of two forces, one deriving from the unaccustomed position of the hero's mother and the other from the long-term effects of the relationship with Virgilia. To put these concepts in psychological terminology, one might say that through his marriage to the emotionally healthy and feminine Virgilia, Coriolanus has had a "corrective emotional experience" and has undergone a partial emotional maturation with a lessening of the need for exhibitionistic, pseudo-masculine behavior, a partial alteration in his concept of woman (mother), and an increase in his capacity for object-love. Under the peculiarly great stress comprising the greater part of the play, the old, morbid influences deriving from Volumnia produce pathological responses in abundance. Yet the healthier influences of the marriage have not been without effect and make possible the relenting which takes place in the final act.

Because of the complexity of ideas here involved, perhaps an attempt at restatement is permissible. Coriolanus' plan to take Rome by force and destroy it is rendered less necessary once he has brought his mother to her knees, according to the previously suggested equation of Rome with mother. Nevertheless, if it had not been for the maturing effect of the relationship with Virgilia, the hostility of Coriolanus would probably have been sufficiently great to have demanded both forms of revenge.

The foregoing speculations are again reminiscent of what Reich has to say regarding therapeutic modification of the phallic-narcissist.

> The analytic treatment of phallic-narcissistic characters is one of the most thankful tasks. Since the phallic phase has been fully reached and since aggression is relatively free, the establishment of genital and social potency, other things being equal, is easier than in other forms. The analysis is always successful if one succeeds in unmasking the phallic-narcissistic attitudes as a defense against passive-feminine tendencies and in eliminating the unconscious tendency of revenge against the other sex.[6]

It appears likely from the evidence the play affords that Virgilia has to a slight but significant extent, increased Coriolanus' awareness of softer tendencies in himself and has reduced his need for revenge against women.

It remains to be asked, what role does guilt play in determining Coriolanus' behavior in the final act of the play? The evidence on this score is somewhat inconclusive, although there can be no question but that such feelings are of significance. Coriolanus' speech of capitulation is the most revealing in this connection.

> *(He holds her by the hand, silent.)*
>
> *Cor.*   O mother, mother!
> What have you done? Behold! the heavens do ope,
> The gods look down, and this unnatural scene
> They laugh at. O my mother! mother! O!
> You have won a happy victory for Rome;
> But, for your son, believe it, O! believe it,
> Most dangerously you have with him prevail'd,
> If not most mortal to him. But, let it come.
> Aufidius, though I cannot make true wars,
> I'll frame convenient peace. Now, good Aufidius,
> Were you in my stead, would you have heard
> A mother less, or granted less, Aufidius?

Auf. I was mov'd withal.
Cor.   I dare be sworn you were;
    And, sir, it is no little thing to make
    Mine eyes to sweat compassion. But, good sir,
    What peace you'll make, advise me: for my part,
    I'll not to Rome, I'll back with you; and pray you,
    Stand to me in this cause. O mother! wife!
                    (*Speaks apart with them.*)

The appellation, "unnatural scene," suggests guilt. More importantly, so does the determination to return to Corioli, inasmuch as
this decision has in it an element of possible suicide. If the implications of this final move were entirely clear, one could make a more
definite statement quantitatively about the importance of the guilt
feelings. The implications are not entirely clear, however. Coriolanus
consults with Aufidius about the terms of peace. He is actually wel-
comed by the Volscian populace on his return to Corioli, and apparently would have come off unscathed but for the treachery of Aufidius. . . . All that one can say with assurance, therefore, is that guilt
feelings are important but probably not decisive in the final crisis.

There remains to be considered the last scene of the play, in which
Coriolanus is taunted by Aufidius and then murdered by the conspirators. The portion of particular interest is the passage between Aufidius
and Coriolanus just before the murder.

Auf. . . . . tell the traitor, in the highest degree
    He hath abus'd your powers.
Cor. Traitor! How now!
Auf.   Ay, traitor, Marcius.
Cor.   Marcius!
Auf. Ay, Marcius, Caius Marcius. Dost thou think
    I'll grace thee with that robbery, thy stol'n name
    Coriolanus in Corioli?
    You lords and heads o' the state, perfidiously
    He has betrayed your business, and given up,
    For certain drops of salt, your city Rome,
    I say "your city," to his wife and mother.
    . . . at his nurse's tears
    He whin'd and roar'd away your victory. . . .

    Cor.   Hear'st thou, Mars?

Auf. Name not the god, thou boy of tears!

    Cor.   Ha!

Auf. No more.

    Cor. Measureless liar, thou hast made my heart
           Too great for what contains it. Boy! O slave!
           Pardon me, lords, 'tis the first time that ever
           I was forced to scold. Your judgments, my grave lords,
           Must give this cur the lie; and his own notion,
           Who wears my stripes impressed upon him; that
           Must bear my beating to his grave, shall join
           To thrust the lie upon him.

First Lord. Peace, both, and hear me speak.

    Cor. Cut me to pieces, Volsces; men and lads.
           Stain all your edges on me. Boy! False hound!
           If you have writ your annals true, 'tis there,
           That, like an eagle in a dove-cote, I
           Fluttered your Volsces in Corioli:
           Alone I did it. Boy!

                                    (V.v.86-117)

It appears worthy of note that, although Shakespeare strives for realism and dramatic effect above lyricism throughout most of the play, at this moment all three qualities are combined superbly to produce a passage which is scarcely excelled elsewhere in his writings and contains a metaphor which has "passed into the common speech of man."

What are the words which stimulate Coriolanus to this eloquent fury? There is the previously effective "traitor," but there is the still more effective "boy." Coriolanus speaks the latter word three times in his outburst, and it is linked with the reference to his mother as "nurse." Doubtless Coriolanus is not aware of the reason for the peculiar effectiveness of this appellation in releasing such a torrent of feeling, but Shakespeare surely is. Taking into consideration the dignity and nobility which find expression in the speech, along with the rage and traces of the old pseudo-masculinity, one can only feel that it is the supremely bitter irony of the situation which stirs Coriolanus: that he should be accused of being a boy in connection with his nearest approach to emotional maturity.[7]

Notes

1. OTTO RANK, *Das Inzest-Motiv in Dichtung und Sage* (1912) (Leipzig: Franz Deuticke, 1926), chap. 6; JACKSON E. TOWNE, "A Psychoanalytic Study of Shakespeare's *Coriolanus,*" *Psychoanalytic Review, 8*:84-91, 1921.

1. W. REICH, *Character Analysis* (New York: Orgone Institute Press, 1949).

2. A. M. MCKENZIE, *The Women in Shakespeare's Plays* (New York: Doubleday, Page and Company, 1924).

3. REICH, *op. cit.*

4. *Ibid.*

5. There is some material suggestive of the hypothesis that Aufidius is unconsciously a father-substitute for Coriolanus, to whom the hero turns after the rejection by mother-Rome.

6. REICH, *op. cit.*

7. Since the Elizabethans and Jacobeans divided the members of society into two categories, men, and women-and-boys, with much emphasis on virile and effeminate qualities, when a Shakespearean character uses the term "boy" in such an instance as this, it carries the additional implication of "effeminate." There is thus the further irony that Coriolanus should be accused of effeminacy in connection with his nearest approach to a compassionate masculinity.

Authoritarian Patterns in Shakespeare's "Coriolanus"

Shortly after the appearance of Hofling's paper, Gordon Ross Smith presented a study of *Coriolanus* based upon the work of Fromm and Adorno. Generally speaking, the methodology of the two papers is similar. The Shakespearean characters, especially Coriolanus, are examined in the light of realistic, psychoanalytical data gathered and interpreted by clinicians and theoreticians. However, the conclusions reached in the two papers are radically different. This does not mean that Reich's phallic-narcissistic character cannot be reconciled in theory with the authoritarian character of Fromm and Adorno, the character that most interests Smith. On the contrary, it can; and in this respect Smith's remarks lend a depth and a richness to Hofling's. What it means, rather, is that Smith's paper tends to play up the *social* aspect of the tragedy, to underscore *political* implications (for Elizabethans as well as for us), to indicate that the hero is a significant cog in a more significant wheel, and thus to differentiate itself from the work of Hofling, which discovers the central interest of the drama in the development of Coriolanus as a son and as a husband.

Smith suggests that the authoritarians in *Coriolanus* are Menenius, Volumnia, Virgilia, and Coriolanus himself, and he suggests this because these characters display to a remarkable degree the traits of the authoritarian as described by Adorno and Fromm. Coriolanus, for example, uses or exploits others, strives to make others suffer and to see them suffering, claims that he should rule over others because he "knows what is best for them," believes that his own intrinsic worth entitles him to a position of authority, shows an unthinking, stereotypical admiration for his parent, and scorns the base-born, the weak, and the defenseless; Volumnia envies men and usurps as much of the masculine role as she can; Virgilia plays the typical role for a woman in an authoritarian community, one of passivity and submission; and Menenius identifies himself with people and institutions of power (something that the other authoritarians also do). By contrast, Aufidius, the Tribunes, and the citizenry present us with the "liberal" element: They are free from authoritarian attitudes; they recognize the complexity of human situations; they consider feelings and potentialities in a realistic way; in short, they are open-minded. The essential conflict in the play develops primarily because Coriolanus "objects to democratic diversity of opinion, for such diversity strikes him as disunity and hence as weakness, and the ambiguities of diversity in opinion are insufferable to one who needs clear and simple formulations. Hence there is no chance of their [the people] pleasing him, for the only way they could all be of one mind would be through the automatisms of authoritarian conformity, and authoritarian is what they are not." Smith concludes by discussing the relevance of this interpretation to the society in which Shakespeare lived and wrote.

M. F.

he purpose of this paper is to try to indicate how closely some of the characters in Shakespeare's *Coriolanus* parallel in their surface appearance certain character syndromes first formulated by Erich Fromm in *Escape from Freedom* and subsequently empirically verified by the studies of Adorno and his associates.[1] I am aware that the philosophical ideas and the unconscious assumptions of mankind may greatly vary from any one time and place to any other, and also that the intellectual revolution of the later seventeenth century has made the habitual content of the commonplace Elizabethan mind seem sometimes as strange to us as that of an ancient Greek or Egyptian. But although assumptions and philosophy sometimes vary so much, I doubt that the character syndromes or innate mental mechanisms which are the framework holding the aforementioned assumptions and philosophy differ much more from age to age than does the human physical form. It is with innate mechanisms and generic responses that I am here concerned. If the range of human character structures and mental mechanisms is finite, however large, then obviously a writer in any age who used direct observation might record a given syndrome quite unaware that a later age might rediscover that syndrome and give it a pejorative name. Such observations would in many ways be comparable to those of Galen or Robert Burton, both of whom recorded signs of physical and mental ailments whose causes they had no modern knowledge of, but which are readily recognizable today.

"Authoritarian Patterns in Shakespeare's *Coriolanus*" by Gordon Ross Smith. Reprinted with permission from *Literature and Psychology*, IX (1959), 45-51.

The chief literary advantage of making such an analysis as this is that we may reduce the great number of incompatible interpretations of this play offered with equal conviction over the last century and a half by ruling many of them out of further consideration on the grounds that they are unsupported by empirical evidence. We will then come much closer to knowing whether the play should be acted, for example, as noble tragedy or as tragic satire.

Before beginning these comparisons, I should like to warn that "authoritarian" and "authoritative" are *not* interchangeable terms. The latter is an approval word; the former, a pejorative one. It seems to me that a rational man must give a certain amount of deference to, say, a nuclear physicist on matters which are a physicist's specialty. Indeed, a rational man owes some kind of deference to anyone who can speak authoritatively, providing we define "authoritative" as able to demonstrate a knowledge greatly superior to that of the common man in that something in which a person is authoritative. A well-informed man who is aware of how many times in history an established, authoritative position has proved to be wrong may entertain some slight reserve with his deference, but if he is aware of his own dearth of knowledge on some subject, he will hardly put it into the balance with the knowledge of someone who is authoritative as I have tried to define that term. An authoritarian opinion or person is altogether different, and therein lies the common confusion. For an authoritarian position may resemble an authoritative one in that it implies superiority and demands acceptance, but differs in having so little that is demonstrable to justify it. Essentially, the words are as different as "sanguine" and "sanguinary." When we recognize that an authoritarian position will commonly be paraded as an authoritative one, we can see that for some people the confusion may become—just dreadful. The cure, I think, lies in one's insistence upon the demonstration of what facts support the position in question.

In analyzing this play for authoritarianism, we shall repeatedly ask in specific ways two general questions. The first is, What harmony or lack of it exists between the characters' declarations about themselves and their actions? Or to put the question in the terms of twentieth century so-called realist Shakespeare criticism, Is character description a cue to the meaning of the action? The second question is, What correspondence is there between the characters of the persons of the drama—where character is determined both by what the person says and by what he does—and modern empirical formulations of authoritarian and nonauthoritarian character syndromes? Instead of summarizing the hundreds of pages of Fromm, Adorno, and subsequent writers, I shall merely mention as I go elements of the authoritarian character as Fromm, Adorno, *et al.,* have determined it, and the appearance of those elements in certain characters. No one parallel constitutes proof of my thesis, but together I believe the accumulation of parallels is compelling.

One of the commonest characteristics of authoritarians is to ally or identify themselves with a person, institution, class, god or other entity which is, or which the authoritarian thinks to be, of great strength. I submit that the chief authoritarians in *Coriolanus* are Menenius, Virgilia, Volumnia, and Coriolanus himself. Menenius' idolized power is the patricians and especially Coriolanus, whom he had "godded" (V.iii.11); Virgilia's is Coriolanus alone; Volumnia's power-idol is primarily the Roman state, which she equates with patricians only, and secondarily her son, who is her support in maintaining her position with those patricians. For Coriolanus the idolization is only secondarily of the Roman patricians; primarily it is of his mother, whose values he has consequently taken over totally. It is for these reasons that Volumnia sacrifices her son for the Roman state, as she had said she would do in her first scene, and that he sacrifices himself for his mother, as the first citizen implies he could do before he has yet appeared. What apparent inconsistencies Volumnia and Coriolanus show are merely logical ones; psychologically they are quite consistent: their logical inconsistencies can always be found explicable in terms of their authoritarian alignments and sado-masochistic tendencies, even to the last extremes of destructiveness in Coriolanus, who from plans to burn Rome and to massacre the inhabitants turns at the behest of his mother to conscious self-destruction. But this extreme development of Coriolanus' character is preceded by many other patterns that are also present in modern formulations of the authoritarian personality.

Fromm divides the authoritarian's sadistic strivings into three types: The first is "to have absolute and unrestricted power over" others. From the first scene until his banishment Coriolanus repeatedly declares the people should have no participation in government, and that what power they have should be taken from them:

> What should the people do with these bald tribunes?
> On whom depending, their obedience fails
> To the greater bench? . . .
> Let what is meet be said it must be meet
> And throw their power i' th' dust.
>
> (III.i.165-171)

The second type is to use or to exploit others. Coriolanus calls the plebs a "musty superfluity" which Rome can "vent" in war (I.i.229-230). He shares his attitude toward them with his mother, of whom he says:

> I muse my mother
> Does not approve me further, who was wont
> To call them woollen vassals, things created
> To buy and sell with groats, to show bare heads
> In congregations, to yawn, be still and wonder,
> When one but of my ordinance stood up
> To speak of peace or war.
>
> (III.ii.7-13)

He admires Aufidius for his valor, flees to him after his banishment in spite of having been told very explicitly that Aufidius hates him, masochistically offers Aufidius his life, and yet once he is allied with him, he dominates over Aufidius, too. Whether domineering or subservient, Coriolanus seems unaware of the unceasing quality of Aufidius' hatred and of its mortal danger to him. Such behavior may be illogical or irrational, but it is not inexplicable, and really all aspects of his relationship to Aufidius are understandable in terms of the modern formulation of the authoritarian personality.

The third type of sadistic striving is to make others suffer or to see them suffer. Such is Coriolanus' attitude toward the starving and toward his banishers, and in his plans to burn Rome not even those sympathizers who had offered to accompany him in his banishment are to be spared.

Not all of these sadistic impulses are overt. Fromm lists five rationalizations of sadistic impulses, most of which Coriolanus at one or another time displays. The first rationalization is, "I rule over you because I know what is best for you, and in your own interest you should follow me without opposition." If for "I" we substitute the patricians, "our best elders" with whom Coriolanus identifies himself so often, the first half of this rationalization is his most persistent demand, as it is that of Menenius also. Coriolanus, of course, does not profess to have any plebeian interests at heart, and the second half is best seen in such lines as these of Menenius:

> I tell you, friends, most charitable care
> Have the patricians of you . . . . you slander
> The helms o' the state, who care for you like fathers.
>
> (I.i.66-79)

I consider these lines rationalization because the play does not contain any examples of benevolent paternalism on the part of patricians, and the chief, patrician of the play openly and consistently displays his contempt.

The second rationalization Fromm cites is, "I'm so wonderful and unique I have a right to expect others to depend on me." Coriolanus declares he should become consul without the public vote, which he thinks the plebeians should be deprived of, however ancient the custom. He constantly asserts his own superiority in virtue and power and the right of his own class, whom he calls eagles, to rule the rest of the populace, whom he calls crows, geese, etc. The third rationalization is, "I have done so much for you I am entitled to take from you what I want." What he calls "Mine own desert" (II.iii.71) and patrician right to what he wants are two of his three insistent themes when he stands for consul and when he harangues the town with his proposal that the plebeians should be deprived of all their established rights. The fourth rationalization, "I have been hurt by others and my wish to hurt them is nothing but retaliation," he makes explicitly when he joins Aufidius, and again when he receives the first Roman embassies. Even if we acknowledge that he has suffered an injustice, it is impossible logically to reconcile his leading the Volscian armies against Rome, which includes the patricians, with his earlier declaration that he owes the Senate and presumably the patricians his life and services. The fifth rationalization, "By striking first I am defending myself or my friends against the danger of being hurt," is his third insistent theme in his denunciations of the tribunes and the people.

Sadism in authoritarians has other characteristic forms of expression which Coriolanus and members of his group also display. Powerlessness arouses the authoritarian's contempt, and Fromm declares, "the very sight of a powerless person makes him want to attack, dominate, humiliate him." Shakespeare has twice juxtaposed Coriolanus' prolonged and supererogatory abuse of the plebeians to his immediately respectful demeanor toward the patricians (I.i.168-255; III.i.1-170). Although he contemptuously abuses plebeians for alleged fickleness, the imagery he employs in the following passage demonstrates that it is plebeian weakness as much as fickleness that has provoked his contempt. He declares,

> . . . He that depends
> Upon your favours swims with fins of lead,
> And hews down oaks with rushes.
>
> (I.i.183-185)

The course of the play proves the plebeians less changeable in loyalties than he.

The Adorno studies declare that typical authoritarians are generally devoid of introspection and insight and tend to project their own unacceptable qualities upon their opponents: "Not oneself but others are seen as hostile and threatening."[2] Although Coriolanus repeatedly accuses the plebeians of rebellion and predatory behavior, and although some of their behavior does lend color to his charges, yet he himself is the most violent, rebellious, and predatory person in the play. The citizenry in comparison are very tractable, and the only people who appear to feed on others are the patricians upon the plebeians. We can quote the Adorno studies in describing Coriolanus: "Moral condemnation serves the purpose of externalization of, and defense against, temptations toward immoral and unconventional behavior."[3] These tendencies Shakespeare makes quite explicit in Coriolanus' later actions.

Aggression in authoritarian persons tends to be moralistic, punitive, explosive, physical, and destructive, whereas in liberal persons it tends to be principled, intellectualized, verbal, and relatively mild and regular in its release. In Coriolanus' harangues, his attack on the unarmed citizenry, and his later march on Rome, we see in action the destructive violence that he had three times threatened in the first act. In comparison the actions the tribunes take against him are, as in liberal persons, governed by persistently held principles (of popular self-interest), and both language and behavior are less violent than those of Coriolanus.

His own internal sense of weakness obliges the authoritarian to be allied with and dependent upon an external source of strength, but, says Fromm, "if the authority in which he believes shows signs of weakness, his love and respect change into contempt and hatred."[4] Thus we can see through Coriolanus' repeated protestations that what he does he does for his country, and through his respect for the patricians. No sooner has he been banished than the patricians, who had not saved him, become "our dastard nobles," deserving of his hatred and revenge against whom he will fight "with the spleen/Of all the under fiends" (IV.v.96-98). There is no remorse, no insight into his own faults, no love of country: only the authoritarian sense of victimization, contempt, and hatred. Clearly his early threat to fight the Roman soldiers who were not supporting him as he demanded was dramatic preparation for this greater reversal. His march on Rome, the breakthrough of his antisocial drives, might have been predicted, so to speak, by the writer of the following passage:

> Display of a rough masculine façade seems to be a compensation for . . . passivity and dependency. Rigid repression of hostility against parents may be accompanied by an occasional breaking through of drives in a crude and unsocialized form; under certain circumstances this may become dangerous to the very society to which there seems to be conformity.[5]

But submission and domination in Coriolanus are for himself, not for the nobler principles he parades, and this also the first citizen had declared in the opening scene.

So far we have seen from the text of the play how closely domination in Coriolanus parallels the nature and forms of sadism in modern authoritarians. The evidences of masochism in Coriolanus are just as complete. Behavior that a psychiatrist would dub masochistic is commonly thought of by the authoritarian himself as love and loyalty, and so Coriolanus is depicted as feeling it. Initially he gives his loyalty to country and patricians, and subsequently to Aufidius, and in opposing the innovation of the tribunes, he gives it to custom also. However, when custom requires that he submit to the weak and lowly by standing publicly in the gown of humility, then he rejects custom as he subsequently does Rome, patricians, and Aufidius. The only person he cannot reject or be rejected by, as said above, is his mother. Both her rejections of him reduce him to tearful obedience.

Other common patterns of authoritarian masochism are a belief in the necessity of catastrophe, love of the conditions limiting human freedom, love for the idea of being controlled by fate, and fear of starvation or of being "devoured" by the strong, all of which appear repeatedly in the lines of the Coriolanus group, but seldom in those of the nonauthoritarian characters. Thus Coriolanus is sure of further rebellion from the plebeians, whereas after his banishment Rome knows the only internal peace it has in the whole play. His love of conditions limiting human freedom is seen in his rejection of Greek precedent in grain distribution and in his demands for the total disfranchisement of the plebeians.

The deliberate conformity characteristic of authoritarian masochism is also explicit. Most important is his adherence to Volumnia and to her values, but also present is evidence of a consciousness of playing a part. He says to his mother at the beginning of the first capitulation scene:

> Why did you wish me milder? Would you have me
> False to my nature? Rather say I play
> The man I am.
>
> (III.ii.14-16)

But actually to say that one is playing a role indicates not spontaneity but conscious conformity to that role and doubt as to the effectiveness of the performance, which doubt suggests a considerable gap between the underlying impulses and the role played. A spontaneous man does not play roles: he behaves as he sees fit and proper, and if he has doubts about his actions, they will be on the score of perception, logic, rightness, but not on whether he properly played a role. It is clear from the above passage that Coriolanus is conforming to a role designed by his mother. Volumnia's answer makes explicit this element of falseness in his character: "You might have been enough the man you are,/With striving less to be so." As if to clinch the matter, in the second capitulation scene Shakespeare has Coriolanus refer to himself as a "dull actor," and I think we are obliged to conclude that Shakespeare thought this tendency a minor but persistent one in the character of Coriolanus, like the tendency of the Nurse in *Romeo and Juliet* to call for *aqua vitae* in any emergency.

The Adorno studies declare the authoritarian's attitude toward his parents "one of stereotypical admiration, with little ability to express criticism or resentment." Parents are thought of as being "wonderful"; emphasis is on "background" and aristocratic superiority. Coriolanus declares his mother "has a charter to extol her blood"; although he says he hates a "promise-breaker," he never directly reproaches her—Hamlet-like—for her recommendations of deliberate deceit, but instead only laments that in using deceit he must by implication kow-tow to the commonalty. He refers to her as "the most noble mother in the world" and as "Olympus" to whom he himself is "a molehill." Such conscious admiration, however, seems inconsistent with his march on Rome and his threats to spare not even his own family. However, identification with the family and the in-group, wrote Adorno, is "one of the main mechanisms by which such people can impose authoritarian discipline upon themselves and avoid 'breaking away'—a temptation nourished continuously by their underlying ambivalence."

The preceding central patterns of authoritarian character are accompanied in Coriolanus by a large number of concomitant patterns that are more or less clearly expressions of the sado-masochistic strivings. Simultaneous tendencies to self-glorification and self-contempt express both kinds of strivings, and Coriolanus shows both. The former appear frequently in harangues upon tribunes and plebeians, as when he speaks against "mingling them with us, the honour'd number,/Who lack not virtue, no, nor power" (III.i.72-73); the latter appear on the battlefield and again in the forum when he depreciates himself and refuses to hear himself praised. In his refusal of praise we may also suspect in him an unwillingness to be submitted even by implication to the judgment of his supposed inferiors. In a later passage Shakespeare has explicitly juxtaposed both of these tendencies:

> . . . City
> 'Tis I that made thy widows: many an heir
> Of these fair edifices fore my wars
> Have I heard groan and drop: then know me not,
> Lest that thy wives with spits and boys with stones
> In puny battle slay me.
>
> (IV.iv.1-6)

The logic is very bad, for why such unaided and successful valor should now fear boys and women is inexplicable. It may be argued that these lines are ironic, and that there is dramatic irony I can grant, for at the hands of these people of whom he is so contemptuous Coriolanus will lose his life. That the lines are irony on Coriolanus' part I cannot see: he is no more given to irony than he is to introspection. Rather, I think they must be considered part of that final revelation of the extremes of character that we so often get toward the end of a Shakespearean play, such revelations as Brutus' unjustifiable quarrel with Cassius or Shylock's sharpening his knife on the sole of his shoe. Both chronologically and in the logic of dramatic development the address to Antium comes between the bad logic of "I banish you" (III.iii.123), and his last and most incredible declaration, "Pardon me, lords, 'tis the first time that ever/I was forc'd to scold" (V.v. 105-6). The address to Antium (IV.iv.1-6) is about as concise a dramatic statement as one could have of the authoritarian's irremediable insecurity which no self-glorification can really allay.

Other concomitant patterns are the following: pseudomasculinity and emphasis on energy, struggle, competitiveness and achievement, as when Coriolanus brags, "like an eagle in a dove-cote, I/Flutter'd your Volscians in Corioli:/Alone I did it" (V.v.15-17); concern with the body, seen in Coriolanus in his consciousness of his own bloody appearance, and of his wounds, in his wanting to wash, and in his detestation of the woolless toga. Concern with the body is seen in Volumnia and Menenius in the absurd catalogue of scars, and in their frequent rejoicings in Coriolanus' physical strength. Intolerance of ambiguity is beautifully explicit; Coriolanus exclaims:

> . . . my soul aches
> To know, when two authorities are up,
> Neither supreme, how soon confusion
> May enter 'twixt the gap of both and take
> The one by the other.
>
> (III.i.108-112)

Sense of victimization and denial of fault are obvious in his complainings about the "dastard nobles" of Rome. The Adorno studies also cite a certain "gullibility" in authoritarians, which may be seen in Coriolanus in the ease with which tribunes and Aufidius play upon his character to their own ends. He never sees through them well enough to counter their moves by behaving otherwise than they all expect; unlike Hamlet, he answers the surface of their comments and never perceives the underlying purposes. His lack of insight is also evident in his attitude toward promises: he professes to be constant and to hate promise-breakers, but he breaks his own major promises, and so we are probably supposed to understand the wager in I.iv. as the first hint that he does not keep his word if doing so would be to his disadvantage.

What the Adorno studies call the "improverished potentialities for inter-personal relationships" characterize Coriolanus in dealing with common soldiers, plebeians, Menenius, and Aufidius. We may also detect impoverishment in his marriage. Whether he be returning from battle, bidding the women goodby, receiving the embassy—upon which occasion he turns from Virgilia to Volumnia with the words, "You gods! I prate"—or finally capitulating, his primary attention is to his mother, not to his wife. In both capitulations it is his mother whom he would please and mollify, not his wife who has little or nothing to do with the contests taking place.

The typical role for a woman in an authoritarian community according to Adorno "is one of passivity and subservience. She is an object of solicitude on the part of the man." Virgilia, with her housebound timidity and her "faint puling" is obviously this to the point of caricature. Since authoritarians idealize family members, she becomes his "gracious silence," and simultaneously an opportunity for him to brace his own uncertain superiority. The subservience of authoritarian women frequently conceals underlying hostility toward men, which may be manifested by "the living out of her thwarted ambitions through the medium of the man"[6] In Volumnia we see caricatured this other extreme of feminine authoritarianism: her envy of men is evident first in her unequivocal usurpation of as much of the masculine role as she can manage and later in her living through Coriolanus to enjoy what she cannot seize for herself.

One of the most remarkable and rewarding things about this play is the precision and economy with which, time and again, Shakespeare has woven typical patterns of authoritarianism into single passages, and those passages into whole scenes. A few examples must suffice at present. Menenius says to the citizens:

> I tell you, friends, most charitable care
> Have the patricians for you. For your wants,
> Your suffering in this dearth, you may as well
> Strike at the heaven with your staves as lift them
> Against the Roman state, whose course will on
> The way it takes, cracking ten thousand curbs
> Of more strong link asunder than can ever
> Appear in your impediment. For the dearth,
> The gods, not the patricians, make it, and
> Your knees to them, not arms, must help. Alack,
> You are transported by calamity
> Thither where more attends you; and you slander
> The helms o' th' state, who care for you like fathers,
> When you curse them as enemies.
>
> (I.i.66-80.)

Here, explicitly or implicitly, we have the invincible power of authority, superhuman forces, necessity of catastrophe, limitation of freedom, the strength and virtues of the superior classes, the alleged perfidy of the weaker and lower classes, the necessity of submission, and factual untruth. Those who disagree he accuses of folly and wickedness; that the plebeians might have any right on their side he does not conceive. Coriolanus presently asks the same citizens,

> . . . What's the matter,
> That in these several places of the city
> You cry against the noble senate, who,
> Under the gods, keep you in awe, which else
> Would feed on one another?
>
> (I.i.188-192)

Here we have again the supposed superiority of rulers, the inferiority of the ruled, supernatural oppression, limitation of freedom, fear of catastrophe, and the implication of folly or malice. When Coriolanus and Aufidius meet in battle, Coriolanus cries, "Let the first budger die the other's slave,/And the gods doom him after!" (I.viii.5-6). Again, sadism in the utter mastery of the winner, masochism in the slavery of the loser, and "fate" in the gods' posthumous decree. Coriolanus declares that the granting of tribunes is an act to "make bold power look pale" (I.i.216), but that bold power should be frightened is a self-contradictory declaration; it suggests that the "bold power" is a front for a permanent state of fright. Of Sicinius Coriolanus declares, "If he have power,/Then vail your ignorance; if none, awake/ Your dangerous lenity" (III.i.97-99). Out of context this passage might be conceived as a plea for the statesmanship of the patricians as against the demagoguery of the tribunes and the incompetence of the populace. But if we examine it in context, what do we find? It is both preceded and followed by lines that are concerned *only* with plebeian power as opposed to patrician. The logic of the passage I have cited then becomes a revelation of character, for it says, "If he have power, give in, but if he has none, he's dangerous." Many more such passages can be cited.

Fromm has remarked that the authoritarian may show courage, activity, and belief, and we can grant Coriolanus the possession of all three of these qualities, although the first two are strictly physical in their manifestations and in no way intellectual or ethical. We can also grant him a reasonable pride in the directness with which he expresses his offensive and often irrational opinions, and we can grant that his "lonely dragon" departure from Rome after banishment is written to be played sympathetically. But the possession of certain virtues does not outweigh his faults and make him a sympathetic hero.

The major antagonists of Coriolanus—Aufidius, the tribunes, and the Roman citizenry—are sharply contrasted with the Coriolanus group, first, by being free of authoritarian compulsions, and second, by their displaying attitudes and behavior which the Adorno studies often label "liberal."

Aufidius and both tribunes pursue their ultimate objectives with a single-mindedness the opposite of the hectic gyrations of loyalty and declared objective in Coriolanus. They approach their problems openmindedly, for Brutus says to Sicinius, "Let's . . ./. . . carry with us ears and eyes for th' time,/But hearts for the event" (II.i.284-286), and Aufidius declares to his associates, ". . . bring me word thither/How the world goes, that to the pace of it/I may spur on my journey" (I.x.31-33), and later when asked what should be done, he answers, "Sir, I cannot tell:/We must proceed as we do find the people" (V.v.15-16). Aufidius and the tribunes consider the feelings and potentialities of the people realistically, and successfully manipulate them; they recognize the complexities of human situations; they discuss and speculate about what their opponents may do, and finally they achieve their objectives. But Coriolanus and his group can only argue or denounce ("a simple, firm, often stereotypical" and moralistic cognitive structure, as the Adorno studies say), and their attempts at control are inept. In the general wrangle preceding the riot, Sicinius tells the citizens that Coriolanus would take away their liberties. Menenius protests his declaration as "the way to kindle," to which a senator adds, "To unbuild the city and to lay all flat" (III.i.198-199). Authoritarians, who customarily think of their property as extensions of themselves, would naturally be prone to think of a city as buildings. Sicinius answers, "What is the city but the people?" and the citizens agree with him, thereby illustrating the liberal's concern with persons rather than with things. Finally, both tribunes are possessed of moral courage and speak out against what they consider wrong, as liberals often will, even though not allied with the prevailing structure of power. Brutus speaks his mind at the ceremonies honoring Coriolanus, and rejects the rebuke of Menenius; Sicinius speaks up for the people's legal rights against the special privileges requested by Coriolanus during the same ceremonies. So also in the marketplace challenge and in the banishment scene. Both initially and later the tribunes pursue their duties in spite of the threat or show of violence which is offered by Coriolanus and which they could not hope to counter physically.

A close scrutiny of the behavior of the plebeians shows that like the tribunes they are chiefly nonauthoritarian. When in the first scene the patricians are preparing to file out in hierarchical order, Coriolanus twice orders the plebeians to "follow," but Shakespeare's stage direction reads, "citizens steal away." Similarly, they refuse to charge for him at Corioli, and his threats prove useless. The voices they give him for consul are frequently reluctant: "The price is to ask it kindly." "But this is something odd." "An't were to give again,—" (II.iii.81-90). Only once do they follow him, and there it is under the combined impulses from Cominius and victory. Both in charging for Lartius and later on the plain before Corioli they prove neither cowardly nor foolhardy but sensibly courageous, as the tribunes are in civic life, and how could it be otherwise when they formed the body of the Roman army? Contrary to the declarations of Coriolanus and Menenius that they riot, feed on one another, and cannot be ruled, the citizens show themselves mild and amenable; it is Coriolanus who commits all the faults he accuses them of having. Though resentful, they are quiet when insults are hurled upon them, whereas Coriolanus is explosive. Even under his provocation they show themselves to be generally fair-minded and gentle, none of which qualities he ever shows toward them. It is true they show inconstancy by reportedly haling Brutus up and down, but although they and Coriolanus share this fault, they are neither so changeable nor so violent as he. Certainly this Roman populace is different from that of *Julius Caesar*. Inevitably the people are many-minded. The authoritarian mentality of Coriolanus objects to democratic diversity of opinion, for such diversity strikes him as disunity and hence as weakness, and the ambiguities of diversity in opinion are insufferable to one who needs clear and simple formulations. Hence there is no chance of their pleasing him, for the only way they could all be of one mind would be through the automatisms of authoritarian conformity, and authoritarian is what they are not.

One of the first questions a person might ask about the interpretation I have offered here is whether Shakespeare might not have been fully in sympathy with Coriolanus because he was authoritarian himself. The answer, if we can rely upon the Adorno studies, is quite easy, for these empirical studies indicate that authoritarians see themselves in an entirely different light from that in which the investigators saw them. The authoritarian's usual concept of himself is of a wellborn, well-bred, courteous, valiant gentleman, loyal, reliable, sturdy, etc. Although the investigators might not think a specific authoritarian individual possessed of all these attributes, the individual would usually find an explanation, as, for example, that the simple virtues of the lower middle classes—known to him as the great middle classes— are obviously superior to the profligacy of the idle rich. The authoritarian portrait of itself or of its ideal might resemble Shakespeare's portrait of Henry V, but never Coriolanus, whose opinions of himself are so often at such odds with his performance. Further evidence of nonauthoritarian attitudes in Shakespeare can certainly be adduced from the sonnets, and in general from Shakespeare's productivity, complexity, subtlety, and lyric power, achievements beyond the scope of the essentially unpoetic authoritarian mind.

It seems obvious that such an interpretation as I have offered should make the play quite effective on the stage for a modern audience—

except, perhaps, for one of professors. The historically minded professors will certainly ask, How can you fit such an interpretation into our knowledge of the London stage and of the early Jacobean climate of opinion? The amount of evidence that can be offered in answer is so very large that I can do little more here than indicate its nature. First, I would cite the section of Fromm's book which discusses the social conditions which gave rise to European authoritarianism in the late middle ages and the Renaissance. Second, I would cite the complexity of philosophical, psychological, and political opinion in Elizabethan and Jacobean times as that opinion has been indicated in such recent surveys as Hiram Haydn's *The Counter Renaissance,* Louise C. Turner Forrest's "Caveat for Critics against Invoking Elizabethan Psychology,"[7] and particularly such studies of political opinion as those of Helen C. White,[8] W. Gordon Zeeveld,[9] and J. W. Allen.[10] Helen White has shown both how social criticism was linked with religion and how equalitarian such criticism often was. Zeeveld has shown how the ancient concept of degree as later epitomized by Ulysses' speech in *Troilus and Cressida* was undermined and indeed contradicted both in practice and in official theory by royal authority in the reign of Henry VIII. J. W. Allen has shown the diversity of the political thought in those times, including the persistence of nonauthoritarian ideas and the rejection of the divine right of kings.

That Shakespeare's political opinion was not static but constantly developing between 1592 and 1605 has been indicated by John Danby's recent study,[11] and that Ulysses' speech on degree is contradicted by the events of the play has been so well demonstrated by Johannes Kleinstück[12] that we are certainly not obliged to interpret *Coriolanus* as a play about the violation of degree. In brief, I don't think that there was a single Elizabethan world picture, I don't believe the theory of humors or any other one psychology was dominant, I do think Shakespeare might have used direct observation in the construction of some of his characters, I deny that anyone has proof that he didn't, and I don't believe Ulysses on degree represents the political acumen of the age or anything more than that segment of political opinion which included the makers of the official mythology. If the play was produced along such lines as I have suggested in this paper, I doubt if any Jacobean audience would have taken Coriolanus for its spokesman. What, then, could have been the relationship of the play to its contemporaneous audiences? I think we can find an historically tenable solution.

Some years ago Dr. Louis B. Wright pointed out the persistent mild hostility that the London middle classes felt toward the aristocracy and its assumption that it was naturally superior;[13] Professor Alfred Harbage has since demonsrated that the Globe audience was quiet, orderly, and chiefly middle class, that representatives of the upper classes were relatively few in number at any one performance, and that the lower classes seldom appeared because they could not afford to go.[14] Now *Coriolanus* contains upper classes and lower, but no middle, and this fact can of course be explained from Plutarch. I suspect, however, that the absence of a middle class in his source has been put to dramaturgic use by Shakespeare. I should like to suggest that *Coriolanus* was written for Harbage's middle-class audience, one that was somewhat apprehensive of the lower classes and their potentiality for disorder, but one that nevertheless felt more sympathy for them than for Stuart absolutism and for the rich, idle, and predatory aristocratic classes. It should be remembered that *Coriolanus* appeared not long after sensational enclosure riots and shortages of grain, that displaced country people had died in London streets from starvation, and that James had shocked Englishmen from the very start with his absolutist pronouncements. Although we may suppose a middle-class audience more sympathetic to the lower classes than to the upper, I think it would not really have liked either; therefore in *Coriolanus* both lower and upper are depicted with serious failings, but the upper classes with much the worse. Professor Oscar Campbell has called the play a tragic satire. I should say rather that it is a realistic and grim satire, that the chief object of reprehension is Coriolanus, and that the play as a whole reflects—as much as official, authoritarian censorship would allow—early Jacobean stirrings of those opinions and feelings which were to grow to flood tide with the Puritan Revolution.

Notes

1. ERICH FROMM, *Escape from Freedom* (New York: Farrar and Rinehart, 1941); T. W. ADORNO et al., *The Authoritarian Personality* (New York: Harper and Bros., 1950).

2. ADORNO et al., op. cit., p. 474.

3. Ibid., p. 420.

4. FROMM, op. cit., p. 172.

5. ADORNO et al., op. cit., p. 482.

6. Ibid., p. 478.

7. LOUISE C. TURNER FORREST, "Caveat for Critics against Invoking Elizabethan Psychology," Publications of the Modern Language Association, 61:651-672, 1946.

8. HELEN C. WHITE, Social Criticism in Popular Religious Literature of the Sixteenth Century (New York: The Macmillan Company, 1941).

9. WILLIAM GORDON ZEEVOLD, Foundations of Tudor Policy (Cambridge: Harvard University Press, 1948).

10. J. W. ALLEN, English Political Thought, 1603-1644 (London: Archon, 1938).

11. JOHN F. DANBY, Shakespeare's Doctrine of Nature: A Study of King Lear (London: Faber, 1949).

12. JOHANNES KLEINSTUCK, "The Problem of Order in Shakespeare's Histories," Neophilologus, 38:268-277, 1954; "Ulysses' Speech on Degree as Related to the Play of Troilus and Cressida," Neophilologus, 43:58-63, 1959.

13. LOUIS B. WRIGHT, Middle-Class Culture in Elizabethan England (Chapel Hill: University of North Carolina Press, 1935).

14. ALFRED B. HARBAGE, Shakespeare's Audience (New York: Columbia University Press, 1941).

Shakespearean Tragedy: "Coriolanus"

Whereas Hofling and Smith play down the oedipal aspect of *Coriolanus* and emphasize the significance of the hero's character structure, Robert J. Stoller makes the relationship—perhaps one should say the warfare—between Coriolanus and his mother the be-all and the end-all of the play. In this respect Stoller's work bears a general resemblance to the earliest, or "original," psychoanalytic approaches to the tragedy, those of Rank and Towne.[1] I say "general resemblance" because, as shall be seen, Stoller's interpretation ultimately regards the classical conception of the oedipal conflict as insufficient to explain the particular kind of parent-child attachment with which *Coriolanus* presents us.

Coriolanus, Stoller maintains, centers about "phalluses and castration." The play is replete with references to swords, pikes, lances, darts, war, wrath, hatred, hardness, piercing, and fighting. Coriolanus himself is socially stiff, hard, muscular, and he can scarcely refrain from penetrating, either with weapons or with words, everyone he meets. Lurching and charging through the drama, he is driven in a "chronic state of misery" that he "cannot understand or control and from which there is no release." Behind this lurching and charging stands Volumnia. Her son, says Stoller, is the "literal embodiment of her phallus which from infancy she had wished to attain" (both Hofling and Smith, it should be noted, touch upon Volumnia's masculine striving, though in not so explicit a way). But Volumnia's psychology not only stands behind the hero's aggressive, penetrating behavior; it also stands behind what that behavior would finally conceal, namely, fear of impotence and homosexual longing. For Stoller, then, Coriolanus' external character has a defensive function, and this is why the accusations that he is a traitor to the mother-land and a "boy of tears" threaten him so profoundly. "It is apparent," writes the author, "that the hatred and destructiveness within Coriolanus cannot simply be explained on the basis of unconscious oedipal desires.

More than just an intrapsychic struggle with oedipal guilt feelings, this tragedy moves swiftly to a mortal combat between mother and son," a combat that Coriolanus loses. As he gives in to his mother for the last time, he knows he is calling destruction down upon his head. Stoller concludes by asserting that the effect of the tragedy lies in "the universality of the threat that every infant senses—his mother's life-and-death power over him." This is what "reverberates in each person of the audience." Thus psychoanalytic criticism, as reflected in the work of Stoller, finds Shakespeare's last tragedy to be rooted, like his first, in the soil of *Oedipus Rex*.

M. F.

A n essence of poetic art, we are told, is ambiguity.[1] There will, for example, never be a definitive theatrical interpretation of Shakespeare's *Hamlet*. To produce such a play, each director chooses among innumerable possibilities and creates a vision of what the protagonist signifies to him. Each version is but one aspect of a character that can never be wholly defined, much less comprehended. As he searches for the play's meaning—"As Shakespeare must truly have intended it to be"—each interpreter believes he will find the clues Shakespeare surely must have given for an astute interpreter to discover. The last notable interpretation will be *the* definitive production—until the next. In the process, Shakespeare, who is as indefinable as life itself, will have suffered an artificial limitation; and so it proves that the poet's art transcends any interpretation be it on a stage or in an essay like this. The story of the play is the play itself.

To modern critical estimation, ambiguity in art is directly proportional to its enduring value (keeping in mind that what is idiosyncracy in one generation may be universality in the next). *Coriolanus* may well be judged a lesser work than many others of the plays because the central character is less imbued with multiplicity and equivocation of motivation than, for example, Hamlet. Men like Coriolanus are deficient in the richness of their personalities. Stereotyped inhibitions, reaction-formations, and the smell of death give their humanity a two-dimensional quality. This is not a defect of the playwright's art but a defect of nature in the hero. While less enigmatic, this drama is still another example of the poet's capacity to hold the mirror up to nature.

"Shakespearean Tragedy: *Coriolanus*" by Robert J. Stoller. Reprinted with permission from *Psychoanalytic Quarterly,* XXXV (1966), pp. 263-274.

One of the greatest skills of a playwright is the progressive revelation of character. The tragic drama is considered the unfolding of a hidden fatal flaw in the character of the hero. This is certainly true of *Coriolanus,* but there is no unfolding; simply a breaking apart as one would break a stick. The protagonist erupts suddenly swollen with rage into the play.

As Coriolanus makes his entrance his friend, Menenius, is striving to reason with a company of mutinous Citizens, armed with staves, clubs, and other weapons.

> *Men.* Hail, noble Marcius! [Coriolanus]
> *Mar.* Thanks. What's the matter, you dissentious rogues,
> That, rubbing the poor itch of your opinion,
> Make yourselves scabs?
> *First Cit.* We have ever your good word.
> *Mar.* He that will give good words to thee will flatter
> Beneath abhorring. What would you have, you curs,
> That like nor peace nor war? the one affrights you,
> The other makes you proud. He that trusts to you,
> Where he should find you lions, finds you hares;
> Where foxes, geese: you are no surer, no,
> Than is the coal of fire upon the ice,
> Or hailstone in the sun. Your virtue is,
> To make him worthy whose offence subdues him,
> And curse that justice did it. Who deserves greatness
> Deserves your hate; and your affections are
> A sick man's appetite, who desires most that
> Which would increase his evil. . . .
>
> (I.i.167-183)

This is a play that centers about phalluses and castration. The references to swords, pikes, lances, staves, darts, war, Mars, charge, beat, wrath, hate, hard, advance, pierce, fight, are beyond count. We feel the great social stiffness, the muscular and psychological hardness of this man, who can scarcely help himself from penetrating everyone he meets either with his explosive words or with his weapons. It is appropriate that the zenith of his career which wins Marcius his epithet, "Coriolanus," is when singlehandedly he penetrates the gates of the city of Corioli and subdues her.

Along with the majority of Shakespearean commentators I am

guilty of ignoring the multiple sources which influenced Shakespeare's writing. Omitting the prevalent political, religious, or moral influences that may have been determinants—the demands of his varied audience that shaped the form of the plays—the restricted perspective here is that of the psychodynamics of Coriolanus. Certainly Shakespeare was not consciously aware of these dynamics. We know that the great writers did not discover the unconscious; it made itself known through them by their genius. Freud freely acknowledged this debt. It is probable, judging by much of the modern American stage, that a conscious knowledge of psychoanalysis is an insuperable barrier to great creativity. It produces at best beautifully described case reports from which the ambiguity and mystery of man's nature have been removed.

In *Coriolanus,* Shakespeare has created a relationship between a mother and her son which reveals with direct clarity the antecedents of the development of the play and the inevitability of the tragedy. Putney has clearly shown the accuracy of Shakespeare's vision of the dynamics of destruction that energize this tragedy.[2] With this I am in complete agreement, as with Seidenberg and Papathomopoulous—who mention *Coriolanus* in a footnote to an essay on Ajax—in the emphasis placed on the relationship between mother and son.[3]

Coriolanus, lurching and charging through this play, is driven in a chronic state of misery he cannot understand or control and from which there is no release. As one of the causes of such arrogance there is the contribution of the prevailing culture that established with the passage of generations the cachet of an arrogant military hero and aristocrat. As a modern instance we may be reminded that from the end of the twelfth century, when the Order of Teutonic Knights was formed to slaughter the pagans, to our present times, the Prussians preserved through generations a minutely scored choreography for their dance of arrogance: each movement of the head and limbs, the flick of facial muscles, the practiced rasp of the voice—and the cataclysmic consequences.

The inculcation of tradition and character begins in the nursery with one's mother. In *Coriolanus,* Shakespeare documents this explicitly.

> *Vol.* I pray you, daughter, sing; or express yourself in a more comfortable sort. If my son were my husband, I would freelier

rejoice in that absence wherein he won honour than in the
embracements of his bed where he would show most love.
When yet he was but tender-bodied, and the only son of my
womb, when youth with comeliness plucked all gaze his way,
when for a day of kings' entreaties a mother should not sell
him an hour for her beholding, I, considering how honour
would become such a person, that it was no better than picture-
like to hang by the wall, if renown made it not stir, was pleased
to let him seek danger where he was like to find fame. To a
cruel war I sent him; from whence he returned, his brows
bound with oak. I tell thee, daughter, I sprang not more in
joy at first hearing he was a man-child than now in first seeing
he had proved himself a man.

Vir. But had he died in the business, madam, how then?

Vol. Then his good report should have been my son; I therein would
have found issue. Hear me profess sincerely: had I a dozen
sons, each in my love alike, and none less dear than thine and
my good Marcius, I had rather had eleven die nobly for their
country than one voluptuously surfeit out of action.

(I.iii.1-28)

For such a mother, a son is the literal embodiment of her phallus
which from infancy she had wished to attain by one means or another.
Subjected to such relentless pressures, her son may either surrender
and become virtually emasculated, or he may be able partially to
salvage his virility by acting out his mother's fantasy as her surrogate
until his repressed (feminine) identification with her—and his guilt
about his repressed hatred of her—lead him to contrive his destruction.

What Khan has called "cumulative trauma" in the relationship of a
child to his mother is a modern elucidation of what Shakespeare knew
intuitively.[4]

Shakespeare perceived the powerful, passive, feminine striving un-
resolved in such a hero's motivations. Two accusations, to which
Coriolanus reacts with violent denial, unhinge him.

Sic. We charge you, that you have contrived to take
From Rome all season'd office, and to wind
Yourself into a power tyrannical;
For which you are a traitor to the people.

Cor. How! traitor!
Men. Nay, temperately; your promise.
Cor. The fires i' the lowest hell fold-in the people!
    Call me their traitor! Thou injurious tribune!
                    (III.iii.62-69)

We now know that no man could more easily have become a traitor than the one portrayed as Coriolanus. This hero and savior of his people cannot hurry fast enough after he is exiled to submit abjectly to his archenemy, Aufidius, and to offer his services for the destruction of his native city. Shakespeare's language understandably conveys the universal consensus of the transitional equivalence of city, home, and mother.

The second indictment, unmanliness, strikes even closer. Battle-scarred, Coriolanus has been required by custom to display to the citizens his wounds to gain the promotion due him. This he intransigently refuses to do. The importance Shakespeare attached to this can be measured by the great number of lines he gives to this mounting controversy of Coriolanus with the citizens. His insensate refusal to display his wounds ritualistically poses for him an insupportable threat. Shakespeare intuitively knew that wounds for such a man signified castration, and that publicly exposing his body was a phallic exhibitionism—borrowed from his mother—that he could not risk. He defends himself, as noted, by reviling and depreciating the male citizenry as hares rather than lions, and as geese rather than foxes.

          . . . He that depends
Upon your favours swims with fins of lead,
And hews down oaks with rushes.
                  (I.i.183-185)

When, however, his mother astoundingly succeeds in coercing him to submit to simulate humility toward this same rabble, he is suddenly stripped of the armor of his overcompensatory defense. "Must I," he demands, "go show them my unbarbed sconce?" (III.ii.98)

Cor.   . . . Well, I must do't.
    Away, my disposition, and possess me
    Some harlot's spirit! my throat of war be turn'd,
    Which quired with my drum, into a pipe

Small as a eunuch, or the virgin voice
That babies lulls asleep! the smiles of knaves
Tent in my cheeks, and schoolboys' tears take up
The glasses of my sight! a beggar's tongue
Make motion through my lips, and my arm'd knees,
Who bow'd but in my stirrup, bend like his
That hath receiv'd an alms! . . .

(III.ii.110-120)

Aufidius, an uncomplicated realist, is a foil to Coriolanus as Fortin-bras is to Hamlet. He brands Coriolanus again with the charge of being a traitor; he further charges him with the intolerable truth that strips from Coriolanus the fruits of a lifetime of struggle by dis-missing him with an attribute of impotence ". . . thou boy of tears . . ." (V.v.100).

Auf. . . . tell the traitor in the highest degree
He hath abus'd your powers.
Cor.   Traitor! How now!
Auf. Ay, traitor, Marcius.
Cor.   Marcius!
Auf. Ay, Marcius, Caius Marcius. Dost thou think
I'll grace thee with that robbery, thy stol'n name
Coriolanus in Corioli?
You lords and heads o' the state, perfidiously
He has betray'd your business, and given up,
For certain drops of salt, your city Rome,
I say 'your city,' to his wife and mother;
Breaking his oath and resolution like
A twist of rotten silk, never admitting
Counsel o' the war, but at his nurse's tears
He whin'd and roar'd away your victory,
That pages blush'd at him, and men of heart
Look'd wondering each at other.
Cor.   Hear'st thou, Mars?
Auf. Name not the god, thou boy of tears.
Cor.   Ha!
Auf. No more.
Cor. Measureless liar, thou hast **made my** heart
Too great for what contains it. **Boy!** O slave!

Pardon me, lords, 'tis the first time that ever
I was forc'd to scold. Your judgments, my grave lords,
Must give this cur the lie: and his own notion,
Who wears my stripes impress'd upon him; that
Must bear my beating to his grave, shall join
To thrust the lie unto him.

First Lord.   Peace, both, and hear me speak.

  Cor. Cut me to pieces, Volsces; men and lads.
Stain all your edges on me. Boy! False hound!
If you have writ your annals true, 'tis there,
That, like an eagle in a dove-cote, I
Flutter'd your Volscians in Corioli:
Alone I did it. Boy!

(V.v.85-117)

Obviously, this shrill arrogance strives to shout down a passive, feminine sense of himself founded on the only infantile object that was provided him, his mother, for Shakespeare chose to exclude the influence of a father from Coriolanus' life.[5]

It is only more evidence of Shakespeare's genius in understanding his characters that the delineation of Coriolanus' character is completed by some indirect expression of homosexual needs. This is revealed in their first meeting, when, after Coriolanus has come to Aufidus and offered up "My throat to thee and to thy ancient malice," Aufidius responds to this gentle surrender.

  Auf.   O Marcius, Marcius!
Each word thou hast spoke hath weeded from my heart
A root of ancient envy. If Jupiter
Should from yond cloud speak divine things,
And say, 'Tis true,' I'd not believe them more
Than thee, all noble Marcius. Let me twine
Mine arms about that body, where against
My grained ash a hundred times hath broke,
And scarr'd the moon with splinters: here I clip
The anvil of my sword, and do contest
As hotly and as nobly with thy love
As ever in ambitious strength I did
Contend against thy valour. Know thou first,
I lov'd the maid I married; never man

> Sigh'd truer breath; but that I see thee here,
> Thou noble thing! more dances my rapt heart
> Than when I first my wedded mistress saw
> Bestride my threshold.
>
> (IV.v.107-124)

Let us examine further the implications of the evidence that Coriolanus is the product of his mother's influence. (Contemplating the overwhelming Volumnia, we admire Shakespeare's good sense in not creating a father for Coriolanus. Such a father would have only cluttered the stage as he scurried around trying to avoid being eaten by his wife.) She gladly wishes her son dead if he will not fulfill her masculine ambition. We see her using him, both as boy and man, as if he were her's to command. "There is," she says, "no man in the world more bound to's mother" (V.iii.159). She relentlessly incites him to a state of sustained tumescence, of virile achievement, from which he is permitted no relief. Volumnia never stops prodding this swollen battering ram to keep it at full salute. It comes as no surprise that she directly incites him to his doom. She is first responsible for his being driven into exile by her emotional blackmail which forced him to try again to submit to the demands of the populace. Yet his mother's inexorable indoctrination from the cradle rendered him incapable for this very task. In exile, his hatred of his mother causes him to submit to Aufidius for their joint annihilation of Rome. The last scene of all is the destruction of a man whose identity was an insubstantial image of his mother's phallic fantasy. The relentless fatality, the inexorable unconscious determinism is played out. No longer the extension and manipulated agent of her virility, Coriolanus becomes for his mother only a threat to be destroyed to preserve herself from his reprisal. Volumnia plays on every emotion to subjugate him, and her witchcraft prevails. When his vengeful intrigue for the assault on Rome encompasses the destruction of his mother, his wife and son, Volumnia reminds him of this fact, at least as far as it includes her.

> *Vol.*   . . . thou shalt no sooner
>   March to assault thy country than to tread,
>   Trust to't, thou shalt not, on thy mother's womb,
>   That brought thee to this world.
>
> (V.iii.122-125)

It is apparent that the hatred and destructiveness within Coriolanus cannot simply be explained on the basis of unconscious oedipal desires. More than just an intrapsychic struggle with oedipal guilt feelings, this tragedy moves swiftly to a mortal combat between mother and son. It has been stated from the start that Volumnia envisions her son's death as a calculated risk. Having lived with her callous detachment throughout his life, his provocative arrogance attempts to shout down his insight into her power over him; that he cannot dispel his sense of being an impostor is revealed in his embarrassed disclaimer of popular renown.

All. Welcome to Rome, renowned Coriolanus!
Cor. No more of this; it does offend my heart:
　　　Pray now, no more.
　　　　　　　　　　(II.i.184-186)

Thus the latent self-destructiveness of this seeming unassailable tyrant is foreshadowed.

This drama is not the gradual evolution of a conflict between a mother and her son. At the outset Shakespeare made it a combat for survival, the mother's exploitation of the son always in the ascendancy.

The universality of the threat that every infant senses (to which we give the name of separation anxiety)—his mother's life-and-death power over him—reverberates in each person of the audience. This is brought into clear focus by having Volumnia openly express her conscious awareness that her son's life is hers to dispose of as her caprice determines. In such an instance, a mother becomes the "Fate" that can drive her son inexorably to his doom.

The development of the drama closes the roads to safety, until at the climax there is no way out. One or the other must die. The issue is exquisitely balanced but conclusively determined. Mother and son confront each other, *both quite aware that the only choice is whether to die or to kill*. Volumnia has no doubt; she has always been ready for this decision. She tells him he cannot kill her (Rome). She has no doubt what Aufidius will then do to her son. Coriolanus knows that his choice means her life or his.

Cor.　　　　　　　　　　　　　O, mother, mother!
　　　What have you done? Behold! the heavens do ope,

> The gods look down, and this unnatural scene
> They laugh at. O my mother! mother! O!
> You have won a happy victory to Rome;
> But, for your son, believe it, O! believe it,
> Most dangerously you have with him prevail'd,
> If not most mortal to him. But let it come.
>
> (V.iii.182-189)

He knows his master's voice, and for the last time obeys, as always, her command, this time that he be killed.

There are those who assess Coriolanus' love for his wife as his motive for sparing Rome; there is little in the play to give support to this opinion. In the second act as he returns victorious from battle, he sees only his mother to whom he kneels until she says to him: "But, O! thy wife." (II.i.192). When he is exiled from Rome he ignores his wife completely (IV,i). In the few additional encounters Shakespeare gives them, Coriolanus is at best perfunctory when he does not ignore her. The poet would have sensed that, having such a mother, her son could not be devoted to any woman.

Coriolanus may provide us with a clue that gives a partial understanding to all tragedy. In the classical definition, tragedy is the flaw in the hero's character that makes the tragic ending inevitable. Is not, then, tragedy the unfolding of the protagonist's need to suicide, "engineered as a murderous response from the environment"?[6] If so, it is a self-destruction determined by a mortal struggle between homicidal hate and helpless dependence.

Notes

1. OTTO RANK, *Das Inzest-Motiv in Dichtung und Sage* (1912) (Leipzig: Franz Deuticke, 1926), chap. 6; JACKSON E. TOWNE, "A Psychoanalytic Study of Shakespeare's *Coriolanus*," *Psychoanalytic Review,* 8:84-91, 1921.

1. ERNST KRIS and ABRAHAM KAPLAN, "Aesthetic Ambiguity," *Psychoanalytic Explorations in Art* (New York: International Universities Press, 1952).

2. Rufus Putney, "Coriolanus and His Mother," *Psychoanalytic Quarterly, 31*:364-381, 1962.

3. Robert Seidenberg and Evangelos Papathomopoulous, "Sophocles' Ajax—A Morality for Madness," *Psychoanalytic Quarterly, 30*:404-412, 1961.

4. M. Masud R. Kahn, "The Concept of Cumulative Trauma," in Ruth S. Eissler *et al.* (eds.), *The Psychoanalytic Study of the Child* (New York: International Universities Press, 1963), Vol. 18, pp. 286-306. "My aim here is to discuss the function of the mother in her role as a protective shield. This role as a protective shield constitutes 'the average expectable environment' (Hartmann, 1939) for the anaclitic needs of the infant. My argument is that cumulative trauma is the result of the breaches in the mother's role as a protective shield over the whole course of the child's development, from infancy to adolescence—that is to say, in all those areas of experience where the child continues to need the mother as an auxiliary ego to support his immature and unstable ego functions."

5. Shakespeare took the plot of *Coriolanus* from Plutarch, who records that Coriolanus never left his mother's house even during the years of his marriage and parenthood.

6. M. Masud R. Kahn, personal communication.

Histories

On "Richard III"

With the exception of the two Parts of *Henry IV*, *Richard III* is the history play of Shakespeare's that has called forth the greatest amount of psychoanalytic criticism. Behind this stands, of course, the character of Richard Crookback, for although Shakespeare endowed his Richard with a good many stereotyped features of the Elizabethan stage-Machiavelli, he still succeeded in creating one of the West's most interesting villains and one that numerous heads have troubled themselves over for a couple of hundred years. However, not all of the psychoanalytic criticism of *Richard III* deals with the protagonist. Otto Rank, for example, has explored the drama for incest themes;[1] Ernest Jones and Robert Fliess have spent some pages analyzing Clarence's nightmare;[2] and Samuel Tannenbaum has discussed what he takes to be a Freudian slip on the part of Brakenbury, the lieutenant.[3] As for Richard, he has been regarded as an antisocial type,[4] as an exemplification of Adler's concept of organ inferiority (bodily defectiveness leads to devaluation of the self, which leads in turn to compensatory striving),[5] and as an example of the type of individual who is ruined by "success," that is, the type of individual who crumbles when he has succeeded in achieving an objective (as King, Richard is guilt-ridden and erratic, something that he was not when he was striving to be King).[6]

In the selection to follow, Freud not only introduces us to the orthodox psychoanalytic explanation of Richard's personality and conduct but also attempts to clarify why a character such as Richard should be so attractive to nonvillainous types in the audience. Freud begins by pointing out the degree to which Richard reminds us of individuals who behave rebelliously, antisocially, and hence neurotically because they believe themselves to be, somehow, "exceptional." He then turns to Richard's opening soliloquy and contends that its "frivolous" surface actually contains a "hint" as to the hero's true motivation, a hint we in the audience are obliged to "fill in." When we do this, however, the "appearance of frivolity vanishes," leaving us with the feeling "that we ourselves might become like Richard, that on a small scale, indeed, we are already like him."

M. F.

hen . . . one asks the patient to make a provisional renunciation of some pleasurable satisfaction, to make a sacrifice, to show his readiness to accept some temporary suffering for the sake of a better end, or even merely to make up his mind to submit to a necessity which applies to everyone, one comes upon individuals who resist such an appeal on a special ground. They say that they have renounced enough and suffered enough, and have a claim to be spared any further demands; they will submit no longer to any disagreeable necessity, for they are *exceptions* and, moreover, intend to remain so. In one such patient this claim was magnified into a conviction that a special providence watched over him, which would protect him from any painful sacrifices of the sort. The doctor's arguments will achieve nothing against an inner confidence which expresses itself as strongly as this; even *his* influence, indeed, is powerless at first, and it becomes clear to him that he must discover the sources from which this damaging prepossession is being fed.

Now it is no doubt true that everyone would like to consider himself an "exception" and claim privileges over others. But precisely because of this there must be a particular reason, and one not universally present, if someone actually proclaims himself an exception and behaves as such. This reason may be of more than one kind; in the cases I investigated I succeeded in discovering a common peculiarity

"Some Character-Types Met with in Psycho-Analytic Work" by Sigmund Freud. Reprinted from *The Collected Papers of Sigmund Freud,* Chapter XVIII of Volume IV, pp. 320-323, edited by Ernest Jones, with permission of Basic Books, Inc. (1959).

in the earlier experiences of these patients' lives. Their neuroses were connected with some experience or suffering to which they had been subjected in their earliest childhood, one in respect of which they knew themselves to be guiltless, and which they could look upon as an unjust disadvantage imposed upon them. The privileges that they claimed as a result of this injustice, and the rebelliousness it engendered, had contributed not a little to intensifying the conflicts leading to the outbreak of their neurosis. In one of these patients, a woman, the attitude towards life which I am discussing came to a head when she learnt that a painful organic trouble, which had hindered her from attaining her aims in life, was of congenital origin. So long as she looked upon this trouble as an accidental and late acquisition, she bore it patiently; as soon as she found that it was part of an innate inheritance, she became rebellious. The young man who believed that he was watched over by a special providence had in his infancy been the victim of an accidental infection from his wet-nurse, and had spent his whole later life making claims for compensation, an accident pension, as it were, without having any idea on what he based those claims. In his case the analysis, which constructed this event out of obscure mnemic residues and interpretations of the symptoms, was confirmed objectively, by information from his family.

For reasons which will be easily understood I cannot communicate very much about these or other case histories. Nor do I propose to go into the obvious analogy between deformities of character resulting from protracted sickliness in childhood and the behaviour of whole nations whose past history has been full of suffering. Instead, however, I will take the opportunity of pointing to a figure created by the greatest of poets—a figure in whose character the claim to be an exception is closely bound up with and is motivated by the circumstance of congenital disadvantage.

In the opening soliloquy to Shakespeare's *Richard III,* Gloucester, who subsequently becomes King, says:

> But I, that am not shap'd for sportive tricks,
> Nor made to court an amorous looking-glass;
> I, that am rudely stamp'd, and want love's majesty
> To strut before a wanton ambling nymph;
> I, that am curtail'd of this fair proportion,
> Cheated of feature by dissembling nature,

Deform'd, unfinish'd, sent before my time
Into this breathing world, scarce half made up,
And that so lamely and unfashionable,
That dogs bark at me as I halt by them;
. . . .
And therefore, since I cannot prove a lover,
To entertain these fair well-spoken days,
I am determined to prove a villain,
And hate the idle pleasures of these days.

(I.i.14-23,28-31)

At a first glance this tirade may perhaps seem unrelated to our present theme. Richard seems to say nothing more than: "I find these idle times tedious, and I want to enjoy myself. As I cannot play the lover on account of my deformity, I will play the villain; I will intrigue, murder and do anything else I please." Such a frivolous motivation could not but stifle any stirring of sympathy in the audience, if it were not a screen for something much more serious. Otherwise the play would be psychologically impossible, for the writer must know how to furnish us with a secret background of sympathy for his hero, if we are to admire his boldness and adroitness without inward protest; and such sympathy can only be based on understanding or on a sense of a possible inner fellow-feeling for him.

I think, therefore, that Richard's soliloquy does not say everything; it merely gives a hint, and leaves us to fill in what it hints at. When we do so, however, the appearance of frivolity vanishes, the bitterness and minuteness with which Richard has depicted his deformity make their full effect, and we clearly perceive the fellow-feeling which compels our sympathy even with a villain like him. What the soliloquy thus means is: "Nature has done me a grievous wrong in denying me the beauty of form which wins human love. Life owes me reparation for this, and I will see that I get it. I have a right to be an exception, to disregard the scruples by which others let themselves be held back. I may do wrong myself, since wrong has been done to me." And now we feel that we ourselves might become like Richard, that on a small scale, indeed, we are already like him. Richard is an enormous magnification of something we find in ourselves as well. We all think we have reason to reproach Nature and our destiny for congenital and infantile disadvantages; we all demand reparation for early wounds to our narcissism, our self-love. Why did not Nature give us the golden curls of Balder or the strength of Siegfried or the lofty brow of genius or the noble profile of aristocracy? Why were we born in a middle-class home instead of in a royal palace? We would carry off beauty and distinction quite as well as any of those whom we are now obliged to envy for these qualities.

It is, however, a subtle economy of art in the poet that he does not permit his hero to give open and complete expression to all his secret motives. By this means he obliges us to supplement them; he engages our intellectual activity, diverts it from critical reflection and keeps us firmly identified with his hero. A bungler in his place would give conscious expression to all that he wishes to reveal to us, and would then find himself confronted by our cool, untrammelled intelligence, which would preclude any deepening of the illusion.

Notes

1. OTTO RANK, *Das Inzest-Motiv in Dichtung und Sage* (1912) (Leipzig: Franz Deuticke, 1926), pp. 69n., 123n., 208, and 211-212.
2. ERNEST JONES, *On the Nightmare* (London: Hogarth Press, 1931), p. 20; ROBERT FLIESS, *The Revival of Interest in the Dream* (New York: International Universities Press, 1953), pp. 134, 152.
3. SAMUEL TANNENBAUM, "Slips of the Tongue," *Shakespeare Studies* (New York: The Author, 1930).
4. See CHARLES A. ADLER, "Richard III—His Significance as a Study in Criminal Life-Style," *International Journal of Individual Psychology*, 2:55-60, 1936.
5. IRA S. WILE, "Some Shakespearean Characters in the Light of Present Day Psychologies," *Psychiatric Quarterly*, 16:62-90, 1942.
6. GERALD H. ZUK, "A Note on Richard's Anxiety Dream," *American Imago*, 14:37-39, 1957.

The Dark Generations of "Richard III"

Murray Krieger's essay is, among other things, a fine example of how Freud's basic insights, usually expressed in brief compass and in a kind of passing fashion, have given rise to detailed, comprehensive treatments of Shakespeare's creations. Although Krieger is concerned chiefly with the character of Richard, his paper ultimately achieves a remarkable integration of elements in that it meticulously traces the impact of Richard's psychology upon the rest of the cast, as well as upon the universe of the play as a whole. In this regard it reminds us of the work of Holland, Barron, Kanzer, and others, where psychoanalytic angles are worked out in such a manner as to deepen our appreciation of the total drama. The implication, of course, is that it may be inadvisable to talk, as many still do, about the "purely literary" or the "purely psychological" dimensions of a play.

According to Krieger, Richard's "will to political power is not merely a substitute for his frustrated will to sexual power," as Freud recognized; it is a "perversion of it" as well, so that "sexual elements become curiously intermingled with political ones." Although Richard is tormented by his "incapacities as a lover," he actually "welcomes" and even "relishes" the torment. "He parades his deformity before women even as he parades it before himself. And he takes an 'underground' delight in both displays." After examining the manner in which Richard woos such women as Anne and Elizabeth (the Queen's daughter), women who are instrumental in his quest for power, Krieger concludes that Richard not only "pursues power as single-mindedly as he would a mistress, but also that he pursues power so that he may coerce a mistress—one who will have to play the game of treating him as a lover and who, though it only aggravates her revulsion, will painfully sport with him as with one 'fram'd in the prodigality of nature.' " But why do the women accept Richard in the first place? Because they too are hypocrites. In the world of *Richard III* "there are no innocents," writes Krieger; and Richard, far from being an alien force in that world, is simply a distillation and purified symbol of its corruption and evil. Richard is a "self-conscious and consistent version of the other characters" who "cannot bear to witness in [him] the logical consequence of their own tendencies." Thus the prophecies and curses that pervade the entire play are linked to the degeneration of England as a nation, not to Richard as an individual. Indeed, Richard must ultimately be regarded as the personification of the interfamilial blood bath that had been going on in England for a good many years. For Krieger, then, the drama's "ritual of lamentation" carries us back "to those other dramas of lust and blood and Nemesis, to those extended cycles about family and domain with which Western tragedy began. Perhaps it is with Greek tragedy, rather than with Marlowe or even Seneca, that *Richard III* has its most essential and most intimate connections."

M. F.

et me begin by remarking that I had half-jestingly thought of calling this essay "Richard III as Scourge and Purge." Not a highly serious way to begin a study of a work of the highest seriousness; but it should immediately indicate that I intend to break radically with the conventional treatments of the play as a Marlovian tragedy, even with those that allow the master Shakespeare a few extensions of the formula in his manipulation of it. For if we call Richard a scourge, then we are assuming that his victims somewhat deserve what he inflicts upon them; that they have been cruelly active themselves even if at the hands of Richard they are now rendered passive. And if we call him a purge, then we are assuming that he is in the service of the gods of a righteous future who must start afresh; that a guilt-ridden past, with all its weighty burdens, must be cast off by one of its own. If we think of Richard in these ways, then it is clear that the play is not uniquely his, nor the power and the evil uniquely his, as the Marlovian formula would have it.[1]

Even looking only at Richard's motivations, however, we find more than is in the world of Marlovian psychology. One need hardly invoke the insights of Freud to see that the lust which impels him is not solely directed toward power. Admittedly, one can point to his opening soliloquy where—in a Marlovian manner which denies the possibility of self-deception and the psychological complexity that goes with it— he announces his villain's role and his prideful assumption of it. Indeed one can strike this note earlier, as early as his perhaps finer soliloquy in *III Henry VI* (III.ii.124-195). Richard, then, does confront his villainy with a consciousness as candid as the actions which ensue from his villainy are consistent. But there is another and a less conscious motive being continually revealed in these speeches. He invariably couples the assertion of political power with the sexual assertion of manliness. And he admits that he embraces the former only because he is, as monster, denied the embrace of sexual love.

Early in the soliloquy from *III Henry VI* Richard despairs of ever attaining the crown as he lists those who would precede him in the line of succession. Well, then, he must turn to another source of masculine satisfaction: "I'll make my heaven in a lady's lap." But the dialectic proceeds:

> O miserable thought! and more unlikely
> Than to accomplish twenty golden crowns.
> Why, love forswore me in my mother's womb:
> And, for I should not deal in her soft laws,
> She did corrupt frail nature with some bribe, . . .
> (III.ii.151-155)

There is no alternative, then. However impossible to attain, it must be power after all: "I'll make my heaven to dream upon the crown." In the opening soliloquy of *Richard III* he notes that the advent of peace demands that the warrior be transformed into the lover. Significantly, it is by a sexual image that he describes the warrior, so that the role as lover may follow naturally from the battle's end. The image tells us something also of Richard's deeper motives in the public life as well as in the private life.

> Grim-visag'd war hath smooth'd his wrinkled front;
> And now, instead of mounting barbed steeds
> To fright the souls of fearful adversaries,
> He capers nimbly in a lady's chamber
> To the lascivious pleasing of a lute.
> (I.i.9-13)

It is clear from Richard's language that he dotes, perhaps perversely, on the sensual abandon in the battle of love—on the "sportive tricks" one plays with "a wanton ambling nymph." And again he decides there is nothing left for him but "to prove a villain" since he "cannot prove a lover."

His villainy seems to him to be chargeable to the heavens since it is but a moral reflection of his deformity.

> The midwife wonder'd, and the women cried
> "O! Jesus bless us. He is born with teeth!"
> And so I was; which plainly signified
> That I should snarl and bite and play the dog.
> Then, since the heavens have shap'd my body so,
> Let hell make crook'd my mind to answer it.
> I have no brother, I am like no brother;
> And this word "love," which greybeards call divine,
> Be resident in men like one another,
> And not in me: I am myself alone.
> (*III Henry VI*, V.vi.74-83)

But if he is not a man among men, neither, of course, is he a beast. He may "play the dog," but he does so as a monstrous perversion of man. As he answers Anne, who insists that even the fiercest beast knows pity, "But I know none, and therefore am no beast" (*Richard III*, I.ii.72). A unique monster, then, excluded from the order of men as from the order of beasts, he sees himself indeed as representing a gap in nature, a lump of chaos thrust into the midst of the natural order. And so he will do the business of chaos in the political and moral order. This dedication to chaos, physical and political, stirs him from his early soliloquy,

> [Love] did corrupt frail nature with some bribe,
> To shrink mine arm up like a wither'd shrub;
> To make an envious mountain on my back,
> Where sits deformity to mock my body;
> To shape my legs of an unequal size;
> To disproportion me in every part,
> Like a chaos, or an unlick'd bear-whelp
> That carries no impression like the dam.
> (*III Henry VI*, III.ii.155-162)

to the speech before his final battle:

March on, join bravely, let us to 't pell-mell;
If not to heaven, then hand in hand to hell.
                    (*Richard III*, V.iii.312-313)

And since force is the arm of chaos even as right is the sometimes feeble arm of order, so must he dedicate himself to force as well. It should be clear, however, that, far from being his essential motivation, force, like the power to which it leads, is a very derivative one. Shakespeare's probing instruments are too delicate to stop, with Marlowe, short of cutting away a little lower layer.

But there is even more psychological complexity than this to Richard. His will to political power is not merely a substitute for his frustrated will to sexual power, but, as his "mounting" warrior may have intimated, is a perversion of it so that sexual elements become curiously intermingled with political ones. His incapacities as a lover continue to torment him, but he welcomes and even relishes the torment. He parades his deformity before women even as he parades it before himself. And he takes an "underground" delight in both displays. His dialogue with Anne is a brilliant manifestation of this strange exhibitionism. Surely we cannot account for Richard's behavior in this scene solely on the grounds of his lust for power. Granted that Richard feels this marriage to be a political necessity (as he tells us, I.i.157-159), that by their union the houses of York and Lancaster can be joined; nevertheless he hardly undertakes his wooing in a way that will ensure success. On the contrary he seems to enjoy this occasion since it presents every conceivable obstacle. It is the most inauspicious moment for him to woo her. Further, he makes it perfectly clear (I.i.160-162) that other foul deeds remain to be done before the marriage can serve its purpose; in other words, that there is no rush about wooing Anne, that he can await a more favorable opportunity.

Let us note the circumstances of the present occasion: Anne is the mourner in the funeral procession of her father-in-law, Henry VI, murdered by Richard, as Anne knows. And it is still but very little more time since the death of her husband whom Richard co-murdered (*III Henry VI*, V.v). Of course, Richard's physical handicaps, in such marked contrast to Anne's murdered Edward—"fram'd in the prodigality of nature," as Richard disdainfully acknowledges—will always damage his chances; but they surely should prompt him to seek out a better time, if success is his primary objective. But both before and after the scene Richard indicates his special pleasure in wooing her at such a disadvantage. And he begins in the worst way possible, by forcibly interrupting the funeral procession, by allowing the conversation to enter those channels which must render him most hateful to Anne, by leading her to engage with him in a repartee that is on his side callously witty. His bantering appears calculated to inspire in her a loathing that must issue in her humiliating outcry, "thou lump of foul deformity." His love of self-torture having accomplished this much, he pursues her, still as her lover lest her revulsion abate. He speaks of the fitness of Henry VI for heaven and she, of Richard's for hell. Richard insists there is one other place for which he is fit:

Anne. Some dungeon.
Rich.   Your bedchamber.
Anne. Ill rest betide the chamber where thou liest!
Rich. So will it, madam, till I lie with you.
(I.ii.111-113)

At this point fair Richard has turned Petrarchan lover. He blames Anne's beauty for his murderous actions, and when she threatens to destroy that beauty, like the sonneteer he answers,

> These eyes could not endure that beauty's wreck;
> You should not blemish it, if I stood by:
> As all the world is cheered by the sun,
> So I by that; it is my day, my life.
> (I.ii.127-130)

When she wishes that her eyes were basilisks to strike him dead, he again has the appropriate retort, even using the appropriate conceit:

> I would they were, that I might die at once;
> For now they kill me with a living death.
> (I.ii.152-153)

Having won her, Richard matches his contempt for her with his pride in himself.

> Was ever woman in this humour woo'd?
> Was ever woman in this humour won?
> I'll have her; but I will not keep her long.

What! I, that kill'd her husband and his father,
To take her in her heart's extremest hate;
With curses in her mouth, tears in her eyes,
The bleeding witness of her hatred by;
Having God, her conscience, and these bars against me,
And I no friends to back my suit withal,
But the plain devil and dissembling looks,
And yet to win her, all the world to nothing!
                                (I.ii.128-138)

And his perverse self-mockery returns. If in spite of all these obstacles he has won the right to succeed his handsome predecessor, then,
he ironically reasons, he must suppose himself to have underestimated
his sexual attractiveness all along. He shall have to get mirrors and
tailors to care for his fine figure and make a proper lover. In the
opening soliloquy of the play he remarked that in this time of peace
he, as a warrior who could not be a lover, had

> . . . no delight to pass away the time,
> Unless to see my shadow in the sun
> And descant on mine own deformity.
>   (I.i.25-27)

Now he closes the soliloquy which follows his success with Anne by
reverting to this idea, this time with the bitterness only renewed by
his amatory conquest:

> Shine out, fair sun, till I have bought a glass,
> That I may see my shadow as I pass.
>   (I.ii.263-264)

   Toward the end of the play there is the similar scene with Queen
Elizabeth when he woos her for her daughter's hand. Again he chooses
the worst possible time since, his murder of her children having only
recently occurred, she has come with his mother to join in cursing him.
Again he seems to succeed and again his success produces in him only
contempt for her. Does it not appear possible, then, not merely that
Richard pursues power as single-mindedly as he would a mistress, but
also that he pursues power so that he may coerce a mistress—one
who will have to play the game of treating him as lover and who,

though it only aggravates her revulsion, will painfully sport with him as with one "fram'd in the prodigality of nature?" And in self-laceration Richard will enjoy it both ways: because his villainous intelligence has forced his mistress to receive him as lover and because his monstrous ugliness increases her horror and his pain in his unnatural role. Surely this is hardly a hero-villain of a single dimension.

I should like now to return briefly to the scene between Richard and Anne in order to ask an obvious question, one answer to which I find most illuminating. How is it, in view of Richard's handicaps of person and occasion and in view of his tactics, that Anne accepts him? We may ask a similar question about Elizabeth in the other scene I referred to—if we assume that she was sincere in her acceptance of him, an assumption that her later acceptance of Richmond makes doubtful for some readers. And we may ask similar questions about many other characters, some of them mostly openly at odds with Richard, who at times seem not to see through his transparent dissembling. Rivers, for example, whom Richard is shortly to dispose of, commends a sentiment of Richard's as "virtuous" and "Christian-like"; and Hastings, just before he learns that Richard has condemned him to death, says of Richard after observing his apparent good humor,

> I think there's never a man in Christendom
> Can lesser hide his love or hate than he;
> For by his face straight shall you know his heart.
> (III.iv.53-55)

The usual answer to these questions seems unacceptable. If we take these characters at their face value, then Shakespeare is asking us to believe the unbelievable: that otherwise intelligent and sometimes brilliant characters (his women, for example, prove their brilliance in their repartee with Richard) are somehow fooled by an open hypocrite who has continually proved a villain even before the events of the play begin. Even if there were no other instance of this but the scene with Anne, does it not seem preposterous that Shakespeare would try to foist it upon his audience? Nor can the insistence upon Shakespeare's youth and inexperience in this early play and upon the improbabilities encouraged by Elizabethan dramatic convention explain away so irresponsible an attitude toward dramatic propriety.

The alternative explanation is obvious. These characters know from first to last that Richard is a villain, so that they are never fooled by him. What they do they do in full knowledge of the truth. If they appear to be convinced by any poses he assumes, it is because they themselves are playing the hypocrite's role. Much of the difficulty in interpreting the play arises from an inability to recognize the villainy that pervades the entire stage. Perhaps once again it is because we have been too quick to see the play as if it were written by Marlowe, with a hero-villain gigantically alone in an inexorable surge which drowns all the innocents in his path. I shall eventually suggest that in *Richard III* there are no innocents; that rather than intruding himself as an alien force into the world of the play, Richard is a purified and thus extreme symbol, a distillation, of that world; that the evil stems not from Richard but from a history he shares with the others even if it finds its essential representative in him. Even the young princes, still children and thus still unsinning, must share with their forebears the burden of guilt.

The answer which common-sense dictates—that the characters are not taken in by Richard but, consciously or unconsciously, must be engaging in deception themselves—finds support at several points in the play. It finds support, for example, in those minor and yet telling scenes in which Shakespeare lets us see what political facts are so obvious that even the common man is aware of them. Thus in a discussion of the affairs of the commonwealth by a group of citizens, one of them simply states, "O! full of danger is the Duke of Glou-cester" (II.iii.27). Even more precisely to the point, we find a scrivener commenting on the published report of Hastings' indictment issued after his execution in order to justify it:

> Here's a good world the while! Who is so gross
> That cannot see this palpable device?
> Yet who so bold, but says he sees it not?
> Bad is the world; and will come to nought,
> When such ill dealing must be seen in thought.
> (III.vi.10-14)

We are evidently being informed here of the deception, however en-forced, which pervades the court. Surely we must acknowledge that what the scrivener and even the "gross" cannot help but see, the high characters of the play must see. Hastings himself, conscious that his pretended trust in Richard, quoted in part above, did not save his head, says in comment and in warning to the still remaining fawners as he is led off to execution, "They smile at me who shortly shall be dead" (III.iv.109). He is recalling, no doubt, his own recent satisfaction in hearing of the execution of Rivers, Grey, and Vaughan, when he, still seemingly beguiled by Richard, could confidently mock (even as we know he himself has already been marked for execution) :

> But I shall laugh at this a twelve-month hence,
> That they which brought me in my master's hate,
> I live to look upon their tragedy.
>
> (III.ii.57-59)

Finally, it is quite likely that the confessed villainy and hypocrisy of Richard's first victim in the play, "false, fleeting, perjur'd Clarence," set the precedent for our moral evaluation of those who follow.

Richard, then, is a fox among foxes. He is wittier than the others and more successful. But his victories can be attributed not so much to the fact that he is more villainous than the rest, as to the fact that he is more consistently and self-admittedly villainous. Whatever reason Anne may give herself or him, she can accept him as successor to her sweet and lovely gentleman, his victim, for but one reason—her self-interest. A widow of the ousted House of Lancaster, she must sense that the ruthless Richard's star is rising. Thus she is serious in her toying acknowledgment to Richard, ". . . you teach me how to flatter you" (I.ii.224). Disdaining the bitter role of her mother-in-law, Queen Margaret, she must instead take Richard, swallowing her curses and pretending to have been successfully wooed—which is of course precisely the game that Richard expects her to play and that his perverseness, as we have seen, demands that she play. It is one of the satisfactions he seeks in power. We must either believe this or believe not only in her apparent conviction that "the murderous Machiavel" has turned Petrarchan lover but also in her apparent desire for him, deformity and all.

Elizabeth is later equally politic in her reception of Richard's addresses to her daughter. One may argue that she is merely putting him off for the moment since she has intended her daughter for Richmond, as we learn in the next scene. But there is no evidence in her scene with Richard that she need fear him, nor does she fear him; for she is as outspoken as she pleases. Why, then, pretend to accept him? Why, having come to curse, does she remain to welcome his addresses?

Is it not more likely that, with Richard still in power and Richmond's venture surely questionable at best, she will play it safe and mother a queen regardless of the victor? So she pretends to be won by Richard's oath (IV.iv.397-417) and by his promised moral conversion.

And so it is with the others of his victims who play at being deceived by him. But like Anne and Elizabeth, these others have moral pretensions as well. We see these pretensions on display frequently: for example, in the solicitous mannerisms of the court (I.iii and II.i) and in the self-righteousness of the lamenting women (IV.iv.). It may be that there is this difference between Richard's seeming hypocrisy and theirs. Richard's is only seeming; theirs is real. When Richard insists that he "cannot flatter and look fair," that as "a plain man" he wants only to "live and think no harm"; when he chides himself for being "too childish-foolish for this world," he knows he is in no danger of being believed. He is laughing at his pose and at their reception of it (often explicitly in an aside), knowing that as deceivers themselves they must play the game with a straight face. His wit enables him to delight in the farce as he forces them to appear to accept the most outrageous of his moralizing utterances. In short, while the others are pretending at being decent, Richard is rather pretending at being a hypocrite. No thorough-going and utterly unscrupulous villain need actually be one.

Richard would seem to be a self-conscious and consistent version of the other characters. They cannot bear to witness in Richard the logical consequence of their own tendencies—which is perhaps another reason that they often rush to accept his pretended pretensions. Nor can they endure to live with this purified reflection of their self-destructive instincts—which may metaphorically justify the fact that so many of them fall prey to him. Each falls prey to his own worst self. Anne is perhaps a perfect symbol here. Early in the action, as we learn more explicitly later, she is led by her personal and political ills to curse Richard and his future wife. It is of course herself she has damned: the torment she suffers while alive, and the unnatural death which it is implied she suffers, are inflicted by Richard only insofar as he is her agent carrying out her curse.

There are yet other indications of the unrelieved ugliness of the world of *Richard III*. Some of those who defend the Marlovian character of the play cite its humorlessness as evidence. No low-comedy vaudeville routines seem to be found here. But this is only a superficial view. For example, the scene between the two murderers as they confront each other and then Clarence (I.iv) has all the earmarks of such a routine. We may miss the similarities because of the morbidity of the occasion: it is, after all, cold-blooded fratricide that is being committed. This stark reality may nag at us and mar our enjoyment of the quips leading to the brilliantly cynical discourse on conscience which may well rival Falstaff's on honor in *I Henry IV*. But this is precisely Shakespeare's point, I take it. While much of the scene takes the form of so-called comic relief, it is a bitter perversion of this device. The scene indicates what has become of humor in the world Shakespeare creates here: it is a humor bitterly transformed to callous irony, a humor too chill to sustain even a suggestion of human warmth.

In the witty dialogue between the murderers all moral values are inverted. Conscience, "a dangerous thing," finally becomes "the devil," so that to obey it and spare Clarence is now a diabolical act. To resist it and murder Clarence is to be "a tall man that respects thy reputation." The lively and biting duels of wit between Richard and Anne and between Richard and Elizabeth are of course other examples of these fearful analogues to comic routines. They may even suggest to us, in an unguarded moment, the brilliance of Benedick and Beatrice in *Much Ado*. Even the terrifying moment of Queen Margaret's systematic and all-inclusive curse is not immune to Richard's ready and deadly wit (I.iii.233-240). He toys with her at the height of her ritualistic fervor until, deflated, she weakly pleads with him, "O, let me make a period to my curse!" And even here his bantering does not stop.

There is bitter humor too in those moments when Richard turns his wit on himself in his public poses, although, of course, always in an aside or a soliloquy. When, responsible for it himself, he speaks forgivingly of those who have caused the imprisonment of his brother Clarence, Rivers congratulates him:

> A virtuous and a Christian-like conclusion,
> To pray for them that have done scath to us.
> (I.iii.316-317)

Richard says aloud, "So do I ever." To himself he adds, "Being well-advis'd; For had I curs'd now, I had curs'd myself." Always there is this final bitter twist. We can argue about whether all this ought to go by the name of humor or comedy, but the term is not important. It is important, however, to note that these passages are analogous to what in many other plays seems more properly comic and, therefore, that this brutal wit is as close to the comic as Shakespeare can come in the infernal world he is creating. It is true to this world and, in its differences from his wit elsewhere, it tells us much about the moral darkness through which his characters wander to their deaths—symbolically self-inflicted through Richard, one of their own.

There is yet a rather evident argument for the general viciousness of the characters; but it is an argument which is conclusive. It asserts its force as early as Act I, Scene iii, when Queen Margaret appears and interrupts the self-righteous and yet haggling claims and counterclaims of the members of the royal court. And since to some extent she is Chorus as well as Nemesis, we must give credence to her characterization of them:

> Hear me, you wrangling pirates, that fall out
> In sharing that which you have pill'd from me!
> Which of you trembles not that looks on me?
> If not, that, I am queen, you bow like subjects,
> Yet that, by you depos'd, you quake like rebels?
> (I.iii.158-161)

There is another reason why we should be especially moved by her words. She is, after all, the widow of the last king of the now deposed Lancastrian line, the line dear to the hearts of the Elizabethans who associated the Tudors intimately with it; and she is addressing the far less favored Yorkists. They are, then, usurpers all, and all fall under her curse. Strangely, although it is Richard whom she most detests and most heatedly condemns, it is he who becomes the instrument of her vengeance. True, she cannot rest content until he is also fallen (IV.iv.71-78). But before this final prayer for his death Margaret has recounted the murderous services which Richard, the Yorkist to end Yorkists, has performed for her; she has, in effect, thanked God for him.

> O upright, just, and true-disposing God,
> How do I thank thee, that this carnal cur
> Preys on the issue of his mother's body,
> And makes her pew-fellow with others' moan.
> (IV.iv. 55-58)

So Richard does serve, in part, as an arm of Lancastrian justice.

But our problem is not so simple or so simply factional. For neither Margaret nor the Lancastrian cause is, after all, much less vicious than the Yorkist. We hear in the play about the previous curse laid on Margaret by Richard's father, the nobler Richard, Duke of York. It is the success of this curse which leads her to match it with her own. When we turn back to *III Henry VI* (I.iv), the circumstances which lead to York's curse frighten us with what they reveal of Margaret's unrestrained cruelty in her days of power. She is a termagant in the earlier play. Hers is a ruthlessness to match the later Richard's: she merits the curses she brings down upon herself as Richard merits his. We can, then, look to the Lancastrian—the injured party, the summoner of vengeance, in *Richard III*—for moral righteousness no more than we can look to the Yorkists for it. If Margaret's curses settle our judgment of the Yorkists, immediate history as revealed in *III Henry VI* makes up our minds similarly about their predecessors.

History indeed holds the answer to all questions about the moral atmosphere of the play—or rather Shakespeare's dramatic version of history in the *Henry VI* plays which precede *Richard III* and in the plays from *Richard II* through *Henry V* to which he turned shortly after *Richard III*. It seems reasonable to assume that Shakespeare, after *Richard III,* followed history back to Richard II in order to trace the origin and the course of the troubles that culminate in the War of the Roses and that—from the viewpoint of the confident Elizabethans—are removed with the death of the remover, Richard III, and with the advent of the Tudors. Shakespeare appears to have viewed English political history from the fall of Richard II until the rise of Henry VII as a single drama; and it is rewarding for us briefly to do so even though Shakespeare produced the first four sections after he had completed the final four. It is the usurpation-theme which dominates the plays. The unruly, destructive forces unleashed by Bolingbroke roar uncontrolled through the land. What the eminently practical and calculating Bolingbroke meant to be a slight and limited blood-letting for the health of the state becomes a blood-bath which drowns generation after generation. Finally Richard III, the blood-bath personified in its purest form, cleanses the land of the last of the guilt-ridden generations, so that with his own bloody end England may begin anew with Henry Tudor, symbol of the conciliation of the past and its feuds. We see, then, why the world of this play must be so unqualifiedly ugly. It is worth noting too that England's salvation, Richmond, must come from outside, from France, like a breath of fresh air, since this world of England is so entirely foul.

As there is this spatial gap between bloody England and the forces of a new day, so in the beginning there was the temporal gap of a generation between the last of those who had a sound view of kingship and those, like Richard II and Bolingbroke, who courted national ill-health. In *Richard II,* only Gaunt and York, the last of the older generation, of the "seven vials" "of Edward's sacred blood," have a full and traditional sense both of the obligations owing to kingship and of the obligations owed by kingship. Richard II, with a decadent version of absolutism, is selfishly aware only of the former of these obligations. Bolingbroke, a modern who has broken with the absolutist principle, has no principle of governmental order to which to appeal except force and expedience; and these are hardly principles conducive to lasting order. Thus he usurps. And, unable to replace the dogma of divine right with another that would equally symbolize the maintenance of the state as an orderly and continuing establishment, he cannot re-order the chaos he has loosed.[2] Nor can those who follow, and blood begets blood.

It may hardly be original to state that Shakespeare relates analogically the traditional views of reason and emotion in the individual to those of order and chaos in the state. But it may be more original to use this analogy in order to establish the extent to which Richard III symbolizes his political and moral milieu. We need say little about the chaos which for Shakespeare must join with usurpation as ruler, upon the deposition of a rightful king—symbol of reason in the state— except to point to Ulysses' famous speech about cosmic, political, and psychological order in *Troilus and Cressida* (I.iii.75-137). Toward the end of this speech is the intimation that when reason is perverted through enslavement to emotion, an overthrow of the proper hierarchy has occurred—a usurpation of mental authority and an introduction of chaos in the individual personality. It is the extremity mentioned in *Venus and Adonis* (792), "When reason is the bawd to lust's abuse." But to return to the words of Ulysses concerned with the loss of order:

> Force should be right; or rather, right and wrong,
> Between whose endless jar justice resides,
> Should lose their names, and so should justice too.
> Then every thing includes itself in power,
> Power into will, will into appetite;
> And appetite, an universal wolf,
> So doubly seconded with will and power,
> Must make perforce an universal prey,
> And last eat up himself.
>   (*Troilus and Cressida*, I.iii.116-124)

But are these lines not a fine description of Richard as I delineated him earlier? Richard is surely the darling of almost a century of English history which has seized upon him and created in him a reflection of itself: he is an incarnation of the spirit of usurpation and thus of chaos. And we saw at the outset that he is, almost literally, a lump of chaos, physical and political, whose very existence defies the natural order. If chaos in the state reflects politically the perversion of the proper government of emotion, then we should expect this perversion in Richard. And we saw earlier too that in Richard the two most forceful emotions, the will to sexual power and the will to political power, are seriously perverted. Finally in Richard we have a brilliance of intellect, but criminally distorted in order to serve his perverse desires—again just what is required of usurpation incarnate.

But if history realizes itself in Richard as its representative, it also uses him—the embodied perfection of its horrors—to purge the world of itself, to end its reign. In a way English history is thus converted to eschatology with Richmond and the Tudors representing a Second Coming which gives birth to the golden world. I have already noted that Richmond returns from another country to be England's salvation. Only under his aegis, according to Elizabeth, can Dorset be safe "from the reach of hell" (IV.i.43). Richmond, who looms throughout the play as a source of help from afar, in effect plays the Saviour, even as the saintly if ineffectual Henry VI has served, like John the Baptist, to prophesy his dominion.

The spirit of usurpation and of chaos has been abroad in varying degrees among all of Shakespeare's characters after the deposition of

Richard II. Thus Richard III, as we have seen, is their symbol too—
a fearful projection of that worst self which they never dare confront.
And for them to confront it reflected in Richard—as many of them
have to—is usually fatal, since they are overcome by the unrelieved
darkness of its aspect.

There is one final way in which the deadly weight of history enters
the play: it asserts itself as ritual. The force of the dark generations
past is felt especially through their curses. And the curse is a formalized affair, as we have seen from Margaret's insistence on giving it a
proper ending. It must be formalized into ritual if, as a form of magic,
it is to be efficacious. It invariably is efficacious. Margaret's extended
curse contributes a structural framework to the play. In it she dis-
penses the fates of almost all the characters. The subsequent action is
constructed largely in order to see her curse realized as, one after
another, its objects succumb. Shakespeare induces us to keep count of
them as her victims by the use of various devices: for example, by
inserting brief pre-execution scenes in which the power of the curse is
explicitly attested, and even once by having her reappear to calculate
her bloody gains. And, in the realm of ritual and magic, the victims
are hers rather than Richard's; for Richard is also her victim, one who
is sufficiently destructive before turning self-destructive. I have already
noted that Anne's earlier curse, of which we do not learn fully until
considerably later, works only too well. Although it comes finally to be
aimed at herself as well as at Richard, the curse once spoken cannot be
unsaid nor its effects neutralized. Even the Duchess of York, the widow
who matches in generation the Lancastrian widow (even as Elizabeth
matches Anne), must add her curse to the others her son must bear.
And the night before Bosworth the ghosts of Richard's victims deliver,
again in proper form, the final curse, the same curse that Faustus had
delivered upon himself: "Despair and die!" They also bless Richmond
and, since they represent York as well as Lancaster, they put the seal
of reconciliation on the House of Tudor. For example, the ghosts of
the Yorkist princes say to the sleeping Richmond,

> Live, and beget a happy race of kings!
> Edward's unhappy sons do bid thee flourish.
>
> (V.iii.157-158)

But Margaret's is not the first curse in the play. We have seen that it is inspired by what has seemed to be the efficacy of York's earlier curse in *III Henry VI*. If his curse has bereft her of power and family, then why should she not answer it with one aimed at those who have been the executioners of his curse? With Margaret's curse reaching for its precedent back into the history that precedes the action of the play, it seems as if we could trace curse upon curse back through the bloody generations to Richard II. And when we turn to *Richard II* (written, of course, not long after *Richard III*), we find at the very start of civil strife speeches by Richard (III.iii.85-100) and by Carlisle (IV.i.136-149) which are half prophecy of the bloodshed ahead and half curse calling for it.

There is another form of ritual in the play—the lamentation of the women and children. It is a competitive telling over of their woes, which, since they are of royal blood, are the woes of history. It takes the form of a stylized, chant-like rivalry of grief among those left by the dark generations to linger on the stage. A simple passage will reveal how rigidly formalized it can be:

Q. Eliz. Give me no help in lamentation;
      I am not barren to bring forth complaints:
      All springs reduce their currents to mine eyes
      That I, being govern'd by the watery moon,
      May send forth plenteous tears to drown the world!
      Ah! for my husband, for my dear lord Edward.
Chil. Ah! for our father, for our dear lord Clarence.
Duch. Alas! for both, both mine, Edward and Clarence.
Q. Eliz. What stay had I but Edward? and he's gone.
Chil. What stay had we but Clarence? and he's gone.
Duch. What stays had I but they? and they are gone.
Q. Eliz. Was never widow had so dear a loss.
Chil. Were never orphans had so dear a loss.
Duch. Was never mother had so dear a loss.
      Alas! I am the mother of these griefs:
      Their woes are parcell'd, mine is general.
      She for an Edward weeps, and so do I;
      I for a Clarence weep, so doth not she;

These babes for Clarence weep, and so do I;
I for an Edward weep, so do not they:
Alas! you three on me, threefold distress'd,
Pour all your tears, I am your sorrow's nurse,
And I will pamper it with lamentation.

(II.ii.66-88)

There is no need to comment at length about the echoes and refrains in the passage, its symmetry, the effective closing of its first and last lines with the word "lamentation." Similar comparisons of sorrows occur among Margaret, the Duchess of York, and Elizabeth (IV.iv) and (though less clearly in the ritual pattern) between Elizabeth and Anne (IV.i). The very impersonality of the lamentation suggests its historic rather than individual authenticity. The characters are taking a recognized role, playing once for their generation a part that has been played many times, borrowing from history words and tears that have rarely gone unused.

In the ritual of lamentation and in the ritualistic curses which successive generations form in answer to one another, we are eventually carried back far beyond Richard II in history and tradition—back to those other dramas of lust and blood and Nemesis, to those extended cycles about family and domain with which Western tragedy began. Perhaps it is with Greek tragedy, rather than with Marlowe or even Seneca, that *Richard III* has its most essential and most intimate connections.

Notes

1. It ought perhaps to be added that, from my unorthodox point of view, Sir Laurence Olivier's film version of the play falls into most of the usual traps of interpretation.

2. For evidence of a similarly corrupt moral atmosphere in the plays about reigns earlier than Richard III's see LEONARD UNGER, "Deception and Self-Deception in Shakespeare's *Henry IV*," in *The Man in the Name* (Minneapolis: University of Minnesota Press, 1956), pp. 3-17.

Richard II and His Shadow World

The psychoanalytic critics of *Richard II* (they are few) devote themselves almost entirely to exploring the flawed, neurotic personality of the King.[1] It may be helpful in understanding this trend to remember that although we now regard *Richard II* as a History, it was originally titled *The Tragedy of King Richard the Second,* and its author probably considered it an example of the "historical-tragical" hybrid to which Polonius so amusingly refers in the second act of *Hamlet.* The point is, the character of Richard should be seen as the product of an early attempt on Shakespeare's part to create a central figure with a potentially tragic psychology.

The following paper by James A. S. McPeek constitutes a full-fledged attempt to illuminate that psychology. Richard, says McPeek, is suffering from what Ernest Jones described as a "God-complex," the central feature of which is "a strong narcissism" that manifests itself in, among other things, self-love, self-pity, and self-dramatization. Resplendent in person and extremely conscious of his appearance in the eyes of other people, Richard continually seizes upon opportunities to "make scenes," to attract attention, to publicly and histrionically lament the circumstances in which he finds himself. Instead of facing reality he regresses to primitive, archaic ways of thinking and takes refuge in a world of narcissistic fantasies, a shadow world. Too, Richard is constantly identifying himself with divine or celestial objects—another aspect of his narcissism and another feature of the God-complex. When he returns to England from his Irish expedition he likens himself to the sun rising in the east; when he is betrayed by his enemies he likens himself to the Son of God. Such fantasies of omnipotence are strikingly at odds with his inability to act. The identification with Christ also reveals his relish for martyrdom and for the glory that springs therefrom. A further aspect of the God-complex as embodied in Richard is his interest in psychology, his tendency to interpret situations, to examine his own and others' thought-processes.

Because his unconscious has come to dominate his ego, he is very perceptive of others' unexpressed urges. He senses, for example, the underlying motives of Bolingbroke, but this is ultimately ironic in that he is completely insensitive to the realities of insurrection as well as to the realities of kingship. Taken as a whole, says McPeek, Richard's behavior falls into one "large unified pattern" and forms "one of Shakespeare's earliest studies of diseased mentality, acutely observed and unerringly integrated."

M. F.

he appeal of *Richard II* to modern audiences may be attributed in part to Shakespeare's constant portrayal of Richard as a character dominated by a set of fantasies[1] which manifest themselves regularly in his actions and speech and which compose a pattern of behavior that Dr. Ernest Jones has named the God complex.[2] Since these fantasies occur to some extent in every man (as Shakespeare appears to realize in that he has Richard identify himself with every man), everyone finds some affinity with Richard as the action develops, and this feeling helps to build the fascination that the antic king arouses. But whereas with normal people the sense of reality controls these fantasies and modifies their expression, with Richard a failing sense of reality weakens his inhibitions and his fantasies tend to become real to him. Just how far Richard's feeling for reality is weakened it is not easy to say, but the evidence suggests that it is feeble. People of this sort who are thus dominated by illusions but who still maintain enough contact with reality to give otherwise a general impression of being normal are today recognized by psychiatrists as having some characteristics of schizophrenia and are known as schizoids or ambulatory schizophrenics.[3]

Was Shakespeare aware of this consistent pattern in Richard or did he simply assemble the pattern without realizing that he was describing a special state of mental disintegration? Shakespeare first of all devises conduct. Though he does not probe deeply into the causes for Richard's condition (as he does later for Coriolanus), he does have him exhibit his symptoms in full before our eyes. The portrait is

"Richard II and His Shadow World" by James A.S. McPeek. Reprinted with permission from *American Imago*, XV (1958), 195-212.

without contradictions, and it is probable that Shakespeare (as always) knew what he was about. As Horace recommends for new and strange characters, the pattern of Richard's strange behavior is sustained from beginning to end.

It is generally agreed that Shakespeare had no literary model or source for this curious portrayal. The Elizabethan psychologists could and possibly did suggest Richard's mercurial qualities,[4] and other features can be perhaps traced separately to like sources. Shakespeare's own observation of Elizabeth or Essex may have suggested even more. Certain accounts of Richard's life indicate that he may have died insane.[5] But though Shakespeare may have known of these views, he does not advert to them: his Richard is clearly not insane, though he is a man of disturbed mentality. In the eyes of York, Richard is one in whom "will doth mutiny with wit's regard" (II.i.28). Gaunt speaks of his behavior as a "rash fierce blaze of riot" destined shortly to burn itself out, and also affirms the illness of Richard (II.i.90-99), though he diagnoses only its political symptoms. In like views, Northumberland, Ross, and Willoughby depict the political behavior of the king (II.i.241-262); and the Archbishop of York later dwells on Richard's disease as one of surfeiting and wanton hours (2 Henry IV.i.54-58). But as with similar estimates of Brutus, Caesar, Hamlet, Othello, and Macbeth made by various characters, none of these statements analyzes Richard's nature, which is to be appreciated only in the full scope of his self-revelation. In speech and action Richard slowly reveals himself as a character dominated by his fantasy world. Some of the features of his complex have long been recognized in him, but the extensive correspondence to its main characteristics does not appear to have been observed.

The most striking feature of Richard's character is, as is well known, a strong narcissism,[6] which manifests itself in many ways and which is also the outstanding and controlling feature of the God-complex. In person resplendent, Richard is extremely self-conscious, oddly preoccupied with his appearance. Even in the most serious situations, instead of immediately considering possible plans of action, Richard is first intent upon his emotional responses, relating them at times to external changes in his complexion. Gaunt's "frozen admonition" makes his royal cheeks pale (II.i.117-119). Hearing of the loss of his armies, he again evaluates the meaning of the disaster in like terms:

> But now the blood of twenty thousand men
> Did triumph in my face, and they are fled;
> And till so much blood thither come again,
> Have I not reason to look pale and dead?
> (III.ii.76-79)

Shakespeare untiringly emphasizes this narcissism, bringing it to its great resolution in the shattering of the shadow-face in the deposition scene.

This narcissism so deeply controls Richard that all his other attributes stem from it, as is characteristic of the complex.[7] It manifests itself in self-love, marked by a love for personal adornment, self-pity and related self-dramatization (defined by Jones as a narcissistic-exhibitionistic tendency). Thus at Flint Castle, as Richard contemplates the imminence of his deposition, his thought, conditioned by his nature, turns first to his jewels and robes which weigh as importantly as his subjects; even his subjects are to be traded for a pair of carved saints, sensed here as objects of personal adornment rather than true symbols of felt religion, and he develops the idea fittingly in a long distributive figure:

> I'll give my jewels for a set of beads,
> My gorgeous palace for a hermitage,
> My gay apparel for an almsman's gown,
> My figur'd goblets for a dish of wood,
> My sceptre for a palmer's walking-staff,
> My subjects for a pair of carved saints,
> And my large kingdom for a little grave,
> A little little grave, an obscure grave; . . .
> (III.iii.147-155)

It may be argued that in using these symbols, Richard is not just playing the poet, but shows a tendency to regress to the primitive or archaic thinking symptomatic of his condition:[8] with him the symbol is a substitute for the reality behind it—that is, the symbol has become the reality. For him kingship has come to mean no more than its trappings.

At the same moment his ever-present self-pity reaches a masochistic pitch in which he relishes the grief that would make a normal man speechless. He will yield his kingdom "for a little grave, A little little grave, an obscure grave"; or they can bury him in the highway, where his subjects, now trampling on his heart, can trample on his head. Seeing pity in his favorite, Aumerle, he addresses him, visualizing himself and his cousin as children playing with their griefs:[9]

> Or shall we play the wantons with our woes,
> And make some pretty match with shedding tears?
> As thus; to drop them still upon one place,
> Till they have fretted us a pair of graves
> Within the earth; and therein laid: "There lies
> Two kinsmen digg'd their graves with weeping eyes."
> (III.iii.164-169)

He is brought back to reality by the pained embarrassment of his nobles:

> Would not this ill do well? Well, well, I see
> I talk but idly and you laugh at me.
> (III.iii.170-171)

Richard's exhibitionistic tendency manifests itself in all his appearances: he delights in attention and self-display. At the trial by combat when the attention is focused on the contesting nobles, he dramatically draws it to himself by throwing down his warder. At Flint Castle his manner suggests that he expects to overawe Bolingbroke and the rebel lords by his mere appearance (III.iii.61-76). That Bolingbroke and York play up the splendor of Richard's appearance emphasizes his love for display. In the deposition scene, though subdued in fact, he dominates the action. The surrender of his crown is a glittering opportunity for his self-dramatization. With his tears, his hands, his tongue, his breath he relinquishes sovereignty. And though this behavior is seemingly renounced with the breaking of the mirror, the gesture itself indicates his disturbed condition, and Richard's vanity, his love for display, is undiminished by grief, as is apparent from his later curiosity about how roan Barbary went under Bolingbroke.

Yet another aspect of Richard's extreme narcissism is his tendency towards fantasies of omnipotence as seen in his special interpretation of his role as vicegerent of God on earth.[10] The merest hint for this development of his character is provided by Holinshed:

> Sir John Bushy in all his talks when hee proponed any matter unto the King, did not attribute to him titles of honour, due and accustomed, but invented unused terms, and such strange names as were rather agreeable to the divine maiestie of God, than to any earthly potentate. The Prince, being desirous inough of all honour, and more ambitious than was requisite, seemed to like well of his speech, and gave good eare to his talke.[11]

In *Richard II* this hint is amplified enormously through two images, both symptomatic of the God-complex, those of the sun-king and the Son of God or Christ.[12] In presenting Richard as a sun-king, Shakespeare is obviously drawing on familiar lore, and in particular on the knowledge that Richard's emblem was the sun emerging from clouds; further, he was to use the same image effectively for Hal. But whereas with Hal the image is felt as simple metaphor, with Richard it becomes a near-obsession. In the scene presenting his return from Ireland he identifies in splendor with the sun. Now that he has returned from the Antipodes, treason and conspiracy will be dissolved by his mere appearance:

> So when this thief, this traitor, Bolingbroke,
> Who all this while hath revell'd in the night
> Whilst we were wand'ring with the Antipodes,
> Shall see us rising in our throne, the east,
> His treasons will sit blushing in his face,
> Not able to endure the sight of day,
> But self-affrighted tremble at his sin.
>
> (III.ii.47-53)

Faced with unpleasant reality, Richard has no plan of action. His ego instead regresses to primitive or archaic thinking, the method of magic as opposed to a normal response which would try to meet this situation and control it with real measures. Here and elsewhere Richard substitutes a more agreeable world of fantasy for distasteful reality.[13] Properly played, the scene makes one aware of the king's resort to fantasy as a release. The other actors stand ill at ease, and little gestures indicate their barely polite tolerance of Richard's fancies. At one moment he exults in the thought that God's angels are his invisible defense against Bolingbroke (III.ii.58-61); in the next his spirits plummet at the news of the dispersed Welsh army (III.ii.64-74). Then with a prompting from Aumerle he instantly recaptures the illusion of his power:

> Is not the king's name twenty thousand names?[14]
> Arm, arm, my name! a puny subject strikes
> At thy great glory. Look not to the ground,
> Ye favourites of a king: are we not high?
> High be our thoughts. ·
>
> (III.ii.85-89).

This cycle of alternate confidence in his omnipotence ("An easy task it is to win our own") and instant, unreasoning despair as reality breaks the illusion is repeated in a vivid pattern throughout the scene. So far is Richard subject to the illusion of his power as God's representative that he apparently believes that forces of nature (storms and pestilence) will destroy those who offend him (III.iii.82-89).[15] In the grasp of this illusion he fancies that he does the earth favor by touching it with his royal hands (III.ii.6-11). Weeping, smiling, like a mother (and matriarchal features are not uncommon in delusions of this sort)[16] he greets *his* earth, and he even conjures small creatures of his earth, spiders, toads, nettles, and snakes to oppose and thwart Bolingbroke (III.ii.14-26). The very normal Bishop of Carlisle gently reproves his presumption, reminding him that men must use the means that God provides:

> Fear not, my lord: that power that made you king
> Hath power to keep you king in spite of all.
> The means that heaven yields must be embrac'd,
> And not neglected; else, if heaven would,
> And we will not, heaven's offer we refuse,
> The proffered means of succour and redress.
>
> (III.ii.27-32)

But Richard is not only a sun-king whose presence he hopes will dazzle and disperse his enemies. As the representative of Christ on earth, he shows a tendency to identify with Christ in his trials and sorrows,[17] and Shakespeare develops the theme at greater length than appears to be commonly realized, and with pointed irony. The image is not necessarily meant to arouse sympathy for Richard, but rather to record the historic view of the Richard faction and at the same time to develop further Richard's complex. Patently the ironic contrast between Richard's true nature and that of Christ, so obvious to us, would be appreciated by the Elizabethan audience. We are prepared for the identification through certain aspects of Richard's view of himself as a sun-king. At his coming, as when Christ comes to judge the sinners, the guilty will "stand bare and naked, trembling at themselves" (III.ii.41-46).[18] It is almost to be expected that in the next breath he would assume that God's deputy has supernatural protection: to every soldier that Bolingbroke has conscripted, a glorious angel will be opposed (III.ii.56-61) in Richard's defense.[19] Some in the audience would perhaps remember that Christ rejected the temptation of claiming supernatural protection: Richard in claiming such aid inverts, as his conduct does throughout the play, the Christ symbol. In the same scene, when Richard mistakes Scroop's ironic report that Bushy, Green, and Wiltshire have made peace with Bolingbroke, he condemns them as Judases:

> Three Judases, each one thrice worse than Judas!
> Would they make peace? terrible hell make war
> Upon their spotted souls for this offence!
>
> (III.ii.132-134)

The inversion of Christ's attitude is recognized by Scroop, who responds:

> Sweet love, I see, changing his property
> Turns to the sourest and most deadly hate.
> Again uncurse their souls; their peace is made
> With heads and not with hands.
>
> (III.ii.135-138)

In the deposition scene his identification with Christ and its ironic implications become yet more apparent. We are prepared for Richard's assumption of the pose of the martyred Christ by the Bishop of Carlisle's ardent but specious defense of Richard in which he predicts that if the deposition occurs, England will be called the field of Golgotha (IV.i.136-144). Richard does not hear and does not need such prompting. Scanning the assembled parliament and the courtiers of Bolingbroke, he finds that while Christ had but one Judas, all are Judases to him:

>   . . . Yet I well remember
> The favors of these men: were they not mine?
> Did they not sometime cry "All hail!" to me?
> So Judas did to Christ: but he in twelve,
> Found truth in all but one; I in twelve thousand, none.
>   (IV.i.167-171)

They are not only Judases, but those who are passively accepting his deposition are Pilates, washing their hands and delivering him to crucifixion:

> Nay, all of you that stand and look upon me,
> Whilst that my wretchedness doth bait myself,
> Though some of you, with Pilate, wash your hands,
> Showing an outward pity; yet you Pilates
> Have here deliver'd me to my sour cross,
> And water cannot wash away your sin.
>   (IV.i.237-242)

As Richard's sweet love turns to sourest hate, as is characteristic of victims of the complex when they are offended,[20] so the redeeming cross becomes a sour cross for him.

At least by strong suggestion, if not by direct allusion, Shakespeare sustains the image with its negative implications in the rest of the action. In Act V, after Richard has been sent to Pomfret, York recounts for his duchess the story of Richard's coming to London (his Jerusalem):

> . . . dust was thrown upon his sacred head,
> Which with such gentle sorrow he shook off,
> His face still combating with tears and smiles
> The badges of his grief and patience,
> That had not God for some strange purpose, steel'd
> The hearts of men, they must perforce have melted,
> And barbarism itself have pitied him.
> But heaven hath a hand in these events,
> To whose high will we bound our calm contents.
>   (V.ii.30-38)

Richard's patience here, together with his strange inability to resort to action against his enemies, might appear to be modeled on the exemplary patience of Jesus. The king of griefs is perhaps meant to imitate the Man of Sorrows in his patient endurance of affliction. But Richard does not maintain this pose. In the closing scene he renounces his patience for despairing violence ("Patience is stale, and I am weary of it"), beats the keeper, and presently kills two servants (Holinshed has four tall men), consigning their souls to Hell, all in marked contrast to the man who died between two thieves with forgiveness for his tormentors. That Piers of Exton interprets Richard's desperation as valiancy only heightens the irony, as likewise does Richard's own certainty of his salvation ("Mount, mount, my soul! thy seat is up on high").[21]

Since Richard has illusions of omnipotence, he shows signs of entertaining fantasies of omniscience, as is characterstic of his complex. A prophet of time to come, he predicts disasters of civil war and pestilence with an assurance that impresses even his enemies (III.iii.85-100). Later, in 2 *Henry IV,* Shakespeare has Warwick attack Richard's supposed prescience with a logical explanation of his "perfect guess" (III.i.80-89).

Another aspect of the complex (as observed by Dr. Jones) is Richard's interest in psychology, his love for interpreting situations and examining his own thought-processes and those of others. People of this sort, in whom the unconscious has come to dominate the ego, may be acutely perceptive in some directions of the unconscious urges of others. Hence Richard's intuitive sensing of the motives of Bolingbroke is characteristic, a perception that is counterbalanced by his complete insensibility to the serious obligations of kingship and a consequent inability to devise any plan of action to oppose the enemy. He is aware of the menace of Bolingbroke from the start:

> How high a pitch his resolution soars!
> (I.i.109)
> A brace of draymen bid God speed him well
> And had the tribute of his supple knee,
> With "Thanks, my countrymen, my loving friends";
> As were our England in reversion his,
> And he our subjects' next degree in hope.
> (I.iv.33-37)

Instead of being intent, as his counselors belatedly are, on how to meet this threat, he helplessly divines Bolingbroke's nebulous purpose and perhaps even shapes that purpose by expressing his willingness to surrender his crown before Bolingbroke, so far as we can see, has consciously entertained the idea of taking it.

His love for examining his thought-processes leads him to interpret in detail each situation, as is illustrated by his speeches in the deposition scene and, better still, by the extensive exposition of his thoughts in prison. Associated with this interest in observation of self and situation is Richard's love for language, shown in his habit of interpreting every situation in terms of rhetorical display (Shakespeare probably did not mean us to admire Richard's rhetorical extravagance any more than his courtiers do). This interest in language for its own sake is a noteworthy trait of the complex.[22]

With Richard's love for rhetoric may be associated his extreme tendency toward ritual, his habit of reducing every situation to ceremony. This use of ceremony, when controlled by reason, is normal, a stabilizing social influence, and most of the characters in the play resort to its devices at times, as Tillyard indicates. But the tendency becomes abnormal when carried to excess, as it is with Richard, who converts every situation to ceremony. With him his devotion to ritual appears to mark a continuing regression to conceptual thinking, an attempt to reconstitute the world of the past as an escape from an oppressive reality.[23] This tendency in Richard is well illustrated in the ceremony of his farewell to his wife, in which the form of love is projected as a substitute for reality (careful analysis of the scene, together with other evidence in the play, suggests that Richard loves only himself).

It is but natural that anyone with these propensities should never seriously question the rightness of his conduct and that he should justify his proceedings simply by virtue of his inherent right. Richard's behavior neatly fits the pattern here. He does not claim infallibility or righteousness, but why should he? As God's deputy, he is a "rightful" king. Criticism arouses anger in him, as when he resents Gaunt's sharp criticism:

> A lunatic lean-witted fool,
> Presuming on an ague's privilege,
> Dar'st with thy frozen admonition

> Make pale our cheek, chasing the royal blood
> With fury from his native residence.
>
> (II.i.115-119)

But he does not attempt to meet or refute Gaunt's charges, nor will he alter his ways. The sense of Gaunt's serious accusations makes no impression, save for his resentment: those who have age and sullens like Gaunt should die (II.i.139-140).

When York in turn reproaches Richard with his faults (some of them crimes), Richard, who has ignored the charges or only idly attended them as matters of no consequence, exclaims, "Why, uncle, what's the matter?" (II.i.186). Moved by Richard's imperviousness, York makes the charge more specific: if Richard seizes Bolingbroke's estates, he violates the laws of succession by which he himself is king. But Richard is above human law; his will is sufficient reason for his action: "Think what you will: we seize into our hands His goods, his money, and his lands" (II.i.209-210). York punctuates his open disapproval by leaving, and in the next moment, after sending Bushy to expedite the plundering of Bolingbroke's estates, this strange king appoints York lord governor of England for the period of his absence in Ireland ("For he is just and always lov'd us well"). Later, in a parallel pattern of behavior, when he reflects on the dispersal of his forces and the death of his favorites, he does not connect his plight with his misdemeanors, but muses instead on the fortunes of kings: kings, he asserts, die in prison or from violence, and none peacefully. His fortunes are the universal lot (III.ii.155-160). It does not occur to him to consider that his lot might be the result of his conduct.

It is manifest that Richard, true to the conditions of his complex, is incapable of really conceiving his guilt or suffering remorse for his sins.[25] Once or twice he seems to recognize his misconduct, but the recognition is superficial and quickly put aside for the vanities that obsess his mind. Thus for a moment he senses reality in the deposition scene as he scans his features (unworn by the cares that would line the face of a good ruler) in the mirror: his glory is a brittle glory; the face in whose glory he believed is a shadow, not a reality. Even his external shows of grief are (he realizes for a moment, with Bolingbroke's help) but shadows of the true grief.

Boling. The shadow of your sorrow hath destroy'd
The shadow of your face.

Rich. Say that again.
The shadow of my sorrow! Ha! let's see:
'Tis very true, my grief lies all within;
And these external manners of laments
Are merely shadows to the unseen grief
That swells with silence in the tortured soul.
(IV.i.292-297)

Though Richard's disease has not progressed to the point that he has lost all contact with reality, his behavior, as recorded in this great key passage, is suggestive of the schizophrenic who attempts to regain contact with the objective world, but who succeeds only in recapturing the shadows of that world, namely the world's representations.[26] Richard has a moment of normal insight here as he perceives that he has been deluding himself with shadows. But in the next moment, as earlier with Northumberland (IV.i.229-236), he transfers the blame:

O, good! Convey? conveyors are you all,
That rise thus nimbly by a true king's fall.
(IV.i.317-318)

And in the prison scene, a discord in the music reminds him that he has wasted time and that time wastes him (V.iv.42-49); but his reflections turn from this seeming realization of personal guilt to his habitual solace in rhetorical self-pity. His time, he says, "Runs posting on in Bolingbroke's proud joy." He has already analyzed the situation to suit his condition: he suffers from discontent, yes; every man is discontented until he becomes nothing (and one must recall Macbeth's soured conclusion that life is vanity). No matter what sort of life I might have led, he rationalizes, I should have still been discontent. His consideration of the lives he might have led is a characteristic evasion of the facts about the life he has led.

This bias has been preserved in Richard through the play. Early he tells us that his subjects, and not he, are to blame for his downfall:

Revolt our subjects? That we cannot mend;
They break their faith to God as well as us.
(III.ii.100-101)

And after his deposition he exclaims to his queen:

> A King of beasts indeed; if aught but beasts,
> I had been still a happy king of men.
>
> (V.i.34-35)

And in prison he is not concerned with his kingdom sick with civil disorder (as Henry IV is at the end of his reign), but with the vanity, as we have seen, that roan Barbary went so proudly under Bolingbroke. He can implore the forgiveness of the absent Barbary for his railing at him, but he has none for Henry of Lancaster.

Richard's fantasy in prison is in itself a special symptom of his disorder. It takes the shape of a rebirth fantasy, which is similar in nature to those experienced by schizophrenics, a fantasy which is based on the patient's unconscious desire to reconstruct his disordered universe.[27] Richard's still-breeding thoughts seek refuge in theology, but find contradictions of his own making (V.iv.11-17); yet other thoughts bearing on possible escape from imprisonment and on the vicissitudes in the lives of kings and beggars, all in themselves barely suppressed queries as to what has gone wrong in his management of his life, end in futility:

> . . . but whate'er I be,
> Nor I nor any man that but man is
> With nothing shall be pleas'd, till he be eas'd
> With being nothing.
>
> (V.iv.38-41)

In this negative way Richard wins reassurance: his search for a solution to his dilemma leads him to the conclusion that all men are discontent till they sink back into nothingness—a conclusion which, since it excuses himself, is obviously not one leading to a better mental health.

Seen from this perspective, all the behavior and the utterances of Richard fall into one large unified pattern, forming one of Shakespeare's earliest studies of diseased mentality, acutely observed and unerringly integrated. Dominated by his complex, Richard continually substitutes his fancies for action. Lost in the dream of his glory, remote from reality, he is equally incapable of either well-considered civil policy or military strategy, and natural prey for flatterers like Bushy and Green. That some people of the time, including Elizabeth herself, should be disturbed by so clinical a portrait and suspect its topical reference is not surprising. Whatever Shakespeare intended, he created in Richard II a haunting character whose case is hopeless from the start.

Notes

1. See, for example, CAROLINE SHRODES, JUSTINE VAN GUNDY, and RICHARD W. HUSBAND (eds.), *Psychology Through Literature* (New York: Oxford University Press, 1943), p. 307; and L. A. G. STRONG, "Shakespeare and the Psychologists," in JOHN GARRETT (ed.), *Talking of Shakespeare* (London: Hodder and Stoughton, 1954), pp. 187-208.

1. I wish to thank Dr. Daniel C. Dawes and Dr. Lydia M. Dawes of the Boston Psychoanalytic Society for their many suggestions and expert counsel, without which I should not have had the courage to attempt this study. Its merits in many ways are theirs: the faults are mine.

2. ERNEST JONES, "The God Complex," in *Essays in Applied Psychoanalysis* (London: Hogarth Press, 1951), pp. 244-265. According to Dr. Jones, the God-complex is "generally the product of an unconscious phantasy in which [people] identify their personality with that of God." The fantasy is widespread, and everyone perhaps has some of its attributes. Some men have them to a marked degree, and if such men become insane, they develop the delusion that their fantasy is reality. More commonly, however, the sense of reality controls its external manifestations. Its major aspects grow out of an embracing narcissism that manifests itself in self-love, a narcissistic-exhibitionistic tendency, and self-pity. Narcissistic exhibitionism (as distinguished from basic exhibitionism) tends to be aloof, inaccessible, surrounded with mystery. In extreme cases this desire to be inaccessible leads to the conception of oneself as a sun god who must be screened from people who might otherwise be destroyed by his magnificence; but in more normal people such fantasies remain in the unconscious. Despite this aloofness such people like to talk about themselves and are always analyzing their thoughts. They love language for its own sake and are keenly interested in psychology. They have omnipotence

and omniscience fantasies, and tend to identify with the god of their religion. They are unforgiving when offended, but lenient in judging offenses against others. They resent authority, crave love and praise, but show indifference to hostile opinion.

Dr. Jones's analysis of the God-complex is necessarily a composite, and for any isolated case correspondence in every detail with his findings is, as he says, not to be expected. Richard as a king will naturally not have the repressions that a common citizen has. Where Richard will use the sun image as a right, the commoner may resort simply to a mysterious aloofness. Richard's aloofness, apart from its indication in his peculiar use of the sun image, may be seen in his avoidance of those who do not flatter his ego, his inaccessibility (as York remarks, II.i.17-29) to good counsel.

3. This term appears to have been first used by Dr. GREGORY ZILBOORG to describe a type of schizophrenia: "The individual may appear normal in all respects, even sane and almost worldly; he may sometimes give the impression of a warm personality. On occasions, admittedly rare, he may even have a position and keep it, doing not very well and not very badly, but keeping it. Intellectually he may not appear brilliant, but he will be adequate, almost always with a cultural beat." "Ambulatory Schizophrenias," *Psychiatry, 4*:152, 1941.

4. See J. W. DRAPER, "The Character of Richard II," *Psychiatric Quarterly, 21*:228-236, 1942.

5. In his edition of Créton, BENJAMIN WILLIAMS considered at length the conjectures or rumors that Richard fled to Scotland and died there in "a state of real or apparent madness." *Chronique de la Traison et Mort de Richard Deux Roy Dengleterre* (London, 1846), pp. i-xix.

6. JOHN PALMER remarks this characteristic, but does not seem to recognize its special implications (*Political Characters of Shakespeare* [London, 1952], p. 152). O. J. CAMPBELL speaks of Richard's sense of the dramatic values of every situation as his most striking feature, a view which emphasizes one aspect of his narcissism (*The Lving Shakespeare* [New York: The Macmillan Company, 1949], p. 180).

7. JONES, *op. cit.,* p. 247.

8. See OTTO FENICHEL, *The Psychoanalytic Theory of Neurosis* (New York: W. W. Norton and Company, 1945), pp. 46-51, 421-422. I am much indebted to this text and its extensive bibliography.

9. The fancies of Richard at this moment and certain other times (in particular, in his invocation of toads and spiders and often his behavior) suggest an obvious infantilism or immaturity. JONES (*op.*

cit., p. 265) calls attention to the resemblance between these characteristics of the complex and those of the "manic" phase of child development described by Melanie Klein.

10. This attitude is of course a characteristic of schizophrenia if carried to the point of actual belief, and represents a regression to primitive thinking. FENICHEL (*op. cit.*, p. 421), citing OTTO RANK, "Der Doppelgänger," *Imago*, *3*:1914, remarks: "The belief in one's own omnipotence is but one aspect of the magical-animistic world that comes to the fore again in narcissistic regressions.

"That narcissistic daydreams are actually believed and become delusions, that the patients feel themselves as king, president, or God is due to the loss of reality testing." See also R. C. BAK, "Dissolution of the Ego, Mannerism, and Delusion of Grandeur," *Journal of Nervous and Mental Disease, 98*:457-463, 1943.

11. *1577 The Last Volume of the Chronicles of England, Scotlande, and Irelande . . .* by *Raphaell Holinshed, at London, Imprinted for John Hosine*, pp. 1094-1905. Somewhat thinner suggestions of the idea may be found in *Woodstock*, in which Richard rebukes the rebels as follows:

> Although we could have easily surprised,
> Dispersed and overthrown your rebel troops
> That draw your swords against our sacred person,
> The highest God's anointed deputy,
> Breaking your holy oaths to heaven and us,
> Yet of our mild and princely clemency
> We have forborne. . . .
>
> (*Woodstock, A Moral History*, ed. A. P. Rossiter, London, 1946, p. 162, V.iii.55-61.)

A chronicle of 1471 also notes a tendency to a mysterious aloofness in Richard:

> After this the kyng in solemne daies and grete festis, in whiche he wered his croune, and wente in his rial array, he leet ordeyne and make in his chambir, a trone, wherynne he was wont to sitte fro aftir mete unto enensong tyme, spekynge to no man, but overlokyng alle menn; and yf he loked on any man, what astat or degre that evir he were of, he most knele.

(*An English Chronicle of the Reigns of Richard II, Henry IV, Henry V and Henry VI. Written before the year 1471* . . . ed. the Rev. John Sylvester Davies, Camden Society, 1956, p. 12.)

12. Though both of these images come naturally to Shakespeare in connection with his basic materials, his special use of the images makes Richard a typical example of the fantasy, which is as old as the nature of man himself and which is at the root of man's original conception of God.

13. FENICHEL (*op. cit.*, p. 50) finds that such people may resort to two types of fantasy, namely "creative fantasy, which prepares some later action, and daydreaming fantasy, the refuge for wishes that cannot be fulfilled." Richard's fantasies seem of the latter type.

14. JONES (*op. cit.*, p. 254) calls attention to this compulsion to fulfill the "obligation of the name."

15. It may be objected that Richard simply reflects here the superstitious awe towards kingship common to the age. But there is a difference between sharing a mass-illusion about someone else and entertaining views of one's own omnipotence. Here again the intensity of the illusion is important: Richard really seems to believe his fantasy.

16. FENICHEL (*op. cit.*, p. 425, citing EDITH WEIGERT-VORWINC-KEL, "The Cult and Mythology of the Magna Mater from Standpoint of Psychoanalysis," *Psychiatry, 1*:1938), remarks: "Deeper than modern man's dependence on the patriarchal father (and on father gods) is every man's biologically determined dependence on the mother, who took care of the infant during his passive-dependent period. Therefore, it is not rare that religious delusions of schizophrenics show matriarchal features and resemble ancient mother religions."

17. I. B. CAUTHEN, JR., studies this aspect of the play in "Richard II and the Image of the Betrayed Christ," *Renaissance Papers* (Columbia: University of South Carolina Publications, 1954), pp. 45-57. He points out that the possible sources only suggest the parallel of Richard and Christ; Shakespeare alone has Richard equate with Christ. Cauthen finds that the equation helps to develop the historic theme of Richard's martyrdom and build our sympathy, and that the extended image serves as a strong unifying device.

18. SAMUEL KLIGER, in "The Sun Imagery in *Richard II*," SP, 45:196-202, 1948, remarks the significance of the sun searching out the sinners here: "So on Judgment Day will the sinner be found out by the eye of God."

19. The difference in tone between Richard's behavior here and that

of a more normal man may be illustrated by Woodstock's remark when he faces death (V.i.131-135):

> Thou canst not kill me villain!
> God's holy angel guards a just man's life
> And with his radiant beams as bright as fire
> Will guard and keep his righteous innocence.
> I am a prince. Thou dar'st not murder me.

Woodstock's claim to God's protection is based on his justice and innocence, not his status as an agent of God. Richard's claims, on the other hand, are part of the mystery with which he cloaks himself, as is characteristic of his complex (JONES, *op. cit.*, p. 251).

20. JONES, *op. cit.*, p. 260.

21. JONES comments on the assurance that people dominated by the complex have regarding their immortality (p. 261).

22. *Ibid.*, pp. 259-262.

23. For a discussion of the tendency to regress to formalistic thinking, see BAK, *op. cit.*, pp. 457-463.

24. Richard's childish resentment of Gaunt is characteristic of the narcissist, who resents a father image, a symbol of authority (JONES, *op. cit.*, pp. 261-262). Richard's characteristically subjective response here may be contrasted with that of Henry IV, who, in a comparable situation, remains intent on the issue even when Blunt is beguiled by Hotspur's appeal (I Henry IV, I.iii.77-92).

25. DRAPER calls attention to this fact about Richard's character (*op. cit.*, p. 230): "He confesses his faults in moments of extravagant remorse, but does not seem actually to realize them . . . in fact he seems incapable of following any policy on anything."

26. See FENICHEL, *op. cit.*, p. 437.

27. *Ibid.*, pp. 424-425. Fenichel (citing FREUD, *The Future of an Illusion* [London: Hogarth Press, 1928]), speaking of the "salvations" achieved by the patient through these rebirth fantasies, observes: "The salvations frequently are experienced in a passive-receptive way, showing signs of the narcissistic *unio mystica,* of the deepest oral reunion of the subject with the universe, and the reestablishment of the original 'oceanic feeling.' "

Prince Hal's Conflict

That the two parts of *Henry IV* have stimulated a good many psychoanalytic criticisms is hardly surprising, for, as everyone knows, these plays contain some of Shakespeare's most brilliant drama, as well as some of his most memorable characters. The criticisms, to speak generally of them, focus upon three main topics: mythic or ritualistic elements, the father-son theme, and the character of Falstaff.[1] However, the majority of the criticisms find it very difficult to treat these topics separately. In other words, a discussion of the father-son problem usually begets a discussion of Falstaff, who enters largely into folkloric and mythic analyses, which in turn are apt to touch upon the theme of father and son, and so forth. The paper to follow is an excellent example, and, in addition, a pioneering contribution to the field.

Focusing upon certain "inconsistencies" in the conduct of Prince Henry—his return to Eastcheap after his "reformation" in Part One, and his harsh treatment of his companions, most notably Falstaff, in Part Two—Ernst Kris maintains that the Prince behaves as he does because he is unable to identify firmly and consistently with his father, Bolingbroke, who has turned out to be not only a regicide but, from the standpoint of the unconscious, a parricide as well in that he was responsible for the murder of his predecessor, King Richard. Prince Henry, as a result, rebels against his father's authority and turns to Falstaff as a father substitute (this comes out clearly in Part One when Falstaff and Hal play father and son for the benefit of the tavern audience). Bolingbroke, in turn, emotionally disowns his son and substitutes Henry Hotspur in his place. Thus Hotspur's rebellion becomes for Kris, as it became for an earlier investigator, Franz Alexander, a representation of Prince Henry's parricidal tendencies. These tendencies are temporarily quelled during the battle of Shrewsbury when Hal defends his father from the rebels' swords and destroys the arch-foe, Hotspur. However, the Prince is still unwilling to associate himself with his father's tainted court; he is still unable to escape the burden of his father's past. Hence, he returns in Part Two to the substitute world of Falstaff and the London taverns. As for the merciless rejection of Falstaff at the close of Part Two when Hal has become King, it derives ultimately from the fact that Bolingbroke and Falstaff have long been associated in Hal's unconscious mind. Yet, even as King Henry V, Hal finds it very difficult to get out from under the emotional shadow of his father's crime and to achieve his own moral identity. It is only when, with a clear conscience and in a righteous cause, he leads his men against the French, it is only when he "proceeds" from "moral scrutiny" to "heroic action" that he finally succeeds in resolving his lifelong "conflict."

M. F.

or well over a century some of Shakespeare's critics have pointed to inconsistencies in the character of Henry, Prince of Wales (later King Henry V), occasionally explained by the poet's lack of interest, whose attention, it is said, was concentrated mainly on the alternate but "true" hero, Falstaff. This seemed the more plausible since most of the puzzling passages or incidents occur in *King Henry IV, Parts I and II* of the trilogy; however, closer examination of three inconsistencies, to which critics are wont to refer as typical of others, seems to throw new light on the psychological conflict with which Shakespeare has invested the hero of the trilogy.[1]

Prince Hal's first appearance on the stage as Falstaff's friend and Poins's companion is concluded by the soliloquy in which he reveals his secret intentions. While he has just made plans to riot with the gang and to rob the robbers, his mind turns to the future.

> I know you all, and will awhile uphold
> The unyok'd humour of your idleness:
> Yet herein will I imitate the sun,
> Who doth permit the base contagious clouds
> To smother up his beauty from the world,
> That when he please again to be himself,
> Being wanted, he may be more wonder'd at,
> By breaking through the foul and ugly mists
> Of vapours that did seem to strangle him.
> If all the year were playing holidays,

"Prince Hal's Conflict" by Ernst Kris. Reprinted with permission from *Psychoanalytic Quarterly*, XVII (1948), 487-506.

To sport would be as tedious as to work;
But when they seldom come, they wish'd for come,
And nothing pleaseth but rare accidents.
So, when this loose behaviour I throw off,
And pay the debt I never promised,
By how much better than my word I am
By so much shall I falsify men's hopes;
And like bright metal on a sullen ground,
My reformation, glittering o'er my fault,
Shall show more goodly and attract more eyes
Than that which hath no foil to set it off.
I'll so offend to make offence a skill,
Redeeming time when men think least I will.
(*I King Henry IV*, I.ii.218-241)

Some critics feel that this announcement deprives the play of part of its dramatic effect: the change in the Prince's behavior should surprise the audience as it does the personages on the stage. The anticipation, we are told, was forced on the poet as a concession to the public. Henry V appeared to the Elizabethans as the incarnation of royal dignity and knightly valor. His early debauches had therefore to be made part of a morally oriented plan; but some critics find the price of justification too high, since it leaves a suspicion of hypocrisy on the Prince's character.

The second inconsistency is seen in the course of the Prince's reformation, which proceeds in two stages. In *Part I*, Prince Hal returns to his duties when the realm is endangered by rebels; at Shrewsbury, he saves the King's life and defeats Percy Hotspur in combat; but while the war against other rebels continues, we find him back in Eastcheap feasting with his companions. His final reformation takes place at the King's deathbed. Critics usually account for this protracted and repeated reformation by assuming that the success of the Falstaff episodes in *Part I* suggested their continuation in *Part II*, an argument supported by the widely accepted tradition that Falstaff's revival in *The Merry Wives of Windsor*, after the completion of the trilogy, was at the special request of Queen Elizabeth. It has nevertheless been emphasized that the concluding scenes of *Part II* follow in all essential details existing tradition.

The third and most frequently discussed inconsistency is King Henry V's treatment of his former companions with merciless severity. Falstaff, who waits to cheer the new King, is temporarily arrested and, while he hopes that Henry will revoke in private his public pronouncement, we later hear that he has hoped in vain. The King's harshness has broken his heart. In the "rejection of Falstaff,"[2] who has won the audience's heart, the dramatist has "overshot his mark"; the King's reformation could have been illustrated by gentler means, and some critics suggest how this could have been achieved without offending the Old Knight. The formula of banishment, however, is only partly Shakespeare's invention since it paraphrases traditional accounts.

This tradition originated soon after Henry V suddenly died in Paris, at the age of thirty-five, crowned King of England and France (1421). The tradition grew in chronicles and popular accounts, hesitantly at first, more rapidly later, when Henry's striving for European leadership and hegemony in the Channel appeared as an anticipation of the political goals of Tudor England. In Shakespeare's time, fact and legend had become firmly interwoven.[3]

Prince Henry (of Monmouth, born 1387) was early introduced to affairs of state. He was twelve years old when, in 1399, his father succeeded Richard II. At fifteen he took personal control of the administration of Wales and of the war against the Welsh. He had shared in this task since 1400, initially guided by Henry Percy, Hotspur, who at that time was thirty-nine, three years older than the Prince's father. In 1405 Hotspur led the rebellion of the Percies and attacked the Prince's forces at Shrewsbury. Supported by the King and his army, Henry of Monmouth carried the day. The rebellion and the pacification of Wales kept the Prince busy until 1408 or 1409. He then entered politics as leader of the parliamentary opposition against the King's council. Repeated illnesses complicated Henry IV's negotiations with Parliament, which at the time of his uprising against Richard II had vested royal power in him. Since 1406 rumors concerning his abdication had been spreading. In 1408 he was thought to have died in an attack of seizures "but after some hours the vital spirits returned to him." From January, 1410, to November, 1411, the Prince governed England through the council, supported by the King's half brothers, Henry and Thomas Beaufort. In November, 1411, Henry IV took over again and dismissed the Prince from the council. One of the reasons for the Prince's dismissal was his desire for an active policy in France. It seems that, initially without the Kng's consent, he had arranged for a small expeditionary force to be sent to the continent in support of Burgundy against the Royal House of France; later the King agreed to the expedition but the Prince had to renounce his intention to lead the forces.

The circumstances that led to Henry of Monmouth's removal from the council are not entirely clear. It seems that Henry IV was motivated by the suspicion that the Prince intended to depose him. The Prince issued public statements denying such intention, and demanded the punishment of those who had slandered him. He finally forced an interview on the King, during which a reconciliation took place. The struggle between father and son was terminated by Henry IV's death in 1413.

According to the chronicle of the fifteenth and sixteenth centuries Henry of Monmouth's character changed after his accession to the throne. The early chronicles do not state in detail wherein the conversion consisted. They familiarize us, however, with two areas in which the Prince's attitude was different from that of the later King. The first of these areas is less well defined than the second: during the conflict with his father, the Prince appeared twice at court "with much peoples of lords and gentles." This show of strength was meant to exercise pressure on King and council. During his reign Henry V never used similar methods; no appeal to forces outside "government" is attributed to him, neither in his dealings with Parliament nor with the baronage. Within the framework of his age he was a rigorously constitutional monarch. Somewhat better defined is the change of the Prince's attitude to the Church. The noble leader of the Lollards, Sir John Oldcastle, was the Prince's personal friend, and at least by tolerance, the Prince seems vaguely to have favored the cause for which he stood. Shortly after Henry V's accession to the throne the persecution of the Lollards was intensified. Sir John was arrested and asked to abandon his error. He refused any compromise, succeeded twice in escaping, but he was finally, in 1417, executed after Parliament had determined on the extirpation of Lollardy as heresy.

The legendary versions of the Prince's reformation elaborated these incidents later on; in their earliest formulation they simply stated: "that the Prince was an assiduous center of lasciviousness and addicted exceedingly to instruments of music. Passing the bounds of modesty he was the fervent soldier of Venus as well as of Mars; youthlike, he was tired with her torches and in the midst of the worthy works of war found leisure for excess common to ungoverned age."[4] Later sources place the Prince's reformation in relation to the conflict with his father: the baronage that had adopted the Prince as leader becomes a group of irresponsible delinquents. Among this group the name of Sir John Oldcastle appears. The fanatic leader of a religious sect thus underwent the transformation into Sir John Falstaff, whose name was substituted by Shakespeare only after Oldcastle's descendants had complained of what seemed a vilification of their ancestor; but various traces of the original name are extant in Shakespeare's text. The banishment of Falstaff then may be considered as an elaboration of Henry V's persecution of the Lollards whom he once had favored. Other elements of the legendary tradition are inserted with clearly moralistic intentions: the Prince's reformation is used to exemplify the nature of royal responsibility. Thus Sir Thomas Elliott in his treatise, *The Book Called the Governor* (1536), introduced the tale of Prince and Chiefjustice according to which the King confirms that Chiefjustice in office who, in the royal name, had once arrested the riotous Prince. The image of Henry V was thus idealized into that of the perfect Renaissance ruler.[5]

Shakespeare borrowed these and similar incidents of his trilogy from a variety of sources, but mainly from the second edition of Raphael Holinshed's *Chronicles of England, Scotland and Ireland* (1587).[6] In addition to historical sources he relied upon a popular play produced a few years earlier. So closely does he follow *The Famous Victories of Henry V* that it seems as if he had set himself the task to retain as many as possible of the incidents familiar to his audience in spite of the total transformation of the context. Without commenting in detail upon this transformation—though such a comparison would permit one to support the hypothesis here to be proposed—it suffices to point to its general direction. The historical facts concerning the conflict between Henry IV and his son and "heir apparent," Henry of Monmouth, had been blurred by legend. The conversion of the Prince became the dominant theme, a conversion modeled after that of the life of the saints. Shakespeare returns to the core of this tradition, or rather rediscovers that core, in the sources accessible to him.

He centers his attention on the conflict between father and son, which is made to account for both the Prince's debauchery and his reformation.

The conflict between father and son appears in *Part I* of *Henry IV* in three versions, each time enacted by one central and two related characters.[7] The theme is manifestly stated by the King in the introductory scene of the trilogy, when he compares Henry of Monmouth with Henry Percy.

> Yea, there thou mak'st me sad, and mak'st me sin
> In envy that my Lord Northumberland
> Should be the father to so blest a son;
> A son who is the theme of honour's tongue;
> Amongst a grove the very straightest plant;
> Who is sweet Fortune's minion and her pride:
> Whilst I, by looking on the praise of him,
> See riot and dishonour stain the brow
> Of my young Harry. O! that it could be prov'd
> That some night-tripping fairy had exchang'd
> In cradle-clothes our children where they lay,
> And called mine Percy, his Plantagenet
> Then would I have his Harry, and he mine.
>   (*I King Henry IV*, I.i.78-90)

The position of the Prince between Falstaff and the King is almost as explicitly stated; he has two fathers, as the King has two sons. When he enacts with Falstaff his forthcoming interview with his father, the theme is brought into the open.[8] It is not limited to court and tavern, the centers of the "double plot," as Empson calls it,[9] but extends to the rebel camp. Henry Percy stands between a weak father, Northumberland, who is prevented by illness from participating in the decisive battle, and a scheming uncle, Worcester, who plans the rebellion, conceals from Percy that the King offers reconciliation and drives him thus to battle and to death.

The three versions of the father-son conflict compelled Shakespeare to deviate from his sources and thereby to enrich the stage: he sharpened the report of the chronicles on the rebellion of the Percies in order to create the contrast of Worcester and Northumberland; he reduced Henry Percy's age from a slightly older contemporary of

Henry IV to a somewhat older contemporary of the Prince—and he invented Falstaff.

The triangular relationships are not only similar to each other, since they all contain variations of the theme of good and bad fathers and sons, but within each triangle the parallel figures are closely interconnected; thus the two Harrys, whom Henry IV compares, form a unit; Hotspur's rebellion represents also Prince Hal's unconscious parricidal impulses.[10] Hospur is the Prince's double. Impulses pertaining to one situation have thus been divided between two personages;[11] but though in the triangles the characters are paired and contrasted, each of the play's personages transcends the bondage to his function in this thematic configuration. They have all outgrown the symmetry which they serve, into the fullness of life.

To appraise Falstaff as a depreciated father figure is to grasp the superficial aspect of a character who, more than any other of Shakespeare, has enchanted readers and audiences since his creation. Franz Alexander finds two principal psychoanalytic explanations for this universal enchantment: Falstaff's hedonism, he says, represents the uninhibited gratification of an infantile and narcissistic quest for pleasure, a craving alive to some extent in every one of us; this hedonism, moreover, is made acceptable by contrast: one turns with relief from the court or the rebel camp to the tavern.[12] In accordance with the last is the traditional antithesis of "tragic King and comic people" used by Shakespeare to emphasize a moral antithesis.[13] From Prince Hal's point of view, Falstaff is a contrast to the King, who represents another version of the unsatisfactory paternal image. Henry IV succeeded his cousin Richard II by rebellion and regicide. The feeling of guilt that overshadowed his life becomes manifest when on his deathbed, in addressing the Prince, he reviews the sorrows that the unlawfully acquired crown inflicted on him.

> How I came by the crown, O God forgive!
> And grant it may with thee in true peace live.
> (*2 King Henry IV*, IV.v.219-221)

In this great scene Prince Henry's mood accords with his father's; he too is burdened with guilt. In the preceding scene he finds his father sleeping, and believes him to be dead. Shakespeare, adapting this scene from the chronicle play, has added a prop device: the crown which lies next to the King's bed.[14] The crown inspires the Prince with awe and apprehension. He longs to possess it, but "the best of gold" is "the worst of gold"; it endangers the bearer. He wages "the quarrel of a true inheritor," controls his desire and, in a mood of contemplation, concludes that royal responsibility is a heavy burden. He has overcome the hostile impulse against the dying King and can now reply to his father:

> You won it, wore it, kept it, gave it me;
> Then plain and right must my possession be;
> (2 *King Henry IV*, V.222-223)

It is an attempt to reassure: "Since I have come guiltless into the possession of the crown, since I refrained from regicide and parricide, I shall rightfully be King"; yet in the greatest crisis of his life, the Prince, now King Henry V, reveals that his apprehension has not been vanquished. The night before the battle of Agincourt, when his outnumbered army is weakened by disease, and confidence is more than ever required, he turns to prayer to avert divine retaliation for his father's crime that, with the crown, seems to have moved to his shoulders.

> O God of battles! steel my soldiers' hearts;
> Possess them not with fear; take from them now
> The sense of reckoning, if the opposed numbers
> Pluck their hearts from them. Not to-day, O Lord!
> O! not to-day, think not upon the fault
> My father made in compassing the crown.
> I Richard's body have interred new,
> And on it have bestow'd more contrite tears
> Than from it issued forced drops of blood.
> Five hundred poor I have in yearly pay,
> Who twice a day their wither'd hands hold up
> Toward heaven, to pardon blood; and I have built
> Two chantries, where the sad and solemn priests
> Sing still for Richard's soul. More will I do;
> Though all that I can do is nothing worth,
> Since that my penitence comes after all,
> Imploring pardon.
> (*King Henry V*, IV.i.306-322)

The essential passages of this prayer follow Holinshed's *Chronicles,* wherein it is reported that after his succession to the throne Henry V had King Richard's body ceremoniously interred in Westminster Abbey and made specified donations in commemoration. Reference to this incident and the place in which it is made invite comment. By reintroducing the theme of the tragic guilt attached to the House of Lancaster, Shakespeare establishes a link between *Henry V* and his older plays that dramatize the downfall of the Lancastrian Kings (Henry VI, Richard III). The victory of Agincourt and the life of Henry V are thus made to appear as a glorious interlude in a tragic tale of crime and doom; however, the King's prayer before the battle reveals the structure of the conflict which Shakespeare embodied in his character: the desire to avoid guilt and to keep himself pure of crime is paramount in Henry V. In one passage of the prayer the King recalls the tears he shed on Richard's coffin, a detail not recorded by Holinshed, and yet obviously suggested by other passages of the *Chronicle.* It may well be considered a hint—the only one we find in the trilogy— that there ever existed a personal relationship between Richard II and the son of his banished cousin Henry of Lancaster—Henry of Monmouth. During the last months of his rule King Richard II sailed for Ireland to quell a local rebellion, and he took Henry of Monmouth with him. The young Prince seems to have attracted the King's attention. The Prince was knighted by King Richard, Holinshed records, "for some valiant act that he did or some other favourable respect." Shakespeare was undoubtedly familiar with this account and very probably familiar with reports of the Prince's reaction to the news of his father's rebellion. Young Henry of Monmouth is said to have replied to a question of Richard's that he could not be held responsible for his father's deed.

In Shakespeare's *King Richard II* no direct reference is made to the relationship between Prince Hal and Richard,[15] but the theme to which we refer is present and clearly emphasized: one entire scene is devoted to it, the first in which the Prince is mentioned. Henry IV, newly enthroned, meets with his Lords—but his son is absent.

> Can no man tell of my unthrifty son?
> 'Tis full three months since I did see him last.
> If any plague hang over us, 'tis he.
> I would to God, my lords, he might be found:

Inquire at London, 'mongst the taverns there,
For there, they say, he daily doth frequent,
With unrestrained loose companions,
Even such, they say, as stand in narrow lanes,
And beat our watch, and rob our passengers.
(*King Richard II,* V.iii.1-9)

The Prince has dissociated himself from the court that his father won by treason. In silent protest he has turned to the tavern rather than to participate in regicide.[16] Regicide dominates the scene that starts with Henry IV's quest for his absent son. The last of Richard's followers and the new King's cousin, the Duke of Aumerle, confesses to Henry IV that he has plotted against his life. Before Aumerle can complete his confession, the Duke of York, his father and the uncle of Henry IV, forces his way into their presence. He doubts whether the purpose of Aumerle's audience be murder or repentance and is prepared to surrender his son.[17] This is the environment from which the Prince withdraws, to which he prefers the vices of Eastcheap and the freedom of Falstaff's company.

In *King Henry IV, Part II,* the contrast between court and tavern is reemphasized in a scene in which Falstaff's carefree vice is juxtaposed with John of Lancaster's virtuous villainy. This younger brother of Prince Hal is in command of the campaign against the still surviving rebels. Falstaff serves in his inglorious army. Lancaster promises the rebels pardon; they accept his offer and he breaks his word to send them to the gallows. We have just witnessed this monstrous perform-ance—taken directly from Holinshed's *Chronicles*—when Lancaster and Falstaff meet. The "sober blooded youth" provokes Falstaff's soliloquy in praise of Sherristack and of Prince Hal, whose valor has not made him addicted to "thin potations."

Falstaff's loving praise of the Prince and what others say when they refer to the Prince in the latter part of *Part II* of *Henry IV* remind us once more of how well he has succeeded in deceiving the world. His conversion upon his accession to the throne comes as a surprise to the court and to the tavern. Only the audience, having been in his con-fidence from his first solilquy, are enabled to understand the contra-dictions in his behavior as being a part of his paramount conflict.

When Shakespeare familiarized himself with the youth of Henry V, this conflict must have imposed upon his mind as one that would unify the various traits and incidents reported. The tendentious accounts in the *Chronicles* had not fully obliterated the traces of antagonism, in the relationship between the Prince and the King. This antagonism, the legends of the Prince's debauchery and conversion, and other elements that the dramatist found in his sources, he wove into a plausible character. The Prince tries to dissociate himself from the crime his father had committed; he avoids contamination with regicide because the impulse to regicide (parricide) is alive in his unconscious. When the King's life is threatened he saves the King and kills the adversary, who is his alter ego. In shunning the court for the tavern he expresses his hostility to his father and escapes the temptation to parricide. He can permit himself to share Falstaff's vices because he does not condone the King's crime; but hostility to the father is only temporarily repressed. When finally he is in possession of the crown, he turns against the father substitute; hence the pointed cruelty of Falstaff's rejection. Both paternal figures between which the Prince oscillates have less meaning to him than appears at first. What he opposes to them is different and of an exalted nature: his ideals of kingship, royal duty, and chivalry. These ideals are with him when he first appears on the stage; they grow in and with him throughout the tragedy, and they dominate throughout the five acts of *King Henry V*.

These ideals, one might speculate, may have been modeled on an idealization of Richard II, the murdered King, whom Prince Hal as a boy had accompanied to Ireland and whose favor he had won. Richard, however, was hardly fit to serve as model of a great king. Shakespeare has drawn him as a weak and irresponsible man, who depended presumptuously on the trappings of royalty for his kingship, on that ceremony that meant so little to Henry V and for which he substituted royal duty. One may conjecture this to have been a further reason why Shakespeare did not explicitly refer to the existence of a personal relationship between Prince Henry and King Richard. But all this is speculative. Opposed to it is solid evidence of the importance of moral conflicts in the personality of Henry V; it would be easy to demonstrate from metaphors and puns alone, with which the poet speaks through the hero, his proclivity to such conflicts. His major actions and interests all indicate too the Prince's search for moral justification.

While living the roistering life of the tavern, his thirst for glory won in battle—but only battle with a moral purpose—and chivalry was great; hence the Prince's bitter caricature of Hotspur.

> . . . I am not yet of Percy's mind, the Hotspur of the North; he that kills me some six or seven dozen of Scots at a break-fast, washes his hands, and says to his wife, 'Fie upon this quiet life! I want work.' 'O my sweet Harry,' says she, 'how many hast thou willed to-day?' 'Give my roan horse a drench,' says he, and answers, 'Some fourteen,' an hour after; 'a trifle, a trifle.'
>
>   (*1 King Henry IV*, II.iv.114-122)

There is jubilant relief when Percy turns to rebellion and the Prince can finally fight an envied rival, and in the service of a just cause liberate and use his own aggressive impulses; hence also, before the invasion of France, the preoccupation with legal points; and finally, on the night before Agincourt, the protracted debate with Williams, the soldier. Assuming that his partner in discussion is "Harry le Roy" an English commoner, the soldier argues

> . . . there are few die well that die in a battle; for how can they charitably dispose of any thing when blood is their argu-ment? Now, if these men do not die well, it will be a black matter for the king that led them to it. . . .
>
>   (*King Henry V*, IV.i.149-154)

Henry goes to great lengths to refute this thesis. He contends that the King is answerable only for the justice of his cause and cannot be answerable for "the particular endings of his soldiers," since "every subject is the King's, but every subject's soul is his own." The moving subtleties of this theological discourse[18] lead to the King's soliloquy on ceremony and royal destiny:

> Upon the king! let us our lives, our souls,
> Our debts, our careful wives,
> Our children, and our sins lay on the king!
> We must bear all. O hard condition!
> Twin-born with greatness, subject to the breath
> Of every fool, whose sense no more can feel
> But his own wringing. What infinite heart's ease

> Must kings neglect that private men enjoy!
> And what have kings that privates have not too,
> Save ceremony, save general ceremony?
> And what art thou, thou idol ceremony?
> *(King Henry V,* IV.i.241-251)

Summoned to battle, the King kneels in prayer in which he disclaims any complicity in his father's crime; thus prepared, the hero can conquer.

Henry V's preoccupation with morals is not glorified by Shakespeare nor presented as the dominant virtue of a "Christian soldier"; it is shown in its dynamic interplay with opposite tendencies, and occasionally—with a slightly ironical smile—exposed as a pretense. While the King is urging the clergy to establish his claim to the throne of France, the audience knows that he has forced the support of the Church by political pressure. The bishops, who have accepted the deal and supplied the garbled justification, are well aware of the King's burning desire for conquest. We are left in doubt as to whether it is political shrewdness or self-deception which prompts the King to pose the question.[19]

> May I with right and conscience make this claim?
> *(King Henry V,* I.ii.96)

Ambiguities and schisms of motivation are characteristic of the King. He flees to the tavern to escape from the evils of the court—but he becomes a past master of licentious living. He strives for humane warfare, and protects the citizens of conquered Harfleur;[20] but when the French break the laws of warfare in attacking the English encampment and killing the boys, Henry has every French prisoner's throat cut. The "friction between flesh and spirit,"[21] between impulse and inhibition, is fully resolved only when from moral scrutiny Henry proceeds to heroic venture, when as leader of men who are determined to fight with a clear conscience against overwhelming odds, he feels himself one among peers:

> We few, we happy few, we band of brothers.
> *(King Henry V,* IV.iii.60)

The inconsistencies in Prince Hal's character that some of Shakespeare's critics thought to have detected are not inconsistencies but attempts to resolve a conflict which is in some of its elements similar to Hamlet's. In Hamlet the Oedipus is fully developed, centering around the queen. In Shakespeare's historical dramas women are absent or insignificant. Prince Hal's struggle against his father appears therefore in isolation, enacted in male society. Hamlet stands between a murdered father and a murderous uncle. Prince Hal's father murdered his second cousin—and predecessor—to whom the Prince had an attachment. Thus the crime is in both cases carried out by the father or by his substitute—the King in Hamlet—while both heroes are battling against the murderous impulse in their own hearts.

The psychological plausibility of Prince Hal as a dramatic character is not inferior to that of Hamlet, whatever the difference in depth and dramatic significance of the two plays may be. While only one part of the oedipal conflict is presented, the defenses which Prince Hal mobilizes in order to escape from his internal predicament are well known from the clinical study of male youths. In our anlysis of the Prince's character we have implicitly referred mainly to two mechanisms: first, to the formation of the superego; second, the displacement of filial attachment onto a father substitute.

The Prince, in his thoughts, compares the King, his father, with an ideal of royal dignity far superior to the father himself. This ideal, derived from paternal figures but exalted and heightened, is his protection in the struggle against his parricidal impulses and against submission to the King. This mechanism operates in some form or other in every boy's development at the time of the resolution of the oedipal conflict. During this process the superego acquires part of its severity and some of its autonomy. It is a process subject to many vicissitudes, as illustrated by a clinical example.

A boy of eight approached his father, a distinguished judge, with a request for advice. He held two one dollar bills and wanted to know whether he might keep them. They had been acquired by the sale to neighbors of pencils which a mail order house had sent him on his request. Upon the receipt of the two dollars he was to be sent a premium to which he now preferred the money. The judge asked to see the advertisement to which the boy had responded and the letter of the mail order house. After reading both he ruled: "You may keep the money; they have no right to make such contracts with minors."

When thirty-five years later the incident was recalled in analysis it appeared that he had not only lost confidence in all authority since that time, but also that when he had asked his father's advice he was testing him. He had grown suspicious that the father did not live up to the principles—sexual and moral—he advocated, and when in his own conflict he sought the father's advice, he had hoped that the father would support his own hesitant moral views. When this expectation was disappointed, he acquired a cynical independence. The compulsion to live up to his ideal became part of a complex neurotic symptomatology.

In one detail only did this patient resemble Prince Hal: His own moral standards assured his independence from all paternal figures and were used as aggressive reproach in every contact with them. Prince Hal uses not only his ideal of moral integrity as reproachful contrast against his father, but also his own playful depravity. The second mechanism of defense the Prince mobilizes is no less common than the first. He adopts an extrafamilial substitute who, true to a pattern frequently observed, is the antithesis of the father. Falstaff is closer to the Prince's heart than the King; he satisfies the libidinal demands in the father-son relation through his warmth and freedom. Yet the Prince proves superior to Falstaff in wit and royal reveling: he triumphs over both father and father substitute.[22] He is paramount in license as he will be paramount in royal dignity.

Literary critics seem of late weary of the intrusion of psychoanalysis. However politely, they assert—and rightly so—their independence.[23] This essay is a psychological analysis which attempts only to underline a few universal, unconscious mechanisms, and is not intended as literary criticism. It suggests that Shakespeare had puzzled about the nature of Henry V's personality, and that already, while writing the last act of *Richard II,* was aware of the conflict on which he intended to center the character development of the King. Shakespeare's plan, suggested in this case by the nature of the tradition about the subject, must have been one of the trends of thought that, on various levels of awareness, directed him in writing the trilogy. It is not suggested that the plan was complete from the beginning; it might have manifested itself to the poet during his work, that is, it might have been preconscious before. Moreover, some elements we here consider part of this plan probably never reached consciousness. What answer Shakespeare might have given if asked why Henry V kills Falstaff by his harshness is comparatively irrelevant. What counts is that he had the King do so, and he surely must have known that this could hardly be popular with his audience. Such internal consistency, the final parricide, can only have been conceived by one who in creating had access to his own unconscious impulses.

If investigations similar to the one here attempted, but more complete and authoritative, were carried out systematically; if they were to comprehend all of Shakespeare's work, and, at least for purposes of comparison, the works of other Elizabethans; if conflicts and their varied or preferred solutions, and those omitted by one author, one group of authors, one period, or one cultural area were collated—such an application of psychoanalysis might be integrated with the work of the literary historian or critic.

Plot and character are clearly not the only, and not always the most important, tools of the dramatic poet. Psychoanalysis suggests other approaches for the study of poetic language, its metaphors and hidden meanings.[24] Systematic investigation in this area may lead to other types of integration than the study of plot or character. The combination of various sequences of such systematic studies might finally lead to a topic in which critics and psychoanalysts are equally interested and about which they are both, each in his own field, almost equally ignorant: the nature of the artist's personality, a question that must be studied in its cultural variations before generalizations can be made.

Psychoanalysis has frequently attempted short cuts, mostly by correlating one of the artist's works with an occurrence noted by his biographers,[25] assumptions that can rarely be verified.

Clinical analysis of creative artists suggests that the life experience of the artist is sometimes only in a limited sense the source of his vision; that his power to imagine conflicts may by far transcend the range of his own experience; or, to put it more accurately, that at least some artists possess the particular gift to generalize from whatever their own experience has been. One is always tempted to look for a cue that would link this or that character to its creator's personality. Falstaff, it has been said, is clearly Shakespeare himself. Why not Percy or Richard II? Are they not equally alive, equally consistent? Could not for each of these characters that very same psychological plausibility be claimed, that we here claim for Prince Hal? Such a quest seems futile and contrary to what clinical experience with artists as psychoanalytic subjects seems to indicate. Some great artists seem to be equally close to several of their characters, and may feel many of them as parts of themselves. The artist has created a world and not indulged in a daydream.

This writer is not exempt from the temptation to detect a neat connection between the artist and one of his characters. I therefore record my own venture in this direction, with appropriate reservations. At the time Shakespeare was working on Richard II, and studying the life of Prince Hal, he reestablished the prestige of the Shakespeare family (which had been lost through his father's bankruptcy) by purchasing a coat of arms. The motto chosen is one that might well have been used to characterize Prince Hal's striving for the crown: *"Non sanz droict."*

Notes

1. For mythic analyses, see J. I. M. STEWART, *Character and Motive in Shakespeare* (London: Longmans, Green, 1949), pp. 132-139; C. L. BARBER, "From Ritual to Comedy: An Examination of *Henry IV*," in W. K. WIMSATT, JR. (ed.), *English Stage Comedy* (New York: Columbia University Press, 1955). pp. 22-51. The father-son theme is best represented by Kris. As for the character of Falstaff, see FRANZ ALEXANDER, "A Note on Falstaff," *Psychoanalytic Quarterly*, 2:592-606, 1933.

1. It is generally assumed that *Part I* of *King Henry IV* was written in 1596 or 1597, immediately or soon after the completion of *King Richard II*, and *Part II* in 1597 or 1598. *King Henry V* must have been completed shortly before or some time during 1599.

2. See BRADLEY (1934), whose censure of Shakespeare is moderate compared to that of HAZLITT (1848).

3. For the legend of Prince Hal, see especially KABEL (1936, pp. 363-416).

4. KINGSFORD, 1901, p. 12.

5. T. SPENCER, 1942.

6. See AX (1912).

7. That the repetition of one theme in various configurations in-dicates its central position was pointed out by JEKELS (1933).

8. The idea of the travestied interview itself is borrowed from *The Famous Victories of Henry the Fifth*. There the Prince and his companions enact the Prince's subsequent interview with the Chief-justice.

9. W. E. EMPSON, 1925.

10. This point was made by ALEXANDER (1933), and by EMPSON (1935, p. 43).

11. ERNEST JONES (1911, 1949) speaks in a similar connection of decomposition.

12. FRANZ ALEXANDER, "A Note on Falstaff," *Psychoanalytic Quarterly* 2:592-606, 1933.

13. EMPSON, *op. cit.*

14. The very crown that literally he had taken from Richard II. See *Richard II*, IV.i.177-221.

15. One might conjecture that Shakespeare preferred not to refer to the personal relationship between Prince Hal and King Richard since he needed a more mature Prince, not a boy of twelve.

16. Only once Henry V states openly his disapproval of his father's actions, and then in a highly restrained fashion. When wooing, some-what abruptly, Katherine of France he says

> . . . I dare not swear thou lovest me; yet my blood begins to flatter me that thou dost, notwithstanding the poor and un-tempering effect of my visage. *Now beshrew my father's ambition! He was thinking of civil wars when he got me.*
> (V.ii.238-243; italics added)

17. York himself had plotted against Richard II and seeks his son's punishment out of a displaced feeling of guilt. Some of the complexities of this relationship were elucidated by TAYLOR (1927).

18. Canterbury says of the newly enthroned Henry V:

> Hear him but reason in divinity
> And, all admiring, with an inward wish
> You would desire the king were made a prelate.
> (I.i.37-40)

19. A somewhat similar analysis of this passage has been given by

TRAVERSI (1941), who in a remarkable essay stresses the importance of "cool reasoning" and "self-domination" in the King's character.

20. TRAVERSI (1941) notes that when the King presents his ultimatum to Harfleur his passion rises, and that in accepting the surrender he regains self-control.

21. *Ibid.*

22. The son's superiority over the father occurs also in other connections in the trilogy. Hotspur is superior to both Worcester and Northumberland, and Aumerle is superior to his father, York, who first betrays King Richard before he betrays his own son.

23. See TRILLING's excellent essay, *Freud and Literature* (1947), or KNIGHT's essay "Prince Hamlet" (1946).

24. See SHARPE (1946).

25. This procedure was initiated in 1900 by a remark of Freud, who envisaged the possibility that Shakespeare's choice of Hamlet as a topic and the treatment of the conflict might have to do with the death of Shakespeare's father and his son Hamnet.

"Henry IV, Part Two"

Norman Holland's essay calls to mind the preceding selection by Kris in that it concentrates intensively upon conflict in *Henry IV* from a perspective that places important historical material, material derived from what we can call the Elizabethan metaphysic of history, upon a realistic psychological foundation. Both Holland and Kris go far beyond mere historical criticism, helping us to understand fully the timelessness of the struggle depicted in the Henry plays. Holland's paper, however, broadens Kris's original insight considerably by including in its analysis of conflict not only the principals but the whole cast of characters who are caught up in the civic turmoil. While Holland regards Hal's struggle as central, he also recognizes the extent to which it derives crucial dramatic strength and meaning from Shakespeare's depiction of the struggles in which all the characters are involved. Individual actions ramify until they are inextricably interlaced. Accordingly, Hal's answer to the question that confronts him makes full dramatic sense only when we view it as an answer to both his personal conflict and to the conflicts of all the characters whose conduct of necessity influences the shape of the nation. What Hal does with Falstaff, and John with the Rebels, is done in an effort to actualize a definition of civil order that is in harmony with nature insofar as it allows the individual to realize his full psychological potential, to escape the pitfalls created by an immature orientation toward one's society, one's fellow men, and one's self.

Mr. Holland begins by pointing out that *II Henry IV* explores a quintessential Shakespearean theme—betrayal. Everywhere in this play characters are suddenly confronted with situations they did not expect. To employ Holland's own terminology, expectation is continually mocked. But *II Henry IV* deals with expectations of a particular nature, expectations that are rooted in egotistic striving for personal aggrandizement, expectations that bluntly ignore the welfare of the social mechanism in which men must live. Thus, the disappointment of these expectations is meted out to characters who have not learned a very basic psychological truth, namely that to fulfill oneself as a human being one must, in trust and generous giving, submit oneself to the larger order that permits the existence of the individual. As for those who are meting out the disappointment, they are coming, gradually and perhaps even painfully, to appreciate the importance of this truth.

M. F.

etrayal, someone has said, is the quintessential Shakespearean theme. Certainly, it would seem to be in *Henry IV* [*Part Two*], for this play hinges on two betrayals. Prince John promises the rebels in a battlefield parley their "griefs shall be with speed redressed. Upon my soul, they shall." Then, once the rebels' troops are discharged, he tells them he will indeed redress their grievances "with a most Christian care"—but executes them as rebels. "God, and not we, hath safely fought today." (Some outraged critics have called the line blasphemous.) Then, at the end of the play, after the death of Henry IV, Falstaff expects to be "one of the greatest men in his realm" in something other than size. He cheers his newly crowned Hal only to be answered by one of the most magnificent and brutal lines in all literature: "I know thee not, old man. Fall to thy prayers." Dismissed, banished, he dies in *Henry V* because "The King has killed his heart."

The ethical rightness or wrongness of these actions constitutes one of the two bones of contention this play has cast among critics.[1] The other is the relation of this play to Part One: are Parts One and Two separate plays or one long ten-act play?[2] The answers to both (like all questions we ask of Shakespeare) must come from a recognition of the significant wholeness of the work of art he has created, for these two seeming betrayals, morally ambiguous as they may appear, make only two among a host of other such incidents in the play.

For example, in an episode that Shakespeare carefully retained

"Introduction" by Norman N. Holland. Reprinted with permission from Norman H. Holland, ed. *Henry IV, Part II* (New American Library, 1965).

from his sources, the old king, believing a prophecy he is to die "in Jerusalem," expects to die on a Crusade. Instead, he finds himself dying, not in the city Jerusalem but in a room in Westminster called "Jerusalem." Once Henry IV is dead, the Lord Chief Justice (who had clapped Hal in prison) thinks himself a man doomed, but instead, the new king creates him Chief Justice anew, "a father to my youth," and puts him in charge of Falstaff. Bringing these and many other such reversals to a fullness and completion is, of course, the reformation of Hal himself from the madcap prince to what he will be in *Henry V*, "the mirror of all Christian kings." "Let the end try the man," he had warned earlier; and at the end he acts

> To mock the expectation of the world,
> To frustrate prophecies, and to raze out
> Rotten opinion, who hath writ me down
> After my seeming.
>
> (V.ii.126-129)

"Expectation mocked" is the key, a theme that pervades and informs the comic scenes as well as the serious ones. To the Lord Chief Justice's amused outrage, Falstaff, who illustrates "all the characters of age," has the gall to set down his name "in the scroll of youth" and —even—call the Justice old. He manages to elude the legal powers of the Lord Chief Justice (roughly equivalent to the Chief Justice of the U. S. Supreme Court), and then he has the effrontery to try to borrow a thousand pounds from him. Mistress Quickly believes Falstaff will marry her (perhaps the silliest of all expectations in a play of silly expectations), and thus Falstaff manages to turn her lawsuit into a cozy dinner party. Old Justice Shallow, in one of the most exquisite moments of the play, turns away from that death that hovers over all the characters to a startling image of vitality and (in Elizabethan English) virility:

Shallow. Jesu, Jesu, the mad days that I have spent! And to see how many of my old acquaintance are dead!
Silence. We shall all follow, cousin.
Shallow. Certain, 'tis certain, very sure, very sure. Death, as the Psalmist saith, is certain to all, all shall die. How [much for] a good yoke of bullocks at Stamford Fair?

> (III.ii.37-43)

Shallow, the classic portrait of the old grad, makes much of "the wild-ness of his youth," but we find that his talk is all an old man's lying. Young Shallow was thin, puny, "ever in the rearward of the fashion," and yet, notes Falstaff ruefully, "Now has he lands and beeves." Everywhere expectation is overturned. Falstaff picks (from Shallow's point of view) precisely the wrong men for his recruits. Yet even so, Francis Feeble of valorous name turns out to have that stoical ac-ceptance of destiny that constitutes (as we shall see) the essential ethic the play puts forward.

The same sense of expecation mocked permeates the language and imagery of the play. What should give hope or security does not. Armor "worn in heat of day . . . scald'st with safety," while, con-versely, "In poison there is physic." Hopes, like ships, "touch ground and dash themselves to pieces," while even houses are "giddy and un-sure." The very buds,

> which to prove fruit,
> Hope gives not so much warrant as despair
> That frost will bite them.
>
> (I.iii.39-41)

Fathers who care for their sons, like bees that gather honey, "are murdered for [their] pains." Sleep, in the King's lovely apostrophe, comes to the least likely, the shipboy suffering a storm in the crows' nest:

> Canst thou, O partial sleep, give thy repose
> To the wet sea-son in an hour so rude,
> And in the calmest and most stillest night,
> With all appliances and means to boot,
> Deny it to a king? Then happy low, lie down!
> Uneasy lies the head that wears a crown.
>
> (III.i.26-31)

The least fortunate are most fortunate—one cannot predict, for prem-onitions themselves run by opposites:

> Against ill chances men are ever merry,
> But heaviness foreruns the good event.
>
> (IV.ii.81-82)

Even the mere dramaturgic content of *2 Henry IV* mocks expectation. The madcap prince of Part Two reverses the reformation we have already seen in Part One. The odd epilogue treats the plays as the unsuccessful payment of a debt—an expectation—and goes on to contract a further debt: "Our humble author will continue the story, with Sir John in it." But Falstaff does not appear in *Henry V*, and further, he is not to be confused with the character you expected him to be; "Oldcastle died martyr, and this is not the man."

Even odder than the epilogue is the induction with Rumor as the presenter. Shakespeare, as always, sets up the internal logic of his work from the very opening lines: Rumor, whatever else he may be, is the creator and defeater of expectations par excellence, bringer of "smooth comforts false, worse than true wrongs." Here, he announces falsely a rebel victory at Shrewsbury and the death of Prince Hal under the sword of Northumberland's son Hotspur. Then, almost the entire first scene of the play deals with expectations created and defeated (even down to the opening lines in which a porter says that Northumberland will be found in the orchard, but then the Earl himself unexpectedly appears). And, of course, no one expected the madcap prince to overcome "the never-daunted Percy." Learning of his son's death, Northumberland says,

> . . . these news,
> Having been well, that would have made me sick,
> Being sick, have in some measure made me well.
>
> (I.i.137-139)

Much later in the play, another old man, King Henry IV, will echo his paradox: "Wherefore should these good news make me sick?" In either case, news—words—seem to have an effect opposite to what one would expect.

The first scene shifts to the second, from one diseased old man to another:

Falstaff. Sirrah . . . what says the doctor to my water [i.e., urine]?
  Page. He said, sir, the water itself was a good healthy water; but, for the party that [owned] it, he might have [more] diseases than he knew. . . .

> (I.ii.1-6)

The Page's response, itself a mockery of what we might expect from a doctor, continues from the previous scene the tension between words and body.

As we might expect from Falstaff's "throng of words" or, indeed, the figure of Rumor, "painted full of tongues," words—"prophecies," "seeming," "rotten opinion," "news"—all play a key role in 2 Henry IV in creating expectations that deeds and persons then defeat in fact, as

>   chances mock,
> And changes fill the cup of alteration
> With divers liquors.
>   (III.i.51-53)

Most notably, Prince John tricks the rebels with his "princely word": "I give it you, and will maintain my word"—though the letter, not the spirit. But there are others whose words create false expectations: Mistress Quickly's malapropisms and Pistol's ranting in garbled quotations make us expect to hear one thing; then, when we hear their blunder, our expectation is mocked. And the rebels, too, create false hopes with words:

> We fortify in paper and in figures,
> Using the names of men instead of men,
> Like one that draws the model of an house
> Beyond his power to build.
>   (I.iii.55-58)

As Lord Bardolph's words hint, this play uses (unusually often for Shakespeare) names that tag their bearers in a manner almost Dickensian: Pistol, Shallow, Shadow, and Moldy; Doll Tearsheet and Jane Nightwork of amorous name; the Sheriff's men, Fang and Snare; Mistress Quickly, whose name, in Elizabethan pronounciation, conceals a ribald pun; Goodman Puff, fat as Falstaff, and hungry Francis Pickbone; Traverse, who, in the opening scene, denies ("traverses") Lord Bardolph's report. Yet, as one would expect in a play of expectations mocked, the actual, physical characters often belie their tags; Sampson Stockfish is a fruiterer, Bullcalf a coward, and Feeble brave.

We would be wrong, though, to conclude that words always build up false expectations, that 2 Henry IV envisions no larger plan that one can trust—such a skepticism would be utterly foreign to Shakespeare and the Elizabethans' sense of cosmic order. There is, as the King says, a plan, though a bitter one, "the book of fate" that lists the defeats of our expectations:

> O, if this were seen,
> The happiest youth, viewing his progress through,
> What perils past, what crosses to ensue,
> Would shut the book, and sit him down and die.
> (III.i.54-57)

And Warwick goes on to make an important statement of the Elizabethans' anecdotal or symbolistic view of history:

> There is a history in all men's lives,
> Figuring the nature of the times deceased,
> The which observed, a man may prophesy,
> With a near aim, of the main chance of things
> As yet not come to life.
> (III.i.80-84)

There is, then, a larger order, and some of the characters find their place in it. Others, notably Falstaff and the rebels who are "betrayed," do not. What is the essential difference between those who find a place and those who are "betrayed"?

As so often in Shakespeare, a peripheral episode tells us, a scene superfluous to the main plot but one which Shakespeare spent some pains to improve from his sources. Hal, thinking his father dead, takes his crown into another room. His father revives and accuses him of wishing parricide. It is, of course, one more episode of expectations mocked, but the King's words tell us more: he accuses Hal of being "hasty," unable to "stay," of wishing his father's death: "What! Canst thou not forbear me half an hour?" Slowly, Hal answers. He did not "affect," that is, crave, desire, the crown. Rather, he took it as an enemy: it "hath fed upon the body of my father." Its gold is no medicine, but rather "hast eat thy bearer up." The King is pleased with his son's "pleading so wisely." Wherein does the wisdom lie?

The King explains in his next speech, "the very latest counsel that ever I shall breathe," presumably, therefore, the most important. He recalls the way he took the crown from Richard in *Richard II,*

How troublesome it sat upon my head.
To thee it shall descend with better quiet.

. . .

It seemed in me
But as an honor snatched with boisterous hand.

. . .

And now my death
Changes the mood, for what in me was purchased
Falls upon thee in a more fairer sort,
So thou the garland wear'st successively.

(IV.v.187-202)

The word "purchased" is important: a legal term, it refers to the
acquiring of land other than by inherited succession ("successively").
The word reflects, as the whole play does, the feudal and Renaissance
prejudice against those who violate the natural order of things by
taking for themselves against the ordained patterns of birth and inheritance. Henry sinned when he "snatched" the crown, but Hal will
wear it free of such sin, for he inherits it. The King's accusations tell
us Hal's wrong in taking the crown from his sleeping father lay in his
inability to "forbear," to "stay," in his "wish," his being "hasty."

Thou hast stolen that which after some few hours
Were thine without offense.

(IV.v.102-103)

Hal's answer is wise in that he says he did not crave the crown, but
rather recognized that the crown is an enemy that feeds on its bearer,
eats its bearer up.

Appetite is both the sin and the danger, that appetite which, as the
Prince had jokingly confessed earlier, "was not princely got." To be
truly a prince, one must not crave and try to take, but rather forbear,
wait, trust, put oneself in that larger order: God's, nature's, his father's.
Appetite governs the common man, not the prince, and, indeed, it was
the common people's appetite that let Henry take the crown from
Richard, though, says the Archbishop,

The commonwealth is sick of their own choice;
Their overgreedy love hath surfeited.

. . .
Thou, beastly feeder, art so full of [Henry]
That thou provok'st thyself to cast him up.
So, so, thou common dog, didst thou disgorge
Thy glutton bosom of the royal Richard;
And now thou wouldst eat thy dead vomit up,
And howl'st to find it. What trust is in these times?
(I.iii.87-100)

The wise monarch provides for his people's appetites. Henry's last counsel—for his expectation was again foiled, his statement of Hal's rightful title was not his "latest counsel"—Henry's last advice is to "busy giddy minds with foreign quarrels," to turn appetite elsewhere, for Henry knows all too well the rebel and vain spirit is one that seeks to take for itself rather than accept the natural order of monarchy.

That larger order is not wholly beneficent, for it includes, as Shallow reminds us, death. "Death, as the Psalmist saith, is certain to all, all shall die," all: Northumberland, the King, Shallow, Silence, Falstaff, the Lord Chief Justice—all the old men in this play of old men are dying. Some try to put it aside, like Falstaff: "Peace, good Doll! Do not speak like a death's head. Do not bid me remember my end." But death cannot be put aside. In Sir Thomas Browne's beautiful sentence, "This world is not an inn but an hospital," not a place to feed but a place to die in. One may consult the doctor as Falstaff does; or, as the Archbishop's rebellion tries to do,

diet rank minds sick of happiness
And purge the obstructions which begin to stop
Our very veins of life.
(IV.i.64-66)

But purges and potions, be they the medicinable gold that the crown so distinctly is not or the sherris-sack whose virtues Falstaff so eloquently proclaims, are of no real use, for death is certain. Though it may be unexpected, in a chamber named Jerusalem instead of the city, death itself is certain.

The play's images of medicines represent one kind of defense against the acceptance of a larger, cosmic order that includes disease and death; words represent another. Thus, the rebels project and plan, emitting words, "publish[ing] the occasion of our arms." They "fortify with the names of men." The Archbishop, so "deep within the books of God," turns himself into "an iron man talking." In general, the rebels emit words and then take them for things, as their predecessor Hotspur did,

> who lined himself with hope
> Eating the air and promise of supply.
> (I.iii.27-28)

They forget their physical selves and ask only for their "articles," "this schedule," their "conditions" in a "true substantial form." And verbal form is all John gives them.

Falstaff, too, emits a "throng of words" that wrench the "true cause the false way." Contrasted with them, taking language in,

> The Prince but studies his companions
> Like a strange tongue, wherein, to gain the language,
> 'Tis needful that the most immodest word
> Be looked upon and learned,
> (IV.iv.68-71)

but once learned, he will no longer speak, emit, such words, but rather take them "as a pattern or a measure" with which to judge the lives of others.

In other words, the Prince will not thrust up a merely verbal reality against the larger order. Rather, he will make himself and his language a part of that larger order, as Prince John does: "God, and not we, hath safely fought today." Pathetically, the rebels themselves try to become part of some larger order: "We are time's subjects."

> We see which way the stream of time doth run,
> And are enforced from our most quiet there
> By the rough torrent of occasion.
> (IV.i.70-72)

But "occasion" is a transitory thing, a creature of time, and time itself is a great betrayer. The King's party fits into a firmer order: "Construe the times to their necessities." When Warwick states the Elizabethan view of history, he speaks of it as a "necessary form." When King Henry disclaims any intent on his part of seizing Richard's crown, he says,

> Necessity so bowed the state
> That I and greatness were compelled to kiss.
>
> (III.i.73-74)

And he accepts the rebel threat—

> Are these things then necessities?
> Then let us meet them like necessities.
>
> (III.i.92-93)

The rebels, however, are responding, not to "necessities," but their "most just and right desires," the "demands" they seek to "enjoy." Appetite is their failure, and John's strategy simply traps them as animals are baited and trapped by their appetites. They drink as token of their wishes granted, but the drink also symbolizes their failure and defeat through appetite. (Indeed, the Archbishop after drinking finds himself "passing light in spirit.")

The real drinker, though, the very essence of appetite, is, of course, Falstaff. "He hath eaten me out of house and home," Mistress Quickly complains. "The old boar" (earlier he had been a sow) doth "feed in the old frank," monetarily, emotionally, and gastrically. At Shallow's, "We shall do nothing but eat, and make good cheer." Falstaff feeds on Shallow, too, taking a thousand pounds from him, promising to turn him into verbal jokes just as he himself ("the cause that wit is in other men") turns himself to words. Hal's succession provokes him into a riot of appetite: "Let us take any man's horses; the laws of England are at my commandment."

Thus, it is supremely appropriate that Hal reject him ("the feeder of my riots") in terms of food, as, earlier, he had taken leave of a Falstaff richly symbolized as a withered apple. In the coronation scene, Falstaff calls out, "My King! My Jove!" (thus identifying himself with Saturn, the titan who devoured his own children). Hal replies:

> I know thee not, old man. Fall to thy prayers.
> How ill white hairs becomes a fool and jester!
> I have long dreamt of such a kind of man,
> So surfeit-swelled, so old, and so profane,
> But, being awaked, I do despise my dream.
> Make less thy body hence, and more thy grace.
> Leave gormandizing. Know the grave doth gape

For thee thrice wider than for other men.
Reply not to me with a fool-born jest.

(V.v.51-59)

Not only does Hal put aside appetite—he fends off Falstaff's word-mongering (even as he himself lapses into two jokes—though he immediately counters, "Presume not that I am the thing I was"). Saddest of all, most brutal but most necessary, he reminds Falstaff of his role as an old man and of the grave's mouth that gapes so widely for him.

The mouth, food and medicine going into it, words coming out, these images dominating a play of appetites and expectations mocked—Shakespeare here harks back to a truth of infancy, to a time when life was a life of the mouth. Psychologists such as Erik Erikson have been stressing in recent years the crucial importance of that time when we must discover our own identities; when we learn, taught by our own appetites, that we must await, trust, expect another to feed us. It is this ability to trust in another that enables the infant to experience that other as an existence separate from his own desires, to experience, therefore, his own separateness, his identity. The paradox continues into later life: it is the ability to give up one's own desires, to trust, even to merge and identify with the "necessity" represented by others, even, in a sense, to tolerate being engulfed by or devoured by it (as King Henry's crown, emblem of the larger order, has eaten its bearer up), that enables us to reemerge, as we did in earliest infancy, into a new sense of identity, a new role. In a paradox almost Biblical, we must lose ourselves to find ourselves.

So with Falstaff: to grow into the new role he should assume now that Hal is king, he must curb his appetites ("Leave gormandizing") and learn to depend on another (the "competence of life" his new king allows him). He must live with the certainty that the grave gapes for him, that he will himself be devoured. As for the rebels, they do not let themselves be merged into the larger necessity represented by the monarch; instead, they try to create roles for themselves out of their own words (or mouths). Necessarily, they fail.

Prince Hal, too, must give up an identity based on his own appetites, that of the madcap prince, and accept an identity set out for him, that of the hero-king. As Ernst Kris points out in a psychoanalytic study of this play, Hal, until his father's death, refuses to fall back into the role his father has planned for him. Rather, he puts aside his father, stained and imperfect as a curber of appetites because he himself "snatched" the crown "with boisterous hand," and he takes an identity from Falstaff, a father-substitute. Once his real father is dead, however, he can put aside Falstaff (ultimately rendering him as dead as his true father) and be taken into the role his father wished for him. Indeed, he can even accept a proper father-substitute in the person of the Lord Chief Justice.

Food is our earliest experience of trust; justice is a later one. Again, we must learn to wait rather than try to grab—we must trust in the larger necessity of law. *2 Henry IV* gives us a pair of justices: a true one in the Lord Chief Justice, a false one in Shallow, who succumbs to his servant's entreaty to "bear out a knave against an honest man." Shallow lets himself merge into a larger order, but one of his servants' making, so that, as Falstaff points out, they become like foolish justices, he a justice-like servingman. The Lord Chief Justice, however, speaks to Hal with "the person of your father"; "the image of his power lay then in me." He justifies his earlier action of imprisoning the Prince by reminding the new young king that he, now, has a new identity— "As you are a king, speak in your state." And Hal responds by assuming his kingly role, merging himself in his father's identity so that "I live to speak my father's words." To the Lord Chief Justice,

> You shall be as a father to my youth.
> My voice shall sound as you do prompt mine ear.
> And I will stoop and humble my intents
> To your well-practiced wise directions.
> . . .
> My father is gone wild into his grave,
> For in his tomb lie my [appetites]
> And with his spirits sadly I survive
> To mock the expectation of the world. . . .
>   (V.ii.118-126)

Thus, Hal merges into his father and contrasts with the Archbishop, who rebelled though he was "the imagined voice of God himself"; he did

> misuse the reverence of his place,
> Employ the countenance and grace of heaven,
> As a false favorite does his prince's name,
> In deeds dishonorable.
> (IV.ii.23-26)

The right people of the play merge into a larger order; the wrong people resist or misuse that larger order. Shallow's very name tells us something about their failure: as Prince John says to the rebels,

> You are too shallow, Hastings, much too shallow,
> To sound the bottom of the after-times.
> (IV.ii.50-51)

The image is of a river, and the Archbishop had earlier compared himself and the other rebels to a river in flood, saying that, if their demands are granted, "We come within our awful banks again." Henry IV, too, is liked to a flooding river: in a detail Shakespeare retained from his sources, Henry (who was himself a rebel) dies as the Thames thrice floods without ebb. As for Hal,

> The tide of blood in me
> Hath proudly flowed in vanity till now.
> Now doth it turn and ebb back to the sea,
> Where it shall mingle with the state of floods
> And flow henceforth in formal majesty.
> (V.ii.129-133)

He has put aside flooding and merged himself into the identity ordained for him by that larger order, vast as the sea. The play can end now, as it began, with a rumor. But now a true rumor, for a bird sings the music of true expectation, the King's will merged into the nation's destiny.

In short, the theme of betrayal permeates and informs the language, incidents, and characters of *2 Henry IV*, but it is betrayal in a special sense: "expectations mocked." That is, the play begins with a sense of hunger or appetite:

Open your ears, for which of you will stop
The vent of hearing when loud Rumor speaks?
(Induction, 1-2)

Then, against selfish or foolish appetite, the play poises a larger, parental plan of justice or monarchy or necessity that threatens to swallow up the characters by danger, disease, or death. And yet this larger necessity offers the paradoxical and unexpected possibility of a new identity, a kind of rebirth into a new self for those who can merge themselves into it. True princeliness calls for this ability to trust in the larger order, to achieve identity by the very act of curbing the self and its appetites and being merged into the greater plan. True rebellion means—in its most primitive sense—feeding oneself, resisting trust in that larger order by substituting one's own medicines, words, appetite, food, plans: "eating the air." And thus, the play itself answers the critics who have been troubled by Prince John's trick on the political rebels and Prince Hal's rejection of the appetitive rebel, Falstaff. These two "betrayals" become necessary and inevitable if we take the play on its own emotional and intellectual terms: the original failure of trust was the rebels' own inability to merge (without wordy conditions) into the larger order of nature.

Again, if we take the play on its own terms, we can see the answer to the second critical issue: the relation of Part Two to Part One. The external evidence from Elizabethan stage-practice that the two plays must have been separate and self-sufficient entities is clear enough. The internal evidence is clear, too. Part One and Part Two are quite different in their essential dramatic ideas, but they make a matched pair.

We can see the difference in the Falstaffs of the two parts. Twinned in avoirdupois, soldiering, and appetites, they nevertheless differ in some important ways. In both parts, Falstaff is a creature who defeats expectation, not only in the action, but also in our response (as Freud notes). From the point of view of the literary historian, as Bernard Spivack has shown, this mocking of our expectations places him in the tradition of the deceptive Vice of the morality plays or the tricky Ambidexter of a *Cambises*. But in Part One, Falstaff seems more triumphant: the Chaplinesque clown who, by his ability to play many parts, triumphs even over death, as (in the final battle) he feigns a death-and-rebirth. In Part Two, Falstaff resists, but succumbs to, the preordained role pointed out by Philip Williams and C. L. Barber. He becomes the slain god, the Lord of Misrule who must be banished to restore health to the land. Hal is absorbed into the role of the hero-king, while Falstaff is engulfed by a mythic significance that demands his rejection and death.

Miss Caroline Spurgeon noted some years ago that the Falstaff of Part One uses many images from books and the Bible, while the Falstaff of Part Two speaks in grotesque, rough, coarse similes drawn from body functions and appetites. We can add that Falstaff One uses a very distinctive figure of speech, the enthymeme: "If I travel but four foot by the squire further afoot, I shall break my wind." "If the rascal have not given me medicines to make me love him, I'll be hanged." "And 'twere not as good a deed as drink to turn true man and to leave these rogues, I am the veriest varlet that ever chewed with a tooth." (These all occur within ten lines in Part One, suggesting the frequency of the figure.) Falstaff Two almost entirely lacks this figure of speech; instead, he has become something of a monologist. He takes in a character, then turns him into a satirical portrait: we see Falstaff Two do this with himself, his page, his tailor, Pistol, Prince Hal, Poins, Bardolph, Shallow, Prince John, and, of course, sherris-sack, in monologues quite different in style from his catechism of honor in Part One (which tests a role). Falstaff Two may be responding to the same taste that led Jonson to put such incidental character sketches into *Every Man Out of his Humor* and *Cynthia's Revels* or that accounts for the popularity of the character-books of Hall, Overbury, and others in the early seventeenth century, but, in any case, he has shifted from acting out different roles (often taken from books and the Bible) to a more passive taking in of what he sees, then spewing it out in words (the image of vomit occurs several times in *2 Henry IV*). Falstaff One's big comic scene is the play-within-the-play in the tavern, when he tries on the roles of King Henry and Prince Hal. Falstaff Two's big comic scene is the recruiting, when he looks at the prospective draftees and coins them into a mint of witty remarks. In short, he becomes the walking embodiment of everything the play rejects: appetite, wordmongering, resistance to one's proper role. He becomes, like Iago in the tragedies, or Autolycus and Caliban in the last plays, Shakespeare's *homo repudiandus,* the character who focuses in himself everything to be rejected. This, then, is the essential difference between the Falstaffs of Part One and Part Two: the earlier Falstaff actively tries on different roles; the later and more passive Falstaff finds himself forced into a pattern laid down for him by his context.

And so does Hal. In Part One, he actively chooses the role of hero; in Part Two, he lapses into kingship. The rest of the characters show the same passivity. Part One gave us an active, scrappy group of rebels; Part Two represents rebellion by talkers and bargainers. Part One sharply opposed characters as good son—bad son; good father—bad father; hot spur and false staff; and Hal forged a role for himself between such extremes. Part Two makes only one such sharp pairing: the good justice, who merges into his master's voice, as against the bad justice, who merges into his servant's. Mostly, Part Two bunches fairly nondescript characters into the roles they must assume—and so the Folio text lists them, in bracketed groups as "Opposites against King Henrie the Fourth," "Of the Kings Partie," "Country Soldiers," "Irregular Humorists," and the women. In the same way, Part Two abounds in references to parts of the body, parts of a house, parts of a kingdom—the later play constantly stresses a sense of role within a larger plan.

These different ways of dealing with role are what make Parts One and Two quite separate but nevertheless a matched pair. In both, the problem is to bring Hal to the role laid down to him by his father, his King, his God. Part One offers the active solution; Part Two, the passive. In the first play, Hal takes from the takers, robs Hotspur and Falstaff of the honors or money they had robbed from others. In the second, Hal is the taker taken: he learns to put down his cravings and appetites and be taken up into the larger plan. Part One is the sunnier version—my pun is intentional—for it looks at the problem of Hal's achieving at-oneness with his father from the point of view of the son who actively battles the rebel within and without. Part Two sees the theme with the eyes of a dying father, in terms of passive expectation, trust, and acceptance of necessity. It is this atmosphere of passivity that keeps the magnificent fighter-Hal of Part One out of the action—what action there is—in Part Two. Finally, in *Henry V*, these active and passive solutions fuse. Hal's active battling fulfills the role he must passively accept. He brings the drives and appetites of others and their roles as Scot, Irishman, Welshman, or French princess into the service of his kingly function:

> Upon the King! Let us our lives, our souls,
> Our debts, our careful wives,
> Our children, and our sins, lay on the King!
> (*King Henry V*, IV.i.247-249)

The King must bear all—but a few traitors and "irregular humorists" who insist on keeping separate. They must die.

Betrayal is the quintessential Shakespearean theme—provided we recognize the special tone that Shakespeare gives it. All his works deal with the taming of shrewishness: the masking over or mastery of hate by love. Betrayal, for Shakespeare, seems to mean a situation in which one can expect love, but in which love falls away and reveals an unsuspected or unmastered hate beneath. Iago is the obvious example, but we can look at all the tragedies as situations in which the love between a man and a woman, love either new or preexisting or expectable, fails to master hate. When love succeeds, the issue is comic, as in *Measure for Measure* and *The Merchant of Venice*, which temper hard justice and feminine mercy. All's well that ends well—that ends in love as Henry V's wars in France will.

So understood, *2 Henry IV*, written near the end of 1597 or early in 1598, occupies a pivotal point in the Shakespearean canon. In the early comedies, romantic love overcomes feuds and hatreds, while in the early histories and tragedies, family or romantic love fails to control political and social aggressions. In the plays of 1598-1601, Shakespeare seems to play with the thought that passivity best counters aggression or romantic assertiveness. Claudio in *Much Ado* lets his Prince do his wooing for him. In *Twelfth Night*, the woman takes the role of wooer, as she does in *As You Like It. 2 Henry IV* also looks forward to the tragedies, the uncurbed and parricidal drives of Brutus and Cassius, and even more, to that character who, more than any other in Shakespeare, resists the role his father had set up for him, putting up instead his own smokescreen of words—Hamlet. In many ways, but notably in the special, paternal way love controls rebellion and aggression, *2 Henry IV* seems closer to the tragedies and "problem plays" than to the earlier histories.

The passivity of *2 Henry IV* may also explain why it has become less popular than the other histories. It was apparently as popular as Part One in the eighteenth century, but, then, eigheenth-cenury audiences were still committed to a larger, hierarchical plan in society. The nineteenth and twentieth centuries prize precisely the acquisitive, assertive behavior that resists inherited patterns and plans, and this particular history play, which so sharply rejects such social individualism, has fallen in popularity. But *2 Henry IV* can look for better days with newer approaches to Shakespeare. Nineteenth-century audiences concentrated on the events represented by the plays rather than on the plays as themselves events and, therefore, they wanted to see in the histories one long epic glorifying England's history—to them, *2 Henry IV* marked a sordid low. Today, however, we recognize that Shakespeare's histories embody Elizabethan political views, not nineteenth-century Whiggery, and we are better at accepting Shakespeare's plays on their own terms, as things-in-themselves. When we do so accept *2 Henry IV*, we find it offers moments as fine as any in the Shakespearean canon: the brilliant and pathetic portrait of Shallow; the grotesquery of Pistol; the Prince's reconciliation with his father; the King's apostrophe to sleep; the rejection of Falstaff. More important, when we accept the play itself as an event, our experience of the play becomes our own act of trust.

Notes

1. Mr. Stanley McKenzie, in an unpublished paper, very skillfully analyzes the ethical problem of the two "betrayals" in terms of the structure and imagery of the play. I am indebted to him for a number of the ideas which follow.

2. "Part Two" in the title of an Elizabethan history play simply means that the play deals with events later in the reign of the king named in the title than those the Part One play deals with. It does not imply that the play in question is an integral part of a series, like a chapter in a novel.

Oedipal Patterns in "Henry IV"

The following essay by M. D. Faber is indebted to the work of Ernst Kris and Franz Alexander. It constitutes an attempt to shed further light on a subject they brilliantly explored.

M. F.

hakespeare's Histories, like all great epics, express more than particulars, more than individual personalities and events, more than Tudor political doctrines or the rising tide of nationalism in the last years of Elizabeth's reign: for Shakespeare's Histories imitate life as all great poetry imitates life, namely, by capturing the universal in the particular, by commenting upon the human condition as it has been, is, and probably will be—in short, by holding the mirror to nature and not shrinking from what appears there. I believe the history plays deserve much more attention from those of us who are concerned with demonstrating the pertinency of psychoanalytic thinking to works of literature. So completely have Shakespeare's tragedies (along with two comedies, *The Tempest* and *The Merchant of Venice*) dominated interdisciplinary discussion that one is not apt to realize just how capable the Histories are of substantiating and clarifying psychoanalytic concepts, and even of affording fresh insights.

Two papers, one by Alexander and one by Kris, vividly point up the extent to which the Shakespeare of *Henry IV* and *Henry V* succeeded in giving expression to some fundamental problems in the emotional growth and maturation of the individual. I regard my work primarily as a continuation of theirs. My attempt is to uncover psychoanalytic significances with which Kris and Alexander were not concerned.

Alexander demonstrates that in *Henry IV, Parts One and Two,* Prince Henry's struggle toward maturity is expressed through his strug-

"Oedipal Patterns in *Henry IV*" by M. D. Faber. Reprinted with permission from *Psychoanalytic Quarterly,* XXXVI (1967), 426-434.

gle with two symbolic or representative characters, Falstaff and Hotspur.[1] "In the history of the metamorphosis of Prince Henry, Shakespeare dramatically describes the characteristic course of the development of the male. There are two difficult emotional problems which must be solved by everyone in the course of his development; the first is the fixation to the early pregenital forms of instinctual life which expresses itself in oral receptiveness and narcissistic self-adoration. This old fellow, Sir John Falstaff, is a masterful dramatization of such an early emotional attitude. The second difficulty to be overcome is the hatred and jealousy directed against the father. Hotspur, the rebel, who strives against the life of the king, is the personification of these patricidal tendencies."[2] Alexander points out that Hotspur is the "exponent of destruction," the "ascetic," "self-restricting" type of individual "often found among political fanatics and exponents of social doctrines for which they sacrifice their lives. Like Robespierre, the fanatic schoolmaster, under the guise of fighting for humanitarian ideals they can take revenge for all their self-imposed restrictions in destroying their opponents en masse."[3] And finally, Alexander maintains that "when [Prince Henry] kills Hotspur on the battlefield, he overcomes symbolically his own destructive tendency. In killing Hotspur, the archenemy of his father, he overcomes his own aggressions against his parent."[4]

Kris tells us that "Hotspur's rebellion represents . . . Hal's unconscious patricidal impulses" and goes on to state that in this respect Hotspur must be regarded as Hal's "double."[5] According to Kris's insightful observation, the two *Henry IV* plays achieve unity and structure as literature largely through their contrasting versions of "the father-son conflict."

Now I believe there are good reasons for talking about father-son conflicts in *Henry IV* in more than one direction and for regarding Hotspur as Hal's "double" in a real as well as in a symbolic way. Shakespeare indicates that the patricidal impulses which Hotspur directs at the Father-King figure of Bolingbroke, impulses with which Hal himself is apparently struggling, are displaced aggressions whose just discharge would be toward Hotspur's own father, the Earl of Northumberland. For if we listen to certain passages of these plays with the third ear of Reik—and we really must listen to all of Shakespeare thus—we will discover in the interactions of Hotspur and his parent a number of features which call to mind a smoldering, largely unconscious oedipal rivalry and which explain the fantastically developed aggressions of Hotspur and his irrational, fathomless abhorrence of Bolingbroke, and finally, which shed further light on the symbolic fabric of Shakespeare's whole design.

That the early acts of *I Henry IV* do not present us with overt expressions of hostility between Hotspur and his father will not surprise anyone, for it is just such expressions that the two men are incapable of. Nevertheless, there is in their relationship as it is depicted in these acts an element which should not go unnoticed. I am referring to the obvious distance between them. Indeed, at no point in the play do Hotspur and Northumberland exchange a single friendly word; at no point do they give us the kind of father-son feeling that Hal and Bolingbroke so often do. Hotspur, as a matter of fact, seems scarcely to be aware of Northumberland's existence. He speaks to him only twice in the entire play, and even in these two instances seems to be pondering data on the King rather than talking to his father (*Part One,* I.iii.157,250). Northumberland, in turn, appears to be totally ineffectual in influencing Hotspur's conduct and is even wont to speak to him indirectly, to address him through someone else: "Brother, the King hath made your nephew mad" (*Part One,* I.iii.138), he says to Worcester while Hotspur fumes in his own private world.

Shakespeare reserves the crucial information about the relationship of Hotspur to Northumberland until the drama approaches its crucial or climactic stage; for it is the significance of the father-son relationship as it bears upon the general problem of rebellion that most interests the playwright and he accordingly waits until the rebellion is at hand before revealing his most arresting truths: only upon the verge of the battle of Shrewsbury do we begin to realize that Northumberland seeks the death of his son; only then do we begin to understand why Hotspur nourishes a bottomless hatred of Henry Bolingbroke, the Father-King figure of the play.

Shortly before the battle of Shrewsbury, Northumberland sends word to his son that he is "grievous sick" (*Part One,* IV.i.16) and cannot therefore come—a message which begets no sympathy from Hotspur.

> 'Zounds! how has he the leisure to be sick
> In such a justling time?
> > (*1 King Henry IV*, IV.i.17-18)

> Sick now! droop now! this sickness doth infect
> The very life-blood of our enterprise.
> > (*1 King Henry IV*, IV.i.28-29)

Hotspur's words tell us that without Northumberland the rebellion has but a slim chance of succeeding. Surely the Earl must be perfectly aware of his importance to the enterprise. Yet for all this he urges his son to rush headlong into the fray without any further consideration.

> Yet doth he give us bold advertisement,
> That with our small conjunction we should on,
> To see how fortune is dispos'd to us.
> > (*1 King Henry IV*, IV.i.36-38)

As everyone knows, it is not long before Fortune makes her disposition clear to Hotspur.

But are we to accept Northumberland's excuse? Are we to believe in his sickness? Kris believes in it. "Northumberland . . . is prevented by illness," he writes, "from participating in the decisive battle . . ."[6] But if we read on into the second part of the play, we realize that something has been overlooked by Kris. For the "Induction" to *2 Henry IV* at once presents us with the rather startling piece of news that Northumberland was not sick at all, that he was lying.

> . . . my [i.e., Rumour's] office is
> To noise abroad that Harry Monmouth fell
> Under the wrath of noble Hotspur's sword,
> And that the King before the Douglas' rage
> Stoop'd his anointed head as low as death.
> This have I rumour'd through the peasant towns
> Between the royal field of Shrewsbury
> And this worm-eaten hold of ragged stone,
> *Where Hotspur's father, old Northumberland,*
> *Lies crafty-sick.*[7]
> > (*2 Henry IV*, "Induction," 28-37)

Shakespeare reveals this information to us just after we have digested the death of Hotspur and the failure of the rebellion.

Thus we are brought to a second question: Why should Northumberland be feigning sickness and thereby consign his son to defeat and death? Professor Baker offers this explanation: Northumberland is, purely and simply, a dastard; a spineless, calculating villain who is not sure the rebellion will succeed and who does not want to commit himself or his troops but is perfectly willing to see others commit themselves and their troops, even when those others include his own child. Writes Baker: "He is not present at the battle of Shrewsbury on account of being sick—which is afterwards found to be feigned—he not being willing to run any risk himself but ready to allow others to fight for him, while simulating an intense interest in their fortunes."[8] The trouble with this explanation is that it does not go far enough; although it accounts for the action through the "Induction" to *Part Two*, it is unable to account for the way in which Northumberland receives news of his son's death. Ultimately, as we shall see, it is the superficial solution.

Both good and bad rumors about the fate of Hotspur and the rebellion are brought to Northumberland from a number of quarters, but the Earl seems extremely reluctant to accept the good rumors. As a matter of fact, he seems almost to insist upon the bad ones. He seems, in short, to be anticipating the destruction of his child. When, for example, Lord Bardolph informs him that the rebellion is successful and Hotspur unscathed, Northumberland replies, "How is this deriv'd? Saw you the field? Came you from Shrewsbury?" (*Part Two*, I.i.23-24). But when Travers enters with bad rumors, rumors which maintain that "Harry Percy's spur" is "cold" (*Part Two*, I.i.42), the Earl pounces upon them and even wants them repeated.

> Ha! Again:
> Said he young Harry Percy's spur was cold?
> Of Hotspur, Coldspur? that rebellion
> Had met ill luck?
>
> (*2 Henry IV*, I.i.48-51)

And when Lord Bardolph breaks in to say that this report of Hotspur's death may well be untrue, Northumberland turns on him snappily with

> Why should the gentleman that rode by Travers
> Give then such instances of loss?
>
> (*2 Henry IV*, I.i.55-56)

At this point Morton enters with a serious expression on his face, an expression which Northumberland immediately takes to be a confirmation of Hotspur's death; indeed, before Morton even has a chance to speak his news, Northumberland begins histrionically to assume the role of bereaved parent.

> Even such a man, so faint, so spiritless,
> So dull, so dead in look, so woe-begone,
> Drew Priam's curtain in the dead of night,
> And would have told him half his Troy was burn'd;
> But Priam found the fire ere he his tongue,
> And I my Percy's death ere thou report'st it.
>
> (*2 Henry IV*, I.i.70-75)

Morton once again attempts to speak his news and once again Northumberland interrupts him to insist upon the death of his son: "Why, he is dead," he says, and continues

> See, what a ready tongue suspicion hath!
> He that but fears the thing he would not know
> Hath by instinct knowledge from others' eyes
> That what he fear'd is chanced.
>
> (*2 Henry IV*, I.i.84-87)

One is reminded of Meerloo's observation that "a sudden foreknowledge and feeling of certainty" about the "death of relatives" often "communicates unconsciously" the desire for their death.[9]

When Northumberland has thoroughly digested Morton's account he speaks his most revealing words. Referring to Hotspur's death he says:

For this I shall have time enough to mourn.
In poison there is physic; and these news,
Having been well, that would have made me sick,
Being sick, have in some measure made me well.
(*2 Henry IV*, I.i.136-139)

In other words, had the report of his son's death come when he was
healthy it would have made him sick; since it comes to him in sickness,
however, its ultimate effect is to make him well. But the fact is, Northumberland is not sick. Thus he is confessing to the members of the
audience, who have heard the play's "Induction," that his son's death
has had an unnatural effect on him, an effect which could not be expected in a normal father-son relationship. He is confessing, in a
word, that the destruction of his child has had the power to make
him well.

. . . as the wretch, whose fever-weaken'd joints,
Like strengthless hinges, buckle under life,
Impatient of his fit, breaks like a fire
Out of his keeper's arms, even so my limbs,
Weaken'd with grief, being now enrag'd with grief,
Are thrice themselves. Hence, therefore, thou nice crutch!
A scaly gauntlet now, with joints of steel
Must glove this hand.
(*2 Henry IV*, I.i.140-147)

The Earl's dramatic return to life, to action, indeed to manliness and
fortitude, appears to derive from Hotspur's death.

From a psychoanalytic point of view all of this is essential to a
thorough understanding of Hotspur's character; for the conduct of
Northumberland, both here and in the early acts, along with, of course,
Hotspur's obvious indifference to his father's health, indeed, to his
father's existence, tells us that the two men have never "cleared the
air" between them, that Northumberland, far from being a father
to his son, has resented and hated him, and that Hotspur has not
known the fatherly affection so crucial to the development of a normal
personality. Thus the Earl has produced a kind of "monster," a
fiercely destructive, fiercely independent sort of person more interested
in war than in women, and driven continually by an enormous appetite

for slaughter. As Hal puts it, and there is, of course, much truth in the parody: ". . . I am not yet of Percy's mind, the Hotspur of the North; he that kills me some six or seven dozen of Scots at a breakfast, washes his hands, and says to his wife, 'Fie upon this quiet life! I want work.' 'O my sweet Harry,' says she, 'how many hast thou kill'd today?' 'Give my roan horse a drench,' says he, and answers, 'Some fourteen.' " (*1 Henry IV*, II.iv.103).

Hotspur's peculiar personality is rooted in his failure to experience a working-through of the father-son conflict; his persistent aggressive urges derive from his anger at his parent for never having been a parent, for wanting him out of the way. Furthermore, and in keeping with this, we must recognize that Hotspur's hatred of Bolingbroke, a hatred which passes all bounds (*1 Henry IV*, I.iii.239-247) and ironically causes his father to adjudge him "mad" (*1 Henry IV*, I.iii.138), stems from this repressed oedipal syndrome. For Bolingbroke, as Father-King, is at once close enough to the heart of Hotspur's conflict to call forth overt expressions of hostility and distant enough to make the display of such aggressions acceptable to Hotspur's superego. And here, it may be said, is the origin and explanation of what Alexander calls Hotspur's desire for "revenge"—it is revenge on the Father, his own father, that Hotspur seeks. When Prince Henry destroys Hotspur on the battlefield, he certainly overcomes a character who embodies "patricidal tendencies."

Finally, it remains to be pointed out that Shakespeare, through his depiction of the relationship between Hotspur and Northumberland, deepens the significance of the Histories as a whole by suggesting that the failure of the rebellion is rooted not only in material considerations but in the very fabric of the rebels' lives, and that those who would disrupt society, who would, through murderous aggression and hatred, split a nation and sow the seeds of civil war, are themselves disrupted and split and at war. Says Worcester just after the news of Northumberland's "sickness" arrives at the rebel camp,

> The quality and hair of our attempt
> Brooks no division.
> (*1 Henry IV*, IV.i.61-62)

The rebels are indeed divided, and in the most basic human way. For let us remember that Hal and his father make peace shortly before the battle of Shrewsbury and that it is Hal who emerges triumphant. Hotspur, on the other hand, does not, indeed cannot make such peace, and it is Hotspur who is destroyed. He rushes to his doom in an old and tragic fashion. Like Oedipus, he does not know what he is doing.

Notes

1. FRANZ ALEXANDER, "A Note on Falstaff," *Psychoanalytic Quarterly*, 2:592-606, 1933.
2. *Ibid.*, p. 599.
3. *Ibid.*, p. 598.
4. *Ibid.*, p. 599.
5. ERNST KRIS, "Prince Hal's Conflict," *Psychoanalytic Quarterly*, 17:493, 1948.
6. *Ibid.*
7. Italics added. Editors are in unanimous agreement that "crafty-sick" can mean only "feigning sickness." *Cf.* Variorum edition.
8. ARTHUR E. BAKER, *A Shakespeare Commentary* (New York: Ungar, 1957), Vol. II, p. 520.
9. JOOST A. M. MEERLOO, *The Two Faces of Man: Two Studies on the Sense of Time and on Ambivalence* (New York: International Universities Press, 1954), p. 97.

Comedies

Jessica, My Child

It is difficult to say why *The Merchant of Venice* has received so much attention from psychoanalytic critics. Norman Holland has suggested that since a great many psychoanalysts are Jewish there would naturally be a good deal of psychoanalytic interest expressed in Shakespeare's most striking Jewish creation, Shylock.[1] Another explanation may lie in the fact that Freud devoted a number of pages to the play in his essay *The Theme of the Three Caskets,* for, as it turns out, the Shakespearean works that begot the interest of Freud also begot, without exception, the interest of his followers. However that may be, *The Merchant of Venice* has called forth a body of analytic criticism as great as that called forth by any other Shakespeare play, with the exceptions of *Hamlet* and *Macbeth.*

The most striking general feature of this criticism is its dualistic methodology, its tendency to treat character and events from, on the one hand, the standpoint of myth or ritual, and from, on the other hand, the standpoint of realistic psychology. Take Shylock for example. He has been regarded by commentators with a ritualistic orientation as a descendant of the jealous father of folklore[2] or as a symbol for Jahweh, the unforgiving God of the Old Testament.[3] By contrast, commentators with a realistic, psychoanalytic orientation have stressed the oral, anal, and sadistic aspects of Shylock's behavior in an effort to establish that Shylock's personality is not peculiarly Jewish but representative of many individuals in the western world who are suffering from misdirected growth.[4]

The following essay by Theodore Reik attempts to capture the archetypal significance of not only Shylock, but also of Antonio, Portia, and Jessica, by focusing upon *The Merchant of Venice* the findings of both history and psychoanalysis. By the time Dr. Reik has concluded his fascinating series of reflections the student of the play is in a good position to appreciate what it is in himself that causes him to respond so deeply to the principals. Of particular interest here is Reik's use of free associations. Throughout this volume it has been taken as axiomatic that drama is able to appeal to the unconscious of the reader or beholder by touching upon specific, significant associations, and that psychoanalytic criticism could shed important light upon the problem of response by shedding light upon the unconscious appeal of the play. Reik's essay is a veritable lesson in this truth. It not only brings together the main lines of psychological action in *Merchant* by finding their equivalents in one particular psychology, namely Reik's, and by demonstrating the way in which that psychology is representative, it also enables the student to bring fresh and important insights to any play.

M. F.

s I consider, in retrospect, the various ways and byways, the many detours and turns through which my thoughts wandered to their destination on that particular evening, it seems to me that we all of us marvel too little at our own mental processes. We are not astonished enough at the wide circle of our own thoughts. We speak most casually of unconscious emotions and impulses and are not ready to admit that the area of the repressed is a state, an underground in which movement and power can be felt and in which continual life and productivity can be observed. Without such an astonishment, psychoanalysis is reduced to a scence without human interest, with technology as its medical application.

As I look back at the meanderings of my thoughts, I am inclined to agree with the sentiment expressed by a patient the other day. This clever man, who had gained insight into his own bizarre obsessional ideas, said, "The mind is an insult to the intelligence." Yet, in my own case, there were no such obsessional thoughts or any other extraordinary mental phenomena. Nothing of this kind; no conspicuous pathological speculations or ideas. Just an everyday train of thought and a fairly average slice of human experience.

It is, of course, necessary to sketch the external situation from which my train of thought emerged. Tired after a long day of psychoanalytic sessions, I relaxed on the couch after dinner. My daughter, Theodora, whom we call "Thody," came into the room and said, "Good night, Daddy," "Where are you going?" I asked. "I have a

date." "Don't come home too late. Good night." I should know better
than to ask her with whom she has a date. It seems she does not like
such questions. Well, she is seventeen years old. . . . In my time children
were not so independent. What does it matter with which boy she has
a date? She is no longer a child. . . . She will be in college very soon. . . .

I turn my attention in another direction . . . to the analytic sessions
of today. My patient Bill comes to my mind.

Bill is a young man from a southern state. He came to analysis because he had tried in vain to overcome his inclination to excessive
drinking, and because of his inability to make any sustained effort. He
is homosexual, snobbish, and in other respects a typical playboy. His
amiability and a concealed shyness seem to enable him to win friends.

While I thought of this patient, I saw, so to speak, in a mental
image, his face which shows little expression. . . . His voice has no rise
and fall when he speaks well-considered sentences. . . . He is rather
rigid and shows that remoteness and flatness of emotions characteristic
of schizoid personalities. . . . He has not done a stroke of honest work
for years, and, it seems, he lives on a strict diet of dry martinis. . . . His
therapeutic chance is not too good, but I shall, of course, do my best.

In his analytic session this afternoon he had spoken of Paris where
he spent some months a few years ago. He had spoken of his wish
to get the leading role in a play soon to be performed on Broadway,
and of his friends, one of whom is an actor. I no longer remember
how he came from there to the subject of race discrimination, but I
believe he mentioned that another of his homosexual friends was a Jew.
He had then said that, in contrast to most citizens of that southern
state in which he was born and bred, he did not feel any race discrimination. But a few minutes later he had spoken contemptuously of "nig-
gers" and Jews. He had said that an art dealer whom he knew had
tried to take him in the day before. The man had tried to sell him an
antique piece of furniture for which he asked a preposterous price.
The patient, expressing his indignation and his dissatisfaction with his
acquaintance, had added, "Once a Jew, always a Jew."

The recollection of these remarks became the point of departure of
my free associations which on a strange detour led me to a new
interpretation of a Shakespearean play, and in a surprising digression

back to a personal problem. While I rested on the couch, smoking cigarettes, I followed this train of thought with, so to speak, impersonal interest. I swam comfortably with the "stream of consciousness" until a certain point was reached at which my thoughts became objects of self-observation. To continue the comparison, it was as if the swimmer had become aware of the kind of waves and of the direction in which they are carrying him. After this point was reached, I came across some odd association whose sequence and meaning I did not understand. I decided to follow them, to investigate them, to find out what they meant and why they emerged from unknown depths. I had become aware of undercurrents in the stream.

I then got up from the couch, took a pencil and paper from the desk and jotted the train of thoughts down together with what occurred to me while I wrote. I regret I did not look at the clock nor did I pay any attention to the time that this process took, but my impression was that not more than a few minutes had elapsed since my daughter had left the room. In a psychological experiment, precise data concerning time and other external factors are, of course, indispensable in the interest of scientific precision. However, my self-observation and self-analysis was not in the nature of an experiment. It had rather the character of an inner experience.

While I remembered what Bill had said that afternoon and while I thought of his emotional disturbance, I was wide awake. The following associations emerged when I felt increasingly sleepy, without, however, yielding to the temptation to fall asleep. The fact that these associations occurred while I was only half awake may have had a bearing upon their character and the rapidity of their succession. I became aware that one thought or word quickly followed the other, as if they crowded the threshold of consciousness. There was, so to speak, a traffic jam at the door.

The words that emerged and astonished me, because I did not understand what they meant and why they occurred to me, were: *Jones . . . Jericho . . . Jephthah . . . Jessica . . . Jehovah . . . Jesus.*

Jones . . . I do not know anyone by this name. . . . Oh yes, of course, Ernest Jones. . . . I have known him for more than thirty years. I remembered him when he was in Vienna. Did I not also meet him in

Holland? I had talked to him at several psychoanalytic congresses, and, of course, we had been invited to lunch at his home when we were in London. . . . I have not heard from him for twelve years. . . . I read his essay on *Hamlet* again a short time ago. . . . I looked something up in his paper on a religious problem. . . . I do not remember what it was. . . . He was already at the time of our visit in England (was this 1929 or 1928?) the most prominent psychoanalyst in the English-speaking countries. . . . I teased him. I said he was the King of the English analysts. . . . Emperor Jones. . . . Of course, the play by O'Neill. . . . What a strange connection! I started from Ernest Jones and arrived at Emperor Jones. . . . Are there any trends besides the name? Perhaps primitive religions with which Jones deals in his *Collected Papers?* . . . I now remember the play. I recall the scene in which the Negro becomes terrified in the forest and how he finally succumbs to the demoniac power of the old tribal gods in which he did not believe and which he had repudiated. The thread leading from the analyst to Emperor Jones was the thought of Negroes. . . . But my patient Bill had spoken of Negroes and Jews.

When I turned my attention away from him, the subterranean continuation of his remarks must have led to Emperor Jones. Even the detour over Ernest Jones must have been significant. But how? Perhaps the study on *Hamlet,* a play such as *Emperor Jones,* and then I had called Jones the King or the Emperor of the English analysts. . . . I liked Ernest Jones, but this comparison itself shows some latent hostility . . . why? Jealousy of the older and superior man? The green-eyed monster? . . . That is from *Othello* . . . The Moor of Venice. . . . Again the Negroes.

I am turning to the following associations. They are, of course, all names—names from the Bible. I must have thought first of Negroes, then of Jews as the patient associated them together in his remark. But each of those names must have its unconscious determination and must have meant something definite in my thoughts. . . . Even their sequence must have a meaning and some psychological significance. . . . I must find why each of them occurred to me. . . . Is there something they have in common besides their being biblical names? . . . The initial sound, the first syllable. . . . Are they only "sound associations" that means thoughts determined by *Klang,* as the German would say, joined together by the same sound at the beginning of the words?

This first syllable . . . I remember that the common first syllable Je is perhaps the abbreviated Hebrew word for God. Je means His ineffable name, otherwise known as Jahweh or Jehovah. . . . Does not Jesus mean "God helps" or "Salvation by God"? . . . But I am suspicious of myself, for this first syllable could not have the same significance in Jericho and Jessica. . . . And is it true that Je is always the abbreviated name of the God of the Israelites? I become aware how much I do not know about those things. . . . Over there is the *Encyclopedia of Religion* on my bookcase. I could look up Jehovah and Jericho, but I am too lazy to get up from the couch. Even if I find what that syllable and each name means, of what importance would that be for the psychological significance of my thoughts? The objective meaning of the names is of no interest, only the meaning I connect with those words is now of consequence. *Jericho* . . . that is, of course, the biblical city. . . . Was I in Jericho when I visited Palestine in 1937? . . . That is nonsense. . . . The ancient city of Jericho does not exist any more.

Suddenly I remember a movie I had seen a few years ago in which a man has the nickname of Jericho. . . . The story of the French film *Les Enfants du Paradis* comes vaguely back to mind. The play takes place in Paris about a hundred years ago. Its milieu is that of the demimonde, theater people, actors, audience, and hangers-on. The leading character is a young man whose misfortunes are presented from the time he acts as a clown to the period when he becomes the celebrated tragedian of the Parisian stage. It is a play of passion and destiny with a tragic ending. There is a girl whom he met in his boy-hood and with whom he fell in love. When he meets her later in life, she always eludes him. It is as if a malicious destiny or that incognito traveling fate, called accident, blocks his way whenever he approaches her. Like Romeo, he is a fool of fortune.

Now the face of the actor who has the part of the leading character appears in my memory. A thin, strangely masklike face, unexpressive and unemotional, but with large luminous eyes. The contrast of this lack of facial expression with his emotional experiences lends the personality of the actor a puzzling kind of interest. . . . What was his name? . . . I now remember: Jean-Louis Barrault. It is not incidental that the movie shows him first in a puppet show in which only auto-maton-like movements and gestures indicate his feelings, while his face does not change at all. The actor's body has the utmost elasticity, while his personality seems rigid, almost frozen. There is a dullness of effect, even in his love of the beautiful girl. No free flow of emotions. A withdrawal from reality and something like a paralysis of will which explains better than external factors why his love object always eludes him or prefers other men, although she is attracted to him. When I saw the film, I got the impression that here was a schizoid type or even a schizophrenic.

At this point I recognized that there were concealed connections between the first subject of my thoughts and their present theme. Did I not think that Bill, my patient, was perhaps schizoid? He spoke of Paris and of plays he had seen there. *Les Enfants du Paradis* takes place in Paris. Bill wants the leading part in a play. His face must have reminded me of Jean-Louis Barrault's.

Jericho is the name of an episodic figure in *Les Enfants du Paradis.* He is an old Jew, doing shady business among theater people, a thief or receiver of stolen goods. I see his crooked nose, his unkempt hair and his pointed gray beard. This old fence is an acquaintance of the actor during his early Bohemian times. He, surprisingly, appears whenever there is a decisive turn in the destiny of the leading character. He seems to know beforehand what will happen, seems to anticipate the future. Yes, he appears to be omniscient. He warns the hero, yet he sometimes seems to bring about the bad fate of this actor. Is he perhaps omnipotent too? This fence, who cheats, whose business shuns the light, has neither wife nor child, but he likes children. He has another nickname: *"couche seul"*—he sleeps alone.

I do not know how and why I thought that this old Jewish criminal presents the disguised God of the Jews, Jehovah, in a degraded form as he would be seen through anti-Semitic eyes. Is it possible that the script writer unconsciously shaped in the episodic figure the reduced Jewish god, a malicious demon—a god who is vengeful and deceiving, associated with crooks and thieves?

The anti-Semitic remark of my patient comes back to mind. Negroes and Jews. . . . In the film there is also a Negro. . . . Oh yes, the actor plays the part of a Negro. . . . Of course, he is presented as Othello, the Moor of Venice. . . . There is a ·scene in which the actor comes into conflict with a high aristocrat, the same man who is his more fortunate rival in the love for the girl. . . . This snobbish character speaks of Shakespeare as an inferior, barbarian playwright who cannot hold a candle to Corneille and Racine. There again appear the threads between my patient's remark and the film. . . . The Negroes and the Jews. . . . Jericho and Othello.

But how does Jephthah come into my train of thoughts? . . . For the life of me, I do not know how the figure of this judge from the Old Testament wandered into my associations. . . . How did just he drift into them? A penny for my thoughts! But even this seems overpaid, because nothing occurs to me . . . Jephthah. . . . Jephthah and his daughter. . . . Did not Jephthah make a vow when he went out to fight the enemies of the Israelites that he would sacrifice the first person he encountered after his victorious return from the battle? And did he not meet his daughter, whom he then had to sacrifice to the cruel god of the Hebrews?

I am trying to reconstruct what I had thought before that. . . . The Negroes and the Jews. . . . The aristocrat who speaks derogatorily of Shakespeare and Othello. . . . Are Jephthah or his daughter perhaps mentioned in Othello? . . . For a moment I thought it must be there, but, no, it can't be. . . . There is some memory stirring within me that Jephthah's daughter is mentioned in one of Shakespeare's tragedies. . . . No, not in *Othello*. . . . Perhaps in *The Merchant of Venice?* . . .

I overcome my laziness, I get up from the couch and get the concordance of Shakespeare's work in order to look it up. . . . There it is. . . . Neither in *Othello* nor in *The Merchant of Venice*. . . . (The Moor of Venice and the Merchant of Venice—is this the common element between the plays? Oh no, it must be again the race discrimination. Negroes and Jews, Othello and Shylock.) The passage is in *Hamlet,* says the concordance, Act II, scene 2. . . . Ah, here! Hamlet runs into Polonius and says: "Oh Jephthah, judge of Israel, what a treasure hadst thou!" The old courtier asks: "What a treasure had he, my lord?" and the Prince answers: "One fair daughter, and no more, The which he loved passing well."

Polonius, who is convinced that Hamlet's love for Ophelia has driven him crazy, thoughtfully remarks, "Still on my daughter . . ." And Hamlet asks, "Am I not i' the right, old Jephthah?" thus identifying the pompous old courtier with the biblical judge.

Jephthah—Jephthah's daughter . . . Jessica. . . . Jessica is the daughter of the Jew Shylock. Here then is the connecting link with

Jephthah's daughter . . . Jephthah loved his child and had to kill her. Shylock loves his daughter and yet he curses her when she elopes with a good-for-nothing fellow. . . . More than this—he wishes to see her dead at his feet when he learns that she squanders the money for which he has toiled and slaved so long.

I remember having read in the book of some Shakespeare commentator or critic that this trait adds to the repulsive picture of Shylock's character. How could a father wish to see his daughter dead merely because she throws money away? Yet, these good people do not understand that it is the Oriental temper, which still lives in the Jews of late times, which bursts forth in Shylock's rage. . . . Such wishes, as well as Jephthah's vow, are expressions of that excitable temper that flares suddenly up and is often enough followed by intense remorse and severe self-punishment. There are hateful outbreaks against objects very much loved, loved not wisely but too well. . . . Yes, those ancient Jews were afraid of themselves and of the intensity of their passions. They had to protect themselves in the love objects. . . . They were so afraid that they had a solemn religious formula in which they asked God to consider oaths spoken in moments of rage as invalid. They anticipated such outbreaks in themselves, and asked God not to oblige them to keep those vows and to forgive them. That formula or prayer is called Kol Nidre and is recited on the High Holiday, Yom Kippur or the Day of Atonement. In it all such oaths and vows taken in the year just beginning are declared invalid. I published a paper on this subject in my book the *Ritual*.

How did I become interested in the Kol Nidre? I am an infidel Jew. . . . Do I have the same inclination to swear away the life of dear persons when I am very angry? Have I some of that hot temper; do I know such sudden flareups and outbreaks as Shylock's? I suddenly feel the urgent wish to read those scenes in *The Merchant of Venice* where Shylock curses his daughter and wishes to see her dead at his feet.

I had tried first to search below the surface for the meaning of those associations and names. I did not get very far, because as soon as I caught a glimpse of the significance of the names of Jericho, Jephthah, and Jessica, my interest became deflected and turned in a new direction.

Investigating those first associations took only a few minutes, and now it is late at night. I wanted to look up some passages in *The Merchant of Venice*. I did that, but then read the whole play again and spent a few hours in thinking about it, daydreaming and pondering about it, following ideas that took me far off. While I read the familiar scenes of Shakespeare's play, I went astray in my thoughts, pursuing fleeting images and impressions. Embryos of ideas, snatches of new thoughts emerged. They were brushed aside, but they recurred and would not let themselves be rejected. These new thoughts all concerned the contrast and conflict of Shylock and Antonio. There was something in the opposition of these two antagonists which I sensed but could not grasp.

This mysterious something transgressed the narrow limitations of the plot about a loan and about a legal argument and counterargument. Something there is unsaid but conveyed. Some concealed meaning is alluded to, but eludes the search of logical and conscious thinking. Shylock and Antonio are, of course, not only this money-lending Jew and that Venetian merchant, in spite of all individual traits and typical features. They are even more than types, more than the kind and noble Gentile and the malicious son of the old tribe. That intangible and elusive element seems to overlap into an area beyond the individual and the typical. It shatters the frame of the two characters and reaches to the sky. In reading the play, Antonio and Shylock grew in my thoughts to gigantic figures standing against each other silently. I did not know what this transformation meant and I first tried to solve the problem by means of conscious analytic interpretation. It was as if a fisherman casts out a net into the deep sea. He brings something up from the depth, but it is certainly not what he wanted and hoped to get. What he tried to bring up to the surface slipped through the meshes of his net.

I am certainly not the first analyst who interpreted Shylock's terms, namely, the condition that he can cut a pound of flesh "in what part of your body pleaseth me" as a substitute expression of castration. When later on in the play the cut should be made from the breast, analytic interpretation will easily understand the mechanism of distortion that operates here and displaces the performance from a part of the body below to above. Only one step is needed to reach the concept that to the Gentile of medieval times the Jew unconsciously typified the castrator because he circumcised male children. Circumcision is, as psychoanalytic experiences teach us, conceived as a milder form of castration. The Jew thus appeared to the Gentiles as a dangerous figure with whom the threat of castration originated. Consciously, to Shakespeare and his contemporaries (as to many of our own time) the Jew appears as a money-making and -grasping figure who takes financial advantage of the Gentiles. Unconsciously, he is the man who threatens to damage them by cutting off the penis. Because his tribe performs the archaic operation of circumcision, the Jew represents an unconscious danger to the masculinity of the Gentiles. The unconscious factor has to be added to the strange features of his different religious rituals, to the unfamiliar dietary customs and the divergent habits of the foreign minority.[1] If Shylock insists upon cutting out a pound of flesh from Antonio's breast, it is as if he demanded that the Gentile be made a Jew if he cannot pay back the three thousand ducats at the fixed time. Otherwise put: Antonio should submit to the religious ritual of circumcision.

The application of the analytic method is really not needed to arrive at this conclusion. It could be easily reached on another route. At the end of the "comedy" Antonio demands that Shylock should "presently become a Christian." If this is the justified amends the Jew has to make for his earlier condition, it would be according to poetic justice that the Jew be forced to become a Christian after he had insisted that his opponent should become a Jew. Such a retaliation corresponds to the oldest law of the world, to the *ius talionis* that demands tooth for tooth, eye for eye.

That bit of insight into the concealed meaning of Shylock's demand remained an isolated and trifling scrap of analytic interpretation until it was blended with other impressions. The first impression concerned the character of Shylock. I remember that I once talked with Freud about what constitutes that quality we call character. He said that in his opinion character is signified by the predominance of one or a few drives over others. While all the drives are, of course, present and operating, one of them is distinguished and superior in intensity. We say, then, that this person has character, a quality we do not attribute to others in whom all drives seem equally developed. While I read the play, Shylock's thirst for revenge impressed me more than any other feature of the man. At the same time half-forgotten lines from the Holy Scriptures began to sound in my mind, fragmentary sentences, snatches of lines. . . . "The Lord will take vengeance on His adversaries" . . . "They shall see My vengeance . . ." "I will not spare them on the day of vengeance," and others. Yes, the God of the Old Testament is a vindictive God. He has perhaps not only the virtues, but also the vices of the worshipers in whose image He is made.

At a certain moment I was, it seemed, carried away by a fancy or an impression that had gained power over me. It seemed to me that the figure of the God of the Old Testament, Jahweh Himself, looms gigantically behind "the Jew that Shakespeare drew." The Mythological figure of the old God reduced to the size of a human creature, diminished and dressed up as a Jewish moneylender? Jahweh, the Lord, who came to earth on the Rialto? But the impression quickly evaporated. It was as if I had, for a moment, seen an apparition in the delusive light of that evening. It reappeared, however, later on.

I then became more interested in another impression that surprised me because it had not been there when I had previously read and seen the play: the lack of characterization of Antonio. If there is a leading character in any Shakespeare play who is less of a personality, is less colorful and less equipped with distinguishing individual traits, I would like to know of it. There is no doubt that Antonio is the leading character. His is the title role of *The Merchant of Venice,* although his opponent steals the show.

What do we know of Antonio? Only that he is kind, loves his friends, is generous to the extent of self-sacrifice and that he is sad. . . . He is kindliness itself, personified. . . . He loves his friends, he wants to give his life for his friends. . . . He is eager to make the supreme self-sacrifice. Greater love hath no man. . . . He not only suffers, he *is* suffering, grief, sorrow themselves. He is sad. Why? Nobody knows, least of all himself. Is this a shortcoming on the part of the greatest playwright of the world or is there something hidden here, unknown even to the Bard?

The play opens with Antonio's entrance and these are his first lines:

> In sooth, I know not why I am so sad:
> It wearies me; you say it wearies you;
> But how I caught it, found it, came by it,

> What stuff 'tis made of, whereof it is born,
> I am to learn;
> And such a want-wit sadness makes of me,
> That I have much ado to know myself.

His friends try in vain to explain his sadness, but he denies that he thinks of his merchandise at sea and answers with a sad "Fie, fie" when Salarino suspects that he could be in love. He is, to all appearances, sad without reason. I now remember that I have read in the book of a Shakespeare commentator that Antonio has "the spleen." It seems to me that this concept is too British. . . . While I still ponder over Antonio's mysterious sadness, a line runs through my mind. "He was despised and rejected of men, a man of sorrows and acquainted with grief." And then: "He hath borne our griefs and carried our sorrows." . . . But those are passages from the Holy Scripture! . . . How do they now emerge? It occurs to me where and when I heard them last. A friend let me have the records of Handel's *Messiah* a few days ago.

In the Fourth Act, Antonio says:

> I am a tainted wether of the flock,
> Meetest for death.
>
> (IV.i.14-15)

Actually, he does not awaken interest and sympathy by the person he is, but by what happens to him; not by his personality, but by his destiny. He is, he says, a tainted wether of the flock, destined to die. He is, rather, a lamb. . . . From somewhere the phrase *"Agnus Dei qui tollit peccata mundi"* comes to mind. Is this not from the Vulgate, the translation of the New Testament? Immediately a passage from the *Messiah* emerges, the passage of "the Lamb of God that taketh away the sins of the world."

Antonio's sadness . . . the man of sorrow . . . the Lamb of God . . . destined to die . . . He was wounded for our transgressions. . . . He was bruised for our iniquities. . . . The scene before the court at Venice. . . . The readiness to die for others. . . . Did He not state, "Greater love has no man than this that a man lay down his life for his friends"? . . . No, I am not the victim of a delusion. Behind the figure of Antonio is the greater one of Jesus Christ. Again the motif "He was despised and rejected" emerges as if the tune wants to confirm my thought, as if the line from the *Messiah* announced that my concept is correct.

Again there is the image of Antonio and Shylock standing opposite each other, the one all charity and the other no charity at all. . . . I know now clearly what was in the background of my mind while I read the play, what were the vague impressions that crowded upon me until they became condensed into one leading thought. I am turning the leaves of the volume, and my glance chances upon the lines of Shylock in the First Act, where he speaks directly to the noble Venetian merchant:

> Signior Antonio, many a time and oft
> In the Rialto you have rated me
> About my moneys and my usances:
> Still I have borne it with a patient shrug,
> For sufferance is the badge of all our tribe.
> You call me misbeliever, cut-throat dog,
> And spit upon my Jewish gaberdine,
> And all for use of that which is mine own.
> (I.iii.107-114)

Here is one of the few occasions in which Antonio shows temperament and hate in contrast to his otherwise gentle and weak attitude. . . . Not a trace of charity and loving kindness here. Not very Christian, as a matter of fact. This seems to contradict my concept that behind the Gentile merchant the figure of his God is concealed.

But then it occurs to me that this feature does not contradict my thesis. It rather confirms it. Did He not go up to Jerusalem when Passover was at hand and abuse and whip the moneychangers and drive them all out of the temple? Did He not pour out their money and overthrow their tables? Behind the treatment Shylock gets from Antonio the features of the primal pattern of the Holy Scripture become apparent.

I do not doubt any more that behind Antonio and Shylock are hidden the great figures of their gods. Here are two small people in Venice, but the shadows they cast are gigantic and their conflict shakes the world. There is the vengeful and zealous God of the Old Testament and the milder Son-God of the Gospels who rebelled against His father, suffered death for His revolt and became God himself afterwards. The two Gods are presented and represented in this play by two of their typical worshipers of the playwright's time.

Shakespeare wanted to present a Jewish figure as he and his contemporaries saw it, but the character grew beyond human measure into the realm of the mythical, as if the God of the Jews stood behind the stage. Shakespeare wanted to shape the destiny of a Gentile merchant who almost became the victim of a vengeful, evil Jew, but the unconscious imagination of this writer shattered the thin frame of his plot. The myth-forming fantasy of this man William Shakespeare, his *imagination complète,* as Taine says, reached so much further than his conscious mind. It reached beyond the thoughts and designs known to him, into the region where the great myths and religious legends of the people are born and bred. He wanted only to write a comedy with a plot about the curious case of a Jew who was outjewed. Unconscious memory traces made him shape the conflict of the two Gods, the holy story as he had absorbed it as a boy. Invisible threads connect *The Merchant of Venice* with the medieval passion plays.

He took the two plots from many sources, the story of the three caskets and the tale of the merchant who got a rough deal from a malicious Jew, and alloyed them into a play. This William saw the Jews as the Toms, Dicks, and Harrys of his time saw them, despised them, and mocked them, and hated them. But something greater than his conscious thought gave that Jew a voice of his own, a rancorous voice that speaks in icy sarcasm, biting and accusing, a voice full of sound and fury, rising in passionate protest and ebbing in utter despair. The creative and re-creative imaginaton of this man Shakespeare poured into the trivial plot of the three thousand ducats something of the stuff the great myths of people, the dreams of mankind, are made on. He added the figure of Antonio, who was to be cut and mutilated, to the mythical figures of Attis, Adonis, and Jesus Christ, who were torn to pieces. Only small inconspicuous traits, little features overlooked and neglected, invisible or only visible under the microscope of psychoanalytic scrutiny, reveal that behind the trivial figures of the comedy are hidden Jehovah and Jesus, that the real *personae dramatis* are overdimensional.

In the battles between the Danai and the Trojans, as Homer describes them, the gods of Olympus fought in the skies above the heads of the combatants. In the fight between the Gentiles of Venice and the Jew Shylock, the greatest conflict of the world is presented in a courtroom scene. I am toying with the plan to publish this new concept. Perhaps in a literary magazine. . . . And why not in a psycho-analytic journal since it is the result of psychological evaluation of small inconspicuous traits in the classical manner of analytic observa-tion of trifles? . . . Perhaps I should entitle the paper with the sentence *"Et hic dei sunt."* Also here are gods.

When I arrived at this concept—or should I say rather when this concept arrived at me?—I felt that glow of thought known to all explorers who first recognize a secret connection, that burning felicity of discovery. It was, to be sure, only a small thing, a trifling contribu-tion to the interpretation of a Shakespearean play, only a little bit of a new construction, yet. . . . The inscription I had often seen on old Austrian cottages, when I was a boy, occurred to me: *"Klein, aber mein."* (Small, but my own.)

It is, I thought, only a trifle of an idea, but it is original. And then came the doubt as to its originality. I had the feeling that I had had this very thought before, a long time ago. . . . Yet, I knew it had oc-curred now, when I reread *The Merchant of Venice.* . . . Is there a phenomenon analogous to the sensation of *deja vu* in the area of think-ing, a feeling of *deja pensé?* . . . Perhaps I did read it once and have forgotten it, and now I thought of it as an original idea of my own. . . . I am trying to remember what various critics and historians of literature wrote on *The Merchant of Venice.* . . . No, there is nothing comparable to my concept. . . . Yet, I know this thought from some-where. . . . When it occurred to me, I nodded, so to speak, to it as you do to all old acquaintances whom you run into on the street and whom you have not seen for many years.

When did I first see *The Merchant of Venice?* That was when I was sixteen or seventeen years old, in Vienna. . . . Wait! I admonished myself. Let me think. . . . I have forgotten who acted a thin man with an iron-gray wisp of beard, a dark gabardine and the black little cap

of the orthodox Jew. His too vivid gestures and his expressive voice
that ran the gamut from cold logic to embittered passion and spoke
the verse of Shakespeare with a Yiddish modulation which was not
at all ridiculous. . . . That was in 1904 or 1905.

The play occupied my thoughts for a long time. . . . I was a boy,
and another still younger boy lived in Vienna then whose name was
Adolf Hitler. . . . At this time, when I was sixteen, I did not love
Shakespeare, but Heinrich Heine. . . . By God, Heine. . . . That is
it. . . . I read then the splendid prose of Heine, and among his writings
the paper *Gods in Exile*. In this essay the writer imagines that the
ancient gods of the Greeks did not perish when Christ triumphed and
conquered the world. They became refugees and left their country.
They immigrated, went underground. Thy disguised themselves and
lived anonymously in exile a pitiful or comfortable life. They tried to
get jobs, incognito, of course. They drank beer instead of nectar.
Apollo, who had once led the cows of Admetos to pasture, became a
shepherd in Lower Austria; Mars became a soldier, and Mercury a
Dutch merchant who was quite prosperous. Bacchus became Father
Superior of a monastery. . . . I must have read that very picturesque
fantasy of the vicissitudes of the ancient Greek gods before or at the
time when I first saw *The Merchant of Venice* in the Burgtheater. . . .
Sometime and somewhere the memory of those pages of Heine's *Gods
in Exile* must have merged with vague ideas and impressions about
the figures of Antonio and Shylock. . . . The two thoughts met and
coalesced. The result of their mixture was the concept, then only
dimly perceived, that Shylock and Antonio, too, are disguised figures
of gods, reduced to very human size, reappearing in the earthly shape
of a noble Venetian merchant and of an old vengeful Jew. . . . This
paper by Heine, therefore, is the birthplace or the source of my
"original" concept or, at least, it stimulated its genesis. Yes, Heinrich
Heine. . . . I suddenly remember that the same great German writer
wrote another short essay on Shakespeare's *Maiden and Women*. . . .
I had, of course, read this paper too, perhaps about the same time I
read *Gods in Exile*. The coincidence facilitated perhaps the meeting
of the two thoughts in my mind after the performance of *The Merchant of Venice*.

I walk over to my bookcase and I take the volume of Heine's collected works. Here is the essay on Shakespeare's women . . . and here

are the passages on Jessica. I begin to read and again I am under the spell of Heine's magnificent diction as once when I was a boy.

Heine writes about a performance of *The Merchant of Venice:* "When I saw this play at Drury Lane, there stood behind in the box a pale, fair Briton who at the end of the Fourth Act fell a-weeping passionately, several times exclaiming, 'The poor man is wronged!' " The poet thinks of this lady when he visits Venice later on: "Wondering dream-hunter that I am, I looked around everywhere on the Rialto to see if I could find Shylock . . . But I found him nowhere on the Rialto, and I determined to seek my old acquaintance in the Synagogue. The Jews were then celebrating their Day of Atonement. . . . Although I looked all around the Synagogue, I nowhere discovered the face of Shylock. I saw him not. But toward evening, when, according to Jewish belief, the gates of heaven are shut and no prayer can then obtain admission, I heard a voice, with a ripple of tears that never were wept by eyes. It was a sob that could come only from a breast that held in it all martyrdom which for eighteen centuries had been borne by a whole tortured people. It was the death rattle of a soul sinking down dead-tired at heaven's gate, and I seemed to know the voice and I felt that I had heard it long ago; then, in utter despair, it moaned out, then as now, "Jessica, my child!"

In these lines, written more than one hundred years ago, Heine has touched the most vulnerable spot of Shakespeare's Shylock. The picture of the old man who has broken down and moans, "Jessica, my child" has the gloomy grandeur of the biblical paintings of Rembrandt.

It is strange that Heine has so little to say about Jessica with whose personality this piece should deal. She is for him just a pleasure-seeking, egocentric female. But he had quite a few things to say about those Venetian young men who are friends of the noble Antonio. He sees them with a critical eye and he is right in looking down on them. Bassanio is a fortune hunter who adds debts to make a luxurious trip, and who does not hesitate to risk the life of his best friend in order to impress Portia by his elegance. How low can you get? There is Lorenzo who elopes with Jessica and lives on the money and jewels she has taken from her father, lives sumptuously, throwing Shylock's money around. There are those other playboys, irresponsible, flippant, crude, and conceited, shallow and out for fun only—such charming people!

Is Shylock not right when he looks down upon those noble Venetian young gentlemen and speaks aside:

> These be the Christian husbands! I have a daughter;
> Would any of the stock of Barrabas
> Had been her husband rather than a Christian!
>
> (IV.i.295-297)

I have two daughters and, considering these young noblemen, I feel as he does. . . .

And Jessica falls in love with one of those guys who talks big and is an empty shell. He will be fed up with her very soon, will soon throw her over and will look down on her because she is Jewish. And the girl herself? She is ashamed of her father, calls herself daughter of his blood, not of his heart. She robs him and leaves him alone and in despair. Farewell, she says:

> . . . and if my fortune be not crost,
> I have a father, you a daughter, lost.
>
> (II.v.56-57)

I begin to wonder how I came to all these thoughts and I am curious. How did I arrive from thinking of an alcoholic patient to an analytic contribution to Shakespeare's play? I fail to recognize any connections in my associations. . . . It is really puzzling, and I would like to find out on which ways my train of thought wandered. I want to discover the truth about them, and about myself, the truth, fair or foul. . . .

I first remembered the remark of my patient Bill, who is a playboy and drunkard, about Negroes and Jews. Then only words came when I was half asleep. Only names: *Jones, Jericho, Jephthah, Jessica, Jehovah, Jesus.* . . . Oh yes, there were thought connections: Emperor Jones, Jericho, that Jewish peddler in the film, who appeared to me as a kind of degraded Jehovah, Jephthah, who had to sacrifice his own daughter, Jessica, the daughter of Shylock. And then Shylock himself as a human representative of the God of the Jews, reduced and despised in his earthly shape, and Antonio, a small-sized edition of the Nazarene. . . . The trial as a miniature of the great conflict of the old and the new God . . . Gods in Exile . . . Heine . . . and Heine's words about Shylock and Jessica.

But what was there before I thought of that patient and of his anti-Semitic remark? . . . Nothing occurs to me. . . . There is a blank. I think only that I am very tired and that I should go to bed. . . . It is long after midnight. Thody is not home yet . . . Thody. . . .

All of a sudden I recognize with full clarity where the whole train of thought started and why it took this direction and what it means. I am amazed, and it is at this point that I repeat wholeheartedly that sentence of my patient, "Our mind is an insult to our intelligence."

When Thody came into the room to say good night and went out for a date, I must have thought some uncomfortable thoughts. I brushed them aside and tried to run away from them. I turned my attention to the analytic sessions of the day and thus arrived at the thought of my patient and his remark about Negroes and Jews. . . . It started there and now all comes back to me, also the thoughts I tried to escape from. . . . Thody's date must have awakened a dormant fear that she could get infatuated or even fall in love with one of those worthless New York playboys, one of the ilk to which my patient Bill or Lorenzo in *The Merchant of Venice* belongs. It occurred to me that she will be eighteen years old next year and that she could take the funds I saved for her education and for which I toiled and worked so hard so many years. She could elope with just such an immature young fellow and give him her money. . . . She could elope as Jessica did . . . and the young ne'er-do-well would use her and the money and would shortly afterwards throw her over and abuse her.

I know, of course, that none of those fears is justified. Thody is not infatuated with any boy and, even if she were, she is quite intelligent and, although she is temperamental and impulsive, she has a lot of common sense. How do I come to have such vain fears and nonsensical thoughts? They must have originated in fleeting impressions I have received lately. The other day Thody expressed her discontent with our very modest apartment. She seems to be ashamed of it and hesitates to invite her girl friends to her house. She is sometimes impatient with my old-fashioned views—and who knows?—perhaps she is somewhat ashamed of me. She is also dissatisfied with me, it seems, because I am always working and I do not explain things to her that she wants to know. The other day when I had no time to explain some psychological terms, she said angrily, "I could just as well be a shoemaker's daughter." She is dissatisfied with her home, its atmosphere, also in other directions. . . . And girls in such moods are sometimes tempted to elope with the first boy with whom they get infatuated.

But this is nonsense, idle fancy and vain fears! . . . I am not Shylock and my daughter is not Jessica. . . . Even if she should want someday to elope with such a playboy and give him the money I saved for her college education, I mused, what could I, an old codger, do? . . . Have I the right to do anything? . . . You cannot teach another human being how to live . . . not even your own child. . . . Perhaps especially not your own child.

It is strange how the idea, or the fear, I ran away from followed me. I tried to escape from it and it pursued me. In my associations I went off on a tangent and was led to the center of the problem that unconsciously preoccupied me. My alcoholic patient took in my thoughts the place of the imaginary playboy who is the future suitor of Thody. From there I drifted into speculations on Shylock, Jessica, and Antonio and then went into a psychological analysis of the secret background of *The Merchant of Venice,* of the second concealed compartment of the play.

How did I come to the new idea? Certainly not by conscious logical conclusions. If there were any, they followed the concept I had already reached. It was an intuitive insight that suddenly emerged. . . . Out of the nowhere into the here. . . . But such intuition is only the sudden perception of an earlier intellectual experience which had remained unconscious and surprisingly reached the threshold of conscious thinking with the help of new impressions. Could I not later on remember some parts of those old thoughts, recognize in retrospect the raw material out of which the new concept was made?

Looking back at the process, I still wonder how the thought about my patient suddenly turned to those names: *Jones, Jericho, Jephthah, Jehovah, Jesus.* Chaotic and yet following its own hidden laws, my associations arrived by a detour at their destination. There is a psychological resemblance between this disjointed way of thinking and the "flight of ideas," to be found in manic states and in the "word salad" of the schizophrenics. The pathological flight of ideas is perhaps also not a flight toward certain things, but a flight away from a pursuing idea. The old German expression *Ideen-Jagd* is more appropriate. From casually progressing associations, my thoughts increased their tempo, began to chase each other. It was as if they first were comfortably pacing and suddenly went into a gallop, like a horse that shies away from its own shadow. Then they changed their pace again when I drifted into those thoughts on Shakespeare's characters. I really reached the phase of objective study, and the origin of my thoughts, their personal sources, were forgotten or submerged. Here is an alloy of aim-directed logical and rational thinking and hidden irrational and emotional thoughts directed by unconscious drives. As far as I know, psychiatry has no name for such composite processes, which are logically progressing but governed by invisible emotions and forces.

While I thus reviewed my own mental process, I felt no emotion except the curiosity of the psychological observer. I asked myself: Did I feel any emotion during the whole process? Oh yes, there was this moment of glow when I discovered traces of the old myth in the plot of *The Merchant of Venice,* but nothing else. Even when I reread the play, there was no strong emotion. Nothing of the cathartic effect Aristotle recognized, no purification of emotions through fear and pity.

But that impression must have been self-deceiving. I grinned to myself ironically: this is certainly not a deep observation. Nothing penetrating about it. . . . Of course, there must have been emotions that directed the course of my thoughts. There was, no doubt, jealousy of my daughter, also possessiveness, fury against the unknown young man who will take her away from me. I sense how intense the rage and revengefulness against that imaginary young man must have been, because it emerged in the substitution displacement of the trial scene between Shylock and Antonio, in the Jew's insistence on cutting a pound of flesh from his opponent. Also an intense anger against my daughter can easily be conjectured, because the thought of Jephthah appeared. The scene in which Shylock wishes to see his disloyal daughter dead at his feet was vividly recalled. There were, I am sure, also love for my daughter and the awareness of my helplessness, if and when a certain situation might endanger her safety, and quite a few other emotions.

But all of them are only suggested by psychological reasoning. All this is only theoretical insight. I don't feel any of those emotions. They are only guessed and not experienced.

But then, all of a sudden, I know that they are there because I hear my own voice moaning, "Thody, my child!"

Notes

1. NORMAN HOLLAND, *Psychoanalysis and Shakespeare* (New York: McGraw-Hill Book Company, 1964), p. 231.
2. OTTO RANK, *Das Inzest-Motiv in Dichtung und Sage* (1912) (Leipzig: Franz Deuticke, 1926), pp. 258, 355.
3. ISADOR H. CORIAT, "Anal-Erotic Character Traits in Shylock," *International Journal of Psycho-Analysis*, 2:354-360, 1921.

1. Study of medieval folklore does not leave any doubt about this character of the Jews in the thoughts of the people among whom they lived. (*Cf.*, for instance, GEORGE LIEBE, *Der Jude in der deutschen Vergangenheit* (Leipzig, 1912).
2. About the unconscious significance of circumcision as castration, see my study "The Puberty Rites of the Primitives" in my book *Ritual* (New York: Farrar, Straus and Company, 1942).

The Mythical Joys of Shakespeare; Or, What You "Will"

Psychoanalytic criticism has paid some attention to Shakespeare's "happy comedies" (John Dover Wilson's convenient expression),[1] but not the sort of attention it has paid to the Tragedies, or even to the Histories. The relatively small body of material that exists, although it contains a number of excellent studies, simply does not present us with a comprehensive picture of this aspect of the playwright's work. The commentators, to speak more specifically of the contributions, have focused upon four main topics: (1) oedipal and sibling rivalries as expressed, for example, in *The Comedy of Errors;*[2] (2) double-disguises (boys who are supposed to be girls are disguised as boys) in relation to patterns of homosexuality and incest as expressed, for example, in *As You Like It;*[3] (3) striking characters, especially those who seem particularly troubled or neurotic, like Jaques or Malvolio;[4] and the psychoanalytic significance of the drama's symbolic surface as expressed, for example, in *A Midsummer-Night's Dream.*[5] The following paper by Leonard F. Manheim touches upon all four of these topics.

Taking up what many critics consider to be the finest of the happy comedies, *Twelfth Night,* Manheim attempts to demonstrate, among other things, the way in which Shakespeare projects into his dramatis personae certain wish fulfillments from his personal experience. Thus the "basic contention" of the paper is that *"Twelfth Night* is an oedipal comedy written from the viewpoint of the father, just as *Hamlet* is an oedipal tragedy written from the viewpoint of the son. The comedy was written between 1598 and 1601; so was the tragedy. Shakespeare's son, Hamnet, died in August of 1596, at the age of eleven, and was survived by his twin sister Judith. In *Twelfth Night* the twin son and daughter are separated by the primal power of the sea, each considering the other dead. The living daughter takes upon herself the sex and appearance of the dead twin son," and, in spite of the fact that brother-and-sister twins are fraternal, not identical, successfully passes for him in the presence of the play's father substitutes. "Here, then," writes Manheim, "is the first and fundamental wish fulfillment of the play. The dead son can be replaced by the living daughter." Now, as the word "first" implies, the expression of this wish fulfillment gives rise to others, and it is to these others that Manheim turns the remainder of his attention. What he discovers, basically, is that the play's subsequent wish fulfillments are of an incestuous or homosexual nature and that, on the surface level, they arise out of Orsino's attachment to Cesario (homosexual), Cesario's attachment to Orsino (incestuous), and Olivia's attachment to her dead brother (incestuous). In his meticulous examination of these attachments Manheim lights up not only the specific play *Twelfth Night*, but also the dreamlike dimension that every work of art contains, the logic of unconscious processes and the unconscious appeal that this play has for us, and, finally, the nature of comedy itself, where "a profound but unacceptable psychodynamic drive" can be "presented as 'a foolish thing,' 'a toy'; indeed, nothing more than a Twelfth-Night frolic."

M. F.

Such tricks hath strong imagination,
That, if it would but apprehend some joy,
It comprehends some bringer of that joy.
>   *A Midsummer Night's Dream,* V.i.18-20
Will will fulfill the treasure of thy love . . . .
>   Sonnet 136

 offer an interpretation of *Twelfth Night* based on accepted Shakespearean scholarship plus the data of psychoanalysis. I shall extrapolate beyond the words assigned to the characters in the play and shall consider these characters as "persons" known to me (and, in all truth, there are few persons whom I meet in the ordinary intercourse of life whom I know as well as I know these characters), and capable of having a former and a future existence of their own, all, of course, wholly within the bounds of the play's basic structure and development. In the same way, and using the same data, I shall attempt to read *out of* (not into) the text evidence of the author's own fears, hopes, and wishes, none of which will at any time contradict or attenuate any accepted biographical facts and documented material. I know that in accepting Freud, Jones, and their school, and rejecting that of Stoll and Sisson, I run the risk of critical condemnation, including the risk of being belabored with the cudgel of Professor Sisson's animadversions on "The Mythical Sorrows of Shakespeare."[1]

I know this so well that I have run to meet it by basing my title on Sisson's. But the reading is different. By "mythical" I mean not that which is mendacious, factitious, untrue, consciously conceived by an irresponsible critic; but rather that which is the product of a non-conscious, "mythopoeic" drive to explain phenomena which are not rationally understood, or which are so understood but are not, on the psychodynamic level, acceptable to the conscious mind.[2] I substitute "joys" for "sorrows," and I mean by "joy" just what Shakespeare meant by the word in his treatise on the ways of the mind which is embodied in the colloquy between Theseus and Hippolyta in the fifth act of *A Midsummer Night's Dream.* As is apparent, I agree with Freud that "Story-tellers are valuable allies, [whose] testimony is to be rated high, for they usually know many things between heaven and earth that our academic wisdom does not even dream of."[3] But I am concerned not only with the intuitions of Shakespeare the creative artist, but with the wish-fulfilling fantasies of Shakespeare the man, and I imply this by adopting, with a possible change of emphasis, his subtitle for *Twelfth Night,* indicating that by the fantasy of this piece of joyous entertainment he is flying in the teeth of certain painful but unalterable facts, giving himself through this fantasy grounds for (irrational) joy. In other words, "What You Will" implies the phenomenon of "the omnipotence of thought"; it means not (or not only) "whatever you prefer" but "that which you *will* into being," "that which you attempt to bring about as a wish-fulfillment."[4] I contend that in *Twelfth Night* Shakespeare was freely expressing a number of such wish fulfillments, some of them conscious, some of them possibly preconscious (that is, not within the area of awareness but capable of being understood directly when they are brought into that area), but most of them completely unconscious; that these wish fulfillments had indeed grown out of the private and personal experience of the author but were also projected into the personal and private experience of the "persons" introduced as characters in the play.

The more conventional Shakespearean critic, apprehensive—not without cause—of the excesses committed by some psychoanalytic investigators (I hesitate to call them "critics"), will ask, "How much do we really know of Shakespeare's private and personal experience?" and "What does that private and personal experience have to do with his works of art?" To the first question I respond that I shall imply nothing concerning Shakespeare's private life which is not in complete harmony with evidence which is acceptable to the most traditional critic; *viz.,* the Shakespearean documents gathered and published by

J. O. Halliwell-Phillips,[5] D. H. Lambert,[6] E. K. Chambers,[7] and B. Roland Lewis.[8] Nor do I intend to imply a one-to-one relationship between documented events and works produced; that, for instance, a shocking event will necessarily be reflected in an attitude or tone in the next succeeding play. I do imply, however, that once an event of importance has been established in point of time, it must be considered as having some influence on some work which follows it, closely or at farther remove. And this makes plain my reply to the second question, for I firmly believe that Shakespeare was a man as well as an artist, and that no man can do, say, or write anything (even—or, rather, particularly—a work of art) that does not reflect his own experience directly or indirectly. The real difficulty is not in finding evidence in a work of art that points clearly to the influence of private experience; on the contrary, the difficulty lies in the fact that created material has its roots in many, seemingly unrelated, elements of personal experience, much of it, I must repeat, unconscious; in other words, much of that material is, as the psychoanalyst puts it, "overdetermined," requiring investigation into many, often inconsistent and seemingly irreconcilable, sources.

The preliminaries thus disposed of, I proceed to my basic contention: *Twelfth Night* is an oedipal comedy written from the viewpoint of the father, just as *Hamlet* is an oedipal tragedy written from the viewpoint of the son. The comedy was written between 1598 and 1601; so was the tragedy.[9] Shakespeare's son, Hamnet, died in August of 1596, at the age of eleven, and was survived by his twin sister Judith.[10] In *Twelfth Night* the twin son and daughter are separated by the primal power of the sea, each considering the other dead. The living daughter takes upon herself the sex and appearance of the dead twin son and is so successful in passing for him that the sea captain Antonio, who has enacted the role of father substitute to the son, can say when he sees the two of them together,

> How have you made division of yourself?
> And apple, left in two, is not more twin
> Than these two creatures. Which is Sebastian?[11]
> (V.i.229-231)

It need not be pointed out (and it could hardly have been unknown to the Elizabethans) that whatever might have been the confusion between male twins in *The Comedy of Errors,* brother-and-sister twins are fraternal, not identical; they do not resemble each other more than ordinary brothers and sisters do.[12]

Here, then, is the first and fundamental wish fulfillment of the play. The dead son can be replaced by the living daughter, who gives up her own sex in order to obtain access, by appearing as a man, or at least "an eunuch," to the bachelor who must be considerably older than she is, for she has "heard [her] father name him" (I.ii.28), and that father "died that day when Viola from her birth/Had number'd thirteen years" (V.i.251-252). The Duke, when informed by Cesario that "he" has been attracted to a woman of about the Duke's age, exclaims,

> Too old, by heaven; let still the woman take
> An elder than herself . . .
>
> (II.iv.30-31)

and stresses the persistent fantasy that women, on losing their virginity, are thereby rendered less attractive to their lovers, a doctrine to which Viola will, of course, not wholly assent:

> *Duke.* Then let thy love be younger than thyself,
> Or thy affection cannot hold the bent;
> For women are as roses, whose fair flower
> Being once display'd, doth fall that very hour.
> *Viola.* And so they are: alas! that they are so;
> To die, even when they to perfection grow.
>
> (II.iv.37-42)

The Duke's attitude toward Viola's masculinity seems to me to be rather ambivalent, and Cesario clearly runs the risk of being accused of a homosexual attachment to the bachelor Orsino. Even in the opening scenes, Valentine comments, "If the Duke continue these favours towards you, Cesario, you are like to be much advanced: he hath known you but three days, and already you are no stranger" (I.iv.1-4). And the Duke himself displaces and condenses his emotional attachments by insisting that Cesario-Viola is the best possible bearer of the tale of his love for Olivia:

> For they shall yet belie thy happy years,
> That say thou art a man: Diana's lip
> Is not more smooth and rubious; thy small pipe

Is as the maiden's organ, shrill and sound;
And all is semblative a woman's part.
. . .

           . . . Prosper well in this,
And thou shalt live as freely as thy lord,
To call his fortunes thine.
(I.iv.30-34,38-40)

Orsino reveals even more when he loses his temper, for he reproaches both Cesario and Olivia when he refers to the former as "this your minion, whom I know you love,/And whom, by heaven I swear, I tender dearly" (V.i.128-129), an obvious projection, for if Cesario is anyone's "minion" it will have to be Orsino's, who "tenders him dearly," rather than Olivia's. And this ambivalence of Orsino is embedded in the speech in which Italianate sadism for once rears its ugly head in the fantasy-land of Illyria:

Why should I not, had I the heart to do it,
Like to the Egyptian thief at point of death,
Kill what I love? a savage jealousy
That sometimes savours nobly. . . .
. . .

Come, boy, with me; my thoughts are ripe in mischief;
I'll sacrifice the lamb that I do love,
To spite a raven's heart within a dove.
(V.i.120-123,132-134)

For a moment it seems that the pattern of Fletcher's Philaster and Bellario is about to be enacted, when Olivia sets matters right by calling in the euphuistic priest to testify to the marriage. But I wonder how many readers and viewers of the play have not suspected, as I did years ago, that Orsino was aware of Viola's secret on some level of marginal consciousness.

But no such logical inference is necessary, for there is no logic in the wish-fulfilling Unconscious, and Viola can be both the lost twin brother and the surviving twin sister, who will provide the mourning dramatist with the male heir he so greatly desires and at the same time be the solacing daughter who will unwaveringly prefer the father figure in spite of all the enticements of normal heterosexual adjustment.[13] In the blithe irrationality of the Unconscious, Viola comes back to life once as her own twin brother, the sea-devoured Hamnet-Sebastian, and then Sebastian (the beautiful martyr, the "hanging god," let it be remembered, of medieval and Renaissance art) also returns to life to wed with most precipitate haste the other virginal figure who is, as we shall note more fully in a moment, another projection of the beloved daughter, leaving the first daughter image, the inviolate Viola, free to devote herself wholly to her beloved father-Duke. And all this happens in Illyria, a fantasy-land like the later Bohemia which had a sea-coast for the same reason that Illyria does; that is, in order that the sea may both engulf and give up its dead. The word-play "Illyria-Elysium" is made at the very outset of the play (I.ii.3-4). In this country of the fulfilled wishes of fantasy it is possible for a sister not only to take the place of her dead brother and thus restore him to life, but also to be, in one guise, a loving daughter to her mourning father, while her *alter ego* is recompensed for the loss of one brother by finding another who is permitted to be her sexual mate.

Note how the legitimized incest fantasies become more and more apparent as we examine the ambivalent intricacies imposed by the plot. Manningham was able to gloss over the implications of an underlying incest theme by forgetting (or never realizing) the occasion of Olivia's mourning and referring to her as the "lady widowe," even though Viola's sea captain says at the very outset that she is

> A virtuous maid, the daughter of a count
> That died some twelvemonth since; then leaving her
> To the protection of his son, her brother,
> Who shortly also died; for whose dear love,
> They say, she hath abjured the company
> And sight of men.
>
> (I.ii.36-41)

to which Viola quite naturally responds,

> O! that I serv'd that lady,
> And might not be delivered to the world,
> Till I had made mine own occasion mellow,
> What my estate is.
>
> (I.ii.41-44)

But Viola is not to be allowed to join her lot with that of her sister in misfortune; instead she goes to serve a living lord and master who "knows her not." And the father-daughter incest theme is betrayed in lines which, through their insistent poetic beauty, have obscured their revealing ambiguity.

Viola. My father had a daughter lov'd a man,
      As it might be, perhaps, were I a woman,
      I should your lordship.
Duke.   And what's her history?
Viola. A blank, my lord. She never told her love,
      But let concealment, like a worm i' the bud,
      Feed on her damask cheek; she pin'd in thought,
      And with a green and yellow melancholy,
      She sat like Patience on a monument,
      Smiling at grief. Was not this love indeed?

      . . . .

Duke. But died thy sister of her love, my boy?
Viola. I am all the daughters of my father's house,
      And all the brothers too: and yet I know not.
                    (II.iv.110-118,122-124)

A moment ago I spoke of Olivia as Viola's *alter ego*. The point might be made without more painstaking demonstration, but there is a pattern in the play which blurts out the secret that even he who runs may read. Let us look for a moment at a piece of deliberate mystification concocted by Maria for the humbling of Malvolio and the delectation of Toby and his companions. In the forged letter which Malvolio believes to have been written by Olivia, there are two sets of verses, the second of which is to convey to the hapless steward, who hardly needs the additional assurance, that it is he and he alone who is the object of his mistress' love:

      I may command where I adore;
        But silence, like a Lucrece knife,
      With bloodless stroke my heart doth gore;
        M, O, A, I, doth sway my life.
                    (II.v.115-118)

Neither Malvolio nor the audience needs much prompting that the code points to him. "M, — Malvolio," he says; "M, — why that begins my name" (II.v.137-138). But he is concerned because "A should follow, but O does" (II.v.142-143). Apart from his reading, we may want to make one of our own, for the letters contribute to a pervasive anagram. The vowels are to be found in the name of every character in the romantic (incest-ridden) plot. All three are to be found in "Viola" and "Olivia" as well as in "Malvolio." Two are to be found in the lesser figures, "Orsino" and "Maria." In the gulled steward whose name furnishes the first clue to the anagram, the "mal-" element points clearly to the "evil" in the presumption of the Puritanical steward who should be the protector of the virginity of his lady-mistress, but instead raises his eyes in unholy desire for her. This is emphasized by the "will" element in "-volio" (*voglio*), substituted in place of the original letters in the "Malevolti" of the source material. All three vowels are to be found in his name, the "o" being used twice, to establish a masculine ending to a rearrangement of both "Viola" and "Olivia." And these two are obvious anagrams for each other, with the latter name carrying a second "i." And, as I have suggested above, she is indeed a second "I" to Viola. As double, therefore, she rejects the substitute father whom her counterpart adores, thus rejecting but also achieving the implied incest. She loses one brother but is recompensed for the loss by her marriage to Sebastian, just as the first "I" loses a brother and finds a father.

The incest taboo is also avoided by what we might term a "purloined letter" technique; the relationships, real and substitute, are made so obvious, so oft-repeated, that they are accepted as innocent, since nothing forbidden could be so patently presented. This is, of course, a pattern not uncommon in Shakespeare, as in other Elizabethan dramatists. Viola and Sebastian, the fatherless twins, each have their respective father-protectors, the sea captains who rescue them from the sea of death and watch over them even after bringing them to rebirth in the land of Illyria-Elysium. Viola's unnamed captain is the sole custodian of her secret, as well as of her "maiden weeds" (V.i.262), but his possible protection for the daughter who turns out to need none is frustrated by the evil "father" Malvolio, who keeps him "in durance" (V.i.281-284). Antonio, Sebastian's faithful father-protector, fares worse, for he is in mortal danger in Illyria (in which he resembles father Aegeon in *The Comedy of Errors*) but braves all dangers for the son who proves to be (or at least seems to be) ungrateful and unfilial. He is saved only by the intervention of the father-paramount, the Duke.

To the fathers who serve, or are served by the twins (the reversal is a dynamic equivalence in the pattern of the Unconscious, in which there is no such word as "not"), there must be added the congeries of fathers who cluster about the second "I." With her real father and brother gone, she avows her intention of remaining unseen—veiled— for seven years, the appropriate period of biblical servitude. She casts aside that veil, however, both literally and symbolically, when brother Cesario makes his appearance and saucily commands her to do so. In the meantime, and until her deliverance by Cesario-Sebastian, she is surrounded by a grotesque set of "protectors," only one of whom, Sir Toby, has designs on her fortune which do not also include threats to her virginity. But they cannot prevail, for if Viola-Cesario has not the swordsman's skill to defend her against the witless Sir Andrew, Sebastian is waiting to act as substitute in the nick of time, and to give Sir Toby a bloody coxcomb (or to make it plain that that is what each of the two false knights really is) and break Sir Andrew's head as well, thus rescuing the virgin "I" from all her unworthy "protectors."

Before concluding, let me repeat my words of warning. I am not describing or attempting to describe the conscious, intentional devices of an artist, appealing to the conscious awareness of the reader or spectator. Any such appeal would arouse anxiety rather than pleasure in both; whereas such anxiety is avoided when "deep calleth unto deep." The analytic critic, like the analytic therapist, avoids this anxiety by a process which I cannot undertake to explain here. In any case, it has become apparent in the years since psychoanalytic criticism first began to function (as criticism, I repeat, not as clinical analysis) that analysis does not "reduce" the work of art nor militate against its full enjoyment; rather, the contrary is true: we perceive in depth what we had formerly missed superficially. In our play we see the disarming nature of the approach through comedy summed up in the song of Feste as epilogue:

> When that I was and a little tiny boy,
>> With hey, ho, the wind and the rain;
> A foolish thing was but a toy,
>> For the rain it raineth every day.
>
> (V.i.398-401)

A profound but unacceptable psychodynamic drive is presented as "a foolish thing," "a toy"; indeed, nothing more than a Twelfth-Night frolic. It could have been masked in the form of tragedy; perhaps the self-same drive would reappear some years later in *King Lear*. But now, at the end of *Twelfth Night; or, What You Will* we rest content, for

> A great while ago the world begun,
>   With hey, ho, the wind and the rain:
> But that's all one, our play is done,
>   And we'll strive to please you every day.[13]
>   (V.i.414-417)

Notes

1. JOHN DOVER WILSON, *Shakespeare's Happy Comedies* (London: Cambridge University Press, 1962). Under this heading Wilson includes *The Comedy of Errors, The Two Gentlemen of Verona, Love's Labour's Lost, A Midsummer-Night's Dream, The Taming of the Shrew, As You Like It, The Merry Wives of Windsor,* and *Twelfth Night; or What You Will.*

2. See A. BRONSON FELDMAN, "Shakespeare's Early Errors," *International Journal of Psycho-Analysis, 36*:114-133, 1955.

3. See CONRAD VAN EMDE BOAS, "The Connection Between Shakespeare's Sonnets and His 'Travesti-Double' Plays," *International Journal of Sexology, 4*:67-72, 1950.

4. See WILLIAM INGLIS DUNN SCOTT, *Shakespeare's Melancholiacs* (London: Mill and Boon, 1962), pp. 61-72; also MELVIN SEIDEN, "Malvolio Reconsidered," *University of Kansas City Review, 28*:105-114, 1961.

5. See WESTON A. GUI, "Bottom's Dream," *American Imago, 9*:251-305, 1952-1953.

1. C. J. SISSON, "The 1934 Annual Shakespeare Lecture of the British Academy," *Proceedings of the British Academy,* Vol. XX (London: Humphrey Milford). Actually, Professor Sisson's fire is not directed against the psychoanalytic critic. The immediate cause of his irritation was Nazi propaganda in guise of criticism, ". . . by dint of which there arises, as from a trap-door at Bayreuth, a dour heroic figure of pure Nordic ancestry, the enemy of all Southern decadences,

faithful to his Leader, the prophet of the new Germany of today" (pp. 3-4). These excesses Professor Sisson ascribes not to the influence of psychoanalysis (under the circumstances, he could hardly do so) but to the example of Coleridge, who carried over into the nineteenth-century German criticism of the brothers Schlegel and their followers, and back into *their* British successors in the later nineteenth and early twentieth centuries.

Not that there is a lack of evidence of Professor Sisson's animosity toward psychoanalytic criticism *per se*. See, for example, his introduction to *Hamlet* in his edition of the *Complete Works* (New York: Harper and Bros., 1953):

> There has been altogether too much throwing about of brains concerning the character of Hamlet himself, both analytic and psycho-analytic. We would do better to consider Hamlet according to his own words, and against the contemporary background of the writings of Thomas More or of John Donne on the problems of his state of mind. (p. 997.)

The psychoanalytic critic—need it be said—does consider the character "according to his own words," and he does not deny the influence of Shakespeare's contemporary background; he does, however, insist on his right and duty to consider the author first as a *man,* then as a Western man, and then as an Elizabethan man.

2. When we consider how much more prevalent the latter meaning of "mythical" has become, it is at least remarkable that the critic who used the word in "mythical sorrow" should not have chosen some expression which is unequivocally indicative of "non-existent" or "grossly exaggerated."

3. S. FREUD, *Delusions and Dreams in Jensen's "Gradiva"* (1803-1895), Standard Edition, Vol. IX (London: Hogarth Press, 1959), p. 8; see also NORMAN N. HOLLAND, "Freud and the Poet's Eye," *Literature and Psychology,* 11:37(n.5) and *passim,* 1961.

4. S. FREUD, "A Case of Obsessional Neurosis" (1909), Standard Edition, Vol. IV (London: Hogarth Press, 1954), 370n. (1923). "The omnipotence of thoughts, or, more accurately speaking, of wishes, has since been recognized as an essential element in the mental life of primitive people." The play on "will" is, of course, closely allied to Shakespeare's word-play on his own name, as, for example, in the "Will" sonnets (135, 136, 143).

5. J. O. HALLIWELL-PHILLIPS, *Outlines of the Life of Shakespeare* (London: Longmans, Green, 1898).

6. D. H. Lambert, *Cartae Shakespeareanae: Shakespeare Documents* (London: George Bell and Sons, 1904).

7. E. K. Chambers, *William Shakespeare: A Study of Facts and Problems* (2 vols.; Oxford: The Clarendon Press, 1930).

8. B. Roland Lewis, *The Shakespeare Documents* (2 vols.; Stanford, California: Stanford University Press, 1940-41).

9. Israel Gollancz, preface to the Temple edition of *Twelfth Night* (London: J. M. Dent and Sons, 1923; first issued in 1894), pp. v-vi; and Sisson, *Complete Works,* pp. 336, 997. Harold Jenkins, "William Shakespeare: A Bibliographical Essay," in Sisson, *Complete Works,* stresses the probable alternation of comedy and tragedy: "As far as one can tell in ignorance of precise dating, *Julius Caesar* and *Hamlet* alternated with *As You Like It* and *Twelfth Night* (p. xiii). Louis B. Wright and Virginia LaMar, in the *Folger Library General Reader's Shakespeare* edition of *Hamlet* (New York: Washington Square Press, 1957), state that ". . . it was performed, probably about 1600," and G. B. Harrison, in *Introducing Shakespeare* (London: Pelican Books, 1939), p. 121, lists both plays in the canon as of the year 1601. For my purposes, I am content with any dating after, but probably not long after, 1596.

10. Much of the biographical information concerning births, marriages, and deaths is taken by the authorities named in notes 5-8 from entries in the parish Register of the Church of the Holy Trinity, Stratford-upon-Avon. This gives 2 February 1585 as the date of the christening of Hamnet and Judith, son and daughter of William Shakespeare, and 11 August 1596 as the date of Hamnet's funeral.

11. I use the Temple edition (see note 9), and I see no need to reproduce old spelling and punctuation.

12. It may be argued that the twins' identical appearance is inherent in Shakespeare's sources. Whether this is so or not is not decisive in the matter of psychodynamic interpretation, for what Shakespeare invented and what Shakespeare adopted by selection from his source material are both indicative of at least some personal predilection on his part for a particular dramatic device. Still, it may be appropriate to glance at the scholarly data concerning the sources. Manningham's diary entry for 2 February 1601 (-2) describes the play as "Much like the Comedy of Errors or Menechmi in Plautus; but most like and near to that in Italian called Inganni" (Gollancz, p. v). "The source for the main plot," writes Sisson (*Complete Works,* p. 356), "is apparently *Apolonius and Sila,* Apolonius being Orsino and Sila Viola. . . . The story came to Riche from Bandello's Italian

novella, and to him from an Italian play, *Gli Ingannati* (The deceived
ones) dating from 1531. . . ." The identity of the Italian source is not
particularly clarified by the fact that "there are at least two Italian
plays called *Gl'Inganni* (The Cheats), to which Manningham may
have referred in his entry as containing incidents resembling those of
Twelfth Night; one of these plays, by Nicolo Secchi, was printed in
1562; another, by Curzio Ganzalo, was first published [in Italian?] in
1592. In the latter play, the sister, who dresses as a man and is mistaken for her brother, gives herself the name of Cesare. . . . A third
play, however, entitled *Gl'Ingannati* (Venice 1537), . . . bears a much
stronger resemblance to *Twelfth Night;* in its poetical induction, *Il
Sacrificio,* occurs the name 'Malevolti,' which is at least suggestive of
the name 'Malvolio' " (GOLLANCZ, pp. vi-vii). To dispose of matters
of source and origin, it seems generally agreed that Malvolio (except
for the suggestion of the name), Sir Toby, Sir Andrew, Fabian, Feste,
Maria, and (at least as far as her name is concerned) Olivia are all
wholly Shakespeare's.

13. I, for my part, have forsworn all temptation to speculative
biographical inferences, but I cannot refrain from marshalling a few
of the well-attested facts, leaving the inferences to the reader.

Both of Shakespeare's daughters were unmarried at the time
Twelfth Night was probably written, Susanna being no more than
eighteen years old and Judith no more than sixteen (if we take the
terminus ad quem, 1601, as the date of the play; it seems more probable that they were both several years younger). Susanna married on
5 June 1607, at the age of twenty-one, and the marriage seems to have
been considered a good one; at all events, William Shakespeare named
John and Susanna Hall the residuary legatees in his will, in addition
to indicating other marked signs of confidence in them. Judith did not
marry until 10 February 1616, being then thirty-one years of age.

Judith's marriage was followed soon after (25 March 1616) by the
execution of Shakespeare's will, and about a month after that by
Shakespeare's death. A few words of comment on some of the less
familiar provisions of the will. (I think I may make them on the
strength of the text of the will alone, for I claim some familiarity
with the Anglo-American law of wills, since I was admitted to the
New York Bar in 1925.) I have already commented on the special
favor shown to John and Susanna Hall. In the will, Judith receives
£100 "in discharge of her marriage porcion" (the words quoted
were added to the original draft of the will), plus £50 in return
for her surrender of her rights as heir-in-law of certain real property

left to Susanna; plus another £150, which is attributable to her only if she survives the testator's death by three years, and which is then to be held in trust with the income alone payable to her "soe long as shalbe marryed and covert baron" (a familiar device to prevent a husband's getting his hands on his wife's property), with a gift over to her children, "if she have anie, and if not, to her executors or assignes, she lyving the saied term after my deceas."

It is plain that the elder daughter was preferred to the younger, even though the latter had remained unmarried and faithful to the father for so many years. The very close order in which her marriage, her father's will, and his death followed one another seems to me most interesting,—but I have sworn to let the reader do the speculating, and I say no more.

The Measure in "Measure for Measure"

Shakespeare's problem plays, or dark comedies, or tragicomedies—
a number of appellations are current—have yet to receive a comprehensive treatment from psychoanalytic criticism. Some very good studies exist, though, and it may be that these can serve as groundwork
for future analyses. For example, Barbara Hannah has examined *All's
Well That Ends Well* from a rather Jungian perspective and has concluded that the play deals with questions of individuation and emotional maturity;[1] Fritz Wittels has suggested that the heroine of
Troilus and Cressida is a narcissist, incapable of love;[2] and Otto Rank,
in an early work, has touched upon the problem of incest motifs in
Measure for Measure.[3] With the exception of the paper to follow,
there is not a great deal more.[4]

Hanns Sachs begins his study of *Measure for Measure* with analysis
of Angelo, a character who is not hypocritical (the usual pronouncement) but involved in a psychological conflict that is precipitated by a
"regression to the sadistic stage of sensuality." Because he is punitive
and cruel, Angelo condemns Claudio to die for fornication; when he
confronts Isabella, however, he is tempted to commit the same crime
that Claudio has committed. Thus (as in *Oedipus Rex*) the criminal
and the judge become one, and the problem of the play as a whole becomes the problem of justice: How can there be justice when the judge
himself is guilty? In *Measure for Measure* this problem is further
complicated by the fact that the Duke, who is the ultimate judge, does
not restrict criminality to guilty deeds but includes guilty thoughts as
well. "If unconscious wishes and drives," writes Sachs, "are not only
in existence, but active in the mind of everyone, if they are kept from
coming to life only by the special grace of destiny, then it follows that
every man who dares to be a judge is a potential Angelo. It means, if
we take it in its full and true sense and set aside as mere accidents the
actual temptations and the outward shapes of our acts and our conscious
thoughts, that no judge can disclaim his identity in guilt with the

criminal before him." Again, although Angelo fully intends to commit an evil deed he is thwarted in this intention by the bed-trick, and it is this that makes *Measure for Measure* a comedy. In tragedy, says the author, "the dreadful crimes are really performed, although unintentionally"; in comedy "there is any amount of bad intentions, but nothing happens." Yet Angelo, because of the Duke's attitude, must still be punished for his evil intentions, and it is fitting, Sachs maintains, that he be punished in the same way that Lucio, another character who thinks maliciously but does no actual malice, is punished, namely, by having to marry a woman he does not want to marry. Nor is the Duke himself entirely free from suspicion, for just as Angelo's wedding "parallels, on a higher level, the enforced marriage of Lucio," so does the Duke's decision to make Isabella his wife parallel in a "legitimate and honorable" way "the crime which Angelo attempted in vain." What is the point? That they (and we) are all sinners; that only mercy can help.

M. F.

t seems that in Shakespeare's time titles were given to new plays in more or less haphazard fashion; some of Shakespeare's own plays are mentioned by his contemporaries under different names. It is therefore advisable to be careful in drawing any conclusion from the title of a play. This caution need not be applied to *Measure for Measure,* since the name forms an intrinsic part of the play; it is taken from the solemn words used by the Duke when, at the end, he condemns Angelo:

> 'An Angelo for Claudio, death for death!'
> Haste still pays haste, and leisure answers leisure,
> Like doth quit like, and Measure still for Measure.
>   (V.i.414-416)

If, therefore, we may feel reasonably sure that the name has been selected by the author, then we have before us the most shattering example of Shakespeare's famous and much discussed irony. Angelo's wrongdoings—blackmail, rape, murder under the mask of justice— are as bad as any committed by any of Shakespeare's villains, Iago or Richard III, for example. And yet, he is let off without any punishment, he keeps his rank and fortune and gets a loving and obedient wife—and that is called "Measure for Measure"!

The smiling indulgence for the failings of an Oliver (*As You Like It*) or a Bertram (*All's Well That Ends Well*) as natural acts of high-strung youths which, after due repentance, may be forgiven and

"The Measure in *Measure for Measure*" by Hanns Sachs. Reprinted from *The Creative Unconscious,* 2nd edition, 1951, pp. 72-98, with permission by Sci-Art Publishers.

forgotten, is an entirely different thing. Shakespeare was not in an indulgent frame of mind when he wrote *Measure for Masure,* nor does he put his audience in a sweet and smiling disposition by the background he gives to Angelo's crimes. This Vienna, reeking with gross sensuality without charm, frothing of frivolity without grace, this city of whores and bawds and fools and knaves, where they "sell men and women like beasts," makes a sex-offender like Angelo appear more disgusting and detestable than any other environment could do. He pretends to others, and tries to believe it himself, that he is the enraged foe and persecutor of its vices, but his own mind is deeply imbued by them.

Angelo has been stamped a hypocrite by general consent of the critics, but this by no means represents his most characteristic trait. He becomes a hypocrite by necessity as soon as he succumbs to temptation, but till then his sternness and gravity cannot be called hypocrisy, that is: conscious dissembling. When Isabella takes up his defense to help Mariana—by the way, the most charming contradiction to the impenetrable armor of her virtuous indignation—she goes so far as to say that she partly thinks "A due sincerity governed his deeds,/Till he did look on me"; and Shakespeare makes it quite clear in more than one passage that this more charitable view is the correct one.

Angelo's inner torment after Isabella's first interview makes him change her harmless farewell words "Save your honour" into an outcry: "From thee—even from thy virtue," and the following monologue shows how amazed he is at the situation. He has not been accustomed to feel temptations and he has evidently never yielded to them before. How else could he be so outraged by his present corruption to compare himself with a carrion and in the same breath with a saint whom the "cunning enemy" baits with a saint?

> . . . never could the strumpet,
> With all her double vigour, art and nature,
> Once stir my temper; but this virtuous maid
> Subdues me quite. Ever till now,
> When men were fond, I smiled and wondered how.
>
> (II.ii.183-187)

This leaves no doubt that Angelo's virtue, as far as conscious and outward acts go, was quite intact. It is true that this virtue did not come from the highest heaven of purity—but that does not stamp it as hypocrisy. As this first monologue shows, Angelo's abstinence was founded on his indifference to ordinary sensuality and to "fondness," that is to love in the form of tenderness. Isabella was his first serious temptation because she aroused something in him to which no other woman had appealed before, a desire that had been slumbering—or rather waiting for its time. The other, secondary motive, was the "pride in gravity" which served to inspire those around him with respect and awe. His eagerness to conceal this vanity ("let no man hear me") is certainly a sign of a disingenuous bent in his character, but his strict morality, on whatever foundation it was built, was not less real for all that. His serious, though unsuccessful, attempt to pray shows that he does not take his fall from grace lightly as an old hypocrite would have done. "When I would pray and think, I think and pray to several subjects."

The outstanding trait in his character, constellating his attitude in all matters, small or great, is cruelty. To his subordinates he is gruff and unfriendly, always ready with a rebuke or a threat. He snubs the simple constable ("Elbow is your name? why dost thou not speak, Elbow?") as well as the kind Provost ("Do you your office, or give up your place, and you shall well be spared"). The unhappy Juliet is to him simply a "fornicatrix." To sit as a judge in court inspires him with the same philanthropic sentiment towards the silly but evidently harmless witness as toward the offender: "hoping you'll find good cause to whip them all." His cruelty is best demonstrated by the fact that he selects Claudio as the victim for the renewed enforcement of the laws against profligacy. In this Vienna of bawds and brothels it would have been easy to find a culprit whose transgressions were of a darker hue than those of Claudio. He seems to be singled out by Angelo just because he was the most innocent offender who came within the scope of the law; his betrothal gave him, according to custom, the right of a legitimate husband, especially since these things happened some time before the revival of the strict law. Indeed, this way of enforcing the old statute does nothing to give it renewed authority, but discredits it by making it appear fantastic and impossible. It is not justice or morality which Angelo tries to establish—though he may persuade himself that these are his aims—but terror, wrath, and cruelty.

This tendency toward cruelty shapes Angelo's life in two ways: first, negatively, by making the ordinary and normal forms of sensuality unattractive to him, or even repulsive. This may be one of the reasons why he pursues them with this cold hate. As the Duke puts it, he

> ... scarce confesses
> That his blood flows, or that his appetite
> Is more to bread than stone—
>
> (I.iii.51-53)

in other words to a free and impartial observer his rigidity seems exaggerated and, therefore, a bit suspicious.

The other, positive, influence is manifested in his bias for meting out punishment, for making others suffer. He loves to wield the sword of justice and to feel entitled, in defending a higher cause, to be severe and uncharitable so long as his own life remains blameless; in this way he satisfies his cravings in a quasi-legitimate way. Through his office he finds an outlet for his dark desire in the form of a social function which has his own approval as well as that of society; in short, he shows what psychoanalysis calls a sublimation, although by no means a perfectly successful one, since his original nature looks through the rents in his gown. This sublimation breaks down with a sudden crash when he meets Isabella. The splendor of her purity, outshining everything to which he has been accustomed, together with the situation which delivers her into his hands, is too much for him.

> ... Can it be
> That modesty may more betray our sense
> Than woman's lightness? Having waste ground enough,
> Shall we desire to raze the sanctuary,
> And pitch our evils there?
>
> (II.ii.168-172)

Thus stimulated and exposed to the storm of desire, his cruelty loses every aspect of sublimation and falls back, regressively, to its original source, revealing its primeval, sensual form. How near these two have dwelled together in Angelo's mind is illustrated by the identity he sees in murder and the sexual sin: " 'tis all as easy/Falsely to take away a life true made/As to put metal in restrained means/To make a false one" (II.iv.46-49). The new temptation, against which Angelo fights in vain, is that of sadism. This psychological picture, the conflict caused by the regression to the sadistic stage of sensuality, would to us moderns who are concerned with the psychic processes in their immediate and intimate appearance, constitute an obsessional neurotic. Shakespeare, who, as the true son of the Renaissance, projected his psychological intuition into the facts and forms of the world outside, made him a judge.

Judge—this is in one word the problem of *Measure for Measure* from which all the rest proceeds. As it often happens with Shakespeare, it looks at first as if he presented only an ephemeral, accidental side of the problem: the evil judge who misuses his power for his own ends, the judge without mercy whose justice is but cruelty. The deeper meaning is not emphasized or advertised to impress the beholder with its profundity, but rather kept in the background and, especially in the comedies, disguised by jokes and scurrility, like a cliff overgrown with grass and shrubs. Whoever takes the trouble to penetrate the dark recesses of this "least attractive" of Shakespeare's comedies, will find that Shakespeare weighed the idea of the man who has assumed the dreadful, superhuman privilege and responsibility of a judge in its deepest sense, as it existed from the beginnings of civilization and will exist as long as men are judged by men and not by the use of machines —verily seen "sub species aeternitatis."

The theme that is harped on constantly in *Measure for Measure* and carried through every possible variation, some straightforward to the point of brutality, some abstract and remote, is this: What happens to justice if the austere judge could commit, would commit, has committed the same crime for which he condemns the offender? What if Angelo is not different from Claudio and deserves to be put in his place—"an Angelo for Claudio?" The question is discussed first in a strictly judicial reasoning at the beginning of Act II by Angelo himself. He excludes the moral side entirely: it does not matter that the judge has the same desires which have led the culprit into crime, so long as he has been able to control them and has not acted on their promptings, even if his successful resistance is to be attributed to mere good luck that shielded him from temptation. ("Had time cohered with place or place with wishing.") He rejects any such plea absolutely: "Tis one thing to be tempted, Escalus,/Another thing to fall." He goes even farther. Since Escalus has dropped a rather broad hint, that even he, Angelo, may have yielded formerly to the common human frailty in the matter of sex, he asserts that a verdict would be just, even if one or two of the jurymen who passed it had actually committed the same crime, provided that their transgressions remained secret. But he does not claim the privilege of unknown guilt for himself. Feeling vainglorious about a life which as yet has been blameless, he waives any such excuse and pronounces his doom:

> You may not so extenuate his offence
> For I have had such faults; but rather tell me,
> When I, that censure him, do so offend,
> Let mine own judgment pattern out my death,
> And nothing come in partial.
>
> (II.i.27-31)

The argument between Angelo and Isabella about Claudio's reprieve starts on the same theme with her words:

> If he had been as you, and you as he,
> You would have slipp'd like him; but he, like you,
> Would not have been so stern.
>
> (II.ii.64-66)

Angelo, touched by the first fire of temptation, does not answer her by nice legal distinctions. He finds no other reply than:

> Pray you, be gone.

Isabella seems to feel that she has come near a vulnerable spot for she softens it by putting Angelo not in Claudio's place but in her own:

> I would to heaven I had your potency,
> And you were Isabel! should it then be thus?
> No; I would tell what 'twere to be a judge,
> And what a prisoner.
>
> (II.ii.67-71)

In the great scene in which Angelo throws all restraint to the winds, this theme is touched on lightly but in such a way that it becomes the climax of the dramatic situation: "Plainly conceive, I love you." "My brother did love Juliet; and you tell me that he shall die for 't."

As a kind of whimsical byplay, Lucio's idle talk toys constantly with the same subject of which he is unable to feel the real import—about the pirate who effaced the commandment against stealing, about Angelo's severity being caused by his being "spawned by a sea-maid," about the Duke who would have been more inclined to condone these faults since he "Would mouth with a beggar, though she smelt brown bread and garlic." All this loose gossip is, in fact, the same melody in counterpoint.

But the *Leitmotiv* breaks forth in full vigor in the Duke's rhymed monologue:

> Shame to him whose cruel striking
> Kills for faults of his own liking!
> (III.ii.281-282)

The Duke, judging Angelo, sees the problem differently than Angelo did when he condemned Claudio. He does not restrict it to the deed but includes the guilty thought. In the first words of the monologue he unfolds its full significance—and turns it against himself as the highest and, therefore, most responsible, judge:

> He who the sword of heaven will bear
> Should be as holy as severe;
> Pattern in himself to know, ...
> (III.ii.275-277)

From now on the theme is given over to the Duke, who uses it ironically, to make it fall in the end with redoubled weight on the head of Angelo:

> . . . his life is parallel'd
> Even with the stroke and line of his great justice:
> He doth with holy abstinence subdue
> That in himself which he spurs on his power
> To qualify in others: where he meal'd with that
> Which he corrects, then were he tyrannous;
> But this being so, he's just.
> (IV.ii.82-88)

This irony becomes even more bitter when the Duke sits in judgment:

> . . . next, it imports no reason
> That with such vehemency he should pursue
> Faults proper to himself; if he had so offended,
> He would have weigh'd thy brother by himself,
> And not have cut him off.
>
> (V.i.108-112)

These words are pronounced before Angelo in whose ears, while they give him the assurance of his safety, they must sound like the knell of doom.

In the end, in the words of condemnation, all disguise is cast off:

> The very mercy of the law cries out
> Most audible, even from his tongue,
> 'An Angelo for Claudio, death for death!'
>
> (V.i.412-414)

Our play shows, at first glance, how in the judicial mind self-restraint for the sake of gaining the respect of others and self-respect break down when temptation takes the form of the suppressed sadistic wishes. The judge, by this resurrection of his primitive, unsublimated sensuality, is driven to repeating the act which he has censured, and thus changes place with the offender. But the scope of the problem grows under the creating hand of the poet and becomes much wider than that of the story. If these possibilities exist generally, if unconscious wishes and drives are not only in existence, but active in the mind of everyone, if they are kept from coming to life only by the special grace of destiny, then it follows that every man who dares to be a judge is a potential Angelo. It means, if we take it in its full and true sense and set aside as mere accidents the actual temptations and the outward shapes of our acts and our conscious thoughts, that no judge can disclaim his identity in guilt with the criminal before him. In the guise of a comedy *Measure for Measure* unfolds one of the tragic conflicts which disturb the peace of mind and the good conscience of mankind since the first foundations of social life have been laid. The identity of the man who judges and the man who is judged, the subject of Shakespeare's comedy, was used two thousand years earlier as the basis of a tragedy which became the everlasting symbol of human guilt.

The citizens of Thebes ask their king to end the dearth and famine which scourges their city; they want him to detect the hidden crime in their midst so that the angry gods can be conciliated by the punishment of the culprit. The king sets out on this search and finds, at the end of a circuitous route of investigation, that he himself is the criminal, the murderer of his father and his mother's husband. It is the fate of Oedipus to be unaware of his guilt and to become his own judge.

Oedipus Tyrannus is the prototype, and probably not the earliest one, of the man who judges himself. It had gone through more than one metamorphosis and appeared in different configurations till Shakespeare distilled it out of the old folklore tale that was handed to him by Cinthio and Whetstone. But its annals are not closed with *Measure for Measure*. Two hundred years later Heinrich von Kleist made a comedy of it which has many traits in common with Shakespeare's comedy, but which also comes near the tragedy by Sophocles. In *Der zerbrochene Krug* (The Broken Jug) the judge tries to misuse the innocence of a girl, by making her believe that her lover is in great danger from which he can protect him. Her lover comes accidentally at the critical moment, but the judge escapes before he is recognized. A jug has been broken in the tussle in the maiden's room, and her mother, believing that her daughter's lover did it, demands satisfaction and punishment. The judge before whom the quarrel is brought next morning would find it easy to condemn the young man, but just at this session a superintendent is present. Pressed by him, the judge has to enter, very much against his will, into the investigation of the merits of the case and, after many comic incidents, is discovered as the culprit. This play, taking a place between *Measure for Measure* and *Oedipus,* has with the first named the element in common that the wicked judge tries to rape a maid by means of a threat to the life of someone dear to her, and that the presence of a higher authority brings the hidden guilt to light and exposes the villain; with the second the fact that judge and criminal are the identical person and the most remarkable technique, the action consisting not in the progression of events, but in a step-by-step revelation of the past which brings about the dramatic development.

The analogy with *Der zerbrochene Krug* demonstrates clearly where the borderline between tragedy and comedy is drawn, that is, which elements in the formation of the plot make a comedy possible and which exclude it. In the tragedy the dreadful crimes are really performed, although unintentionally; in the comedies there is any amount of bad intentions, but nothing happens. Our mind seems to be built that way, ready to welcome it when mental acts are not taken too seriously and come and go airily without leaving any visible trace, whereas everything that has happened in the world of outward reality produces indestructible consequences and cannot be reversed or undone. This is, of course, mere semblance and sophistry, since mental acts, the offspring of the immortal drives and desires, inheriting partly at least the immortality of their progenitors, are as permanent and unchangeable as any part of reality; they can be supressed, or even totally repressed, but not destroyed or nullified. To strengthen our belief in this falsification and to make our mental acts appear as something negligible and superficial, looks like a humiliation of our pride; it may well be so, but at the same time it does us a good service by lightening the burden of our social responsibility. If thoughts, wishes, and intentions don't count, then our conscience has so much less right to make us suffer for them. This appears to be one of the most important, although never openly avowed, functions of comedy in general: the poet, by various enticements and inducements, makes us enter into the spirit of his work: we take part in his world which he constructed to suit this purpose. As long as we dwell in it, we are ready to mistake it for the one in which we live ordinarily and to accept it gladly when it is implied by the way things are shaping out finally, that thoughts without a practical consequence are just "airy nothings." Our thoughts and emotions move then in this better—or at least lighter—world as if they were at home in it: this produces the so-called illusion of the audience or readers. Thus the load that conscience—or to put it for once into psychoanalytic parlance, the Super-Ego—has laid on our shoulders, is made to press less heavily. We may sit for a while on the roadside and look around till we resume our weary pilgrimage.

Shakespeare, when he decided to write *Measure for Measure* as a comedy, although his mind was far removed from the humor and sprightliness of his earlier plays, respected this fundamental rule by sheer intuition. Whetstone, as we have seen, had already eliminated the unjust execution, but the other crime had to be relegated to the realm of mere intentions as well. The trick by which a legitimate spouse is substituted so that the rape becomes the consummation of marriage had been used by Shakespeare in *All's Well That Ends Well*.[1] It came in handy here, and for this purpose a lady who had been betrothed to Angelo and deserted by him was incorporated in the play. In this manner the original, sinister, and bloody story was turned inside out. Angelo's character was much involved in these alterations. As pointed out before, it would have been easy to go the whole length with him, to make him the funny, stupid dupe who gets tripped up at every step. The usual way to make him ridiculous would have been to bring him together with the disguised Duke in such a manner that the unrecognized master is slandered in his face by the deceived deceiver. Lucio, who is the shadow without the substance of Angelo's wickedness, is put in this situation instead. The meeting between the Duke and Angelo is not avoided out of regard for the probability that Angelo would see through the disguise, since Escalus actually speaks to him (III.ii. 226-274). Besides, no comedy worth its salt has ever respected this sort of improbability. What made such a comic meeting impossible is Angelo's character. Shakespeare eliminated all the dreadfulness of the crimes by having none of them committed actually, but he retained, he even deepened, thir appalling effect as far as Angelo's mind is concerned. He was unwilling to sacrifice the character problem to the comedy.

Angelo obtains his pardon in the end, this is a foregone conclusion. All that happens to him is to be found out and exposed; his pride is turned into humility. He had been tormented not only by the fear of detection, but also by the cruel pangs of his guilty conscience:

> . . . Would yet he had lived!
> Alack! when once our grace we have forgot,
> Nothing goes right: we would, and we would not.
> (IV.iv.35-37)

This wish, that Claudio might still live, is fulfilled. Indeed, the pangs of his conscience must have been greatly alleviated when he learned that he, with all his villainy and cunning, had done no wrong at all. Isabella with her clear and unerring intellect grasps here, as she always does, the true merit of the situation and presents it with her usual lucidity. Poor Mariana of the Moated Grange, evidently never a specially bright person, can say no more in his defense than that his badness promises well for his becoming a good husband. But when Isabella, out of her sisterly love for Mariana, consents to beg for the life of the man who tried in vain to defile her, she pleads his cause better than the best lawyer could do:

> For Angelo,
> His act did not o'ertake his bad intent,
> And must be buried but as an intent
> That perish'd by the way. Thoughts are no subjects,
> Intents but merely thoughts.
>
> (V.i.455-459)

So Angelo the mighty demon has been, in fact, a perfectly harmless creature. In his sin he saw himself as Lucifer and felt the pride of Lucifer, so that this relief of his guilt feeling is, at the same time, his deepest humiliation. This shame is for the proud man a worse punishment than "immediate sentence then, and sequent death" for which he begs as a grace. His sins turn out to be of the same low order as those of Lucio: idle words and bad intentions, and he is punished in exactly the same way as Lucio, by being constrained to marry a woman whom he can neither love nor esteem.

The contradiction between human justice and sinfulness is not restricted to the theme of the judge who judges himself. Its universal significance is expressed in the words of the Gospel: "Judge not that ye be not judged." It is especially closely bound up with the Oedipus-crime. Shakespeare by no means neglected or overlooked this most universal and most general of human problems. In *Measure for Measure* there is hardly a hint of it, but he had treated it some years before in *Hamlet* and—as Freud demonstrated (first in his *Traumdeutung*) transmuted the mythological form of antiquity into the modern psychological one. This new form which puts psychic conflicts in the place of fate and inhibition in the place of act, marks the transformation from the classic and medieval spirit to a new era. Only one man has penetrated even farther than Shakespeare into this darkest region of the mind, Dostoyevsky in his *Brothers Karamazov*. He showed a group of brothers each of whom killed the father in his own way—in fact, in intention, in phantasy or in overcompensation of unconscious wishes—and thus created the greatest novel of all time.

The central problem of the guilty judge, as Ivan expounds it to Alosha, is this: Can you find forgiveness in your heart for all crimes? Can you forgive wanton cruelty, the torturing and killing of innocent children? If you knew that their suffering is necessary to form a part in an universal harmony which could not come into existence without it, would you accept this harmony? And Alosha being still, in spite of his kindness, the "little Karamazov," to the delight of his tempter, answers with a vehement No. The Staretz Sossima's answer is different: We can forgive the worst sin, the most hideous crime, we can even ask the sinner to forgive us (as Sossima kneels before Dimitri), when we are aware that we ourselves are guilty of his crime and responsible for it. The identity between judge and criminal is reaffirmed in a new sense. For Dostoyevsky this new sense became the cornerstone of his mystical religiosity, yet it can be conceived in a purely human, untranscendental way, and then it coincides to a great extent with the disclosures, made many years later, by Freud. With him it rests on the experience that our entire personality comprehends not only what we want to know about ourselves, but our Unconscious as well. Since unconscious, repressed desires and wishes are essentially the same everywhere, we are all linked together by the bond of common guilt, and it matters little whether we call it by its Christian name of Original Sin or by the psychoanalytic term: Oedipus complex.

Dostoyevsky, being a poet, not a philosopher, abstained from working out systematically the consequences of his teachings for the social reality. He contents himself with pointing out in a general way that the Russian orthodox church takes no part in the judging of the delinquent but tries to help him out of his isolation into which he has put himself by his wrong-doing. "For it is impossible for the criminal to say: I alone am right and all the world is wrong." The trial of Dimitri, although the simple minds of the jurymen resist the wicked sophistry of the lawyer, shows that human intelligence, working in the service of law and order, is not sufficient to reveal the truth, and it ends with a miscarriage of justice. Dostoyevsky had his own experience of justice when he was sentenced to death and reprieved on the scaffold. He prostrated himself from then on in passivity before a higher will and tried to find the way to redemption by suffering. But self-abnegation and obedience to the mysterious decrees of a higher master were not a sufficient answer to his creative will and the *Brothers Karamazov* remained a fragment. Would the second part which Dostoyevsky planned have come nearer a solution? He died before he could write it and we will never know.

This is one of the few occasions on which the paths of the two men who knew more about the human mind than all the rest of us approached each other. They both look at the problem of universal guilt, shared by judge and criminal alike, but the Russian of the nineteenth century is swept away into mysticism, whereas the Elizabethan, although he approaches the abyss, never gets out of touch with the realities of life. He takes it for granted that human society has to go on and will continue even if it be found that justice is, of necessity, bound to be a failure. He never loses himself in the quest of man as he ought to be and is willing to accept man and man's life as they are. But he is not willing to be hoodwinked. When he looks at the world, he finds it, at this time of his life, to be rotten and full of evil and he paints it exactly as he sees it.

That *Measure for Measure* was conceived in a period of pessimism is not a mere conclusion from the chronological propinquity to *Lear* and *Othello;* it is attested by the play itself. The two characters that come nearest to Shakespeare's ideals and who, therefore, more than the others may be taken to be the representatives of the author's own attitude, are deeply imbued with this pessimistic outlook on life. The admonition of the Duke, disguised as a friar, to Claudio to resign himself to death, contains not a particle of religious argument, not a word about the submission to the will of God or the hope of eternal bliss. It is nothing less than an execration of life, of its insecurity, its illusions, its sufferings, its evils, which no Schopenhauer could surpass, and made still more impressive by the pure beauty, the slow falling cadences of its language. Escalus, a sincere admirer and well-wisher of the Duke, calls him "Rather rejoicing to see another merry, than merry at any thing which professed to make him rejoice." When Angelo's corruptness is revealed to the Duke, the latter is not astonished; indeed, he seems to have suspected it from the beginning.

Isabella's pessimism is hardly less deep. When the Duke tells her of the deserted Mariana, her natural reaction is: "What a merit were it in death to take this poor maid from the world! What corruption in this life that will let this man live!" (III.i.240-243) This contempt for life and everything it has to offer is, not less than her desire for perfect purity, the cause of her wish to spend her life behind the walls of a convent. Her disgust that her brother should cling to a life bought at the price of infamy appears less harsh, her forbidding severity is not quite so awe-inspiring, since she herself considers life as a thing that is hardly worth having. She is absolutely sincere when she says:

> O! were it but my life,
> I'd throw it down for your deliverance
> As frankly as a pin.
> (III.i.104-106)

The Duke and Isabella are, therefore, well matched in every respect: they are both good and virtuous and not much in love with life. A caricature of their attitude must not be missing in this bitter comedy. It is furnished by Barnardine who carries the contempt of life to the point where it becomes inhuman:

> A man that apprehends death no more dreadfully but as a drunken sleep; careless, reckless, and fearless of what's past, present, or to come.
> (IV.ii.145-147)

The duke calls him "unfit to live or die." In the end Barnardine is pardoned with the rest.

Shakespeare's pessimism not only speaks through the mouths of his hero and heroine, it pervades the whole play and imparts to it the pungent and bitter taste that aroused the displeasure of the critics. In showing up all sorts of depravity, he tears away the last shred of pretense from them and mocks their repulsive nakedness with exultant despair. It is all so ugly and distressing, but just for this reason he does not want to delude himself about the truth. Life is not good —then let us find out how bad it can be! Lust and cruelty, one is as horrible as the other, as long as one takes man seriously. Don't take him seriously and the horrible thing becomes a comedy—the bitterest comedy ever written.

One question remains. id Shakespeare really want to except his hero, the Duke, from all contamination of the wickedness around him? Of course, the part allotted to him as the defender of virtue and chastity makes it impossible to expose such frailties. But are there not slight innuendos? That Lucio says of him that "he had some feeling of the sport; he knew the service and that instructed him to mercy," means nothing, for Lucio's words are but a projection of his own salaciousness. It is somewhere more to the purpose that Friar Thomas suspects him of a love-intrigue, so that he has to protest:

> Believe not that the dribbling dart of love
> Can pierce a complete bosom.
>
> (I.iii.2-3)

In the monologue at the end of Act III he speaks, without further explanation, of "my vice." Maybe a distant inkling of the feeling that he would not be unable to commit the same crime as Angelo is at the bottom of the somewhat obscure words with which he proclaims Angelo's pardon: "I find an apt remission in myself."

The most instructive fact is the manner in which the Duke woos Isabella and the way in which she reacts. He proposes to her, taking her acceptance for granted. Yet there is not the slightest indication that she is in love with him, and she who in the most difficult situation has always "le mot juste" on her lips, finds not even one poor syllable for the acceptance of his offer. Would she not prefer to go back to her convent from which she was drawn, much against her inclination, by her brother's peril? Any constraint is out of the question, but it is not easy to decline an offer of marriage which comes from your lord and master, from the man who saved your brother's life. As Angelo's wedding parallels, on a higher level, the enforced marriage of Lucio, so commits the Duke, in a legitimate and honorable way, the crime which Angelo attempted in vain.

The moral is: they all are sinners. Even the highest and purest judge is not better than the villain whom he judges. But what of that? If this world is so full of horrors, if life is a thing without real value, what does it matter if a man tries to take away his brother's life? Even if he succeeds, he cannot succeed in robbing him of anything that is worth while. We are sinners all, but impotent sinners, deceivers deceived by our own passions. Condemning each other, we are "like an angry ape."

Not justice, only mercy, may bring some rays of light into the abysmal darkness while it "will breathe within your lips."

If this measure is applied, the pardon of Angelo, which seems such a flagrant injustice, is not irony but really and truly "Measure for Measure."

Notes

1. BARBARA HANNAH, *"All's Well That Ends Well,"* in *Studien zur analytische Psychologie C. G. Jungs,* Festschrift zum 80 (Zurich: Rasher Verlag, 1955), Vol. II, pp. 344-363.

2. FRITZ WITTELS, "Psycho-Analysis and Literature," in SANDOR LORAND (ed.), *Psycho-Analysis Today* (New York: Covici-Friede, 1933), pp. 342, 375.

3. OTTO RANK, *Das Inzest-Motiv in Dichtung und Sage* (1912) (Leipzig: Franz Deuticke, 1926), p. 394.

4. See also ROBERT FLIESS, *Erogeneity and Libido* (New York: International Universities Press, 1957), pp. 109-110; JOHN F. ADAMS, *"All's Well That Ends Well:* The Paradox of Procreation," *Shakespeare Quarterly, 12*:261-270, 1960.

1. This substitution-trick is as old as the hills—or at least as old as the fairy tale of Snow White.

Shakespeare's "Tempest": A Psychological Analysis

Shakespeare's last plays (especially *The Tempest*) have called forth a good many discussions from psychoanalytic critics, discussions that, for the most part, concentrate intensively upon the psychology of the plays' protagonists. Psychoanalytic treatments of *The Winter's Tale,* for example, tend to develop around the figure of Leontes, particularly in his relationship with his wife and in his attitude toward his daughter. As might be suspected, the specific question of the hero's sudden, "inexplicable" fit of jealousy in Act I has received a good deal of attention on both the ritualistic and realistic levels of analysis.[1] Psychoanalytic readings of *Pericles* also tend to explore the hero's character as it reveals itself through his relations with his wife and daughter. The consensus here seems to be that *Pericles* deals largely with the protagonist's attempt to integrate the various sides of his personality. Worth noting too is that Antiochus' incestuous attachment to his daughter has provoked some psychoanalytic discussion.[2] *Cymbeline* is the late play of Shakespeare's that has attracted the least attention from the psychoanalytic critics; often one comes upon it while reading criticism of *The Tempest* (the paper to follow is an example), and when one does, one finds that it is the husband-wife, father-daughter aspects of the play that are taken to be especially significant.[3] As for *The Tempest,* it completes the pattern. Prospero, particularly in his role as father, absorbs the interest of the psychoanalytic commentator, and discussions of the other characters in the drama invariably refer back, in one way or another, to him. More so than with *Pericles* and *The Winter's Tale,* psychoanalytic readings of *The Tempest* develop on the level of psychic realism, the level of myth and ritual. This can hardly come as a surprise, however, when one thinks on the obviously symbolic or mythical creatures that dot the play's "supernatural" landscape.[4]

In his analysis of *The Tempest,* an analysis that reflects the influence of Jung as well as Freud, K. M. Abenheimer maintains that we behold in this play "a dramatic representation of Prospero's inflated loneliness and paranoid isolation into which he had retired after his expulsion from Milan and of his attempt to overcome it and return to the social world." As Duke of Milan, Prospero expected to live in the "parentlike care and shelter of his brother." Even then, however, he displayed a tendency to isolate himself, to reduce human contacts as much as possible and to substitute intellectual pursuits in their place. Betrayed by his brother, and living upon his island, he still longs for the kind of security his brother offered. As a result of this longing, he introjects "the images of caring and protective parents" and plays their role. "Instead of being mothered he now mothers Miranda and he also identifies himself with the image of the omnipotent and omniscient father. Such identification with archetypal images leads inevitably to isolation, for no longer can such a person react to events as his own heart and feelings would demand; he has to hide his own personality and play the part of being nothing but a good and protective parent." The other creatures on the island, Ariel and Caliban, represent further aspects of Prospero's personality. The asexual, childlike Ariel comprises his spiritual side, his "anima," to use the Jungian term, and Prospero's possessive, domineering treatment of Ariel speaks for his need to make every loved figure comply with the "ideal of the kind and asexual parent." Caliban, by contrast, represents Prospero's animal, his physical being and physical needs, as well as his incestuous interest in his daughter. Because Prospero wants "the Madonnalike kind mother, or the pure immaterial spirit, but fears and hates the earth mother who appears to him as an evil witch," he fears and hates and abuses her son, Caliban. With the coming of the tempest, however, Prospero's transformation, which is the play's chief concern, begins. "He lays aside his magic isolating mantle and tells his daughter the story of his life." Next, he "loses Miranda to Ferdinand and his parental domination over her ends." Again, "he revenges himself on his enemies, giving vent for the first time to self-assertive feelings other than those needed to ensure his domination and aloof superiority," and acknowledging "the existence of forces outside his ego and ego domination." Too, he frees Ariel, thus repudiating on the symbolic level his dependent, isolating feelings toward the mother archetype. Yet Prospero's return to human life and intercourse never becomes, in Abenheimer's view, complete. Perhaps after such isolation a full embracing of the "common progeny of mankind" is simply too much to expect. At any rate, Prospero toward the end of the play is still somewhat aloof, somewhat cold, somewhat aristocratic. There is no hint that his contempt for Caliban has slackened. He is thinking primarily of his retirement, of his death. He is, in short, somewhat "depressed." Abenheimer's paper concludes with a brief discussion of *Cymbeline* and *The Winter's Tale* as they bear upon the significance of *The Tempest*.

M. F.

hat strikes one as most puzzling on reading *The Tempest* is that Shakespeare, at the height of his mastery as a playwright, suddenly seems to have violated all the basic rules of dramatic art. In a play, one ought to see what happens as action on the stage and the unfolding of the action ought to awake the spectator's sympathetic interest. He should be able to fear and rejoice with the persons on the stage and to share their emotions. In *The Tempest,* an unusually large part of the story is only recounted, not acted. How Prospero was deprived of his dukedom by his treacherous brother; how he and his daughter came to the island on which the play is set; and how he managed to live there for twelve years, we only hear narrated. And the same is true of the story of Ariel's enslavement by the witch Sycorax, and his liberation through Prospero, or the history of Sycorax' son Caliban, and his meeting with Prospero. When Shakespeare does present happenings on the stage, such as the shipwreck and the fate and reactions of the ship's company after the shipwreck, our sympathetic participation in their feelings is hindered by our knowledge that they are victims of magic deception. No sooner has our pity and anxiety for the ship on the storm-beaten sea been awakened than we meet Prospero telling his daughter that the tempest was caused by him and that he made sure that nobody came to harm in it. From then onward we constantly know that the mourning of the king for his son, or of the son for his father, are unnecessary, and that all the plotting of the courtiers against the king, or of Caliban

"Shakespeare's *Tempest*: A Psychological Analysis" by K. M. Abenheimer. Reprinted with permission from *Psychoanalytic Review,* XXXIII (1946), 399-415.

and the drunkards against Prospero, will come to nothing, because the omnipotence and omniscience of Prospero and Ariel will interfere in time. What is the dramatic meaning of this play in which the dramatic sympathy of the spectator is nipped in the bud since he partakes in all the action on a double level, that of the people who are the objects of Prospero's magic, and that of Prospero who controls all external events? Yet, do we really take part in all that happens in this double role? There is certainly one person in the play whose weight and importance overshadows every other figure, and in his fate we can sympathetically participate without being disturbed by knowledge from another level. This one person is Prospero himself. He is certainly not the God of Destiny where his own fate is concerned, and he is as much exposed to the transforming influence of the tempest as any other mortal person. Prospero's transformation may well be the dramatic core of *The Tempest*.

Prospero, when he was Duke of Milan, lived the life of a recluse and indulged his predilection for mystical studies. He turned away from the outside world to a world of invisible powers and magic.[1] The affairs of the world and the actual reign of his dukedom he left to his brother. He completely trusted his loyalty. This childlike trust was disappointed when his brother, together with the King of Naples, betrayed him. Deprived of all power and help, he was exiled and exposed to the play of the elements on the stormy sea in a small boat. Lear, in a similar situation, perished. Prospero, however, managed to survive this first tempest. Nevertheless, the manner in which he succeeded in withstanding catastrophe was not altogether satisfactory. He certainly saved his own and his daughter's life; he acquired full mastery over the outer circumstances of life and gained magical powers far beyond the mere necessities of life. Yet, at the same time, he became completely isolated, living on a small island ("isola") away from all human contact (save that of his child-daughter). The psychological cause of this isolation is clearly visible. Prospero, who as duke expected to live in the parentlike care and shelter of his brother, did not succeed in giving up his longing for such care completely when he was betrayed. He introjected the images of the caring and protecting parents and played their role himself. Instead of being mothered he now mothers Miranda, and he also identifies himself with the image of the omnipotent and omniscient father. Such identification with archetypal images leads inevitably to isolation, for no longer can such a person react to events as his own heart and feelings would demand; he has to hide his own personality and play the part of being nothing but a good and protective parent. There is a striking example of this in the second scene of the first act. Prospero has raised the tempest because he wanted to revenge himself on his enemies and because the stars told him that his own fortunes would decline unless he seized the chance offered to him. Yet when Miranda is upset by the sight of the ship struggling with the storm, Prospero does not tell her his true motives for causing the tempest but tries to quiet her with the remark:

> I have done nothing but in care of thee,
> Of thee, my dear one! thee, my daughter!
> (I.ii.16-17)

This is a sentimental pretence of having no interest of his own and acting only out of care of others, which conforms to the wishful fantasy of the loving parent. Prospero, the magician, patronizes others or rules over them and orders them about, but does not expose his own personality to the reactions and the influence of others, and thus is isolated. The breaking down of this isolation is the central dramatic theme of *The Tempest*.

The same dominating and patronizing relationship as with Miranda exists between Prospero and Ariel. Ariel is a figure not easily understood. Superficially, he seems to be a nature spirit like Puck in *A Midsummernight's Dream*, but this similarity is deceptive.[2] Ariel's rather human feelings, his longing for freedom, his compassion with Gonzalo's suffering, and his often expressed wish to please his master contradict this assumption. When Prospero asks him about the sea storm:

> My brave spirit!
> Who was so firm, so constant, that this coil
> Would not infect his reason?
> (I.ii.206-208)

he, too, presupposes human feelings and a human psychology in Ariel.

We come nearer the understanding of this figure if we remember that this male spirit has to appear in a female disguise (as a nymph, or as Ceres) several times. Thus he is reminiscent of many ambisexual girls and sweethearts in Shakespeare's other plays. (It is not by chance that Ariel is often played by actresses on the modern stage.) He is most akin to the male beloved in the *Sonnets*. Ariel, like him, has "A woman's face, a woman's gentle heart" (Sonnet 20), and Prospero constantly addresses him in various terms of endearment like a sweetheart. When Ariel asks "Do you love me, master?" Prospero answers "Dearly, my delicate Ariel," and later he confesses that he will miss his dainty Ariel when he is set free. Of Ariel, as of the male addressee in the *Sonnets,* it can be said:

> The other two, [i.e., elements] slight air and purging fire,
> Are both with thee, wherever I abide.
>
> (Sonnet 45)

He represents Prospero's spiritual love, cleansed and divorced from material and physical aspects. He is childlike and impish as befits the anima of so inflated and pompous a man as Prospero.

Like all anima figures, Ariel was originally connected with the mother image. He was Sycorax', the witch-mother's, servant. She imprisoned him in a cloven pine but Prospero broke this material entanglement and freed him as Eros freed Psyche. Yet Prospero's relation to this anima figure has become ambiguous. In the *Sonnets* the young nobleman is the idol to whom Shakespeare looks up and whom he admires and praises most self-effacingly and submissively. Prospero's attitude toward Ariel is quite different. He keeps him as his slave and is his absolute master. He masks this possessiveness, however, with sentimental justifications. When Ariel impatiently asks for release from his slavery, Prospero maintains that he has a rightful claim to it because Ariel owes him gratitude for his liberation from Sycorax' tortures. How spurious this claim is becomes apparent when Prospero adds the menace that he will torture Ariel in the same way as Sycorax did if he refuses to obey. He will force him back into the material prison of a cloven tree where he would share in the contempt with which Prospero treats everything material. In subjects whose love still follows the pattern of the child-parent relationship we can often observe how submissive dependence on a greatly overvalued love object changes into open possessiveness as soon as the lover passes from a self-effacing phase into an inflated, megalomaniac phase. They then try to force the beloved one into submission by open threats or by the expression of utter contempt, self-deceptively justifying their claims with the debts of gratitude which the other owes them. This is the nature of Prospero's relationship to Ariel. His love of Ariel is insincere and only a thin veil over frank possessiveness. This also explains why he constantly has to repeat his promise to set Ariel free after two days. It sounds as if neither Ariel nor Prospero himself had much faith in his given word.

The paradox of this situation in which Prospero wants to master the anima is that he himself becomes possessed by her. The anima who always is supposed to be obedient and is never allowed a will of her own is identical with the ego ideal. She is not an independent being outside Prospero's ego but the image of the immaterial spirituality, justness, and goodness to which he aspires himself. Prospero is so lonely and isolated because he tries to force the ego as well as every beloved figure to comply with the same ideal of the kind and asexual parent. Anima and ego are enslaved by the same emotional anima image of perfection. Any deviation from it arouses Prospero's contempt and utter rejection.

Ariel and Miranda are very much akin, particularly in the time before Miranda meets Ferdinand. She is an image of "woman" as Prospero desires women to be, all-pleasing, all-obedient, all-submissive. In consequence she is as unsubstantial and impersonal as Ariel himself. Prospero's relationship to her is also cleansed of physical aspects through the incest taboo. Thus she is as childlike, pure, and immaterial an anima as Ariel. Yet she, as a human being, has the potentiality of transformation into something completely human which is lacking in Ariel. This is probably the deeper reason for the duplication of the anima in the play.

Caliban's name is an anagram of the word "cannibal," but his character has very little to do with that of aborigines. He is Prospero's shadow, the personification of all those qualities which Prospero in his identification with the kind and omnipotent parental images and with the spiritual anima excludes from his ego. This is why Prospero despises him so utterly. He is only half-human like all the personifications of dissociated complexes. He is lecherous and his sexual desires are turned to Miranda (who, as the only woman on the island, cannot have escaped some subconscious incestuous interest on Prospero's part). He is earthy and dirty and stinking (anal), animalic and selfish, all those qualities which are opposed to the good, loving parent with whom Prospero is identified.

His arch-crime, however, is that he does not repay kindness with kindness and unfaltering goodness. This seems to Prospero to justify every form of abuse and utter contempt. People who, like Prospero, are isolated and unable to make contact often try to establish a semblance to a relationship by an exchange of kindness according to the principle of "do ut des." They try to bribe others into conforming to their ideal of kindness and spirituality and thus, of course, achieve the very opposite of their intention. Instead of creating relationships with independent beings, they try to impose the superego figures by which they themselves are enslaved. Every kindness on their part justifies in their eyes a claim not only for equal kindness in return, but for absolute perfection on the part of the other. Any imperfection in the other is a sign of ingratitude and a justification for unqualified rejection. No personal relationship exists in which one person as a whole reacts with differentiated feelings to another person as a whole and experiences his defections in the setting of the total personality. As a result, kindness seems to produce impersonal claims for gratitude, claims as abstract as legal claims are. If they remain dissatisfied, every form of punishment seems permissible. Thus the overdone longing for kindness leads to a world where only cold and impersonal obligations exist, sanctioned by the threat of disproportionate punishment. Shakespeare's writing is full of such demands for gratitude and of disproportionate threats or reactions in the case of frustration. Examples are to be found not only in Prospero's behavior toward Ariel and Caliban, but also in Lear's behavior toward Cordelia, or in Timon or in Coriolanus.

Caliban's useful qualities, which Prospero cannot help exploiting do not diminish Prospero's contempt. Caliban, like a true god of the material, chtonic world, has both physical strength and a deep knowledge of the earth and its helpful forces, fresh springs, brine pits, fertile places, and all the qualities of the island. Prospero contemptuously rejects everything material. He wants the Madonnalike, kind mother, or the pure, immaterial spirit, but fears and hates the earth mother who appears to him as an evil witch. Caliban, the son of the evil witch Sycorax, is her heir and representative in the play.

Here, however, we come again across a curious paradox in Prospero's character, a paradox quite common in men like Prospero. In spite of their attempt at identifying themselves with the good parents, they begin in their inflated state to display some qualities of the very opposite, that is, the witch. Prospero rules over his two slaves by menacing them with exactly the same type of cruel punishment which Sycorax used to employ. This cruelty clashes curiously with Prospero's role as the all-providing benevolent wizard. Yet, if one tries to protect oneself against disappointments by absolute superiority and control of everything, one just cannot help assimilating and using some of those hated, aggressive qualities which one wanted to ward off. If one starts to play the role of God one cannot avoid playing the role of the Devil as well. When Prospero became the magician by identifying himself with the omnipotent and omniscient father, he simultaneously took possession of the witch's island and made his home there. As little as Apuleius could Prospero remain unaffected by such an excursion into the country of the witch.

The wreck of Naples' ship exposes the ship's company to a plight similar to that which Prospero had to master twelve years ago. We take part in their anxiety and grief but share at the same time Prospero's knowledge that the catastrophe may turn out to be the beginning of psychic progress and moral development. Now we can understand this double knowledge not as a violation of the rules of dramatic art, but as a most daring attempt at representing dramatically the truth that the tempests which separate us from the shelter of family and social security have a double aspect, a horrifying and a beneficial one. They may lead into emotional crises but can result in progress and conversion.

The different reactions of the various members of the ship's company also provide Shakespeare with an opportunity to show some other aspects of the problem of separation from the sheltering parental world which the main hero, Prospero, by-passed and avoided. Thus

Shakespeare accompanies the main theme by a counterpoint of variations on the same theme.[3]

The King is another representative of the all-powerful father image. He, in his aloof superiority, had never realized the injustice and injury done to Prospero. Now under the influence of his grief over the loss of his son he opens his mind to the sufferings of others and repents his treachery toward Prospero.

Gonzalo, too, is a believer in the ideal of a world where everybody behaves like good parents and good children and he gives this vivid description of how the world according to his ideal should be:

> I' the commonwealth I would by contraries
> Execute all things; for no kind of traffic
> Would I admit; no name of magistrate;
> Letters should not be known; riches, poverty,
> And use of service, none; contract, succession,
> Bourn, bound of land, tilth, vineyard, none;
> No use of metal, corn, wine, or oil;
> No occupation, all men idle, all;
> And women too, but innocent and pure;
>
> . . .
>
> All things in common nature should produce
> Without sweat and endeavour: treason, felony,
> Sword, pike, knife, gun, or need of any engine,
> Would I not have; but nature should bring forth,
> Of its own kind, all foison, all abundance,
> To feed my innocent people.
>
> (II.i.147-155, 159-164)

No experience can shake Gonzalo's wishful optimism that there will always be good fathers whom one can serve, and nothing can shake his own kindness and helplessness. He does not react to disappointment with self-isolation and the attempt to force the world into his ideal pattern by masterly superiority, as Prospero does. Shakespeare knows that unfailing loyalty toward parental figures can be achieved only at the expense of the loyalty which one owes to oneself and to other values, and thus is found together with a shallowness of personality and a certain cynicism about all other values than parental and filial loyalty. Gonzalo shows these traits not so sharply as Polonius does and is not as free of them as Kent and Belarius, but all these figures are creations which arise from the same emotional source.

Ferdinand, too, gets over the presumed death of his father without Prospero's self-isolation. On the contrary, he is now able to turn his love to the other sex and finds a new love in Miranda. This can be the beginning of a healthier development than that of Prospero's if Ferdinand is able to concede to Miranda some independence and to maintain some measure of independence for himself as well. Certainly Ferdinand's sudden infatuation is based on a projection of the anima image onto Miranda, but all youthful love begins like that. Whether it will be the first step of a healthy development or of a development in the direction of Prospero's difficulties depends on Ferdinand's reactions to the realization that the real Miranda does not fully coincide with his image of the longed-for woman, a realization which has inevitably to come one day. If he then can stand the tension between her and himself without retreating into himself and without trying to crush Miranda's independence or forcing her to conform with his fantasies, or without self-effacement, he will have succeeded in avoiding Prospero's isolation. It is for this reason that Prospero's problems are preeminently those of the middle age (after 35 years); at Ferdinand's age they usually have not yet fully crystallized.

Antonio and Sebastian rebel against paternal authority. When they are freed from the restrictions which the stable social world imposes on them they plan regicide. Shakespeare abhors such a treacherous attack upon authority. Prospero circumvented it in his own case by identifying himself with the omnipotent father image after the world had refused to shelter him like a child. He jumped the gap between the small child and the outsized father, whilst in a healthy development the gap would disappear through the growing up of the child and the transformation and deflation of the father image. The first step in a transformation of this kind is the imaginary attack on the father and patricide; for symbolically death does not annihilate but transforms the father image. Maybe, the very lenient treatment which Sebastian and Antonio receive from Prospero is explained by Prospero's dim awareness that their crime has not been so alien to his own subconscious tendencies and that he should have dealt better with these tendencies in a less repressive way.

Trinculo and Stephano, too, enter into a homicidal conspiracy but on a different level from that of the two noblemen. They are simple men who do not live in a hierarchical world; they are blind to the different dignities of people and are interested only in animalic pleasures which are common to all human kind. Because of this common animalic nature they are identified with Caliban, the personification of Prospero's shadow, and are despised like him. Their conspiracy is the rebellion of the suppressed shadow, the attempt of the evil forces to seize power and to overwhelm and destroy those who want to be only good. The believer in the hierarchy of absolutely good parental figures, obedient servants or children, and despised shadows, stands in constant fear of rebellion; and he has all reason to do so, not because the power of evil is so much greater than the power of goodness, but because he is hostile not only to the purely evil but also to the mature man who has made peace with the animal in himself and gained confidence and strength by the assimilation of his shadow.

There is at least one figure among the ship's crew who seems to be definitely more mature than the noblemen and who nevertheless is treated by the noblemen without the respect that is his due. . . . The boatswain has weathered so many storms that the present tempest and his landing on a deserted island in no way unbalance him and he goes to sleep as soon as the ship is safe in harbor.

Yet Prospero, too, is affected by the tempest. His transformation begins when he realizes that he is being offered a chance that will not return, and that his fortunes will ever after droop if he misses it. And here he recognizes, for the first time since his isolation, the existence of forces outside his ego and ego domination.

He causes the storm and he revenges himself on his enemies, giving vent for the first time to self-assertive feelings other than those needed to ensure his domination and aloof superiority.

This is followed immediately by his first friendly contact with a human being when he lays aside his magic isolating mantle and tells his daughter the story of his life. He conceals no longer that he, too, is a suffering human being who made grave mistakes and, without Gonzalo's help, would have lost everything through the neglect and carelessness with which he treated the affairs of the world. The depth of his loneliness and how unaccustomed he is to open out and converse with others on the same level is shown by the three questions with which he interrupts his narrative. Again and again he has to make sure that Miranda is listening, for it is more than twelve years since he has asked anybody to be a sympathetic listener and he can scarcely believe that such personal contact is still possible.

Next he loses Miranda to Ferdinand and his parental domination over her ends. The awakening of Ferdinand's and Miranda's love is only indirectly Prospero's doing. He gave Miranda an opportunity to meet Ferdinand, but the love between them sprang up as a free reaction in them. Miranda, the anima, got the freedom to act on her own.

Then Prospero's two slaves get somewhat out of hand. Caliban sees a chance to rebel when he meets Trinculo and Stephano, a rebellion which, unfortunately, ends in nothing and leads to no revision of Prospero's attitude toward his shadow. Ariel, however, finally does get his freedom. As long as Prospero kept his anima in slavery, and deluded himself that he treated her lovingly, and demanded nothing but what Ariel owed him in gratitude, he had no chance of establishing healthier and freer relations with other people. Not only is love impossible as long as the anima is enslaved, one also deceives oneself about one's isolation by imagining that the domination over the anima is something in the nature of relationship. People often believe that they love most passionately when they really are only in a half-demanding, half-domineering dependence on another person. They cannot begin a real relationship until they break this dependence and give back the freedom to their love objects.

At the same time as he frees Ariel, Prospero promises that he will renounce his magic, break his staff, and drown his book, thus ending the inflation caused by the identification with the image of the omnipotent and omniscient father.

He does not carry the revenge against his enemies to its ultimate possibility by annihilating them, which would have left him again isolated, but he forgives them and returns to contact with others.

The result of Prospero's transformation is described in the Epilogue in these words:

Now my charms are all o'erthrown,
And what strength I have's mine own;
Which is most faint.

(319-321)

Too little attention has been paid to these verses with the result that the most unsound theories were propounded about the meaning of Ariel's emancipation and Prospero's drowning of his magic book. Prospero really describes here Shakespeare's last ideal and aim of personal development, an aim which found similar expression again and again in the history of the human mind. Goethe, at the end of the second part of *Faust,* lets the hero burst out into expressing nearly the same longing and desire:

Noch habe ich mich ins Freie nicht gekämpft.
Könnt ich Magie von meinem Pfad entfernen,
Die Zaubersprüche ganz und gar verlernen,
Stünd ich, Natur! vor dir ein Mann allein,
Da wär's der Mühe wert, ein Mensch zu sein.
(*Faust,* Part II, 5. Act, 6. Scene)

Modern psychotherapy repeatedly defined its aim in similar terms, when Freud and his followers wanted to help the patient to overcome archaic, magical forms of thinking and lead him to a realistic outlook about himself. Jung in his essay, "The Relation of the Ego to the Unconscious," describes developments very similar to that of Prospero, for example, how the archetype of the "magician" takes possession of the ego because the ego dreamt of a victory over and an enslavement of the "anima."[4] He, however, points out that a formulation of the aim of development which contains no mention of something in us which transcends the realm of the ego is not quite satisfactory. Goethe mentions this "something" by contrasting the ego with the transcendent "Natur." Shakespeare does not recognize anything transcendent and remains areligious to the end, and that is the point where our doubt begins whether Prospero actually managed to overcome his isolation and to return to society as a freer and more mature man than he was twelve years ago. Has the development which *The Tempest* describes only the character of a dreamlike vision which anticipates something that was not yet accessible for active use in Prospero's life (something which had not yet been "worked through") or does it indicate that Prospero can now live humbly, using nothing but his own strength, no longer relying on charms and magics?

I am inclined to answer this question according to the first alternative. When Prospero joins the ship's company at the end of the play he meets them in an entirely conventional manner and not as a man who has found a relationship to other human beings on a more personal level than mere conventions. He immediately is identified with the noblemen, no matter how personally unworthy they are, and he finds no kind word for those socially inferior. His approach to Gonzalo seems to me particularly stilted and out of focus. He calls him "holy," says, "Let me embrace thine age whose honour cannot/Be measured or confined," and he promises, "I will pay thy graces home, both in words and deed." All this is both too much and too little. Too little, because it is aloof and we expect some warmth of friendship and love, not only "paying home" and reverence for honorable old age. And too much because Gonzalo, this kind but shallow old man, is not holy. Prospero meets Gonzalo not as a man who matures and was made wise through his own sufferings, but as a young man who looks up to the old man because he represents the unfailing loyalty and helpfulness of the good father.

What Prospero's future relationship to Caliban will be remains unclear in the play, but certainly there are no signs that his contempt has slackened and that he is about to realize that Caliban is a part of himself and a necessary one.

He goes on with his witchcraft to the very end of the play, arranging calm seas and auspicious gales for the King's journey home (contrary to his previous promise to abjure this rough magic as soon as he had lifted the spell from the senses of the King and his company). On the other hand he envisages his own future as a retirement where every third thought shall be his grave. This sounds far too similar to his state of mind before his expulsion from Milan, the only difference being that he will indulge in depressed instead of magical fantasies in his retreat. It is here that Jung's criticism comes in. If one tries to eliminate the magician (and the anima) and to put nothing else in their place, one will remain suspended between three dangers: (1) of beginning to do magic again, (2) of overvaluing other people and expecting them to have magical powers and to play the parents role, or (3) of falling into an abyss of depression. All three dangers are visible in the last act of the play.

Last but not least, Prospero's attitude toward women shows no change. The only woman who appears in the play (apart from The Masque) is Miranda. She is the image of the all-pleasing child as Prospero may wish her to be. As such the aspects of the earthy mother which Prospero abhors are absent in her also. She is, like Athene, the product of her father's wishful thought; she grew up without the influence of a mother and does not remember her mother at all (whilst remembering servant women in Milan). The mother aspect of woman is under a peculiar tabu in *The Tempest*. The only mother of whom we hear in any detail is Sycorax, the evil witch-mother of Caliban. Ferdinand never mentions his mother, nor do the men of the King's ship's company mention his wife or his mother. Kindness is expected from men or given by men such as Prospero, his brother, and Gonzalo. A mental outlook which is quite intolerant to the realistic woman, which fears and avoids women as horrible witches unless they are Mirandas, is, of course, still archaic and magical. As long as Prospero keeps to it, his statement that he has overthrown his charms remains incorrect and an anticipation of an aim which he actually has not yet reached.

We read *The Tempest* as a dramatic representation of Prospero's inflated loneliness and paranoid isolation into which he had retired after his expulsion from Milan and of his attempt to overcome it and to return to the social world. It remains to be discussed whether the other plays of the same period, *Cymbeline* and *The Winter's Tale* tally with this interpretation. It seems to me that the motive force for writing these two plays was already the same as that for *The Tempest*, but it was not yet clear enough to find more than a dim expression.

The Winter's Tale shows how the King of Sicily through a sudden fit of jealousy isolates himself from wife, children, and friends, and how after sixteen years this isolation is miraculously undone. This action takes up four-fifths of the play, but the love intermezzo between Perdita and Florizel surpasses the rest of the play so much in charm and liveliness that the first three acts read like a mere exposition of the idyll in Bohemia. The King's jealousy remains psychologically incomprehensible; and his liberation from his isolation is the result of mere outer circumstances and miraculous events so that it becomes nearly impossible to take a sympathetic interest in him and his fate. Nevertheless, he is intended to be the hero of the play. This is confirmed by a comparison between the play and its source. The play is a dramatization of Greene's novel, *Pandosto or The Triumph of Time*. Pandosto, the jealous king of the novel, is the King of Bohemia, and his friend, whom he suspects unjustly, is the King of Sicily. Shakespeare reverses their parts and lets the jealous King reign and reside in Sicily. It is easier for an English audience to identify themselves with a king of an island and to take a sympathetic interest in his fate than to look upon the king of a remote continental country as the hero of the play. Pandosto commits suicide after the return of his daughter, in desperation over his previous mistakes which caused so much harm. Shakespeare changes this because he is concerned with the problem of the salvation from paranoid self-isolation. He did not want to write another "Othello" or "Lear" where jealousy or paranoid estrangement led to the death of the hero. He, therefore, also removes one of the motives of Pandosto's death. Pandosto's wife dies in grief over her husband's unjust jealousy whereas Hermione remains alive and joins her husband after Perdita's return. The only permanent victim of Leontes' jealousy in his own family is his young son who could not survive the separation from his mother. It seems rather symbolic that the mother-fixed youth has to disappear for good, for this is the problem in all the three late comedies: how the mother-fixation can effectively be conquered without paranoid sham solutions.

Perdita, like Miranda, grows up without a mother. She has not even a foster-mother, and the shepherd who brings her up is a widower. In Greene's novel he was married to Mopsa, who took the mother's place in Perdita's life. Shakespeare transforms Mopsa into a mere playmate of Perdita's.

In *Cymbeline* the interest in the hero of the play is completely swamped by the side actions of Posthumus' test of Imogen's fidelity and of Belarius' and his foster-sons' life in the woods. Nobody who reads the play without knowing its title would regard Cymbeline, who appears only five times on the stage in a completely passive role, as the hero. He obtained this position because his fate mirrors the problem with which Shakespeare was occupied at that time, for Cymbeline, by his unjustified banishment of Belarius and his undue trust in his second wife, had lost his children and true friends. . . . The same basic motive of isolation through paranoid folly is repeated in Posthumus' loss of his wife through the foolish test of her fidelity and in Belarius' retreat into the woods. There Belarius plays the part of the faithful father to the King's sons after the King had betrayed his parental obligations towards him; thus he introjects the father image which he could not find outside. He anticipates Prospero more than either Cymbeline or Leontes does. The Queen and her son, Cloten, are the forerunners of Sycorax and Caliban. Imogen is related both to Miranda and Ariel. Significant is her description of the "Sooth" as "tender air," or "mollis aer=mulier," which, in addition to her ambisexual part, connects her with Ariel whose name is also chosen for its aural connection with "air" and not for its possible Hebrew meaning of "Lion of God." Again, hatred of women is rampant in *Cymbeline*. None of the four youthful heroes and heroines of the play is brought up by his or her mother. Imogen, a fantastic paragon of goodness, contradicts as little as Miranda the rejection of women, and only confirms that women who are not born out of the *wishes* and *thoughts* of man are unbearable.

The comparison of these three plays gives us an opportunity to observe the unfolding and clarification of a set of ideas in Shakespeare's mind. In the two plays which precede *The Tempest* the return from the isolation marks but the end of an action in which the circumstances that cause the isolation, or events that have no direct connection with the hero, take up most of the action. Only in *The Tempest* does Shakespeare find a most artful way of making the hero's transformation from an isolated magician to a humble human being within the social world the center of the play. Only in *The Tempest* does he gain considerable insight into the psychological causes both of the hero's isolation and of his liberation. In the previous plays he only states the problem, and does not see through it with psychological understanding. For in spite of the superficial impression that *The Tempest* is more full of magic, spirits, and fairy-tale motives than the other plays, it surpasses them incomparably in psychological realism and insight.

This insight was, of course, not of the kind which modern psychology has; it resulted not from scientific reflection, but from Shakespeare's inner necessity of struggling with these problems. The depths of his insight is unique and commands our admiration, in spite of our criticism that Prospero only saw but did not reach the final aim of self-realization.

It is equally unique how this insight finds immediate expression in the dramatic events of a play which does not strike us either as strange or mystical nor as a mere allegory of ideas which could be equally well expressed in an abstract rational form. Shakespeare's best plays are truly symbolic in Jung's sense, that is, they are the best possible expression of some insight for which no more rational formulation had yet been found. Shakespeare was the creator of a mythology of modern man.

Notes

1. See L. A. G. STRONG, "Shakespeare and the Psychologists," in JOHN GARRETT (ed.), *Talking of Shakespeare* (London: Hodder and Stoughton, 1954), pp. 202-203; J. I. M. STEWART, *Character and Motive in Shakespeare* (London: Longmans, Green, 1949), pp. 20-37; W. H. AUDEN, "The Alienated City: Reflections on *Othello*," *Encounter*, August, 1961, pp. 3-14.

2. OTTO RANK, *Das Inzest-Motiv in Dichtung und Sage* (1912) (Leipzig: Franz Deuticke, 1926), p. 350; A. BRONSON FELDMAN, "Imaginary Incest," *American Imago*, *12*:117-155, 1955; W. I. D. SCOTT, *Shakespeare's Melancholiacs* (London: Mills and Boon, 1962), pp. 131-144.

3. HANNS SACHS, "The Unconscious in Shakespeare's *Tempest*," in *The Creative Unconscious* (Cambridge, Massachusetts: Sci-Art Publishers, 1951), pp. 289-323.

4. See SACHS, *op. cit.;* also HARRY SLOCHOWER, "Hamlet: The Myth of Modern Sensibility," *American Imago*, 7:197-228, 1950; THEODORE REIK, *Fragment of a Great Confession* (New York: Farrar, Straus, and Company, 1949), p. 336; OTHAR MANNONI, *Prospero and Caliban,* trans. Pamela Powesland (New York: Frederick A. Praeger, 1956), pp. 97-109.

1. He, therefore, is not an introvert who turned to himself and accepted himself. Extroversion and introversion are a pair of opposites not of the same logical nature as "a" and "non a," where everything which is not "a" must of necessity be "non a" and vice versa. If one is not extrovert one need not necessarily be introvert. A man may be turned away from the outside world and from himself as well, and his whole interest may be taken up by an imaginary world and by introjected objects, but not by his own self, which may remain rejected and unknown to him. Such a man is neither extrovert nor introvert.

2. *The Tempest* has far less connection with *A Midsummer Night's Dream* than is often assumed. *A Midsummer Night's Dream* is the vision of a state outside time (Midsummernight) and outside social and moral bounds. It is the vision of an ecstatic state of liberty in a world where action has no irreversible consequences and where everything is mere play; the world of nature spirits as opposed to the human world of tragical consequences and moral demands. *The Tempest,* on the other hand, is the symbol of the fateful storms which cause the deepest moral crises, such as being driven out of the shelter of the family and social tradition or the crisis which brings Prospero back into social contact. Therefore, *The Tempest* is far more the epilogue to the great tragedies than a play on the free level outside human tragical entanglements.

3. The linking together of various solutions of the same problem is often found in dreams. It is probable that the accompaniment of the main theme in *The Tempest* by these variations is the result of Shakespeare's autonomous creative fantasy and not of conscious deliberations of the author.

4. C. G. JUNG, *Two Essays on Analytical Psychology* (London: Bollingen Foundation, 1928).

Caliban's Dream

We have seen in the section on *Romeo and Juliet* what Norman N. Holland can do with the inconspicuous little dreams of Shakespeare's characters, and we now have another opportunity to sample his work. Three things must be mentioned, however, before we begin. First, whereas the preceding essay on *The Tempest* by Abenheimer is indebted to Jungian concepts and techniques, "Caliban's Dream" derives entirely from the Freudian school of psychoanalytic psychology, and especially from its tendency to stress that the development of the child proceeds in "stages" (oral, anal, genital) and that the psyche of the chronologically adult human being can remain unconsciously arrested or fixated at one of these earlier stages. Second, whereas Abenheimer is prone to emphasize the archetypal or mythic elements that stand behind character and event, Holland is committed to what we have called realistic analysis, and indeed, grounds his arguments not only in realistic psychological data but in realistic historical data as well. Third, just as Holland used Romeo's dream to light up the dramatic significance of the whole play *Romeo and Juliet,* so does he use Caliban's dream to illuminate the underlying dramatic preoccupations of *The Tempest.* For Caliban's dream leads us, ultimately, to a consideration of the problem of freedom versus authority, as it relates to Prospero's role on the island, to the marriage of Miranda and Ferdinand, to the drunken antics of Stephano and Trinculo, and to the Renaissance ideal of education or "nurture" that enters importantly, though implicitly, into the action.

M. F.

Caliban. Art thou afeard?
Stephano. No, monster, not I.
Cal. Be not afeard: the isle is full of noises,
    Sounds and sweet airs, that give delight and hurt not.
    Sometimes a thousand twangling instruments
    Will hum about mine ears; and sometimes voices
    That, if I then had wak'd after long sleep,
    Will make me sleep again; and then, in dreaming,
    The clouds methought would open and show riches
    Ready to drop upon me, that when I wak'd,
    I cried to dream again.
  Ste. This will prove a brave kingdom to me, where I
    shall have my music for nothing.
Cal. When Prospero is destroy'd.
                      (*The Tempest,* III.ii.142-155)

reud found in his study of *Gradiva* that "invented dreams can be interpreted in the same way as real ones,"[1] naturally enough, I suppose, for invented dreams represent a kind of midpoint between dreaming itself and artistic invention in general. The usual way to interpret a dream is by means of the dreamer's free associations, but Caliban, alas, gives us none— and, after all, few dreams dreamed in literature are reported from a couch. For a fictional dreamer, Freud suggests "we shall have to content ourselves with referring to his impressions, and we may very tentatively put our associations in place of his."[2] Robert Fliess notes that an analyst can contribute, independently of the dreamer's associations, two elements to the interpretation of a dream: (1) the interpretation of symbolism, and (2) associations known to the analyst which the dreamer—for whatever reason—may not supply.[3]

If we look simply at the manifest content of this recurring dream in the manner suggested by Erikson[4] it reveals an unusual style. Verbally, the report uses primitive words and sentences like a child's and sensorily, the dream is a simple visual one. Spatially, the dream moves along one line, up and down. Temporally, as Robert Graves has noted about this dream, "The illogical sequence of tenses creates a perfect suspension of time."[5] The only somatic phenomena the dream touches on are vision and sleeping and dreaming themselves. There are no interpersonal relations, only relations to an environment, and simple pleasure is the only affect. Caliban's is a very limited dream, and we can admire Shakespeare's fine intuition in giving so primitive a dream to so primitive a dreamer.

We may admire his intuition even more, though, for making this primitive dream a handsome instance of the most primitive of dream mechanisms—the dream screen, represented here by the clouds.[6] The dream, in fact, scarcely progresses beyond its screen; the clouds "would open," would "show riches/Ready to drop." But the cloud does not open and the riches do not directly appear—they are only expected. The timelessness of his verbs suggests Caliban's longing to merge ("sleep again," "dream again") into this benevolent environment of vaguely human "voices" and "noises," "sweet airs." It is not too difficult to see in the clouds a breast symbol and in the "riches" the longed-for, nurturing milk. And when the dream ends, Caliban's response is to cry for the loss of his dream, as though to lose the dream were to lose the breast. "Though the wishes of life become progressively more complex and subtle, this ['the ever-recurring wish for a primary breast experience'] remains as the deepest substrate occasionally to be revealed in regressive experiences during the course of analysis or other intense psychological vicissitudes."[7]

There may be, in Caliban's phrasing, "The clouds methought would open," the faintest sign of a differentiation of self from object that matches the significance of the clouds as dream screen and breast. That is, as soon as Caliban says, "The clouds," he immediately adds, "me-thought," as though to assert the continued existence of his separate self. Contrast his actual phrasing in this respect with, say, "I thought the clouds would open. . . ." Similarly, the accusative *me* faintly suggests a continued dependency: "The clouds thought me." But perhaps 'twere to consider too curiously to consider so.

Fliess says we may supply the interpretation of symbolism to a dream when free associations are absent. If we do, we find in this dream a well-nigh universal symbolism—riches standing for feces. If so, then the clouds about to open and drop them would be the buttocks, and lest this equivalence of breast and buttocks seem too far-fetched, it might be well to remember Caliban's mother was

> The foul witch Sycorax, who with age and envy
> Was grown into a hoop.
>
> (I.ii.258-259)

Even so, despite this convenient, if uncomfortable, confirmation, the reading seems forced.

Riches may have a different meaning for Caliban, or at least in *The Tempest*. If we follow the word through the play, we find it associated primarily with gifts: the "rich garments" given to Prospero on his exile from Milan (I.ii.164); Prospero's "rich gift" of his daughter Miranda to Ferdinand (IV.i.8); the gifts of the goddesses to the young couple (IV.i.60,106).

Another meaning the play associates with *rich* is change, as in the description of Ferdinand's supposedly dead father's body:

> Nothing of him that doth fade
> But doth suffer a sea-change
> Into something rich and strange.
>
> (I.ii.399-401)

Similar associations would be with the old courtier Gonzalo's fantasy of an ideal state in a peaceful unchanging golden age; there, "riches, poverty,/And use of service, none." Conversely, Ferdinand's being forced basely to carry logs is transformed by Miranda's presence so that "most poor matters point to rich ends."

Clouds, too, seem to be associated in the comedy as a whole with transformations, as in the description of Venus, who is to be kept from the masque celebrating the young lovers' betrothal:

> I met her Deity
> Cutting the clouds towards Paphos and her son
> Dove-drawn with her. Here thought they to have done
> Some wanton charm upon this man and maid.
>
> (IV.i.92-95)

But they are prevented from enticing them to pay the bed-right before marriage. Again, Prospero's speech at the end of the wedding-masque (often taken to be Shakespeare's own farewell to the stage) associates clouds with transformation:

> Our revels now are ended. These our actors,
> As I foretold you, were all spirits and
> Are melted into air, into thin air;
> And, like the baseless fabric of this vision,
> The cloud-capp'd towers, the gorgeous palaces,
> The solemn temples, the great globe itself,
> Yea, all which it inherit, shall dissolve
> And, like this insubstantial pageant faded,
> Leave not a rack [a wisp of cloud] behind.
> We are such stuff
> As dreams are made on, and our little life
> Is rounded with a sleep.
>
> (IV.i.148-158)

The play as a whole, then, associates images of clouds and riches with (1) a gift which (2) transforms. We recognize more specific versions of familiar anal themes: the gift of feces, this first sense of something precious later to be transformed to true riches or airy nothings.

Yet none of these speeches does Caliban speak or even overhear—they can hardly be considered part of his associations to the dream. There is, however, one speech about clouds that he does overhear and which seems almost a version of his own recurring dream, and that speech is followed by events which act it out. About a half-hour before recounting the dream, Caliban had been carrying firewood for Prospero and grumbling at an environment that is not only not the benevolent one he dreams of; controlled by Prospero's magic, it bites him, pricks him, stings him, and hisses at him. At this point, Trinculo appears, a jester shipwrecked with the rest of Prospero's visitors. Fearing Trinculo is one of Prospero's spirits, Caliban cowers under his gaberdine, and there he hears Trinculo soliloquize a version of his own recurring dream: "Yond same black cloud, yond huge one, looks like a foul bombard [a big leather liquor bottle] that would shed his liquor. . . . Yond same cloud cannot choose but fall by pailfuls" (II.ii.22-25).

Then, complaining of Caliban's fishy smell, Trinculo clambers in under the monster's buttocks. Now comes Stephano, the cook from the shipwreck, who has salvaged a literal leather bottle, not a metaphorical one. Caliban mutters terrifiedly at these spirits, and Stephano soothes him by pouring liquor down his throat. When Trinculo exclaims in recognition, Stephano pours drink into his mouth which seems the monster's "other mouth." "His forward voice now is to speak well of his friend; his backward voice is to utter foul speeches and to detract." And then Stephano discovers Trinculo: "How cam'st thou to be the siege [i.e., shit] of this moon-calf? Can he vent Trinculos?"

In effect, shortly before Caliban tells his new-found masters his recurring dream, they have recited and acted out for him a "black," "foul," smelly, and backward—in short, anal—version of that dream. And Caliban does indeed take the two clowns as versions of his dream:

> That's a brave god, and bears celestial liquor:
> I will kneel to him.
>
> (II.ii.120-121)

"I'll swear, upon that bottle, to be thy true subject; for the liquor is not earthly." "I will kiss thy foot; I prithee, be my god." "I'll kiss thy foot; I'll swear myself thy subject."

He sees these creatures from the clouds as bringing him transformation from what Prospero calls his slave: "Thou earth." "Filth as thou art." "This thing of darkness." Instead, adopting new masters, he thinks, will give him freedom.

No more dams I'll make for fish;
  Nor fetch in firing
  At requiring;
Nor scrape trencher, nor wash dish;
  'Ban, 'Ban, Ca Caliban
  Has a new master; get a new man.
Freedom, hey-day! hey-day, freedom! freedom!
  hey-day, freedom!

                                        (II.ii.184-191)

He gleefully capers, unconsciously confirming what Erikson and others have suggested are the central issues of anality: control and autonomy. It is, I suppose, one of the ironies of the play that Caliban would not so eagerly take the clowns as agents of his transformation from filth to a free man if he were as aware as we are that they represent more the anal level of his dream than the oral. They lead him ultimately into "th' filthy mantled pool" where "the foul lake/O'erstunk their feet." Poor Trinculo complains, "I do smell all horse-piss."

Caliban's identification of Stephano, however, shows an even more specific correspondence to his dream and one at a still higher level than either oral or anal.

Cal. Hast thou not dropped from heaven?
Ste. Out o' th' moon, I do asure thee: I was the Man
      i' th' Moon when time was [i.e., once upon a time].
Cal. I have seen thee in her, and I do adore thee: my
      mistress [Miranda] showed me thee, and thy dog and thy
      bush.

                                        (II.ii.140-144)

That which, in the dream, was about to drop from the heavens, now seems to have a very specific meaning.

Stephano had described Caliban as a moon-calf and, much later in the play, Prospero tells of his parentage:

              This misshapen knave,
His mother was a witch; and one so strong
That could control the moon.

                  (V.i.267-269)

Like all witches in that day and age, Sycorax had intercourse with the devil, so that Prospero can curse Caliban,

> Thou poisonous slave, got by the devil himself
> Upon thy wicked dam, come forth!
> (I.ii.319-320)

Caliban himself can speak of Prospero:

> . . . his art is of such power,
> It would control my dam's god, Setebos.
> (I.ii.372-373)

And, again, late in the play, he associates Setebos with Prospero, when he comes upon him in his Milanese robes and exclaims,

> O Setebos! these be brave spirits indeed.
> How fine my master is!
> (V.i.261-262)

In other words, what Caliban hears and knows allows us to guess at long chains of associations for him: clouds, heavens, moon, and mother; that which drops from the heavens; the man in the moon ("I have seen thee in her"; "My mistress showed me thee"); Setebos as his father but also a god and devil (pagan gods being Christian devils).

The ultimate meaning, then, of his recurring dream that riches are about to drop from the clouds is a wish for mother to give him a father with godlike powers who will transform him. And Caliban seems in reality to be about to gratify this wish by his eagerly greeting Stephano as his king and god.

It is questionable, I suppose, to supply associations this way, because, first, the dream is a recurring dream, and, second, Caliban gives us no associations to the dream—rather, he tells the dream as itself the association to a richly charged psychological event. At the moment he tells the dream, Caliban is planning to kill a father, Prospero, who is not only Miranda's father, but also king, magus, stage manager, master of slaves and spirits, and English teacher—all positions of godlike authority. Further, it was Prospero who disrupted Caliban's earlier life —he had been alone on the island that represented his mother.

The planning of the murder involves a number of suggestive details. Caliban, we have seen, accepted Stephano as his god and vowed to serve him. The next scene we see him, there has been a good deal more drinking, and Caliban feels free to broach his plan to his new master— they will steal upon Prospero sleeping and brain him, leaving Stephano king of the island with Miranda for his bed.

During this planning, Ariel, invisible, keeps saying, "Thou liest," and Stephano, taking the voice to be Trinculo's, beats him for being disrespectful to the king's new "subject," Caliban. The plan made, the three conspirators sing a song, which Ariel interrupts by playing the tune. Thus, at the moment of planning the archetypal oedipal crime (killing the father and taking his woman), the invisible Ariel, Prospero's agent, threatens the father's punishment. It is he who provokes Caliban's question, "Art thou afeard," and his reassurances: "Be not afeard" and the recital of the dream.

Later Ariel tells us that at this moment,

> they were red-hot with drinking;
> So full of valour that they smote the air
> For breathing in their faces; beat the ground
> For kissing of their feet.
>
> (IV.i.171-174)

The conspirators are attacking not only a father, but their very environment. Caliban's recital of his dream then serves as a reassuring reversal of his own massive hostility—there will be no punishment; the environment, sounds and clouds, is benevolent. At the moment he is about to murder a sleeping father he recalls a dream in which the rich prize of a benevolent father will drop upon a sleeping Caliban, transforming him and freeing him.

Caliban's recurring dream, then, serves him as a wish-fulfilling reversal of his own long, deep-seated hostility to Prospero. His wish is for a good father who would make him free, and thus his dream leads us back to a major theme in *The Tempest:* freedom and servitude. Ariel, who faithfully serves Prospero, is set free, and Prospero himself escapes the island. Those who rebel, however, Ferdinand against Prospero, Sebastian and Antonio against their king, are paralyzed, rendered helpless, and led through educative ordeals. The play as a whole acts out a traditional Renaissance idea: true freedom is submission to the authority of God and his agents. Caliban parodies the theme: submission to the rule of Stephano, "dropped from heaven," gives him the power to get his peer Trinculo beaten and the father-figure Prospero murdered.

Caliban in his own way, then, acts out a basic motif for Shakespeare himself, as does this whole play (which is often thought of as Shakespeare's own freeing himself—retiring from the stage). "So often his plays contrast the private man and the public one . . . he seems to enjoy seeing two sharply different characters in a similar situation, often with one merging into a larger matrix or order, the other thrusting loose from it: Hal and Hotspur, Laertes and Hamlet, Macbeth and Banquo, Edmund and Edgar, and so on."[8] "Shakespeare's application for a coat of arms and his purchase of New Place . . . show how in life he placed his aggressive, phallic drives toward business success at the service of oral wishes to be accepted into a larger, nurturing social order."[9] Over and over again in Shakespeare's works, we see a sonlike man finding through submission to a father figure the strength to fight outsiders, as here Caliban thinks he will gain from benevolent, liquor-giving "King Stephano" the strength to fight the hostile father Prospero.

But to see Prospero as hostile is to see him from Caliban's point of view. Prospero himself has submitted to higher forces—God, providence, destiny—and it is this submission and identification that give him his magic powers. He can call down spirits and goddesses from the heavens to act a wedding masque, blessing his daughter's betrothal: "Sweet aspersion shall the heavens let fall." Similarly, old Gonzalo at the end of the play can look at the young lovers and say,

> Look down, you gods,
> And on this couple drop a blessed crown.
> (V.i.201-202)

By contrast, Caliban can only wish—dream—for riches to drop on himself—or curses on others:

> As wicked dew as e'er my mother brush'd
> With raven's feather from unwholesome fen
> Drop on you both!
> (I.ii.321-323)

In short, Caliban's dream parodies Prospero's great wedding-masque: both invoke blessings from the heavens.

Similarly, Caliban ends his recital of his dream by wishing to sleep again. "When I waked,/I cried to dream again" (III.ii.151-152). By contrast, Prospero ends his masque by saying:

> ... We are such stuff
> As dreams are made on, and our little life
> Is rounded with a sleep.
>   (IV.i.156-158)

The brute longs for pleasure; the old man can contemplate not only pleasure but all of life as a passing fantasy.

In recognizing that Prospero's masque is the mature and superlative version of Caliban's wishful dream, we are finding from the special point of view of dream analysis what many critics have said about this play. "The main opposition is between the worlds of Prospero's Art, and Caliban's Nature. Caliban is the core of the play . . . he is the natural man against whom the cultivated man is measured. But we are not offered a comparison between a primitive innocence in nature and a sophisticated decadence. . . . Caliban represents . . . nature without benefit of nurture; Nature, opposed to an Art which is man's power over the created world and over himself."[10] Now, however, we can see this contrast from a psychological point of view.

Prospero is the mature man, willing to give up his daughter to her young lover, willing, too, to give up his kingly power and retire a private citizen to Milan "where/Every third thought shall be my grave" (V.i.310-311). If Prospero speaks for Shakespeare, he speaks for a man writing of himself at the last of the psychosocial stages, accepting the fact his life is lived, giving up to the next generation the power and the woman he has achieved.

Even so, opposed to the mature Prospero, Shakespeare has left a spokesman for his childhood: the ugly, brutish Caliban eager to kill the father and rape his woman. Prospero's masque is a rich, artistic ceremony in which he passes his power of procreation on to the next generation.The dark underside of that ceremony is Caliban's dream, the child's unruly, sexual hunger to be fed by another. Yet, *The Tempest* brings even the brute child to temper his cravings—to seek riches from the clouds in another sense. As Caliban says in his last words: "I'll be wise hereafter/And seek for grace" (V.i.294-295).

To sum up, if we analyze Caliban's dream as hard as we can, we find it expresses three levels of wish. At the oral level he longs for nurture from a breast. At an anal level he seeks transformation from the earthly, smelly filth he is to an autonomous individual. At the oedipal level he wishes his mother would give him a father, identification with whom would transform him from a slave. He tells his dream as a way of protecting against punishment for his own hostile wishes toward a father.

More generally, as Freud suggested, we can interpret invented dreams in a literary work like real ones, and, when we do, even the more recondite concepts of psychoanalysis (such as the dream screen) enrich the unity of the whole work of art. The play's moral contrast of Art and Nature acts out in an intellectual way the contrast between the integrity of age and the dependency of childhood, as in all art—and life, too—mature significances fulfill and inherit the conflicts of infancy.

Notes

1. S. FREUD, *The Interpretation of Dreams* (1900), Standard Edition of the Complete Psychological Works of Sigmund Freud, Vol. IV (London: Hogarth Press, 1953), p. 97; *An Autobiographical Study* (1925), Standard Edition, Vol. XX (1959).

2. S. FREUD, *Delusions and Dreams in Jensen's Gravida* (1907), Standard Edition, Vol. IX (1959), p. 73.

3. ROBERT FLIESS, *The Revival of Interest in the Dream: A Critical Study of Post-Freudian Psychoanalytic Contributions* (New York: International Universities Press, 1953), pp. 123-124.

4. ERIK H. ERIKSON, "The Dream Specimen of Psychoanalysis," *Journal of the American Psychoanalytic Association,* 2:5-56, 1954.

5. ROBERT GRAVES, *The White Goddess* (New York: Random House, 1960), p. 477.

6. BERTRAM D. LEWIN, "The Forgetting of Dreams," in RUDOLPH LOEWENSTEIN (ed.), *Drives, Affects, Behavior* (New York: International Universities Press, 1953), pp. 191-202; "Reconsideration of the Dream Screen," *Psychoanalytic Quarterly,* 22:174-199, 1953.

7. ROY M. WHITMAN, "Remembering and Forgetting Dreams in Psychoanalysis," *Journal of the American Psychoanalytic Association,* 11:752-774, 1963.

8. NORMAN N. HOLLAND, *Psychoanalysis and Shakespeare* (New York: McGraw-Hill Book Company, 1966), p. 141.

9. *Ibid.*, p. 142n.

10. FRANK KERMODE (ed.), *"The Tempest,"* in *The Arden Shakespeare* (6th ed.; New York: Random House, 1964), p. xxiv.

Contributors

M. D. Faber, Ph.D., who edited this anthology, is Professor, Department of English, University of Victoria, Victoria, British Columbia, Canada. He teaches the university's Shakespeare course.

Karl M. Abenheimer, LL.D., is a Fellow of the British Psychological Society, and practices psychotherapy in Glasgow, Scotland.

David B. Barron, M.D., is Senior Attending Psychiatrist, Forest Hospital, Des Plaines, Illinois.

William H. Desmonde, Ph.D., is Chairman, Department of Philosophy, Psychology, and Sociology, Nassau Community College, Garden City, New York.

Sigmund Freud, M.D. (1856-1939), Psychoanalyst.

Neil Friedman, Ph.D., is Assistant Professor, Department of Sociology, Brandeis University, Waltham, Massachusetts.

Alexander Grinstein, M.D., is a practicing psychoanalyst and Clinical Associate Professor of Psychiatry, Wayne State University School of Medicine, Detroit, Michigan.

Charles K. Hofling, Ph.D., is Professor, David P. Wohl Memorial Mental Health Institute, St. Louis University, St. Louis, Missouri.

Norman N. Holland, Ph.D., is Professor, Department of English, State University of New York, Buffalo, New York.

Ludwig Jekels, M.D., practiced psychoanalysis in Vienna for many years before coming to live and work in New York City.

Ernest Jones, M.D. (1879-1958), was a practicing psychoanalyst in London, England, the founder of the American Psychoanalytic Association, the British Psychoanalytic Association, and at one time President of the International Psychoanalytic Association.

Richard M. Jones, Ph.D., is Professor, Harvard University Graduate School of Education, Cambridge, Massachusetts.

Mark Kanzer, M.D., is Clinical Professor of Psychiatry, State University of New York, Downstate Medical Center, Brooklyn, New York.

Murray Krieger, Ph.D., is Professor, Department of English and Comparative Literature, University of California, Irvine, California.

Ernst Kris, Ph.D. (1900-1957), former editor of *Imago* and Lecturer at the New York Psychoanalytic Institute, practiced psychoanalysis in Vienna and New York.

F. L. Lucas, M.A. (1894-1967), was for many years Reader at King's College, Cambridge University, Cambridge, England.

Leonard F. Manheim, Ph.D., founder and for many years editor of *Literature and Psychology,* is Professor, Department of English, University of Hartford, Hartford, Connecticut.

James A. S. McPeek, Ph.D., is Professor, Department of English, University of Connecticut, Storrs, Connecticut.

Theodor Reik, Ph.D., President of the National Psychological Association for Psychoanalysis, practiced in Vienna and Berlin before coming to New York City.

Hanns Sachs, LL.D. (1881-1947), former editor of *Imago,* practiced psychoanalysis for many years in Berlin and Boston.

Stephen A. Shapiro, Ph.D., is Assistant Professor, Department of English, University of California, Irvine, California.

Gordon Ross Smith, Ph.D., is Professor, Department of English, Temple University, Philadelphia, Pennsylvania.

Robert J. Stoller, M.D., is Professor, Department of Psychiatry, University of California School of Medicine, Los Angeles, California.

Martin Wangh, M.D., practices psychoanalysis in New York City.

Frederic Wertham, M.D., practices psychoanalysis in New York City.

Cynthia Kolb Whitney, Ph.D., is Staff Engineer, Massachusetts Institute of Technology, Cambridge, Massachusetts.

Andrew M. Wilkinson, Ph.D., is Director of the Oracy Research Unit, School of Education, University of Birmingham, Birmingham, England.

Index

To differentiate between persons, plays, and characters, often with the same names, persons are set in regular type (Julius Caesar), plays in italics (*Julius Caesar*), and characters in caps and small caps (JULIUS CAESAR).

EDWARD, PRINCE OF WALES (ED-
WARD V) (*Richard III*), 352
Edward the Confessor, King, 235
Ego psychology, 63
Eissler, K. R., 147, 281
ELBOW (*Measure for Measure*),
483
ELECTRA, 143
Eleusinian Mysteries, 28–29
Eliot, T. S., 97
ELIZABETH (*Richard III*), 347,
354, 357, 363, 366
Elizabeth I, Queen, 107n., 234,
236, 246, 381, 390
Elliott, Sir Thomas, 393
Elze, Karl, 2
EMILIA (*Othello*), 158, 160, 161,
165, 171, 173, 180, 191
Empson, William, 7, 394, 406n.
Enfants du Paradis, Les, 445
ENOBARBUS (*Antony and Cleo-
patra*), 282
Erikson, Erik, 13, 122, 128, 132,
135, 140, 141, 145n., 146n.,
421, 523, 527
Eros and Civilization (Marcuse),
146n.
ESCALUS (*Measure for Measure*),
486, 491, 494
Escape from Freedom (Fromm),
309
ETEOCLES, 216
*Every Man Out of His Own
Humor* (Jonson), 425

F

Faber, M. D., 1–20, 21–22, 33–
34, 41–42, 55–56, 63–64, 79–

80, 87–88, 111–112, 121–122,
147–148, 155–156, 169, 183–
184, 193–194, 207–208, 219–
220, 233–234, 251–252, 281,
287–288, 307–308, 327–328,
341–342, 347–348, 367–368,
387–388, 409–410, 429, 430–
438, 439–440, 463–464, 479–
480, 499–501, 521
Fairy Tales (Grimm Brothers),
199
FALSTAFF, SIR JOHN (*Henry IV,
Parts 1 and 2*), 124, 181, 387,
388, 389, 393, 394, 395, 398,
404, 411, 412, 413, 414, 416,
418, 420, 421, 422, 425, 428,
431
*Famous Victories of Henry V,
The*, 393, 406n.
FANG (*Henry IV, Part 2*), 415
Fanny's First Play (Shaw), 152
FATAL SISTERS, 241
FATES, 200, 205, 209
Faust (Goethe), 513
FEEBLE (*Henry IV, Part 2*), 413,
415
Feldman, A. Bronson, 185
Feldman, Harold, 63
Fenichel, Otto, 161, 385n.
FERDINAND (*Tempest*), 510, 515,
521, 524, 529
Fergusson, Francis, 7, 124, 127–
129, 132, 135
"Figure in the Carpet, The"
(James), 221
FLEANCE (*Macbeth*), 230, 236,
242, 243, 245, 258, 271